Model-Driven Power System Automation

IEEE Press

445 Hoes Lane

Piscataway, NJ 08854

Model-Driven Power System Automation

An Object-Oriented Approach Based on IEC 61850

Iony Patriota de Siqueira
Tecnix Engineering and Architecture Ltd
Recife
Brazil

IEEE Press
WILEY

Published by John Wiley & Sons, Inc., Hoboken, New Jersey.

Library of Congress Cataloging-in-Publication Data:
Names: de Siqueira, Iony Patriota author
Title: Model-driven power system automation : an object-oriented approach based on IEC 61850 / Iony Patriota de Siqueira.
Description: Piscataway, NJ : IEEE Press, [2026] | Includes bibliographical references and index.
Identifiers: LCCN 2026006139 | ISBN 9781394413966 hardback | ISBN 9781394413980 adobe pdf | ISBN 9781394413973 epub | ISBN 9781394413997 online
Subjects: LCSH: Electric power systems–Automation
Classification: LCC TK1005 .P36 2026
LC record available at https://lccn.loc.gov/2026006139

Cover Design: Wiley
Cover Image: Generated with AI using ChatGPT open-source AI

To Gislaine

Table of Contents

List of Illustrations

List of Tables

List of Abbreviations

ACSI	Abstract Communication Service Interface
AMQP	Advanced Message Queuing Protocol
ARP	Address Resolution Protocol
ATM	Asynchronous Transfer Mode
BI	Business Intelligence
BRCB	Buffered Report Control Block
C/S	Client/Server
C/SS	Client–Server System
CDC	Common Data Class
CHESF	Hydroelectric Company of San Francisco
CIA	Confidentiality, Integrity, and Availability
CID	Configured IED Description
CIGRE	International Council on Large Electric Systems
CORBA	Common Object Request Broker Architecture
CSMA	Carrier Sense Multiple Access
CT	Current Transformer
CU	Control Unit
DBMS	Database Management Systems
DCS	Digital Control System
DER	Distributed Energy Resource
DERMS	Distributed Energy Resource Management Systems
DII	Dynamic Invocation Interface
DMZ	Demilitarized Zone
DNP	Distributed Network Protocol
DOS	Distributed Object System
DoS	Denial of Service
DRTS	Distributed Real-time Systems
DS	Distributed System

DTD	Document Type Definition
DUT	Device Under Test
ECT	Electronic Current Transformer
EMC	Electromagnetic Compatibility
EMS	Energy Management System
ERP	Enterprise Resource Planning
ESB	Enterprise Service Bus
EVT	Electronic Voltage Transformer
FAT	Factory Acceptance Test
FCD	Functionally Constrained Data
FCDA	Functionally Constrained Data Attribute
FMEA	Failure Modes and Effects Analysis
FTP	File Transfer Protocol
GIS	Gas Insulated Substation
GOOSE	Generic Object-oriented Substation Event
GPS	Global Positioning System
GSE	Generic Substation Event
GSSE	Generic Substation State Event
GW	Gateway
HAZOP	Hazard and Operability Analysis
HMI	Human–Machine Interface
HTTP	Hypertext Transfer Protocol
I/O	Input/Output
ICCP	Inter-control Center Communication Protocol
ICD	IED Capability Description
IDL	Interface Definition Language
IEAEI	Indian Electrical and Electronics Manufacturers Association
IEC	International Electrotechnical Commission
IED	Intelligent Electronic Device
IEEE	Institute of Electrical and Electronics Engineers
IGMP	Internet Group Management Protocol
IID	Instantiated IED Description
IP	Internet Protocol
IRIG	Inter-range Instrumentation Group
ISO	International Organization for Standardization
IT	Information Technology
ITAI	Institute for Innovation and Applied Technology
KEPRI	Korean Electric Power Research Center
LACP	Link Aggregation Control Protocol
LAN	Local Area Network
LCAP	Link Aggregation Control Protocol

LCB	Log Control Block
LD	Logical Device
LN	Logical Node
MAU	Medium Attachment Unit
MCAA	Multicast Application Association
MICS	Model Implementation Conformance Statement
MMS	Manufacturer Message Specification
MSTP	Multiple Spanning Tree Protocol
MSVCB	Multicast-sampled-value-control-blocks
MU	Merging Unit
NTP	Network Time Protocol
OCL	Object Constraint Language
OMG	Object Management Group
OPC	OLE for Process Control
ORB	Object Request Broker
OSI	Open Systems Interconnection
OSPF	Open Shortest Path First
OT	Operation Technology
P2P	Peer-to-peer
PAS	Power Station System
PD	Physical Device
PDC	Phasor Data Concentrator
PERA	Purdue Enterprise Reference Architecture
PICOM	Piece of Information for COMmunication
PICS	Protocol Implementation Conformance Statement
PIXIT	Protocol Implementation eXtra Information for Testing
PLC	Programmable Logic Controller
PMU	Phasor Measurement Unit
PTP	Precision Time Synchronization Protocol
QoS	Quality-of-service
RARP	Reverse Address Resolution Protocol
RAS	Remote Access System
RBAC	Role-based Access Control
RCB	Report Control Block
RIP	Routing Information Protocol
RMI	Remote Method Invocation
RPC	Remote Procedure Call
RSTP	Rapid Spanning Tree Protocol
RTSP	Real-time Streaming Protocols
RTU	Remote Terminal Unit
SA	Substation Automation

SAS	Substation Automation System
SAT	System Acceptance Test
SAT	Site Acceptance Tests
SCADA	Supervisory Control and Data Acquisition
SCD	Substation Configuration Description
SCL	Substation Configuration Language
SCSM	Specific Communication Service Mapping
SED	System Exchange Description
SGCB	Setting Group Control Block
SGML	Standard Generalized Markup Language
SIPS	System Integrity Protection Schemes/Systems
SMTP	Simple Mail Transfer Protocol
SNTP	Simple Network Time Protocol
SOA	Service-oriented Architecture
SOAP	Simple Object Access Protocol
SOE	Sequence-of-event
SOS	Service-oriented System
SQL	Standard Query Language
SSD	System Specification Description
STP	Spanning Tree Protocol
SUT	System Under Test
SV	Sampled Values
SVCB	Sampled Value Control Block
TCP	Transmission Control Protocol
TPAA	Two-party Application Association
UA	Universal Architecture
UCA	Utility Communications Architecture
UDDI	Universal Description, Discovery and Integration
UDP	User Datagram Protocol
UFPE	Federal University of Pernambuco
UML	Universal Modeling Language
UNIBRATEC	Brazilian Technology University
UPE	Pernambuco State University
UPS	Unified Power System
URCB	Unbuffered Report Control Block
USVCB	Unicast-sampled-value-control-Blocks
VLAN	Virtual Local Area Network
VPN	Virtual Private Network
VT	Voltage Transformer
WAMPAC	Wide-area Monitoring, Protection, Automation and Control

WAMS	Wide-area Measurement Systems
WAN	Wide-area Network
WS	Web Service
WSDL	Web Services Description Language
XML	Extensible Markup Language

About the Author

Iony Patriota de Siqueira holds a PhD in Electrical Engineering (National Award), an MSc (Honors) in Industrial Engineering, an MBA in Information Systems, and a BSc in Electrical Engineering, with over 40 years of experience in protection, automation, and maintenance management in the power industry.

Dr. Siqueira is a CIGRE Fellows, IEEE Senior Member, a Strategic Advisor, and a Former Chairman of the Study Committee on Protection and Automation of the International Council on Large Electric Systems. He is also a permanent member of IEC Technical Committee 57 on Power Systems Management and Associated Information Exchange, a permanent member of the Brazilian National Academy of Engineering, and the convenor of the ABNT Study Commission on Management and Information Exchange in Power Systems.

He is an invited post-graduate teacher at UFPE, UFCG, UPE, and PUC Minas universities, a recipient of the National Engineering Award for the best PhD thesis on Energy Processing, and has received several commendations, including the Technical Committee Award, Honorary and Distinguished Member from CIGRE, the CIER Special Award, and a Vote of Praise from the Brazilian Chamber of Deputies for his contributions to Engineering. A former advisor of ABRAMAN, Director of the Maintenance Institute of Brazil (IMAB), Vice President and Technical Director of CIGRE-Brasil, and President of Tecnix Engineering and Architecture Ltd., he has authored four books on maintenance, management science, automation, and critical infrastructure networks; co-authored one book on operations research; and edited two books on system automation.

Preface

This book presents a model-driven approach to understanding and implementing power system automation. By model-driven approach, we mean an approach in which models provide formal representations of the structure, behavior, requirements, and implementation of automation schemes and artifacts. For modeling purposes, the Unified Modeling Language (UML), standardized and maintained by the Object Management Group, is the obvious choice to describe all modeling components and their interactions, employing an object-oriented approach that is suitable for studying automation systems in an agnostic manner, independent of manufacturers and solution providers.

For power system automation, IEC 61850, the international standard for communication networks and systems in power utility automation, standardized and maintained by the International Electrotechnical Commission (IEC), serves as the ideal companion to UML, as it is currently the preferred object-oriented approach for new and future deployments of digital substations and power plant automation systems.

The book uses these two standards to present an integrated view of power system automation, comprising a top-down chain of models that covers all design decisions throughout its development, based on IEC 61850. It originated from class notes initially prepared for an advanced course and from workshops on the IEC 61850 standard presented by the author at the Korean Electric Power Research Institute (KEPRI) and later at the Itaipu Binational Power Plant, under the sponsorship of the Institute for Innovation and Applied Technology (ITAI). The book content was further developed for workshops in Kuala Lumpur (Malaysia), sponsored by Tenaga Nasional Berhad; tutorials in Saint Petersburg and Moscow (Russia) during the International Scientific and Technical Conference on Actual Trends in the Development of Power System Protection and Automation, under the sponsorship of the Russian System Operator of the Unified Power System (UPS); and Elecrama in Mumbai (India), sponsored by the Indian Electrical and Electronics Manufacturers Association (IEEMA), focusing on the specification, commissioning, and functional testing of IEC 61850-based systems. Finally, it was also refined for a cybersecurity tutorial on digital substations and electrical power systems, held in Rio de Janeiro (Brazil) and sponsored by the Brazilian National Committee of CIGRE.

Much of the material of the book was developed while the author served as convener of CIGRE Work Group B5.32 on Functional Testing of IEC 61850-Based Systems; Special Reporter for the CIGRE Biennial Session on Life Cycle Management of Protection and Control Systems; convener of CIGRE Work Group B5.64 on Methods for Specifying Functional Requirements for Protection, Automation, and Control; convener of CIGRE Work Group B5.88 on the Implementation Guide for Fully Digital IEC 61850-Based Protection, Automation, and Control Systems; strategic advisor for CIGRE Study Committees D2 (Information Systems, Telecommunication and Cybersecurity) and B5 (Protection and Automation), and later as Secretary and Chairman of CIGRE Study Committee B5 on Protection and Automation.

Concepts related to functional testing were also drawn from the author's experience as Protection and Automation Manager at the Hydroelectric Company of San Francisco (CHESF); President and CEO of Tecnix Engineering and Architecture Ltd.; Technical Director and Vice President of CIGRE-Brazil; and from his post-graduate students in software development, power plant automation, and asset management at the Brazilian Technology University (UNIBRATEC), the Catholic University of Minas Gerais (PUC Minas), the Federal University of Pernambuco (UFPE), and the Pernambuco State University (UPE). The teaching material has also been used in lectures and seminars about IEC 61850 delivered by the author at PACWorld, OMICRON, CIGRE, and IEEE congresses, and at the symposia organized by the Brazilian, Colombian, Mexican, Malaysian, Indian, and Russian National Committees of CIGRE, and several in-company workshops for introducing IEC 61850 to automation engineers at CHESF, ITAIPU Binational, and the IEEE Region 9 student chapter.

Acknowledgments

Many ideas and contributions to this book were drawn from documents and standards developed by Technical Committee 57 of the International Electrotechnical Commission (IEC) and its Working Group 10, of which the author is a member, particularly during the development of IEC 61850—Communication Networks and Systems for Power Utility Automation. Additional contributions came from *PACWorld* magazine and his colleagues on the editorial board, as well as from the Study Commission on IEC 61850, which he convenes at the Brazilian Standardization Organization, and from numerous working groups, symposia, discussion sessions, and colloquia conducted during his tenure as Chairman of CIGRE Study Committee B5 on Protection and Automation and as a strategic advisor for CIGRE Study Committee D2 on Information Systems, Telecommunication, and Cybersecurity.

Although many manufacturer products and documentation were consulted during the writing of this book, the concepts included are agnostic to any specific or proprietary implementation, with a focus on the desired models and functionality, as defined by the applicable standards. The author is deeply grateful for the friendships formed with professionals met through these forums, whose shared knowledge contributed to this book. In particular, the author is indebted to CIGRE for permission to use some pictures of the documents he convened or presented at their respective conferences, and to all colleagues and friends who contributed to his apprenticeship in these activities. Of course, any misinformation or mistakes remain the author's sole responsibility.

The author expresses his sincere gratitude to the students in his classes, as well as to those participating in in-company training and open tutorials and panels organized by CIGRE and IEEE, whose insightful questions, thoughtful discussions, and creative perspectives significantly contributed to the development of the ideas presented in this book. Their curiosity and engagement not only enriched the learning environment but also inspired many of the concepts explored in these pages. This work is, in many ways, a reflection of our shared intellectual interest.

He extends his sincere gratitude to Brett Kurzman, Nandhini Karuppiah, Arunraj Subramanian, and Ryan Couch, his editorial team at Wiley; to Margaret Cummins, Senior Editorial Director for Advanced Engineering at IEEE; and to the anonymous reviewers from Wiley-IEEE Press for their meticulous attention to detail, insightful suggestions, and unwavering dedication throughout the editing process.

The author is also profoundly grateful to his family for their constant support, patience, and encouragement throughout this journey. Their understanding and love have been the foundation that made this work possible.

1

Introduction

1.1 Introduction

The introduction of multifunctional ***Intelligent Electronic Devices*** (***IEDs***) in Substation Automation Systems (SAS) and power plants has revolutionized how these systems are designed, operated, and maintained by manufacturers, integrators, consultants, utilities, and the energy industry. From simple electromechanical analog relays to static relays, and now to modern digital and virtual devices connected through high-speed communication networks both inside and outside substations, automation engineers have seen a shift from pure hardware to firmware and current software-based systems. Today, SAS are complex, wide-area distributed systems that must interact in real time not only with humans and the industrial processes they oversee and control but also with other substations, power plants, distributed generation sources, remote Supervisory Control and Data Acquisition (SCADA) systems, and Asset Management systems. Unlike earlier SAS technologies, which rely on localized hardware and software with synchronous, time-dependent components, these newer systems utilize distributed hardware and software characterized by asynchronous, real-time behavior that challenges traditional design, testing, and operational methods.

This evolution was mainly driven by the introduction of the IEC 61850 standard (Communication Networks and Systems for Power Utility Automation). This standard defines an object-oriented, model-based software approach for interacting with ***IEDs***, both within and between electric substations, power plants, and distributed resource stations. Although it did not standardize the functions to be performed by an SAS, it standardized how these functions should communicate, not only among themselves and with the controlled process but also with other stations and distributed power plants. Standardization occurred at a high abstraction level, related to the application layer—the highest level of the Open Systems Interconnection (OSI) communication stack defined by the International

Organization for Standardization (ISO)—paving the way for its adoption in many other fields.

From a designer, system architect, or integrator perspective, engineering an SAS based on IEC 61850 involves choosing and connecting various hardware, software, services, and data structures (or `logical nodes`) provided by relay manufacturers or software providers. These components are linked through high-speed local and wide-area networks that follow a common standard. This standardization, in principle, guarantees that `logical nodes` or servers from different vendors can communicate and work together when connected via an appropriate network. Standardized conformance tests are available, and interoperability has been demonstrated by major suppliers, integrators, and utilities, with these solutions deployed in numerous countries and projects worldwide.

From a utility or maintenance engineer's perspective, the distributed nature of these systems makes it challenging to use most traditional commissioning, maintenance, and testing methods. Isolating a single relay or function for testing is no longer as simple as it was with electromechanical, static, or digital monofunctional relays. Functions may now be spread across multiple `IEDs` that can participate in several functions, requiring a systematic approach to their design, testing, and maintenance. These and other requirements are thoroughly addressed by CIGRE, IEC, and IEEE working groups and in recent editions of IEC 61850, and are the focus of this book.

1.2 Learning Objectives

Understanding the complexity of IEC 61850 can be challenging for researchers, engineers, integrators, and especially students. Many users need a clear, educational explanation of its layered models, abstractions, and communication mechanisms, along with practical examples that turn the standard's theory into effective engineering practice. This textbook combines these concepts into a straightforward framework, offering a top-down learning path that supports classroom teaching, professional training, and everyday engineering tasks. It presents a structured and formal approach for specifying, designing, commissioning, and maintaining automation systems based on IEC 61850. The process remains independent of any specific or proprietary implementation, focusing instead on the intended functionality. It relies on formal modeling of the system to be designed, which is also used for conformance testing of the specification. A hierarchy of layered abstract classes is introduced to model the complete IEC 61850 application.

The book uses a simplified set of graphical symbols from Unified Modeling Language (UML) and Systems Modeling Language (SysML), as defined by the Object Management Group (OMG). UML use cases, shown in both graphical and tabular forms, describe the intended functions of any SAS from a user's perspective. UML class and object diagrams illustrate the logical structure of their nodes. Messages among objects are easily shown using UML communication diagrams, reflecting message exchanges in the process and station network.

UML state and activity diagrams also depict the dynamic behavior of ***logical nodes*** and their interactions. UML sequence diagrams are used to show performance requirements, such as network latency and relay trip timing. Time requirements are shown as constraints on events and messages within these diagrams. For readers unfamiliar with these standards, the book includes a summary in Annex 16.7 for easy reference. A functional specification template (Annex 16.9) is provided to help users prepare specifications using this method.

1.3 Target Audience

This book is intended for electrical, communications, automation, and software students, engineers, and instructors involved in the teaching, design, commissioning, maintenance, and operation of SAS systems based on IEC 61850. It targets power system engineers with some knowledge and experience in Protection, Automation, and Control (PAC) systems, but who are not experts in software and communication systems.

For software engineers skilled in modern model-based and object-oriented methods, the book aims to link their expertise to the specialized field of PAC systems by providing specific examples of designing and specifying distributed SAS based on IEC 61850.

Communication systems have also undergone a similar transition toward software-defined networks (SDN) and intent-based networks (IBN). Therefore, the book is expected to support the coexistence and integration of these technologies in substation and power plant automation.

For undergraduate and graduate teachers and researchers, the book offers an integrated view of current power system automation technologies, bridging the gap to the large-scale implementation of the standard IEC 61850 and its derivatives. Depending on the course, it is suitable for a one- or two-semester university syllabus or for one- or two-week intensive seminars on selected topics for experienced professionals.

The widespread adoption of these technologies has drawn hackers' attention, increasing the power system's vulnerability to cybersecurity threats both nationally and internationally and requiring targeted countermeasures by security professionals.

For senior undergraduate and graduate students in electrical, automation, and cybersecurity engineering, this book can serve as both a reference and a textbook for educators and researchers involved in smart grid research and teaching. Chapter 15 includes numerous examples suitable for discussion seminars or lab exercises, supplemented by the review questions at the end of each chapter.

1.4 Prerequisites

At the undergraduate level, students are expected to have some prior knowledge of electric power systems, substation and power plant protection and automation, communication networks, and software architecture. This knowledge is limited to the structure of substations and power plants, as well as the functions of key switchyard equipment, including transformers, circuit breakers, switches, bus bars, and turbine generators.

A basic understanding is essential for automation systems, focusing on the primary functions of protective relays, SCADA systems, and engineering stations used in substations and power plants. Basic knowledge of IEC 61850 is useful but not mandatory for the book.

Readers are assumed to have a basic understanding of telecommunication and communication networks at the conceptual or functional level. Chapters 3 and 4 serve as introductions and refreshers on these topics. Concepts such as local area networks (LANs) and wide-area systems will be introduced as needed in each chapter. No specific technology, such as wired networks, optical fiber, microwaves, or satellite communication, will be described. These topics will be discussed from an abstract functional perspective, consistent with IEC 61850.

At the architectural level, rudimentary knowledge about software is assumed based on the UML and SysML modeling languages. Annex 16.7 (UML and SysML graphical symbols) summarizes a reduced profile, including the main graphical symbols from these standards used in the book and their meanings, for easy reference.

1.5 Book Contents

The book takes a constructive approach to lowering the learning barrier for IEC 61850 due to its novel concepts. It is divided into 15 chapters and 10 annexes. Each chapter is self-contained and can be read independently, depending on the reader's interest, with occasional references to other chapters. However, a sequential reading is recommended for a structured course on power system automation and modeling of IEC 61850-based systems. Chapters 3 and 4 are suggested as refresher courses on communication aspects, before the remaining chapters. In nonsequential reading, a core must-read is Chapter 5 (IEC 61850 Models), as it provides a structured top-down overview of the standard and a summary of the models discussed in the book. The annexes provide easy reference data on the standards used in the chapters, primarily the UML artifacts that describe the models. The following paragraphs summarize each chapter's contents.

Chapter 1, **Introduction**, presents the history and central aspects of IEC 61850, including its capabilities, documentation, modeling, interoperability, engineering, and quality assurance related to SAS.

Chapter 2, **Automation Evolution**, summarizes the technological evolution of power system automation, including communication protocols, the introduction of Ethernet and LANs in substations, and the latest developments in software-based power plants.

Chapter 3, **Network Models**, reviews the different system topologies for equipment and functions that can be deployed in SAS, from the process level to the bay, station, and corporate levels, relevant to IEC 61850-based systems.

Chapter 4, **Architecture Models**, reviews the software characteristics of distributed SAS, reflecting the evolution of local and wide-area communication networks, important to IEC 61850-based systems.

Chapter 5, **IEC 61850 Models**, introduces a hierarchical view of the main models defined by the standard, including substation, product, type, communication, functional, data, and service models, which are detailed in subsequent chapters.

Chapter 6, **Communication Models**, reviews how SAS equipment can communicate in accordance with the IEC 61850 standard and the roles of local and wide-area utility-level communication networks.

Chapter 7, **Functional Models**, reviews the functional modules defined by the IEC 61850 standard for the composition of SAS functions, including logical nodes, devices, servers, proxies, and gateways deployed in ***IEDs***.

Chapter 8, **Data Models**, reviews the different data classes and sets specified by the IEC 61850 standard, with their types and attributes, to compose functional modules that implement SAS functions.

Chapter 9, **Service Models**, reviews the services available from the IEC 61850 standard for communication, control, reporting, logging, setting, and timing functions in SAS.

Chapter 10, **Time Models**, presents the main service models available in IEC 61850 for timing management, including the requirements for real-time systems, time sources, protocols, clock synchronization, and the specific ***logic nodes*** for time modeling and management.

Chapter 11, **Message Models**, reviews the various message types that can be exchanged between functional modules and equipment conforming to the IEC 61850 standard for SAS, including those at the process, substation, and wide-area network levels.

Chapter 12, **Engineering Models**, reviews the design cycles used to develop digital substations and the role of the Substation Configuration Language (SCL), an XML-based language defined by the IEC 61850 standard for describing and configuring components in SAS.

Chapter 13, **Testing Models**, reviews the test specifications defined by the IEC 61850 standard for quality assurance, conformance verification, and certification of equipment in SAS. The UML Test Profile, as determined by the Object Management Group (OMG), is a conceptual framework that describes the test components, simulators, and their behavior as needed for testing protection and automation systems based on IEC 61850.

Chapter 14, **Security Models**, presents a hierarchical view of power network cybersecurity based on the Purdue Enterprise Reference Architecture and Methodology (PERA). It spans from lower field levels and process domains to higher levels of business and corporate utilities, using IEC standards to protect IEC 61850-based systems.

Chapter 15, **Automation Models**, reviews examples of case studies of equipment and functions that can be deployed in substation and power plant automation systems in accordance with IEC 61850. It covers typical applications in protection, teleprotection, interlocking, breaker failure, hydro and wind power plants, and distributed energy resources.

Annexes contain summaries of possible implementations for the automation of substations, hydropower, wind power, and distributed energy resources using IEC 61850. An integrated UML class diagram of IEC 61850 is introduced, followed by a reference list of the logical nodes and acronyms defined in the standard, along with profiles of UML, SysML, network, and security graphical symbols used in the book. Forms are included to specify functional requirements and test requirements for IEC 61850-based systems.

The **Bibliography** lists publications related to the standard IEC 51850 and power system automation, organized into tutorials, books, standards, reports, papers, videos, and websites for easy reference.

1.6 Book Conventions

The following typographic conventions are used in this book:

- ***Courier New Bold Italic***: Due to the large number of abbreviations, acronyms, and words introduced by the standard IEC 61850, they are formatted in this book using a distinct italic style (e.g., ***IED***, ***LogicalNode***, ***Server***). Note that, besides the syntactic format, they usually convey some specific semantic meaning introduced by the standard, as listed in Annex 16.6, in addition to their traditional meaning.

- ***Times New Roman Bold Italic***: Used to name reserved keywords and symbols of programming languages such as C++ or Python (e.g., ***class, structure, {,}***).
- **UML Symbols**: A profile of stylized shapes is used to draw UML and SysML pictures, as defined in Annex 16.7.
- **Network Symbols**: Annex 16.8 defines a profile of stylized shapes used to draw communication networks and cybersecurity countermeasures.

1.7 Excluded Contents

Due to the complexity and scope of the IEC 61850 standard, the book focuses on the main concepts and modeling artifacts in an agnostic, implementation-independent manner. No specific proprietary solution, manufacturer product, technology, commercial design tool, or implementation language is described, except those defined in the IEC 61850 standard, or references to open-source software and other documents from standardizing bodies.

1.8 Summary

Modern power systems are automated with software-based intelligent devices that are either centralized or physically distributed across local and wide-area networks and supplied by various vendors. To ensure their interoperability and seamless integration, designing, operating, and maintaining these systems require a structured approach grounded in modern techniques, supported by standardized, model-based methodologies.

This chapter introduces the topics and conventions of the book and summarizes the upcoming chapters. After discussing the evolution of automation in the next chapter, the remaining chapters will explore different perspectives for various stakeholders, each supported by conceptual models to provide a comprehensive view of power system automation.

1.9 Review Questions

The review questions at the end of each chapter help identify key concepts, reinforce main ideas, check understanding, encourage active learning, support self-assessment and reflection, and improve retention. This prepares students for real-world practice, exams, or self-study, starting with the next chapter.

They are clear questions (not just yes/no answers) or suggestions for further exploration of the chapter's topics, serving multiple educational and cognitive purposes. For instructors and teachers, they provide ready-made tools for discussions, seminars, quizzes, and assignments, helping students focus on the key parts of the chapter. They can also be used with examples from Chapter 15 to support discussions.

2

Automation Evolution

2.1 Introduction

Since the introduction of the IEC 61850 (Communication Networks and Systems for Power Utility Automation) standard, the way substations and automation systems are designed, built, commissioned, operated, maintained, and refurbished has undergone significant changes. The traditional method of selecting relays and control systems has evolved into a systematic process of specifying and integrating components across distributed software, hardware, and communication networks. Testing has also progressed from checking isolated relays to a hierarchical approach that ranges from unit and standard conformance to integration and performance evaluation of distributed functions.

2.2 Learning Objectives

This chapter reviews the main facts related to this evolution, from historical to technological events, and how they led to the development of the IEC 61850 standard. This section introduces the standard capabilities, documentation, engineering, interoperability, and quality assurance requirements of modern Substation Automation Systems (SAS). The following topics are covered in sequence:

- Substation Evolution
- Protocol Evolution
- Ethernet in Substations
- Interoperability Requirements
- Modeling Requirements
- IEC 61850 Capabilities
- IEC 61850 Documentation

These topics are essential for understanding the motivation behind the development of the IEC 61850 standard.

2.3 Substation Evolution

The history of substation automation and protection systems mirrors the evolution of significant technological advancements in electronics, power systems, and telecommunication over the last few decades. Drastic reductions in bandwidth constraints were introduced in serial communication technologies (from 1200 b/s to 500 kbps), in local area network (LAN) technologies (from 1 Mb/s to 100 Gb/s), and in new technologies such as frame relay, asynchronous transfer mode, and optical fibers. These reductions were followed by significant cost declines, driven by standards such as Ethernet and Transmission Control Protocol/Internet Protocol (TCP/IP), the explosive growth of the communications market, and advances in hardware capabilities.

In the same decades, data management capabilities were affected by reduced memory constraints. Storage media have evolved from tape to disk and, more recently, to static memories, changing the measure of capacity from KB to GB and TB. In contrast, technology has evolved from magnetic to optical, and ultimately to flash and nano memory. Access methods shifted from sequential to direct and parallel access to files, disks, and databases, while software constraints shifted from sequential to structured and object-oriented designs. Programming languages evolved from Assembler to scripted and object-oriented languages, shifting the programming paradigm from procedural to functional and object-oriented.

These facts were reflected in the evolution of power system automation, motivating the birth of four distinct generations of relays and automation systems and their standard devices:

- **First generation**—electromechanical devices
- **Second generation**—static devices
- **Third generation**—digital devices
- **Fourth generation**—virtual devices

Built initially from pure electromechanical devices, the first generation of relays relied primarily on the known principle of iron armature attraction by a current flowing through a coil. This attraction was activated by the movement of an electric contact, which closed the control circuit to execute a typical action on a switchgear device, such as opening or closing a circuit breaker, when the current in the coil exceeded a predefined value. The value could be based on a calculated short-circuit current on a substation feeder or an overvoltage on a bus, due to a sudden load rejection. These devices were typical of electromechanical relays that protected and controlled most of the electric substations worldwide for decades. The technology is known as the first generation of protection systems, also referred to as the age of electromechanical relays. It is also characterized by a direct metallic connection between the devices and the process equipment, forming a single hierarchical level of control.

The second generation of automation systems came with the evolution of power electronics. The widespread use of transistors and diodes made it possible to control large amounts of energy with a very low-power signal, without requiring mechanical parts to be moved. Further evolution of these technologies enabled the construction of smaller devices, using static units with increasing processing capacity. This technology was typical of the second generation of protection systems, or the age of static relays. It is also characterized by introducing an intermediate level of control between the station control and the process equipment, forming two hierarchical levels of control.

The third generation of relays followed the introduction of microprocessors as a substitute for analog static devices. Built from a highly dense integration of transistors and based on the processing of digital signals, these devices enabled the execution of multiple functions by a single relay. The functions were encoded in firmware memory and processed by a microprocessor, allowing, for the first time, the change of the functions (or their versions) performed by a given relay, without requiring a change to its hardware. This generation is characterized by digital, multifunctional relays and controls, typically organized into three levels of control, with the introduction of remote control centers.

The fourth generation resulted from developments mainly in telecommunications and software systems. The availability of high-speed local and wide-area networks, based on optical, metal, or radio media, enabled the distribution and integration of functions from different locations in real time. Simultaneously, software development evolved to a mature level, with tools and methods that enabled the design of much larger, broader, and more complex systems. It was now possible to design a sophisticated SAS entirely based on software. These facts characterize the fourth generation of automation systems, which utilize virtual or object-oriented objects. These systems are based on distributed, asynchronous, and real-time functions, with capabilities defined by the IEC 61850 standard set. It is also typical of a four-level hierarchical control, introducing a virtual process level that isolates the ***IEDs*** from the real signals of process equipment.

The status of today's SAS challenges current methods for specifying and testing such systems. Their complexity can be visualized along three axes representing communication, space, and time, as shown in Figure 2.1. Current SAS utilizes asynchronous methods along the communication axis, rather than traditional synchronous approaches, which introduces challenging nondeterministic behaviors and concurrency requirements. The difficulty is amplified along

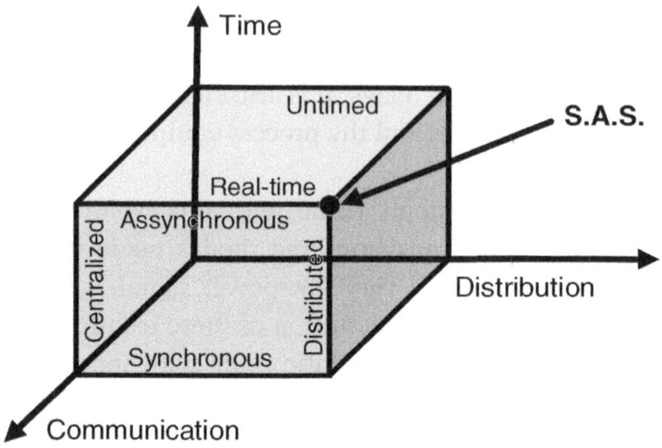

Figure 2.1 Complexity of SAS.

the distribution or space axis due to their dispersed physical allocation, limited knowledge of automation tools, and the need for nonconventional (software) testing techniques. Finally, the real-time aspect along the time axis introduces challenging temporal and functional requirements that are difficult to meet with conventional approaches.

Parallel with the evolution of substation technology, communication protocols have reflected advancements in connecting devices and networks, ensuring efficient and secure data exchange, as described in the following paragraph.

2.4 Protocol Evolution

Since the introduction of the ARPANET network in the 1960s and 1970s, one of the predecessors of the Internet, computers have been connected using the Network Control Protocol and later X.25, enabling packet data transmission across networks and laying the foundation for the development of wide-area networks.

This was led in the 1980s by the introduction of the TCP/IP protocol, which revolutionized networking by allowing different networks to interconnect. This period also saw the rise of LANs and the development of the Ethernet protocol, which enabled efficient short-range communication.

The 1990s witnessed the introduction and widespread adoption of the Hypertext Transfer Protocol (HTTP), which enabled the transmission of web pages and made information accessible through the World Wide Web. The first security protocols, such as Secure Sockets Layer (SSL), also emerged, laying the foundation for HTTPS, which secures web transactions.

The next decade, the 2000s, introduced wireless networks and mobility protocols, such as Wi-Fi (IEEE 802.11) and Bluetooth, enabling mobile device connectivity and supporting the Internet of Things (IoT). Voice over IP (VoIP) and Session Initiation Protocol (SIP) allow voice calls over the Internet, advancing multimedia communication.

In the 2010s, due to IPv4 address exhaustion, IPv6 was widely adopted, allowing for an almost unlimited number of IP addresses. Additionally, several security-focused protocols, such as Transport Layer Security (TLS) and Quick UDP Internet Connections (QUIC), developed by Google, have improved HTTP security and efficiency on mobile networks. Redundant Ethernet architectures, such as Parallel Redundancy Protocol (PRP) and High-Availability Seamless Redundancy (HSR), were developed to ensure continuous operation, even during network failures. Precise time synchronization using the IEEE 1588 Precision Time Protocol (PTP) is now possible for applications that require time accuracy within microseconds for protection and automation.

In this decade, the 2020s and beyond, new low-latency protocols have been introduced for use in IoT (such as MQTT and CoAP) and 5G, enabling real-time communication on mobile networks. Further security developments are occurring with protocols like DNS over HTTPS (DoH) and DNS over TLS (DoT), which enhance privacy in browsing.

The evolution of communication protocols reflects technological advancements and emerging needs. They continually adapt to support growing data volumes, ensure security, and cater to an increasingly diverse range of devices. These evolutions were reflected in the increasing use of Ethernet in substations.

2.5 Ethernet in Substations

The evolution of Ethernet in electrical substations, which followed the natural adoption of new protocols, reflects the growing importance of digital communication in power systems. It enables faster, more reliable, and more efficient operation and monitoring.

The first noticeable change was the introduction of Supervisory Control and Data Acquisition (SCADA) systems in the 1980s, which utilized protocols such as Modbus, DNP3, and proprietary solutions. Ethernet technology was not widely adopted in this decade, as most communication used serial connections (RS-232, RS-485). SCADA systems enabled remote monitoring and control of substations; however, communication bandwidth and speed were limited, and interoperability among devices from different manufacturers was challenging.

The late 1990s to 2000s saw the transition to IP-based networks, with Ethernet gradually replacing serial connections to integrate substations with other utility systems. IEC 61850, a global standard for substation communication networks, was introduced in the early 2000s. This protocol facilitated the adoption of Ethernet and standardized the data exchange between devices, improving interoperability.

In the 2010s, the IEC 61850 standard gained widespread adoption, and Ethernet networks were increasingly deployed in substations for all critical applications, including protection, control, and monitoring. SAS became increasingly digital, with Ethernet backbones replacing copper wiring in many cases, simplifying design and enabling more flexible architectures.

In the current decade, the 2020s and beyond, modern Ethernet technology, including 10 Gbps and beyond, is being explored to accommodate the growing data needs of advanced monitoring and control systems, such as synchro phasors and wide-area monitoring systems. Software-defined networks and intent-based networks are beginning to emerge in substations, offering improved network management, flexibility, and programmability. Security has become a critical focus as Ethernet-enabled substations become more connected. Standards such as IEC 62351 and cybersecurity practices are being implemented to protect against cyber threats, as described in Chapter 14.

Today, Ethernet forms the backbone of modern substation automation, providing the speed, scalability, and reliability required for advanced digital protection, automation, and control in the evolving power grid. Over this backbone, numerous additional protocols have been developed, raising concerns about interoperability.

2.6 Interoperability Requirements

Interoperability refers to the ability of two or more devices, whether from the same vendor or different vendors, to exchange information and use that information to cooperate correctly (Figure 2.2).

This concept can be extended to an entire utility or corporate enterprise, covering (1) the needs of communication at the business level with their processes and external entities; (2) the interchange of information among internal processes and functional domains; (3) the transmission of information between actors and stakeholders; (4) the needs of communication using different protocols; and finally (5) the requirements for information exchange among different components in different locations in the utility. Figure 2.3 illustrates the layered interoperability requirements for a typical utility.

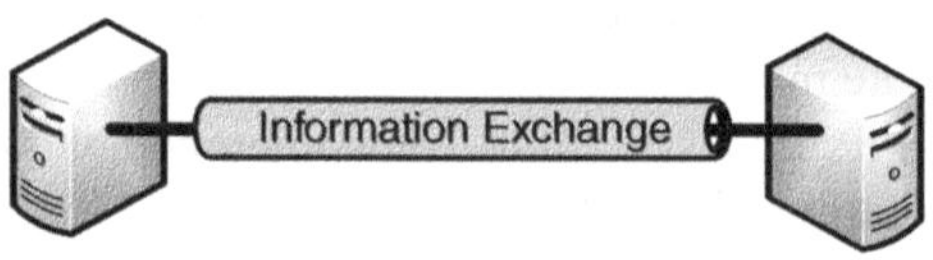

Figure 2.2 Interoperability definition.

The adoption of IEC 61850 has been the primary standard for

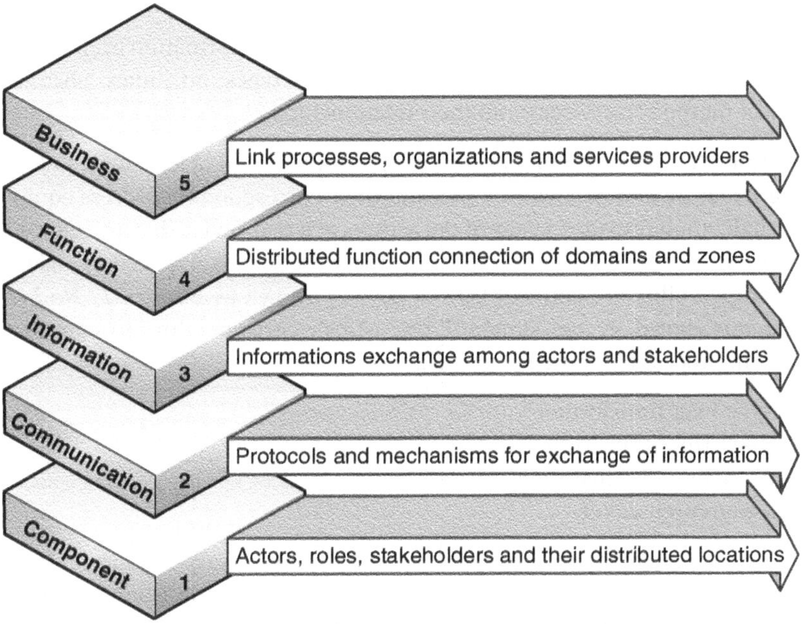

Figure 2.3 Layered interoperability model.

achieving utility-level interoperability across all major communication layers, introducing the concept of model-based development.

2.7 Modeling Requirements

All recent developments in protocols and software-based devices require a structured approach to designing and maintaining substation automation solutions. Three main approaches have emerged to use models to represent the standard requirements of SAS:

- **Functional decomposition**
  - To understand the logical relationship between components of a distributed function
  - Presented in terms of `logical nodes` describing the functions, subfunctions, and functional interfaces
- **Data flow**
  - To understand the communication interfaces supporting the exchange of information between components
  - To special functional performance requirements

- **Information modeling**
  - To define the abstract syntax and semantics of the information exchanged
  - Presented in terms of data object classes and types, attributes, abstract object methods (services), and their relationships

These principles embody a process of virtualization of real objects used to represent the structure and behavior of SAS and their corresponding process equipment. Virtualization provides a view of the aspects of a real device that are relevant to information exchange with other devices. Only the details required to ensure device interoperability are defined. Virtual devices known as ***Logical Nodes*** (***LN***) were introduced by the standard IEC 61850, corresponding to common power system process equipment, such as:

- ***YPTR***—power transformer
- ***TCTR***—current transformer
- ***TVTR***—potential transformer
- ***XCBR***—circuit breaker

Each virtual device contains details about the data necessary to represent the standard functionality of the real devices, as well as their communication requirements with other real and virtual devices. The data contents of an ***XCBR logical node***, for instance, can be represented as:

- ***XCBR1***
  - ***Position***
  - ***Mode***

Position and Mode are data objects representing the position and operational mode of the circuit breaker modeled by the ***logical node XCBR1***. They are modeled using a set of ***common data classes*** (***CDC***) to express common data objects of logical nodes.

Besides these data objects, IEC 61850 ***logical nodes*** provide external services (Figure 2.4) that can be accessed by other ***logical nodes***, human beings, and clients, such as the following:

- ***GetLogicalNodeDirectory***—for getting the data directory of a ***logical node***
- ***GetAllDataValue***—for getting the data contents of a ***logical node***

These also include specific commands for real devices, such as the ***Close*** and ***Open*** commands for circuit breakers sent over a communication network using a client human–machine interface ***logical node*** (***IHMI***), as shown in Figure 2.4.

A primary goal of any SAS is to attain acceptable levels of interchangeability among functions and devices. Hardware or device interchangeability refers to

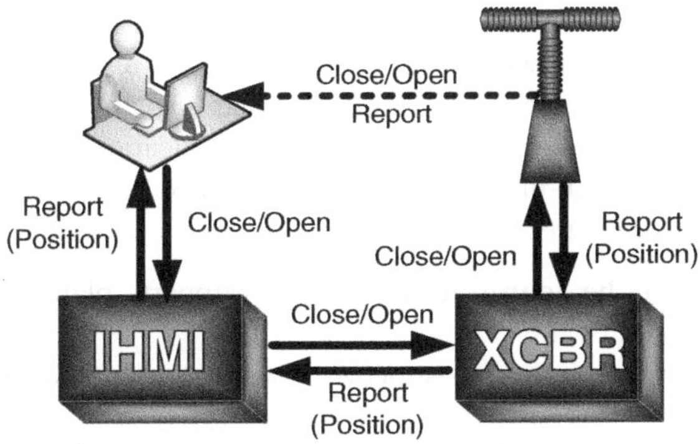

Figure 2.4 Commands for circuit breakers.

replacing a device supplied by one manufacturer with one from another, without altering any other system elements. Replacement implies physical similarity, while no change implies logical similarity among the exchanged functions and devices.

A lower requirement can be attained by functional interoperability. This refers to the ability of two or more ***IEDs***, from the same vendor or different vendors, to exchange information and use it to execute specified functions correctly. A common language is required in this case. To exchange information, the devices shall be connectable to a common bus with a standard protocol (language syntax), while to use the information, the devices shall understand the information provided by other devices (language semantics). To retain functionality, the devices shall perform a common or joint function (language pragmatics) if applicable.

In addition to these requisites, to attain the desired levels of interoperability, some static requirements must be met by any SAS:

- **Free allocation of functions to devices**—supported by communication, allowing any function to occur in any device. Devices are not required to support all functions
- **Functions and communication independent of devices**—functions and their communication shall be described independently of the device, with no reference to any proprietary implementation in ***IEDs***
- **Functions described only by exchanged information**—only as far as necessary for the identification of the information to be exchanged
- **Function interaction described by logical interfaces**—freely allocated to physical interfaces or LANs for implementation
- **Open for future communication requirements**—arising from future functions

These static requirements should be complemented by dynamic ones, so that the receiving node's reaction must align with the overall requirement of the distributed function to be performed. The behavior in the degraded case, including scenarios such as erroneous messages, lost data due to communication interruptions, resource limitations, and out-of-range data, must be specified. These resulted in several dynamic requirements:

- **Generic information to be communicated**—to support planned functional extensions
- **Generic communication behavior**—to support future extensions with generic rules
- **Information transfer with standard content**—*`Pieces of Information Communication`* (*`PICOMs`*)
- **Exchanged data with all attributes**—for an unambiguous understanding of the receiver
- **Data transfer with guaranteed and defined time**—acceptable overall transfer time is guaranteed in any situation

As shown in Figure 2.5, vendor tools for design and maintenance are now available and deployed with the SAS and embedded in engineering stations.

To support these requirements, IEC 61850 was conceived to provide a consistent set of capabilities for designing and exploiting distributed real-time systems across all power system applications.

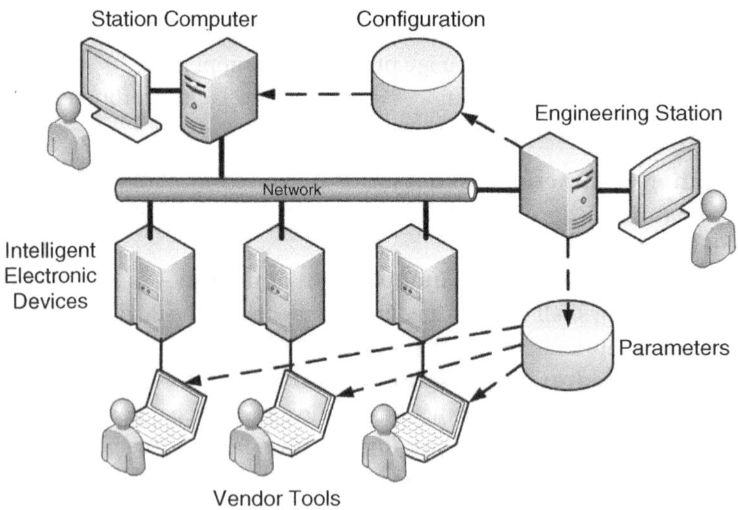

Figure 2.5 Vendor tools and engineering station.

2.8 IEC 61850 Capabilities

The original goals of the IEC 61850 standard were to provide a single protocol for communication in substations, capable of modeling and storing data using a standard method and format, and to provide basic data transfer services. It should primarily promote high interoperability among systems from different vendors through appropriate conformance tests.

The first edition of IEC 61850 expanded these objectives to ensure that communication profiles were based on existing IEC/IEEE/ISO/OSI standards, utilizing open, expandable protocols that support self-descriptive devices, including data objects, syntaxes, and semantics tailored to the needs of the electric power industry. Additionally, it should be possible to model the SAS as a single element within the overall power control system.

The current capabilities of IEC 61850 encompass not only the exchange of information within substations and power plants but also among substations and distributed generation, and from substations and power plants to control centers. It is being applied not only to protection and automation but also to various other applications, such as metering, condition monitoring, and engineering configuration. These capabilities are provided using a set of common resources comprising:

- **Data modeling**—by `logical nodes` grouped under `logical devices`
- **Reporting schemes**—for reporting through a client–server relationship
- **Fast transfer of events**—for a peer-to-peer communication mode
- **Setting groups**—switchable active group according to the requirement
- **Sampled data transfer**—to handle the transfer of `sampled values`
- **Commands**—commands with standard and enhanced security
- **Data storage**—of the configured data of the substation in a specific format

To achieve interoperability, communication among functions and devices within a substation must be based on standardized protocols. These standards must govern both the physical means of linking devices and the format and contents of exchanged messages. Existing standards define adequate means to connect physically, address, and route messages among devices. Communication in a distributed real-time system can be viewed as a hierarchy of stacks, ranging from physical devices to high-level functional requirements. This is best viewed using the ISO communication stack, also known as the Open Systems Interconnection (OSI) Reference Model, as shown in Table 2.1.

IEC 61850 addresses the need for a standard set of syntactical and semantic rules that define the format and meaning of these messages for SAS. These rules are detailed in the standard documentation published and maintained by IEC.

Table 2.1 IEC 61850 mapping to OSI Reference Model.

Layer	Use
Application	Protection and control application
Presentation	SAS data representation and encryption
Session	*IED* or interhost communication
Transport	End-to-end *IED* connections and reliability
Network	Path and logical addressing on the substation
Data link	*IED* physical addressing
Physical	Media and signal transmission in a substation

To standardize the communication requirements of SAS, the following aspects are defined by IEC 61850:

- What functions and information are network-visible
- How are they named and described
- How functions can be accessed
- How information can be exchanged
- How communication networks can connect devices

Depending on the information being transferred, communication needs within and outside a station occur across multiple layers, as shown in Figure 2.6, ranging from the field and Process Network levels to the Station Network and the corporate and utility Wide Area Network levels.

The Process Network, located near the field level, connects primary equipment directly involved in power system operation, such as circuit breakers, switchyards, current transformers, voltage transformers, and protection relays. It transmits real-time signals with strict latency and reliability standards. This layer acts as the interface between the physical power system and the digital automation system.

The Station Network at the substation level connects switches to link relays, bay controllers, HMIs, gateways, and engineering workstations. Latency requirements are less strict than at the process level but still need to support substation automation reliably.

The Wide Area Network at the control center and interstation level connects substations, control centers, regional dispatch centers, external users, and other enterprise systems. It supports wide-area protection schemes, SCADA/EMS data exchange, synchrophasor transport, and utility Information Technology/Operational Technology (IT/OT) integration. This layer typically uses routed, redundant, high-bandwidth telecom infrastructure and must ensure strong cybersecurity and quality of service to maintain grid-level situational awareness and coordinated operation.

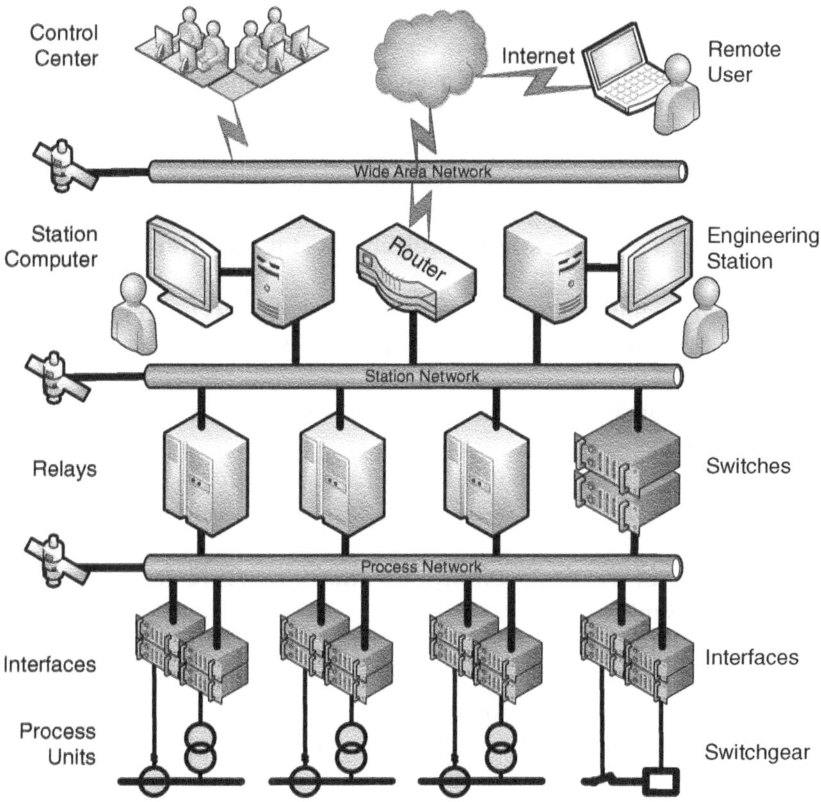

Figure 2.6 Utility communication networks.

To support and standardize many aspects of communication, IEC 61850 depends on a comprehensive set of documentation maintained by the International Electrotechnical Commission.

2.9 IEC 61850 Documentation

The original standard documentation of IEC 61850 is composed of 10 parts, with the following titles and subparts:

- **IEC 61850-1: Introduction and Overview**
  This document provides a high-level overview of the entire IEC 61850 standard, including its objectives, scope, and general structure.
- **IEC 61850-2: Glossary**
  Contains a glossary of terms used throughout the standard, which is crucial for understanding specific technical language and concepts in IEC 61850.

- **IEC 61850-3: General Requirements**
  Specifies the general requirements for the communication systems used in substations. This includes environmental and electromagnetic compatibility requirements to ensure reliable operation.
- **IEC 61850-4: System and Project Management**
  This section covers guidelines and requirements for system management and project planning, including configuration and testing processes for SAS.
- **IEC 61850-5: Communication Requirements for Functions and Device Models**
  Describes the communication requirements for the specific functions and devices used in substation automation, such as protective relays and control equipment.
- **IEC 61850-6: Configuration Language for Communication in Electrical Substations**
  Defines the Substation Configuration Language (*SCL*), a standardized XML-based language used to describe configuration information in substations.
- **IEC 61850-7 Series: Basic Communication Structure for Substation and Feeder Equipment**
  This series includes multiple parts that describe the data models and communication services for different equipment:
  - **61850-7-1**: Principles and Models
  - **61850-7-2**: *Abstract Communication Service Interface*(*ACSI*)
  - **61850-7-3**: Common Data Classes
  - **61850-7-4**: Compatible Logical Node Classes and Data Classes
  - **61850-7-410**: Hydroelectric Power Plants—Communication for Monitoring and Control
  - **61850-7-420**: Distributed Energy Resources (DER)
- **IEC 61850-8 Series: Specific Communication Service Mapping (*SCSM*)**
  Details of how the abstract communication services described in the 61850-7 series are mapped to specific protocols:
  - **61850-8-1**: Mapping to MMS (Manufacturing Message Specification) and ISO/IEC 8802-3 (Ethernet)
  - **61850-8-2**: Mapping to XMPP (Extensible Messaging and Presence Protocol)
- **IEC 61850-9 Series: Process Bus**
  Focuses on process bus communication, defining how data from sensors and other process equipment is transmitted:
  - **61850-9-1**: *Sampled Values* (*SV*) over Serial Unidirectional Multidrop Point-to-Point Link
  - **61850-9-2**: *Sampled Values* over ISO/IEC 8802-3

- **IEC 61850-10: Conformance Testing**
  Specifies the testing requirements and methods to verify conformance to IEC 61850, ensuring that equipment and systems are interoperable and function as specified.

Each part of the IEC 61850 documentation provides detailed guidance on aspects of substation automation and defines the relationship between a specific substation component and a data object class, as illustrated for a circuit breaker and an operator in Figure 2.7.

To extend its application to new areas, domain-specific extension numbers were defined by the IEC, such as:

- ***x0*0**: Substation automation
- ***x1*0**: Hydropower plants
- ***x2*0**: Distributed energy resources

to name documents that extend the original intended application, such as:

- **IEC 61850-7-410**: Hydroelectric power plants
- **IEC 61850-7-420**: DER

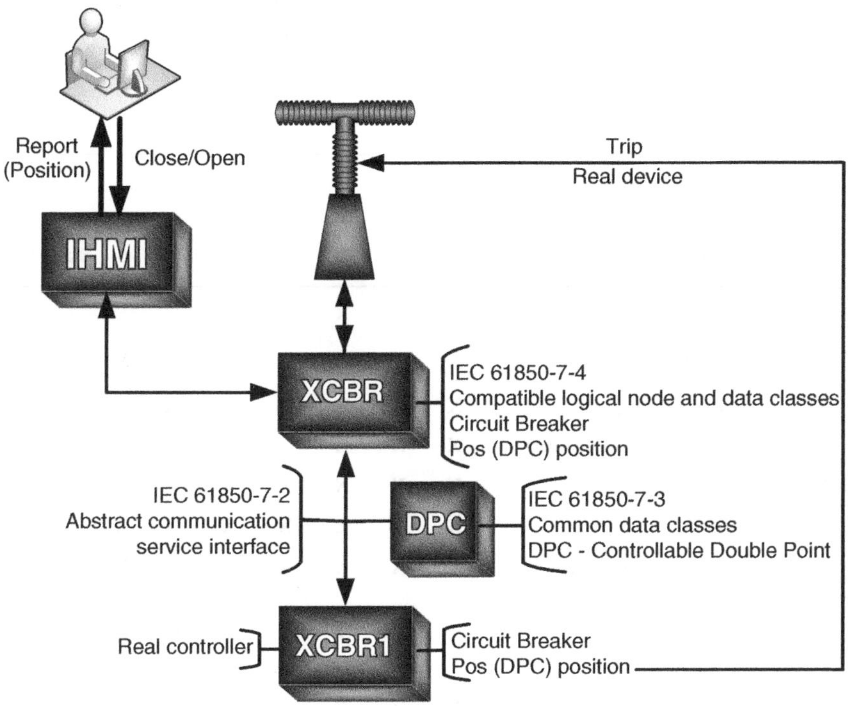

Figure 2.7 Relation between parts of IEC 61850 series.

Many new documents were also developed to extend the standard further:

- **IEC 62445-1**: Communication between substations
- **IEC 62445-2**: Communication between control centers and substations
- **IEC 61400-25**: Wind turbines
- **IEC 62271-3**: Switchgears
- **IEC 61850-7-500**: Use of **`logical nodes`** for substation automation
- **IEC 61850-80-1**: Guideline for information exchange of IEC 61850-based ***`CDCs`***, information addressing, and services using IEC 60870-5-104/101
- **IEC 61850-90-1**: Using IEC 61850 for communication between substations
- **IEC 61850-90-2**: Using IEC 61850 for communication between substations and control center

IEC 62445 extends IEC 61850 to applications such as wide-area interlocking, line-distance protection, and line-differential protection that depend on information exchange between substations. Due to its size (exceeding 1000 pages in the original version), the standard suggests which parts are likely to interest utilities, vendors, and SAS consultants, as shown in Table 2.2.

The widespread adoption of IEC 61850 paved the way for digital substations as the standard solution for expanding and modernizing power systems.

Table 2.2 Guide for the reader.

		IEC 61850							
	↓User module→	1	5	7-1	7-4	7-3	7-2	6	8 and 9
Utility	Manager	X		X					
	Engineer	X	X	X	X		X	X	
Vendor	Application engineer	X	X	X	X	X	X	X	X
	Communication engineer	X	X	X			X		X
	Product manager	X	X	X	X	X	X	X	
	Marketing	X	X	X	X	X	X	X	
Consultant	Application engineer	X	X	X	X	X		X	
	Communication engineer	X		X			X	X	X
All others		X	X	X					

2.10 Digital Substations

The digitalization of control and protection systems, along with the associated communication, has consequences for the safety and operation of the electrical system. The main change is replacing deterministic communication using metallic wires with probabilistic communication in Ethernet networks. Therefore, several advantages can be listed for the digitalization of substations compared with conventional protection and automation technologies. The main benefits result from the new features introduced, such as:

- Unification of protocols
- Interoperability between devices
- Reduced cabling and hardware footprint
- Reduction of thermal losses in cables
- Ease of data transfer and copying
- Simplification of the adjustment and calibration process
- Ease of software update
- Unification of configuration software
- Remote testing
- Remote configuration
- Automatic diagnostics
- Improved magnetic compatibility (with optical cables)
- Standardization of hardware and software
- Unification of the time reference
- Greater operational efficiency

These advantages are also expected to affect maintenance, operations, projects, and security. The maintenance of digital substations is particularly affected by how human interventions are processed. The main changes are viewing adjustment via software only, frequent version changes, and the possibility of distributed, remote maintenance. These benefits introduce risks and opportunities associated with new modes of human error, cyber risks, and accidental shutdowns, thereby impacting the installation's reliability and operation.

Remote access and data transfer can affect system operation and increase cybersecurity vulnerabilities. In addition to shutdowns, these events can result in accidental or intentional changes to the configuration of the protection systems, affecting reliability and security.

The engineering of digital substations has undergone significant changes, primarily due to technological advancements and the tools designers use. The technological shift from electromechanical or static devices connected by metallic wires to smart devices connected by local or remote communication networks is accompanied by the adoption of digital configuration and engineering tools. The physical design changed from a set of device interconnection drawings to a set of standardized textual files that define each device's configuration and its communication with other devices through communication networks. The configuration and engineering model of Chapter 12 will address these aspects.

2.11 Summary

IEC 61850 strongly supports the digitalization and virtualization of substation and power system automation. This standard was one of the first international norms developed, well before manufacturers implemented it, thereby guaranteeing universal acceptance within the industry. Finding SAS devices on the market that do not support this standard is now almost impossible.

Many utilities are now pursuing the concept of a fully digital substation, which poses implementation challenges and introduces new demands for commissioning, maintenance, and security. Chapter 3 will introduce the main concepts of network models, a foundational aspect required by IEC 61850.

2.12 Review Questions

1 List the four generations of SAS and describe their main differences.

2 What are the main types of information exchanged inside a SAS according to IEC 61850?

3 Which standard part defines the ***Substation Configuration Language*** (***SCL***), and what is its primary purpose?

4 What are ***Logical Nodes*** in IEC 61850?

5 Which redundant Ethernet protocols ensure high availability of communication?

6 Explain the concept of interoperability and the difference between hardware interchangeability and functional interoperability.

7 Why did the introduction of microprocessors significantly change the design and functionality of protection devices?

8 Describe the relationship between information modeling, functional decomposition, and data flow in the design of IEC 61850-based systems.

3

Network Models

3.1 Introduction

The increased digitalization of the power grid and the integration of distributed energy resources have added complexity to power systems by introducing many new power sources and diverse green technologies. The use of distributed control across large geographic areas has also made cyberattacks on electrical infrastructure a concern. The main challenge in managing this complexity is developing secure and reliable network solutions for communication, control, and automation systems.

3.2 Learning Objectives

This chapter reviews the main network models used for power system automation, focusing on communication redundancy and reliability within a substation, as required by IEC 61850. It discusses system models for a utility communication architecture that supports distributed functions at the process, bay, station, and corporate levels. These models will also help introduce the system-wide architecture models covered in Chapter 4, starting with the seven layers of the Open Systems Interconnection (OSI) model.

3.3 Open Systems Interconnection Model

The OSI model is an abstract framework standardized by the International Organization for Standardization (ISO) that divides network communication into layers, enabling communication using standard protocols. According to Figure 3.1, the OSI model is formed by seven layers. Each layer uses the lower-stacked layers

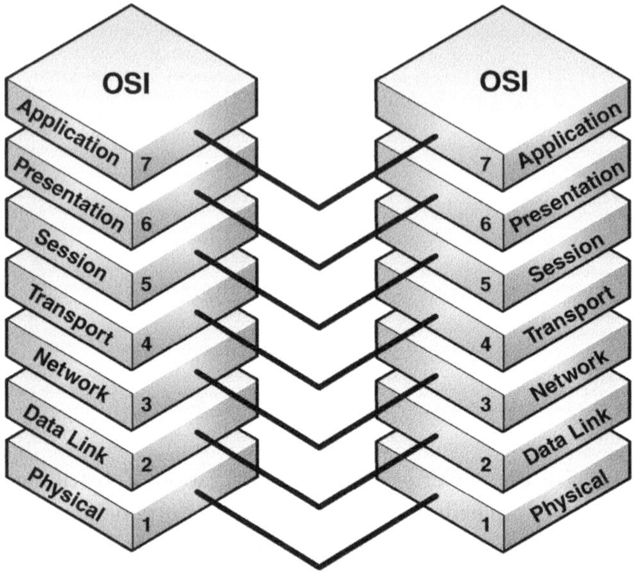

Figure 3.1 OSI communication model.

to communicate with the corresponding layer on another server, while providing communication services to the upper layers.

The upper Application layer defines partner identification, quality, authentication, and privacy for the application services. This layer uses services provided by the Presentation layer, which converts between visualization and syntax formats used by the connected applications. Each connection is initiated by the Session layer, which coordinates the start and completion of conversations and dialogs, utilizing the Transport layer for end-to-end control and error checking during data transfer. The Network layer routes and forwards data to the correct destination, using the Data Link layer for synchronization and bit-stuffing of binary strings into message packets, which are transferred through the network using the Physical layer. Figure 3.2 summarizes the primary function of each layer of the OSI model.

To compose the message, layers 2–7 add headers to the data string submitted by the Application layer, followed by a Data Link layer closing header, forming the packet of strings transmitted by the Physical layer. Figure 3.3 shows how these headers are added to create the packets transmitted by each OSI layer.

Network equipment is connected using a physical (or wireless) communication channel to deliver the messages among the OSI layers. Servers can be directly connected to the Physical layer using hubs, metal or optical cables, or wireless electromagnetic signals. At the Data Link layer, switches

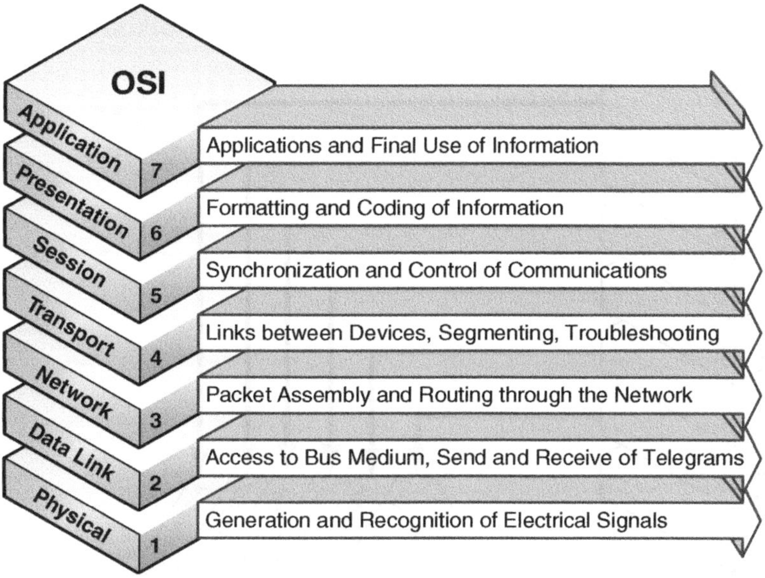

Figure 3.2 OSI communication model mapping.

deliver messages in a local area network. Routers deliver messages between local users or networks, while ATM routers usually route messages at the Transport layer, with retransmission and reassembly of lost packets. Figure 3.4 illustrates the connections among the seven OSI layers of two remote servers. This stacked architecture operates using a set of standard protocols that run at each layer.

3.4 Protocol Models

Several open and proprietary protocols are commonly used to implement each layer of the OSI reference model. At the upper layers—Application, Presentation, and Session—many mail and file transfer protocols are available, including the Simple Mail Transfer Protocol (SMTP), Telnet, and the File Transfer Protocol (FTP), as well as Telnet for remote administration. Most implementations use the Transmission Control Protocol (TCP) or the User Datagram Protocol (UDP) for the Transport layer. These are supported by several protocols at the Network layer, such as the Internet Protocol (IP), the Address Resolution Protocol (ARP), and the Reverse Address Resolution Protocol (RARP). Message addressing is encoded by several protocols at the Data Link layer, such as Ethernet and Token Ring, and delivered to the Physical layer, which is available through various technologies, including optical fiber, structured cabling, and

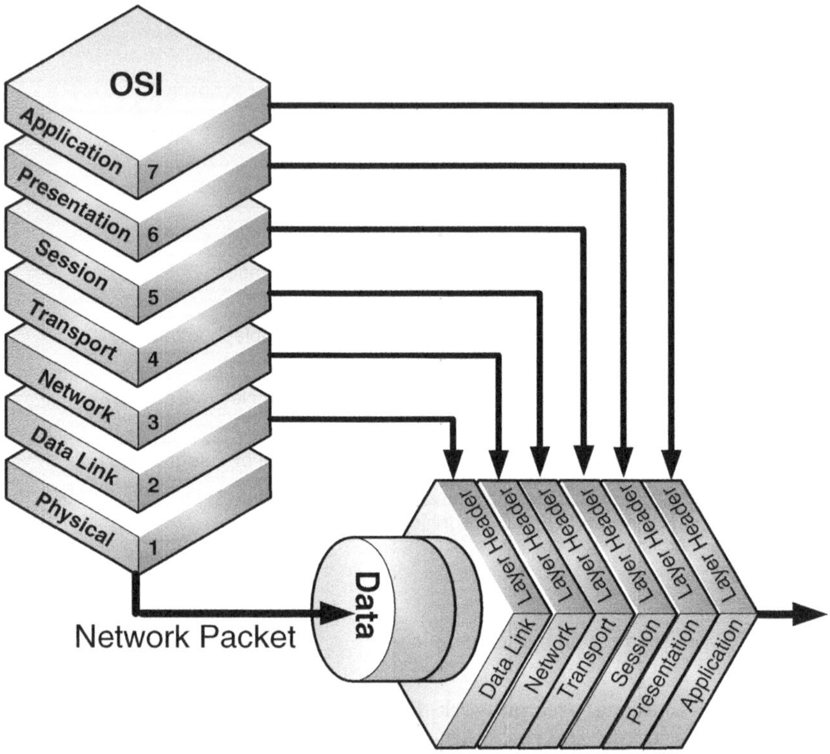

Figure 3.3 Message composition on the network.

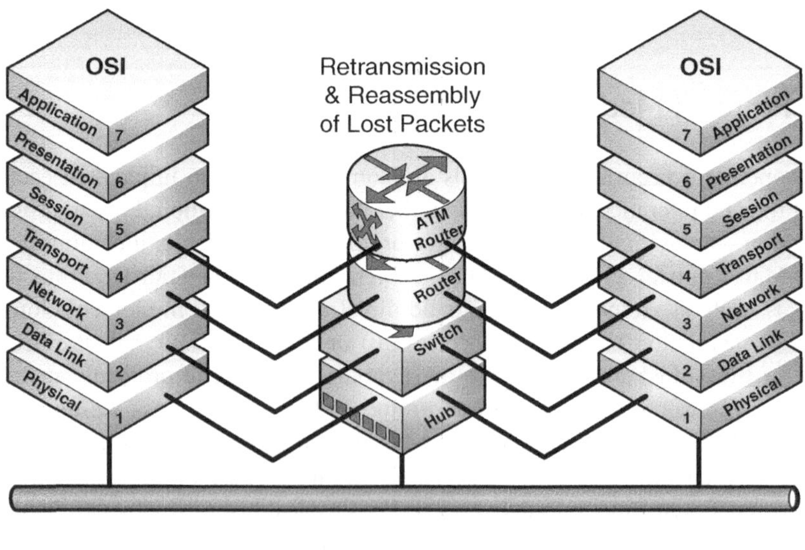

Figure 3.4 OSI communication at the Transport layer.

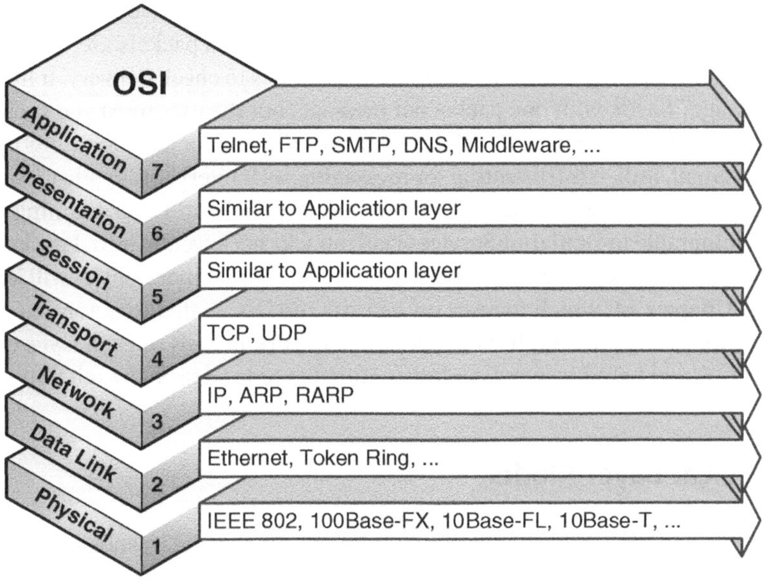

Figure 3.5 OSI model and protocols.

wireless networks based on standards like IEEE 802. These technologies include 100Base-FX (100 Mbps over fiber), 10Base-FL (10 Mbps over fiber), and 10Base-T (10 Mbps over twisted-pair copper). Figure 3.5 summarizes the protocols associated with each layer of the OSI reference model.

IP is the most widely used Network layer protocol on local Ethernet networks. IP can be used in unicast mode to transmit packets of data to a specific host, in multicast mode to transmit packets to a group of hosts, or in anycast mode to transmit packets to one of a group of hosts (typically the nearest). In IP, the destination and source of a message are identified by their IP addresses. All services are unreliable, and packets may be dropped, duplicated, and received out of order.

At the Transport layer, TCP runs above IP, using port numbers and checksums (like UDP) to ensure reliable message routing. The service is provided in order by stream, so the application does not know how the bytes are packed into packets. It includes flow and congestion control, as well as connection setup and teardown phases. It can introduce a considerable delay between bytes at the source and those at the destination due to timeouts and retransmissions. Contrary to IP, it works only with unicast (not multicast or anycast).

Similarly, UDP runs above IP, offering the same unreliable service as IP. Packets can get lost anywhere, in the outgoing buffer at the source address, at the router or link in the network, or at the incoming buffer at the destination. However, it adds port numbers used to identify "Application layer" protocols or processes, as well as an optional checksum to preserve message integrity.

For power system automation and IEC 61850 use, it is instructive to compare TCP to UDP as transport protocols. UDP is more real-time, as packets are sent or dropped without checking, but are not delayed by routines to check delivery. It has a more "message" flavor, with one packet per message, but the user must add their reliability mechanisms on top. TCP is ideal for transferring files or large amounts of data, such as email. Still, it is frustrating for messaging, as it interrupts applications that don't conform to message boundaries and lack "Application Layer Framing." TCP is also vulnerable to Denial-of-Service (DoS) attacks because the initial packet consumes resources at the receiver. Further communication vulnerabilities will be discussed in Chapter 14, which focuses on security models related to automation systems. The following paragraphs address some network models of each layer of interest to IEC 61850-based systems, mainly required to redundancy and reliability.

3.5 Physical Layer Model

The Physical level (layer 1) is the lowest layer of the OSI model, responsible for establishing the physical connection between devices and for transmitting raw data bits over a network medium. Physical redundancy can be introduced primarily at the lower layers of the OSI model. Figure 3.6 shows a duplicate channel

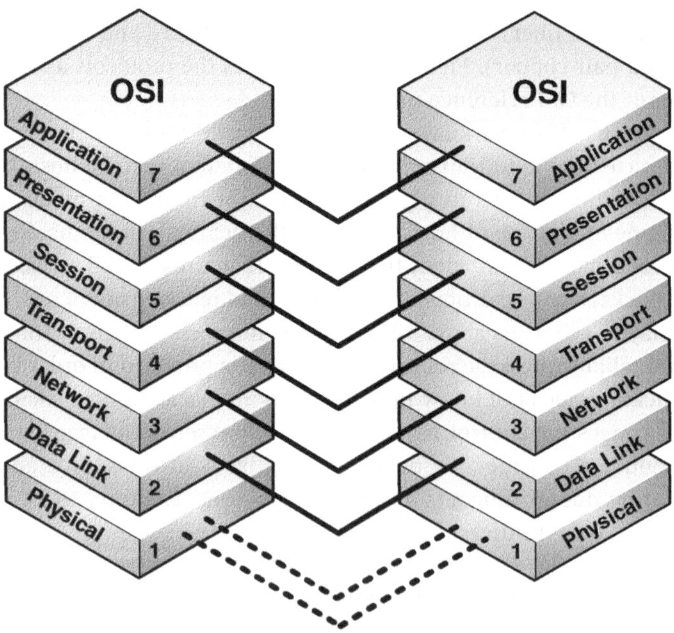

Figure 3.6 Redundancy at the Physical layer.

deployed at the Physical layer between two pieces of equipment in a local network. Routing cables through multiple conduits can achieve this, with various wires distributed across them to prevent complete connectivity loss if a conduit is damaged. It can also use redundant hardware, with multiple controllers and connections on each, to avoid a total loss in the event of hardware faults.

Figure 3.7 Bus network architecture.

Several physical architectures are possible for a local network, with varying levels of redundancy. The most basic scheme is a bus network, as shown in Figure 3.7, in which all switches (SW) are connected in a linear chain, forming a single bus to which all servers or Intelligent Electronic Devices (***IEDs***) of an automation system can be connected. Profibus DP is a typical example of this architecture. It is inexpensive, but a bus failure will affect all connected servers.

Figures 3.8 and 3.9 show examples of a typical SAS configuration employing a duplicated bus network architecture, both with two switches. The former connects a Human–Machine Interface (HMI) and a ***Gateway*** (for external communication) with three ***IEDs***, and a separate bus with two ***merging units*** (***MUs***) and ***control units*** (***CUs***) for monitoring and controlling switchyard equipment. The latter is a variant of the former in which all ***IEDs*** are connected to a shared, duplicated bus network.

The following physical basic scheme is a ring network, as shown in Figure 3.10, where the switches are connected in a circular formation, creating a single bus to which all ***IEDs*** can be connected. The advantage is that the integrity of the bus connection is kept even if one of the connections is broken.

Figures 3.11 and 3.12 show examples of typical SAS configurations employing ring network architectures with six switches. The former depicts a single station and ***process bus*** with an HMI and a ***Gateway*** for external communication connected to four ***IEDs***. The latter implements redundancy in a typical station and process bus with two rings, each with two switches, and an HMI and a ***Gateway*** connected to four ***IEDs***.

Another basic architecture is a star network, as shown in Figure 3.13, with switches connected radially to form a single bus that connects all substation ***IEDs***. A variant of this architecture is the tree network, as shown in Figure 3.14. The main disadvantage of these networks is that the integrity of the bus connection may be broken by the loss of just one of the connections.

Figure 3.15 illustrates a typical SAS configuration utilizing a double-star network, with each branch having a single switch. It depicts a single station and ***process bus*** with HMI and ***Gateway*** connected to four ***IEDs***. Redundancy results from each ***IED's*** connection to both networks, with an HMI and a ***Gateway*** for external communication.

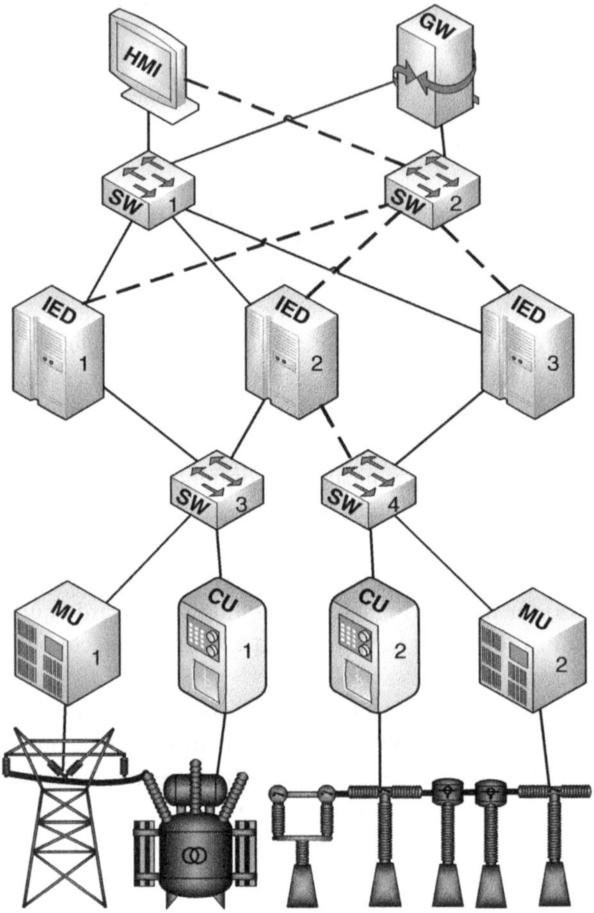

Figure 3.8 Double station and process networks.

A more elaborate architecture is a mesh network, as shown in Figure 3.16, where switches are connected freely, forming a meshed bus topology. The main advantage of these networks is that they can be tailored to different needs, offering alternative pathways for messages. Depending on the mesh topology and its redundancy protocol, the integrity of the bus connection can be preserved even when multiple connections are lost.

In addition to parallel physical paths, alternative paths at the Data Link layer of the OSI model can enhance network reliability, which is of interest to IEC 61850.

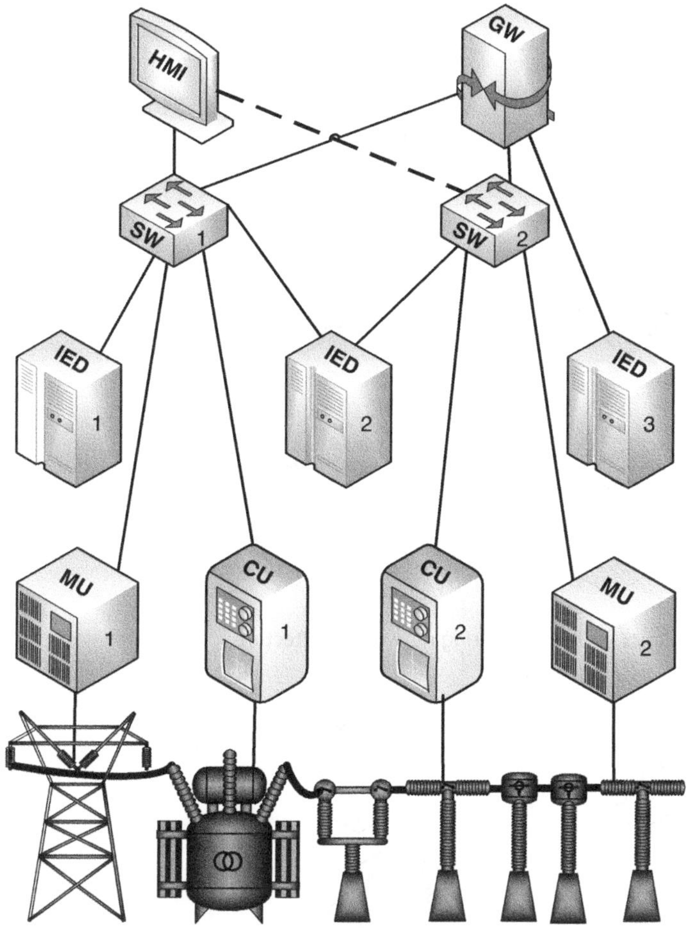

Figure 3.9 Redundancy of common process and station bus.

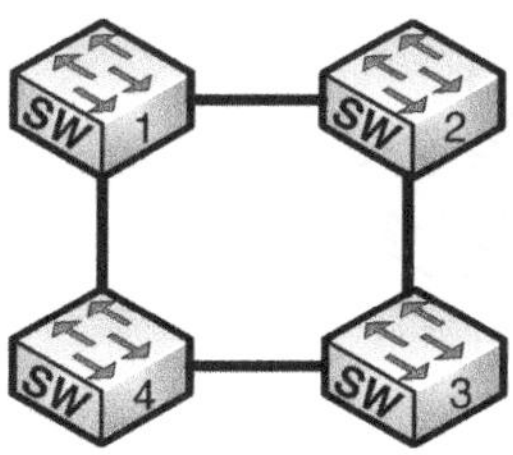

Figure 3.10 Ring network architecture.

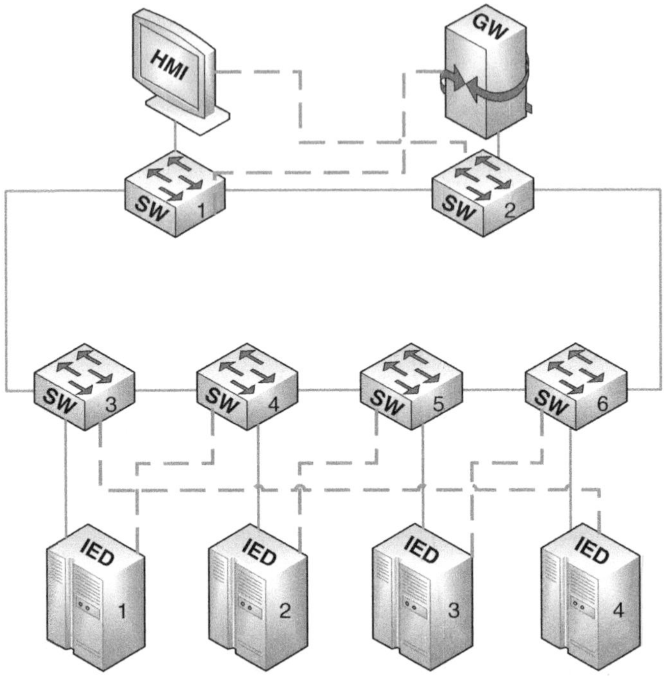

Figure 3.11 Redundancy with a single-ring network architecture.

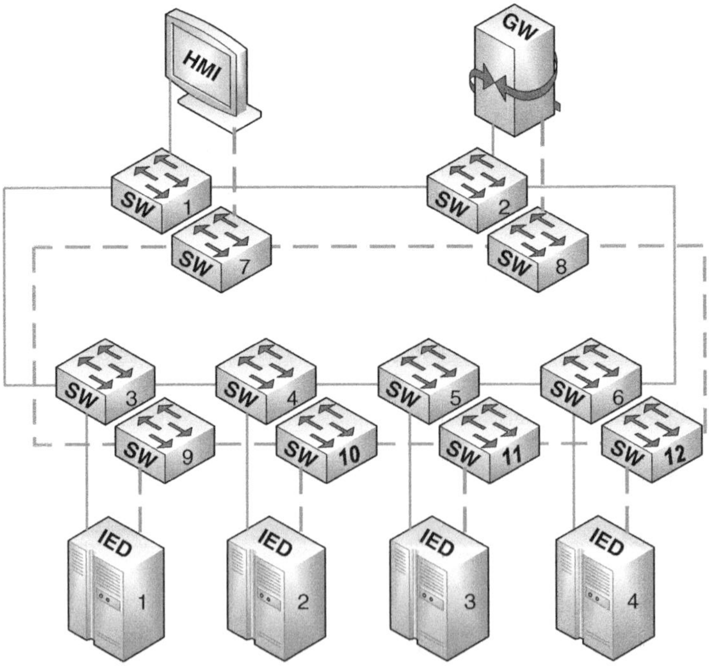

Figure 3.12 Doubled parallel-ring redundant network.

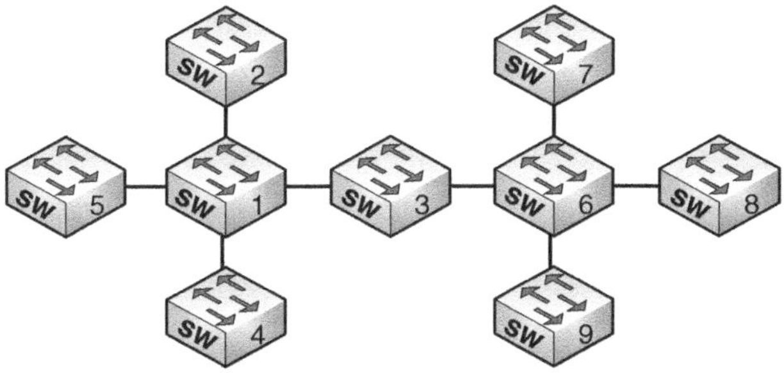

Figure 3.13 Star network architecture.

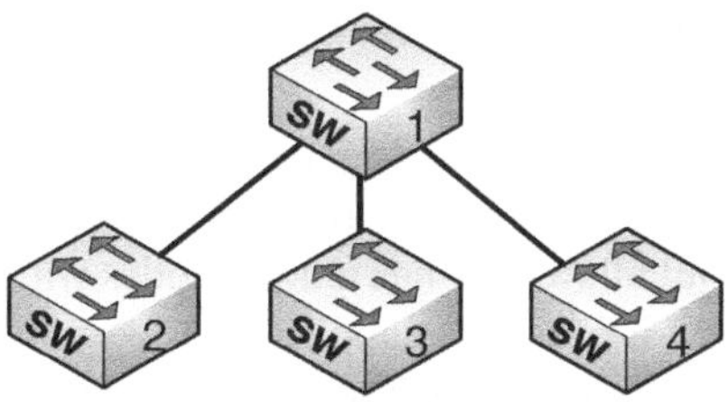

Figure 3.14 Tree network architecture.

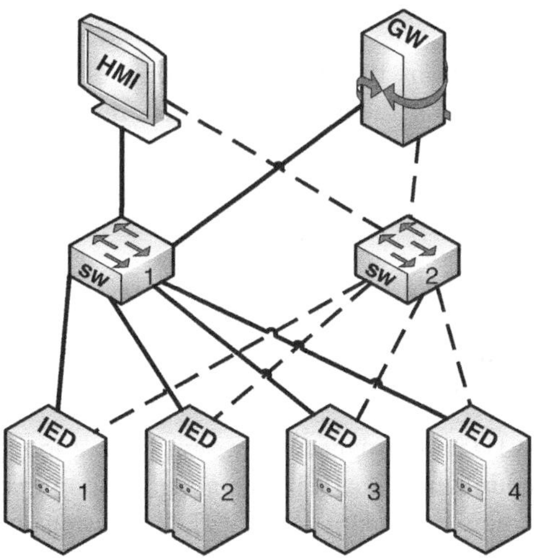

Figure 3.15 Redundant star network architecture.

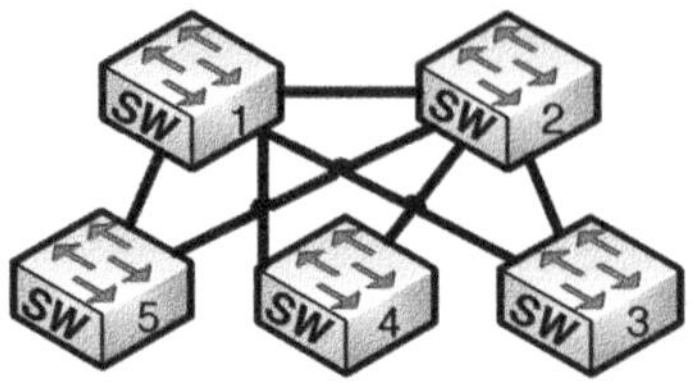

Figure 3.16 Mesh network architecture.

3.6 Data Link Layer Model

The Data Link (layer 2) of the OSI model is responsible for data transfer between two directly connected nodes on the same network segment. Path redundancy must be introduced at this layer to fully exploit the inherent reliability of a tree or mesh network, as shown in Figure 3.17.

The selection of the best path for messages in a mesh or ring network, a spanning tree, or an undirected graph must be mapped across the network, covering all nodes (switches) with a unique bus, without allowing rings among nodes with conflicting paths. Figures 3.18 and 3.19 show a possible mapping of links in a mesh and ring network, by dynamically selecting those switch ports assigned with a forward state (F), and those with a blocked state (B), so that the ports in the F state form a spanning tree over the network. In contrast, the B ports are blocked and assigned to state F when necessary, after a network failure.

In addition to physical replication of the various network segments, the management of the forward and blocking states of the Data Link layer ports can be accomplished using several algorithms that implement functional and recovery schemes to increase reliability. Among the most common are the following protocols:

- **STP**—Spanning Tree Protocol
- **RSTP**—Rapid Spanning Tree Protocol
- **MSTP**—Multiple Spanning Tree Protocol
- **PRP**—Parallel Redundancy Protocol
- **HSR**—High-availability Seamless Ring
- **LACP**—Link Aggregation Control Protocol

STP was standardized by IEEE 802.1D and designed to prevent layer 2 loops in Ethernet networks by disabling redundant links. It builds a logical loop-free tree by electing a Root Bridge and blocking redundant paths. RSTP is a faster version of STP, standardized by IEEE 802.1w, which provides enhanced port roles and handshake mechanisms to achieve faster topology convergence. The RSTP

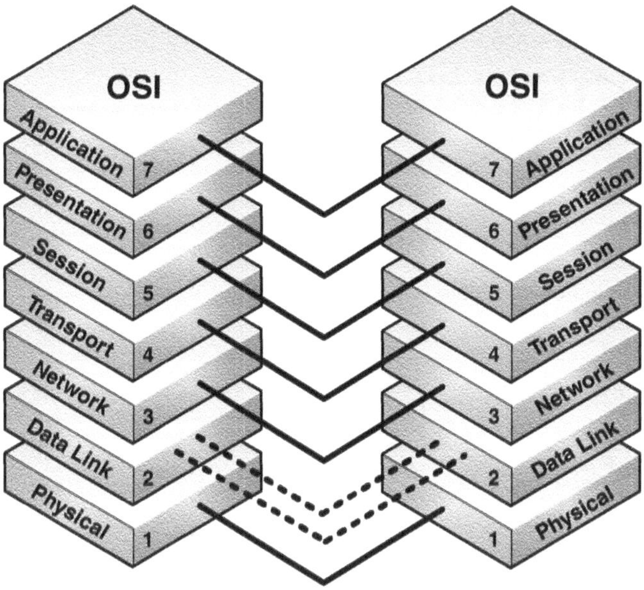

Figure 3.17 Redundancy at the Data Link layer.

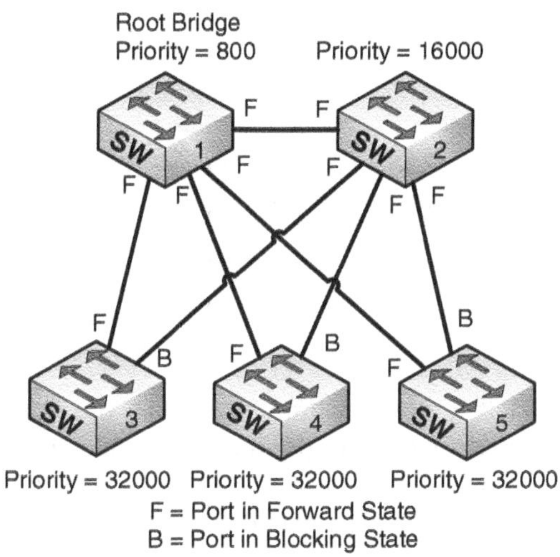

Figure 3.18 Spanning tree in a mesh network.

implements an algorithm (on the switches) that determines the best path between the source and destination of a message on the network, using alternate paths (Figure 3.20). If one of the paths fails, traffic will be automatically switched

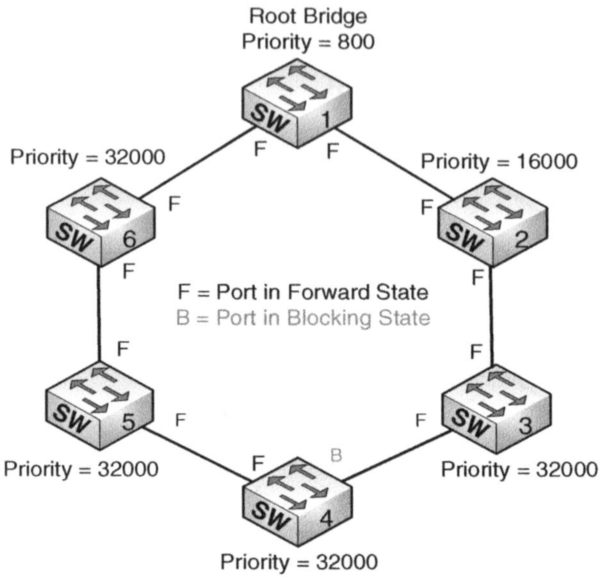

Figure 3.19 Spanning tree in a ring network.

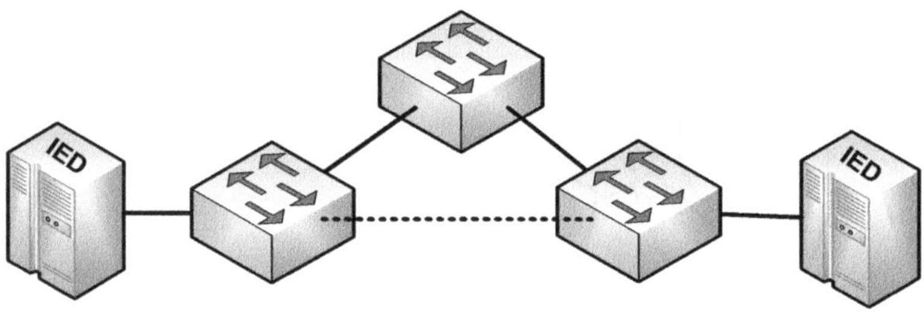

Figure 3.20 Spanning Tree Protocol.

to the alternate route. This switching will necessarily introduce a delay or recompositing time of a few milliseconds into the latency of trip messages, which must be added to the function's end-to-end operating time. If the network is used to transmit sampled analog values, packet loss may occur during the switching period, compromising the function. These aspects need to be considered and evaluated mainly for protection systems. Fault tolerance is achieved with a non-zero recovery time of approximately 1 second. The switches exchange Bridge Protocol Data Units (BPDUs) to decide the active topology, so that no duplicate frames are transmitted, but blocked links are underutilized until a failure. MSTP is standardized by IEEE 802.1e to allow multiple Virtual Local Area Networks (VLANs) to share a single spanning tree instance, optimizing link usage. It maps VLANs to Multiple Spanning Tree Instances (MSTIs), reducing CPU load and enabling load balancing, providing efficient use of redundant links with VLAN-based load distribution.

The PRP, defined in IEC 62439-3, introduced an alternative to the layer 2 management: redundant links operating on independent parallel paths, which would result in a null recovery time if one of the paths failed (Figure 3.21). This alternative can be implemented in *Mesh* (hybrid star ring) networks. PRP sends identical frames simultaneously over two independent LANs, enabling zero-recovery time—if one path fails, the other frame still arrives. It requires two separate, parallel networks, with duplicate frames transmitted on both, resulting in double bandwidth usage.

Finally, the HSR protocol, defined in IEC 62439-3, implements a particular case of the PRP for ring networks, guaranteeing a zero-restoration time if one of the ring arcs fails (Figure 3.22). In this case, each node is connected in a ring; frames are sent in both directions simultaneously, with zero recovery time if data arrives

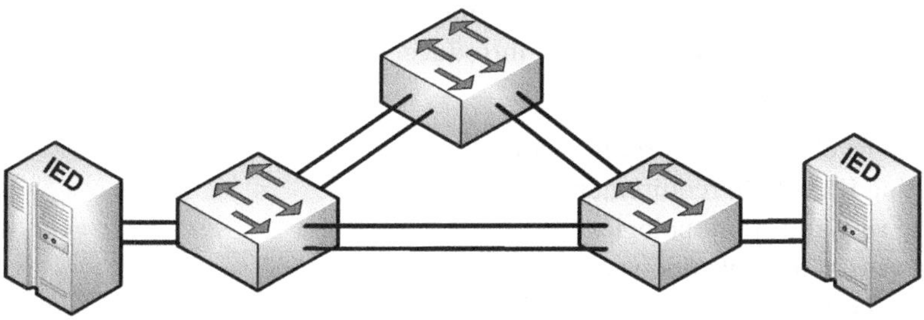

Figure 3.21 Parallel Redundancy Protocol.

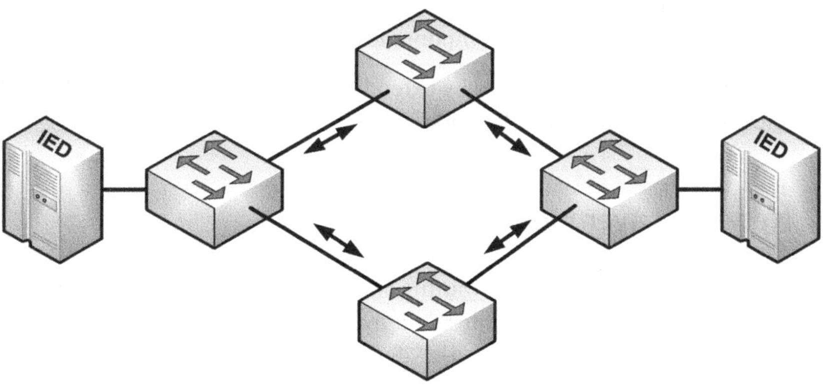

Figure 3.22 High-availability Seamless Ring.

Figure 3.23 LCAP-based Ethernet connection.

on the surviving path after one link fails. It requires a ring or a meshed network with multiple rings, where every switch forwards frames in both directions, using typically only 50% of available bandwidth.

LACP, as defined by IEEE 802.3ad, combines multiple physical links into a single logical link (Link Aggregation Group [LAG]) to provide higher bandwidth and redundancy. It dynamically negotiates and manages link aggregation across switches or devices, increasing throughput while providing layer 2 fault tolerance.

The distinguishing feature of each protocol is its failover time, or the time it takes to reroute messages after a link failure, forming a new spanning tree. STP takes an average of 30 seconds to recover, while RSTP takes 0.25–12 seconds. Additionally, the LACP manages virtual links of multiple ports among switches (Figure 3.23), allowing the definition of virtual spanning trees.

Both the PRP and HSR protocols introduce the following advantages for connected functions in local networks:

- Device-level Ethernet port duplication
- Meeting IEC 61850 requirements
- Using ring and star topologies
- Transparent to applications using the network
- Simple network functional fault tolerance
- Zero restoration time in the event of failure
- Independence from high-level external protocols
- RSTP compatibility
- Use of conventional network components (tools, switches, links).

Further reliability can be achieved by extending redundancy higher in the OSI communication stack, up to the Network layer.

3.7 Network Layer Model

The Network layer is responsible for routing and forwarding data packets between networks. Additionally, it encapsulates data into packets, handles fragmentation if needed, and reassembles them at the destination. Redundancy can also be deployed by the routing protocols at the Network layer of the OSI communication stack, as shown in Figure 3.24.

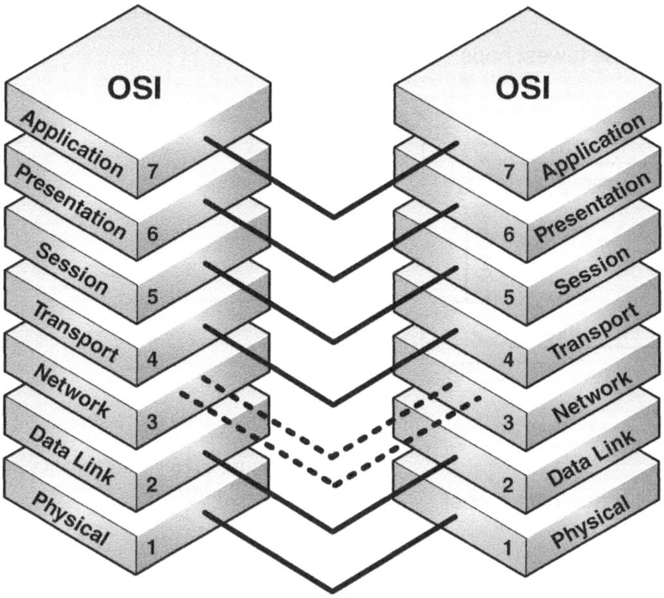

Figure 3.24 Redundancy at the Network layer.

Some specific routing protocols have been standardized to deploy redundancy at the Network layer, for instance:

- **RIP**—Routing Information Protocol
- **OSPF**—Open Short Path First

These protocols are distinguished by the priority assigned to the dynamic path used to route a message between two points in the network. RIP prioritizes the path with the fewest hops (Figure 3.25), while OSPF prioritizes the path with the lowest cost, exploring higher-bandwidth links (Figure 3.26).

Reliability can be further increased by deploying redundancy at the Transport layer of the OSI model.

3.8 Transport Layer Model

The Transport layer of the OSI model is responsible for reliable end-to-end data delivery between applications on different hosts. It manages communication between specific ports on devices, handles data segmentation and reassembly, and uses protocols such as TCP and UDP to provide services to the upper layers, including error control, flow control, and congestion control. Transport layer

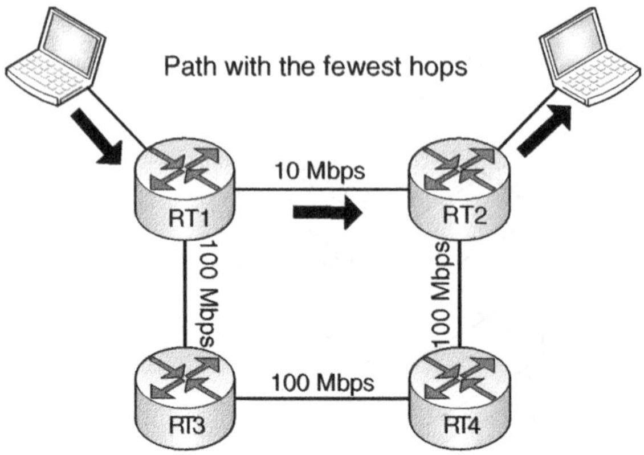

Figure 3.25 Redundancy by RIP.

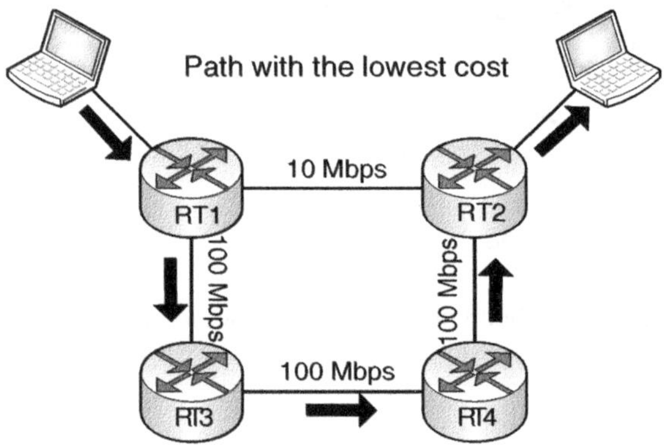

Figure 3.26 Redundancy by OSPF protocol.

redundancy focuses on ensuring continuous end-to-end communication even if a lower-layer network path, interface, or connection fails (Figure 3.27).

Several redundancy mechanisms are employed at this layer, such as:

- Multihoming via SCTP
- Redundancy via parallel TCP connections
- Multipath TCP
- UDP redundancy
- Transport layer redundancy
- Multiprotocol Label Switching (MPLS) Transport layer redundancy

Multihoming is a mechanism implemented using the Stream Control Transmission Protocol (SCTP), in which each endpoint can have multiple IP addresses. If one path fails, SCTP automatically switches to a secondary path without breaking the association. SCTP uses heartbeat signals, such as ***GOOSE*** messages, at layer 2 to test all paths. If the primary path fails (due to missing

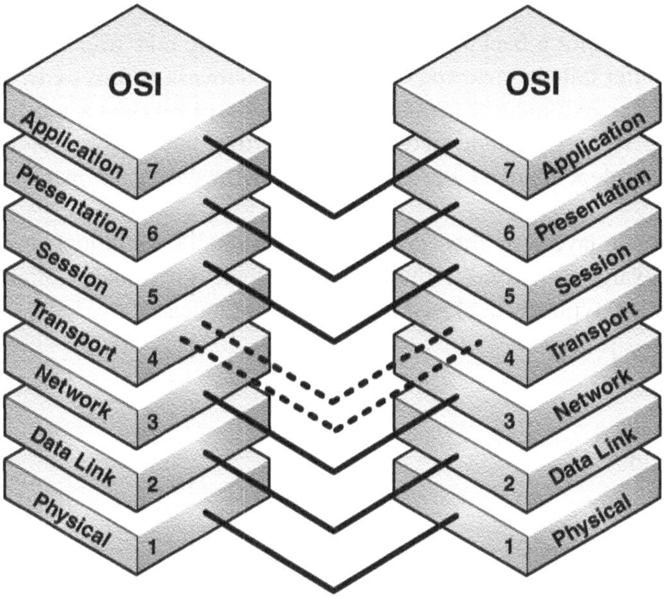

Figure 3.27 Redundancy at the Transport layer.

ACKs), SCTP activates an alternative route. Additionally, it utilizes multi-streaming to prevent head-of-line blocking by separating data into independent, ordered streams.

Redundancy via parallel TCP connections (Transport Bonding) can be implemented in the upper layers using parallel TCP sessions, since TCP has no native support for multihoming or multipath. It opens two or more TCP connections simultaneously to guarantee redundancy.

Multipath TCP (MPTCP) is a Transport layer redundancy extension of TCP that uses subflows within a single logical connection. If a path dies, MPTCP keeps the session alive through other sub-flows.

UDP redundancy (via Multipath or N-Duplication in applications) is an externally added mechanism, as UDP has no connection state and no native reliability mechanism. It is deployed by sending duplicate packets over multiple interfaces or using redundancy blocks such as Reed-Solomon, so that lost packets can be reconstructed.

Transport layer redundancy is a mechanism that typically uses protocols such as Virtual Router Redundancy Protocol (VRRP) or Hot Standby Router Protocol (HSRP). VRRP is a networking protocol that provides automatic default gateway redundancy for a local network. It allows multiple routers to form a virtual router with a single IP and MAC address, ensuring that if the primary router fails, a backup router automatically takes over, preventing network outages. HSRP is a network feature that enables a backup router to automatically take over in the event of a primary router failure, ensuring uninterrupted network connectivity.

MPLS Transport layer redundancy (Transport Profile—MPLS-TP) is a mechanism typically used in carrier-grade networks, supporting bidirectional path protection switching independent of the IP layer, and is heavily used in telco networks.

The remaining upper layers of the OSI model (Session, Presentation, and Application) are software layers used to implement the logic functionality of an IEC 61850-based system, typically deployed into four-level models:

- Process-level model
- Bay-level model
- Station-level model
- Corporate-level model

3.9 Process-level Model

According to IEC 61850, a process network directly connects ***MUs*** and ***CUs*** to process equipment, such as instrument transformers, circuit breakers, and power transformers. Figure 3.28 illustrates the typical connections of two ***MUs*** and two ***CUs*** to high-voltage disconnecting switches, circuit breakers, and instrument transformers in the process network of a transformer bay substation.

Being near high-voltage equipment, ***process networks*** must comply with strict requirements for primary systems, such as electromagnetic compatibility, temperature, and shock resistance, where applicable. Sometimes they are deployed inside the main container of the controlled equipment. To transport fast-transient messages, adequate bandwidth must be provided for continuous data streams and highly prioritized trip signals to transmit data from the protection device to the circuit breakers, while also transmitting data to the station bus/data filtering at the coupling point. This includes simultaneous TCP/IP traffic for standard control and status signal transmission, process bus reports, a download/upload channel for setting and parameterizing

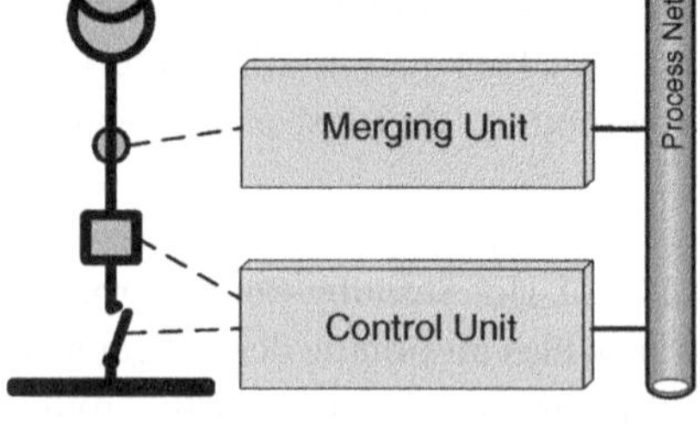

Figure 3.28 Process network example.

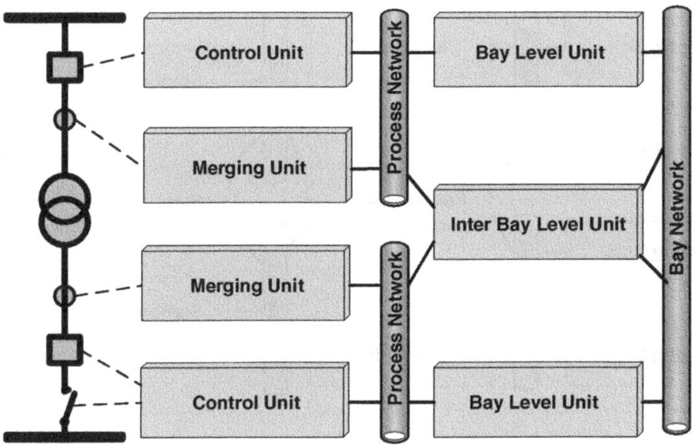

Figure 3.29 Multiple bay-level network architecture.

functions, exact time synchronization, and redundancy to enhance the bay-level network's reliability.

3.10 Bay-level Model

A substation automation network can also be structured into several segments, one per bay or feeder. This helps isolate each bay from the others and organizes the ***IEDs*** in network segments and cybersecurity domains. Figure 3.29 illustrates a typical architecture for a bay-level network for a transformer bay in a substation.

In this example, a bay network connects bay-level units specific to the high- and low-voltage sides of the transformer, and possibly an inter-bay unit to process functions common to both sides. In this example, two process networks connect the merging and control units on each side to support the station-wide level functions.

3.11 Station-level Model

At a higher level, bay-level networks can also be coordinated by a station-level network. This level is dedicated to communication between bay-level networks and among ***IEDs*** with functions related to the whole station. Figure 3.30 illustrates a typical configuration for a ***station network*** that connects three station units (***IEDs***) for station-level functions, as well as the bay and process networks of the transformer bay introduced in the previous paragraph.

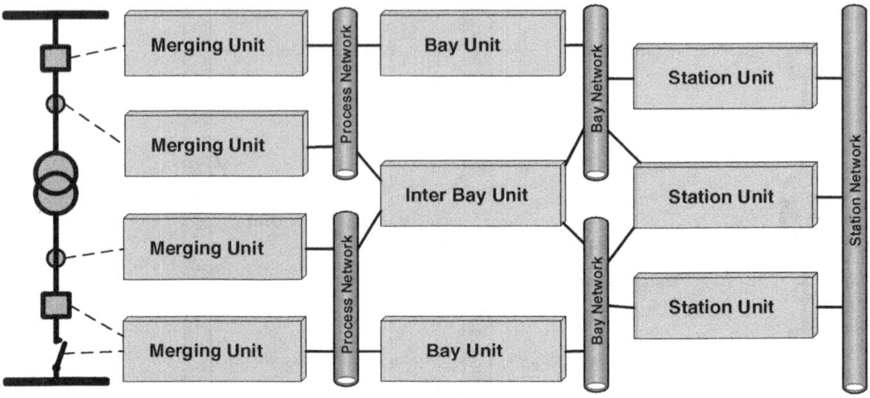

Figure 3.30 Station-level network.

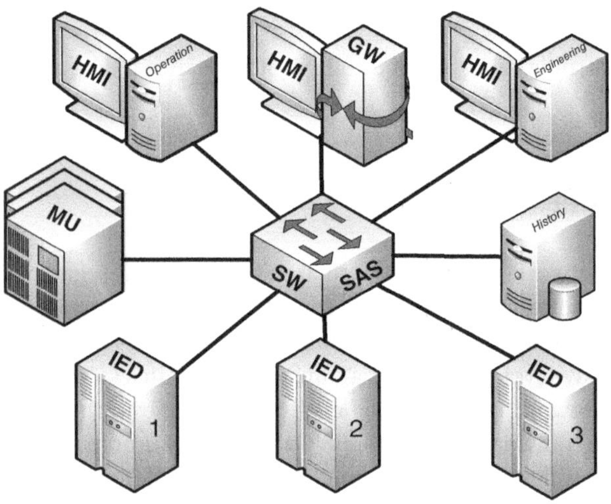

Figure 3.31 Typical substation physical architecture.

Physically, all these networks can be deployed as logical segments using a single switch or centralized network, as shown in Figure 3.31, connecting several HMI units and ***gateways***, a historian, and all substation ***IEDs***. The deployment depends on hardware availability and the security requirements enforced.

Alternatively, for reliability and security reasons, the physical network can be split into two parallel networks, as shown in Figure 3.32, requiring duplicate network ports in some ***IEDs***. For the same reasons, the network can be further segmented into two redundant ***station networks*** and ***process networks*** for different substation parts, as shown in Figure 3.33.

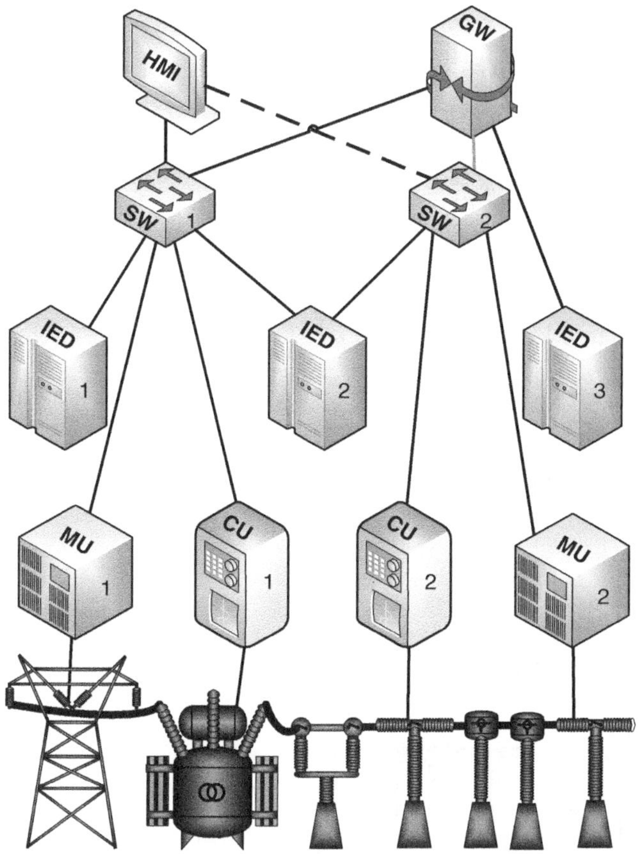

Figure 3.32 Redundancy of common process and station bus.

Outside the substations, several architectural models are possible for connecting the local systems to the corporate-level networks.

3.12 Corporate-level Model

The corporate-level architecture defines the connection between the substation network and corporate network, allowing the exchange of messages between the station and remote SCADA systems using IEC 61850. Several arrangements are possible for this architecture:

- Dual-homed HMI computers
- Dual-homed historian server with firewall

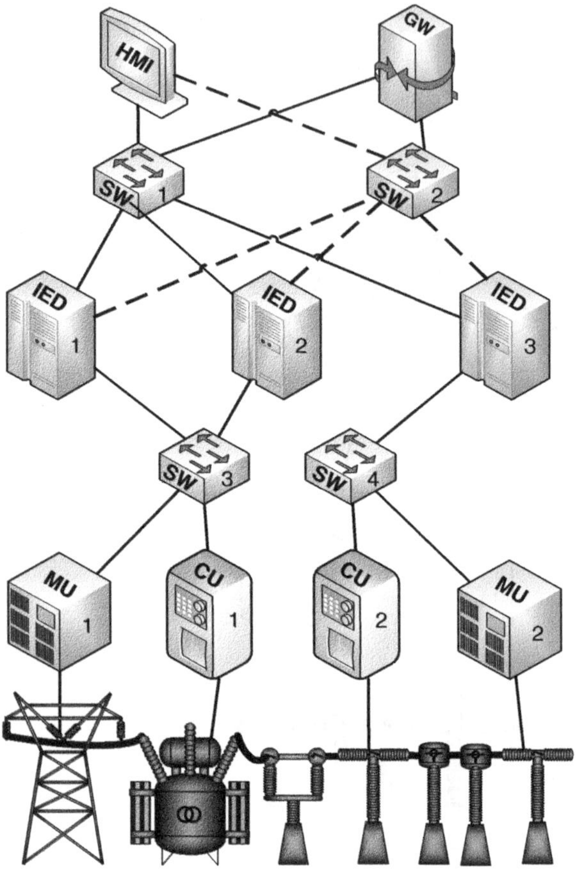

Figure 3.33 Double protection and station and process networks.

- Packet filtering between networks
- Firewall with historian
- Firewall with bridge/router
- Firewall with demilitarized zones (DMZs)
- Double firewall with DMZs
- Double firewall and DMZ and VLAN

A dual-homed HMI architecture uses an HMI server as a `gateway` (*GW*) with two network ports to connect the `station network` to the external network switch and router, as shown in Figure 3.34. It is a low-cost arrangement with only two Network Interface Cards (NICs), making it easy for the HMI to implement and administer locally. The main disadvantages are the single point of failure at the `gateway` and the difficulty of remotely administering `IEDs` and historians.

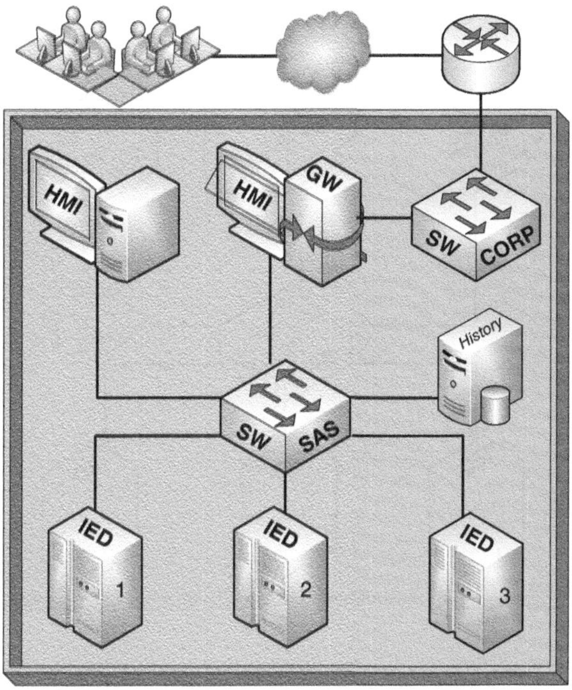

Figure 3.34 Dual-homed HMI computers.

The dual-homed historian server with firewall of Figure 3.35 shows a slightly different architecture. Instead of an HMI, a historian with two NICs runs specific software to interface the local network to the external switch/router. It is also a low-cost, easy-to-implement arrangement with added security. Again, the main disadvantages are the single point of failure at the historian and the difficulty of remotely administering `IEDs` and firewalls.

A different architecture can be built using packet filtering between the networks, as shown in Figure 3.36. A dedicated bridge connects the local `station network` to the external switch/router. The advantages are similar to the dual-homed historian server with firewall architecture, but with reduced protection provided by the bridge/router connection.

Figure 3.37 depicts a variant of this architecture in which the firewall and historian are connected to the `station network`. Like the previous arrangement, it offers enhanced security but requires opening external gates to remotely access the historian.

As shown in Figure 3.38, the historian can be connected directly to the external network to circumvent this restriction. However, in this case, the gates need to be open to connect the `IEDs` to the historian.

A bridge provides a variation of this arrangement with a firewall to connect the local network to the corporate external network, as shown in Figure 3.39. This

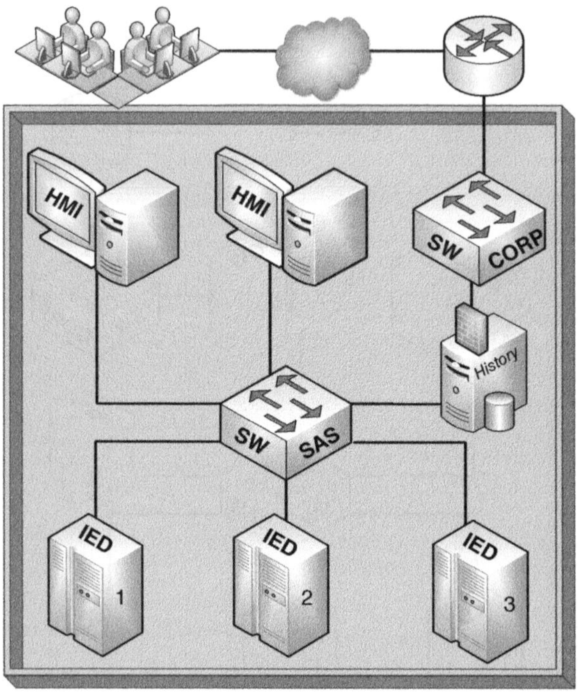

Figure 3.35 Dual-homed historian server with firewall.

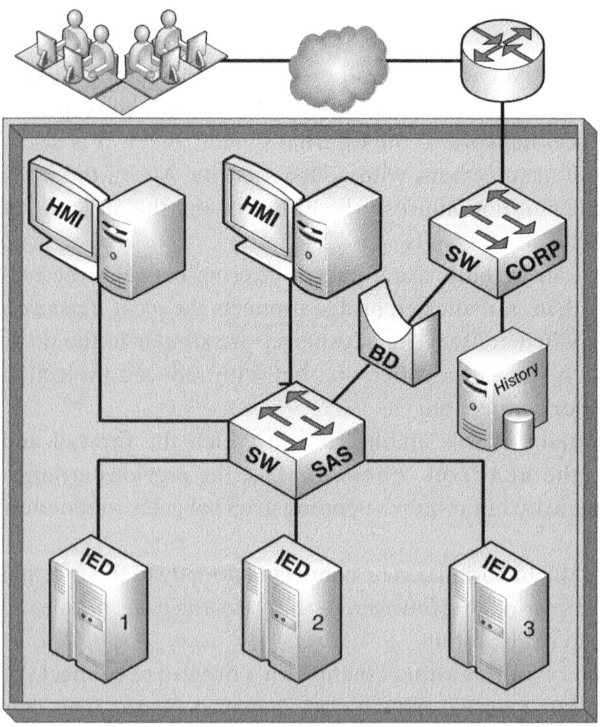

Figure 3.36 Packet filtering (bridge) between networks.

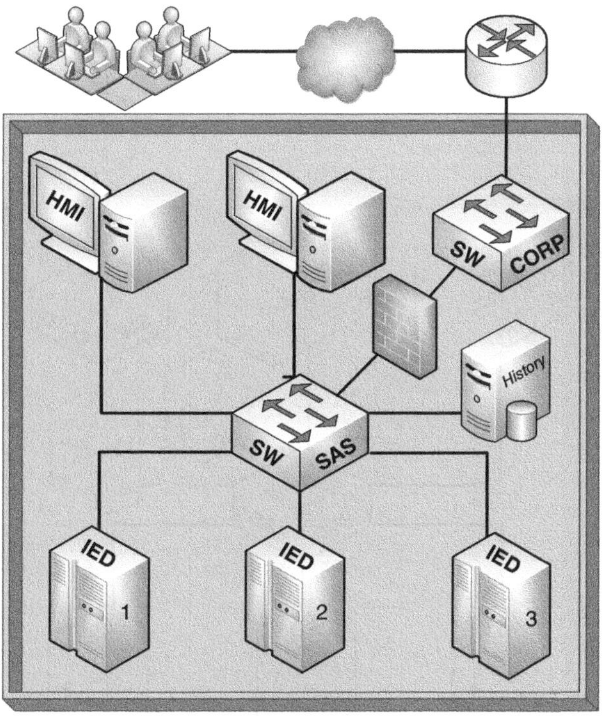

Figure 3.37 Firewall with historian on substation network.

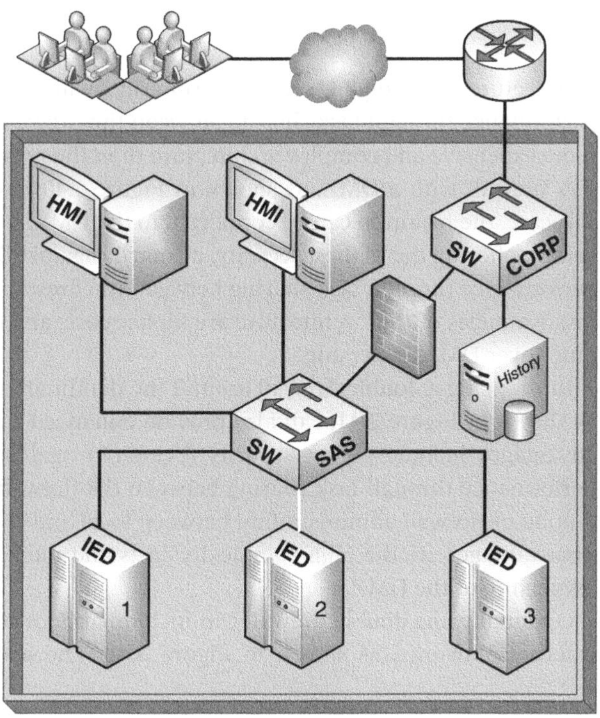

Figure 3.38 Firewall with historian on corporate network.

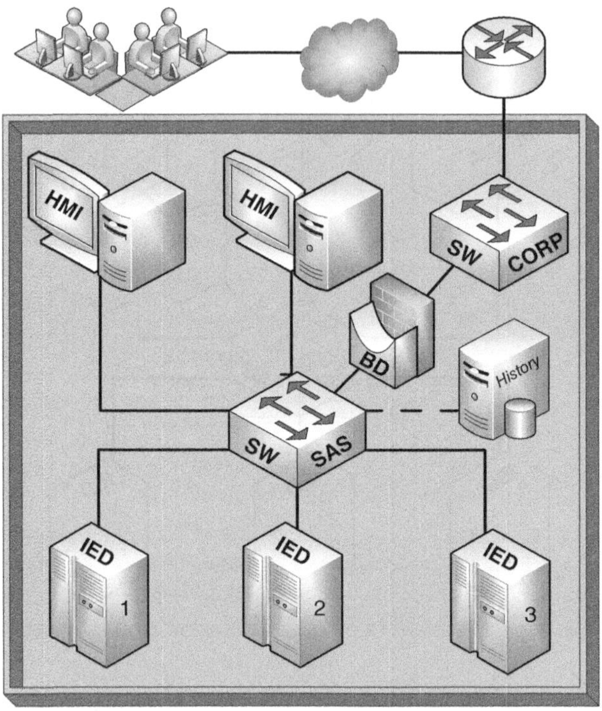

Figure 3.39 Firewall with bridge/router.

architecture offers higher security, primarily against DoS attacks, and improved performance through task sharing between the firewall and the router. But it is a more expensive and complex architecture than the previous one.

A firewall with a DMZ, as shown in Figure 3.40, provides higher security. In this case, the historian can be connected to the DMZ, integrated into the firewall/bridge, offering the highest security, primarily against DoS attacks, and improved performance through task sharing between the firewall and the router. The main disadvantages of this architecture are higher costs and complexity, as well as disputes over DMZ ownership.

Introducing a double firewall around the demilitarized zone in the substation, as shown in Figure 3.41, can also provide enhanced security. This architecture's advantages include higher security (primarily against DoS attacks), improved performance through task sharing between the firewall and the switch, and separation of firewall administration between local and remote networks. The main disadvantages are the high complexity costs and the potential for a dispute over ownership of the DMZ.

Optionally, the double firewall can include bridges connecting to the local and external networks, as shown in Figure 3.42. The advantages include extreme

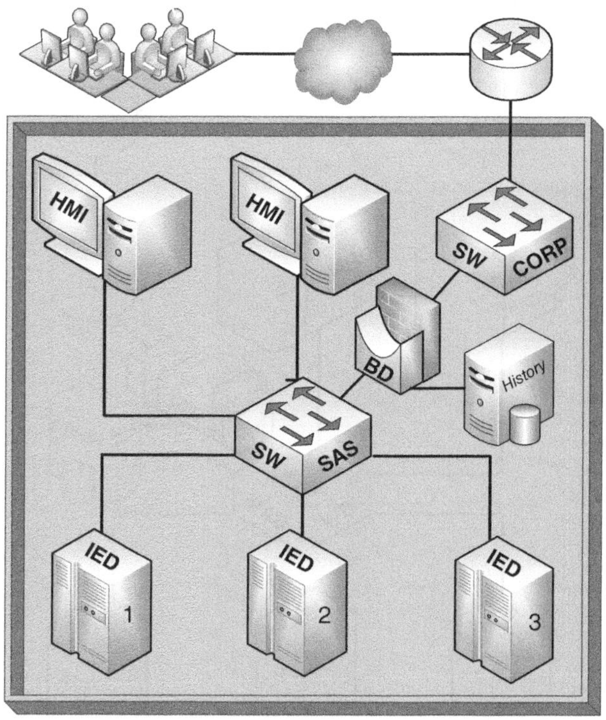

Figure 3.40 Firewall with demilitarized zone.

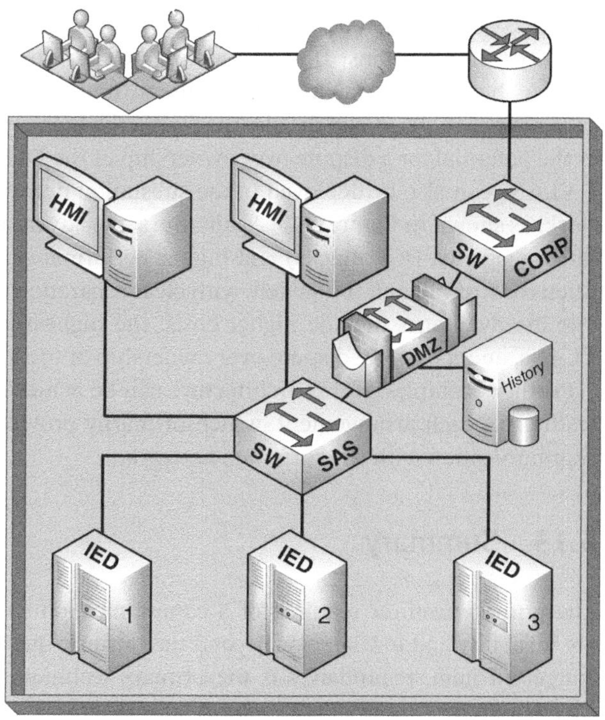

Figure 3.41 Double firewall with demilitarized zone.

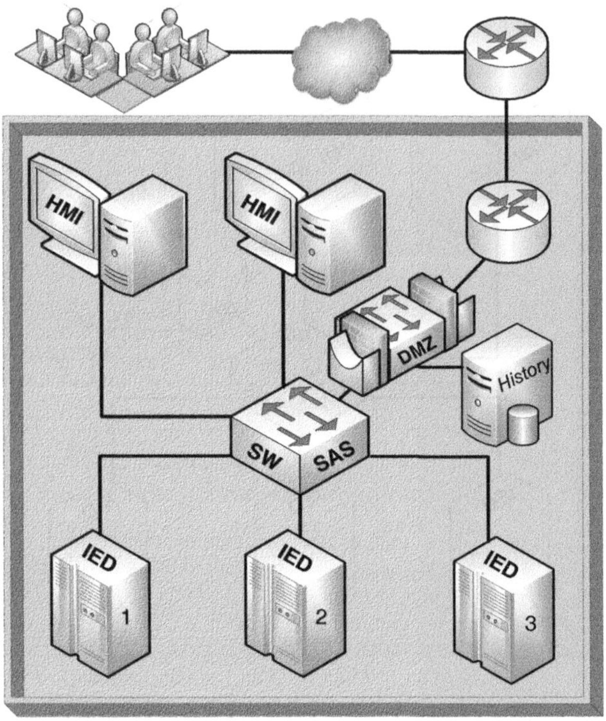

Figure 3.42 Double firewall and router with demilitarized zone.

security (mainly against DoS attacks), higher performance through task sharing among the firewall, switch, and routers, and a clear separation of firewall administration. The main disadvantages are the high costs and complexity, as well as the potential for a dispute over ownership of the DMZ.

VLANs can also be deployed in the substation network to secure the local network, as shown in Figure 3.43. Again, the same advantages apply: higher security (mainly against DoS attacks) and higher performance through task sharing between the firewall and the switch, with clear separation of firewall administration. The disadvantages include higher costs, the highest level of complexity due to VLANs, and a possible dispute over ownership of the local DMZ.

Further examples of this architecture can be achieved by replicating the main features of each arrangement, which primarily provide additional reliability for communication with the corporate network.

3.13 Summary

The primary features required of a communication structure in a power system are reliability and low latency. Beyond the intrinsic quality and technology of each connected item, redundancy is the primary technique for ensuring higher data

Figure 3.43 Double firewall and demilitarized zone with VLAN.

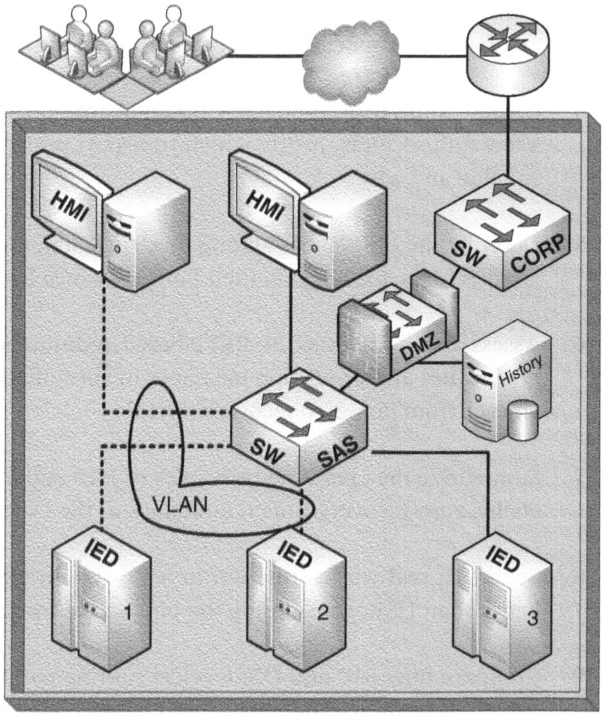

transmission reliability. Redundancy can be achieved by duplicating the communication network, replicating connections from ***IEDs*** to the network, or using redundant applications, such as duplicated protection systems for each piece of equipment.

Low latency is achieved by IEC 61850 by mapping real-time messages to the lower layers of the OSI communication model. Redundancy is implemented by duplicating hardware and routing software in the upper layers. As described in this chapter, various architectural models can support communication inside and outside the substation in accordance with IEC 61850. These aspects will also influence the distributed architectures discussed in Chapter 4, which are mainly based on software models.

3.14 Review Questions

1 List the seven layers of the OSI model and briefly explain the main function of each layer.

2 Explain how headers are added to a message during OSI layer encapsulation and discuss why this process is crucial for reliable communication.

3 Compare TCP and UDP as transport protocols in IEC 61850 applications, emphasizing latency, reliability, and cybersecurity risks.

4 Given a substation protection function that must send trip signals within a few milliseconds, justify which transport protocol (TCP or UDP) is more suitable and why.

5 Describe the differences among bus, ring, star, and mesh physical network architectures, focusing on their fault-tolerance features.

6 Assess the limitations of RSTP-based redundancy for transmitting sampled values and protection messages in substations. What operational risks emerge from non-zero recovery times?

7 Summarize the operating principles of PRP and HSR and explain how they enable zero-recovery-time redundancy at the Data Link layer.

8 Suggest a real-world situation in a substation where using PRP would be better than HSR, considering the physical setup and device features.

9 Compare how RIP and OSPF select routing paths in layer 3 networks and explain how these differences could impact communication performance in environments with multiple substations.

10 Assess how Transport layer mechanisms such as SCTP multihoming or multipath TCP enhance end-to-end reliability compared to traditional TCP alone.

11 Examine the process-, bay-, station-, and corporate-level models in IEC 61850-based systems. Provide an example of a communication function that depends on coordination between at least two of these levels.

12 Compare the security and reliability trade-offs among different corporate-level architectures, such as dual-homed HMI, DMZ-based firewalls, and VLAN-segmented designs. Determine the conditions where a utility would need the most complex configuration.

4

Architecture Models

4.1 Introduction

Distributed systems have evolved as a technological trend since the rise of personal computers and local networks. From administrative offices to factory floors in major industrial plants, mainframe computers have been replaced by portable, affordable platforms, marking the beginning of the distributed systems era. This change was made possible by new software paradigms for implementing distributed systems, based on the network models discussed in Chapter 3. This trend was further extended with the automation of the power grid, which faced the challenge of managing a large number of geographically dispersed power plants.

4.2 Learning Objectives

After a brief introduction to physical and virtual computers, this chapter describes the various models of dispersed systems and their evolution toward either a distributed or centralized system, also supported by IEC 61850. The following types of distributed architectures will be discussed, with their acronyms:

- Distributed Systems
- Remote Access Systems (RAS)
- Client–Server Systems (C/SS)
- Remote Procedure Calls (RPCs)
- Distributed Object Systems (DOS)
- Peer-to-Peer (P2P) Systems
- Service-Oriented Systems (SOS)
- Distributed Real-time Systems (DRTS)
- Distributed Systems Based on IEC 61850
- Centralized Systems Based on IEC 61850

4.3 Physical Machines

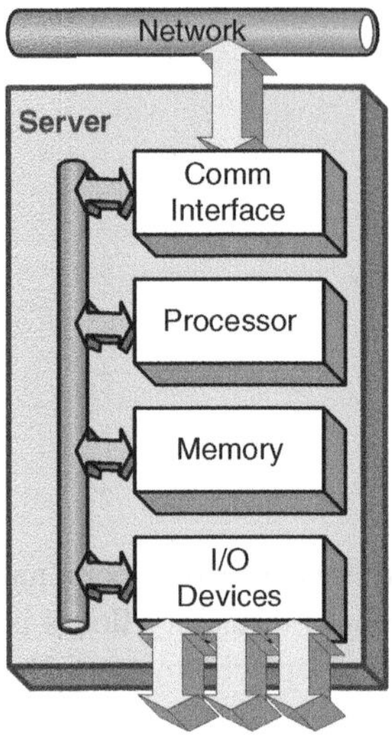

Figure 4.1 Hardware overview of a computer.

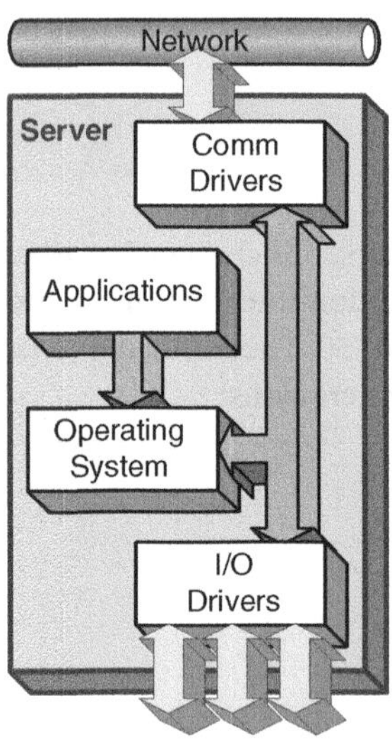

Figure 4.2 Software overview of a computer.

In a conventional computer, each application server requires dedicated physical modules that include a processor (CPU), memory, Input/Output (I/O) devices, and communication interfaces to connect to external networks. Figure 4.1 illustrates the hardware overview of a typical computer. These physical devices support the operation of several pieces of software, including the operating system, applications, I/O drivers, and communication drivers, which connect to external networks. Figure 4.2 illustrates the corresponding software overview of a typical computer. In this view, applications run under an operating system, which manages I/O and communication drivers, as well as all computer resources, making it a natural model for implementing automation systems.

As IEC 61850 was designed to be independent of hardware implementation, it is a natural evolution to be deployed in virtual machines (VMs).

4.4 Virtual Machines

Virtualization is a technique that enables more efficient use of physical computer hardware by creating an abstraction layer over the hardware, mimicking multiple physical computers dedicated to various applications. It is considered a long-lived architecture, providing flexibility and evolvability for virtual ***Intelligent Electronic Device*** (***vIED***) servers. Two common architectures utilize VMs (Figure 4.3) and containers (Figure 4.4). VMs operate under an orchestration layer known as a hypervisor, which allows the hardware elements of a single computer—such as processors, memory, storage, networking, and more—to be partitioned into multiple VMs. Each VM runs its own operating system and behaves like an independent computer, even though it runs on only a portion of the underlying hardware. A container is a lightweight, portable unit

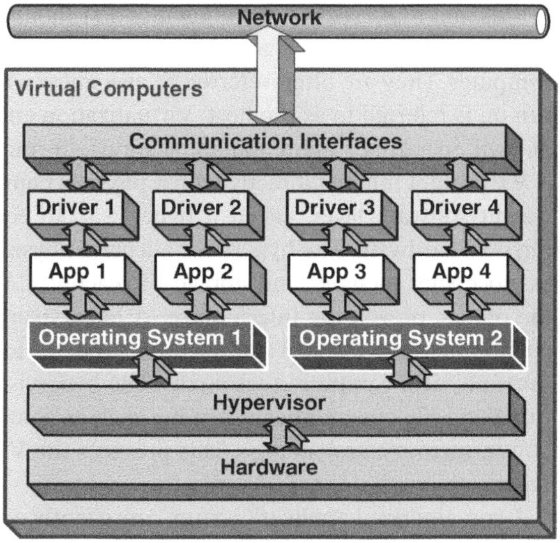

Figure 4.3 Virtual machines.

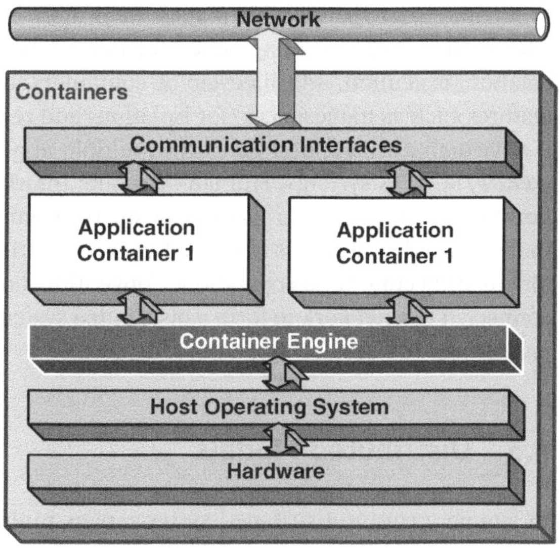

Figure 4.4 Containerization.

that packages an application together with everything it needs to run—such as operating system, libraries, system tools, and configuration files—in an isolated environment. Each container runs its own operating system and behaves like an independent computer, even though it runs on just a portion of the underlying hardware, under an orchestration layer known as a container engine.

VMs and hypervisors, also known as VM monitors, are two essential concepts in virtualization. A VM is a simulated representation, or emulation, of a physical computer. They are often referred to as a guest while the physical machine they run on is referred to as the host. Virtualization enables multiple VMs, each with its own operating system and applications, to run on a single physical machine. A VM cannot interact directly with a physical computer. Instead, it needs a lightweight software layer, called a hypervisor, to coordinate with the underlying physical hardware. The hypervisor allocates physical computing resources—such as processors, memory, and storage—to each VM. It keeps each VM separate from the others, preventing interference. A hypervisor is a small software layer that enables multiple instances of operating systems to run concurrently, sharing the same physical computing resources. The hypervisor manages these VMs as they run alongside one another, assigning each its share of the underlying computing power, memory, and storage. This prevents the VMs from interfering with each other.

A containerized application runs consistently across different environments—from a developer's laptop to production servers or cloud platforms, because all dependencies are included. They share the same operating system kernel but run in separate user spaces. This makes them more efficient than VMs, which each require their own operating system instance. The container engine manages the creation, execution, and lifecycle of containers, utilizing host operating system features such as namespaces (for isolation) and resource control.

A virtualized computer can host multiple applications or services, including ***vIEDs***, SCADA systems, Human–Machine Interfaces (HMIs), and databases, in flexible, scalable, and hardware-agnostic environments. They are primarily used in centralized systems, as described in Section 3.13, where redundancy is crucial for ensuring continuous operation. Conventional or virtualized computers can be connected to a network to form a distributed system, as described in the following paragraph.

4.5 Distributed Models

In simple terms, a distributed system spans multiple computers. Some components may reside on computers in the same room, an adjacent office, another city, or on the other side of the world—in other words, a collection of autonomous computers linked by a network, with software designed to produce an integrated computing facility. A well-designed distributed system should be perceived as a single, integrated computing facility. As a result, designing and testing these systems is more complex than designing and testing a monolithic system. The introduction of Local Area Networks (LANs) at the beginning of the 1970s triggered the development of distributed systems with six key characteristics:

- Support for resource sharing
- Openness
- Concurrency
- Scalability
- Fault tolerance
- Transparency

Resource sharing refers to the range of valuable resources that can be shared in a distributed system. It includes items such as printers, disks, CD-ROMs, and data. A resource manager is a software module that manages a set of resources of a particular type.

Openness is the characteristic of a system that can be extended in various ways, such as through hardware and software additions. Historically, computer systems were largely closed until the UNIX operating system broke that mold.

Concurrency in a distributed system does not necessarily mean concurrency within a single program. It can be achieved by allowing multiple users to invoke similar commands or by enabling multiple different server processes to run simultaneously. Synchronization, of course, is an issue that needs to be solved in these systems.

Scalability is the property of a distributed system that operates across multiple scales, ranging from two workstations and a file server to several client–server computers. Often, the more important question is not if you can scale, but if you can scale well. The Internet is the ultimate example of the unlimited scalability of distributed systems.

Fault tolerance refers to a system's ability to recover from failures. It is required in some systems but may be a nuisance value in others. Fault-tolerant design is based on two approaches: hardware redundancy and software recovery. Hardware redundancy occurs when two computers are employed for a single application, one acting as a standby. It is a very costly, but often very effective solution. Redundancy can be planned at a finer grain when individual servers are replicated, or redundant hardware is used. On the other side, software redundancy can be designed so that the state of permanent data can be recovered or "rolled back" when a fault is detected, using some transaction processing.

Transparency refers to the concealment of component separation in a distributed system. It can be related to access, location, concurrency, replication, failure, migration, performance, and scaling. Access and location transparency are the two most important forms of transparency, sometimes referred to as network transparency, and can be demonstrated through e-mails and web addresses.

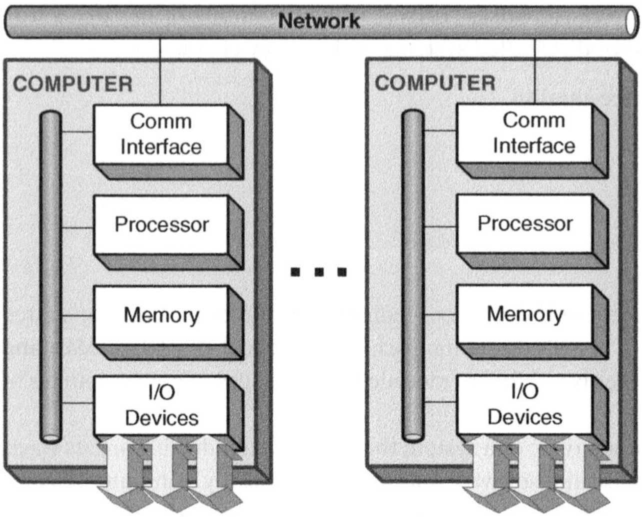

Figure 4.5 Hardware overview of a distributed system.

Specific design issues in distributed systems include naming conventions (assigning names to resources), communication, software structure, and workload allocation. Figure 4.5 depicts a hardware overview of a distributed system. One network links several computers, each composed of a communication interface, a processor, memory banks, and I/O devices.

Figure 4.6 depicts a software overview of the same distributed system. One network links several software nodes, which are composed of communication drivers, applications, an operating system, and I/O drivers.

Besides all its advantages, distributed systems also have some disadvantages:

- **Complexity**—typically, distributed systems are more complex than centralized systems
- **Security**—more vulnerable and susceptible to external attack
- **Manageability**—more effort required for system management
- **Unpredictability**—erratic responses depending on the system organization and network load

These disadvantages may come from some fallacious assumptions in the operation of distributed systems, such as the following:

- The network is reliable.
- Latency is zero.
- Bandwidth is infinite.

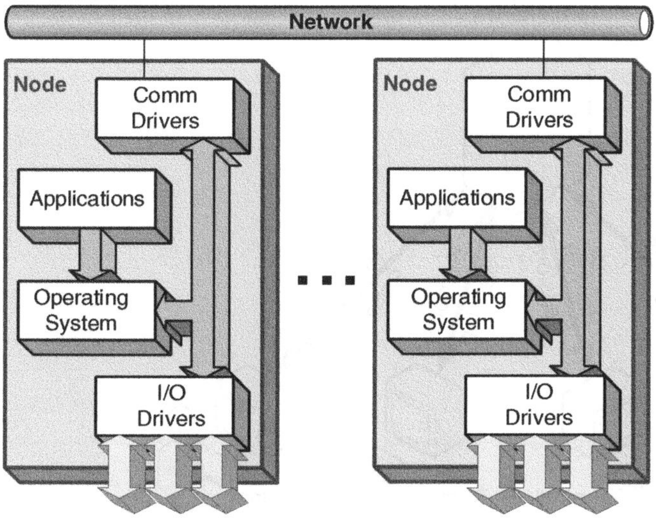

Figure 4.6 Software overview of a distributed system.

- The network is secure.
- Topology doesn't change.
- There is one administrator.
- Transport cost is zero.
- The network is homogeneous.

The following paragraphs outline the primary characteristics of each type of distributed system, which in turn lead to the core concepts of IEC 61850 systems.

4.6 Remote Access Models

RAS were the first distributed architecture to be developed, aiming to provide distributed access to central processing facilities. These were formed by mainframes with processors, memory, files, and applications, shared by users connected to remote terminals that consisted of dumb monitors and keyboards linked to the central facility via communication lines. Figure 4.7 shows the general architecture of a RAS.

As a natural evolution, lightweight processors replaced the dumb terminals, giving rise to C/SS.

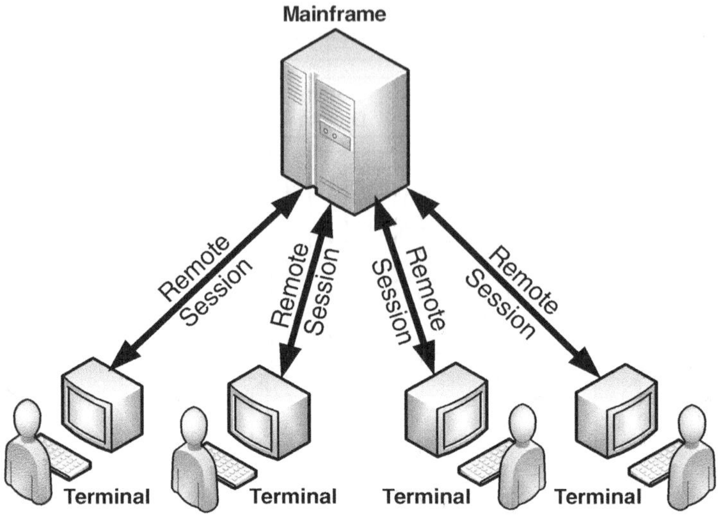

Figure 4.7 Remote access system.

4.7 Client–server Models

In a client–server architecture, the application is modeled as a set of services provided by servers and a set of clients that use these services. Clients are aware of servers, but servers do not need to be mindful of the clients. Clients and servers are logical processes, but the mapping of processors to processes is not necessarily one-to-one.

Figure 4.8 illustrates the communication process in a client–server architecture. Typically, a server with database access handles requests from multiple clients. Each request is sent from the client to the server, which accesses the database, formats a response, and sends it to the requesting client. Each request–response pair is treated independently from the others, so there is no mechanism to synchronize these communications.

A C/SS does not necessarily require a hierarchical architecture. For example, a network of C/SS may be assembled as depicted in Figure 4.9. In this architecture, each computer can act as either a client or a server for several other computers connected to the network.

Sometimes, the system can be composed of a server network, as depicted in Figure 4.10. Each server is responsible for attending to the requests of a subset of clients, typically those located near it. The data can be distributed across servers or specialized for each client.

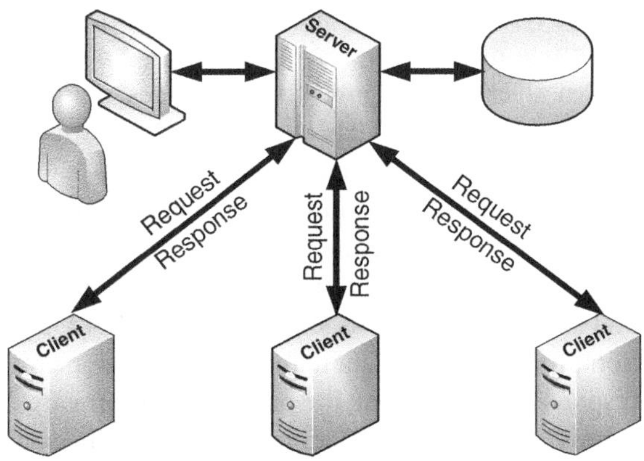

Figure 4.8 Client–server communication.

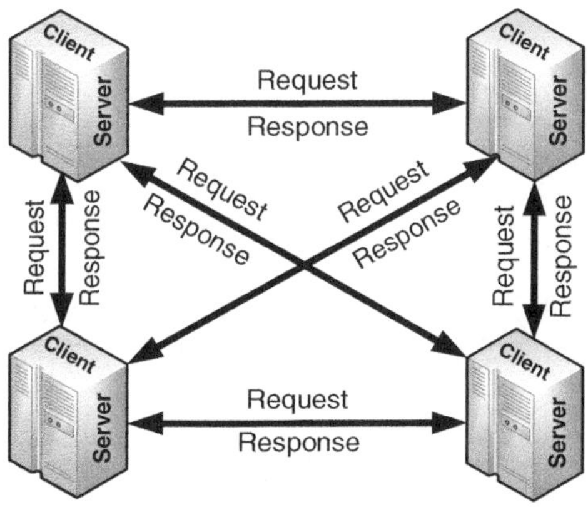

Figure 4.9 Network of client–servers.

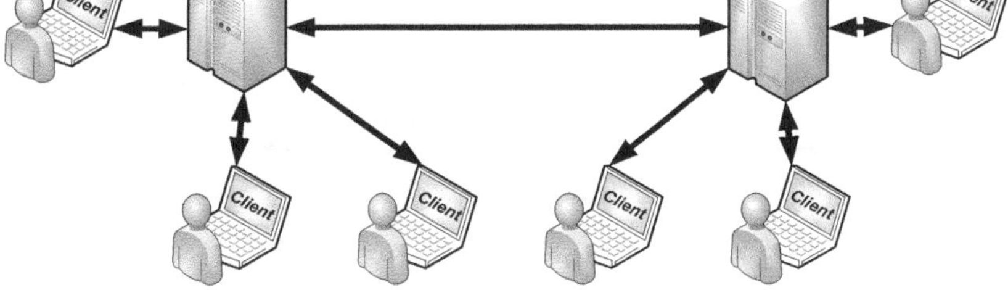

Figure 4.10 Network of servers.

C/SS typically employ a layered application architecture, dividing the software into three distinct layers: Presentation, Application, and Data. These layers are shown stacked in Figure 4.11. The Presentation layer displays the results of a computation and collects user inputs. The Application Processing layer provides application-specific functionality, e.g., in a banking system, banking functions such as opening an account, closing an account, etc. The Data Management layer manages the system databases.

Variants of pure C/SS may support different client types, including thin-client and fat-client models, as shown in Figure 4.12. In a thin-client model, all application processing and data management are done on the server. The client is simply responsible for running the presentation software. In a fat-client model, the server is only responsible for data management. The software on the client implements the application logic and the user interface.

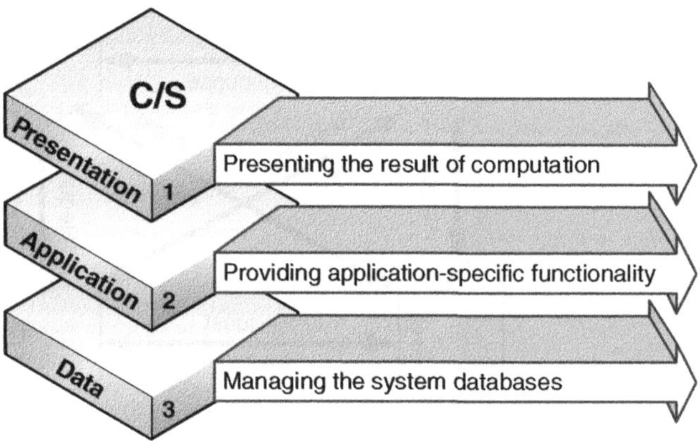

Figure 4.11 Layered application architecture.

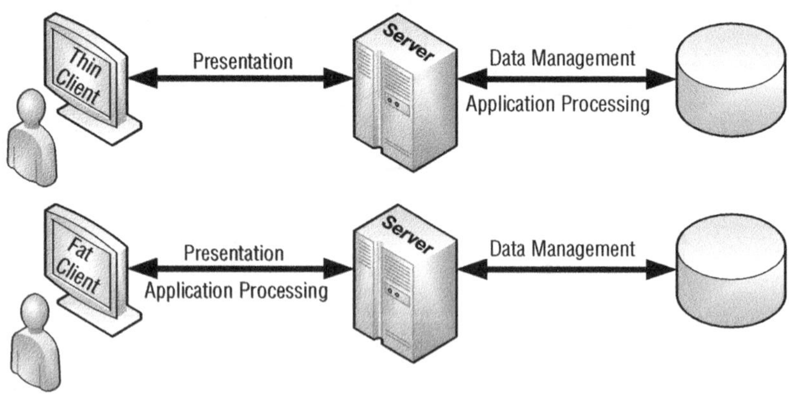

Figure 4.12 Thin and fat clients.

Thin-client models are typically used when migrating legacy systems to client–server architectures. The legacy system acts as a server, and the graphical interface runs on the client. A significant disadvantage is that it places a heavy processing load on the server and network. Figure 4.13 shows a typical client–server ATM system, where each ATM terminal is a thin client. In this example, the account server serves as a teleprocessing monitor, managing data and processing applications on the custom account database.

In fat-client models, more processing is delegated to the client. They are most suitable for new C/SS where the client system's capabilities are known. However, they are more complex than a thin-client model, particularly for management, as new application versions must be installed on all clients.

Besides the fat and thin clients, C/SS may be structured in a three-tier architecture formed by a Presentation layer, an Application Processing layer, and a Data Management layer, as shown in Figure 4.14. Each Application Architecture layer in this system may execute on a separate processor. This typically yields better performance than a thin client and is simpler to manage than a fat client,

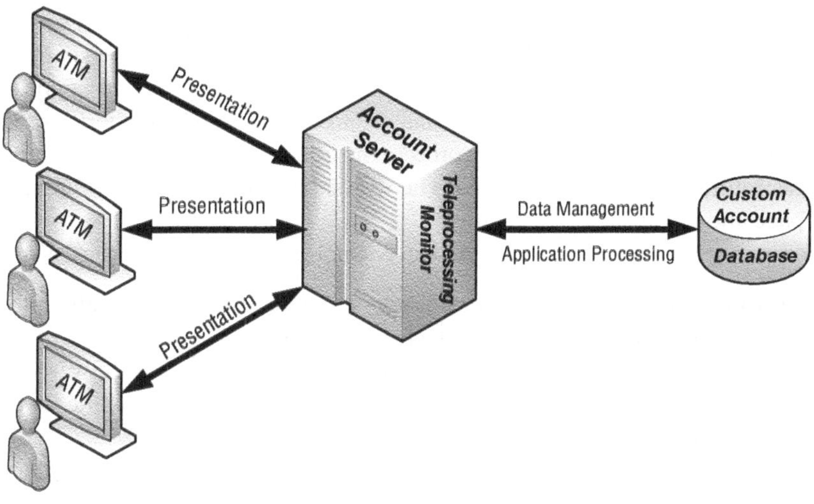

Figure 4.13 Client–server ATM system.

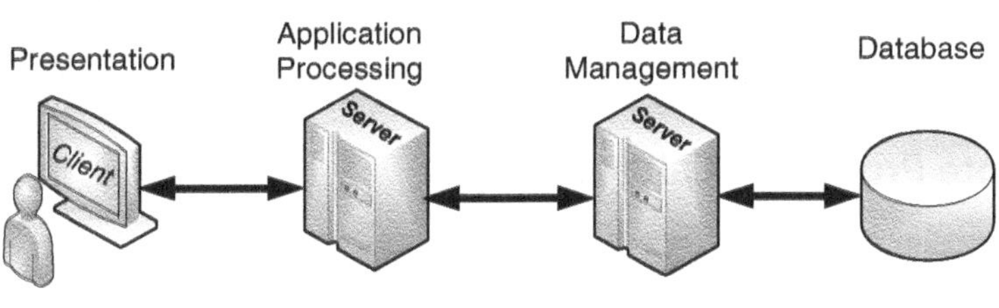

Figure 4.14 Three-tier client–server architecture.

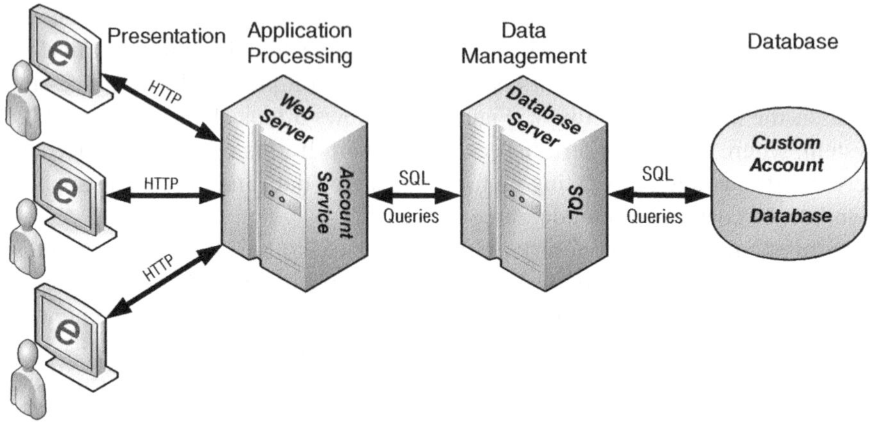

Figure 4.15 Three-tier Internet banking system.

leading to a more scalable architecture. As demand increases, additional servers can be added.

Figure 4.15 shows a three-tier Internet banking system in which a web server responds to requests from multiple web browser clients using the Hypertext Transfer Protocol (HTTP). The same server runs an Account Service application to verify user access rights and translate user requests into SQL queries submitted to the database server. This will process the queries over a Custom Account Database, returning the requested data. The web server formats this data into an HTTP page and returns it to the client.

In summary, client–server architectures can be implemented in three basic flavors:

- **Two-tier systems**—usually for legacy systems, using computationally intensive applications and data-intensive applications
- **Two-tier with fat client**—usually for off-the-shelf application software on the client and computationally intensive processing of data, which needs to have a stable end-user functionality
- **Three-tier**—usually for large applications with many clients, with data integration from many sources

The next level of distributed systems was achieved with the introduction of the RPC concept.

4.8 Remote Procedure Call Models

Distributed systems that use RPC mask distributed computing with a "transparent" abstraction of a procedure call that resembles a standard procedure call but hides all aspects of distributed interaction, thereby supporting an easy programming

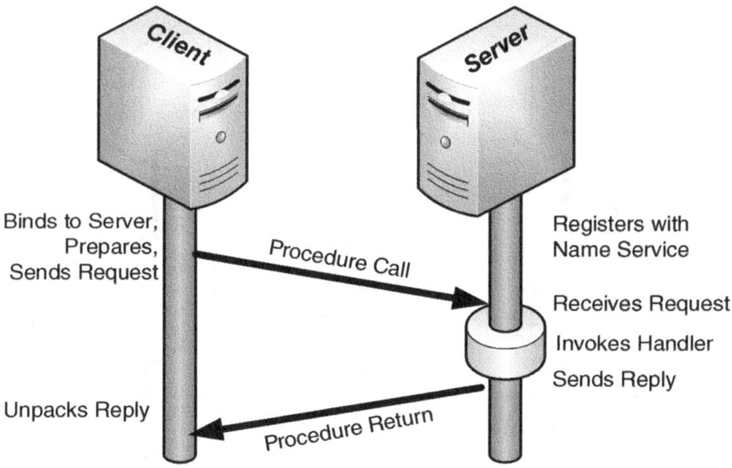

Figure 4.16 Basics of RPC.

model. Introduced in 1985, when most applications were built directly on the Internet, RPC is now the core of many distributed systems, including CORBA, Java RMI, HTTP, and web services.

Figure 4.16 shows the basic mechanism of an RPC between a client and a server. To initiate communication, the client establishes a binding with the server, registering itself with a name service. Once bound, the client begins a procedure call by preparing and sending a request to the server. This, in turn, receives the call and invokes a handler to process the request, using available databases. The result is sent as a reply to the client, which then unpacks and consumes it.

RPC strives for distribution transparency, though this is rarely fully achieved due to server and network failures. It is primarily based on client/server technology and is well-supported by modern programming languages. Further developments in software led to the replacement of RPCs with distributed objects as an alternative model for distributed systems.

4.9 Distributed Object Models

Distributed object architectures make no distinction between clients and servers. Any object in the system may provide and use services from other objects. Each distributable entity is an object that provides services to different objects and receives services from them. Object communication is facilitated through a middleware system known as an Object Request Broker (ORB). Distributed object architectures are more complex to design for all these functionalities than C/S and RPC systems.

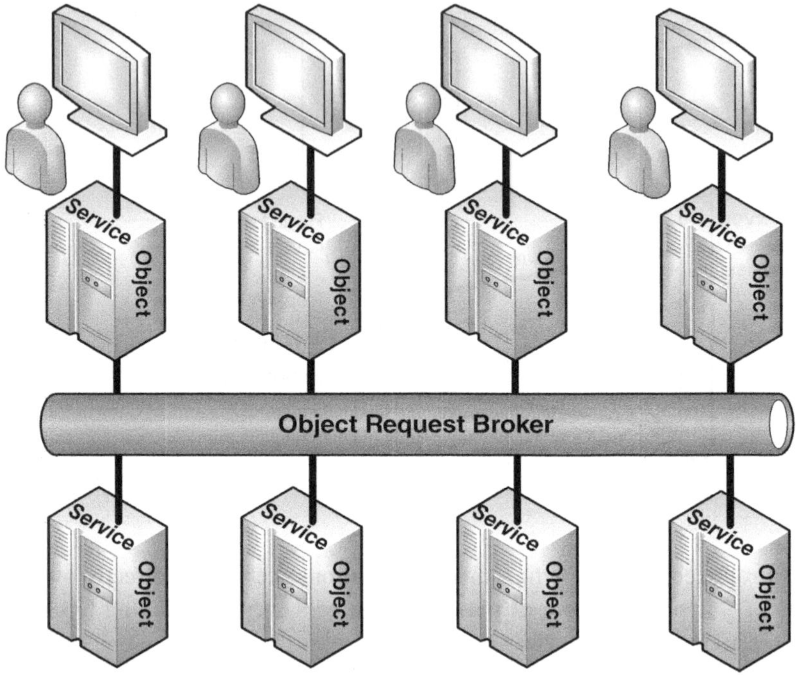

Figure 4.17 Distributed object architecture.

An ORB is software that intermediates the request and reply between distributed objects, as shown in Figure 4.17. Every object is a piece of software running on servers that expose one or more services that users or other objects can request.

An advantage of a distributed object architecture is that it allows the system designer to delay decisions on where and how services should be provided. It features a highly open system architecture that allows new resources to be added as needed, in a flexible, scalable manner. It is also possible to dynamically reconfigure the system, with objects migrating across the network as required. As such, it is used mainly in two circumstances:

- As a logical model to structure and organize the system, providing application functionality solely in terms of services and combinations of services
- As a flexible approach to a C/SS, the logical model is a C/SS, with both clients and servers realized as distributed objects communicating through a common communication framework

As an example of a distributed object architecture, Figure 4.18 illustrates the structure of a data mining system comprising three distributed databases, two

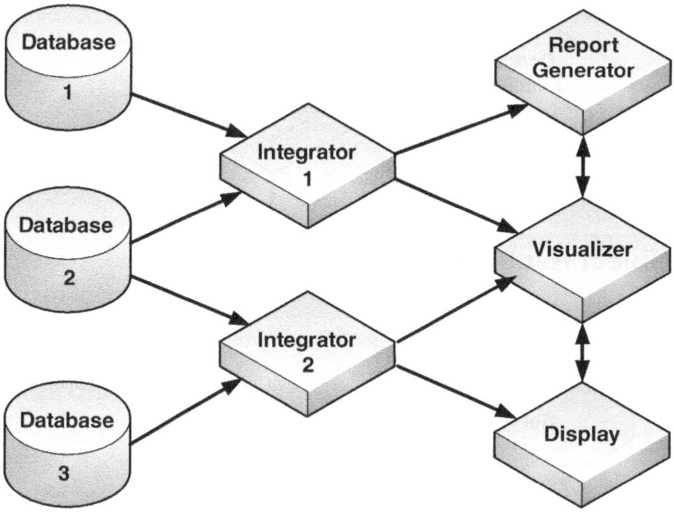

Figure 4.18 Example of a data mining system.

data integrators or data warehouses, and a display module that responds to users' requests.

In this data mining system, the logical model is not one of service provision, as it includes distinguished data management services. It allows the number of accessed databases to be increased without disrupting the system, and new relationship types to be mined by adding new integrator objects. For example, the Common Object Request Broker Architecture (CORBA) is an Object-Oriented Middleware for DOS. It is an international standard from the Object Management Group (OMG) for an ORB, a middleware component that manages communications between distributed objects. Figure 4.19 shows the CORBA application structure.

CORBA application objects are standard modules defined by the OMG for a specific domain, e.g., insurance. Fundamental CORBA services include standard distributed services, such as directories and security management. Horizontal facilities encompass services across various applications, including user interface facilities. CORBA standard defines an object model for application objects as an encapsulation of state with a well-defined, language-neutral interface defined in an Interface Definition Language (IDL) and an ORB that manages requests for object services. It also establishes a set of general object services helpful in many distributed applications, as well as a set of standard components built on top of these services. As such, CORBA objects are comparable, in principle, to objects in C++, Python, and Java. They must have a separate IDL interface definition that can be mapped to programming languages (C++, Python, Java, etc.). Therefore, objects written in different languages can communicate with each other.

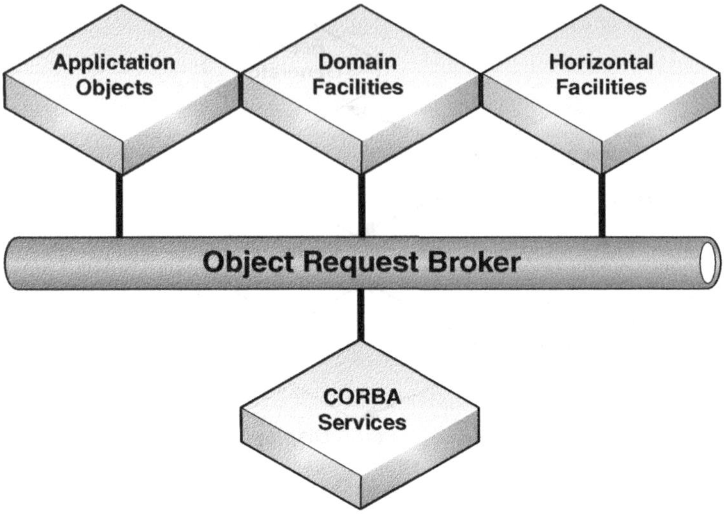

Figure 4.19 CORBA application structure.

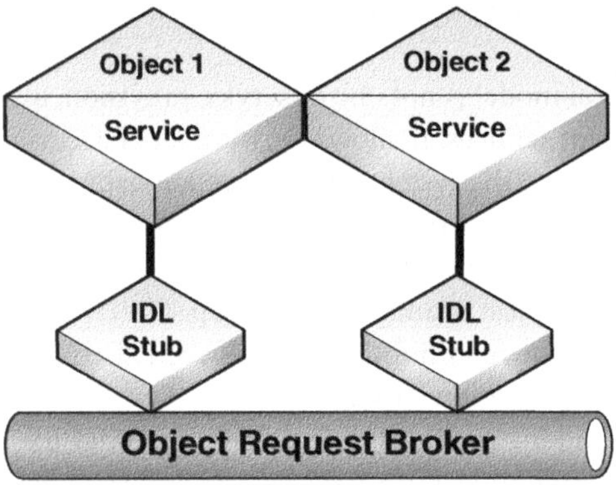

Figure 4.20 ORB-based object communications.

The ORB handles object communication and maintains a list of all objects in the system and their interfaces. Using an ORB, the calling object binds an IDL stub that defines the interface of the called object. This stub results in calls to the ORB, which then calls the required object through a published IDL skeleton that links the interface to the service implementation. Figure 4.20 illustrates the communication between two objects using IDL stubs and an ORB.

ORBs are not usually separate programs, but rather a set of objects in a library linked with an application during its development. They handle communications between objects executing on the same machine. Several ORBS may be available,

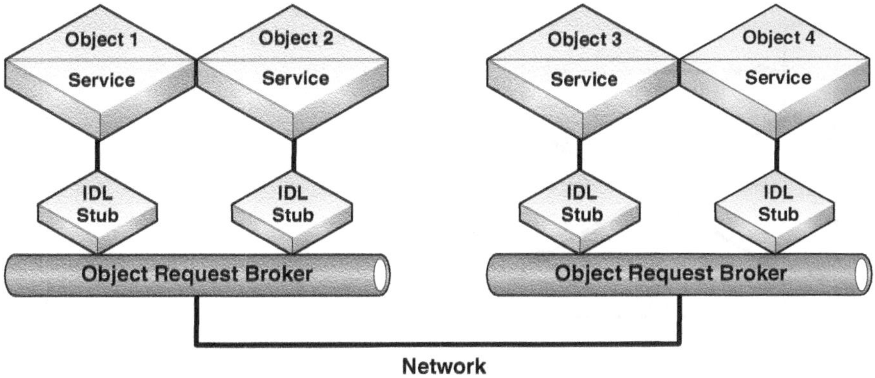

Figure 4.21 Inter-ORB communications.

and each computer in a distributed system will have its own ORB. Inter-ORB communications are used for distributed object calls, as shown in Figure 4.21.

CORBA services include (i) naming and trading services, to allow objects to discover and refer to other objects on the network; (ii) notification services, to allow objects to notify other objects that an event has occurred; and (iii) transaction services, to support atomic transactions and rollback on failure.

These resources ultimately led to the concept of P2P communication and service exchange among servers, which in turn gave rise to an additional model for distributed systems.

4.10 Peer-to-peer Models

P2P architectures are decentralized systems in which any network node may perform computations. They aim to use the computational power and storage of many networked computers. Figure 4.22 shows the general architecture and communication of a P2P system.

Two general logic architectures are common in P2P systems: decentralized and semi-centralized architectures. Decentralized P2P architectures are built from multiple computers that communicate with one another, as shown in Figure 4.23.

In a semi-centralized P2P architecture, servers can communicate bilaterally; however, a centralized discovery server is responsible for discovering and distributing information among them. This architecture is shown in Figure 4.24.

Eventually, P2P systems evolved to the point of abstracting servers entirely, giving rise to the concept of SOS.

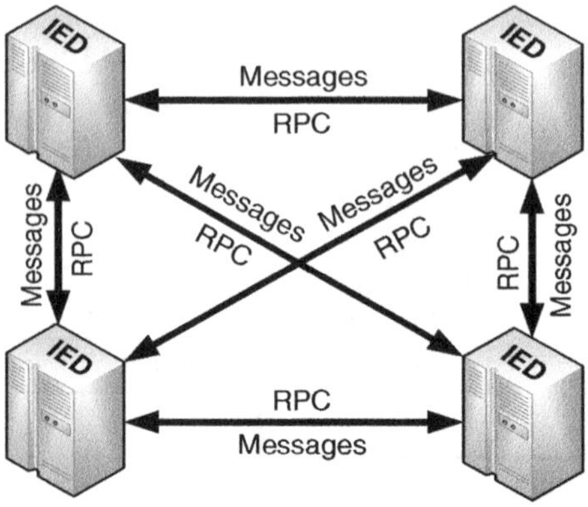

Figure 4.22 Peer-to-peer communication.

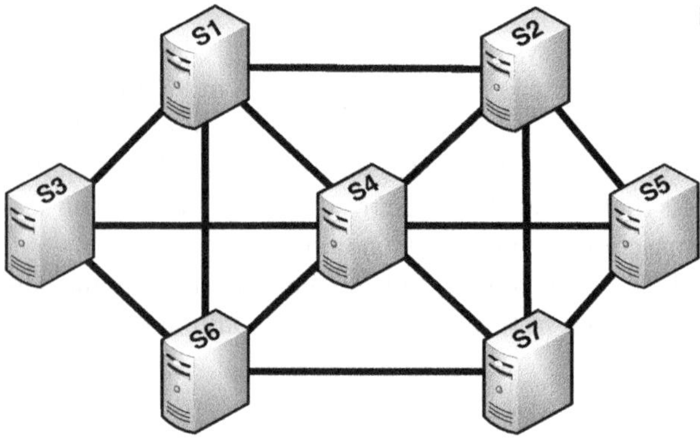

Figure 4.23 Decentralized P2P architecture.

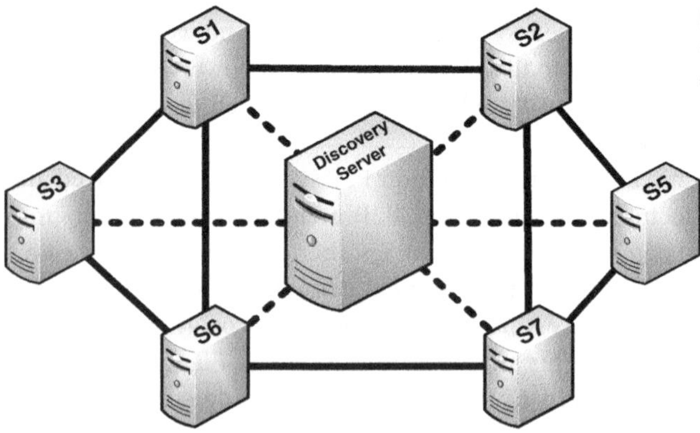

Figure 4.24 Semi-centralized P2P architecture.

4.11 Service-oriented Models

A Service-Oriented Architecture (SOA) is a distributed system based on externally provided services (web services). A web service is a standard approach to making a reusable component available and accessible across a network. Figure 4.25 shows the mechanism for publishing, discovering, and binding web services. A Service Registry is a repository of descriptions of available services in these systems. Every Service Provider publishes the service descriptions on the Service Register. After locating the desired service in the Service Registry and obtaining the required information, a Service Requestor binds to the Service Provider.

Services from Distributed Service Systems are provided independently. For this, they must adhere to a public advertising of service availability. The service provider and the requester bind at runtime to maintain their independence. This also allows for a pay-for-use of services. New services can be built as needed by combining existing services, enabling smaller, more compact, reactive, and adaptive applications. To achieve these goals, services are based on agreed XML standards that can be provided on any platform and written in any programming language. Key standards for web services include Simple Object Access Protocol (SOAP), Web Services Description Language (WSDL), JavaScript Object Notation (JSON), and Universal Description, Discovery, and Integration (UDDI). An automotive information service is a typical SOS, as shown in Figure 4.26.

An in-car information system provides drivers with information on weather, road traffic conditions, and local information. This is linked to a car radio, which delivers information as a signal on a specific radio channel. The car is equipped with a Global Positioning System (GPS) receiver to discover its position, and based on that position, the system accesses a range of information services. Information may be delivered in the driver's specified language.

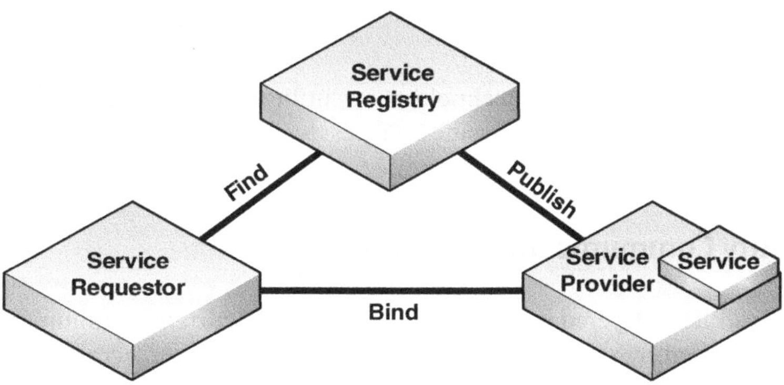

Figure 4.25 Web services.

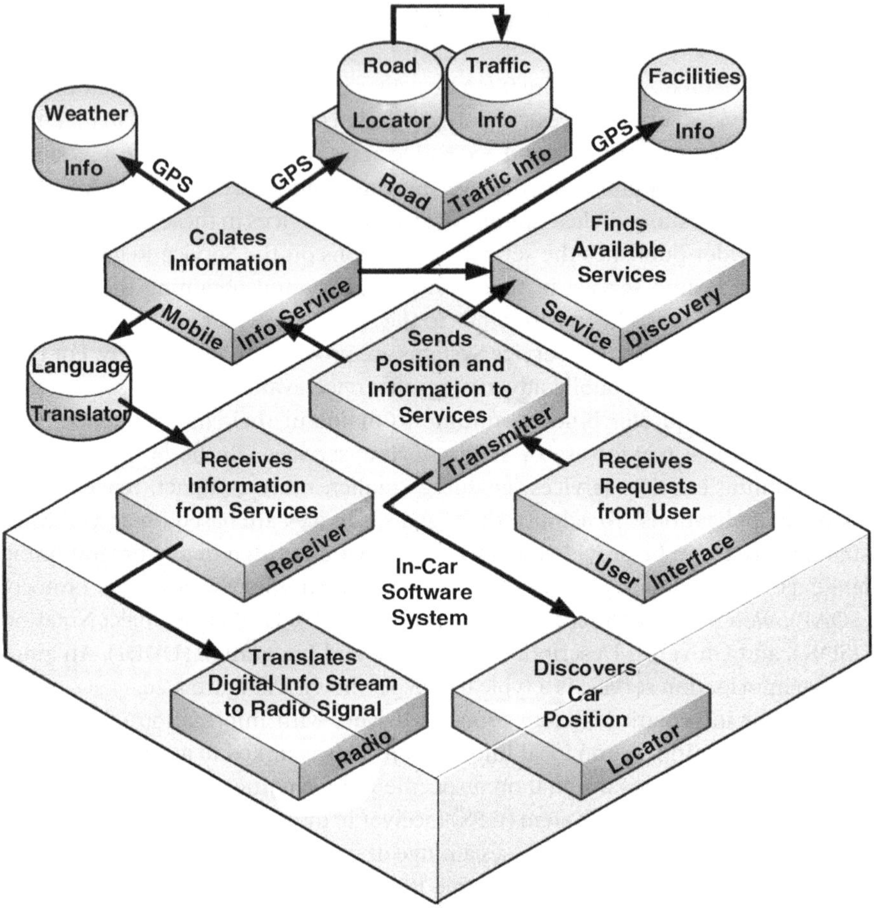

Figure 4.26 Automotive information service.

SOA is currently the preferred technology for utility-wide communication, encompassing both operational and business processes.

4.12 Utility Communication Models

Figure 4.27 illustrates a layered matrix view of the trend in current communications systems adopted by electric utilities, ranging from the lower Access layer near the power process to the Transport layer connecting the substations, the Control layer at the corporate level, and up to the Service layer for connection to

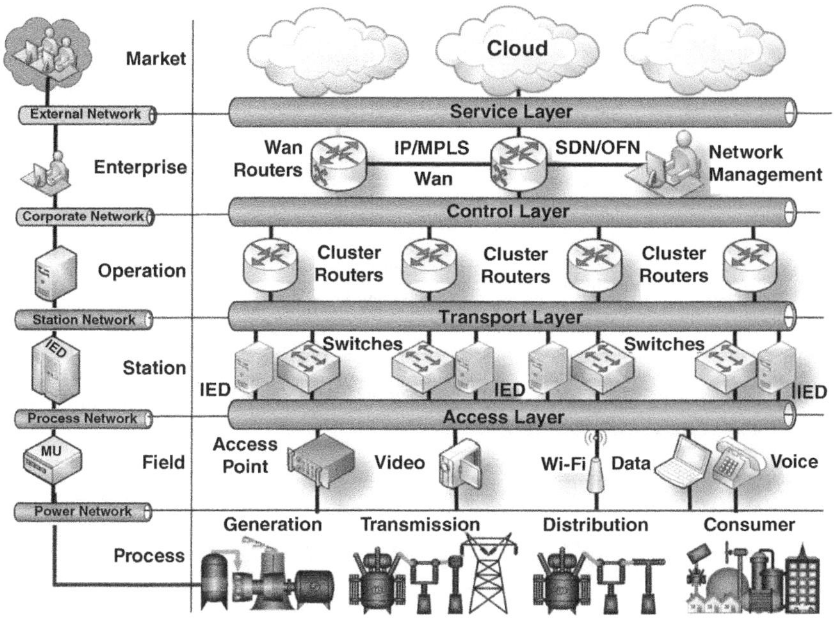

Figure 4.27 Utility network telecom convergence.

external market entities. Note that the upper web Service layer not only enables utility-wide communication, but also serves as the standard bus for external communication to the market and the cloud.

Following this principle, a typical utility communication system is divided into four layers:

- **Level 0**—Access layer
- **Level 1**—Transport layer
- **Level 2**—Control layer
- **Level 3**—Service layer

Each layer is organized as a service bus, providing middleware for data exchange among processors and repositories distributed in all hierarchical levels (Figure 4.28):

- **Level 0**, the Access layer, provides a Real-Time Event Bus with a Message-Oriented Middleware to exchange phasor and sample values of status and analog signals for monitoring and control.
- **Level 1**, the Transport layer, provides a Logic Message Bus with Procedural Middleware to exchange ***GOOSE*** and client–server messages among local concentrators for automation processes.

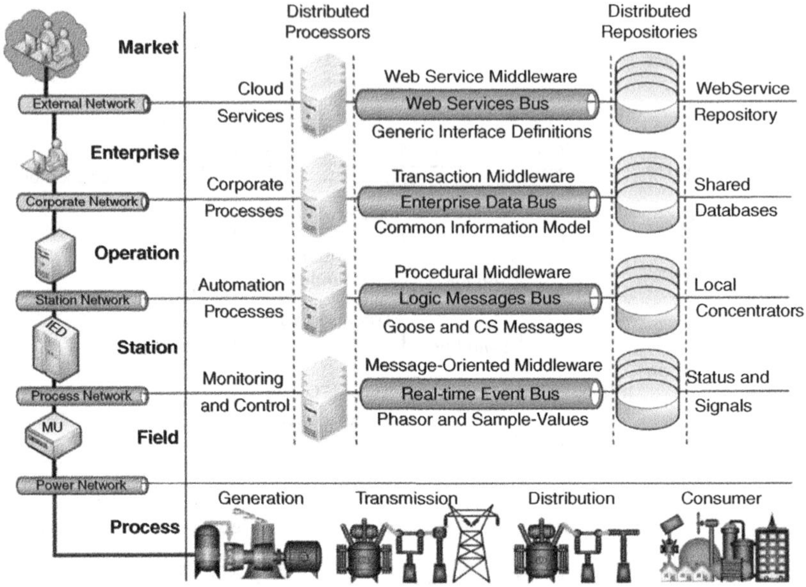

Figure 4.28 Utility network services buses.

- **Level 2**, the Control layer, provides an Enterprise Message Bus with Transactional Middleware to exchange Common Information Model data and messages among shared databases for corporate processes.
- **Level 3**, the Service layer, provides a Web Service Bus with a Web Service Middleware, using Generic Interface Definitions to exchange data and messages among Web Service Repositories for the corporation's cloud services.

Each layer provides services to the users at the same level and to upper or lower layers, granting access, transport, control, and information exchange for the distributed business and automation systems required by the utility. Ideally, these services should be agnostic to communication technology and provided in a standardized form by different providers. This applies mainly to DTRS used for utility automation.

4.13 Distributed Real-time Models

A DTRS is a distributed system with defined response time requirements for some real-world events. It may be located on computers in the same room, in an adjacent office, in another city, or on the other side of the world. As a result, designing and testing these systems is even more complex than developing and testing other distributed systems.

Suppose a system accomplishes some real-time requirements and operates on distributed servers. In that case, it can utilize any communication architecture, such as P2P, client–server, network of client–servers, or distributed computing. The complexity of these systems can be accessed by referencing the axis of Figure 2.1.

Along the communication axis, the simplest systems usually use synchronous communication, which is easier to implement and operate. Real-time systems require asynchronous communication, which is more complex to implement and manage because they must respond in real time to asynchronous events. As its name implies, DTRS, along the Distribution axis, are composed of distributed servers and services, allowing for faster responses to real-time events than a localized or centralized system. And finally, along the Time axis, real-time systems must respond to real-time events while adhering to strict time requirements, unlike offline systems.

Substation Automation Systems (SAS) are systems with requirements similar to those of DTRS, as they must respond to asynchronous, distributed real-time events. These requirements are part of the objectives of distributed systems based on the IEC 61850 standard, as described in the following paragraph.

4.14 Distributed Models Based on IEC 61850

To address the needs of electric power system automation, the International Electrotechnical Commission released, in 2004, the first edition of a standard entitled IEC 61850—"Communication Networks and Systems in Substations," now titled "Communication Networks and Systems for Power Utility Communication." It is a standard for object-oriented communication and organization in Power Utility Automation distributed systems.

According to this standard, a Real-Time Distributed System (RTDS) for an SAS comprises several ***IEDs*** operating in a linked configuration, as shown in Figure 4.29. Every ***IED*** is itself a server formed by several modules, such as a communication interface to exchange data with other ***IEDs*** through the network; one or more processor modules for managing all ***IED*** activities; a memory module, for storing specific ***IED*** data; an internal data network for linking all internal ***IED*** modules; and one or more I/O devices for connecting the ***IED*** to the power system process equipment or HMI. The plant equipment connected to these ***IEDs*** typically includes instrument transformers, circuit breakers, power transformers, and other similar devices.

A software overview of an SAS is shown in Figure 4.30, based on the IEC 61850 standard. The set of ***IEDs*** and networks is now a set of software modules defined

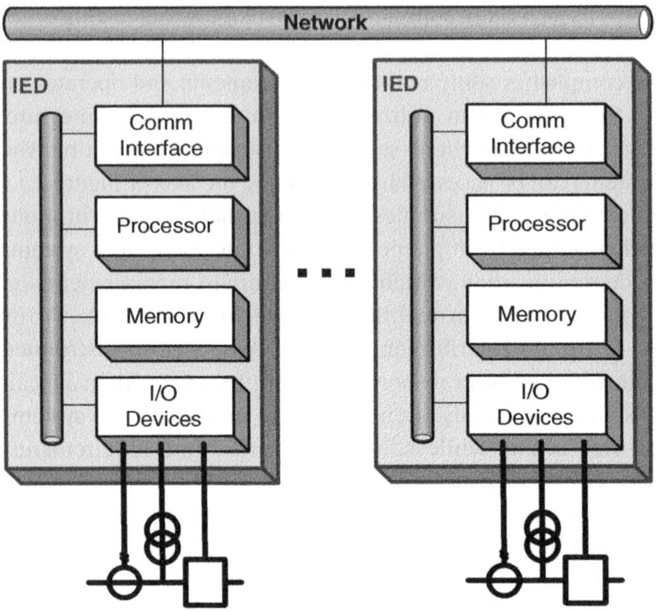

Figure 4.29 Hardware overview of IEC 61850 systems.

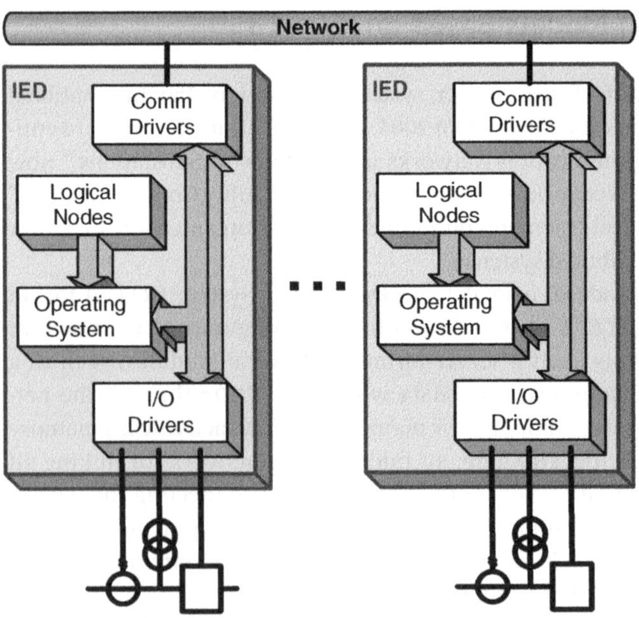

Figure 4.30 Software overview of IEC 61850 systems.

by the standard. The network comprises a middleware that links several ***IEDs*** through their communication drivers. Each ***IED*** consists of one or more server modules. Each server is guided by an operating system that distributes actions across several logical nodes, or software components that implement specialized actions required by the ***IED***. Each ***IED*** also has a set of I/O drivers that communicate with external physical equipment or an operator via an HMI and are formed by one or more communication drivers that exchange data with other ***IEDs*** and servers.

As a software and communication standard, IEC 61850 proposes to structure a distributed SAS as a set of specialized models that include the following:

- Communication Model
- Functional Model
- Data Model
- Service Model
- Message Model
- Timing Model
- Testing Model
- Configuration Model
- Conformance Model
- System Model

The main requirement of this system concerns the free allocation of objects (or ***Logical Nodes***) across a distributed network of servers, as shown in Figure 4.31. Because the input and output of every logical node are formatted data according to IEC 61850, all functionality exposed by a ***logical node*** can be physically located on any server connected to the network. The servers are a

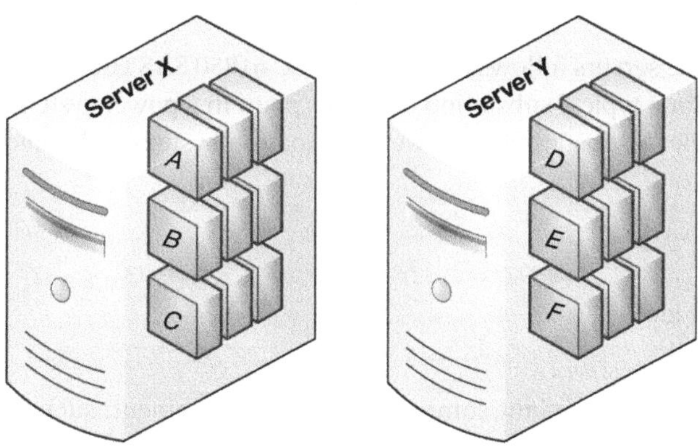

Figure 4.31 Free allocation of objects (Logical Nodes).

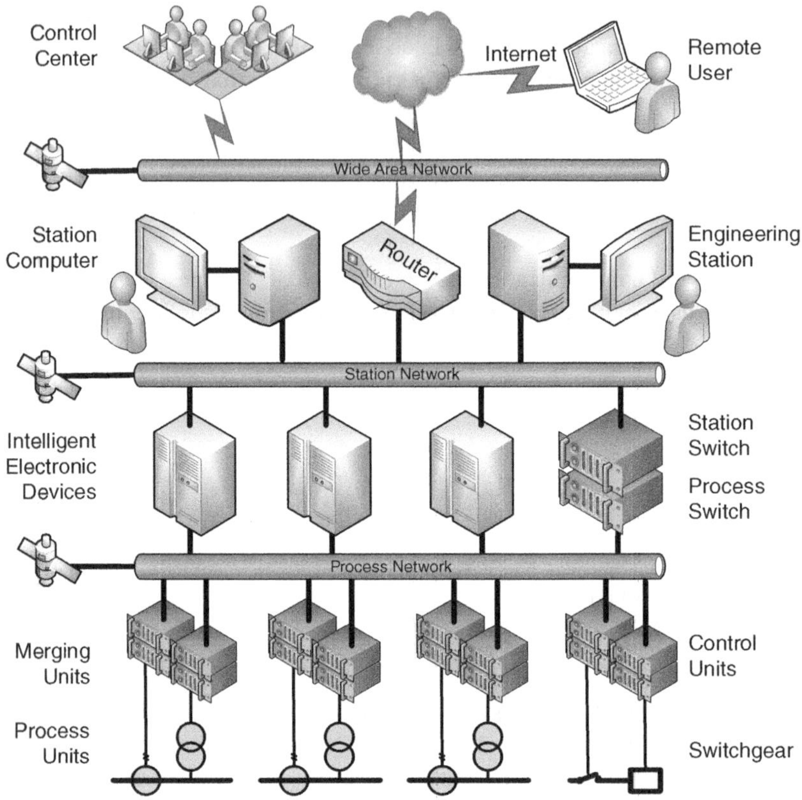

Figure 4.32 General IEC 61850 SAS hierarchy.

collection of `logical nodes` that expose services to other logical nodes, accessible over the network.

The organization of these servers follows the General IEC 61850 SAS Hierarchy, as shown in Figure 4.32, for a typical substation or power plant in a power system. According to this principle, a substation or power automation system is divided into four levels:

- **Level 0**—Process level
- **Level 1**—Bay level
- **Level 2**—Substation level
- **Level 3**—System level

At the Process level (0), a power plant comprises primary equipment, such as breakers, transformers, generators, turbines, and transmission lines. Sensors and instrument transformers collect information about the status of each equipment, while actuators change their status in response to external signals. These signals are collected, formatted, and distributed by specialized servers, called ***Merging Units*** and ***Control Units***, via a ***Process Network*** to several ***IEDs*** at the Bay level (1). One or more Process Switches may control this network or be jointly operated with a ***Station Network***, controlled by one or more Station Switches. The ***Station Network*** links the ***IEDs*** to one or more station computers and engineering stations at the Substation level (2), using their HMIs. Routers connect the station to the world outside the power plant at the System level (3), typically through a Wide-Area Network (WAN) and the Internet, allowing remote users and control centers to access it. Synchronizing signals can be captured directly from satellite or utility-based clocks at any network level and distributed to the servers and ***IEDs*** connected to that network level.

Due to their complexity, SAS based on IEC 61850 share many common traits with the following types of distributed systems:

- Client–Server System (CSS)
- Peer-to-peer System (P2P Systems)
- Object-oriented System (OOS)
- Service-oriented System (SOS); and
- Real-time Distributed System (RTDS).

These traits explain the standard's colossal size, complexity, and broad applicability in meeting the requirements of modern power system automation. A promising alternative to distributed systems is to concentrate all processing required by an automation system in a centralized system using IEC 61850.

4.15 Centralized Models Based on IEC 61850

A Centralized Protection, Automation, and Control (CPAC) system for a substation based on IEC 61850 represents a modern approach, where Virtual Protection, Automation, and Control (***vPAC***) functions are consolidated in a central platform—typically a redundant virtualized server (paragraph 4.4), a cluster or group of interconnected host machines providing a unique environment or a high-performance (mainframe) computer—instead of being distributed across numerous ***IEDs***. Figure 4.33 illustrates the typical architecture of a CPAC system.

The central units host all protection algorithms, control logic, automation functions, monitoring, disturbance recording, engineering, and operation functions. Depending on local regulations, separate hosts may be required for metering, security, and other purposes. Typically, they consist of two or more synchronized servers running real-time virtualization or redundant computing nodes to ensure high availability. The distributed functions are limited to HMIs,

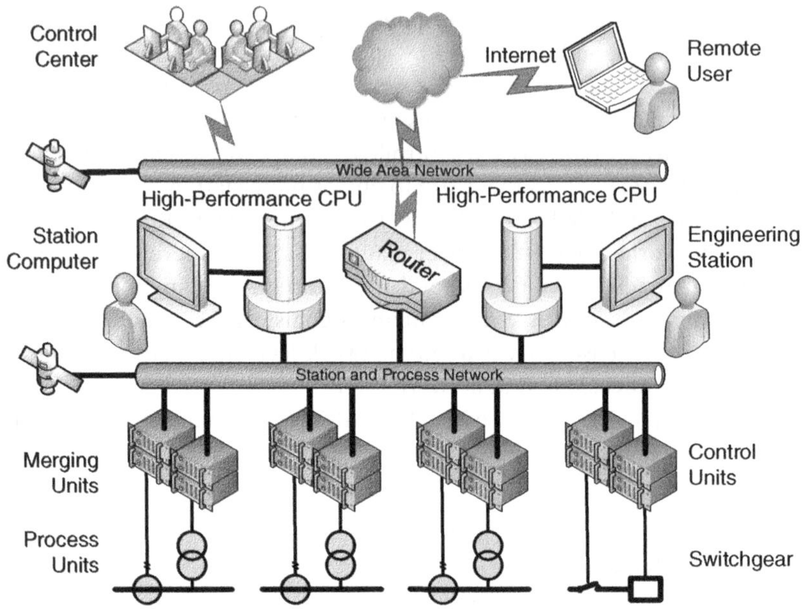

Figure 4.33 IEC 61850 centralized architecture.

sensors, merging units, and control units that are directly connected to the controlled process. A redundant Ethernet network forms the substation LAN, running a process bus connecting merging units, control units, and switchgear, and a station bus connecting SCADA, HMI, gateways, operation, and engineering stations.

The advantages of this architecture include reduced numbers of physical ***IEDs*** and their associated hardware maintenance, as well as flexible, software-based deployment of new protection and automation functions, with ***SCL*** management in a single container, enabling easier central supervision and disturbance analysis. The challenges include a high dependency on network reliability and central computing availability, typically supplied by independent software and computer manufacturers (not by relay vendors), which require extensive configuration, redundancy, and mandatory cybersecurity measures.

4.16 Summary

Distributed systems support several requirements necessary for SAS, including resource sharing, openness, concurrency, scalability, fault tolerance, and transparency. Among these, client–server architectures deliver services from servers to programs running on clients, with user interface software typically running on the client. In contrast, data management software runs on the server. Application functionality may be on the client or the server. In a distributed object architecture, however, there is no distinction between clients and servers. Every server can be a client of a service provided by other servers.

DOS also require middleware to handle object communications and add and remove system objects. CORBA is an example of a set of middleware standards that support distributed object architectures. P2P architectures are examples of decentralized architectures that lack a distinction between clients and servers. At the same time, SOS are built by linking software services from different service providers.

This chapter presented an overview of distributed systems, covering the following architectures:

- Distributed Systems (DS)
- Remote Access Systems (RAS)
- Client–Server Systems (C/SS)
- Remote Procedure Calls (RPC)
- Distributed Object Systems (DOS)
- Peer-To-peer Systems (P2P)
- Service-oriented Systems (SOS)
- Distributed Real-time Systems (DRTS)
- Distributed Systems Based on IEC 61850
- Centralized Systems Based on IEC 61850

The following chapter will present the several distributed models that IEC 61850 defined and their application to SAS.

4.17 Review Questions

1. Describe the six main characteristics of distributed systems and explain why each is essential for modern automation environments.

2. Explain the function of a hypervisor in VM architectures and compare how resource sharing varies between VMs and containers.

3. Evaluate the primary disadvantages of distributed systems (such as complexity, security vulnerabilities, and manageability). How do the "fallacies of distributed computing" contribute to these challenges?

4 Consider a substation undergoing digitization. Provide a well-supported recommendation on whether virtualization (using VMs or containers) should be employed to run its automation servers.

5 Summarize the operational principles of RAS and explain how they shaped the development of client–server architectures.

6 Compare thin-client, fat-client, and three-tier client–server models, emphasizing how their processing responsibilities and scalability vary.

7 Discuss how RPCs try to achieve distribution transparency. What limitations stop complete transparency in real-world systems?

8 A utility needs to combine different software components written in multiple programming languages. Explain why a distributed object architecture based on CORBA might be a suitable solution.

9 Describe the structural differences between decentralized and semi-centralized P2P architectures, and specify scenarios where each model is most effective.

10 Compare SOA and distributed object models regarding interoperability, scalability, and independence between components.

11 Examine the four levels of the IEC 61850 SAS hierarchy (Process, Bay, Substation, System). Provide an example demonstrating how a protection or control function depends on collaboration across multiple levels.

12 Evaluate the benefits and challenges of implementing a centralized IEC 61850-based PAC architecture. In what operational scenarios could a centralized model outperform a distributed ***IED***-based model?

5

IEC 61850 Models

5.1 Introduction

Among the many features of IEC 61850, abstraction and modeling are perhaps the core ideas that link all its traits. Abstraction and modeling are fundamental concepts in many fields, especially in computer science, engineering, and science overall, and they are often used together. While an abstraction simplifies complex systems by emphasizing the most important parts and ignoring details not relevant to the immediate task, a model represents a system or idea built to understand, predict, or communicate how something works. It can be physical (such as a scale model of a building) or abstract (such as mathematical or computational models). Abstraction is a step in creating a model that involves choosing which parts of reality to include and which to leave out. The level of abstraction determines how detailed or simple the model will be.

5.2 Learning Objectives

This chapter employs a top-down approach to introduce the abstractions and object-oriented modeling for Power System Automation based on the IEC 61850 standard. Paralleling the traditional seven layers of the Open Systems Interconnection (OSI) model for network communication, this chapter develops a unified chain of models of all major software classes defined by IEC 61850, grouped in stacked layers, ranging from the higher slices seen from users and integrators to the lower layers interfacing network communication and middleware. These models compose four concurrent views, as seen by different stakeholders, that summarize the architecture of a station and its automation system in accordance with IEC 61850. Each view refers to several standardized abstract classes, which will be detailed in the remaining chapters, gathered in the following topics:

- IEC 61850
- Unified Modeling Language (UML) Views
- Substation Model
- Product Model
- Type Model
- Communication Model
- Functional Model
- Data Model
- Service Model

The remaining paragraphs will cover these topics, using a top-down UML model that connects all major classes in the standard (please refer to Figure 16.1 in Annex 16.1) to provide a hierarchical overview of IEC 61850's capabilities. The details of each model and the use of each class will be addressed in subsequent chapters.

5.3 IEC 61850

One challenge with IEC 61850 is its large size and complexity. Consisting of thousands of pages of textual and graphic content, the standard has been difficult for protection and automation engineers, including manufacturers, utilities, and integrators, to understand. Since its initial release, which mainly focused on substations, new functionalities and logical nodes (LNs) have been added and continue to be added, expanding its use to areas like wind power, hydropower, distributed energy, inter-substation communication, and electrical mobility. Future updates are also planned for condition monitoring, testing, logic, and to align with other standards.

Lack of a digital version has also created difficulties for tool makers, integrators, and software developers, leading to differences and uncertainties in interpretation and reducing the interoperability of models compiled by different tools. This scenario has motivated Technical Committee 57 of the IEC to develop a digital version, which will be available online as a machine-readable UML model. To minimize interoperability and conformance issues, the UCA International Users Group (UCAIug), a not-for-profit corporation focused on assisting users and vendors in the deployment of standards for real-time applications, works closely with standardization bodies to provide a forum in which the various stakeholders in the energy and utility industry work cooperatively to accredit product/system-testing programs that facilitate the interoperability of products and systems based upon these standards. This process eases the work of relay and software developers, but does not reduce the difficulty that automation and protection engineers and students face in understanding and applying the standard.

A traditional way to understand a complex process is to visualize or abstract it into hierarchical views, allowing step-by-step modeling with more details. To apply this method to IEC 61850, the UML model described in the following section mimics the OSI communication model, offering a layered, top-down perspective of its standardized objects organized into class package layers. Each layer is supported by lower layers and supports upper layers, mimicking a hierarchical, organized middleware service that ranges from low-level message classes to high-level classes. This modeling approach gives an overall view of all abstract classes, shown in a single UML Class Diagram (located in Annex 16.1), suitable for a classroom poster or a personal reference to the entire standard.

The models are formed by classes organized in seven layers or packages (by coincidence, the same number of the OSI communication levels), also called models, comprising, from top to bottom, the Substation Model, the Product Model, the Type Model, the Communication Model, the Functional Model, the Data Model, and the Service Model. The upper level, or Substation Model, comprises all classes that describe a Substation Automation System (SAS) and its external and inter-substation communication. These classes are expanded and interfaced with lower-level classes, increasing the model's detail regarding data types, communication, and services. The deepest layer comprises all low-level service and message classes, like Client-Server, ***GOOSE***, and ***`Sampled-Value`*** messages, used to interface with network middleware. These layers are described using UML views and class diagrams. Annex 16.7 resumes the UML graphical notation used to model these classes.

5.4 UML Views

The UML, defined by the Object Management Group, is a graphical language for specifying, visualizing, constructing, and documenting software systems. As a modeling language, it enables users to define multiple system models, each representing a distinct view of the same subject or business area, tailored to the user's specific interests and needs. In UML, a model captures a view of a system with a particular purpose. It provides a comprehensive description of aspects relevant to the model's purpose at an appropriate level of detail. Models can be used to provide different views of a system to other stakeholders, to focus on a single aspect of a system at a time, or to express the results of various stages in a software development process. To define a model, one needs to clearly define its purpose and provide a comprehensive picture of the system, while omitting irrelevant

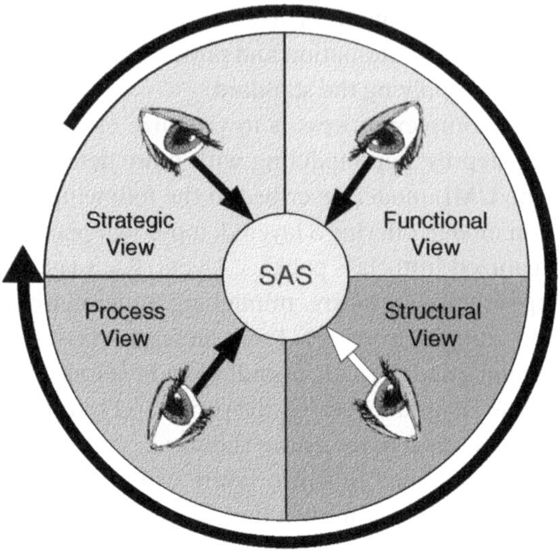

Figure 5.1 Different views of an SAS.

details. Typically, four generic views are used to model a business or technical project in UML: the Strategic, Structural, Functional, and Process Views. For an SAS, these views are shown in Figure 5.1.

The views are usually built sequentially, shown clockwise in Figure 5.1, starting with a Strategic View. When applied to an SAS project, a Strategic (or Business) View contains an external/integrator or owner/stakeholder perspective and a conceptual model of the overall organization and objectives of the design. Clients and software toolmakers also benefit from this external view for modeling user requirements for a new project.

This is further detailed in a Functional View, which outlines the logic and operational blocks that form the main SAS functions, enabling the attainment of the strategic objectives. Users, operators, and maintainers are among the stakeholders who use this operational view to manage the substation.

The Structural View offers a more detailed perspective, highlighting the building blocks of static objects and data that comprise each functional block of the previous view. Manufacturers and Intelligent Electronic Device (***IED***) suppliers are responsible for the modules and data structures provided by the devices used in the substation that support interoperability.

Finally, the Process View details the methods, services, dynamic data, and messages exchanged among the building blocks and the external environment to attain the desired SAS functions. Messages classes are modeled as a sub-package of the Service package from this view, or as part of the middleware used to support communication among ***IEDs*** specific to each application. In an SAS context, the environment encompasses all electrical, mechanical, and process equipment in the substation or power plant, as well as local and remote operators, control centers, and other relevant components. Field engineers, network administrators, and communication personnel provide the network and middleware to support this view.

To implement these views, IEC 61850 uses instantiated objects from a collection of seven packages of classes, defined in the standard and named and numbered in this chapter and book according to the following models:

1. Substation Model
2. Product Model
3. Type Model
4. Communication Model
5. Functional Model
6. Data Model
7. Service Model

According to the four UML views defined earlier, these packages can be associated and organized in a hierarchical layered structure, with their corresponding stakeholders, as shown in Figure 5.2, using the aforementioned package numbering.

A Strategic View of the SAS can be built from instantiated classes in the Substation, Product, Type, and Communication Models, and specified in *SCL*, the XML (eXtensible Markup Language)-based Substation Configuration Language of IEC 61850. This is followed by a Functional View of the SAS, built from objects instantiated from the Functional Model defined by IEC 61850, mainly using

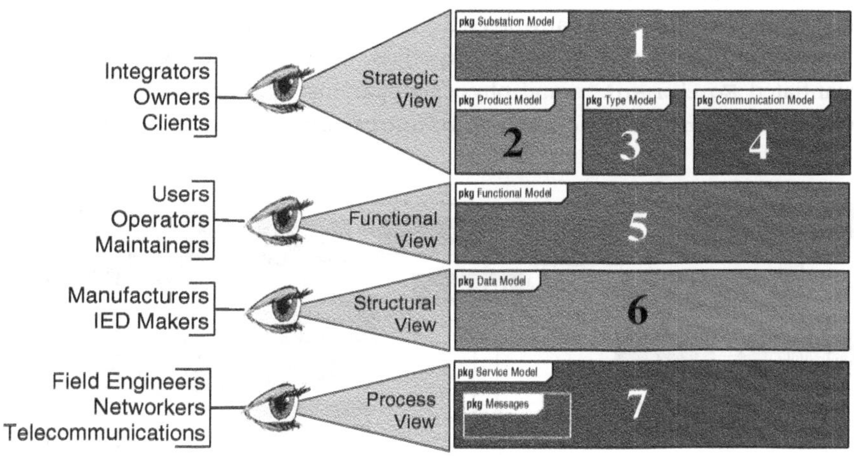

Figure 5.2 Hierarchical layered organization of SAS views and models.

logical nodes. The next Structural View details all data objects used by ***logical nodes*** and functional objects, inherited from classes defined in the IEC 61850 Data Model. Finally, the Process View collects all objects derived from classes defined on the Service Model and its Messages package to support the methods of the above layers. These views, as collections of packages of classes, are organized by hierarchical, layered dependency relations defined in a unique UML Class Diagram, shown in Figure 16.1 in Annex 16.1, and described in the subsequent paragraphs. The packages in this figure follow the same numbering and color scheme as Figure 5.2, utilizing the UML graphical conventions outlined in Annex 16.7, summarized in the following paragraphs and chapters.

5.5 Substation Model

The Substation Model is the highest level of object hierarchy, based on the functional structure of the substation. It is configured using ***SCL*** to describe a Strategic View of an SAS. It links the automation functions to substation functions and equipment and derives functional designations for the ***logical nodes*** from the substation structure. Its objects are instantiated from the abstract classes ***Substation***, ***VoltageLevel***, ***Bay***, ***Equipment***, ***SubEquipment***, ***ConnectivityNode***, and ***Terminal***. These classes are related in the UML Class Diagram in Figure 5.3, composing the Substation Model package, part of the Strategic View at the upper Layer 1 of the general UML model of Figures 5.1 and 5.2. The IEC 61850 documentation provides a detailed description of these classes in this and the subsequent packages.

Using these classes, a substation can be modeled physically, by objects instantiated from the class ***VoltageLevel***, containing electrically connected substation parts instantiated from the ***Bay*** class, as part of the switchyard, with instantiated ***Equipment's*** and physical apparatus; or functionally, by instantiated ***Equipment's*** performing ***Subfunctions*** of the main ***Functions***

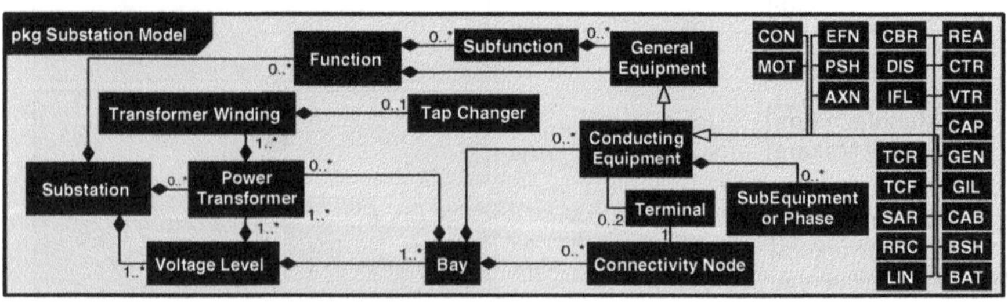

Figure 5.3 Substation Model package.

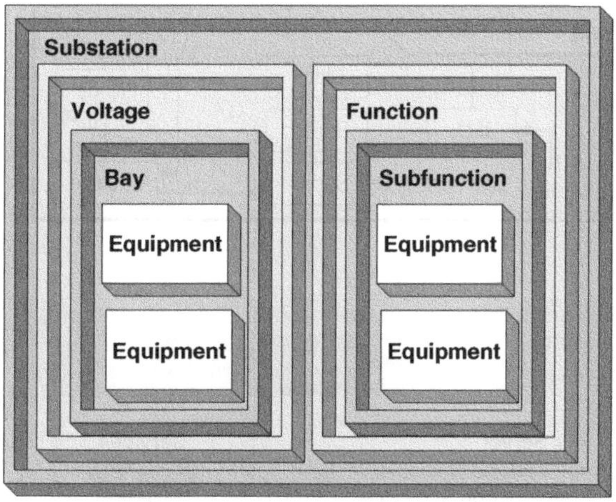

Figure 5.4 Typical substation instantiated objects.

attained by the ***Substation***. These are linked by ***ConnectivityNode*** and ***ConductingEquipments*** objects between primary devices and ***Terminals***, as well as by electrical connection points of a primary apparatus at a single voltage level. Figure 5.4 shows an example of a hierarchical composition of a typical substation, with a physical and functional model of the objects instantiated from these classes.

These objects are implemented using classes defined in a Product Model, in the second layer of the integrated model of IEC 61850, as part of an SAS's Strategic or Business View.

5.6 Product Model

The Product Model is used to specify the characteristics of all ***IEDs*** within a Strategic View of the SAS. It describes the configuration of each ***IED***, with its ***access points***, ***logical devices***, and ***logical nodes***. It also defines the capabilities of each ***IED*** by the communication services offered, with default or configuration values. The following abstract classes are described in IEC 61850 for the Product Model: ***IED***, ***Server***, ***LDevice***, ***LNode***, ***LN0***, ***Router***, and ***Clock***. These classes are related to the UML Class Diagram in Figure 5.5, which forms the Product Model package, part of the Strategic View on Layer 2 of the general UML layered model shown in Figure 5.2.

According to IEC 61850, ***IEDs*** are substation automation (SA) devices that perform SA functions using LNs residing on servers, the communication entities within an ***IED***. Within a ***Server***, an ***LDevice*** models a ***logical device*** (***LD***) composed of ***LNodes***, or ***logical nodes*** (***LN***), which contain

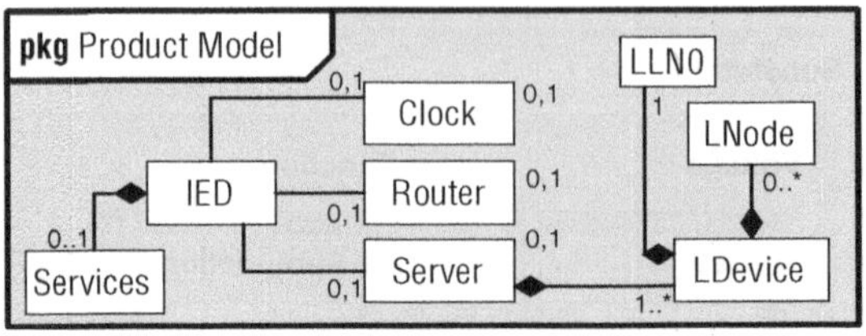

Figure 5.5 Product Model package.

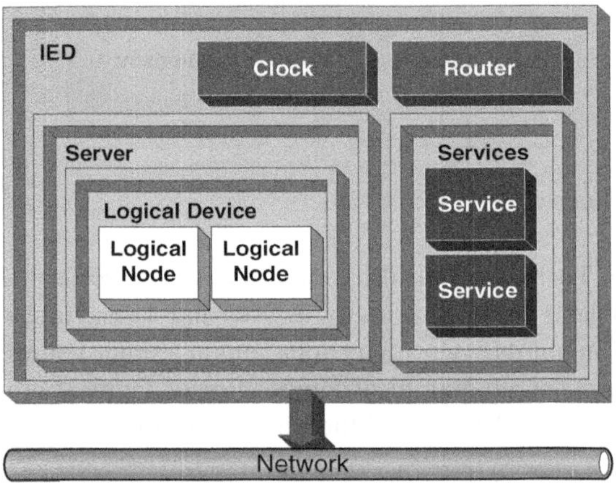

Figure 5.6 Typical IED instantiated objects.

objects that carry their data. ***Routers***, a component of a communication network, connect different subnetworks and block real-time messages outside the standard scope. A clock indicates the location of a subnetwork's master clock. Figure 5.6 illustrates the general composition of a typical Product Model, featuring these instantiated objects.

Figure 16.1 in Annex 16.1 illustrates how this layer relates to the upper layer through the association of the ***LNode*** class with the corresponding Substation View classes in the upper layer, which model their deployment by ***logical nodes*** in specific ***IED***s. These objects are also implemented in ***SCL***, referring to data classes defined in a Type Model, which is part of the third layer of the integrated model, as well as the Strategic View of an SAS.

5.7 Type Model

The Type Model represents an external view concerning substation information and its formatting types as part of a Strategic View of the SAS. It describes, in abstract terms, the type of each piece of data used in SAS and declared in ***SCL***.

Only two abstract classes are included in the Type Model by IEC 61850: **`Data`** and **`Type`**. All concrete data types are derived from these classes, as shown in the UML Class Diagram in Figure 5.7, which forms part of the Type Model package on Layer 3 of the leveled model in Figure 4.32. Specific types of data for each application are modeled in the next layer.

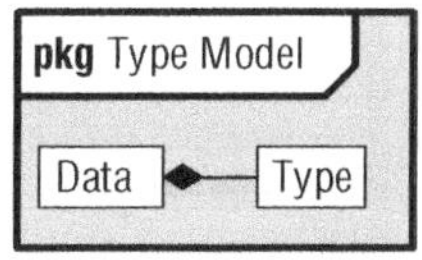

Figure 5.7 Type Model package.

Figure 16.1 in Annex 16.1 illustrates the relationship between this layer and Layer 2 by associating the **`Data`** class with the **`LNode`** class of the Product Model, which models the structuring of each **`logical node`** in **`Data`** objects by their **`Type`**. The behavior of these objects depends on classes from the Communication Model, in Layer 4 of the integrated model, as part of a Strategic View.

5.8 Communication Model

The Communication Model is used to specify the characteristics of local networks and their ***access points***, completing the Strategic View of the SAS. It includes the direct communication capabilities between logical nodes via logical buses (**`SubNetworks`**) and **`IED`** access points, as well as which **`logical devices`** and nodes are reachable via an **`access point`**. The Communication Model also describes which **`IED access points`** are connected to each subnetwork. The following abstract classes are included in the IEC 61850 Communication Model: **`SubNetwork`**, **`PhysConn`**, **`Address`**, **`GSV`**, and **`SMV`**. These classes are related to the UML Class Diagram in Figure 5.8, which comprises the Communication Model package on Layer 4 of the general UML layered model of Figure 5.2.

In this model, a **`Subnetwork`** object serves as a connecting node for direct (link-layer) communication between ***access points***. It contains all **`access points`** that can (logically) communicate with the **`SubNetwork`** protocol without an intervening router. It defines a logical connection with a specific protocol. An **`Access point`** is a communication point of the **`logical device`**(s) of an **`IED`** to a subnetwork. A **`Router`** class in the Product Model extends access to servers connected to another subnetwork at another access point of that **`IED`**, which hosts the router function. In contrast, a **`Clock`** class in the second layer synchronizes the internal clocks of all (other) **`IEDs`** connected to this subnetwork. A **`PhysConn`** class models the server's physical address, while an **`Address`** class defines the server's logical address. **`GSVs`**

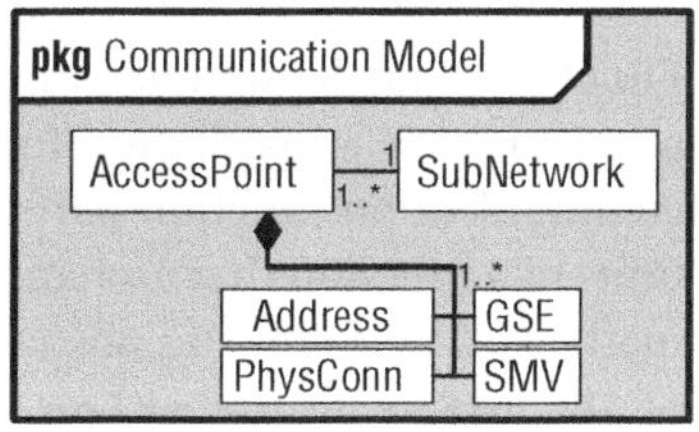

Figure 5.8 Communication Model package.

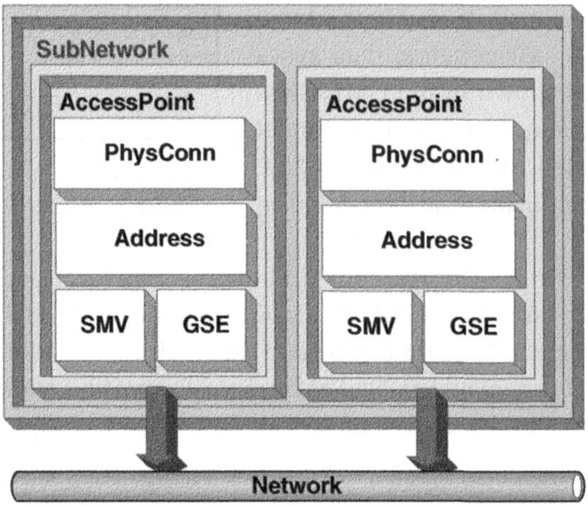

Figure 5.9 Typical SubNetwork instantiated objects.

and ***SMVs*** are classes that represent the addresses of ***GOOSE*** and ***GSSE control blocks***, respectively, as well as the addresses of ***Sampled Value control blocks***. Figure 5.9 shows a pictorial composition of a typical Communication Model using instantiated objects.

Figure 16.1 in Annex 16.1 illustrates how this model relates to the upper layers by associating the ***AccessPoint*** class with the ***LNode*** and ***Router*** classes of the Product Model, which models the access points of ***logical nodes*** and routers within each ***IED***. These classes and the remaining objects of the Strategic View are all described in ***SCL*** and implemented using classes defined in Layer 5 of the integrated model as part of the Functional View of an SAS.

5.9 Functional Model

A Functional Model defines the task(s) performed by the SAS, i.e., by application functions, or the system's characteristic that guarantees the attainment of a specific objective, as part of a Functional View of the SAS. Generally, functions exchange data with other functions performed by ***IEDs*** (physical devices). Functions may be split across different ***IEDs***, but they communicate with each other to form a distributed function and with parts of other functions. These communication-function parts are modeled by Logical Nodes, the most minor units of a function that exchange data, software objects defined by their data and methods. The following abstract classes are included in the Functional Model of IEC 61850: ***Substation***, ***Automation System***, ***Function***, ***Network***, ***IED***, ***Server***, ***Proxy Gateway***, ***Logical Device***, ***LDO***, ***Compatible Logical Node***, and ***PICOM***. These classes are related in the UML Class Diagram shown in

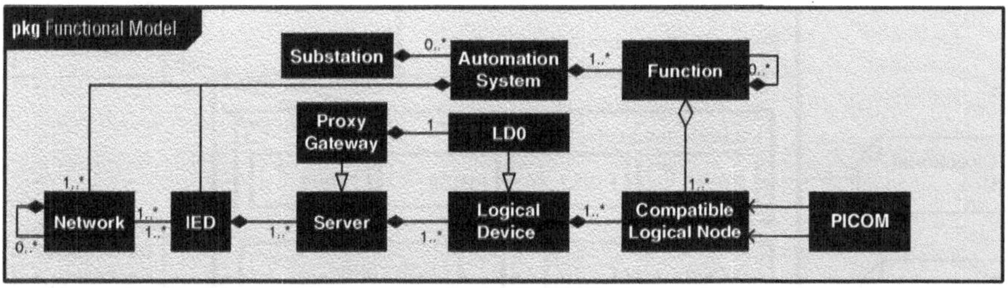

Figure 5.10 Functional Model package.

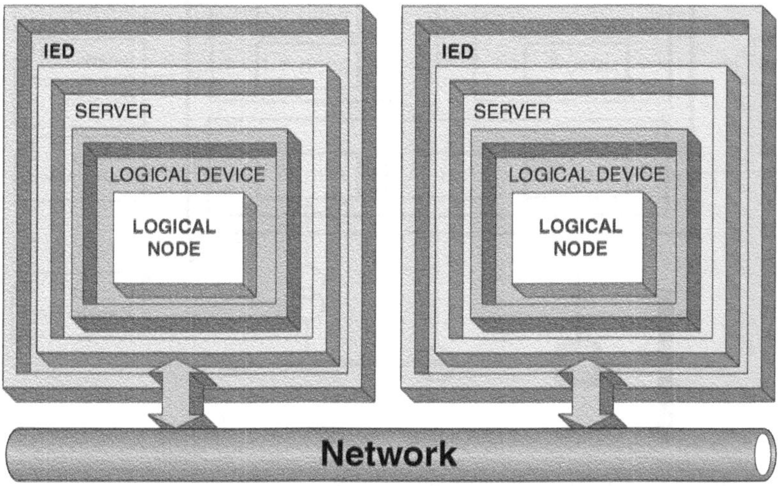

Figure 5.11 Typical functional instantiated objects.

Figure 5.10, forming the Functional Model on Layer 5 of the UML layered model shown in Figure 5.2.

Instantiation from these abstract classes enables the construction of a functional view of an SAS, comprising ***IED***s that contain ***Servers*** with one or more ***Logical Devices***. Each ***Logical Device*** may include several instances of ***Logical Nodes*** as containers of ***Data*** objects. Figure 5.11 shows a pictorial composition of a typical functional model with these instantiated objects.

Figure 5.12 illustrates a functional model for a protection ***IED***, constructed from objects inherited from classes in the Functional Model. It includes ***logical devices*** for distance protection, overcurrent protection, measuring, recording, and merging units.

Figure 16.1 on Annex 16.1 illustrates the relationship between this layer and the upper layers by associating the classes ***Substation***, ***Function***, ***Network***, ***IED***, ***Server***, ***Logical Devices***, ***Compatible Logical Node***, and

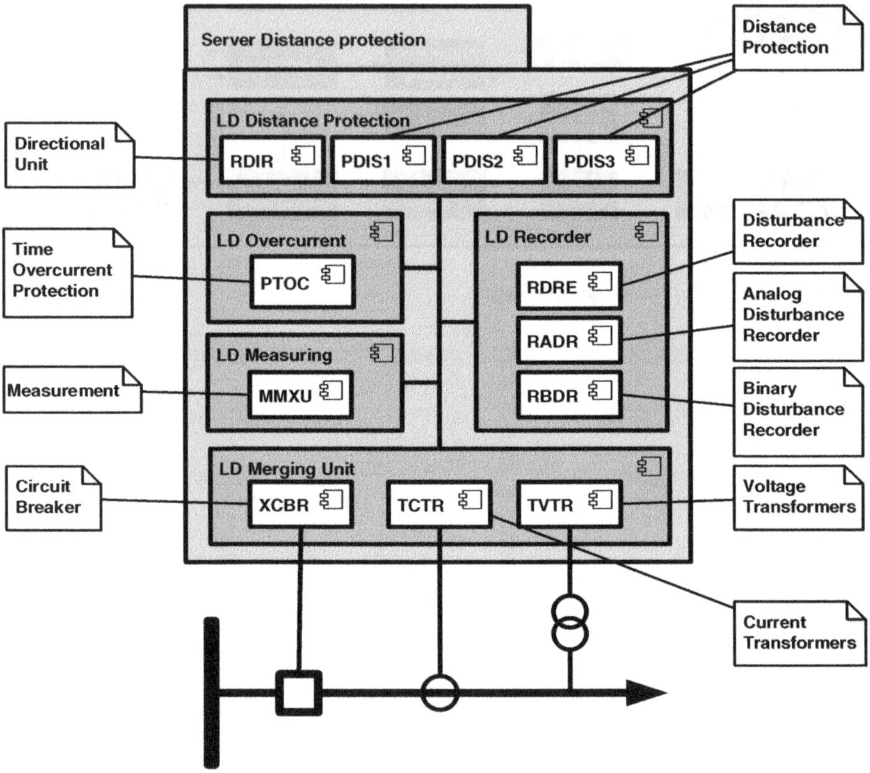

Figure 5.12 Functional Model for distance protection.

Access Point with their corresponding classes in the upper layers. This model is the concrete implementation of the SAS described by ***`SCL`*** in the upper models. These objects are implemented using data classes defined in a Data Model, in Layer 6 of the integrated model, as part of the Structural View of an SAS.

5.10 Data Model

A Data Model represents concrete knowledge concerning substation information and its class representation, forming a Structural View of an SAS data. It describes abstractly the information used by any real function or device in the substation. The following abstract classes are included in the Data Model of IEC 61850: ***`Namespace`***, ***`Data`***, ***`Composite CDC`***, ***`Common Data`***, ***`Simple CDC`***, ***`Primitive Component`***, ***`Composite Component`***, ***`Basic Type`***, ***`Data Type`***, ***Data Attribute***, and ***`Functional Constraint`***. These classes

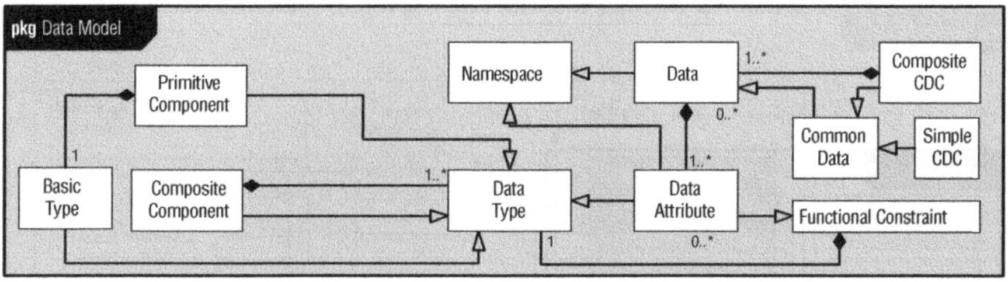

Figure 5.13 Data Model package.

are related to the UML Class Diagram of Figure 5.13, which comprises the Data Model package on Layer 6 of the UML layered model.

A key element of the IEC 61850 Data Model is the ***Namespace***, an abstract container environment that groups unique identifiers (i.e., names). It provides context and disambiguation of items with the same name residing in different namespaces. An identifier defined in a namespace is associated with that namespace, allowing the same identifier to be independently defined in multiple namespaces with different meanings.

Figure 16.1 in Annex 16.1 illustrates the relationships between this layer and the upper layers: through class associations, the ***Logical Device*** inherits a ***Namespace*** and all ***Compatible Logical Nodes*** of the Functional Layer on the upper level, and through containment relations, this layer contains the ***Data*** class. The methods supported by these objects are implemented using data classes defined in a Service Model, which is part of the seventh and lowest layer of the integrated model, as shown in Figure 5.2, within the Process View of an SAS.

5.11 Service Model

A Service Model is a set of functions and procedures made available for the user of a Data Model to access or change its data components and configurations as part of a Process View of the SAS. IEC 61850 defines two types of services: abstract services, which are functions and procedures described for the model's classes, and concrete services, which are functions and methods implemented in objects derived from the model's classes. These services encompass functions for reading and writing values and attributes, controlling devices, reporting and logging events, accessing directory information, uploading and downloading files, and transferring ***GOOSE/SV*** messages. An abstract communication service interface (***ACSI***) and a specific communication service mapping (***SCSM***) provide interfaces to these services. The following abstract classes are defined in this model by IEC 61850: ***Two-Part Application Association***, ***Multi-Part***

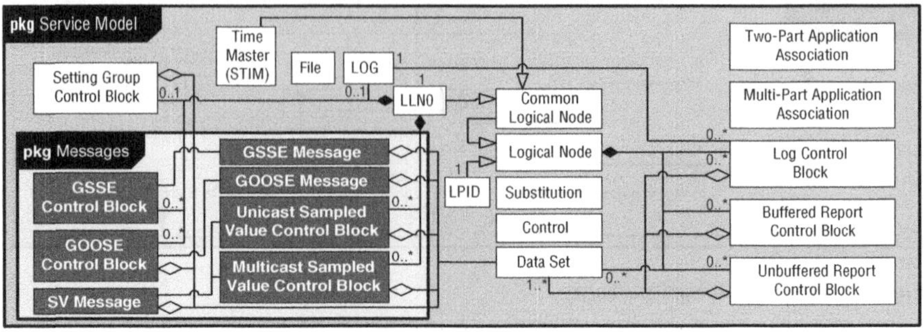

Figure 5.14 Service Model package.

Application Association, ***Log Control Block***, ***Buffered Report Control Block***, ***Unbuffered Report Control Block***, ***Common Logical Node***, ***Logical Node***, ***Substitution***, ***Control***, ***Data Set***, ***LPHD***, ***LLN0***, ***LOG***, ***File***, ***Time Master***, ***Setting Group Control Block***. Additionally, the following message classes are defined in the Messages subpackage: ***GSSE*** Message, ***GOOSE*** Message, ***Unicast Sampled Value Control Block***, ***Multicast Sampled Value Control Block***, ***GSSE Control Block***, ***GOOSE Control Block***, and ***SV Message***. These classes are related to the UML Class Diagram of Figure 5.14, which comprises the Service Model package on Layer 7 of the UML layered model of Figure 5.2. Message classes are grouped into subpackages of this layer, including ***GSSE/GOOSE Control Blocks*** and Messages, ***SV Message***, and ***Unicast/Multicast Sampled Value Control Blocks***, depending on the network middleware.

Abstract services include client–server request/reply of information, peer-to-peer real-time multicasting, and Simple Network Time Protocol (SNTP) time synchronization. Figure 5.15 illustrates how these services function as middleware, providing network access to data on the distributed ***logical nodes*** and the mapped physical equipment of substations and power plants.

Logical Nodes and their services have been defined by IEC 51850 for almost any conceivable power system equipment and function, including substations, hydropower plants, wind power, and distributed energy resources. Many others are being defined currently. Services have been mapped to the Ethernet protocol stack, Web Services, Common Object Request Broker Architecture (CORBA), and other middleware for communication.

Figure 16.1 in Annex 16.1 illustrates how this layer relates to the upper layers through a class association that enables the composition of messages with data from the Data and Functional packages. These messages are routed directly to the middleware used for communication in the SAS network.

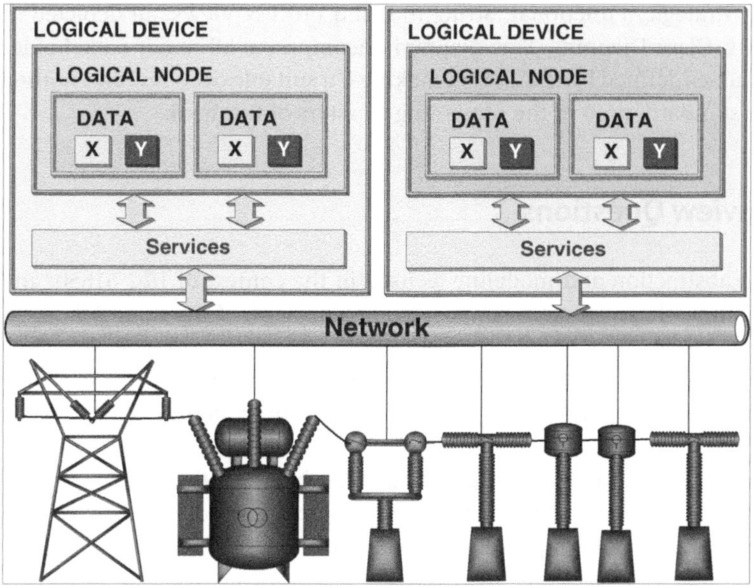

Figure 5.15 Typical service instantiated objects.

5.12 Summary

Despite its complexity and scale, IEC 61850 can be studied and understood through a hierarchical model structure, similar to the standard OSI model for network communication. This allows it to be partitioned into layers that provide services to upper levels while using services from lower levels. Other stakeholders can utilize specific layers to understand and specify SAS systems, while developers can leverage the entire stack to implement devices and complete automation systems.

Specifically, the format of the user requirements is not covered by IEC 61850, motivating CIGRE to propose a domain-specific language to formally specify the required functionality, published as a brochure number 926 entitled "Methods for Specification of Functional Requirements of Protection, Automation, and Control," available at the digital platform eCIGRE.org.

This chapter presented a top-down object-oriented model of the IEC 61850 standard, analogous to the traditional seven-layer OSI model for network communication. In this model, all major software classes defined by IEC 61850 are organized in stacked layers, ranging from the higher slices visible to users and integrators to the lower layers that interface with network communication middleware and field process equipment. These seven models comprise four concurrent views of an SAS: the Strategic, Functional, Structural, and Process Views, all depicted in a single UML Class Diagram. This diagram encompasses all major stakeholder needs and classes defined by IEC 61850, making it a suitable overview and unified guide to the standard, used in the remaining chapters of this book.

5.13 Review Questions

1 Define abstraction and modeling as used in the context of IEC 61850, and explain how these concepts support the organization of the standard.

2 Explain why IEC 61850 can be organized into seven stacking models. How is this layered structure similar to the OSI communication model?

3 IEC 61850 is described as complex and extensive, with thousands of pages of content. Analyze how creating a digital, machine-readable UML version of the standard could improve interoperability and tool integration.

4 A utility engineer must model a new substation using ***SCL***. Describe how the Substation Model, Product Model, and Type Model each contribute to creating the Strategic View needed for this task.

5 Compare the roles of the Product Model and the Functional Model in representing ***IED*** capabilities and SAS functional behavior. How do these models complement each other?

6 List the abstract classes that make up the Type Model and summarize its role within the IEC 61850 architecture.

7 Consider a scenario where a protection function is distributed across three ***IEDs***. Explain how the Functional Model and Communication Model together ensure the proper operation of this distributed function.

8 Examine the importance of ***Namespaces*** in the Data Model. Why are namespaces crucial for ensuring consistency and preventing ambiguity in large, multi-vendor IEC 61850 projects?

9 Explain the difference between Abstract Services and Concrete Services in the Service Model. Give an example of how each one supports SAS operation.

10 Assess how message classes like ***GOOSE***, ***GSSE***, and ***Sampled Values*** are arranged in the Service Model to support the Process View of an SAS.

11 The four UML views—Strategic, Functional, Structural, and Process—serve different stakeholders. Analyze how aligning these views enhances communication among engineers, integrators, and system operators during an SAS project.

12 Considering all seven IEC 61850 models, suggest how a novice engineer could use the layered UML Class Diagram as a learning roadmap to gradually understand the standard from high-level concepts down to service and message classes.

6

Communication Models

6.1 Introduction

Distributed systems operate by exchanging data over communication networks that connect all servers, clients, and users, forming what is commonly called a network. In an automation system, the networks connecting all Intelligent Electronic Devices (IEDs) act as a communication backbone, enabling messages to be exchanged among distributed objects and services necessary to complete distributed functions.

6.2 Learning Objectives

This chapter discusses the main communication requirements for IEC 61850 as applied to Substation Automation System (SAS) and Power Plant Automation System. The following topics are covered:

- Communication Profiles
- Communication Requirements
- Real-time Requirements
- Abstract Interfaces
- Specific Interfaces
- Mapping to Manufacturing Message Specification (MMS)
- Mapping to Common Object Request Broker Architecture (CORBA)
- Mapping to Ethernet

No specific technology, such as a wired network, optical fiber, microwaves, or satellite communications, will be described, except for those that are standardized. The topics will be covered from an abstract functional perspective, in accordance with the IEC 61850 standard.

6.3 Communication Profiles

A communication profile, as defined by IEC 61850, is used to map the specific needs of ***IEDs*** and to exchange messages within a SAS. The upper Application layer of the Open System Interconnection (OSI) model is mapped to protection and control application requirements for information exchange. These are represented by specific SAS data representation and encryption, mapped to the Presentation layer of the OSI model. ***IED*** and Interhost communication are facilitated by messages exchanged at the Session layer, primarily to establish publisher–subscriber (P/S) and peer-to-peer relationships. These are provided by Transport layer services, enabling end-to-end ***IEDs*** to establish reliable connections. The Network layer provides logical and path addressing inside the substation network, mapped to ***IED*** physical addresses supported by the Data Link layer. The Physical layer of the OSI communication model supports all media and signal transmission inside the substation. This setup is summarized in Figure 6.1.

This framework is consistently used to support all communication messages of IEC 61850, both inside and outside a digital substation.

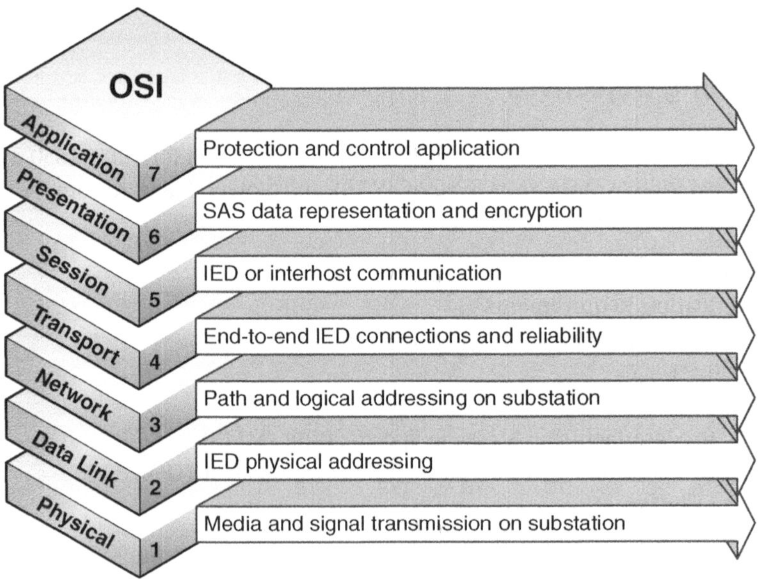

Figure 6.1 IEC 61850 mapping to OSI reference model.

6.4 Communication Messages

The primary communication requirements in an SAS system concern the various types of information transfer needed for the engineering, maintenance, and operation of a power plant or substation. These can be described in seven distinct classes, related to the kinds of messages exchanged among servers at different layers of a utility communication architecture, as shown by the circled numbers in Figure 6.2.

1. Sampled value exchange for current transformers (CTs) and voltage transformers (VTs)
2. Fast Input/Output (I/O) data for protection and control

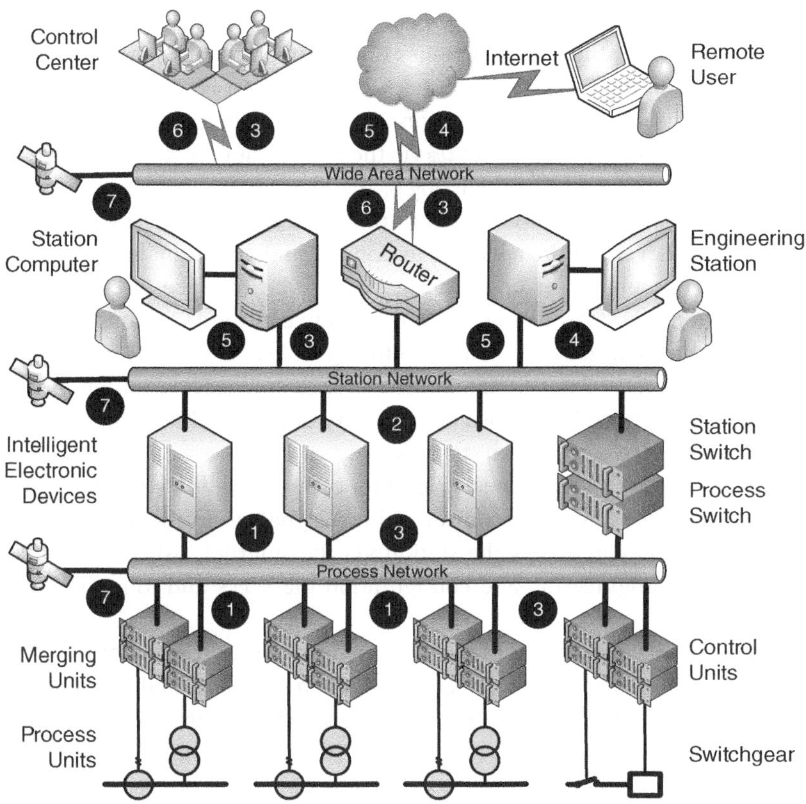

Figure 6.2 General information transfer requirements in SAS.

3. Control and trip signals
4. Engineering and configuration
5. Monitoring and supervision
6. Control center communication
7. Time synchronization

At the Process Level (0), sampled values of current, voltage, and the status of switchgear units must be exchanged from ***CTs***, ***VTs***, and any other analog or discrete sensor on primary equipment. This is shown as interface 1 in Figure 6.1. At the same level (0), the control and trip signals, as shown in interface 3, can be exchanged with the switchgear and upper levels to control primary equipment, such as circuit breakers and generators. A time synchronization interface 7 is also necessary at this level to orchestrate the merging and control unit sampling processes.

At the Bay Level (1), the sampled values and trip/command signals from the process level, transmitted through interfaces 1 and 3, must be communicated to and from ***IEDs*** for bay logic and protection. Fast I/O data for protection and control must also be exchanged among ***IEDs*** via the bay or station network to support decision-making and bay/station-wide logic. A time synchronization interface 7 may also be necessary at this level to orchestrate the ***IED*** logic processes.

At the Station Level (2), in addition to control and trip signals transmitted from the station computer or engineering station via interface 3, engineering and configuration messages can be exchanged between the IEDs and the engineering station through interface 4, or monitoring and supervision signals can be transmitted via interface 5 to the station computer or engineering station. A time synchronization interface 7 may also be necessary at this level to orchestrate the signals exchanged between the two stations.

At the System Level (3), interface 6 is used for communication with the control center, while interface 3 receives control and trip signals from the utility control center. Remote users can access the station via the Internet, using interfaces 4 and 5 to exchange engineering and configuration messages and to monitor and supervise.

The main challenge for the IEC 61850 standard is meeting all these information-exchange requirements with current communication standards and technologies. Previously, common substation protocols were primarily Modbus, DNP, and IEC 870-5-1. Modbus is a widely used master-slave protocol among industrial users and has gained popularity in substations and power plants. It issues simple read/write commands to addresses inside an ***IED***. Distributed Network Protocol (DNP) is a widely used master–slave protocol, primarily employed in North America. DNP can run over multiple media, such as RS-232 and RS-485, and issue various Read/Write messages to an ***IED***. Finally, IEC 870-5-101 is considered the

European counterpart to DNP. It differentiates itself from DNP with its slightly different messaging structure and the ability to access object information from the **IED**.

To understand how IEC 61850 meets all the information exchange requirements of substations, reference will be made to the OSI communication model depicted in Figure 6.3. Starting at the Physical layer, the standard defines the generation and recognition of coded signals that model the events and variables of standard substations, such as secondary AC and voltage derived from CTs and VTs. These signals are distributed by the process network, with standardized access to the bus medium defined at the Data Link layer. If necessary, packet assembly and routing through the process, station, and wide-area network are determined at the Network layer. The Transport layer establishes links between **IEDs** and external users, granting message segmentation and necessary troubleshooting. Synchronization and control of communications are defined in the Session layer for both process, station, and wide-area networks. Formatting and coding information is perhaps the strongest feature of IEC 61850, which is implemented at the Presentation layer of the OSI model, for the **logical nodes** and messages exchanged among **IEDs**. Finally, the substation applications and final use of information are defined by standardized services exposed by **logical nodes** and servers at the Application layer.

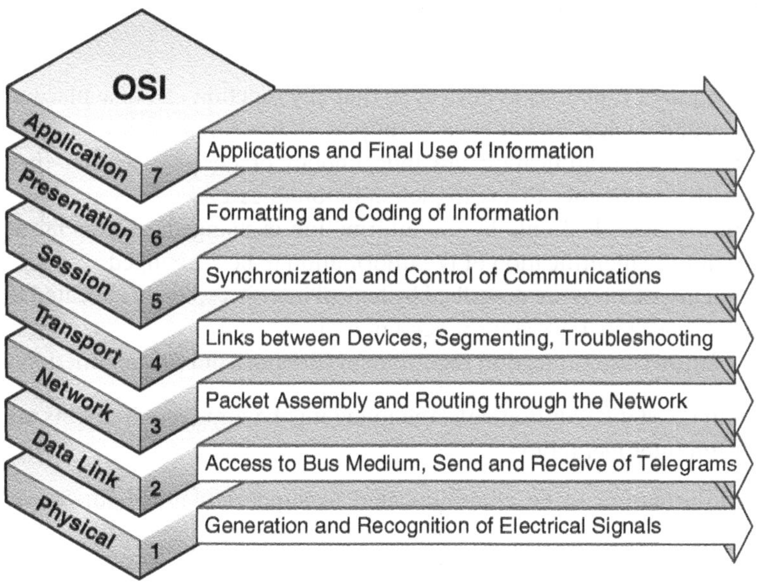

Figure 6.3 OSI communication model.

6.5 Communication Requirements

To attain these functions, four main requirements are usually expected from a communication system in an automation project:

- Reliability
- Interoperability
- Interchangeability
- Performance

Reliability refers to the communication system's ability to perform its required functions under stated conditions for a specified period. In computer networking, a reliable protocol provides reliable delivery of data to the intended recipient(s). In contrast, an unreliable protocol does not notify the sender when transmitted data is delivered. Reliability is vital in automation systems, as communication failures can damage equipment and even harm people.

Besides reliability, interoperability refers to the ability of two or more ***IEDs***, from the same vendor or different vendors, to exchange information and use it to execute specified functions correctly. The devices should connect to a common bus with a standard protocol (syntax) to exchange information. To use the received information, the devices shall understand the information provided by other devices (semantics). The devices shall perform a common or joint function (if applicable) to retain functionality. Full interoperability requires the attainment of several static requirements, such as:

- Free allocation of functions to devices so that any function can take place in any device, and devices do not need to support all functions
- Functions and communication are independent of devices, so that they operate with no reference to any implementation in ***IEDs***
- Functions are described only by the information exchanged, only as far as necessary for the identification of the information to be exchanged
- Functional interactions are described by logical interfaces, freely allocated to physical interfaces or LANs for implementation
- Open for future communication requirements arising from future functions.

In addition to the static requirements, the following dynamic requirements are also listed for full interoperability:

- Generic information to be communicated to support planned functional extensions
- Generic communication behavior to support future extensions with generic rules
- Information transfer with standard contents such as ***Pieces of Information Communication*** (***PICOMs***) defined by IEC 61850

- Exchanged data with all attributes for an unambiguous understanding of the receiver
- Data transfer with guaranteed and defined time, with an acceptable overall transfer time defined and guaranteed in any situation

Finally, the following requirements are listed related to the response as related to interoperability:

- The reaction of the receiving node must fit into the overall requirement of the distributed function to be performed.
- The behavior in a degraded state must be specified in case of erroneous messages, lost data due to communication interruptions, resource limitations, out-of-range data, etc.

Interchangeability refers to the ability of automation and communication systems to replace a device supplied by one manufacturer with a device provided by another, without changing the other elements in the system. Replacement implies physical similarity, whereas no change implies logical similarity.

In summary, interoperability impacts performance, requiring every data message to be self-contained and independent of external information. This may result in significant overhead and inefficient communication, but it is usually not a problem at 10 Mb/S or 100 Mb/s. The requirements for real-time communication further constrain this.

6.6 Real-time Requirements

The real-time term refers to the allowed (upper limit) delay in transmitting or responding to a message, or in performing an action resulting from a command. To cover most requirements found on SAS related to time, IEC 61850 classifies messages into seven types, according to the maximum delay in their transmission:

- **Type 1**—Fast messages (<1 ms)
- **Type 2**—Medium-speed messages (<100 ms)
- **Type 3**—Low-speed messages (<100 ms)
- **Type 4**—Raw data messages (>100 ms)
- **Type 5**—File transfer functions (>1000 ms)
- **Type 6**—Time synchronization (application-dependent)
- **Type 7**—Command messages with access control (application-dependent)

Current restrictions on standard network technology pose the primary design challenge in meeting these requirements. Packet collisions in conventional network technologies, such as Carrier Sense Multiple Access/Collision Detection

(CSMA/CD), result in delays as messages are retransmitted. When the sender (station) is ready to transmit data, it checks if the physical medium is busy. If so, it senses the medium continually until it becomes idle, then transmits a piece of data (a frame). In the event of a collision, the sender waits for a random period and then attempts to transmit again. To circumvent these difficulties, current Ethernet switches employ several alternative technologies, such as the following:

- IEEE 802.3x—Full Duplex Operation
- IEEE 802.1p—Priority Queuing
- IEEE 802.1Q—VLAN
- IEEE 802.1w—Rapid Spanning Tree
- IGMP Snooping (Multicast Filtering)

These techniques try to avoid or minimize, to some extent, the trial-and-error method of conventional CSMA/CD. In a Full Duplex Operation (IEEE 802.3x), switches use different ports for sending and receiving messages from ***IEDs***, avoiding collisions on the channels between servers, as shown in Figure 6.4.

Priority tagging with virtual LANs (VLANs) is a switching method that adds new fields to the standard Ethernet frame (Figure 6.5), enabling the partitioning and isolation of servers and ***IEDs*** in VLANs and assigning priorities to their messages (Figure 6.6). These allow the assignment of priority tagging to mission-critical frames, so that the switch processes them first before processing low-priority frames. SAS can now group ***IEDs*** and messages by intended application, using different priorities and VLANs.

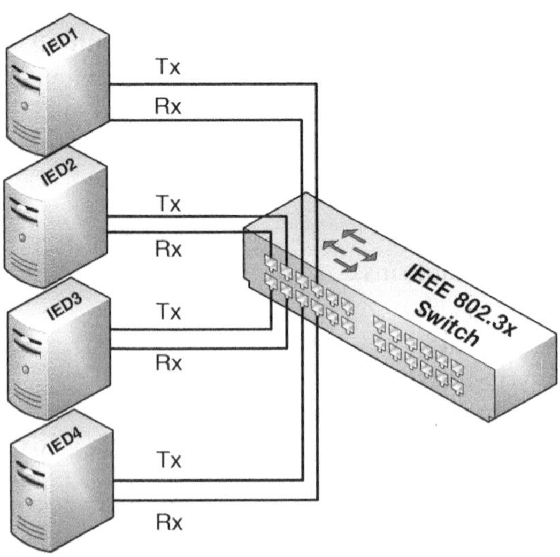

Figure 6.4 Collision avoidance with full duplex ports.

Figure 6.5 Standard Ethernet frame.

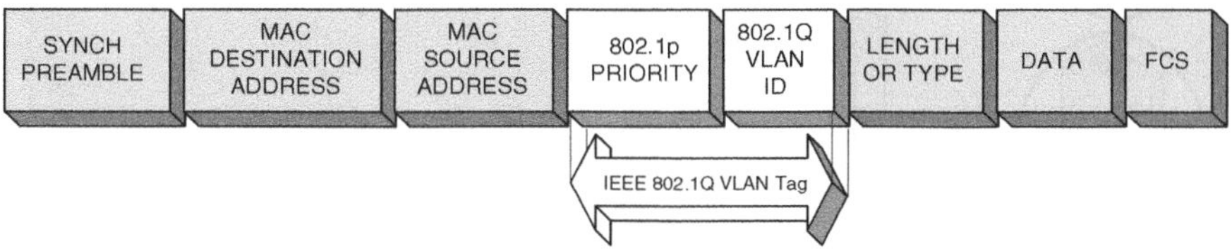

Figure 6.6 Priority tagging with VLANs.

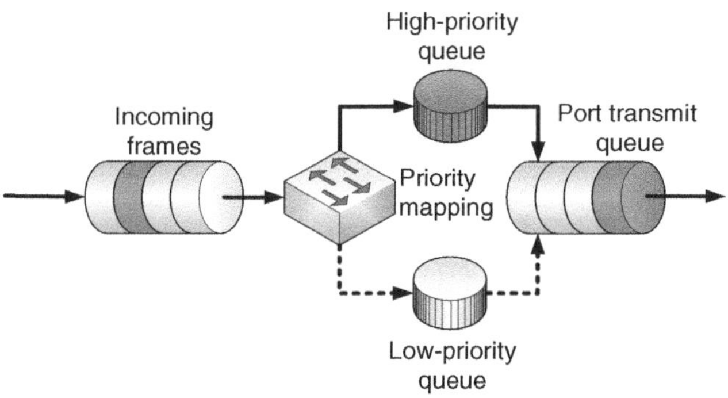

Figure 6.7 Frame processing inside a switch.

Inside the switch, the incoming frames are queued in an incoming queue by their order of arrival, as shown in Figure 6.7. Subject to the queue size, it avoids collisions at the incoming port by quickly removing frames from the port and placing them in the queue. The switch uses priority mapping to separate incoming frames into high-priority and low-priority internal circular queues before reordering them in the port transmit queue. The outgoing frames are ordered according to the priority tag on the incoming frames.

VLAN tags on the Ethernet frames allow the switch to segregate ***IEDs*** and servers into different virtual networks, as shown in Figure 6.8. VLAN1 is dedicated to protecting ***IEDs***, while VLAN2 is dedicated to supervising ***IEDs***. Frames arriving at the switch from ***IEDs*** from VLAN1 are replicated only to ***IED1*** and ***IED2s*** on the same virtual network. The same is true for VLAN2, ***IED3***, and ***IED4***. This reduces the risk of collisions and speeds up frame routing in the switch while providing some level of security for these signals.

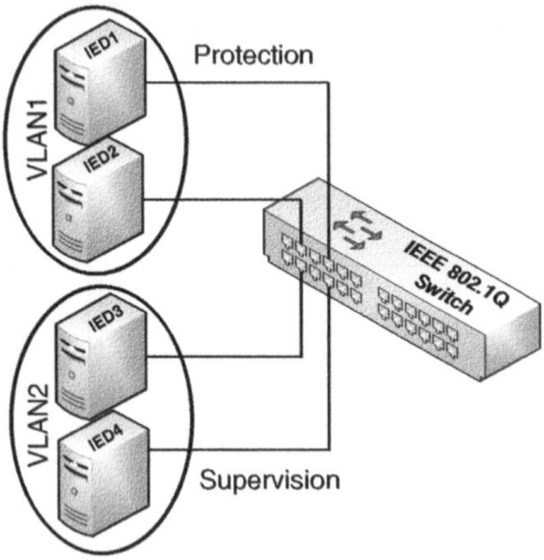

Figure 6.8 Segregation of IEDs into different VLANs.

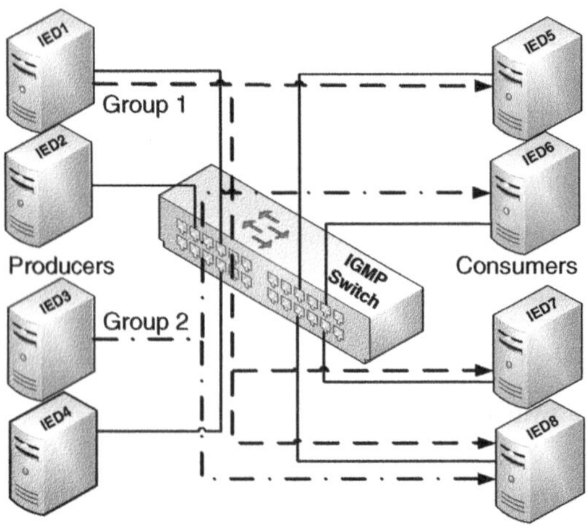

Figure 6.9 Management for multicast messaging.

The Internet Group Management Protocol (IGMP) is a protocol for IP multicasting that transmits an IP datagram to a "host group"—a set of zero or more hosts identified by a single IP destination address. The datagram is not guaranteed to arrive at all destination group members or in the same order as other datagrams. Several host groups can be defined on the same network, as shown in Figure 6.9. A host does not need to be a group member to send datagrams to it. A permanent group has a well-known, administratively assigned IP address and may have any number of members, even zero. On the other hand, a transient group is assigned an address dynamically when the group is created, at the request of a host. A transient group ceases to exist, and its address becomes eligible for reassignment, when its membership drops to zero.

Another recent technology has enabled real-time operation in Ethernet networks. Introduced by Isochronous Real-Time Ethernet (IEC 61784), it allows frames to be synchronized by the highly accurate time synchronization mechanism of IEEE P1588 (transparent clock mode). In this method, the Ethernet bandwidth is time-sliced into slices, for example, 1 ms each, with the slice time parameterized. Among the advantages of real-time Ethernet add-ons, the primary one is the ability to reserve real bandwidth for guaranteed response times. The maximum transfer time for each frame can now be predicted and used in time-sensitive processes. Another advantage is the redundancy of the no-dropout ring, which ensures no telegram is lost even in the event of an interruption. And finally, most importantly, it enables less than 1 μs time synchronization between events over Ethernet using IEEE 1588 Precision Time Protocol Redundancy.

All these network requirements are simplified by IEC 61850, separating the application from the detailed communication aspects by defining abstract interfaces for most of its services.

6.7 Abstract Interfaces

The concept of abstract interfaces is well established in software development, particularly in client–server (C/S) systems. According to it, only those aspects needed to describe the requested actions on the receiving side of a service request are defined. In IEC 61850, this concept is implemented through the ***Abstract Communication Service Interface (ACSI)***, which clients use to request services from servers. Figure 6.10 shows the virtualization principle of ***ACSI***.

The IEC 61850 ***ACSI*** models comprise a set of services and responses that regulate identical network behavior for all ***IEDs***. The services are defined in ***ACSI*** class definitions, following a standard template depicted in Table 6.1.

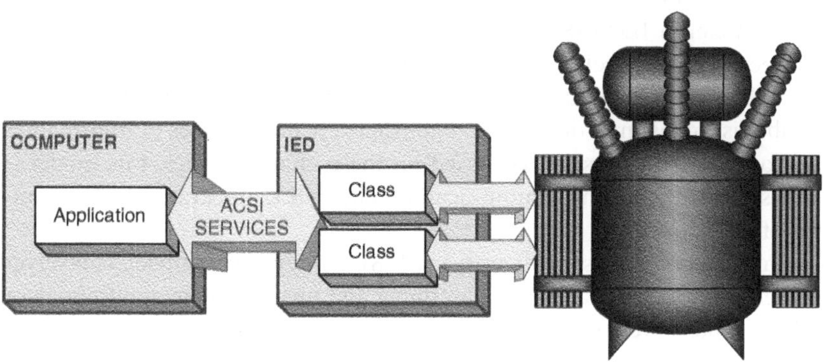

Figure 6.10 Virtualization of ACSI.

Table 6.1 ACSI class definition template.

ABC Class		
Attribute Name	**Attribute Type**	**Value/Range/Explanation**
Attribute1[1..N]	Type1	
Attribute1[1..N]	Type1	
Services		
Service1		
Service2		

IEC 61850 defines two ***ACSI*** Models: C/S and P/S. Two types of ***ACSI*** messages serve these models: broadcast and unicast messages. Figure 6.11 shows the ***ACSI*** models and messages it exchanges.

Broadcast messages are placed onto a communication network intended to be read and acted on, as appropriate, by any ***IED***. A broadcast message typically contains the sender's and global recipient addresses, e.g., time synchronizing. In comparison, unicast (or point-to-point) messages are unidirectional, connection-less communication between a server and a selected set of clients. The C/S model of IEC 61850 uses synchronous messaging, where the client is blocked until the reply arrives. It helps access centralized information and configure parameters of servers and ***IEDs***. It is also used for transaction processing between ***IEDs***, as shown in Figure 6.12. C/S communication offers built-in redundancy features, including connection awareness (with session states, failure detection, and reconnection), failure mechanisms (switching to backup servers), and supervision (of server health and redundancy states).

The P/S model in IEC 61850 uses asynchronous, many-to-many communication between servers. It relies on the preferences of P/S, which deliver messages to many subscribers. A publisher is like a producer or sender of messages, while a subscriber is a consumer or receiver. Publishers create instances of information that get forwarded to subscribers. Based on these characteristics, this model is used in distributed real-time communication. Figure 6.13 illustrates the key components of this model.

An Event Server is used as middleware in a P/S communication model. This server exposes services and interfaces for subscribing and unsubscribing applications or subscribers. A push event service pushes all published events to all subscribers who have registered for that event type. P/S models offer distinguishing advantages over other communication models. They are practical and efficient distributors of large volumes of time-critical information, even when unreliable delivery mechanisms

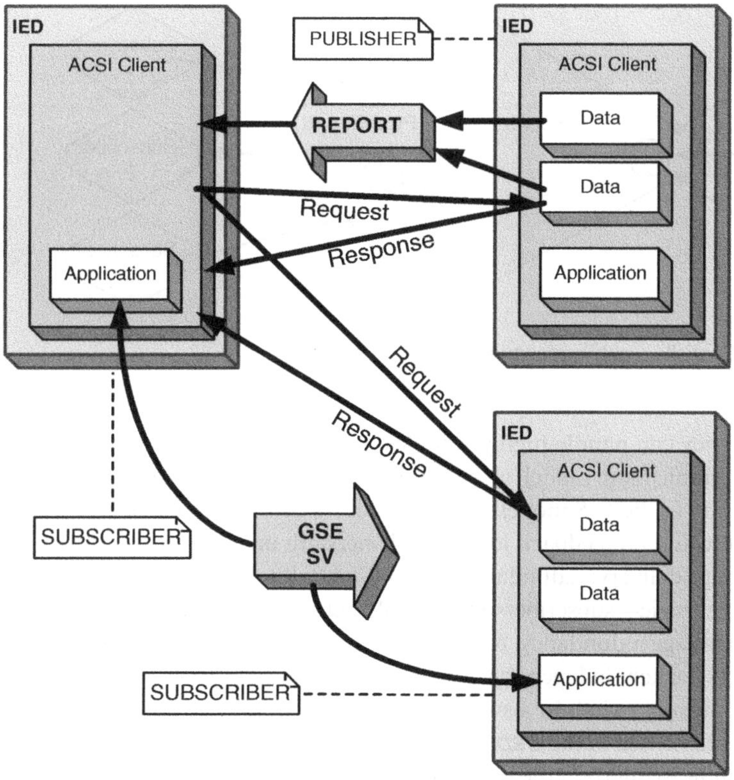

Figure 6.11 ACSI models.

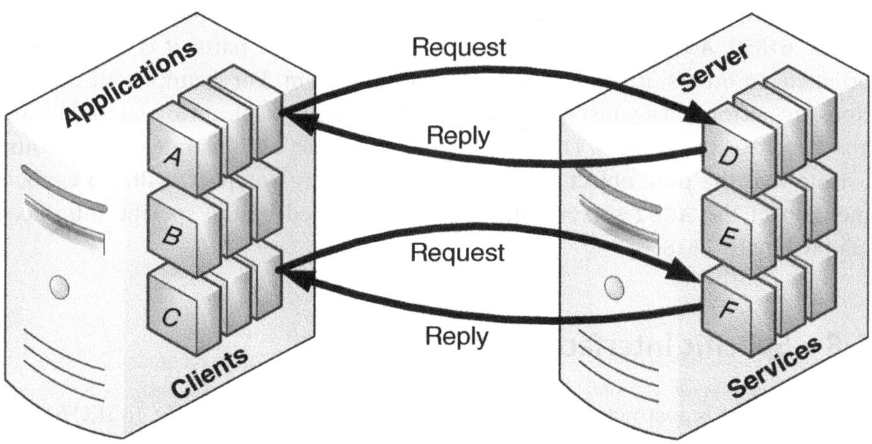

Figure 6.12 Client–server communication model.

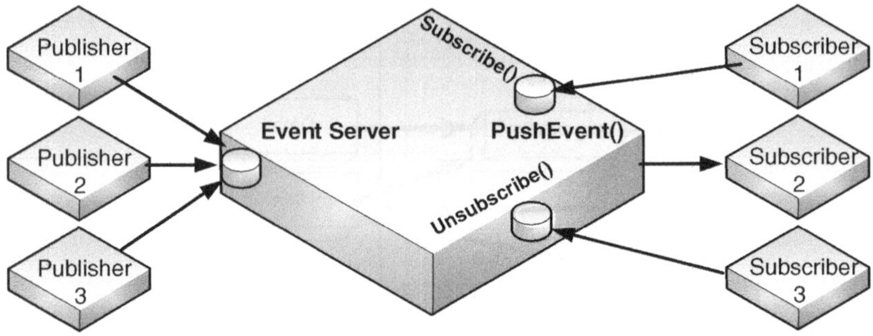

Figure 6.13 Publisher–subscriber communication model.

are in place. They can handle highly complex data flow patterns, and their many-to-many communication model is highly efficient in terms of bandwidth and latency. Contrary to the C/S model, the P/S model is connectionless and acknowledged, guaranteeing no feedback loop—publishers are unaware of the subscriber status or message delivery; redundant streams—multiple publishers, with identical data; switchover logic—subscribers must implement logic to validate data, handle failover, and manage redundancy. Additionally, applications running on publishers and subscribers are kept independent and can be developed by separate entities. For example, to control a switch in a switchyard, an HMI needs to know the name of the switch implemented in the ***IED***, how to express its request to change the switch position, and how to interpret the reply data. IEC 61850 addresses this issue by standardizing abbreviated names for substation functions and equipment, specifying naming conventions for functions and information, and outlining procedures for accessing and exchanging information via ***ACSI*** functions.

Despite these advantages, the ACSI specification still has problems. As defined in IEC 61850, ***ACSI*** is not fully object-oriented. In some parts, it is truly object-oriented. In others, it is a classical procedural system. For example, all interactions are performed against one object, the ***ACSI*** server. Objects to manipulate are also passed as parameters. The code fragment in Table 6.2 illustrates these points:

Note that the pure object-oriented version is more compact, with no explicit mention of the ***ACSI*** server. This is further detailed by the specific interfaces adopted by IEC 61850.

6.8 Specific Interfaces

Because ***ACSI*** is abstract, it needs concrete realizations to be usable. In IEC 61850, they are referred to as ***Specific Communication Service Mapping (SCSM)***. Specific interfaces define all the concrete aspects needed to describe

Table 6.2 ACSI ObjectNameList service example.

sequence <ObjectName> ObjectNameList;
// Strict 61850 version
ObjectNameList Server:: DataObjectDirectory(in DataObjectName name) raises (DirectoryFailed,NoSuchObject);
// More OO version
ObjectNameList DataObject::Directory() raises (DirectoryFailed);

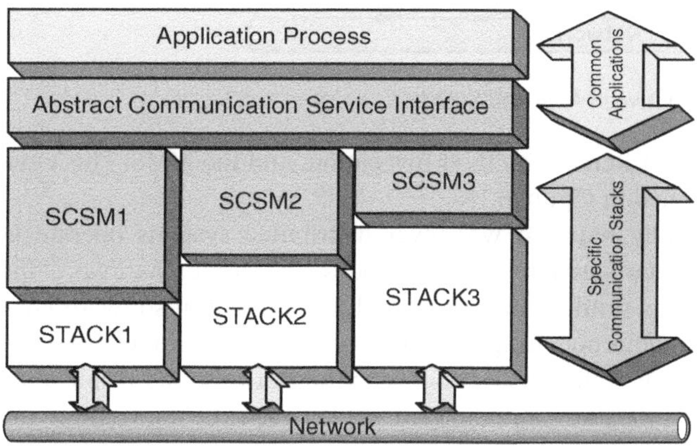

Figure 6.14 IEC 61850 reference model mappings.

the actions required by a particular protocol. Among its objectives, ***SCSM*** maps individual objects from the data model to specific communications technology or middleware. For instance, Part 8-1 of IEC 61850 maps data objects and network services to the MMS protocol, defined by ISO 9506. Figure 6.14 illustrates the IEC 61850 reference model, which maps applications to various ***SCSM*** services and their relationship to the network.

SCSM is a standardized procedure that maps ***ACSI*** services and objects onto a protocol stack/communication profile. For interoperability, a minimum number of profiles and corresponding ***SCSM*** are required. Special application subdomains, such as "station bus" and "process bus," may require multiple mappings. An ***SCSM*** shall detail the instantiation of abstract services into a protocol or middleware-specific single services. It shall detail the mapping of ***ACSI*** objects into objects supported by the specific protocol or middleware. Typical object-oriented middleware

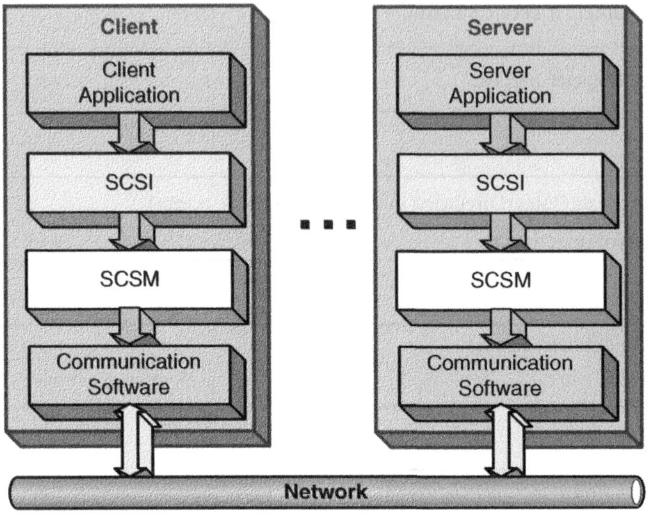

Figure 6.15 Interaction between ACSI and SCSM.

includes the CORBA, Java Remote Method Invocation, and the MMS. This environment can be envisioned in Figure 6.15.

Middleware is generally required whenever distributed systems operate in heterogeneous environments, where different nodes run various hardware and operating systems. In this setting, there is a need for a common software layer that sits above heterogeneous operating systems to provide a uniform platform for distributed applications, as well as a layer between the Network and Application layers. Figure 6.16 illustrates how middleware sits between the application and the operating system, as well as its communication software.

To attain its objective, IEC 61850 requires the following functions from a middleware:

- C/S communication model
- P/S communication model
- Fine-grained time synchronization
- Ability to trade off delivery reliability against delivery delay
- Support for differing quality-of-service requirements of the different message types

The following mappings to existing middleware have been published or are works in progress at the IEC Technical Committee 57, with more to come:

- MMS
- *SV* over Serial Link
- *SV* over ISO/IEC 8802-3

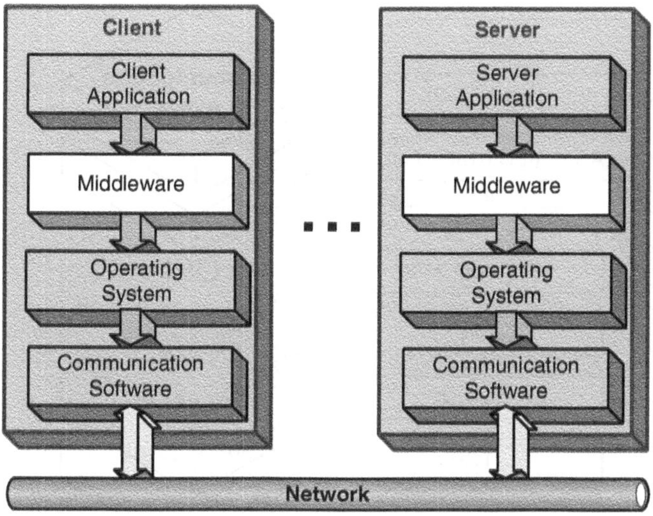

Figure 6.16 Protocol stack incorporating middleware system.

- Web services
- OPC XML DA
- IEC 60870-5-104
- IEC 60870-5-101
- DNP3
- CORBA

Profiles define all these mappings of ***ACSI*** to ***SCSM***. Profiles are agreed-upon format(s) used by a particular protocol or middleware to transmit data objects, commands, etc. ISO recognizes Application Profiles (A-Profiles) and Transport Profiles (T-Profiles). A-Profiles represent the protocols and agreements for the upper three layers of the OSI reference model (Application, Presentation, and Session). In comparison, T-Profiles represent the protocols and agreements for the lower four layers of the OSI reference model (Transport, Network, Data Link, and Physical). Figure 6.17 depicts these definitions on the OSI stack.

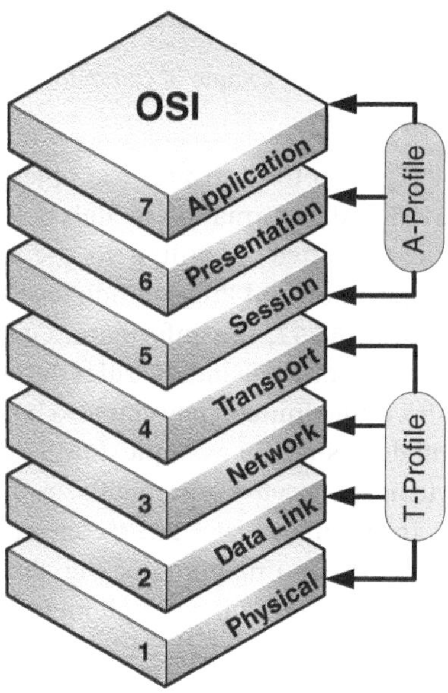

Figure 6.17 Communication profiles.

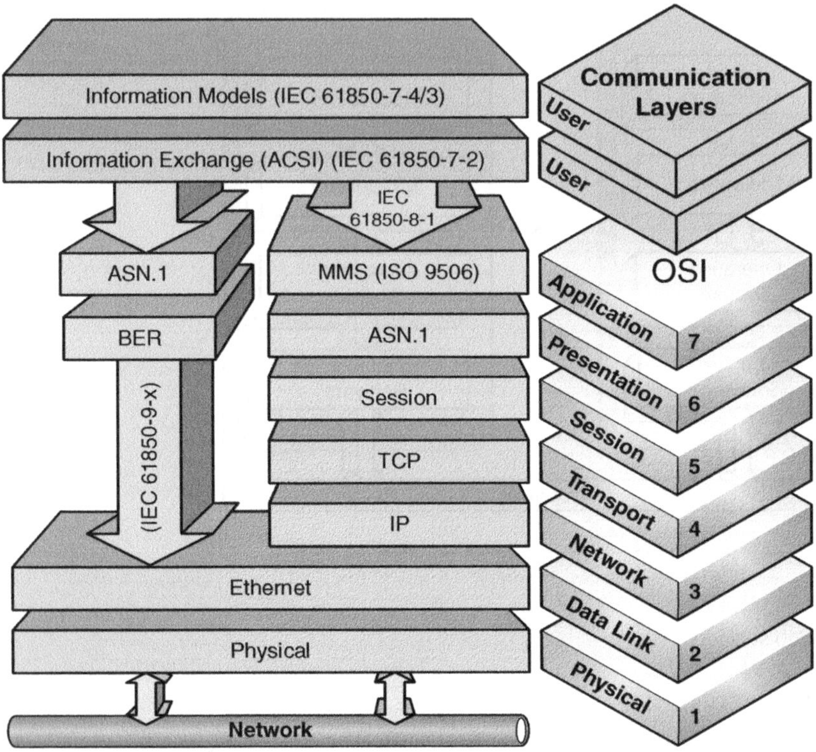

Figure 6.18 Example of communication mapping.

Figure 6.18 illustrates examples of communication mappings defined in IEC 61850. All information models defined on modules IEC 61850-4 and IEC 61850-3 are formatted according to the information exchange rules of ***ACSI***, at the Application and Presentation levels of the OSI communication layers. Once specified in ***ACSI***, this information can be mapped directly to the Ethernet layer of the OSI model using the rules defined in IEC 61850-9-x, for messages that require strict time limits. They can also be mapped to the entire stack of layers in the OSI model, using, for example, MMS as the middleware for that information, with less stringent speed requirements, as in C/S communication.

In summary, each ***SCSM*** comprises a specification of the communication stack being used, a mapping of the abstract IEC 61850-7 specifications to the stack's real elements, and an implementation specification for functionality not covered by the stack. The following paragraphs describe some typical mappings defined in the standard.

6.9 Mapping to MMS

IEC 61850 describes mapping from IEC 61850 ***ACSI*** services to the Manufacturing Message System (MMS) model. MMS is not a standalone communication protocol. It defines the message that an unspecified network must transport. MMS services and protocols are specified to operate over full OSI and TCP-compliant communications profiles. Their use enables provisions for both centralized and distributed architectures.

Developed in 1980 for the MAP project (General Motors' flexible manufacturing initiative), it was initially tied to the OSI communication stack and the Token Bus (IEEE 802.4) by unfortunate circumstance. It was reputed to be heavy, complicated, and costly due to poor implementations. After being adopted by Boeing in the project TOPs (MMS on Ethernet)—a wise step indeed—it was also adopted by the automotive, aerospace, and major manufacturing industries, which used programmable logic controllers. In 1993, it was standardized and updated as ISO/IEC 9506-1: Industrial Automation Systems—Manufacturing Message Specification, Part 1: Service Definition, and ISO/IEC 9506-2: Industrial Automation Systems—Manufacturing Message Specification, Part 2: Protocol Specification. MMS comprises a set of standard objects that must exist in every conformant device, on which operations can be executed (e.g., reading and writing local variables, signaling events, etc.). A set of standard messages is exchanged between a client and a server station to control these objects. These messages are encoded by a set of encoding rules (which map values and parameters to bits and bytes when transmitted) and a set of protocols (which govern the exchange of messages between devices). The main MMS components are variable and type objects, program control objects, event objects, semaphore objects, journal objects, operator station objects, and files.

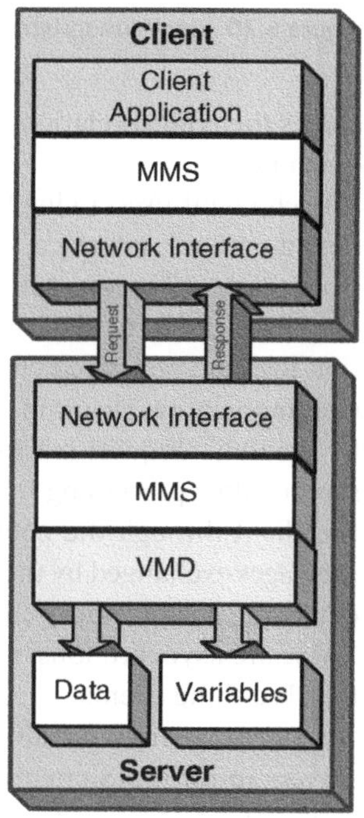

Figure 6.19 Virtual machine device of MMS.

One of MMS's intended objectives is interoperability, which refers to the ability of network applications to exchange data among themselves without requiring a specific communication environment. This requires independence, so interoperability must be achieved independently of the application developer, network connectivity, and the type of function performed. The significant drawbacks of MMS include its lack of explicit support for P/S architectures, its complexity, poor performance, and the high cost of ISO protocol stacks. Figure 6.19

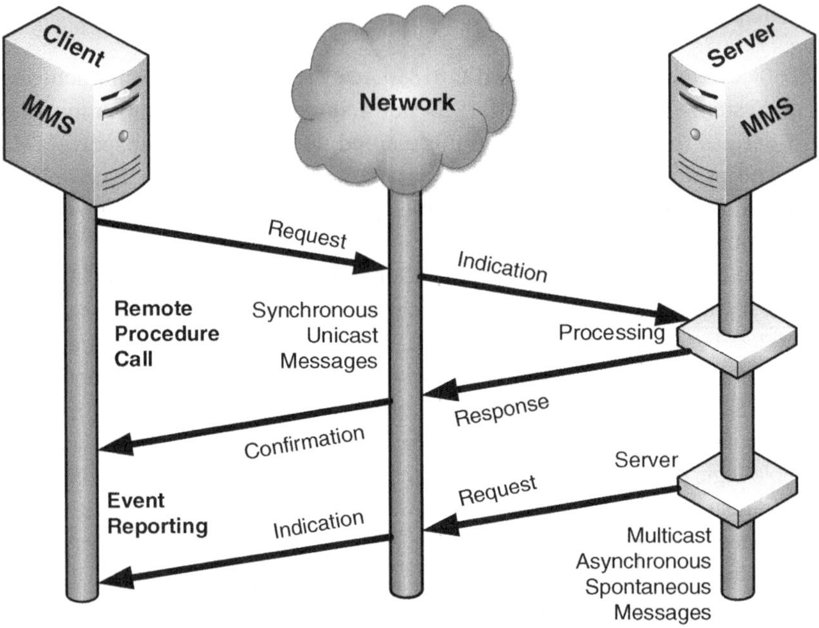

Figure 6.20 MMS underlying mechanism.

shows the typical relationship between a client application and the MMS virtual machine.

Each client uses a client layer of MMS to communicate with an MMS server over a network interface, sends requests in a C/S model, and receives responses from the MMS server. An MMS server is implemented as a virtual machine that maintains a set of data and variables representing the status of communication for each registered client. The underlying mechanism is shown in the UML Communication Diagram of Figure 6.20. A client initiates a remote procedure call by sending a request message over the network, which is forwarded to the MMS server. After processing by the MMS server, a response is generated and sent to the client through the network as confirmation. These are synchronous unicast messages exchanged by the MMS client and server. Simultaneously, the server can detect the need to notify clients about the occurrence of some programmed event. These are asynchronous, multicast, spontaneous messages from the MMS server to subscribing clients.

To start communication, associations must be established among clients and servers in an MMS environment. Figure 6.21 shows the UML Communication Diagram for MMS connection establishment and release mechanism. To establish an association with a server, a client sends a request over the network and

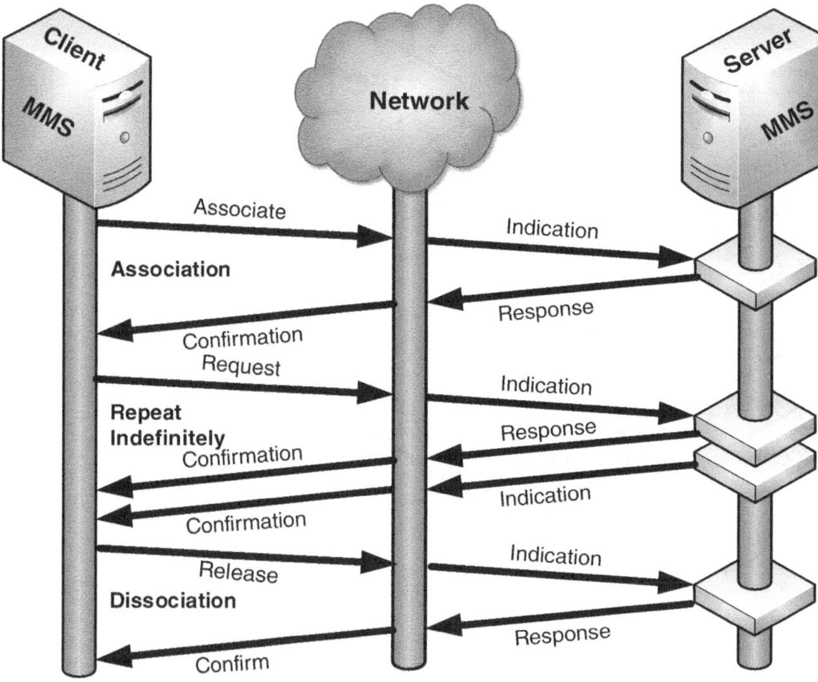

Figure 6.21 MMS connection establishment and release.

waits for the server's response. After the association is accepted, the client can initiate and repeat a series of remote procedure calls with synchronous requests and responses from the server indefinitely. The server can also send asynchronous events at any time during the association's lifetime. To finalize the association, the client sends a message requesting the release, thereby ending the communication.

Only the slow messages are mapped to MMS by IEC 61850. As shown in Figure 6.22, fast messages, such as sampled measured values (***SMVs***) from the process and ***GOOSE*** messages, are mapped directly to the data link or Ethernet layer of the OSI model. Slow messages correspond to C/S requests between ***IEDs*** for reporting, parameterization, file transfer, and other purposes.

The similarities between these two standards facilitate the mapping of IEC 61850 and MMS. Figure 6.23 shows their main objects and the corresponding mappings.

Logical devices from IEC 61850 are mapped to the MMS domain as a repository of data structures. A ***Dataset*** is naturally mapped to a ***Named Variable List***, while ***Control Blocks*** are mapped to ***Control Blocks*** and ***Named Variable Lists*** in MMS. A ***Log*** is mapped to its equivalent Journal in MMS. Table 6.3 shows the detailed map of ***ACSI*** to MMS, as defined by IEC 61850.

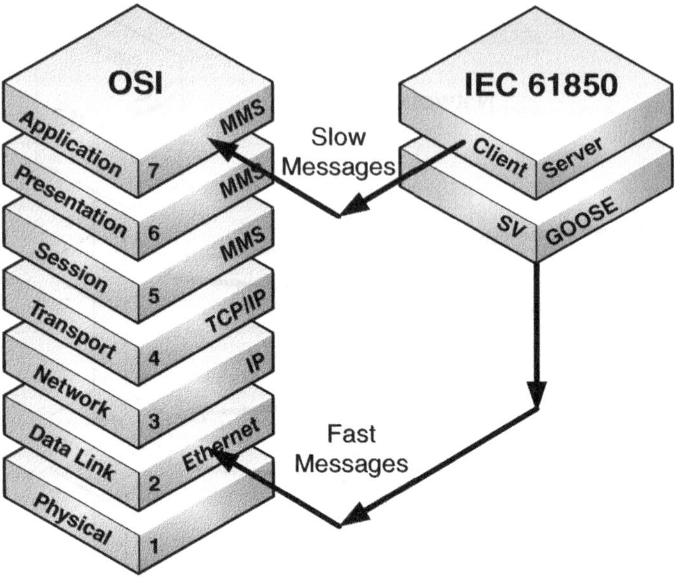

Figure 6.22 IEC 61850 mapping to MMS.

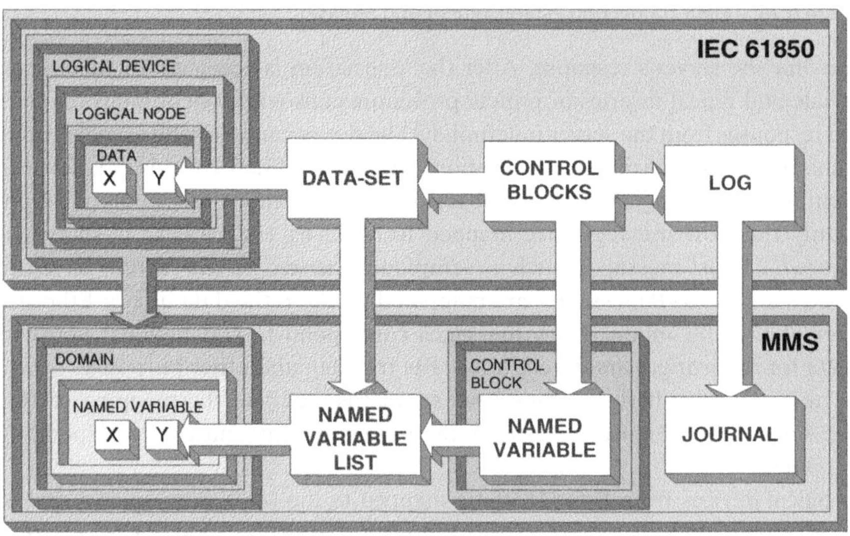

Figure 6.23 Mapping approach from SCSI to MMS.

Table 6.3 Detailed map of ACSI to MMS.

IEC 61850	MMS
Logical Device	MMS Domain
Logical Nodes	MMS Named Variables
Data	MMS Named Variables
Data Attribute	MMS Named Variables
Control Blocks (attributes)	MMS Named Variable List
Control Blocks (behavior)	Needs to be programmed
Log	MMS Journal

The mapping of a specific data (*POS*) from a *logical node* (*Q0CSWI*) of a *logical device* (*K03*) would be done as shown in Figure 6.24. Note the change in the name separator used in IEC 61850 and MMS. A variable referenced in IEC 61850 as *K03/Q0CSWI/ST/POS/stVal* would be named *K03/Q0CSWISTPOS$stVal* in MMS, using the name separator "*$*."

This process can map the entire hierarchy of data modeling for any equipment or SAS function, from IEC 61850 to MMS. Figure 6.25 illustrates the mapping to MMS of data related to a circuit breaker.

This mapping is shown in Table 6.4, between MMS objects and services defined by *SCSM*.

Even as a widely adopted C/S middleware, MMS is not immune to criticism. Its recognized complexity and poor performance are among these, mainly for real-time environments. The lack of explicit support for P/S architectures is also a primary reason for objection. This explains why mappings to CORBA and Ethernet were also proposed.

6.10 Mapping to CORBA

A mapping also exists between IEC 61850 *ACSI* services and CORBA, defined by the Object Management Group (OMG). CORBA is a medium that enables software components written in multiple computer languages and running on various platforms to work together. A mapping from the standard IEC 61850 abstract specification of communication service to a concrete communication infrastructure based on CORBA was submitted to the IEC Technical Committee 57. It defines how the concepts, objects, and services of *ACSI* can be implemented

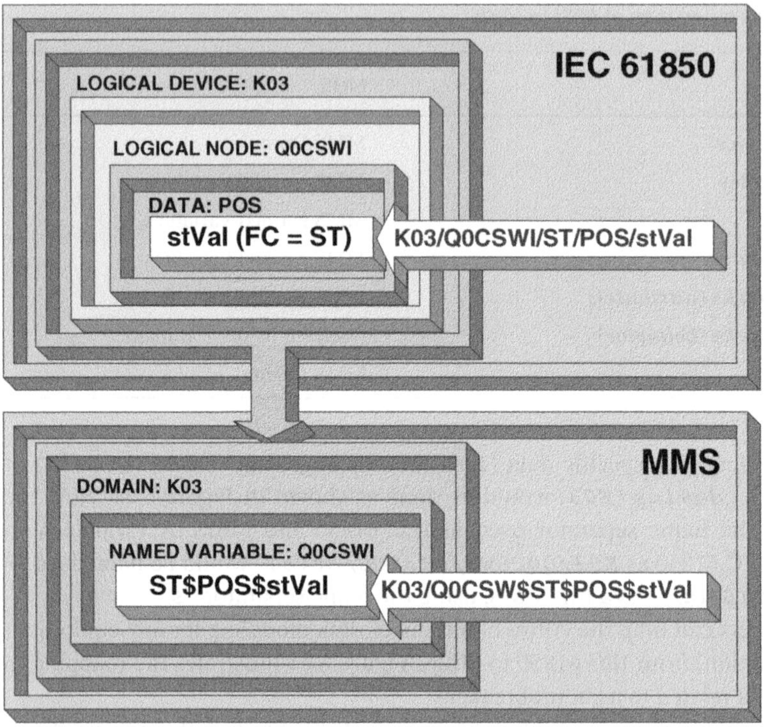

Figure 6.24 Mapping detail to an MMS named variable.

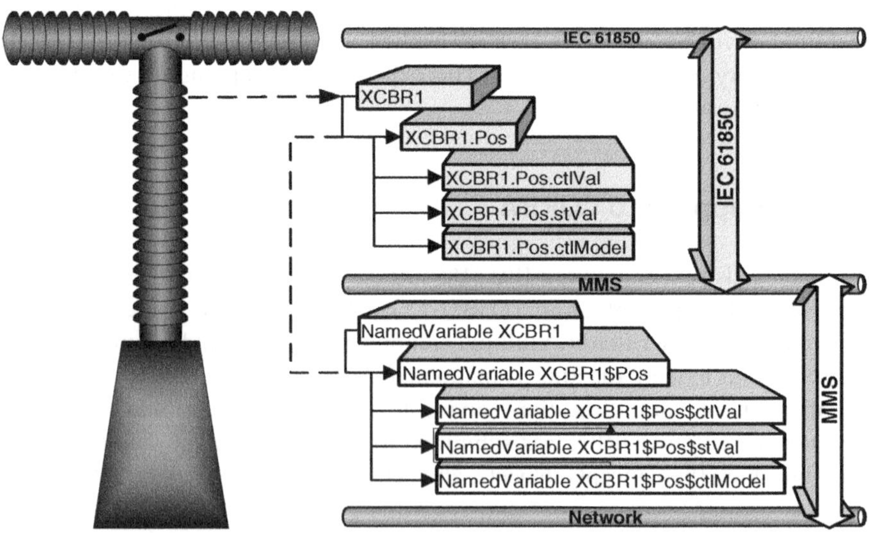

Figure 6.25 MMS mapping example.

Table 6.4 MMS objects and services used by SCSM.

MMS Object	IEC 61850 Object	MMS Services
Application Process VMD	***Server***	***Initiate*** ***Conclude*** ***Abort*** ***Reject*** ***Cancel*** ***Identify***
Named Variable Objects	***Logical Nodes and Data***	***Read*** ***Write*** ***InformationReport*** ***GetVariableAccessAttribute*** ***GetNameList***
Named Variable List Objects	***Data Sets***	***GetNamedVariableListAttributes*** ***GetNameList*** ***DefineNamedVariableList*** ***DeleteNamedVariableList*** ***GetNameList*** ***Read*** ***Write*** ***InformationReport***
Journal Objects	***Logs***	***ReadJournal*** ***InitializeJournal*** ***GetNameList***
Domain Objects	***Logical Devices***	***GetNameList*** ***GetDomainAttributes*** ***StoreDomainContents***
Files	***Files***	***FileOpen*** ***FileRead*** ***ObtainFile*** ***FileClose*** ***FileDirectory*** ***FileDelete***

using CORBA distributed objects technology. The following main components form CORBA:

- **An Object Request Broker (ORB)**—resolves object references to locations and marshalling/unmarshalling of parameter and return values when invoking a method on a remote object

- **An Interface Definition Language (IDL)**—specifies the interface of an object so that stubs for the client applications and skeletons for the server applications can be created
- **A Dynamic Invocation Interface (DII)**—permits clients to access the underlying request mechanisms at run time directly
- **Interface and Implementation Repositories**—definitions of interfaces for type-checking remote method calls
- **Object Services**—comprise different aspects of a distributed computing environment without support for critical real-time requirements

As shown in Figure 6.26, each server in a distributed CORBA system uses an ORB to communicate with other servers.

ACSI data types are mapped directly to CORBA data types, as shown in Table 6.5.

Similarly, ***ACSI*** services are mapped directly to CORBA services, as shown in Table 6.6.

The complete mapping of ***ACSI*** to CORBA is formed by several sections, as follows:

- Mapping of Server Model
- Mapping of Association Model
- Mapping of Logical Device Model
- Mapping of Logical Node Model
- Mapping of Data Object Model
- Mapping of Data Attribute Model
- Mapping of Publish and Subscribe Data Transfer
- Mapping of Generic Object-Oriented System-Wide Events
- Mapping of Control Model

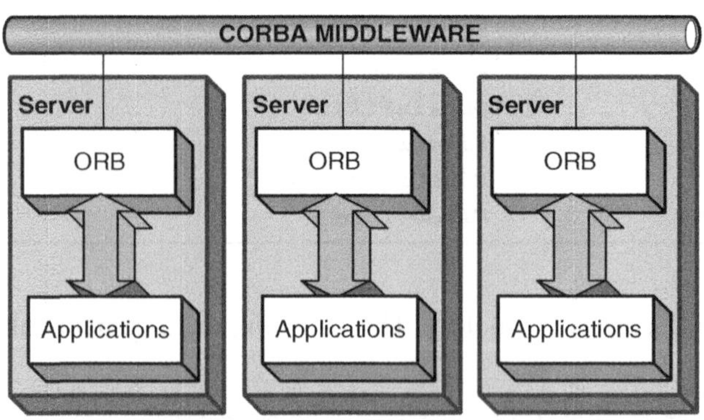

Figure 6.26 CORBA object request broker.

Table 6.5 ACSI and CORBA fundamental types.

IEC 61850 ACSI Data Type	CORBA Data Type
OCTET STRING	sequence <octet>
VisibleString	String
BIT STRING	sequence <boolean>
INTEGER	long
REAL	float
Sequence	struct
Array	Array
ENUMERATED	enum
NULL	Nil

Table 6.6 ACSI and CORBA fundamental services.

IEC 61850 ACSI	CORBA
Request response	Request
Request / no response	One-way request
GOOSE message	Push event channel
Sampled value transmission	Push-pull real-time event channel

- Mapping of Substitution Model
- Mapping of Transmission of SMVs
- Mapping of Time Synchronization Model
- Mapping of File Transfer

The following IDL code exemplifies the declaration of an IEC 61850 server for communication to a CORBA ORB:

```
interface Server {
        attribute ObjectName ServiceAccessPoint;
        attribute LogicalDeviceList LogicalDevices;
        attribute FileList Files;
        attribute ClientAssociationList ClientAssociations;
        any ServerDirectory (in ClassTypeCode classtype)
        raises (FailedDirectory,NoSuchType);
};
```

Although CORBA offers a complete set of object-oriented middleware services that can meet IEC 61850 requirements, strict time requirements for SAS led to the definition of a direct mapping to Ethernet.

6.11 Mapping to Ethernet

To offer specific speeds for different types of needs and to explore the services available in the OSI model, IEC 61850 is also mapped to the Ethernet model. IEC 61850 defines seven types of messages that need to be mapped by ***SCSM***, required by the real-time requirements listed in Section 6.6, repeated as follows:

- **Type 1**—Fast messages (<1 ms)
- **Type 2**—Medium-speed messages (<100 ms)
- **Type 3**—Low-speed messages (<100 ms)
- **Type 4**—Raw data messages (>100 ms)
- **Type 5**—File transfer functions (>1000 ms)
- **Type 6**—Time synchronization messages (application-dependent)
- **Type 7**—Command messages with access control (application-dependent)

The mapping is to different layers of the OSI communication stack, as shown in Figure 6.27, where the numbers correspond to the message types conveyed by each layer, as listed earlier.

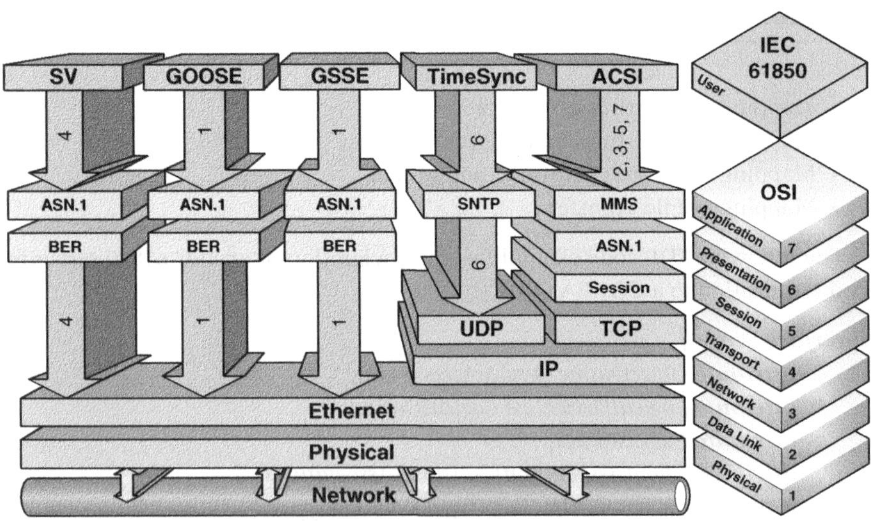

Figure 6.27 Overview of functionality and profiles.

Fast messages (Type 1) are typically used to transfer protection-tripping, interlocking, and switch-position data and are mapped directly to the Data Link layer (Ethernet) after being structured using Abstract Syntax One (ASN.1) at the Application layer, and coded into the Ethernet frame using some Basic Encoding Rules defined by IEC 61850, at the Presentation layer. The same is done for raw data messages (Type 4) that transfer sampled values from instrument transformers to ***IEDs***. These mappings are selected to bypass the upper five layers of the OSI stack (Application, Presentation, Session, Transport, and Network) to enable faster delivery. Time messages (Type 6) synchronize other messages and processes, using a broadcast mechanism mapped directly to the Transport layer via User Datagram Protocol (UDP), which encapsulates and sends datagrams without delivery guarantees. It does not require prior communications to set up special transmission channels or data paths. UDP is sometimes referred to as the Universal Datagram Protocol. Medium- and low-speed messages (Types 2 and 3), file transfer (Type 5), and command messages are mapped to the Application layer, using a C/S mechanism, typically based on MMS. The choice of a direct mapping of ***GOOSE*** and ***SV*** messages to the Data Link layer (Ethernet) can be better understood by comparing it with MMS, as shown in Table 6.7. The IP protocol is not fast enough with current technologies. Of course, this can change shortly, with the availability of ultra-fast IP networks.

One example is mapping IEC 61850 ***ACSI*** services related to ***Sampled Values*** (***SV***) to serial links. It specifies a mapping of the abstract service for transmitting ***SV*** over a serial unidirectional multidrop point-to-point link built on a mixed stack, with direct access to an ISO/IEC 8802-3 network. Figure 6.28 illustrates the communication stacks involved.

It applies to communication between merging units of ***CTs*** or ***VTs*** and bay devices, such as protection relays. Transformer technology can be based on optical

Table 6.7 *GOOSE/SV* and MMS comparison.

GOOSE/SV	MMS
Publisher–subscriber	Client–server
Multicast to multiple consumers	Unicast to one specific consumer
IP is not fast enough	IP is fast enough and provides Transport and Network layers
No addressing	Addressed by the Network layer
Not routable	Routable on LAN or WAN

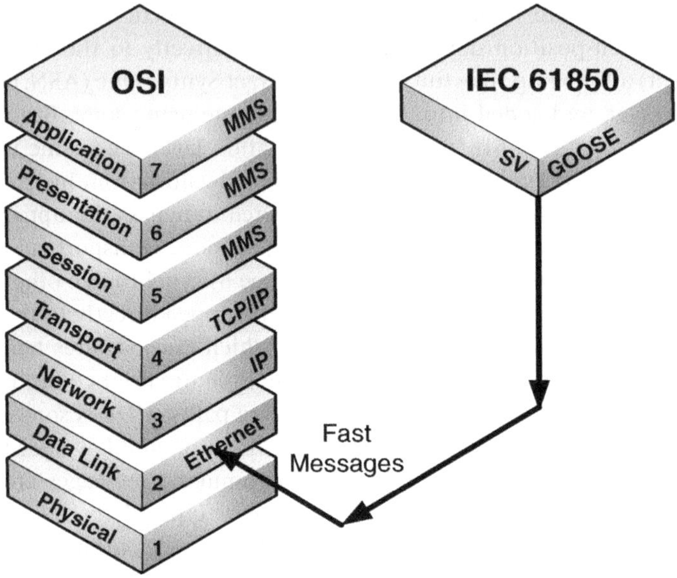

Figure 6.28 ***GOOSE*** and ***SV*** communication stack.

arrangements with electronic components, air-core coils (with or without an integrator), or iron-core coils with an integrated burden. It can be used as a current-to-voltage converter. The standard addresses a point-to-point connection from the merging unit to electronic measuring instruments and electronic devices that provide digital output. Figure 6.29 shows the general arrangement for this application as a UML Package Diagram.

The Physical layer specification includes the Medium Attachment Unit (MAU) for connecting the merging unit to the secondary equipment, possibly by an optical fiber transmission system. By considering and solving electromagnetic compatibility requirements, a copper-based transmission system is a viable option. The preferred version of the fiber optic transmission system is IEEE 802.3 100Base-FX. Two fibers are always required in an optical fiber transmission system to support link supervision. A twisted-pair medium, as specified in IEEE 802.3 10Base-T, can be used as an option if appropriate electromagnetic shielding measures are implemented.

At the Data Link layer, the mapping to the Ethernet broadcast address shall be used as the default destination address. Priority tagging and virtual LAN, as specified in IEEE 802.1Q, separate critical and high-priority bus traffic, protecting relevant applications from low-priority bus loads. The sampled analog

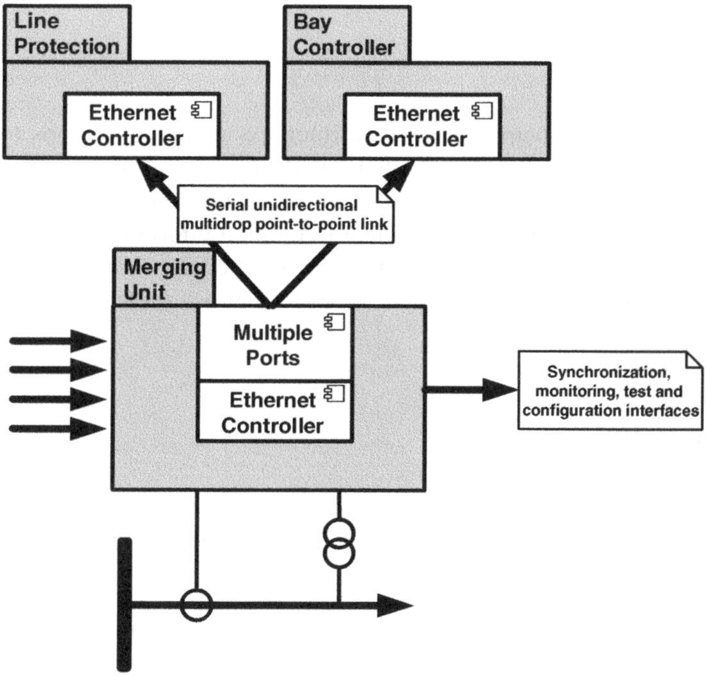

Figure 6.29 Serial unidirectional multidrop point-to-point link.

value buffer update is directly mapped to the reserved Ethertype and the Ethertype PDU.

6.12 Summary

Rapid and secure communication is the core requirement for digital substation and wide-area automation of power systems. IEC 61850 does not define any specific communication technology, but requires several requisites for the supporting network, which are defined in other standards. This chapter introduced the main topics of communication models related to IEC 61850, including:

- Open Systems Interconnection
- Communication Requirements
- Real-time Requirements
- Abstract Interfaces
- Specific Interfaces

- Mapping to MMS
- Mapping to CORBA
- Mapping to Ethernet

Many more mappings are being specified to interface digital substations to industrial protocols and control centers, such as DNP, to ease their migration to IEC 61850. Eventually, this movement will culminate in the complete merging and harmonization with the IEC-defined standard Common Information Model, covering the entire spectrum of power system data and models. Chapter 7 will introduce the functional blocks defined by IEC 61850 that use these models to exchange information in SAS.

6.13 Review Questions

1 Describe the seven types of information exchange needed in an SAS and identify which layers of the utility communication architecture they mainly function in.

2 Explain how IEC 61850 maps its communication needs onto the OSI reference model. Discuss the role of at least three OSI layers in supporting SAS communication.

3 Assess how the ideas of reliability, interoperability, interchangeability, and performance collectively influence the design of communication systems in IEC 61850-based substations.

4 Considering the static and dynamic requirements for interoperability listed in the chapter, suggest a practical scenario where failing to meet one of these requirements could compromise a protection function.

5 Compare the purpose and communication behavior of the C/S and P/S `ACSI` models. How does each model meet specific SAS communication needs?

6 Explain how modern Ethernet features such as VLAN tagging, IEEE 802.1p priority queuing, and IGMP snooping enhance a substation network's ability to meet IEC 61850 real-time requirements.

7 List the seven IEC 61850 message types categorized by real-time constraints and describe the typical applications of two of these types.

8 A protection engineer must guarantee sub-millisecond delivery of tripping signals. Explain why ***GOOSE*** messages are mapped directly to the Data Link layer instead of being transported over MMS.

9 Summarize how the ***ACSI*** promotes standardized behavior among ***IEDs*** despite variations in vendor-specific implementations.

10 Compare the advantages and limitations of MMS as a middleware for IEC 61850. Why does IEC 61850 depend on mappings to CORBA and direct Ethernet in addition to MMS?

11 In a diverse automation environment with multiple operating systems, examine how middleware helps ensure reliable distributed communication, referencing the requirements listed in the chapter.

12 Considering the mappings to MMS, CORBA, and Ethernet, suggest criteria a utility might use to choose the most appropriate SCSM for a new substation design, taking into account latency, scalability, vendor integration, and long-term maintenance.

7

Functional Models

7.1 Introduction

Substation Automation Systems (SAS) include functions that protect, supervise, and control the power grid. Modern technologies allow these functions to be implemented in both software and hardware in different ways. To illustrate how functions are organized within an SAS, the IEC 61850 standard provides a comprehensive set of software building blocks that depict the logical structure and enable communication among these components.

7.2 Learning Objectives

This chapter presents the main modeling blocks available in IEC 61850 as applied to Substation and Power Plant Automation Systems. The following topics are covered:

- Functions
- Logical Nodes
- PICOM Model
- Logical Devices
- Servers
- Proxies and Gateways
- Intelligent Electronic Devices (IEDs)
- Networks

These topics will be covered in accordance with the IEC 61850 standard specifications, following a review of general concepts in functional modeling. Further details about the data and services provided by these models will be covered in Chapters 7 and 9, respectively.

7.3 Functional Modeling

A model is a representation of some aspects of reality. It helps to understand, describe, or predict how things work in the real world. In power system automation, a functional model represents the knowledge of substation functions and devices, described abstractly to facilitate communication in an objective function or device. In an SAS, an information model provides data that can be exchanged among process equipment, human operators, and SAS equipment. Figure 7.1 shows the general concept of an SAS and its information exchange, represented by a network of functional blocks that model the controlled process.

An SAS model can also be viewed from three different perspectives, related to the structure of (1) functions performed in the power system by the functional blocks, (2) the data used and interchanged among these building blocks, and (3) the services provided by these blocks to the power system. Figure 7.2 shows these perspectives in a Venn diagram.

SAS functions can be modeled by instantiating objects from abstract classes defined in IEC 61850. These classes can be organized into packages by their

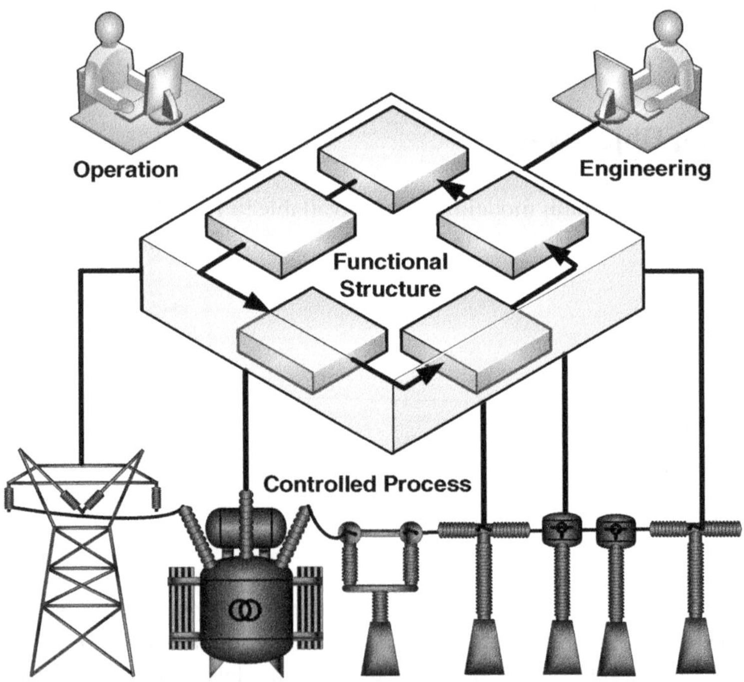

Figure 7.1 General concept of an SAS.

primary objectives and stacked into a hierarchical pyramid of functional layers, as described in Chapter 5. Seven general packages were defined to contain all classes defined in the standard, as shown in the UML Package Diagram reproduced in Figure 7.3, derived from the hierarchical views in Figure 5.2.

These UML packages contain abstract classes that model the substation, product items, and their types used on the SAS, as well as communication resources, implemented functions, data available to each function, services provided by

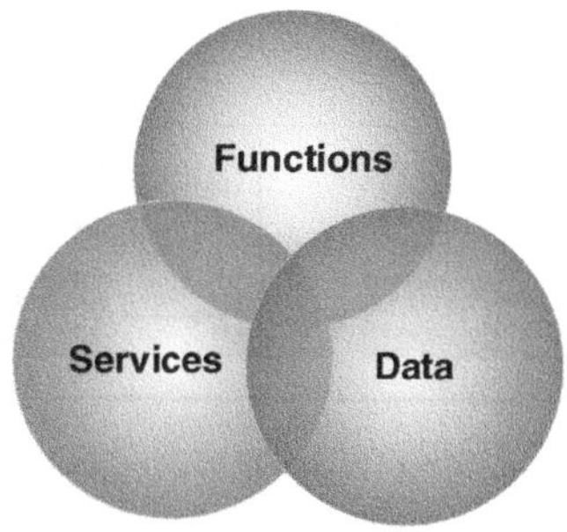

Figure 7.2 Three views of an SAS.

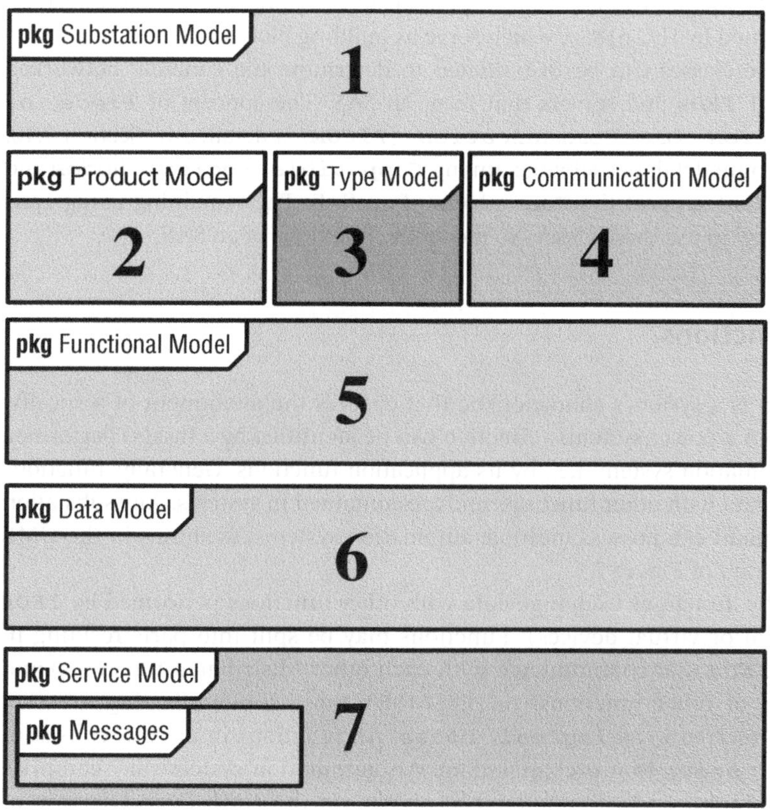

Figure 7.3 IEC 61850 Package Diagram.

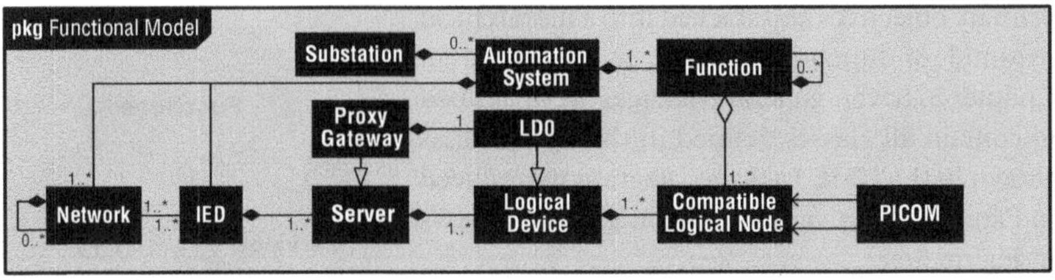

Figure 7.4 UML functional model for IEC 61850.

each function, and messages exchanged by each functional block. The complete UML Class Diagram, with all packaged classes, is reproduced in Figure 16.1 of Annex 16.1. This chapter will focus on the abstract classes packaged in the functional model, as detailed in the UML Class Diagram of Figure 7.4.

This UML diagram illustrates the relationships among the standard abstract classes defined by IEC 61850, which serve as building blocks for functional modeling. These classes can be instantiated to determine the concrete networked structure of ***IEDs*** and servers that form an SAS. The concept of ***Piece of Information for Communication*** (***PICOM***) is detailed in Section 7.10. It is used to model data exchange among ***Compatible Logical Nodes*** and ***Devices*** that support the ***Functions*** of an SAS. The remaining paragraphs describe how to use these classes to model the functions of an SAS.

7.4 Functions

A function is a system's characteristic that ensures the attainment of a specific objective. In a power system, a function can be identified by a task(s) performed by an automation system, i.e., by its application functions. Generally, functions exchange data with other functions and are contained in systems. Any substation or power plant can possess multiple automation systems, as shown in the UML Class Diagram of Figure 7.5.

Generally, functions exchange data with other functions performed by ***IEDs*** (in physical or virtual devices). Functions may be split into parts residing in different ***IEDs*** that communicate with each other (distributed functions) and with parts of other functions. In IEC 61850, these communicating function parts are referred to as ***logical nodes***. All functions in an SAS consist of ***logical nodes*** that exchange data. An automation system may comprise several functions and subfunctions, as shown on the UML Class Diagram of Figure 7.6.

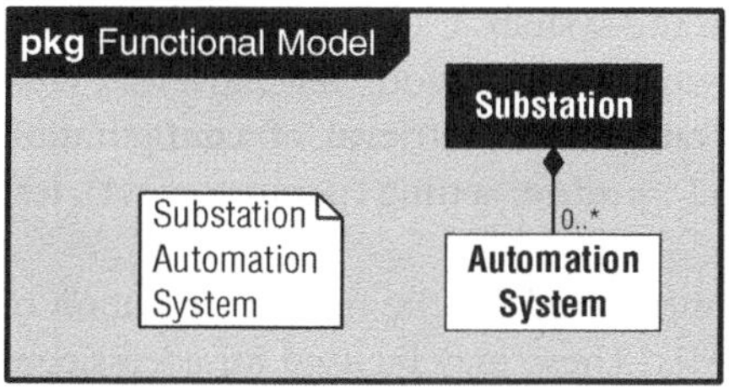

Figure 7.5 UML model of an automation system.

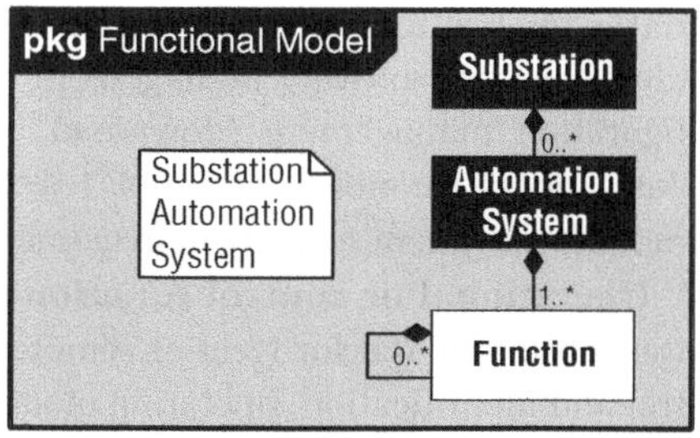

Figure 7.6 UML model of automation functions.

Automation functions may be classified into three levels in a substation or power plant, such as:

- **Process level functions**—functions interfacing to the controlled process
- **Bay level functions**—functions using mainly the data of one bay and acting primarily on the primary equipment of that bay
- **Station level functions**—further divided into:
  - **Process-related functions**—using the data of more than one bay or of the complete substation and acting on the primary equipment of more than one bay or of the complete substation
  - **Interface-related functions**—representing the interface of the SAS to the local station operator Human–Machine Interface (HMI), to a remote control center, or to the local or remote engineering for monitoring and maintenance

Automation functions may further be categorized into six general classes:

1. System support functions
2. System configuration or maintenance functions
3. Operational or control functions
4. Local process automation functions
5. Distributed automatic support functions
6. Distributed process automation functions

System support functions are primarily used to manage the automation system itself and, as such, have no direct impact on the process. Common instances of system support functions are network management, time synchronization, and node self-checking.

System configuration or maintenance functions are used to set up or evolve the system, including setting and changing configuration data and retrieving configuration information from the system. Usual examples are node identification, software management (download, activation, and retrieval), configuration management (download, activation, and retrieval of configuration data), operative mode control of `logical nodes`, setting (parameter set), test mode, and system security management.

Operational or control functions are required for the regular operation of the substation and for local or remote HMIs. These may be used for access control and identification, operating mode control, switchyard control, management of spontaneous indication changes, parameter set switching, alarm management, event management, data retrieval, disturbance recorder/fault data retrieval, and log management.

Local process automation functions operate directly on the process without operator intervention. Examples include primary protection functions, protection-related functions, local automatic functions, and metering functions.

Distributed process automation functions automate processes and system data without operator interference. Distributed functions occur when two or more `logical nodes`, located in different physical or virtual devices, perform a function together. Since all functions communicate somehow, the definition of a local or distributed function is not unique but depends on the definition of the functional steps to be performed. Typical examples are breaker failure, automatic protection adaptation, voltage and reactive power control, load shedding and restoration, infeed or transformer change, and automatic switching sequences.

Although standardization of functions is not the intention of the IEC 61850 series, many known functions have been informally described in IEC 61850-5 by the following external data and objectives:

- **Task of the function**—description to understand its task within the SAS
- **Starting criteria for the function**—event causing its execution
- **Result or impact of the function**—some change in the process, or another function, or notification for the human operator
- **Performance of the function**—total requested response time
- **Function decomposition**—how the function may be decomposed in LNs
- **Interaction with other functions**—data exchanged with different functions

The following example illustrates the functional description of a differential protection, similar to a UML Use Case specification:

- **Task**—The differential protection function is used to protect one transformer. It monitors the transformer using the input and output currents. The differential protection starts and trips the transformer if changes in the input and output currents do not match.

- **Starting criteria**—The monitoring part of the function is set into operation if the function is started. The function issues a trip in case of an emergency.
- **Result**—The transformer is protected by switching off the related circuit breakers.
- **Performance**—To reach an accurate fault selection, the relative accuracy of current samples should be ≤25 μs. The response time (tripping time) should be in the order of 5–20 ms.
- **Decomposition**—Logical nodes ***IHMI***, ***TCTR***, ***PDIF***, ***TCTR***, ***XSCI***, ***XCBR***, and other primary equipment-related ***LNs***.
- **Interaction**—Alarm management, event management, disturbance/fault record retrieval, and other protection functions.

In IEC 61850-based systems, the building blocks or ***logical nodes*** describe the complete structure of a function.

7.5 Logical Nodes

An IEC 61850 function may be split into parts called ***Logical Nodes***, which may optionally reside in different ***IEDs*** or virtualized servers, communicating with each other (distributed function) and with parts of other functions. Contrary to ***Functions*** that may be part of only one ***Automation System***, ***Compatible Logical Nodes*** can be part of more than one ***Function***. This is illustrated in the UML Class Diagram shown in Figure 7.7.

It should be emphasized that a ***logical node*** (***LN***) is not a physical equipment itself—it's a wrapper for its communication, providing the meaning of the data (semantic definition), the structure of the data (how it's organized), and the access methods (how to interact with it). Its functionality is described informally by the standard, but it is not a formal specification for its internal behavior. This is left for the concrete implementation by the manufacturer or developer. Its role is to serve as a standardized data container for all information and functions related to a specific device function, aiming for interoperability among different suppliers.

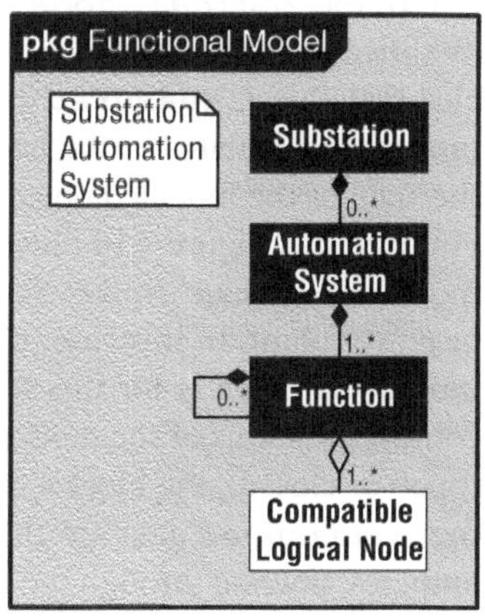

Figure 7.7 Definition of compatible logical nodes.

A ***Logical Node*** may be viewed as the most minor component of a function that exchanges data. It is an object defined by its ***Data Objects*** and ***Methods***. ***Data Objects*** are constructed from ***Common Data Classes***.

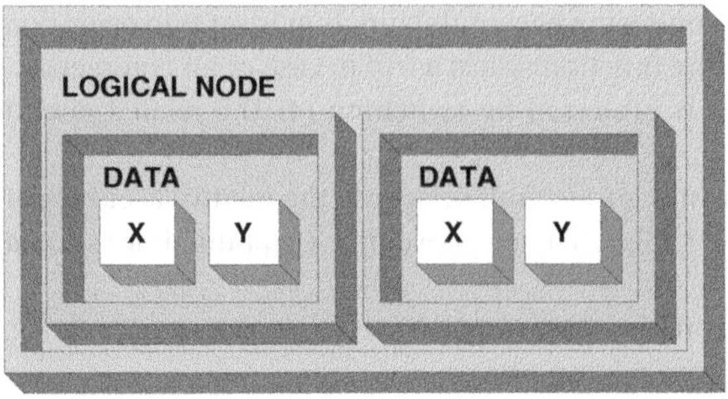

Figure 7.8 Logical nodes and data objects.

Figure 7.8 illustrates the typical composition of a ***Logical Node***, featuring two ***Data Objects***, each with two data elements, X and Y.

For each ***LN***, IEC 61850 suggests a textual description of its task within the overall function. In particular, the context required to execute the ***LN*** should be specified. This includes (i) the starting criteria and other inputs of the ***LN*** from a communication point of view; (ii) the input and outputs by the data to be exchanged; (iii) the operation modes, such as which other ***LNs*** should be informed about any degradation; and (iv) performance requirements for the communication.

Logical Nodes may represent functional models of real devices. Different protection, control, and monitoring functions are implemented by aggregating multiple ***LNs***, which are data containers that represent meaningful, exchangeable information about the modeled object. ***Data*** is exchanged between ***IEDs*** and functions using ***LNs*** from the functions implemented in the ***IED***. Four types of data are associated with a typical ***logical node***, as shown in the UML Package Diagram of Figure 7.9.

Settings are configuration parameters that enable the adjustment or selection of the ***logical node***'s functionality. ***Controls*** are ***LN*** data that can be modified by commands sent to the ***Logical Node***, thereby controlling the modeled real object. ***Measured*** data are values read or monitored from the modeled process or calculated by the ***Logical Node***. ***Statuses*** are data reflecting either the state of the modeled object or the function allocated to the ***logical node***. For example, Figure 7.10 illustrates the UML Package Diagram with data used to model a ***Logical Node XCBR***, which denotes a circuit breaker in a substation or power plant. In this case, no ***Settings*** are necessary, as there are no configuration parameters for this breaker. ***Controls*** are the data required to set or control the status of the modeled process, such as the breaker's switched position (open or closed), the block's opening or closing, and the charger motor's enablement. ***Measured*** data are the sum of switching operations and the current, in amperes, flowing through the breaker. The ***Status*** is monitored by the operating capability, the point of wave operating capacity, and the fully charged operating capability.

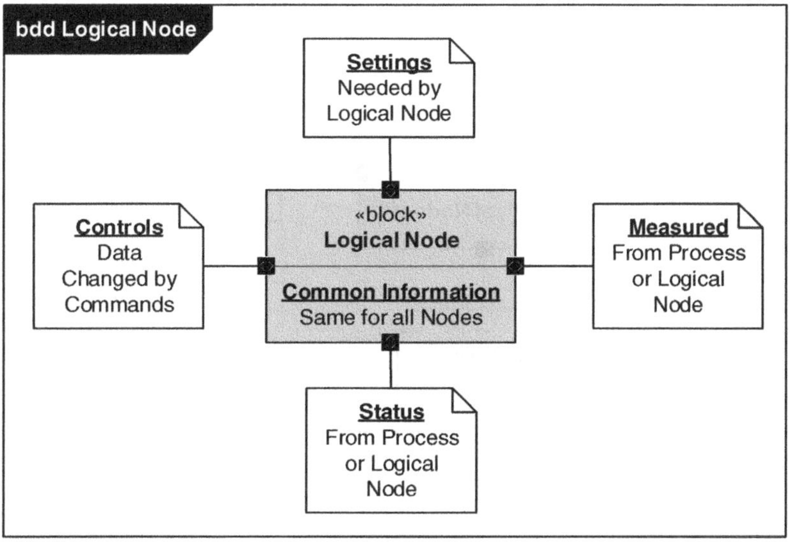

Figure 7.9 Logical node information.

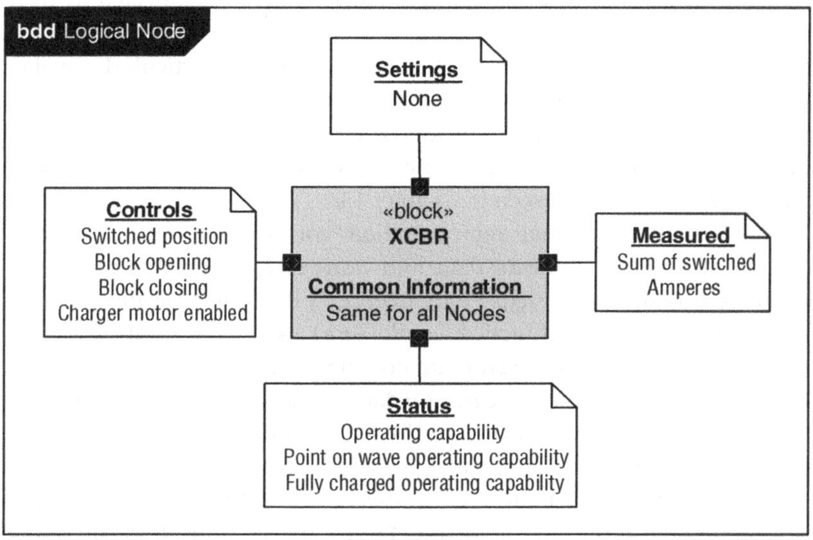

Figure 7.10 Logical node XCBR information.

`Logical Node` data can also be classified according to their role in the input–output function performed by the modeled object. This function can be represented in the UML Package Diagram of Figure 7.11, relating to the Output data generated by the Logical Node, as a function of the `Input` and `Process`

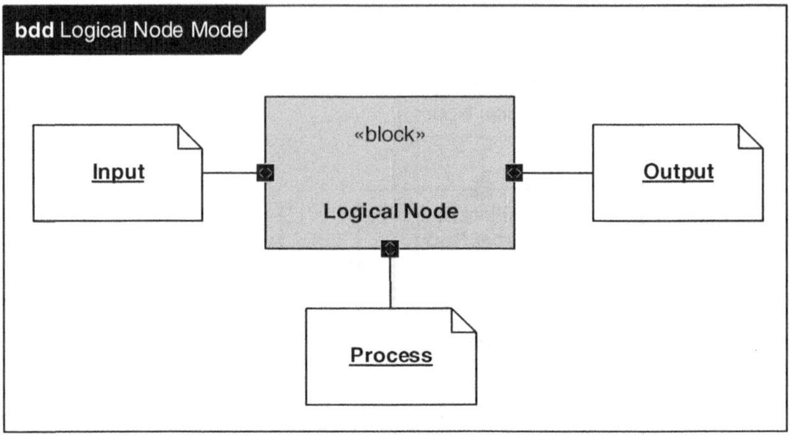

Figure 7.11 Logical node functional model.

data. This representation clarifies the real function of the ***logical node*** in a complex process: the **Output** data can be ***Input*** data to other ***LN*** within the same function, while the Process it represents can affect or be affected by it. In this architecture, the ***inRef*** (Input Reference) attribute plays a crucial role in defining logical connections between ***Logical Nodes***, particularly in data flow and interlocking logic across devices and functions. It specifies references to external data (from other ***LNs*** or devices) used as inputs to the ***LN's*** internal logical processing. Additionally, they also play a vital role during the testing and simulation of ***IEDs***, as will be seen in Chapter 13.

The input–output functional representation corresponds to the standard classification of ***logical node*** data into ***Control***, ***Status***, ***Settings***, and ***Measured***, as shown in Figure 7.12. ***Control*** data can typically affect the ***Process*** and ***Output*** of a function, while ***Status*** data can only affect the ***Output***. ***Logical Node Settings*** do not affect the ***Process*** but influence the function's ***Output***. Finally, ***Measured*** data impacts only the ***Output*** of the modeled function, which is impacted only by the ***Process*** it represents.

This representation can be illustrated by several typical ***logical nodes*** found on SAS, as shown in Figure 7.13. In this figure, a ***PDIF logical node*** models a differential protection, with the ***Input*** data coming from measured differential and restraint currents, while the ***Output*** data is generated by status information from its start, operate, and active curve characteristics. The ***TCTR logical node*** models a current transformer, with no ***Input*** and ***Setting*** data, where the ***Process*** data generates the output function from the ***Measured LN*** data. The ***logical nodes XCBR*** and ***XSWI*** model circuit breakers and switches, respectively, with ***control*** data as ***inputs*** and ***outputs***.

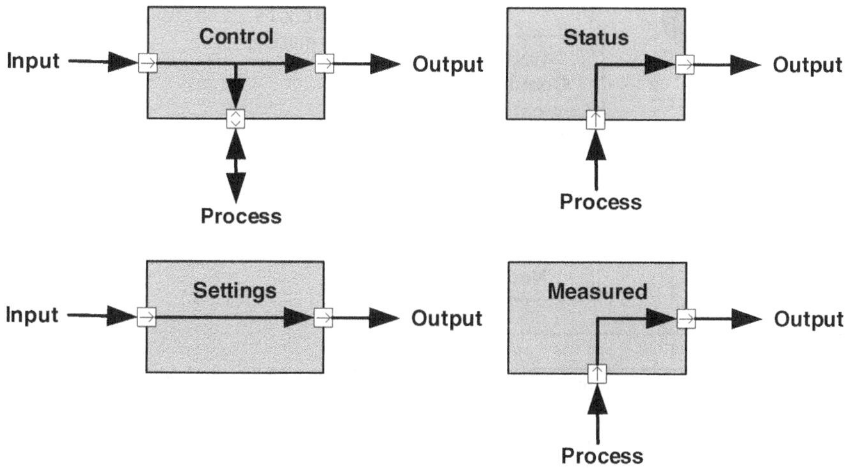

Figure 7.12 Logical node data classification.

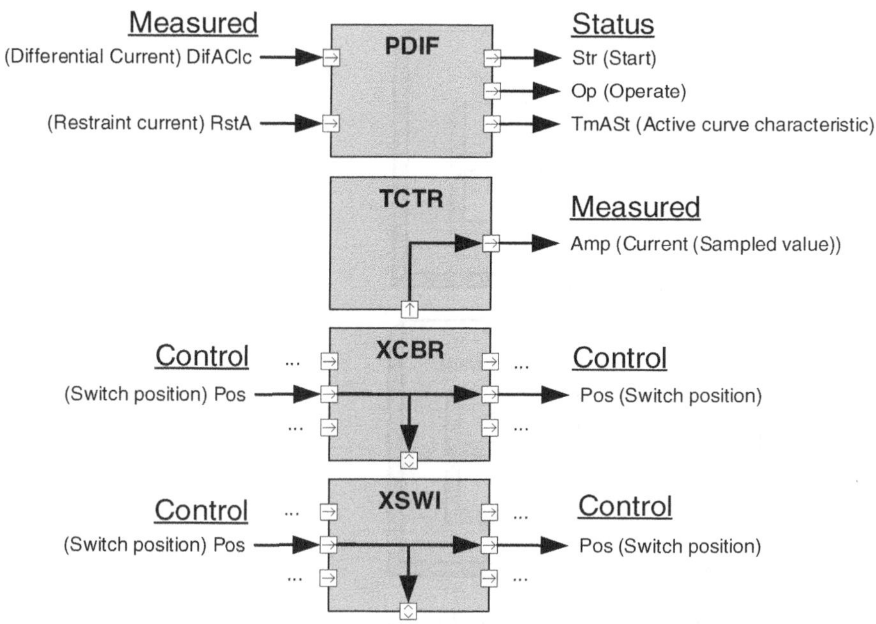

Figure 7.13 Logical node information modeling examples.

Besides the specific data used by each ***LN***, particularly of the real object it models, some common data is necessary for every instance of a ***Logical Node***. These data are inherited by every class of ***Logical Node*** from an abstract ***Common Logical Node***, as shown in the UML Class Diagram in Figure 7.14. Data

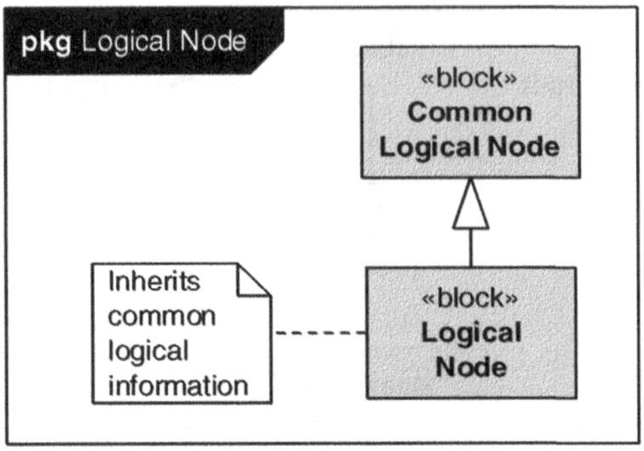

Figure 7.14 Common logical node information.

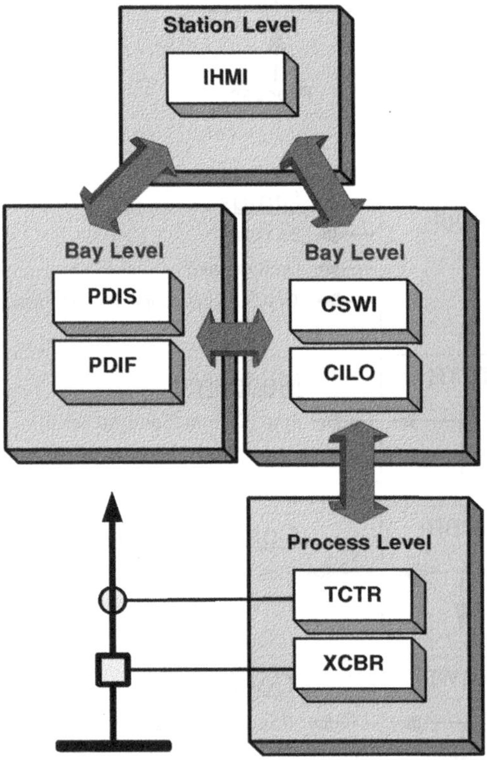

Figure 7.15 Logical nodes allocation in substations.

inherited from this mechanism includes, for instance, information independent of the modeled function, such as the ***mode***, ***health***, ***nameplate***, etc.

Typically, the ***Logical Nodes*** in an automation system can be grouped into three levels, as exemplified in Figure 7.15:

- **Station level**—comprising HMI (e.g., ***IHMI***), station-wide interlocking (e.g., ***CILO***), alarm and event handling (e.g., ***CALH***), station-wide voltage control (e.g., ***ATCC***), etc.

- **Bay level**—including control, automatic, measuring, and protection functions (e.g., ***CILO***, ***ATCC***, ***MMXU***, ***CSWI***, ***PDIS***, ***PZSU***, ***PDOC***, ...).
- **Process/switchgear level**—representing the power (primary) system, i.e., the power system apparatuses as seen from the secondary system via the I/Os (e.g., XCBR, TCTR, etc.).

The interaction of functions and ***Logical Nodes*** in an automation system can also be classified into two types: *informative interactions*, where the exchanged data provides some information not as a prerequisite for the function, often called local or stand-alone functions; and *functional interactions*, where the exchanged data are needed to perform the functions, often called distributed functions. These interactions occur independently of the physical location of each ***logical node***, as IEC 61850 allows for their free allocation in servers and ***IEDs***, provided they are reachable on the network. Additionally, each ***LN*** can be part of several functions, as illustrated in Figure 7.16. That is, a function is performed by a set of non-exclusive ***Logical Nodes***, which may be shared by other functions and distributed across several servers or ***IEDs***.

To allow their instantiation into an SAS, ***Logical Node*** classes are identified by four uppercase letters, with the first letter identifying the type of its intended function. The following list identifies the sets of ***LN*** types defined by IEC 61850:

- ***L***—System LN
- ***P***—Protection

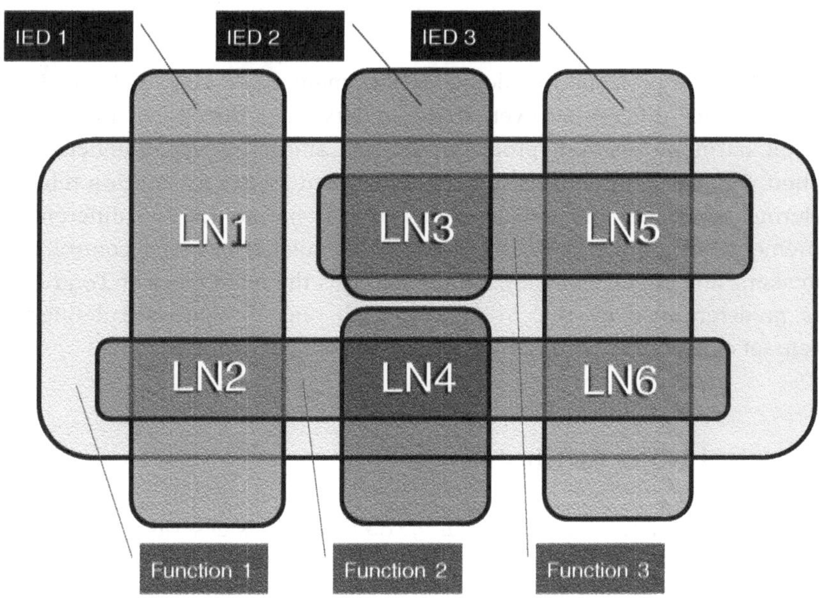

Figure 7.16 Free allocation of functions to IEDs.

- *R*—Protection-related
- *C*—Control
- *G*—Generic
- *I*—Interfacing and archiving
- *A*—Automatic control
- *M*—Metering and measurement
- *S*—Sensor and monitoring
- *X*—Switchgear
- *T*—Instrument transformers
- *Y*—Power transformers
- *Z*—Further power system equipment

Some examples of ***Logical Nodes'*** names, following the aforementioned rules, are:

- *PDIF*—Differential protection
- *RBRF*—Breaker failure
- *XCBR*—Circuit breaker
- *CSWI*—Switch controller
- *MMXU*—Measurement unit
- *YPTR*—Power transformer

The user can further edit the instantiated ***logical node*** name in a project by changing the ***logical node*** prefix or suffix, or by instantiating it from an existing library and adapting it to their rules, all within the standard's character limit for LN naming.

The standard for protection modeling defines many more ***logical nodes***, including distance, differential, overcurrent, undervoltage, directional, frequency, earth fault, harmonic restraint, protection scheme, and zero-speed or underspeed protection. Similar definitions exist for measurement ***logical nodes*** related to metering, sequence, and imbalance, as well as harmonics and differential measurement. For control, ***logical nodes*** are available for switch control, circuit breakers, and circuit switches. Annex 16.5 lists the main types of ***logical nodes*** predetermined by IEC 61850. For each one, the standard defines a complete set of attributes, as described in the following paragraph.

7.6 Logical Node Attributes

In the standard documentation, each ***Logical Node*** is described by a short textual description of its functionality, a device function number, if applicable, its attributes, the relationships between ***LNs*** and functions, and its most common

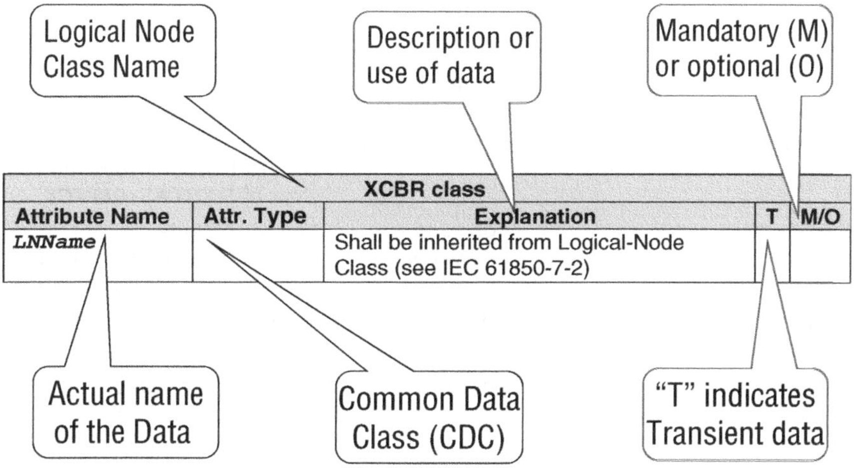

Figure 7.17 Table structure of logical node class definition.

application area. A table format is used in IEC 61850, as shown in Figure 7.17, which contains the name, type, and explanation of each attribute for every `logical node`, indicating whether it is mandatory or optional (*M/O*) in each instance of the *LN*. Attributes may also be transient (*T*), meaning their data is momentary and must be logged or reported to keep evidence of their state.

Attribute types are selected by inheritance from a `Common Data Class` that defines the data structure common to all `Logical Nodes`. Table 7.1 lists the attribute names and types of the abstract `Logical Node` class, with their corresponding explanation.

These attributes are inherited from a `Common Logical Node` class, which contains additional data common to all `Compatible Logical Nodes` defined by IEC 61850. The common characteristics are described in Table 7.2. The `Common Logical Node` is an abstract class that collects the common attributes needed by every `logical node`. All `Compatible Logical Nodes` are specializations of this class.

Using these common attributes and the template of Figure 7.17, the standard IEC 61850 defines each attribute present in each `logical node` in a format similar to Table 7.3, illustrated for the logical node *XCBR*.

The same information can be coded as an expandable tree, as shown in Figure 7.18, a visual representation commonly adopted by most IEC 61850 tools.

These classes are inherited from the `Compatible Logical Node` *class*, which in turn inherits from the `Common Logical Node` class, and this class is

Table 7.1 Attributes of the logical node class (LN).

Attribute Name	Attribute Type	Explanation
LNName	*ObjectName*	*Logical Node* name: identify *LOGICAL-NODE* within the scope of *LOGICAL-DEVICE*
LNRef	*Object Reference*	*Logical Node ObjectReference*: unique pathname of a *LOGICAL-NODE*
Data [1..n]	*DATA*	Identify *DATA* that is contained in the *LOGICAL-NODE*
DataSet [0..n]	*DATA-SET*	Identify a *DATA-SET* that is contained in the *LOGICAL-NODE*
BufferedReport ControlBlock [0..n]	*BRCB*	Identify a *BRCB* that is contained in the *LOGICAL-NODE*
UnbufferedReport ControlBlock [0..n]	*URCB*	Identify an *URCB* that is contained in the *LOGICAL-NODE*
LogControlBlock [0..n]	*LCB*	Identify an *LCB* that is contained in the *LOGICAL-NODE*
SettingGroup ControlBlock [0..1]	*SGCB*	Identify the *SGCB* that is contained in a *LLN0*
Log [0..1]	*LOG*	Identify the *LOG* that is contained in the *LLN0*
GOOSEControlBlock [0..n]	*GoCB*	Identify the *GoCB* that is contained in the *LLN0*
GSSEControlBlock [0..n]	*GsCB*	Identify the *GsCB* that is contained in the *LLN0*
MulticastSampled ValueControlBlock [0..n]	*MSVCB*	Identify a *MSVCB* that is contained in the *LLN0*
UnicastSampled ValueControlBlock [0..n]	*USVCB*	Identify a *USVCB* that is contained in the *LLN0*

Table 7.2 Attributes of the common logical node class.

Common Logical Node class				
Attribute Name	**Attr. Type**	**Explanation**	**T**	**M/O**
LNName		Shall be inherited from Logical-Node Class (see IEC 61850-7-2)		
Data				
Mandatory Logical Node Information (Shall be inherited by ALL LN but LPHD)				
Mod	*INC*	Mode		*M*
Beh	*INS*	Behavior		*M*
Health	*INS*	Health		*M*
NamePlt	*LPL*	Name plate		*M*
Optional Logical Node Information				
Loc	*SPS*	Local operation		*O*
EEHealth	*INS*	External equipment health		*O*
EEName	*DPL*	External equipment name plate		*O*
OpCntRs	*INC*	Operation counter resettable		*O*
OpCnt	*INC*	Operation counter		*O*
OpTmh	*INC*	Operation time		*O*
Data Sets (see IEC61850-7-2)				
Inherited and specialized from ***Logical Node*** class (see IEC 61850-7-2)				
Control Blocks (see IEC 61850-7-2)				
Inherited and specialized from ***Logical Node*** class (see IEC 61850-7-2)				
Services (see IEC 61850-7-2)				
Inherited and specialized from ***Logical Node*** class (see IEC 61850-7-2)				

Table 7.3 Example of logical node (XCBR).

XCBR class				
Attribute Name	**Attr. Type**	**Explanation**	**T**	**M/O**
LNName		Shall be inherited from Logical-Node Class (see IEC 61850-7-2)		
Data				
Common Logical Node Information				
		LN shall inherit all Mandatory Data from *Common Logical Node* Class		*M*
Loc	*SPS*	Local operation (local means without substation automation communication, hardwired direct control)		*M*
EEHealth	*INS*	External equipment health		*O*
EEName	*DPL*	External equipment name plate		*O*
OpCnt	*INS*	Operation counter		*M*
Metered Values				
SumSwARs	*BCR*	Sum of Switched Amperes, resettable		*O*
Status Information				
CBOpCap	*INS*	Circuit breaker operating capability		*M*
POWCap	*INS*	Point On Wave switching capability		*O*
MaxOpCap	*INS*	Circuit breaker operating capability when fully charged		*O*

itself an inheritance from the ***Logical Node*** class, as shown in the UML Class Diagram of Figure 7.19.

As a concrete example, consider the ***logical node PDIF***, for describing differential protections. Figure 7.20 shows a ***PDIF*** package with the UML Class Diagram illustrating inheritance from the ***Compatible Logical Node*** class.

Table 7.4 shows its definition in table format. All kinds of current differential protection use this ***LN***.

LPHD and ***LLN0*** are two special ***Logical Nodes*** that inherit directly from the ***Logical Node*** and ***Common Logical Node*** classes, respectively, to describe

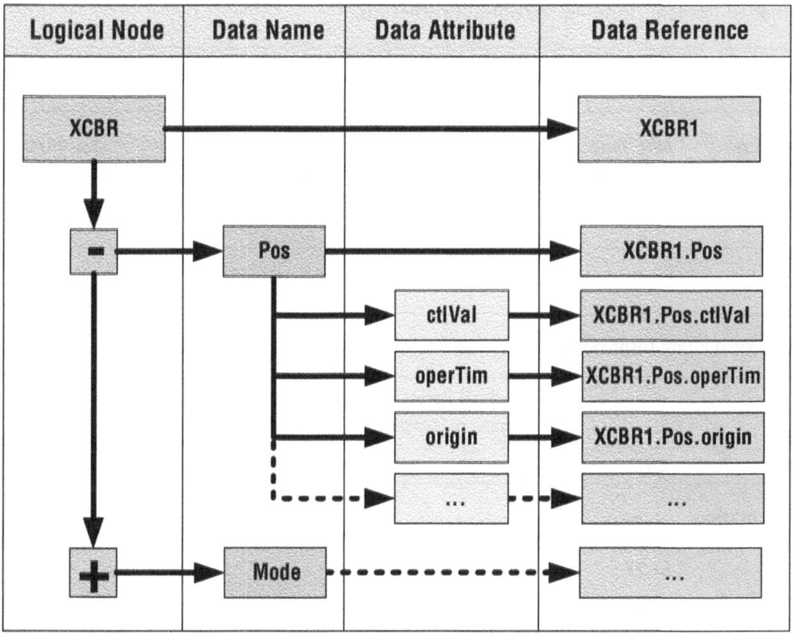

Figure 7.18 Tree structure of logical node XCBR.

Figure 7.19 Logical node inheritance relationship.

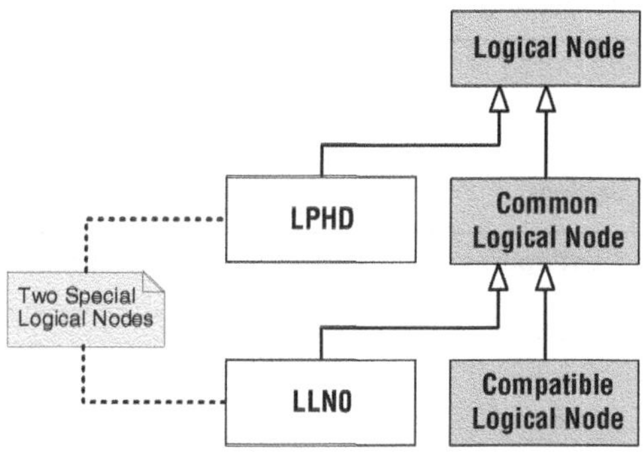

Figure 7.20 Logical node class of a differential protection.

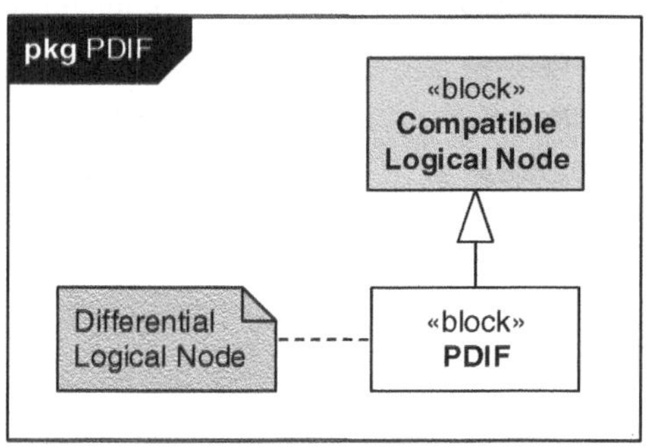

Table 7.4 PDIF logical node—differential protection.

PDIF class				
Attribute Name	**Attr. Type**	**Explanation**	**T**	**M/O**
LNName		Shall be inherited from ***Logical-Node*** class (see IEC 61850-7-2)		
Data				
Common Logical Node Information				
		LN shall inherit all mandatory data from ***Common Logical Node*** class		*M*
OpCntRs	*INC*	Resettable operation counter		*O*
Status Information				
Str	*SCD*	Start		*O*
Op	*ACT*	Operate	T	*M*
TmASt	*CSD*	Active curve characteristic		*O*
Measured Values				
DifAClc	*WYE*	Differential current		*O*
RstA	*WYE*	Restraint current		*O*
Settings				
LinCapac	*ASG*	Line capacitance (for load currents)		*O*
LoSet	*ING*	Low operating value, percentage of the nominal current		*O*
HiSet	*ING*	High operating value, percentage of the nominal current		*O*
MinOpTmms	*ING*	Minimum operate time		*O*
MaxOpTmms	*ING*	Maximum operate time		*O*
RstMod	*ING*	Restraint mode		*O*
RsDlTmms	*ING*	Reset delay time		*O*
TmACrv	*CURVE*	Operating curve type		*O*

Table 7.5 LPHD logical node–physical device information.

LPHD class				
Attribute Name	**Attr. Type**	**Explanation**	**T**	**M/O**
LNName		Shall be inherited from Logical-Node class (see IEC 61850-7-2)		
Data				
PhyNam	*DPL*	Physical device name plate		*M*
PhyHealth	*INS*	Physical device health		*M*
OutOv	*SPS*	Output communications buffer overflow		*O*
Proxy	*SPS*	Indicates if this *LN* is a proxy		*M*
InOv	*SPS*	Input communications buffer overflow		*O*
NumPwerUp	*INS*	Number of power-ups		*O*
WrmStr	*INS*	Number of warm starts		*O*
WacTrg	*INS*	Number of watchdog device resets detected		*O*
PwrUp	*SPS*	Power up detected		*O*
PwrDn	*SPS*	Power down detected		*O*
PwerSupAlm	*SPS*	External power supply alarm		*O*
RsStat	*SPS*	Reset device statistics	*T*	*O*

physical devices and server characteristics. Table 7.5 lists the attributes of the ***LPHD Logical Node***.

Logical Node LLN0 addresses common issues for ***Logical Devices***, as shown in Table 7.6.

A special ***LN*** model simulates the ***IED*** front-panel operator interface at bay level for configuration, local control, and other purposes, as shown in Table 7.7. The same ***LN*** class can be used to model the local operator interface at the station level, serving as the station operator's workplace. The roles of the different HMIs are not fixed for most functions and are defined during the engineering phase.

Even with most of the standards' ***logical nodes*** already covering the usual automation functions in substations and power plants, there is still the possibility of user-defined extensions to cover specific cases.

Table 7.6 LLN0—logical node zero.

LLN0 class				
Attribute Name	**Attr. Type**	**Explanation**	**T**	**M/O**
LNName		Shall be inherited from logical node class (see IEC 61850-7-2)		
Data				
Common Logical Node Information				
		LN shall inherit all mandatory data from the common logical node Class		*M*
Loc	*SPS*	Local operation for a complete logical device		*O*
OpTmh	*INS*	Operation time		*O*
Controls				
Diag	*SPC*	Run diagnostics		O
LEDRs	*SPC*	LED reset	*T*	*O*

Table 7.7 IHMI logical node—human-machine interface.

IHMI class				
Attribute Name	**Attr. Type**	**Explanation**	**T**	**M/O**
LNName		Shall be inherited from ***Logical-Node*** Class (see IEC 61850-7-2)		
Data				
Common Logical Node Information				
		LN shall inherit all Mandatory Data from ***Common Logical Node*** class		*M*

7.7 Logical Node Extension Rules

To maximize its applicability, while keeping uniformity, the standard defines specific extension rules for **`Logical Node`** and data usage, such as:

- If there is any **`Logical Node`** class that fits the function to be modeled, an instance of this **`Logical Node`** shall be used with all its mandatory data (***M***).
- If there are dedicated versions of this function with the same basic data, different instances of this **`Logical Node`** class shall be used.
- If there are no **`Logical Node`** class that fit the function to be modeled, a new **`logical node`** shall be created.
- If, in addition to the mandatory data (***M***), there is also optional data (***O***), which fit the function to be modeled, these optional data shall be used.
- If there are some data (***M*** or ***O***) that are needed more times than defined in the **`Logical Node`** class, additional data with number extensions shall be used.
- If, in the **`Logical Node`** class, data is missing for the allocated function, the first choice shall be to use one of the data listed.
- If none of the data listed covers the requirements, new data shall be created according to the rules for new data.
- Other extensions are not allowed.

For instance, these rules can be used to extend the use of **`Logical Node PDIS`** to model different distance-protection zones, as shown in Table 7.8.

Similarly, the rule of data specialization by number extension can be used to define additional winding hotspot temperature measurements on **`LN YPTR`** for power transformers, as shown in Table 7.9.

Table 7.8 Extension for distance protection zones.

Logical Node Class Name: *`PDIS`* (Distance)	
Instance name (without prefix)	**Meaning**
`PDIS1`	Zone 1 of the distance protection
`PDIS2`	Zone 2 of the distance protection
`PDIS3`	Zone 3 of the distance protection
Etc.	Etc.

Table 7.9 Specialization of data by number extension.

Logical Noce Class Name: YPTR (Power Transformer)	
Data name: *HPTmp* (Winding hotspot temperature in °C)	
HPTmp1	Winding hotspot 1 temperature (in °C)
HPTmp2	Winding hotspot 2 temperature (in °C)
HPTmp3	Winding hotspot 3 temperature (in °C)
HPTmp4	Winding hotspot 4 temperature (in °C)

Table 7.10 Examples for new logical nodes.

1. Character	1. Character	2. Character	3. Character	New LN
A Automatic Control	Door	Entrance	Control	***ADEC*** Automatic door entrance control
Z Further Equipment	Fire	Protection	Transformer	***ZFPT*** Fire protection of a power transformer

New logical nodes can also be created using these rules. Table 7.10 lists examples of names that can be used to develop ***Logical Nodes*** for automatic door entrance control and fire protection of power transformers.

Once selected or defined, ***Logical Nodes*** can be used to model complete functions and ***IEDs*** in an SAS, as shown in the subsequent paragraph.

7.8 Logical Node Usage

The following is a short list of typical automation and protection functions that can be modeled using ***logical nodes***:

- Merging units
- Distance and overcurrent protection functions
- Automatic functions
- Breaker and voltage control functions
- Telecontrol functions
- Measuring and metering functions

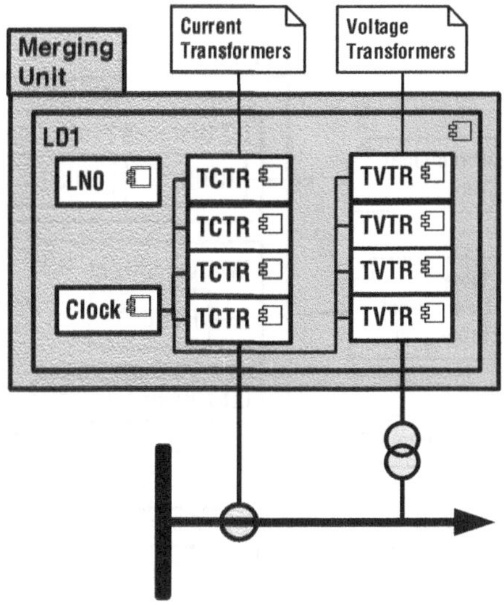

Figure 7.21 Typical merging unit.

Merging Units can be modeled by instantiating from the abstract classes of ***Logical Nodes TCTR*** and ***TVTR***, depending on the number of CT and VT signals digitized, as shown in the UML Deployment Diagram of Figure 7.21 for a three-phase ***merging unit***. A ***Clock*** and an ***LN0*** are also included to model the synchronizing signal and the common data for the ***logical device***.

Distance and overcurrent protections can also be modeled by instantiating from the abstract classes of ***Logical Nodes RDIR***, ***PDIS***, and ***PTOC***, based on the number and types of protection units, as shown in the UML Deployment Diagram in Figure 7.22 for a three-zone distance protection with a time-overcurrent protection unit. Disturbance recording and ***merging units*** for the instrument transformers and circuit breakers can also be modeled on the same ***IED***.

Hierarchical levels can be used to model breaker and voltage control functions, as shown in Figure 7.23. This UML Deployment Diagram models the interlocking functions at the bay and station levels, as well as the breaker and tap changer at the bay and process levels.

Measuring and metering functions can also be modeled by assigning ***Logical Nodes*** to hierarchical levels, from revenue and operational meters at the bay level to archiving and human–machine tasks at the station level, as shown in the UML Deployment Diagram in Figure 7.24.

All these examples are built using specialized ***logical nodes***, with roles defined in the standard that correspond to common substation automation functions. Requirements not covered by these ***LN*** can be modeled using generic ***logical nodes***.

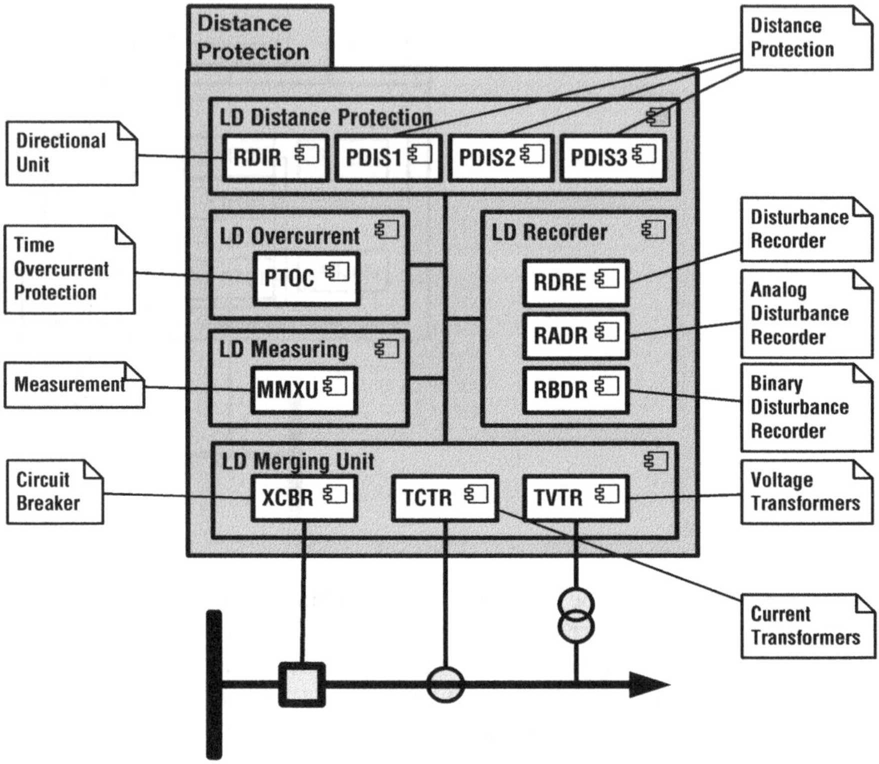

Figure 7.22 Typical distance protection.

7.9 Generic Logical Nodes

Although most of the required functions are already modeled by `logical nodes` in the standard IEC 61850, two `logical nodes` have more generic or auxiliary roles for modeling functions that are not yet standardized:

- *GGIO*—Generic process I/O
- *GAPC*—Generic automatic process control

The `GGIO logical node` represents generic digital and analog inputs and outputs that don't fall under any specific `logical nodes` defined in the IEC 61850 standard. It handles digital and analog input/output signals that model auxiliary I/O signals, such as contact status (open/closed), equipment alarms without a specific `logical node`, non-critical analog measurements, and devices with custom signals that don't match standard `logical nodes`. They

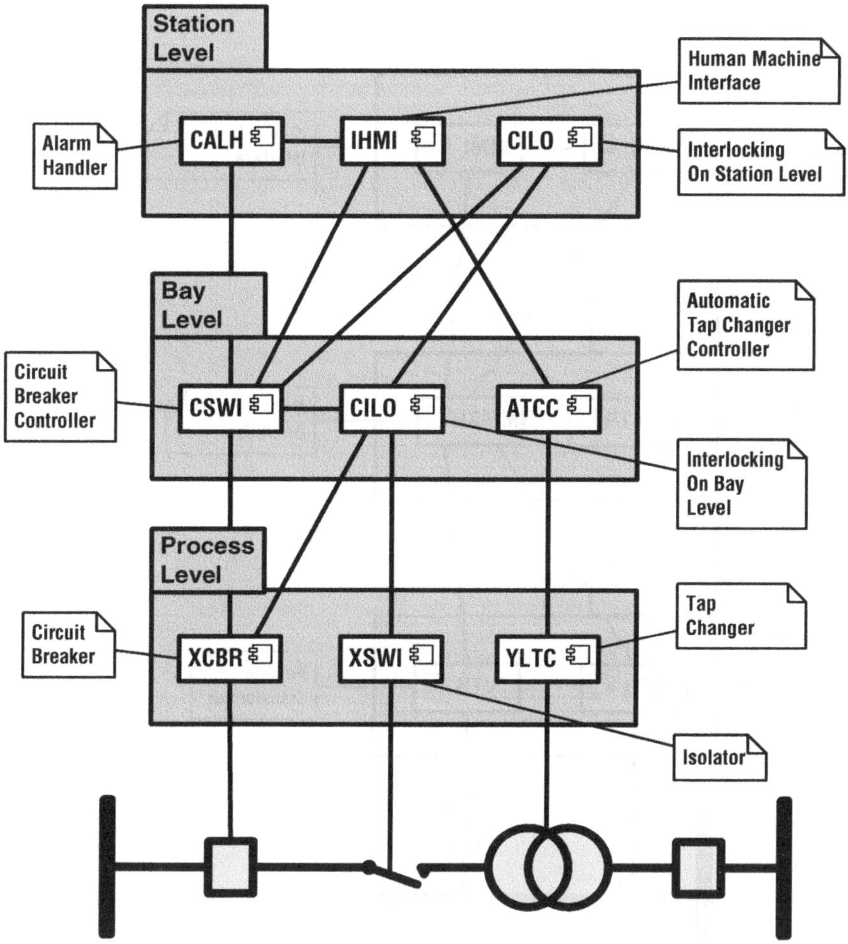

Figure 7.23 Breaker and voltage control functions.

can be used, for example, to model the alarm for an open panel door, the ambient temperature in a room, or the status of a pump or fan, among other applications. Table 7.11 lists the data objects of this ***logical node GGIO***.

The ***GAPC logical node*** represents generic automatic process control functions, mainly when no specific predefined ***logical node*** exists in the standard. It handles automatic control functions, such as timing logic, interlocking, regulation, sequential control, and custom automation logic, and integrates user-defined control functions within the IEC 61850 framework. They can be used, for example, to model automatic cooling control based on measured temperature,

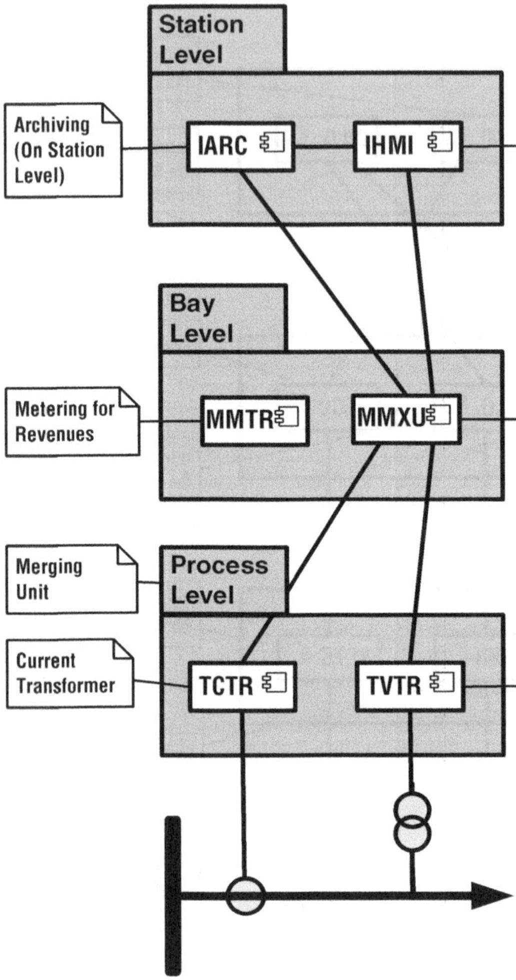

Figure 7.24 Measuring and metering function.

breaker switching sequences, and complex interlocking conditions involving multiple inputs. Table 7.12 lists the data objects of this logical node.

Table 7.13 summarizes the main features and applications of ***GGIO*** and ***GAPC logical nodes***, related to their application, customization, and use.

Following good engineering practices, the last line of this table lists the recommended restricted circumstances when these ***logical nodes*** are used. When necessary, generic automatic functions can be modeled by hierarchical layers of these generic ***Logical Nodes***, from the process level using ***LN GGIO*** (Generic Input and Output), to the bay level using ***LN GAPC*** (Generic Automatic Process

Table 7.11 GGIO logical node class.

GGIO class				
Attribute Name	**Attr. Type**	**Explanation**	**T**	**M/O**
LNName		The name shall be composed of the class name, the LN-Prefix and LN-Instance-ID according to IEC 61850-7-2		
Data				
Mandatory Logical Node Information (Shall be inherited by ALL LN but LPHD)				
Mod	*INC*	Mode		*M*
Beh	*INS*	Behavior		*M*
Health	*INS*	Health		*M*
NamePlt	*LPL*	Name plate		*M*
Data Objects				
Status Information				
Loc	*SPS*	Local control behavior		*O*
EEHealth	*ENS*	External equipment health		*O*
LocKey	*SPS*	Local or remote key		*O*
Intln1	*INS*	Integer status input		*O*
Alm1	*SPS*	General single alarm		*O*
Wrn1	*SPS*	General single warning		*O*
Ind1	*SPS*	General indication (binary input)		*O*
Measured and Metered Values				
AnIn1	*MV*	Analog input		*O*
AnOut1	*APC*	Controllable analog output		*O*
CntRs1	*BCR*	Counter, resettable		*O*
Controls				
OpCntRs	*INC*	Resettable operation counter		*O*
LocSta	*SPC*	Switching authority at the station level		*O*
SPCSO1	*SPC*	Single-point controllable status output		*O*

(Continued)

Table 7.11 (Continued)

Controls				
Attribute Name	**Attr. Type**	**Explanation**	**T**	**M/O**
DPCSO1	*DPC*	Double-point controllable status output		*O*
ISCSO1	*INC*	Integer status controllable status output		*O*
Services				
Inherited and specialized from **Logical Node** class (see IEC 61850-7-2)				

Table 7.12 GAPC logical node class.

GAPC class				
Attribute Name	**Attr. Type**	**Explanation**	**T**	**M/O**
LNName		The name shall be composed of the class name, the LN-Prefix and LN-Instance-ID according to IEC 61850-7-2		
Data				
Mandatory Logical Node Information (Shall be inherited by ALL LN but LPHD)				
Mod	*INC*	Mode		*M*
Beh	*INS*	Behavior		*M*
Health	*INS*	Health		*M*
NamePlt	*LPL*	Name plate		*M*
Data Objects				
Status Information				
Loc	*SPS*	Local control behavior		*O*
EEHealth	*ENS*	External equipment health		*O*
LocKey	*SPS*	Local or remote key		*O*
Auto	*SPC*	Automatic operation		*O*
Str1	*ACD*	Start		*O*
Op1	*ACT*	Operate		*O*

Status Information				
Attribute Name	**Attr. Type**	**Explanation**	**T**	**M/O**
Alm1	*SPS*	Generic single alarm		O
Ind1	*SPS*	Generic single indication		O
Controls				
OpCntRs	*INC*	Resettable operation counter		O
LocSta	*SPC*	Switching authority at station level		O
SPCSO1	*SPC*	Single-point controllable status output		O
DPCSO1	*DPC*	Double-point controllable status output		O
ISCSO1	*INC*	Integer status controllable status output		O
Settings				
StrVal1	*ASG*	Start value		O

Table 7.13 Generic logical nodes.

Feature	*GGIO*	*GAPC*
Function type	Generic I/O	Generic automatic control
Typical application	Sensor states, analog signals	Logic, sequences, and timing control
Customization	High	High
When to use	No suitable I/O node available	No suitable control node available

Control), up to the station level using the ***LN IHMI*** (human–machine interface), as shown in the UML Package Diagram of Figure 7.25.

The use of these generic solutions should be limited to specific cases not covered by the predefined standard ***logical nodes***, with detailed documentation of their functions and data communication, as provided by the ***PICOM*** concept.

7.10 PICOM Model

Communication and data transfer between ***logical nodes*** can also be modeled using the ***PICOM*** concept, introduced in Technical Brochure 180 of CIGRE Working Group 34.03 and adopted in IEC 61850. ***PICOM*** describes an information

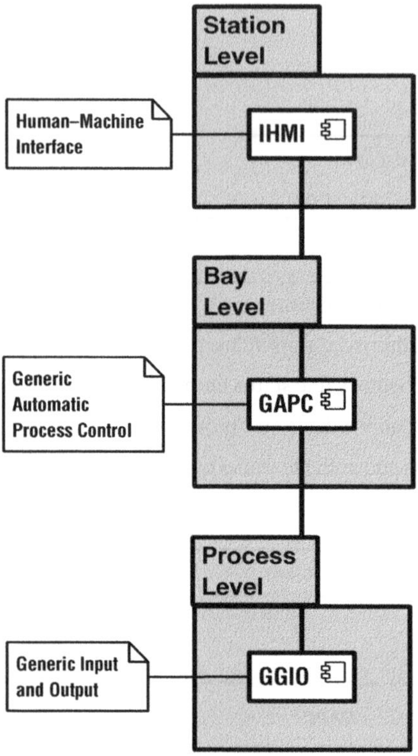

Figure 7.25 Generic automatic function.

transfer on a logical connection with communication attributes between two `logical nodes` (Figure 7.26).

It also contains information to be transmitted and requirement attributes, such as performance. However, it does not define the structure or format of data exchanged over the communication network. The ***`PICOM`*** concept can be used to understand or specify the flow of information related to different functions in an SAS, as shown in Figure 7.27.

A UML Class Diagram can describe the relationships between ***`PICOMs`*** and other abstract classes defined in IEC 61850. Figure 7.28 shows a ***`PICOM`*** as a UML class with a bidirectional relation to the ***`Compatible Logical Node`*** class, modeling the information transfer necessary to accomplish a function.

A ***`Logical Node`*** can be modeled according to the ***`PICOM`*** types it exchanges with other ***`LNs`***. ***`Measured`*** values, ***`Status`*** information, ***`Control`*** signals, and ***`Settings`***, which comprise all information associated with a ***`Logical Node`***, are communicated to and from an ***`LN`*** using ***`PICOMs`***, as shown in Figure 7.29.

Even the services provided by ***`Logical Nodes`*** are modeled by the exchange of ***`PICOMs`*** between the client and server, as shown in Figure 7.30. This includes messages requiring control and substitution actions, parameter get and set operations, directory definitions, and reports.

The following types of components form a typical ***`PICOM`***:

- **Data**—meaning the content of the information and its identification as needed by the functions (semantics)
- **Type**—describing the data structure, i.e., if it is an analog or a binary value, a single value or a set of data, etc.
- **Performance**—meaning the permissible transmission time (defined by performance class), the data integrity, and the method or cause of transmission (for example, periodic, event-driven, or on request)
- **Logical connection**—containing the logical source (sending `logical node`) and the logical sink (destination or receiving `logical node`).

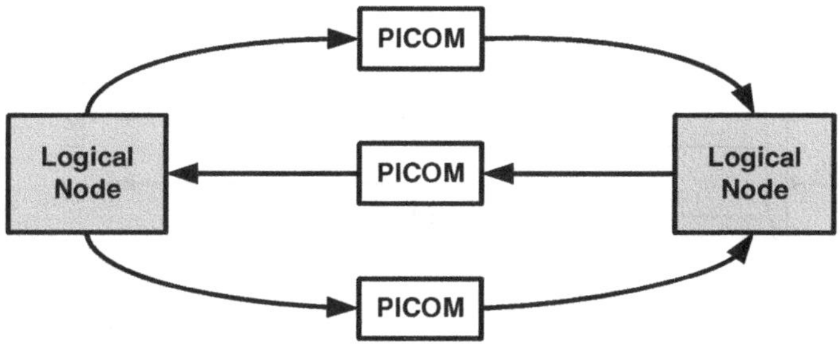

Figure 7.26 Exchanged data in functions using PICOM.

Figure 7.27 Flow of PICOMs between logical nodes.

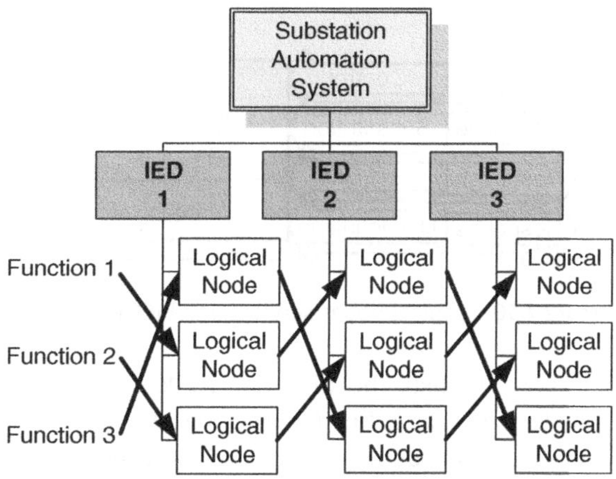

Figure 7.28 Modeling PICOMs.

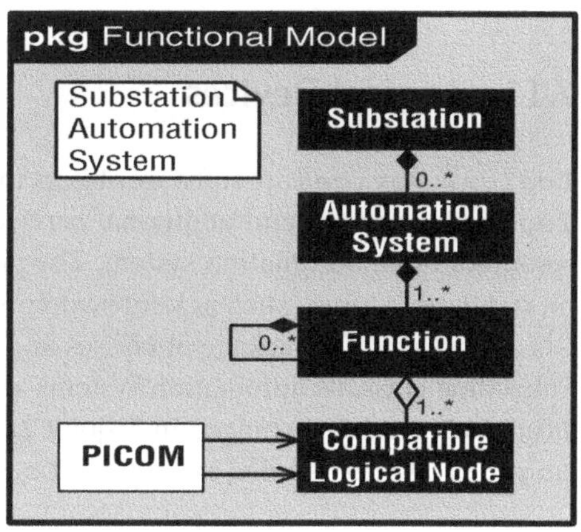

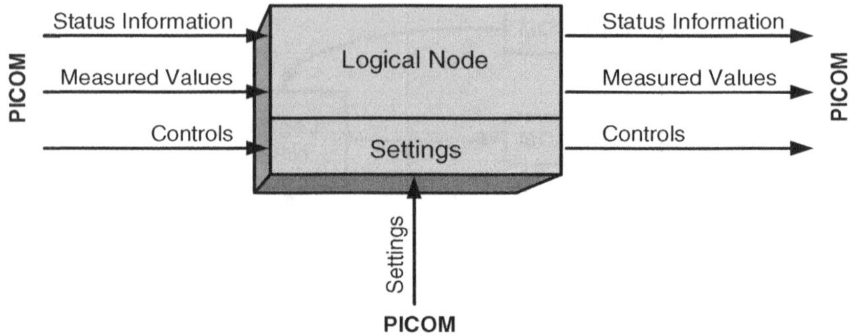

Figure 7.29 Logical node representation by PICOMs.

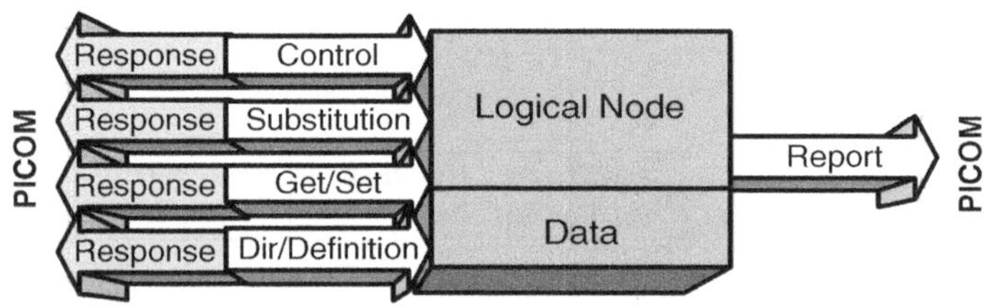

Figure 7.30 Logical nodes services and PICOMs.

Table 7.14 lists the different ***PICOM*** types, their meanings, attributes, and transfer times, as defined by IEC 61850.

Once they are defined, ***logical nodes*** are organized in ***logical devices*** that share standard services and resources in an SAS, as described in the following paragraph.

7.11 Logical Devices

Logical Devices are software objects that model the composition of functions, ***logical nodes***, and additional services that share common objectives and resources in an automation system. The grouping of ***logical nodes*** is based on standard features, such as joint switching on and off. Figure 7.31 shows a UML Class Diagram of a package of classes and the hierarchical relationship among a Substation class, its automation systems and functions, formed by ***Compatible Logical Nodes***, arranged in disjoint ***Logical Devices***. This means that a ***Logical Node*** pertains to a unique ***Logical Device***.

Table 7.14 PICOM types and meanings.

PICOM TYPE	Meaning of PICOM and its value attribute	Type mode	Number of value attributes combined (range/-typical)	Size in bit of value attribute	Transfer time (range/typical) (ms)	Message type
1	Process value (sample)	Value Cyclic	1–8 1, 2, 3, 5	6	• 10 • 0,1; 0,5; 1; 2; 5; 10	**4**
6	Report (calculated) such as energy list	File Request	1	1024	• 1000–5000 • 1000; 5000	**5**
7	Fault value (calculated) such as fault distance	Value Request	1–2 1	16	• 1000–5000 • 1000; 5000	**3**
10	Event/alarm	Event Spontaneous	1–16 1	1	• 100–1000 • 100; 500; 1000	**3**
12	Trigger (calculated) for example for start of another function	Event Spontaneous	1	1	• 10–1000 • 10; 50; 100; 1000	**1**
22	Trip	Cmd. Spontaneous	1	1	• 1	**1**
24	ID Data, setting	File Spontaneous Request	1	1024	• 1000–5000 • 1000; 5000	**5**
17	Calculated state	Status Request	1	1	• 1–100 • 1; 10; 20; 50; 100	**2**
19	Mode of operation	Status Request Cyclic	1	1 16	• 10–100 • 10; 100	**3**
26	Acknowledge by operator or auto	Cmd. Spontaneous	1	1	• 10–1000 • 10; 100; 1000	**3**

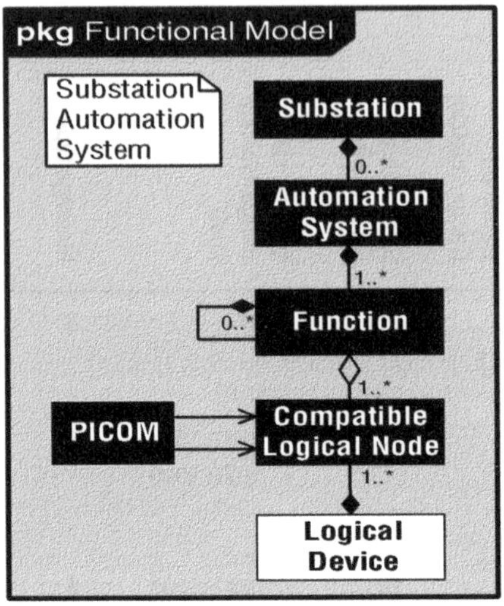

Figure 7.31 Definition of logical devices.

These classes aim to provide information describing the relevant device functionality. They present the standard device-view modeling and implementation aspects, as well as related services, define reusable parts of industrial devices, and represent groups of functions or ***logical nodes***. In addition, ***Logical Devices*** represent information about the host's visible resources, the equipment connected to that host, and the common communication aspects applicable to several contained ***LNs***.

A ***Logical Device*** can also function as a ***gateway*** (***proxy***), making itself transparent from a functional point of view so that it can be identified independently of its location (in a separate device connected to the network or in a ***proxy*** device). They provide information about the physical devices they use as host (***nameplate*** and ***health***) or about controlled external devices.

Logical Devices reside within physical or virtualized devices, usually defined and modeled as ***Servers***. They form a group of functions, each defined as a (set of) ***Logical Nodes***. They contain a single ***LLNO*** (***Logical Node Zero***), a single ***LPHD*** (***Logical Node Physical Device***), and at least one ***Compatible Logical Node***, as shown in the UML Class Diagram of Figure 7.32.

A ***Logical Device*** class is formed by three main attributes that identify its instance name, pathname, and a set of embedded ***Logical Nodes***. This class provides a unique service, ***GetLogicalDeviceDirectory***. Table 7.15 shows the general specification of a ***Logical Device*** class by IEC 61850.

Attribute ***LDName*** contains the ***logical device*** name to identify a ***LOGICAL-DEVICE*** within the scope of a system unambiguously. The ***LDName*** attribute identifies a ***LD*** within the scope of a system. ***LDRef*** is a ***logical device ObjectReference***, a unique pathname of a ***LOGICAL-DEVICE***. Finally, ***LogicalNode [3..n]*** is used to identify the ***LOGICAL-NODEs*** contained in a ***LOGICAL-DEVICE***, plus ***LLN0*** and ***LPHD***.

The ***Server*** class can list the available ***Logical Devices*** via the service GetLogicDeviceDirectory by polling on a per-request/response basis. Clients use this service to retrieve the ***ObjectReferences*** of all ***LNs*** within the referenced ***LN***. It provides client-server communication for selective reading/writing of data

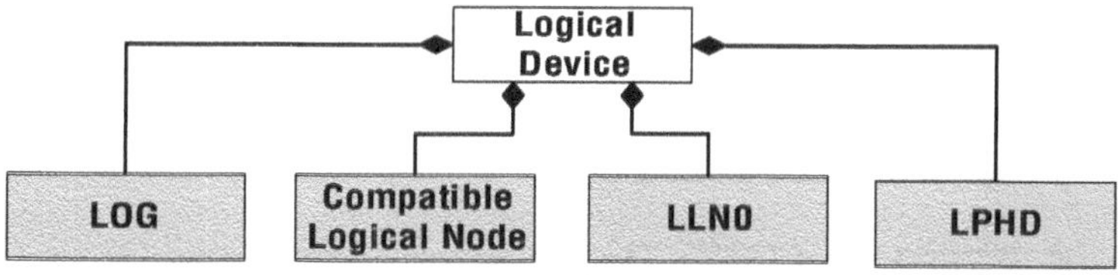

Figure 7.32 Logical device composition.

Table 7.15 Logical device class definition.

LOGICAL-DEVICE class		
Attribute name	**Attribute type**	**Value/value range/explanation**
LDName	*OjectName*	Instance name of an instance of *LOGICAL-DEVICE*
LDRef	*ObjectReference*	Pathname of an instance of *LOGICAL-DEVICE*
LogicalNode [3..n]	*LOGICAL-NODE*	IEC 61850-7-4 specifies specialized classes of *LOGICAL-NODE*

Figure 7.33 Logical device model.

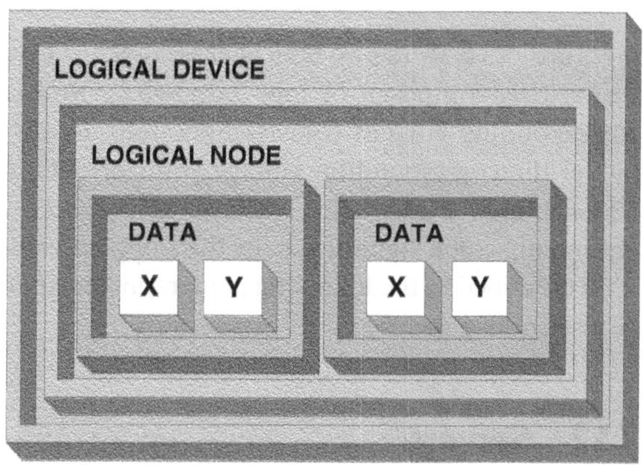

on the server. In this arrangement, the data volume is limited to the amount required for the client, while a connection monitor is implicitly included. The disadvantage is the transmission of large data volumes over point-to-point links, which results in one message per recipient and limits its suitability for time-critical applications. Also, the behavior for establishing the connection must be defined on the client side. The hierarchical organization of data in a *Logical Device* is shown in Figure 7.33.

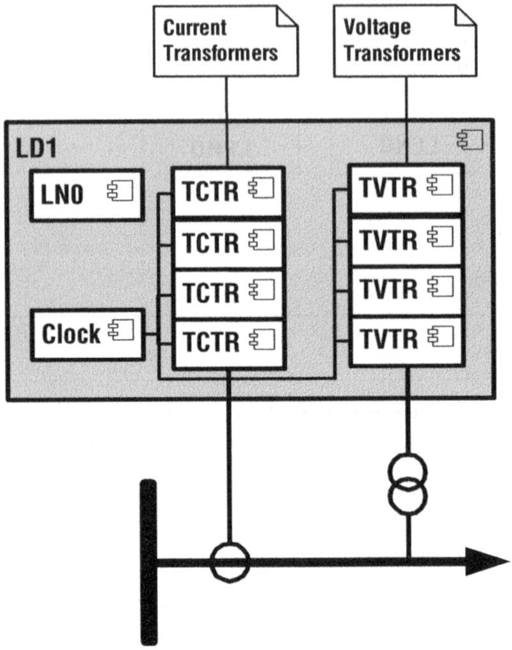

Figure 7.34 Typical logical device of merging unit.

Figure 7.34 shows a typical ***Logical Device*** (LD1) for a ***Merging Unit***. It is composed of four ***Logical Nodes*** of type ***TCTR*** to model the corresponding current transformers, four ***Logical Nodes*** of type ***TVTR*** to model the corresponding voltage transformers, a mandatory ***LLN0 Logical Node*** to model the device characteristics, and a Clock class to model the synchronizing clock signal used for the sampled values.

As described in the following paragraph, one or more ***Logical Devices*** may be present in a ***Server***.

7.12 Servers

A ***Server*** represents a device's external visible behavior. All other ***ACSI*** models are part of the server. The ***server*** resides within a physical (or virtual) device, representing the application data modeling view of the outside world. A public service, ***ServerDirectory***, provides the list of internal server objects. Any physical or virtual device with a communications interface can be considered a ***server***. It has an IP address accessible over a network by an external client. Figure 7.35 shows how ***servers*** are interconnected in a station network.

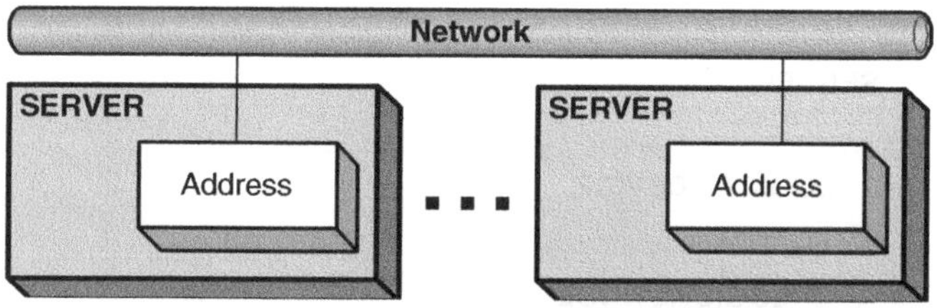

Figure 7.35 Servers in a station network.

A ***Server*** can accept a connection from one or more external clients, authenticate that connection, synchronize its ***clock*** with the client, and transfer files to and from the client. A ***server*** contains one or more ***logical devices***, which comprise one or more ***logical nodes*** that represent the basic building blocks (objects) that provide various functionalities of the ***logical device***. ***Servers*** are composed of ***Logical Devices***, grouped by their standard features. Figure 7.36 illustrates the UML Class Diagram showing the relationship between servers and other SAS objects in the IEC 61850 Functional Model.

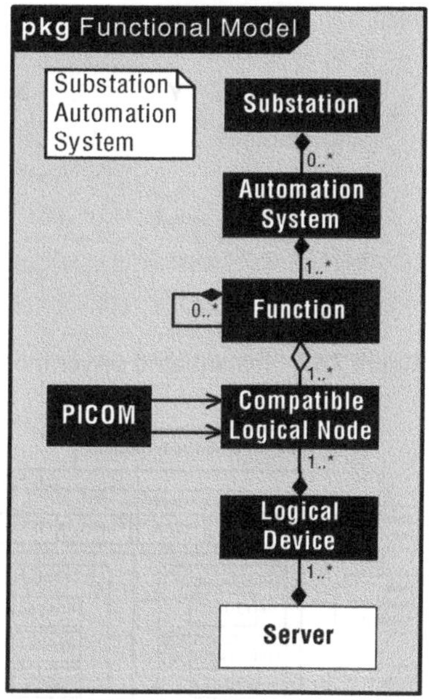

Figure 7.36 Servers in an SAS.

When instantiated, a ***Server*** can be viewed as a container object with one or more ***Logical Devices***, each comprising one or more ***logical nodes*** and various ***data*** objects, as illustrated in Figure 7.37.

These definitions enable ***servers*** to be modeled for various automation devices, such as distance protection and ***merging units***. Figure 7.38 shows examples of UML Deployment Diagrams of these models. The ***Server*** Distance Protection comprises five ***Logical Devices*** for distance protection, overcurrent protection, measuring, recording, and a ***merging unit***. The ***Server Merging Unit*** shall consist of four ***LN*** for the current and potential transformers, including the three phases and neutral, and the ***LN LN0*** and ***Clock*** to synchronize the sampled values.

Information hosted by ***Servers*** includes (i) ***logical nodes*** and ***data*** representing the fundamental application functions and associated information visible from the communication network; (ii) information about real or virtual devices representing the resources of the host itself and (if applicable) about the field equipment connected to the host device; and (iii) communication services

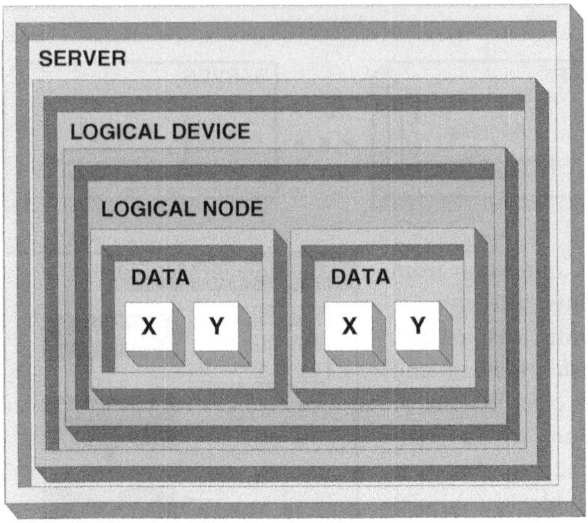

Figure 7.37 Instantiated server model.

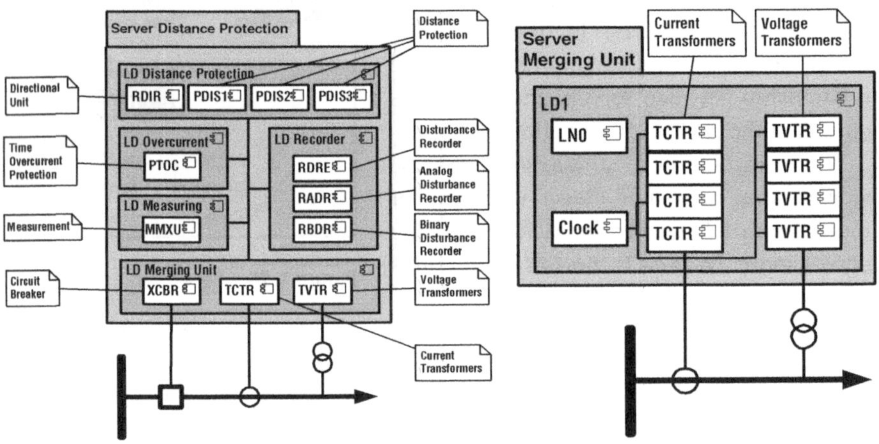

Figure 7.38 Typical server models.

and mapping to specific communication systems representing the supported exchange services.

A ***Server*** can be further described by its composition, as shown on the UML Class Diagram of Figure 7.39. Besides ***Logical Devices***, ***Servers*** may contain ***File*** structures and ***Two-Part*** and ***Multi-Part Application Association***. A server comprises all ***ACSI*** models, at least a ***Logical Device Node***, and an Association model to establish and maintain connections

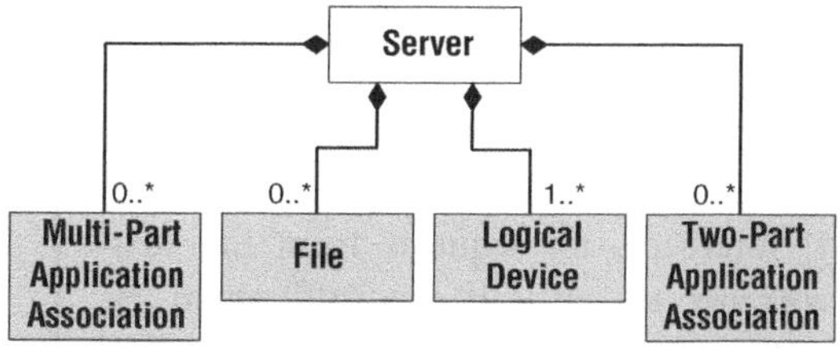

Figure 7.39 Server composition.

Table 7.16 Server attributes.

Attribute	Meaning
`ServiceAccessPoint`	Identifies a ***SERVER*** within the scope of a system
`LogicalDevice [1..n]`	Identify a ***LogicalDevice*** contained in a ***SERVER***;
`File [0..n]`	Identify a ***File*** contained in a ***SERVER***
`TPAppAssociation [0..n]`	Identify a client with which a ***SERVER*** maintains a two-party application association
`MCAppAssociation [0..n]`	Identify a subscriber with which a ***SERVER*** (publisher) maintains a multicast application association.

between devices and implement access control mechanisms. ***Servers*** also include a time synchronization model that synchronizes their clocks with a time server to improve time-tagging accuracy in applications such as reporting and logging. Finally, ***servers*** also provide file transfer models to manage file stores and the ability to transfer files between them.

Table 7.16 lists the attributes provided by any server class.

To support self-description, any ***server*** class provides a ***ServerDirectory*** service. Clients use this service to retrieve the names of all ***LDs*** or ***Files*** within the referenced ***Server***. A client shall use these services to retrieve the definition of the complete hierarchy, as well as the definition of all accessible information, and of all instances of all underlying classes in each ***server***. This service can be used for polling on a per-request/response basis, as well as for client-server communication, allowing for selective reading/writing of data on the ***server***. The advantage is that the data volume is limited to the amount required by the client, and the connection monitor is included implicitly. The disadvantages include the transfer of large data volumes over point-to-point communication, resulting in one message per recipient, and limited suitability for time-critical applications. Of course, the connection's behavior must be defined on the client side.

Besides regular ***servers***, two special types of ***Servers*** are defined by IEC 61850 to function as ***Proxy*** and ***Gateways*** in substation automation.

7.13 Proxies and Gateways

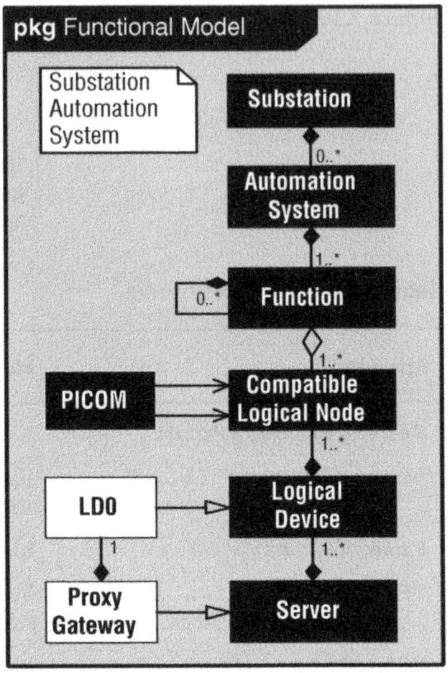

Figure 7.40 Definition of proxy and gateway.

A ***Proxy*** is a ***server*** that sits between a client application and a real ***server***. It intercepts all requests from the real ***server*** to see if it can fulfil them. If not, it forwards the request to the real ***server***. A ***Gateway*** server provides access to a different network with a different network address, possibly using various protocols.

Proxies and ***Gateways*** are ***Server*** specializations that mirror the ***Logical Devices*** of other physical devices. A ***Logical Device*** named ***LD0*** represents information about the ***Proxy/ Gateway***. Figure 7.40 shows the UML Class Diagram for the specialization of ***servers*** that function as ***Proxy*** or ***Gateway*** in an SAS.

Proxy and ***Gateway*** inherit all services from the ***Server*** class, primarily the ***GetServerDirectory*** service. Figure 7.41 shows the relationship between a ***Proxy*** or ***Gateway*** and the corresponding ***Server*** and components. A direct mapping is defined among their ***Logical Devices***, ***Logical Nodes***, and ***Data***, so the ***Proxy*** or ***Gateway*** can answer requests directed to the real ***server***.

A typical application of a ***Proxy*** is integrating legacy devices into an IEC 61850-based project. These devices can be, for instance, electromechanical or electronic relays that lack native IEC 61850 support and may not have an Ethernet interface. This requires their connection to a substation LAN through a ***Gateway*** or ***Proxy*** server, as shown in Figure 7.42. This ***Proxy*** will typically:

- Convert the legacy communication (ex. RS232/485) interface to the Ethernet
- Convert the legacy communication protocol (ex., Modbus, DNP) to IEC 61850
- Map the data from the legacy device database into IEC 61850 object models
- Interface the messages to/from the legacy device to IEC 61850 ***IED***s

The modeling of these devices will require a ***logical device*** (***LD0***) for the ***Proxy*** itself, and ***Logical Devices*** (***LD1 ... LDN***) for the legacy devices interfacing to the IEC 61850-based system, as shown in Figure 7.43. The functions of

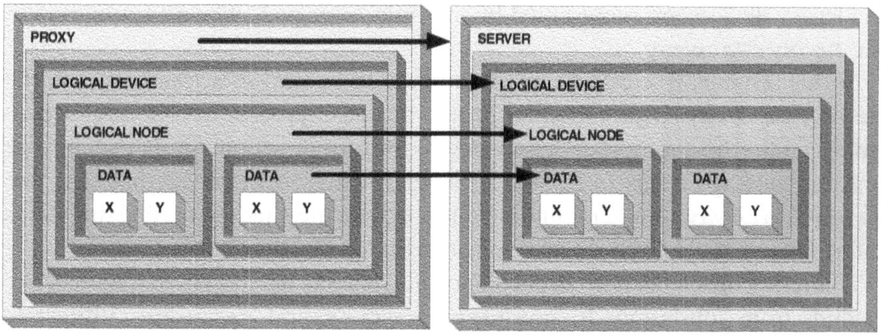

Figure 7.41 Proxy and gateway.

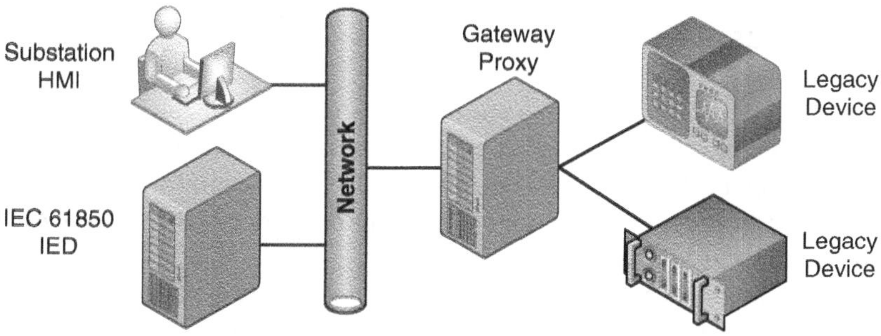

Figure 7.42 Communication architecture with legacy devices.

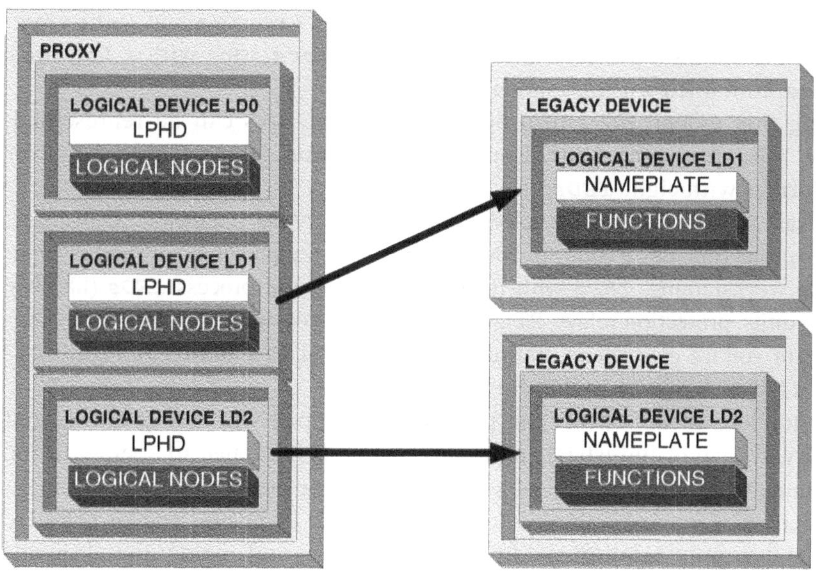

Figure 7.43 Modeling of legacy devices on the proxy.

the legacy devices are represented by multiple ***Logical Nodes*** configured in the ***Proxy/Gateway***.

In this scheme, if a ***GOOSE*** message needs to be sent to a legacy device, the ***Proxy/Gateway*** must subscribe to this message, process it, and send a control signal to the appropriate legacy device for further action. Similarly, suppose a status message needs to be sent to other IEC 61850 ***IEDs***. In that case, the ***Proxy/Gateway*** should monitor it, and a ***GOOSE*** message containing this status information should be configured for subscription by other ***IEDs***.

This class specialization and composition chain, as shown in Figure 7.40, extends from substations to ***servers***, ***proxies***, and ***gateways***, ultimately leading to the concept of an ***IED*** as introduced by IEC 61850.

7.14 Intelligent Electronic Devices

IED refers to any device incorporating one or more processors capable of receiving or sending data/control from or to an external source (for example, electronic multifunction meters, digital relays, controllers, etc.). As for composition, an ***IED*** may host one or more ***Servers***, have one or more network cards, and have one or more IP addresses (one per hosted ***server***).

An ***IED*** provides a place for ***Servers***. As such, they don't have their services. The contained ***Servers*** offer their services. Figure 7.44 illustrates the UML Class Diagram that relates ***IEDs*** to the ***Servers*** they are included in.

Note that an automation system can contain one or more ***IEDs***, which may in turn contain one or more ***Servers***, including ***Proxies*** and ***Gateways***. Figure 7.45 shows a possible model of two ***Servers***, each with a ***Logical Device***, contained within a single ***IED***.

Using this model, the entire deployment of an SAS can be represented. Figure 7.46 shows the UML Deployment Diagram for protecting a power transformer with eight ***IEDs***.

Typical ***IED*** types include telecommunication ***IEDs*** (gateways, converters, RTUs), protection ***IEDs*** (relays), HMI ***IEDs*** (gateways, personal computers, engineering workstations, ***IEDs*** with integrated HMIs), and process ***IEDs*** (like bay control units, protection relays, RTUs on the process side, meters, autonomous controllers or voltage controllers, transducers, and digital ***VTs*** and ***CTs***). Figure 7.47 shows a typical hardware architecture of an ***IED***.

The nucleus of an ***IED*** is the processor, equipped with a digital bus and memory, typical of industrial computers, which is hardened to operate in the electromagnetic environment of substations and power plants. Depending on its function, it may contain specialized hardware, firmware, and/or software for human communication and input/output of external analog/digital signals

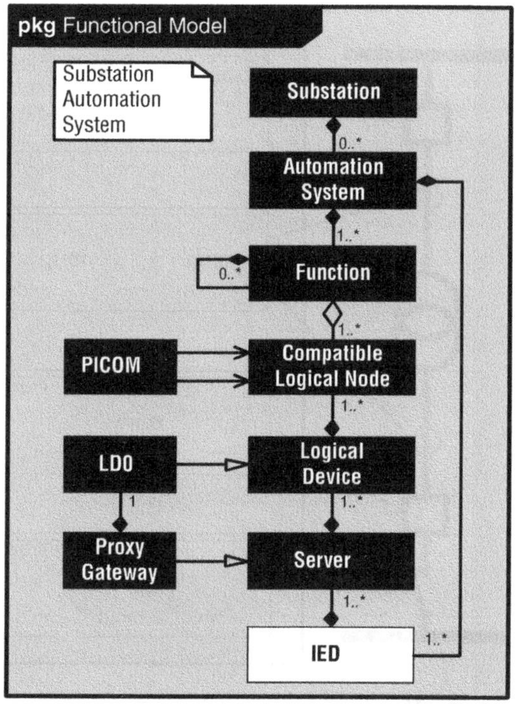

Figure 7.44 Intelligent electronic devices.

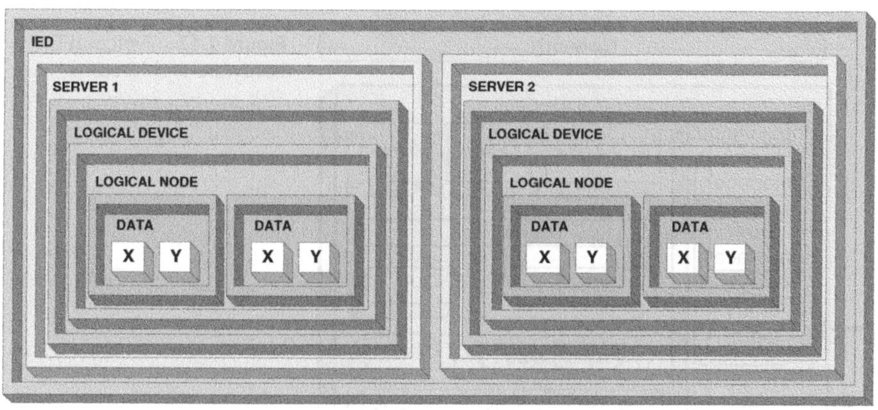

Figure 7.45 IED model with two servers.

from/to field equipment, such as ***CTs***, ***VTs***, and physical contacts. Finally, an ***IED*** must include means to synchronize its events with a time reference source and communicate with other ***IEDs***. One or more network cards enable this connection to the communication networks that form the automation system.

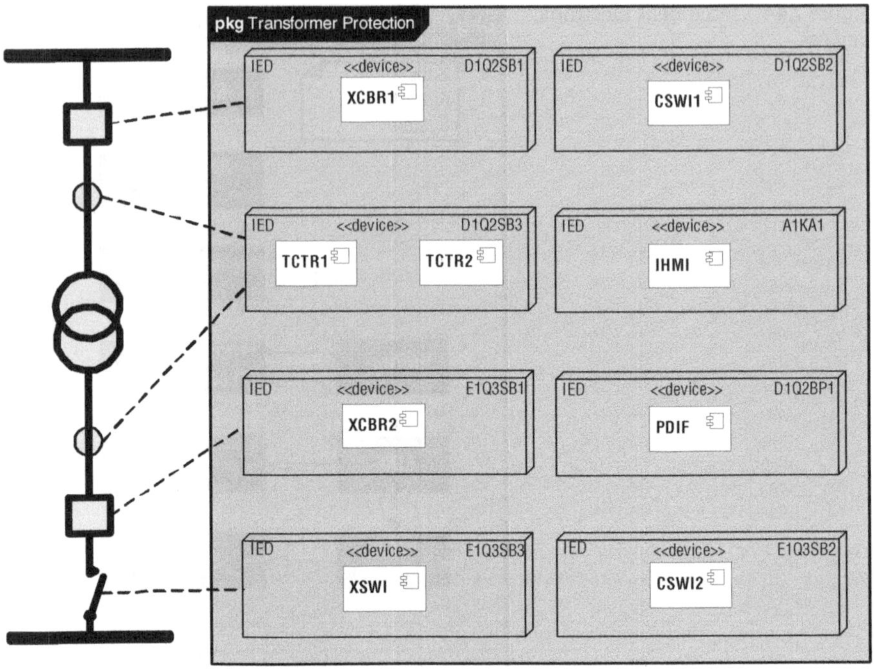

Figure 7.46 IED deployment diagram.

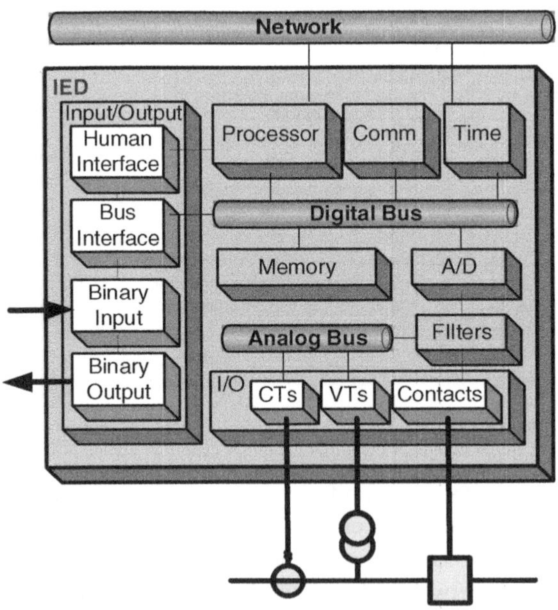

Figure 7.47 Typical IED hardware architecture.

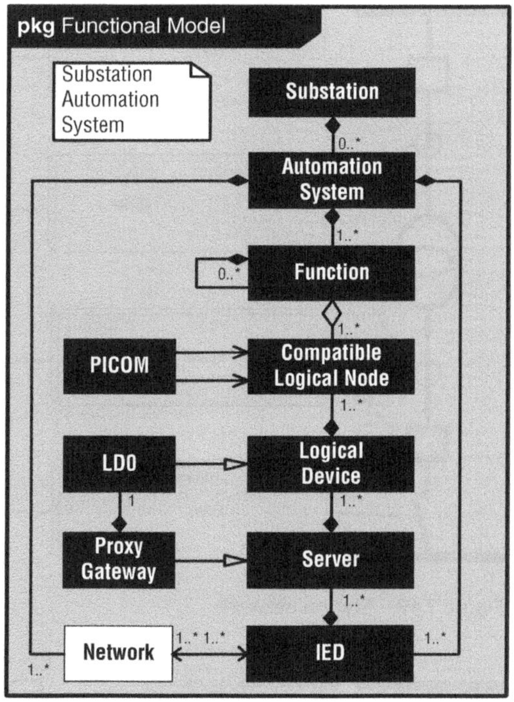

Figure 7.48 Definition of a network.

7.15 Networks

The concept of a network, as applied to the SA and IEC 61850 standard, refers to a physical (LAN) or virtual (VLAN) connection of ***servers*** in an SAS. Network services are provided by the Specific Communication Service Model (***SCSM***) used on the SAS. Their services are provided by the middleware used on the SAS. So, a network is formed by any logical connection among the ***Servers*** of a station that the SAS's specific ***SCSM*** uses. It comprises various network components, including switches, hubs, repeaters, bridges, and routers. Figure 7.48 illustrates how a network closes the loop, linking all classes in an SAS, in a UML Class Diagram.

Note that an automation system can contain one or more ***networks*** that connect several ***IEDs***, each with multiple ***servers***, including ***Proxies*** and ***Gateways***. Each ***IED*** can connect to one or more ***networks***, depending on its number of communication ports.

An SAS can be deployed using a single ***network***, the station network, that links all IEDs, as shown in the UML Deployment Diagram in Figure 7.49.

Optionally, the network can be split into a process network and a station network, as shown in the UML Deployment Diagram on Figure 7.50. A process

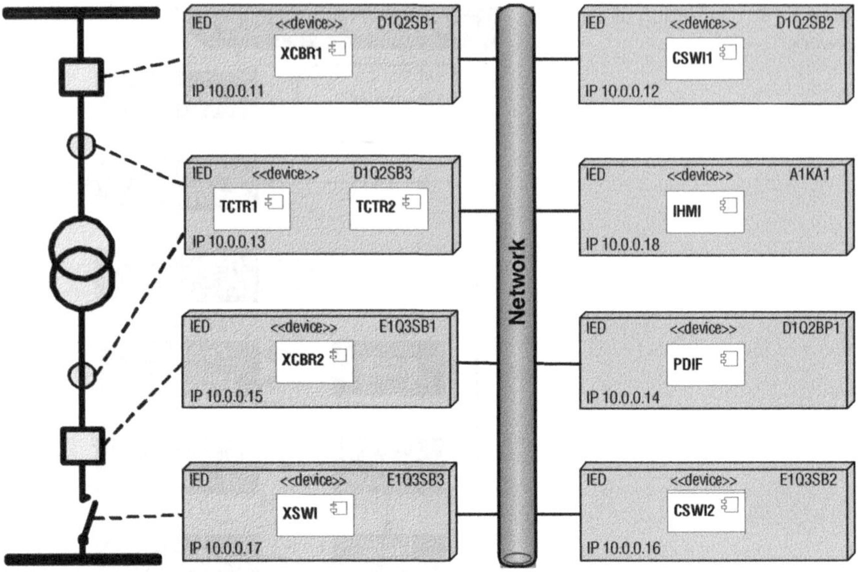

Figure 7.49 Station network.

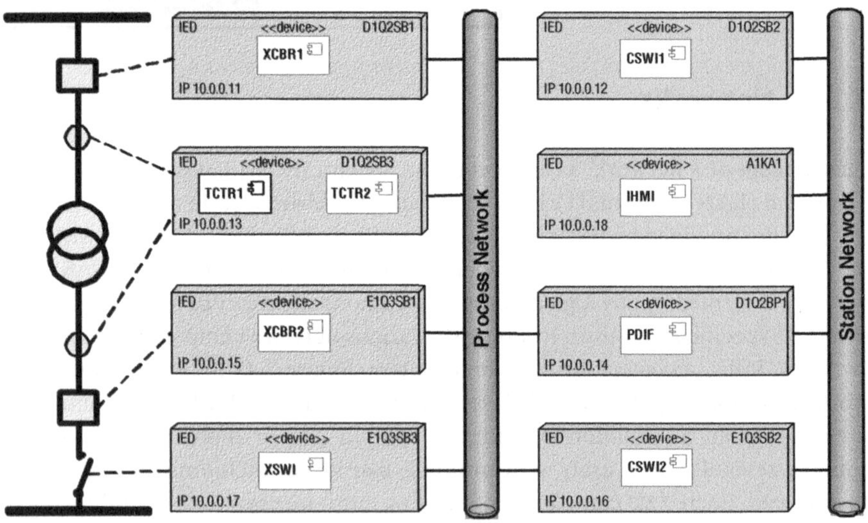

Figure 7.50 Process and station network.

network links all **IEDs** directly connected to the substation's switchyard or process equipment.

An SAS can be composed of any number of station and process networks, further divided into logical or physical segments according to the automation and security requirements. Chapter 14, which covers security models, will discuss these topics in further detail.

7.16 Summary

A functional view of an SAS comprises a stack of UML classes related by inheritance and containment associations, as specified in the IEC 61850 standard. The upper layer of this stack includes the ***Substation***, a container for several **Automation Systems**, ***IEDs***, and **Networks**. Each automation system comprises one or more functions and is composed of ***compatible logical nodes*** that exchange information defined by ***PICOMs***, grouped into one or more ***logical devices*** (***LDs***). ***LDs*** are further grouped into ***servers***, including `proxies` and ***gateways***, and deployed as ***IEDs***. These ***IEDs*** are connected by communication ***Networks*** forming the distributed SAS. Chapter 8 offers a more detailed examination of the data structure and attributes that comprise each SAS function's data model.

7.17 Review Questions

1 Explain the main purpose of functional modeling in an SAS based on IEC 61850. What issues does functional modeling solve, and why is it crucial for system interoperability?

2 Describe the three perspectives of an SAS shown in the chapter's Venn diagram. How do the function, data, and service views work together to shape automation system models?

3 Differentiate between a function and a ***logical node*** in the IEC 61850 framework. In your explanation, emphasize their roles and how they work together within distributed automation functions.

4 Classify automation functions into their respective levels (process, bay, station) and provide an example of a function implemented at each level. Discuss what distinguishes these levels in terms of scope and objectives.

5 Using the example of the differential protection function, explain how the standard's functional description elements (task, starting criteria, result, performance, decomposition, and interaction) support the modeling of protection behavior. Explain why each element is necessary.

6 Discuss the role of **`Logical Node`** data categories (Settings, Controls, Measured, Status). How does this classification enhance both semantic clarity and standardized data exchange?

7 In a scenario where a new protective behavior needs extra measurements not supported by current ***`LN`*** attributes, outline the steps and rules you would follow to extend a **`Logical Node`** or its data.

8 Compare the common use cases of ***`GGIO`*** and ***`GAPC`*** **`Logical Nodes`**. When should each be used, and why should their use be limited?

9 Explain how ***`PICOM's`*** model information flows between **`Logical Nodes`**. Choose one ***`PICOM`*** type and demonstrate how its transfer characteristics influence the performance of an SAS function.

10 Analyze how **`Logical Devices`**, **`Servers`**, and ***`IEDs`*** form a hierarchical structure within an SAS. Using this structure, describe how a protection ***`IED`*** hosting multiple **`logical devices`** would be modeled and accessed by external clients.

8

Data Models

8.1 Introduction

To perform their essential functions, Substation Automation Systems (SAS) need access to data that shows the status and properties of the modeled power system, as well as the automation functions. This data can be organized in various formats, using current communication middleware and information frameworks. To demonstrate how functions use data in an SAS, the IEC 61850 standard offers a comprehensive set of building blocks for representing data exchanged by ***logical nodes*** and for modeling and communicating with other Intelligent Electronic Devices (***IEDs***) and switchyard equipment.

8.2 Learning Objectives

This chapter addresses the role of data models and structures in SAS and their organization in accordance with IEC 61850. The following topics are covered:

- Data Modeling
- Data Hierarchy
- Primitive Elements
- Namespaces
- Data Classes
- Common Data Classes
- Data Attributes
- Data Types
- Functional Constraints

How different functions use these data will be discussed in Chapter 9, about Service Models.

8.3 Data Modeling

A model represents some aspects of reality. It helps understand, describe, or predict how things work in the real world. According to IEC 61850, a data model represents knowledge about substation information and its representation in classes, abstractly describing the information used by the automation functions and devices.

Data sources for automation systems can be analog, providing continuous information about the current condition or behavior of a component or system, or state, providing information about the component or system's state. Derived information from these sources can include cumulative data, such as statistics for a specific period, historical records, or prior data.

Analog information can be a measured value, like (sampled) value of a process quantity, a processed value derived from an estimated value, a three-phase value calculated from a three-phase electric power quantity, a setpoint as a controllable target (demanded) for a process quantity, or a parameter such as a controllable value for system behavior (adjustment).

Digital or state information can include, for instance, a component or system status condition, an alarm or statement of a safety intervention, a command for a controllable status of system behavior, or an event or state transition (status, alarm, command). Information can also be cumulative, like a timing value for the total time duration of a specific state; a counting value, like the total number of occurrences of a particular event; or characteristic values, like signal properties of analog information. Historical data can take the form of simple logs, such as a chronological list of source information for a period; transient logs containing events triggered during a short period (event-driven reports); or a report with periodical notifications comprising statistical information and overall performance.

Besides the capability to represent all these types of information, a data model must attain a set of requirements, such as (i) self-description, provided by all devices regarding functions; (ii) standardized rules for extensions, to avoid the need of private ranges in the IEC 61850; (iii) information for HMIs in ASCII text even if presentation of the information itself by the HMI is out of the scope of the IEC 61850 series; and (iv) data understandable by machines and humans, for data exchange without operator interference.

Additionally, a data model for SAS should attain a set of semantic requirements. In this regard, all data and data attributes should have standardized names and references. The names shall be self-descriptive, using standardized abbreviations derived from typical applications intended for the data objects. According to IEC 61850, all ***Data*** and ***Attributes*** shall be retrievable from their clients and structured into standard, reusable data classes and attributes, as described in the layered class hierarchy of the standard.

8.4 Data Hierarchy

To attain these objectives, IEC 61850 data models are structured into a hierarchy of classes, as illustrated in the UML Class Diagram in Figure 8.1.

In this view, a substation comprises one or more automation systems, each formed by several `IEDs`. Each `IED` is composed of one or more `Servers`, each formed by `Logical Devices` that contain compatible `Logical Nodes`, with their `Data` and respective `Attributes`. Their behavior is inherited from a hierarchical set of packages of abstract classes, as illustrated in the UML Package Diagram in Figure 8.2.

At the top of this hierarchy is a package of root classes for modeling data and functions needed by SAS. These are inherited from a package of standard classes, serving as building blocks for more specialized data structures known as compatible data classes. Finally, these are built from concrete primitive data objects, inherited by all data used by the standard. Figure 8.3 shows a typical UML data class composition for describing a circuit breaker, modeled by a compatible ***logical node XCBR*** class.

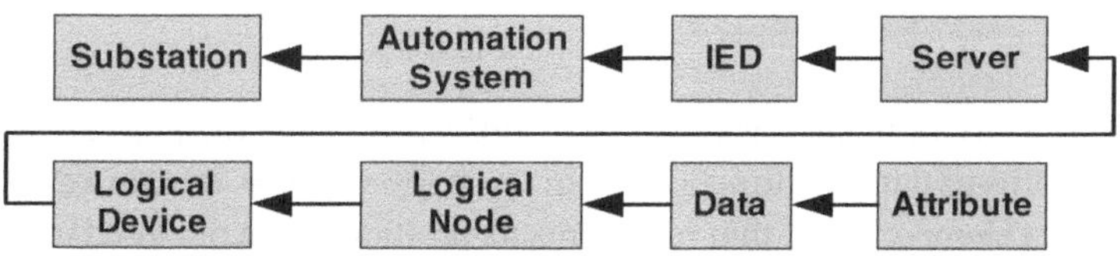

Figure 8.1 UML classes for IEC 61850.

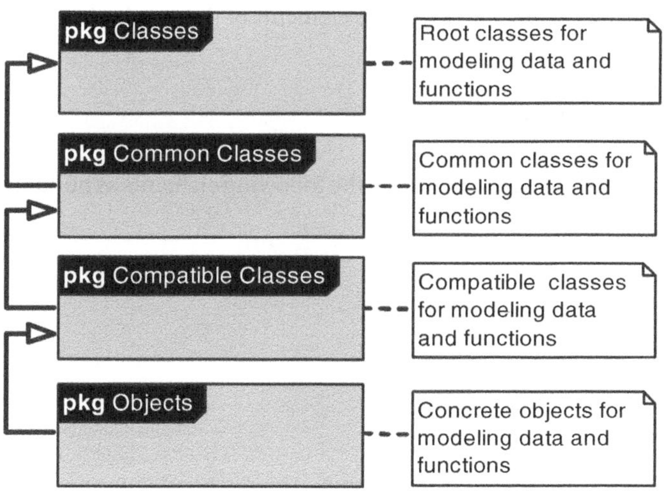

Figure 8.2 UML data packages for IEC 61850.

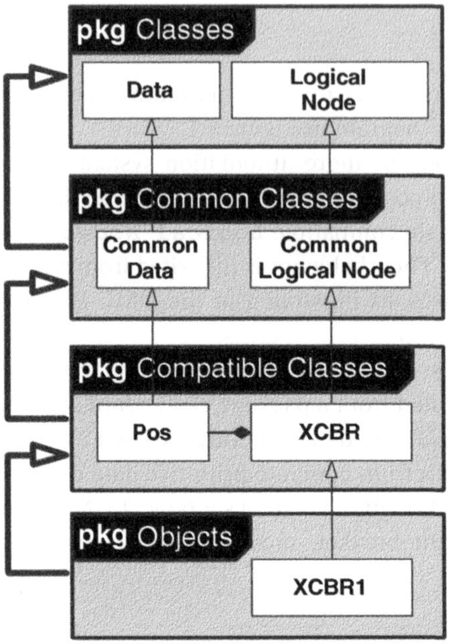

Figure 8.3 Samples of UML data packages.

In this example, a circuit breaker is modeled in IEC 61850 using the object class ***XCBR1***, which inherits its data and functions from the ***Compatible Class XCBR***. This class has a data element, ***Pos***, that represents its position (open or closed) and is inherited from the ***Common Data*** and ***Common Logical Node*** classes. These classes are derived from the upper classes for ***Data*** and ***Logical Node***, respectively, which allows the definition of all primitive elements of the standard.

8.5 Primitive Elements

For representing data in an SAS, IEC 61850 uses the following elements as building blocks for data structures:

- ***Namespaces***
- ***Physical devices***
- ***Logical devices***
- ***Logical nodes***
- ***Data classes***
- ***Data attributes***

Using these elements, it is possible to construct a hierarchical data model of substation automation that spans function deployment through implementation, grouping, modeling, and representation, down to every elementary data property. Figure 8.4 illustrates the hierarchical data organization and the role of each primitive data structure of IEC 61850.

These data models are part of Layer 6 in the hierarchical structure of IEC 61850, as introduced in Chapter 7 and illustrated in Figure 7.3, which links the upper Functional Model to the lower Service Model. This layer comprises several classes related by inheritance and composition, as shown in the UML Class Diagram in Figure 8.5. These include classes to model primitive and composite components, standard and basic data attributes and types, namespaces, and functional constraints. The comment boxes in this figure list possible data objects that can be instantiated from these classes.

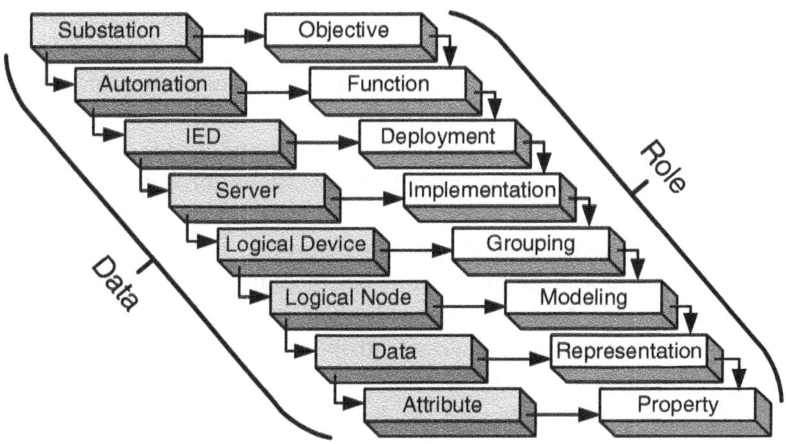

Figure 8.4 Data model hierarchy.

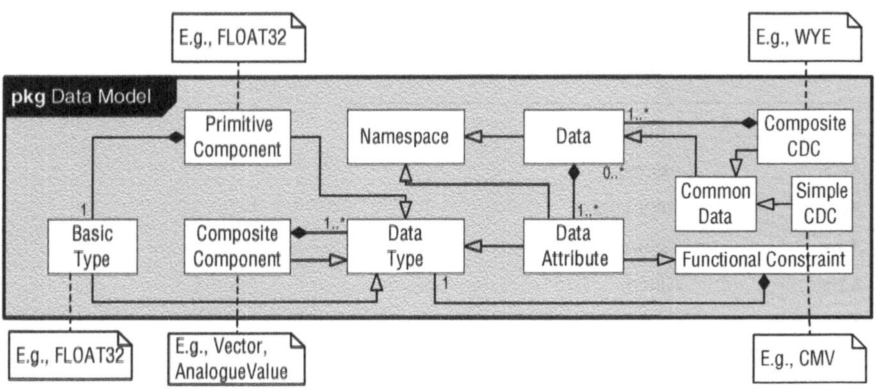

Figure 8.5 IEC 61850 data model.

The following paragraphs describe these models, starting from a ***Namespace*** definition.

8.6 Namespaces

A ***Namespace*** is an abstract container environment created to hold a logical grouping of unique identifiers (i.e., names), providing context and disambiguation of items with the same name residing in different ***Namespaces***. An identifier defined in a ***Namespace*** is associated with that ***Namespace***. The same identifier can be independently defined in multiple ***Namespaces***, each with a different meaning.

A requisite for substation automation is that all substation data must be identified unambiguously. IEC 61850 standardizes the names of ***Compatible Logical Nodes***, ***Data***, and ***Attributes***. A manufacturer may predefine some prefixes, postfixes, and the name of ***Logical Devices***, as allowed by IEC 61850. A customer usually specifies their plant and device designation scheme. Table 8.1 lists some standardized abbreviations for data names, as defined in IEC 61850.

Several data model classes inherit their name definitions from a ***Namespace***, as shown in the UML Class Diagram on Figure 8.6, including ***LogicalDevices*** and ***Compatible Logical Nodes***, along with their ***Data*** and ***Attributes***. ***LogicalDevices***, for instance, have an attribute for ***logical device namespace*** (***ldNs***) that references the prime technical specification used for the ***logical device***. ***Logical Nodes*** also have an attribute, ***logical node namespace*** (***lnNs***), that references the ***logical node's namespace***.

Table 8.1 Standardized abbreviation for data names.

Term	Description
A	Current
ACS	Access
Acu	Acoustic
Age	Ageing
Alm	Alarm
Amp	Current non-phase-related
An	Analog
Ang	Angle

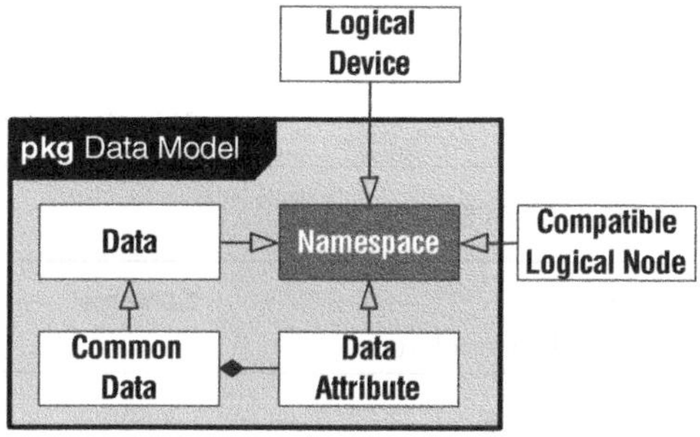

Figure 8.6 *Namespace* class.

A similar attribute is used in every data ***namespace*** (***dataNs***) to reference the data ***namespace*** of a single instance of ***DATA*** and in every ***common data class namespace*** (***cdcNs***) to reference the ***namespace*** used for the definition of a single instance of ***DATA***.

Each instance of a ***Namespace*** class has two main components: ***Object Names*** (***ObjectNames***), commonly called ***Instance Names*** (***Instance Names***), or the unique names given to instances of a class; and ***Object References*** (***ObjectReferences***) constructed by the concatenation of all the ***ObjectNames*** comprising the whole pathname of an instance, identifying the instance uniquely. Table 8.2 presents typical examples of concatenating ***ObjectNames*** for several objects defined in IEC 61850.

Figure 8.7 illustrates an example of reference naming for a data attribute in a ***logical node*** within a ***logical device***, adhering to the rules mentioned earlier.

This scheme allows referencing any attribute of a data class defined in a ***logical device*** or ***logical node***, as described in the following paragraph.

8.7 Data Classes

Information internal to every ***logical node*** and ***logical device*** is modeled by several classes that encapsulate ***DATA*** structures representing meaningful information for applications in an automation system. The values of ***DATA*** instances can, for example, be written by predefined services like ***SetDataValues*** and read by ***GetDataValues***. These classes provide a means to specify typed information, for example, the position of a switch with quality information, and a timestamp. They also specify ways to enter information, such as switching positions, accessing previously entered information, assessing information quality, and associating information with timestamps.

A ***Data*** class is a composition of ***Data Attributes*** that may be part of a ***Composite Common Data Class (CommonCDC)***, which is inherited from

Table 8.2 List of ***ObjectReferences***.

ACSI class	ObjectReference of instance
LOGICAL-DEVICE	
LDRef (logical device reference)	*LDName*
LOGICAL-NODE	
LNRef (logical node reference)	*LDName/LNName*
DATA	
DataRef (data reference)	*LDName/LNNName. DataName[. DataName[...]]*
DataAttribute	
DataAttributeReference (data attribute reference)	*LDName/LNName. DataName[. DataName[. ...]] DataAttributeName[.DaComponentName[. ...]]*
DATA-SET	
DsrEF (data set reference)	*LDName/LNName.DataSetName* (persistent), or *@DataSetName (non-persistent)*

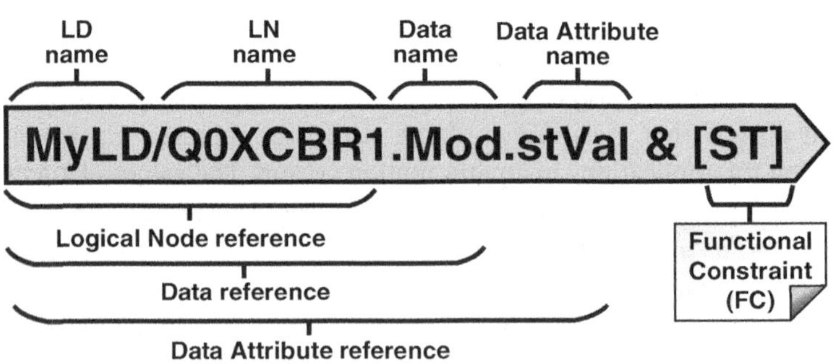

Figure 8.7 Name reference example.

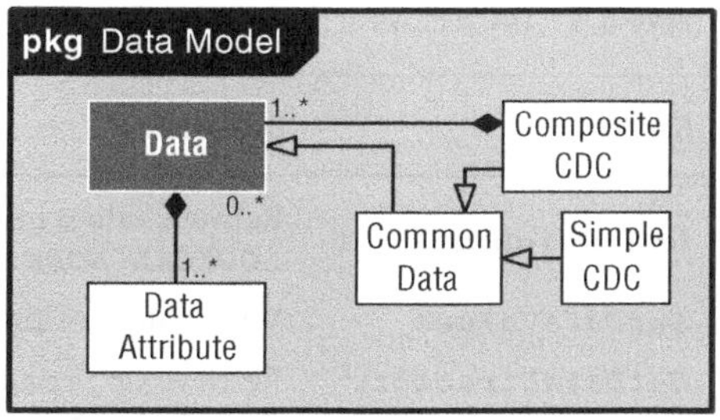

Figure 8.8 Composition and specialization of data classes.

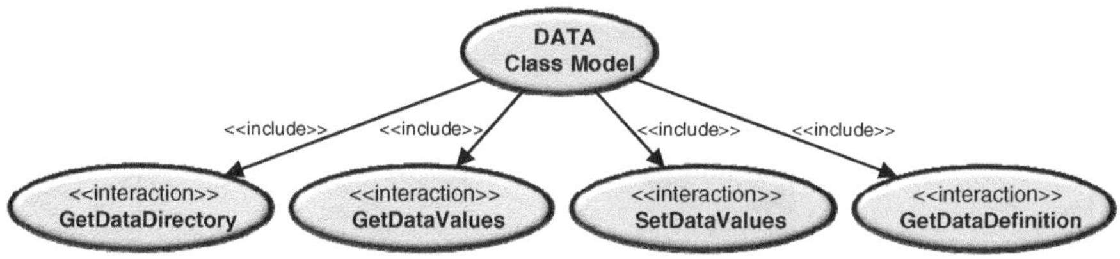

Figure 8.9 Data model use case.

a ***Common Data Class (CDC)***. This class inherits behavior and data from the ***Simple CDC*** and ***Composite CDC*** classes, as shown in the UML Class Diagram in Figure 8.8.

In IEC 61850, every ***Data*** class has several attributes such as:

- ***DataName***–to identify a ***DATA*** within the scope of a ***LOGICAL-NODE***
- ***DataRef***–data ***ObjectReference*** with unique pathname of a ***DATA***
- ***Presence***–to specify if a ***DATA*** within a ***CompositeCDC*** or a ***LOGICAL-NODE*** is mandatory (***TRUE***) or optional (***FALSE***)
- ***DataAttribute***–to specify a data attribute
- ***CompositeCDC [0..n]***–for specialization of ***DATA***
- ***SimpleCDC [0..n]***–for specialization of ***DATA***

In addition to the attributes, a ***DATA*** model includes four services to manipulate them, as shown in the UML Use Case Diagram in Figure 8.9.

Table 8.3 summarizes the description of each service of this use case. Together, they enable sequencing or polling on a per-request/response basis through client–server communication, allowing for selective reading/writing of data on the server. It has the advantage that data volume is limited to the portion required for the client, and the connection monitor is included implicitly. The disadvantage remains the large volume of data generated by point-to-point communication, which requires a separate message for each recipient and is thus unsuitable

Table 8.3 DATA class services.

Service	Description
GetDataValues	Retrieve values of ***DATA*** contained in the ***LOGICAL-NODE***
SetDataValues	Write values of ***DATA*** contained in the ***LOGICAL-NODE***
GetDataDirectory	Retrieve ***ObjectReferences*** of all ***DataAttributes*** contained in the ***DATA***
GetDataDefinition	Retrieve definitions of all ***DataAttributes*** contained in the ***DATA***

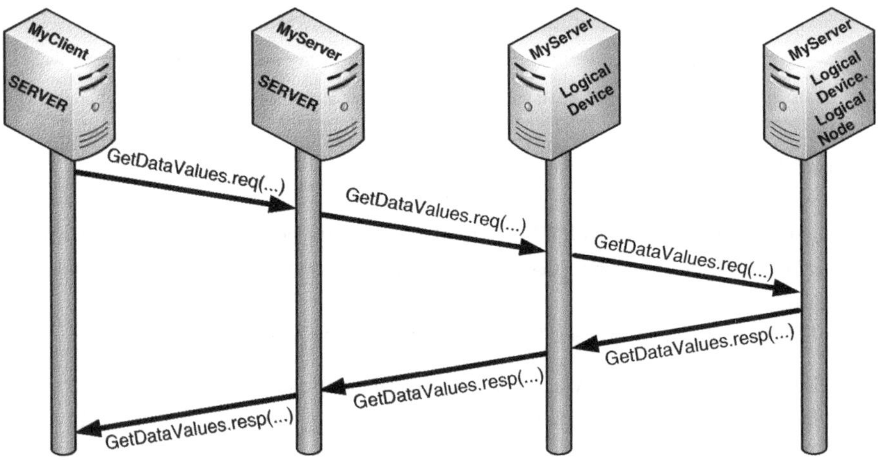

Figure 8.10 Normal GetDataValues interaction.

for time-critical applications. As is typical of a client–server architecture, the behavior for establishing the connection must be defined on the client side.

As a rule, all these services require an ***ObjectReference*** to the ***DATA*** class, of type DataRef, as an input parameter. The method returns, as output, an indication of the process's success (Response+) or failure (Response−), along with the requested data, typically as a vector of items whose addresses are supplied by the input parameter ***DataAttributeValue [1..n]***. Figure 8.10 shows a typical UML Sequence Diagram for the method GetDataValues, with a normal return from the server.

Using UML, a data class can be declared as a structure, as shown in Table 8.4, and implemented in an object-oriented language such as C++, C#, Java, or Python.

Several other classes inherit the attributes and methods from ***DATA***, such as the ***CDC***.

Table 8.4 Data class structure for programming.

DATA
+ DataName: CosNaming::NameComponent + DataRef: **char**[1..255]([255]) + Presence: **bool** + Data_att: **DataAttribute*** + CompositeCDC: **DATA*** + SimpleCDC: **COMMON_DATA***
+ GetDataValues(): **void**** + SetDataValues(): **void** + GetDataDirectory(): **void** + GetDataDefinition(): **void**

8.8 Common Data Classes

CDC define attribute classes to build data objects that include, for instance, standard names, standard data types, and attribute classifications such as measurands, status, and configuration, as needed by other IEC 61850 classes. They provide a valuable means to reduce the size of data definitions (in the standard and any implementation language) so that the data definition need not list all its attributes; instead, it references the ***CDC***. ***CDC*** are also helpful in maintaining consistent definitions of data attributes across an application. Figure 8.11 illustrates a UML Class Diagram with the inheritance relationship between this class and the **`Data`** class within the Data Model package.

CDC are used to model several types of data used in applications, including ***Status Information***, ***Measured Information***, ***Controllable Status***, ***Controllable Analog***, ***Status Settings***, ***Analog Settings***, and ***Description Information***. Typical classes derived from ***CDC*** include:

- **Control**
  - Controllable Double Point (***DPC***)
  - Controllable Single Point (***SPC***)
  - Controllable Integer (***INC***)
  - Binary-controlled Step Position (***BSC***)
  - Integer-controlled Step Position (***ISC***)
- **Measured Information**
  - Measured Value (***MV***)
  - Complex Measured Value (***CMV***)
  - Three-phase WYE Connection (***WYE***)

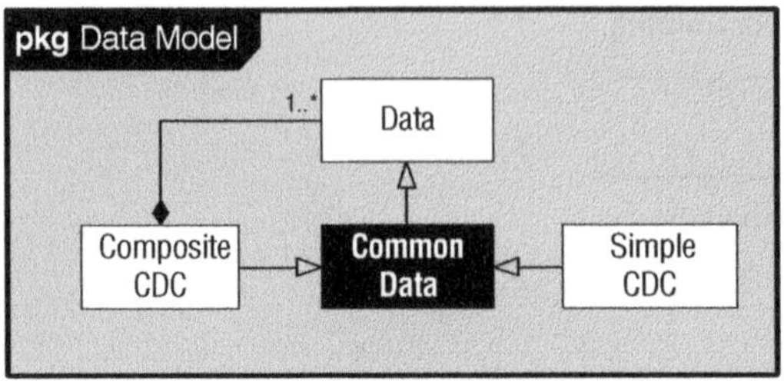

Figure 8.11 Common data class.

- Three-phase DELTA Connection (***DEL)***
- Sequence (***SEQ***)
- Sampled Analog Values (***SAV***)

- **Status Information**
  - Single Point Status (***SPS***)
  - Double Point Status (***DPS***)
  - Integer Status (***INS***)
  - Status Indication Group (***SIG***)
  - Integer Status (***ISI***)
  - Protection Activation Information (***ACT***)
  - Directional Protection Activation Information (***ACD***)
  - Security Violation Counting (***SEC***)
  - Binary Counter Reading (***BCR***)
- **IED Settings**
  - Controllable Analog Set-Point Information (***APC***)
  - Analog Setting (***ASG***)
  - Setting Curve (***CURVE***)
  - Single Point Setting (***SPG***)
  - Integer Status Setting (***ING***)
- **Name Plate Description**
  - Device Name plate (***DPL***)
  - Logical Node Name Plate (***LPL***)
  - Curve Shape Description (***CSD***)

All these classes inherit attributes and functionalities from a ***COMMON-DATA*** class. Table 8.5 shows the UML definition of a ***COMMON-DATA*** class, following the IEC 61850 standard for ***CDC***, in a format suitable for implementation in any object-oriented language (C++, C#, Java, Python, etc.).

In this class, the attribute ***DataName*** identifies a ***DATA*** within the scope of a ***LOGICAL-NODE*** or a nested ***DATA***; the ***DataRef*** contains a data ***ObjectReference*** or a unique pathname of a ***DATA***. ***Presence*** is an attribute that specifies whether a ***DATA*** is mandatory (***TRUE***) or optional (***FALSE***). And

Table 8.5 Common data class structure for programming.

COMMON-DATA
DataName: **ObjectReference** DataRef: **ObjectReference** Presence: **BOOLEAN** DataAttribute: **DataAttribute**[1..*]
GetDataValue (in Request: **GDVReq**, out Response+: **GDVResp+**, out Response-: **GDVResp-**) SetDataValue (in Request: **GDVReq**, out Response-: **SDVResp-**) GetDataDirectory (in Request: **GDDiReq**, out Response+: **GDDiResp+**, out Response-: **GDDiResp-**) GetDataDefinition (in Request: **GDDeReq**, out Response+: **GDDeResp+**[0..*], out Response-: **GDDeResp-**)

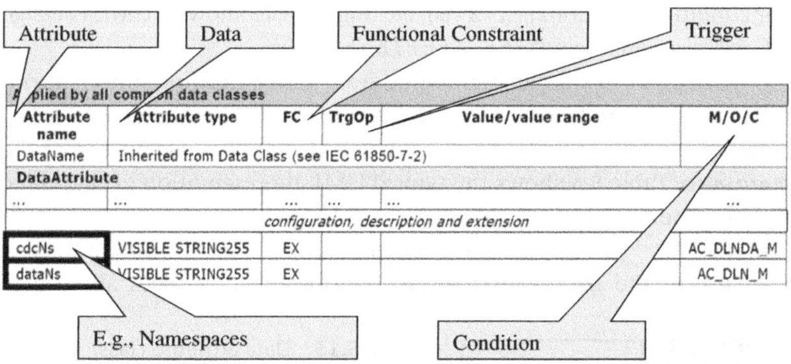

Figure 8.12 Excerpt of common data class specification.

DataAttribute contains the attributes of the common data modeled by this object. In addition, the following services are inherited from the Data class:

- ***GetDataValues***—retrieve values of ***DATA*** contained in the ***LOGICAL-NODE***
- ***SetDataValues***—write values of ***DATA*** contained in the ***LOGICAL-NODE***
- ***GetDataDirectory***—retrieve ***ObjectReferences*** of all ***Data Attributes*** in the ***DATA***
- ***GetDataDefinition***—retrieve definitions of all ***DataAttributes*** in the ***DATA***

Figure 8.12 shows the table format used by IEC 61850 to specify the contents of ***Common Data***.

In addition to the methods inherited from the *CDC*, **Data** classes are further specialized by the data attributes they own.

8.9 Data Attributes

Attributes define characteristics of data classes, such as name, range, type, and special constraints applied to services and states. Several categories of attributes are defined by IEC 61850, including **Control** for status, measured/metered values, or settings; ***Substitution*** for setting replacements; and ***Configuration*** for description and extension. Additional information provided by attributes include the services allowed on the data such as ***Functional Constraints*** (e.g., *FC=CO* means control service allowed), trigger conditions that cause a report to be sent (e.g., *TrgOp=dchg* means a change causes a report), value or value range, indication if the attribute is optional (*O*), mandatory (***M***), conditional mandatory (***X_X_M***), or conditional optional (***X_X_O***), etc. Figure 8.13 shows a UML Package Diagram of classes related to a **Data Attribute** class.

All **Data Attributes** derive their names from a ***Namespace***, inherit attributes from **Data *Type*** and ***Functional Constraint*** classes, and form, by composition, the attributes of a **Data** class, which also derives its name from the same ***Namespace***. Table 8.6 shows the typical UML representation of this class, suitable for implementation in an object-oriented language.

In this model, *FC [1..2]* denotes the functional constraints that specify the expected use of the ***DataAttribute***, indicating the services allowed to

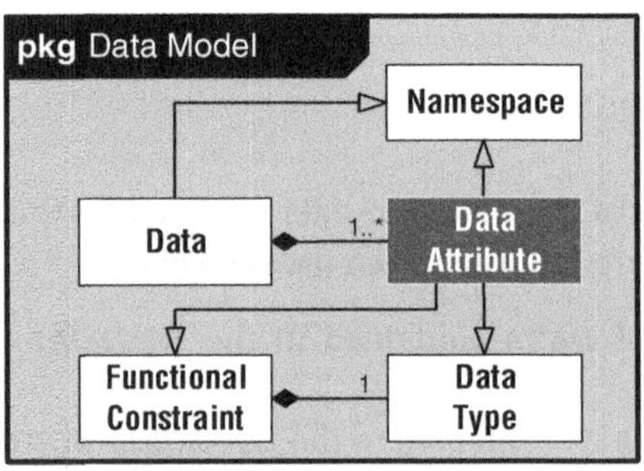

Figure 8.13 Data attribute class.

Table 8.6 Data attribute model.

DataAttribute
FunctionalConstraint: **FC** [1..2] TrgOp: **TriggerConditions** [0..1]

be operated on a specific `DataAttribute`. The attribute `TrgOp [0..1]` denotes the trigger option that specifies the trigger conditions (associated with a `DataAttribute` of a `DATA`) that may cause a report to be sent or a log entry to be stored in a log. Table 8.7 lists the trigger possibilities defined by the IEC 61850 standard.

Additionally, a `Data Attribute` class has several other attributes, as listed in Table 8.8.

IEC 61850 defines several templates for describing attributes of status information, measured information, controllable status information, controllable analog set-point information, status settings, analog settings, and attribute types used in the standard data classes. These are inherited from `Data Type` classes defined in the standard.

Table 8.7 Data attribute trigger options.

TryOp	Semantic	Services Allowed
dchg	data-change	A report or a log entry shall be generated due to a change of the value of the data attribute.
qchg	quality-change	A report or a log entry shall be generated due to a change of the value of the quality attribute.
dupd	data value update	A report or a log entry shall be generated due to freezing the value of a freezable attribute or updating the value of any other attribute. An updated value may have the same value as the old value.

NOTE: The trigger conditions, integrity, and general interrogation of the TriggerConditions type are used independently of instances of `DATA`; they can be set remotely by services and thus trigger sending reports or placing log entries into logs.

Table 8.8 Semantics of data attributes.

DAName	Semantics
`actVal`	Binary counter status is represented as an integer value.
`addInfo`	Additional information may be provided to clarify the most recent detected violation.
`addr`	The address of the remote source that last incremented the count. NOTE 1: The kind of address stored (application address, IP address, link address, etc.) is whatever the server can detect. This may depend on the specific mapping.
`angRef`	Angle reference. Indicates the quantity that is used as a reference for the phase angle. The fundamental frequency (index = 1) is used as a reference by convention for the amount stated.

8.10 Data Types

`Data Type` classes provide definitions of basic data types for the composition of more complex and composite data classes. They inherit their attributes from four major IEC 61850 classes: ***Basic Type***, ***Data Attribute***, ***Composite***, and **`Primitive Components`**, as shown in the UML Class Diagram of Figure 8.14.

Table 8.9 presents the primary attributes of a **`Data Type`** class, as defined in IEC 61850. In this table, a **`DATName`**–data attribute type name, identifies a **`DAType`** within the scope of a **`DataAttribute`** or a nested **`DataAttribute`**; a **`DATRef`**–data attribute type **`ObjectReference`**, denotes a unique path-name of a **`DAType`**; **`Presence`** specifies if a **`DataAttribute`** is mandatory (***`TRUE`***) or optional (***`FALSE`***); **`CompositeComponent`** *`[0..n]`*–composite component, denotes a specialization of **`DAType`**; and **`PrimitiveComponent`** *`[0..n]`*–primitive component, denotes a specialization of DAType.

Table 8.10 lists all major Basic **`DataTypes`** specified by IEC 61850, which can be mapped to the native types of numbers of any object-oriented language used for implementation.

Additionally, IEC 61850 defines **`Composite Component Types`** for several power system data such as **`Quality`**, **`TimeStamp`**, **`AnalogValue`**, **`ScaledValueConfig`**, **`RangConfig`**, **`Vector`**, **`Unit`**, **`Originator`**, **`PulseConfig`**, **`CtlModels`**, **`SboClasses`**, and **`ValueWithTrans`**. For example, a ***`TimeStamp`*** type represents a UTC with the epoch at midnight (00:00:00) on 1970-01-01, as defined in Table 8.11 of IEC 61850.

To limit the use of **`Data Types`**, **`Data Attributes`** are restricted by ***`functional constraints`*** defined in IEC 61850.

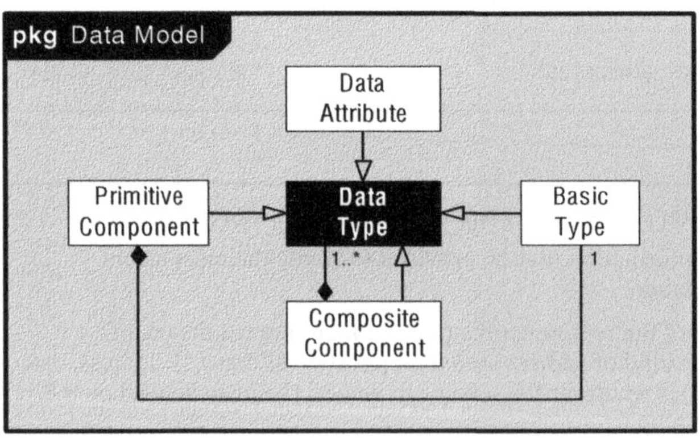

Figure 8.14 Data type class.

Table 8.9 DAType definition.

DAType		
Attribute name	**Attribute type**	**Value/value range/explanation**
DATName	*ObjectName*	Instance name of an instance of ***DAType***, for example, ***cVal*** (first level), mag (second level), **f** (third level)
DATRef	*ObjectReference*	Pathname of an instance of ***DAType*** E.g., ***MMXU1.PhV.phsA.cVal*** E.g., ***MMXU1.PhV.phsA.cVal.mag*** or E.g., ***MMXU1.PhV.phsA.cVal.mag.f***
Presence	*BOOLEAN*	Indicates mandatory/optional
Specializations of DAType		
CompositeComponent [0..n]	*DAType*	Example, ***mag*** in Vector class of IEC 61850-7-3 Example, ***f*** in AnalogueValue of IEC 61850-7-3
PrimitiveComponent [0..1]	*BasicType*	Example, ***FLOAT32*** class of IEC 61850-7-3 for ***f***

NOTE 1: An instance of a **DAType** may contain 0 or more instances of a **ComositeComponent** or a **PrimitiveDAT**. However, they cannot both be absent, so at least one of these elements must be present.

NOTE 2: The structure of a DAType is recursive since a **CompositeComponent** is also of type **DAType**. SCSM may restrict the recursion level, so the number of levels of recursion of **CompositeComponents** usually is no greater than 2.

8.11 Functional Constraints

FCs specify the restrictions on the attributes and the services that data objects can provide. They are data structures and rules that regulate how each data attribute can be set and changed. Each set of rules defines a class of ***Functional Constraint*** that shows its use. ***Data*** attribute classes inherit the procedures and restrictions determined by a specific ***Functional Constraint*** class. Figure 8.15 shows this relationship by a UML Package Diagram of Classes.

Table 8.10 Basic data types.

BasicTypes			
Name	**Value range**	**Remark**	**Used by**
BOOLEAN			IEC 61850-7-3 IEC 61850-7-2
INT8	−128 to 127		IEC 61850-7-3 IEC 61850-7-2
INTI6	−32 768 to 32 767		IEC 61850-7-3 IEC 61850-7-2
INT24	−8 388 608 to 8 388 607	For ***TimeStamp*** type	IEC 61350-7-2
INT32	−2 147 483 648 to 2 147 483 647		IEC 61850-7-3 IEC 61850-7-2
INT128	−2**127 to (2**127)-1	Required for counters	IEC 61350-7-3
INT8U	Unsigned integer, 0 to 255		IEC 61850-7-3 IEC 61850-7-2
INT16U	Unsigned integer, 0 to 65 535		IEC 61850-7-3 IEC 61850-7-2
INT24U	Unsigned integer, 0 to 16 777 215		IEC 61850-7-2
INT32U	Unsigned integer, 0 to 4 294 967 295		IEC 61850-7-3 IEC 61850-7-2
FLOAT32	Range of values and precision as specified by IEEE 754 single-precision floating point		IEC 61850-7-3
FLOAT64	Range of values and precision as specified by IEEE 754 double-precision floating point		IEC 61850-7-3
ENUMERATED	Ordered set of values, defined where type is used	Custom extensions are allowed	IEC 61850-7-3 IEC 61850-7-2
CODED ENUM	Ordered set of values, defined where type is used	Custom extensions shell not be allowed. Type shall be mapped to an efficient encoding in a SCSM	IEC 61850-7-3 IEC 61850-7-2

BasicTypes			
Name	**Value range**	**Remark**	**Used by**
OCTET STRING	Maximum length shall be defined where type is used[a]		IEC 61850-7-3 IEC 61850-7-2
VISIBLE STRING	Maximum length shall be defined where type is used[a]		IEC 61850-7-3 IEC 61850-7-2
UNICODE STRING	Maximum length shall be defined where type is used[a]		IEC 61850-7-3

a. The length suffix shall have the format "...*STRINGnn*" where "*nn*" is the length in characters.

Table 8.11 TimeStamp class.

TimeStamp type definition			
Attribute name	**Attribute type**	**Value/value range/explanation**	**M/O**
SecondSinceEpoch	*INT32*	(0..MAX)	*M*
FractionOfSecond	*INT24U*	Value = SUM from i=0 to 23 of bi*2**-(i+1); Order = b0, b1, b2, b3, ...	*M*
TimeQuality	*TimeQuality*		*M*

Figure 8.15 Functional constraint class.

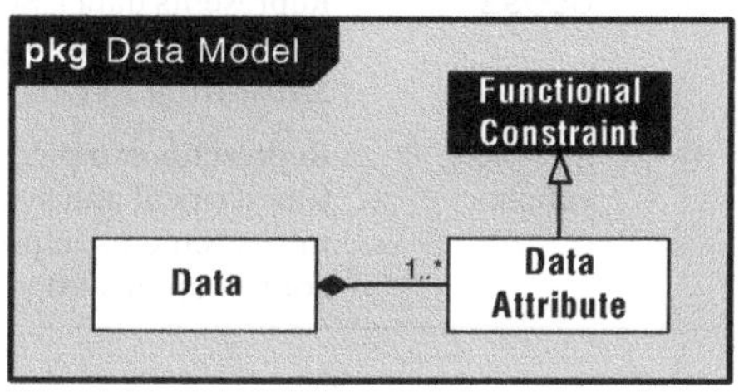

IEC uses a two-letter code to designate each ***Functional Constraint*** class, such as those listed in Table 8.12.

FCs define and categorize the data types associated with ***logical nodes*** and their data objects. They help determine how data is accessed, processed, and communicated. ***FCs*** serve as filters or categories for grouping data based on its role or usage within a device or communication. They categorize data for clarity and

Table 8.12 Functional constraints.

Type	Meaning	Description	Example
ST	Status information	Represents the current state or status of a device or process	Switch position (On, Off), circuit breaker status
MX	Measured values	Represents measured or calculated analog values	Voltage, current, frequency
SP	Set-point information	Represents target values or parameters that can be set	Desired voltage level
CF	Configuration information	Represents configuration parameters that are usually set during commissioning and rarely changed afterward	Rated power of a transformer
DC	Description information	Provides descriptive or documentation information about the logical nodes or data objects	Names, comments, or textual descriptions
SG	Setting group	Represents values that belong to specific setting groups for devices that can operate under different settings	Protection relay settings
SE	Service parameters	Represents parameters related to service or maintenance	Firmware version, diagnostics
CO	Control	Represents control actions or commands issued to devices	Open/close command for a breaker
EX	Extended data	Represents extended data not covered by other functional constraints	
GO	*GOOSE*	Represents data associated with ***GOOSE*** (***Generic Object-Oriented Substation Events***) communication	
SV	Sampled values	Represents sampled data for time-critical and synchronized measurements in protection and control applications	

efficient access, define which data can be read, written, or subscribed to, optimize data exchange by sending only the necessary data types based on functional constraints, and ensure that devices from different vendors can interact seamlessly by adhering to a standard data structure and classification. Additionally, they can be used by language compilers and implementation tools to check their correct usage in a project.

8.12 Summary

`Data` represents the status and characteristics of the modeled power system and its automation and can be organized in various ways using current communication middleware and information frameworks. **`Data`** models defined in IEC 61850 provide an extensive set of building blocks for representing data exchanged by ***`Logical Nodes`*** and for modeling and communicating with other ***`IEDs`*** and switchyard equipment. They are described in the standard with sufficient detail to be implemented in any object-oriented language.

This chapter introduced the role of data models and structures in SAS and their structure according to the IEC 61850 standard, including ***Namespaces, Data Classes, Data Attributes, Data Types***, and ***`Functional Constraints`***. The following chapter addresses how the standard's service models process this data.

8.13 Review Questions

1 Explain the concept of a data model within the IEC 61850 standard. How does it facilitate the representation and exchange of information in an SAS?

2 Describe the hierarchy of IEC 61850 data, from substation-level entities to primitive elements. Why is this hierarchy important for maintaining consistency and interoperability?

3 Differentiate between analog, digital, cumulative, and historical information within SAS data sources. Provide an example of how each type can be used in an automation function.

4 Discuss the role of ***`Namespaces`*** in IEC 61850 data modeling. How do ***`Namespaces`*** prevent ambiguity, and what types of elements inherit their naming from them?

5 Using the example of the ***`XCBR Logical Node`***, analyze how ***`Data Classes`*** and their associated attributes model the behavior and properties of real-world equipment. Explain how composition and inheritance contribute to this representation.

6 Compare ***`Simple Common Data Classes`*** (***`Simple CDCs`***) and ***`Composite Common Data Classes`*** (***`Composite CDCs`***). In what situations would each be necessary, and how do they support reusable modeling?

7 Examine the structure and purpose of ***Data Attributes*** within a ***Data Class***. How do characteristics such as trigger options (***TrgOp***) and ***FCs*** influence data exchange mechanisms?

8 A protection engineer wants to model a new configurable parameter for a differential protection ***LN***. Outline the steps needed to extend the data model according to IEC 61850's rules for ***Data Classes*** and ***Data Attributes***. Discuss potential impacts on ***Namespaces***, ***Data Types***, and ***FCs***.

9 Evaluate how ***Data Types***, including both primitive and composite components, enable the standard to be mapped into any object-oriented implementation language. Provide an example showing how a composite type (e.g., ***TimeStamp*** or ***Vector***) supports structured data exchange.

10 Explain the importance of ***FCs*** in organizing and managing data within IEC 61850. How do ***FCs*** affect communication, filtering, and the behavior of services such as reporting and control?

9

Service Models

9.1 Introduction

Distributed functions carried out by Substation Automation Systems (SAS) rely on essential support services from the automation and communication framework. These services can be provided through various methods, using available middleware or utilizing resources from IEC 61850. To model how functions are carried out in an SAS, the IEC 61850 standard provides a comprehensive set of service models that facilitate data transformation and enable functionality within equipment models.

9.2 Learning Objectives

This chapter describes the main service models defined by IEC 61850, including the abstract services and association model standardized for all data classes. It covers services from ***Generic Logical Node*** and ***Data Set*** models, as well as from a specific ***Logical Node 0***. Service models are designed to meet common operational and maintenance needs, including configuration settings, substitution, association, file transfer, reporting, logging, control, and timing. The services provided by the time model will be discussed in the next chapter.

9.3 Abstract Services

In an object-oriented environment, a service model is a set of functions and procedures made available to the user of a data model and class, allowing them to access or modify its data components and configurations. These can be further classified as abstract services—functions and procedures defined for the classes of a model—or concrete services—functions and methods implemented in objects derived from the model's classes.

In an IEC 61850-based SAS, abstract services are provided via a virtual interface named ***Abstract Communication Service Interface (ACSI). ACSI*** is a virtual interface to ***Intelligent Electronic Devices (IEDs)*** that provides abstract communication services, such as connection, data access, unsolicited data transfer, device control, and file transfer, independent of the actual communication stack and profiles used by the communication middleware. The ACSI specification includes a hierarchical class model of all information accessible via a communication network. The term "abstract" means that only those aspects required to describe the actions on the receiving side of a service request are defined. IEC 61850 clients use it to request services from IEC 61850 servers.

Abstract services provide IEC 61850 with the isolation of object models from communication-specific details by mapping standard utility services to multiple protocols. It is "future-proof," allowing adoption of future technologies and middleware without changing the abstract services. The services are provided by parametrized ***logical devices***, built from ***logical nodes*** that define how the data is organized in data objects.

Abstract services provided by ***ACSI*** are implemented by mappings to concrete communication services, using the Specific Communication Service Mapping (***SCSM***) defined by IEC 61850. These standardized procedures provide the concrete mapping of ***ACSI*** onto a particular protocol stack/communication profile. According to the application, the mapping requires a minimum number of ***SCSM*** to grant interoperability. Special subdomains such as "station bus" and "process bus" may require multiple mappings. However, only one ***SCSM*** and profile should be used for each protocol stack, detailing the instantiation of abstract services/objects into protocol-specific services/objects used by the middleware. Services provided by ***ACSI*** include a control service for grouping data into ***datasets*** for reporting or logging, a substitution service for replacing values of ***DataAttributes*** in data, and ***Get/Set*** and ***Dir/Definition*** services for reading and writing data values and retrieving directory/definition information. Figure 9.1 shows how ***ACSI*** services operate on data stored in a ***Logical Node***.

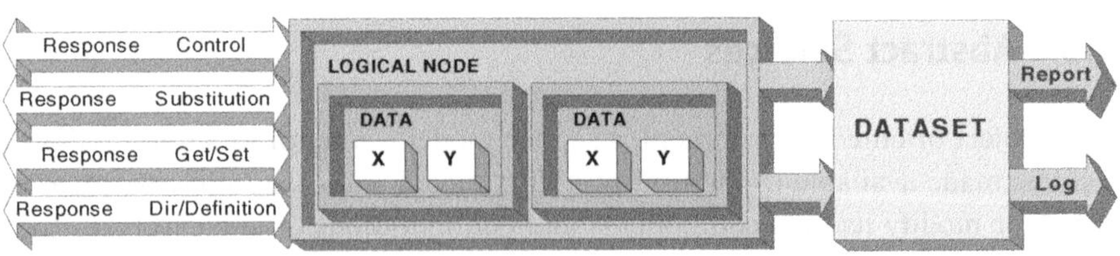

Figure 9.1 Services operating on data.

These services are classified into three main types: (i) client–server (C/S), whose information exchange model is mainly request/reply; (ii) peer-to-peer, over Ethernet, used for fast real-time multicasting within a single LAN (i.e., publish/subscribe model); and (iii) time synchronization service, where no operations are defined in the standard, just the description of the expected functionality. The recommended protocols are Simple Network Time Protocol (SNTP) or IEEE 1588—Precision Time Protocol (PTP). Figure 9.2 shows the relationship between a process and the configuration interface provided by **ACSI**.

Two primary **ACSI** abstract interfaces are provided by IEC 61850: one for communications between a client and a server for real-time data access and retrieval, device control, event reporting and logging, publisher/subscriber, self-description of devices (device data dictionary), data typing and discovery of data types, and file transfer, and one for fast and reliable system-wide event distribution between an application in one device and many remote applications in different devices (publisher/subscriber) for transmission of trip signals and sampled measured

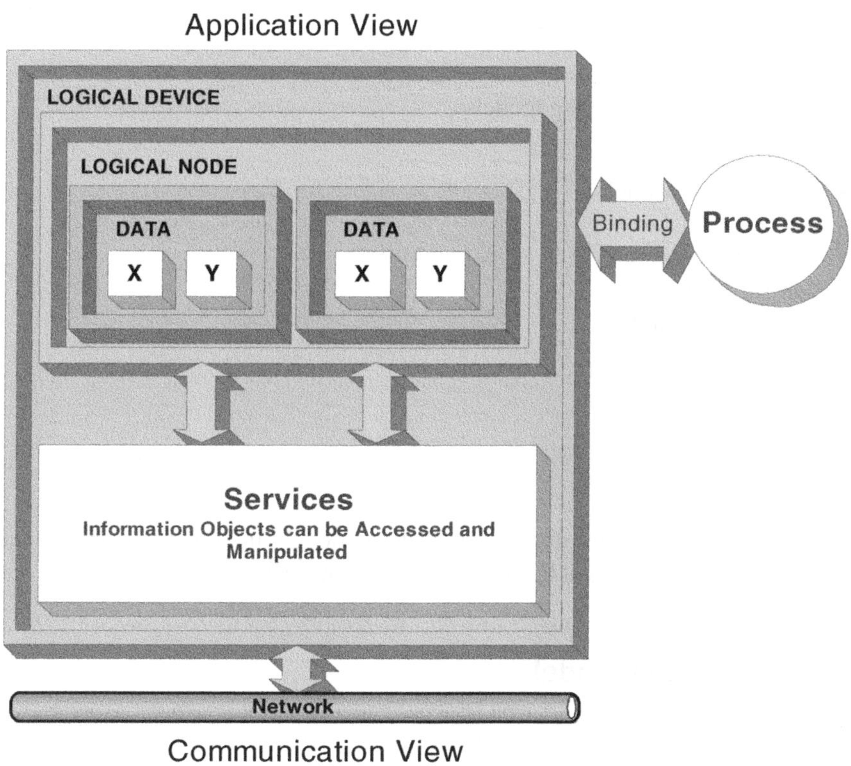

Figure 9.2 Relation of process and configuration interface.

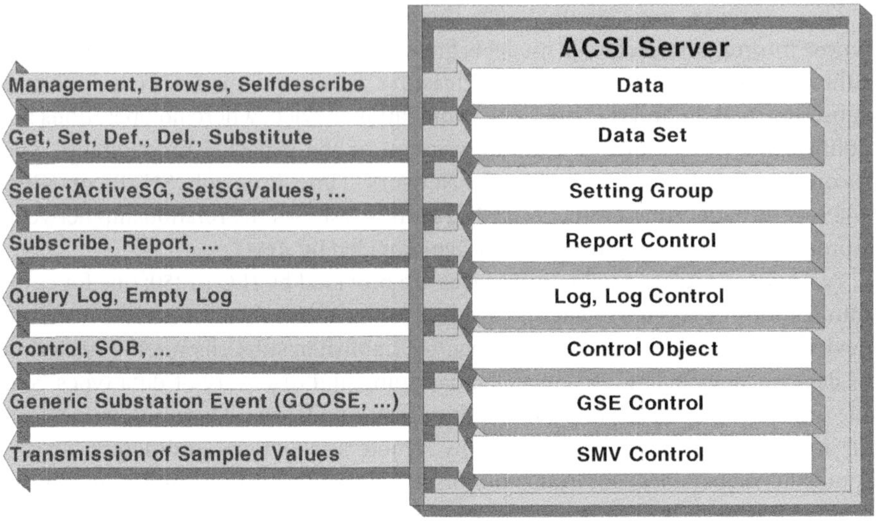

Figure 9.3 ACSI C/S service models.

values. Figure 9.3 illustrates how C/S services are connected to an ***ACSI*** server that implements the following models:

- Association Model
- Logical Node Model
- Server Model
- Data Set Model
- Control Model
- File Transfer Model
- Reporting Model
- Logging Model
- Setting Model
- Time Model
- Substitution Model

The following paragraphs detail each of these models and their associated data objects. The Time Model will be described in Chapter 10.

9.4 Association Model

The Application Association Model defines how two or more devices can be connected and establishes communication between them. This is done by class of associations (two-party/multicast) or access control concepts (restrict). The

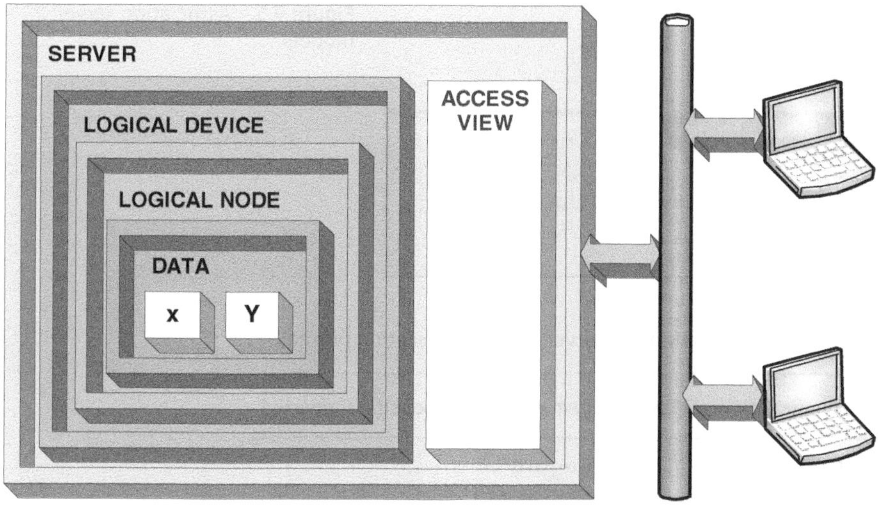

Figure 9.4 Access views of a server.

services provided include ***Associate***, ***Abort***, and ***Release*** associations among devices. A typical sequence in an Application Association consists of polling per request/response and C/S communication for the selective reading/ writing of data on the server. This sequence has the advantage that data volume is limited to the portion required for the client, and the connection monitor is included implicitly. The disadvantage is the large volume of data resulting from point-to-point communication, which requires one message per recipient, as well as its limited suitability for time-critical applications. The behavior for establishing the connection must be defined on the client side.

The Association model implements Access Views to restrict a specific client's access to class instances, class instance attributes, and ***ACSI*** services that act upon class instances of a particular server, as shown in Figure 9.4.

Associations are defined by two types of ***Server Association*** classes: a ***Two-party application association*** (TPAA) class that provides service requests and responses (thereby transferring both unconfirmed and confirmed services) and a Multi-party ***application association*** class that provides unconfirmed services (in one direction only). Figure 9.5 shows a UML Package Diagram of this relationship.

Table 9.1 summarizes these communication profiles with their corresponding association models.

The ***TPAA*** is used mainly for C/S communication, ***GSE*** messages among servers, and bi-directional connection-oriented information exchange. It shall be reliable, and the information flow shall be controlled end-to-end, so that the

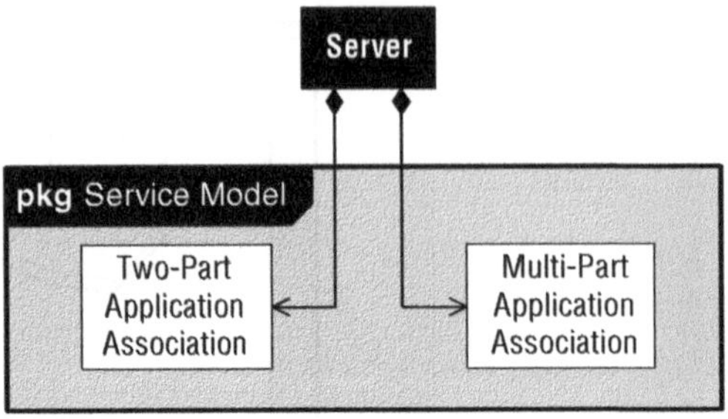

Figure 9.5 Association server models.

Table 9.1 Association model versus communication profiles.

Communication profile	*ACSI* association model(s) supported
Client/server	Two-party
GSE Management	Two-party
GOOSE	Multicast
GSSE	Multicast
Time Sync	Two-party or multicast

connection provides measures to promptly notify of reasons for data non-delivery. The sources of information do not send more than the destination can buffer. Two class attributes are used to qualify this association:

- ***AssociationId***—identification used to identify the application associations
- ***AuthenticationParameter***—information required to grant permission to access instances of a specific access view to a server, like user identification, view, and password. Details are defined in the ***SCSMs***.

At least three services shall be provided to support the functioning of a ***TPAA*** class:

- ***Associate***—to establish an association
- ***Abort***—to end an association
- ***Release***—to release an association.

Figure 9.6 shows a UML Sequence Diagram for the typical operation cycle for a ***TPAA*** class communication.

A ***Multicast Association Application (MCAA)*** is achieved through the multicast transmission of ***GOOSE*** and ***GSSE*** messages, while time synchronization can be performed using either two-part or multicast transmission. It is based on unidirectional information exchange between a single source (the publisher) and one or more destinations (the subscribers). The publisher should provide

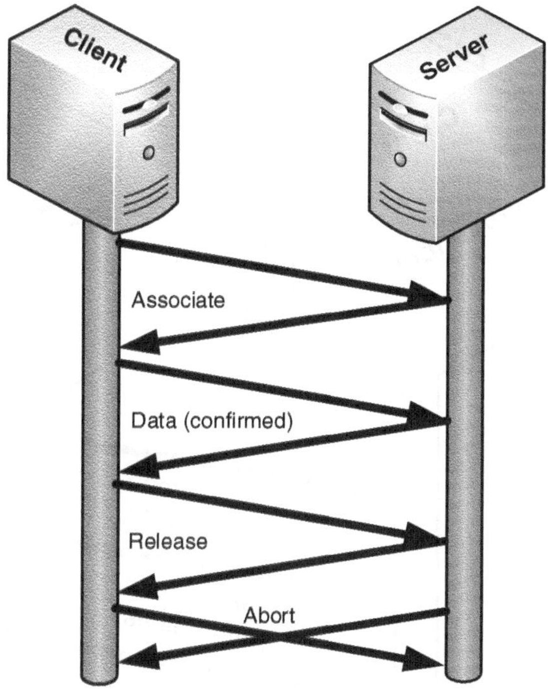

Figure 9.6 Two-party operation.

sufficient information for the recipients to interpret its meaning. A subscriber shall be capable of detecting loss, discarding duplicate information received, and notifying the user of any lost data.

The primary attribute of an ***MCAA*** class is the ***AuthenticationParameter***, which contains information that grants a client permission to access instances of a specific access view. Each multicast service shall provide a service parameter for this data exchange so that if an ***AuthenticationParameter*** does not match a valid parameter, the service request shall be rejected. Figure 9.7 shows a UML Sequence Diagram of the typical operation cycle for an ***MPAA*** class communication.

These associations are used primarily for fast data and message transfer, as defined by the ***logical node*** model in IEC 61850.

9.5 Logical Node Model

A ***Logical Node*** is a class used by IE 61850 to represent a specific type of function of the substation or automation system as described in Chapter 7. It contains logs that can be queried and data written to or read individually and in groups (***Data Sets***). These sets store measured data and status information that

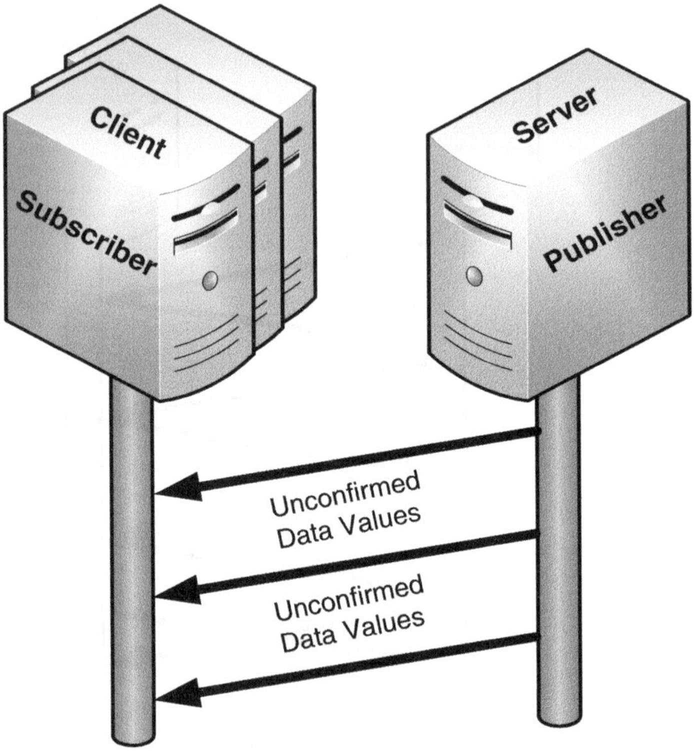

Figure 9.7 Multicast operation.

are typically read-only, as well as control and configuration information that is generally read and written. A ***Logical Node*** can also respond to control inputs and provide solicited and unsolicited reports.

In addition to its role for functional modeling, these classes provide services for sequencing operations, such as polling per request/response and C/S communication for selective reading/writing of data on the server. An advantage of this approach is that the data volume is limited to the client's requirements, and connection monitoring is implicitly included. As a disadvantage, it requires a large data volume due to point-to-point communication, resulting in one message per recipient, which limits its suitability for time-critical applications. The client must define the behavior to establish the connection.

Every ***Logical Node*** class inherits common attributes and services from a ***Common Logical Node*** class, inheriting compatible attributes and services from a ***Compatible Logical Node*** class, as illustrated on the UML Class Diagram in Figure 9.8.

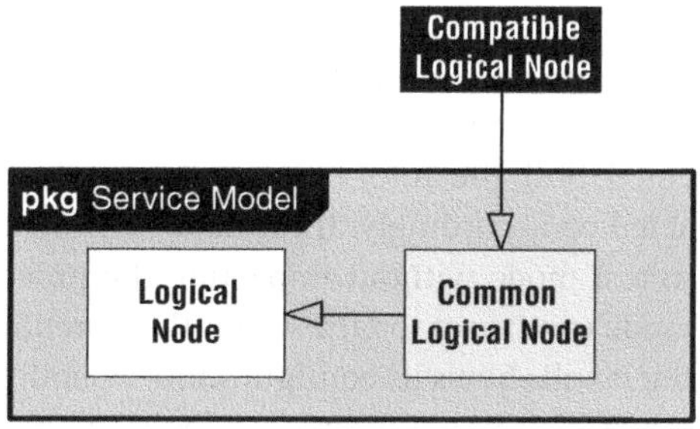

Figure 9.8 Logical node model.

Table 9.2 Common logical node class.

CLN class				
ATA Class	**Attr. Type**	**Explanation**	**T**	**M/O**
Mandatory Logical Node Information (Shall be inherited by ALL LN but LPHD)				
Mod	*INC*	Mode		*M*
Beh	*INS*	Behavior		*M*
Health	*INS*	Health		*M*
NamPlt	*LPL*	Name plate		*M*
Optional Logical Node Information				
Loc	*SPS*	Local operation		*O*
EEHealth	*INS*	External equipment health		*O*
EEName	*DPL*	External equipment name plate		*O*
OpCntRs	*INC*	Operation counter resettable		*O*
OpCnt	*INS*	Operation counter		*O*
OpTmh	*INS*	Operation time		*O*
Data Sets (see IEC 61850-7-2)				

A ***Common Logical Node*** (*CLN*) class provides mandatory and optional data, attributes, and behavior common to all logical node classes, such as nameplate, health, and operating time. Table 9.2 lists the characteristics common to this class.

Among the mandatory node information, the ***Mod*** attribute defines the node's expected behavior regarding its availability to the automation system. Five modes are possible for this attribute, ranging from the normal state (*ON*), where functions are performed as designed, to the blocked (***BLOCKED***) state, in which the **`logical node`** passively supervises the process but has no active function on the system. If this attribute is set to ***TEST***, the logical node's function is executed. Still, the automation system indicates the results as test results and can be acted on accordingly. If the state is set to ***TEST/BLOCKED***, the function operates in test mode without impacting the process. Otherwise, the **`logical node`**'s mode can be set to OFF when the function is inactive in the automation system, but it still shows its configuration capability. These modes will be decisive for testing of distributed functions, described in Chapter 13—Testing Models. Table 9.3 summarizes the **`logical node's`** behavior based on its ***Mode*** attribute.

The **`Health`** attribute is a standard parameter that defines the state of the **`logical node`**'s hardware and software. The ***OK*** state signals the node is normal, with no hardware or software problems detected. When set to the ***WARNING*** state, minor issues are detected, but the automaton's operating state remains safe. In the ***ALARM*** state, severe problems were detected that prevent the node from operating in the automation system. **`Logical node zero`** (***LLN0***) data reflects the worst

Table 9.3 Mode and behavior of logical nodes.

State	On	Blocked	Test	Test/Blocked	Off
Description	Normal state	The process is passively supervised	The function is operated, but the results are indicated as test results	Function is operated in test mode, but with no impact on the process	Function is inactive, but shows its configuration capability
Value	1	2	3	4	5
Output (to process)	Generated	No	Generated	No	No
Reporting (to client)	Yes	No	Flagged as test	Flagged as test	No
Control (from client)	Accepted	Rejected	Accepted	Accepted	Rejected
Functional (process-related) data	Visible	Visible	Visible	Visible	Not visible
Configuration (capability) data	Visible	Visible	Visible	Visible	Visible

Table 9.4 Health state of logical nodes.

Health State	Value
Ok ("green")—no problems, normal operation	1
Warning ("yellow")—minor problems, but in safe operation mode	2
Alarm ("red")—severe problem, no operation possible	3

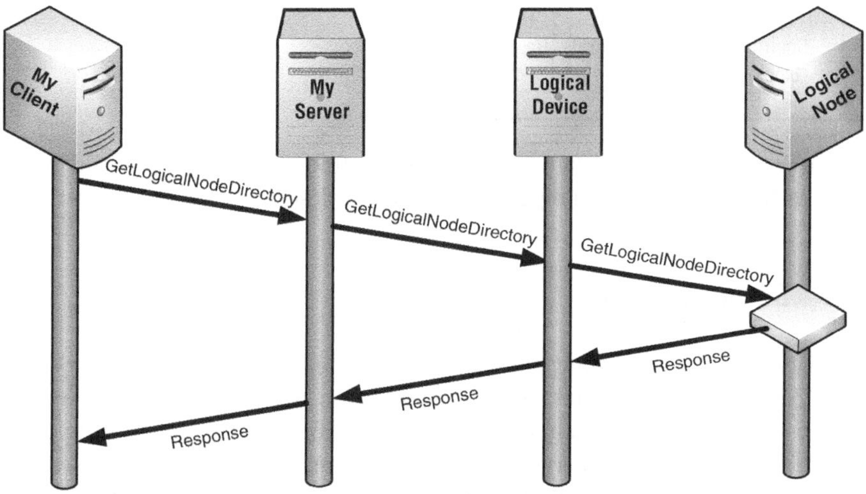

Figure 9.9 Normal GetLogicalNodeDirectory interaction.

value of `Health` of the `logical nodes` that are part of the `logical device` associated with `LLN0`. Table 9.4 summarizes the behavior of the `logical node` based on its `Health` attribute.

A `logical node` class provides two services: `GetLogicalNodeDirectory`, to retrieve the object references of a specific `ACSI` class contained in the `logical node`, and `GetAllDataValues`, to retrieve all data attributes in the `logical node`. Figure 9.9 shows a UML Sequence Diagram of a client's (MyClient) interaction to retrieve the directory of a `logical node` residing on the server's `logical device`. The request originates from the MyClient server to the MyServer, which then forwards it to the `Logical Device`, which passes it to the specific `Logical Node`. The response travels in the opposite direction, from the `Logical Node` to MyClient.

A composition with three `Control Block` classes supports the control and reporting functions, as additional services provided by `logical nodes`. Figure 9.10 expands this composition in a UML Class Diagram.

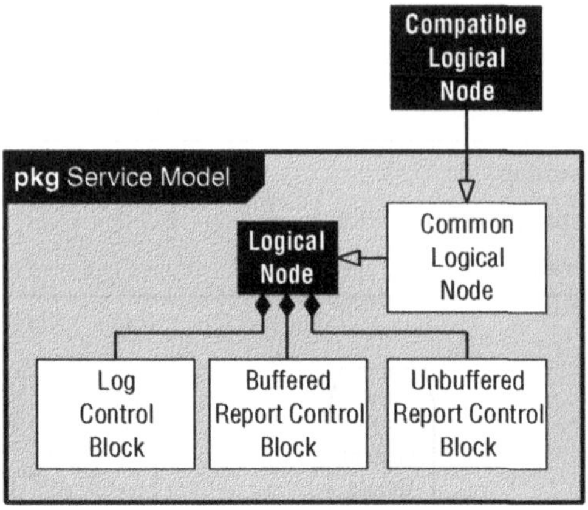

Figure 9.10 Logical node composition.

Control Blocks are data structures that define the content produced by the ***Logical Node's*** logging and reporting services, as described in the server model.

9.6 Server Model

To enable data storage about physical servers in an automation system, Logical Node Zero (LLN0) is a special LN that retains data related to each server's Physical Device (PD). These data include the device identification and name plate, messages from device self-supervision, etc.). ***LLN0*** may also be used for services common to all ***logical nodes***, like mode setting, settings, etc. It does not restrict the dedicated access to any single ***LN***. Figure 9.11 illustrates the UML Class Diagram of the relationship between ***LLN0*** and the ***logical device***, which inherits its properties and data from the ***Common Logical Node*** in the IEC 61850 service model.

The composition of the ***Logical Node Zero*** includes inherited data from the ***Common*** and ***Logical Node*** classes, services from the ***Generic Object-Oriented Substation Event (GOOSE)*** and ***Sampled Values (SV)*** exchange classes, and data setting groups. Among the ***Data*** components of ***LN0*** the following are listed and represented in the UML Class Diagram of Figure 9.12:

- Attributes and operations inherited from ***LN*** class
- ***Setting-Group-Control-Block*** (***SGCB***)
- ***LOG***
- ***GOOSE-Control-Blocks*** (***GoCB***)
- ***GSSE-Control-Blocks*** (***GsCB***)
- ***Multicast-Sampled-Value-Control-Blocks*** (***MSVCB***)
- ***Unicast-Sampled-Value-Control-Blocks*** (***USVCB***).

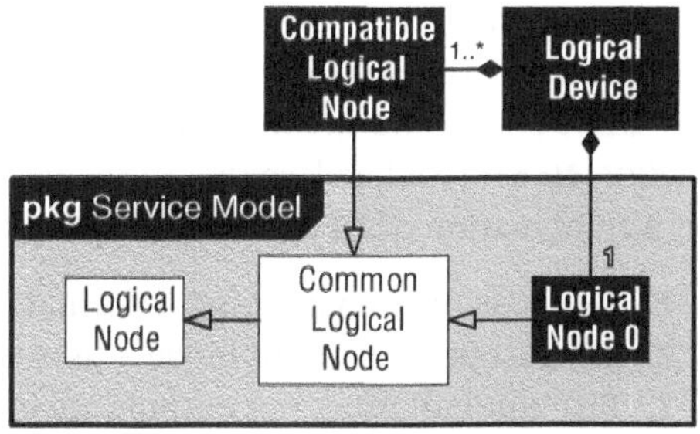

Figure 9.11 Logical node 0 model.

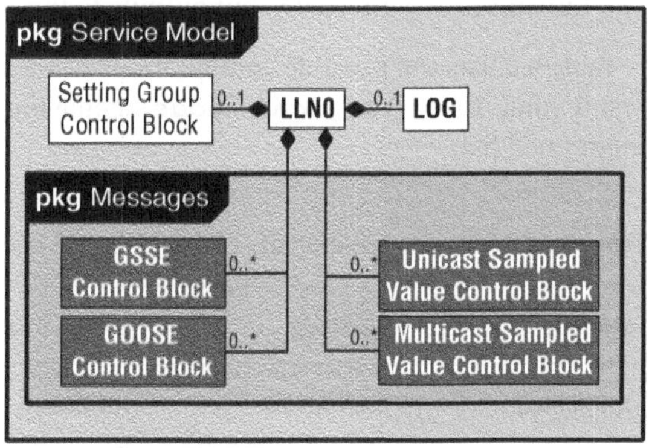

Figure 9.12 Logical node 0 composition.

Table 9.5 lists the elemental composition of the ***LLN0*** class:

Table 9.5 LLN0 class.

LLN0 class				
***DATA* Class**	**Attr. Type**	**Explanation**	***T***	***M/O***
Common Logical Node Information				
		LN shall inherit all Mandatory Data from Common Logical Node Class		*M*
Loc	*SPS*	Local operation for complete logical device		*O*
OpTmh	*INS*	Operation time		*O*
Controls				
Diag	*SPC*	Run Diagnostics		*O*
LEDRs	*SPC*	LED reset	*T*	*O*

Among the roles of the ***LLN0*** class is controlling the behavior of the **`logical device`** and its **`logical nodes`**. The mode of the **`logical device`**(***LDMode = LLN0.Mod***) and the mode of a specific **`logical node`** XXXX (***LNMode = XXXX.Mod***) are related, so that the behavior of the **`logical node`**(***XXXX.Beh***) is a combination of ***LLN0.Mod*** and ***XXXX.Mod***, selected from the following list:

1. ***LN/LD*** is fully operational—normal control and data exchange allowed
2. ***LN/LD*** operates in test mode—uses test data, with simulated behavior only
3. Test input allowed, but outputs are blocked—no effect on process
4. ***LN/LD*** inactive—no function execution, no output
5. Function runs internally, but outputs to the process are blocked

Table 9.6 lists the possible combinations of these modes and the corresponding result value for the **`logical node`**'s behavior, as determined from the aforementioned list.

Table 9.6 Mode combination of LLN0 and logical nodes.

LNMode	**LDMode**	**LNBeh (read only)**	**LNBeh**
XXXX.Mod	**LLN0.Mod**	**XXXX.Beh**	**Value**
On	On	On	1
On	Blocked	Blocked	2
On	Test	Test	3
On	Test-blocked	Test-blocked	4
On	Off	Off	5
Blocked	On	Blocked	2
Blocked	Blocked	Blocked	2
Blocked	Test	Test-blocked	4
Blocked	Test-blocked	Test-blocked	4
Blocked	Off	Off	5
Test	On	Test	3
Test	Blocked	Test-blocked	4
Test	Test	Test	3
Test	Test-blocked	Test-blocked	4
Test	Off	Off	5
Test-blocked	On	Test-blocked	4
Test-blocked	Blocked	Test-blocked	4

LNMode	LDMode	LNBeh (read only)	LNBeh
XXXX.Mod	**LLNO.Mod**	**XXXX.Beh**	**Value**
Test-blocked	Test	Test-blocked	4
Test-blocked	Test-blocked	Test-blocked	4
Test-blocked	Off	Off	5
Off	On	Off	5
Off	Blocked	Off	5
Off	Test	Off	5
Off	Test-blocked	Off	5
Off	Off	Off	5

A similar behavior is defined for the ***Loc*** state data. This data indicates the switchover between local and remote operation: ***local*** = ***TRUE***, ***remote*** = ***FALSE***. This changeover is always performed locally on the server using a physical key or toggle switch that can be read. At the bay level, ***local*** means operation from the bay unit, and ***remote*** means operation from a station unit or SCADA system. At the process level, ***local*** refers to operations directly on the process device, such as a circuit breaker, and ***remote*** refers to operations from a bay unit. If in a ***Logical Device***, the ***Loc*** data of ***LLN0*** contradicts the ***Loc*** of any contained ***LN***, ***local*** is always dominant.

Most of these data can be collected and referred to as a nominated set by several services using the IEC 61850 data set model.

9.7 Data Set Model

A ***Data Set*** defines a data collection in a ***logical node*** to be processed as a single entity in SAS. It allows grouping of various kinds of data so that specific services can use them as a single object. This concept can be viewed by considering Figure 9.13.

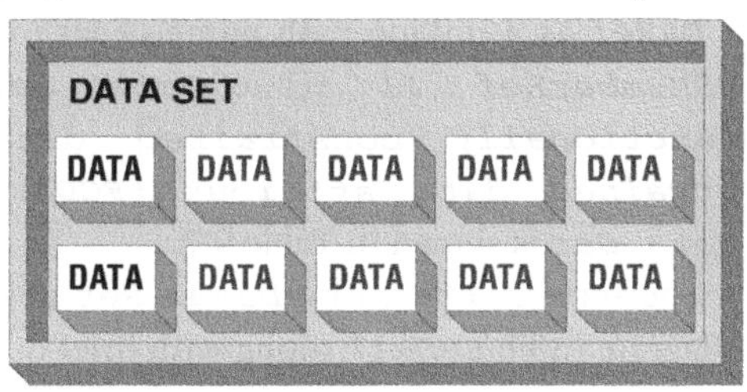

Figure 9.13 Data set composition.

A ***Data Set*** enables the sequential execution of services, such as polling per request/response and C/S communication, to selectively read/write data on the server. The advantage of this

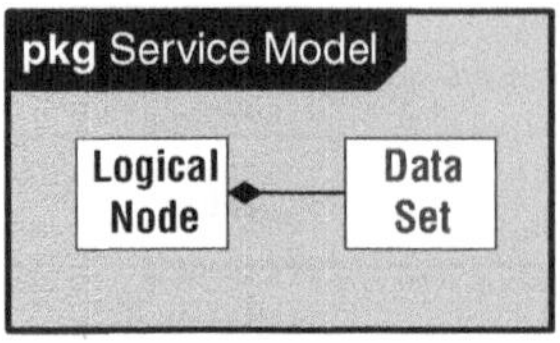

Figure 9.14 Data set model.

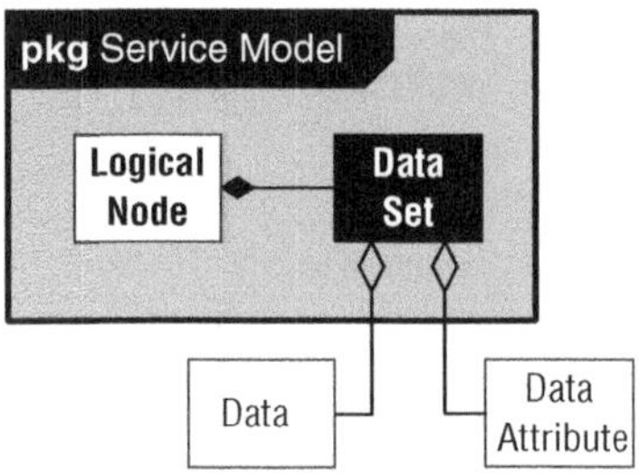

Figure 9.15 Data set aggregation.

method is that the data volume is limited to the portion required for the client, and the connection monitoring is included implicitly. The disadvantage is that a large data volume is transmitted over point-to-point links, resulting in one message per recipient and making it unsuitable for time-critical applications. The client must define the behavior to establish this type of connection. The UML Class Diagram of Figure 9.14 shows the relationship between a ***Data Set*** and its containing logical node.

Among its capabilities, a ***Data Set*** can be defined and given a name, offering services to create, delete, list, read, and write data into and from a ***logical node***. Clients can define collections of data attributes commonly needed by their processes, comprised of references to data objects, accessed with a single name. Any ***Data Set*** may be predefined in the project or created during process execution. In both cases, clients may interrogate it.

A ***Data Set*** is implemented as an ordered group of ***ObjectReferences*** of ***DATA*** or ***DataAttributes*** organized as a single collection. Figure 9.15 illustrates this concept using a UML Class Diagram.

The client and the server shall know their ***Data Set*** members and order so that only the name and current values need to be transmitted. This capability permits more efficient use of communications bandwidth. With this arrangement, a ***Data Set*** can be used multiple times as the building block for several data structures used by IEC 61850, like ***Control Blocks*** and ***Messages***, as shown in the UML Package Diagram of Figure 9.16.

The attributes of a ***Data Set*** include a ***DSName***, to identify a ***DATA-SET*** within the scope of a ***LOGICAL-NODE*** or a ***two-party-application-association***; a ***DSRef*** as a unique path-name of an instance of a ***DATA-SET***; one or more ***DSMemberRef [1..n]*** as ***Data Set*** member references to specify the ***functionally constrained data*** (***FCD***) or ***functionally constrained data attribute*** (***FCDA***) of ***DATA***. The internal structure of a ***Data Set*** is shown in Table 9.7.

The services offered by ***Data Set*** objects are listed in the UML Use Case Diagram in Figure 9.17, along with brief descriptions in Table 9.8.

Clients can use the ***CreateDataSet*** service to request that ***servers*** create or configure ***DataSets***. It uses a ***DataSetReference*** to specify the

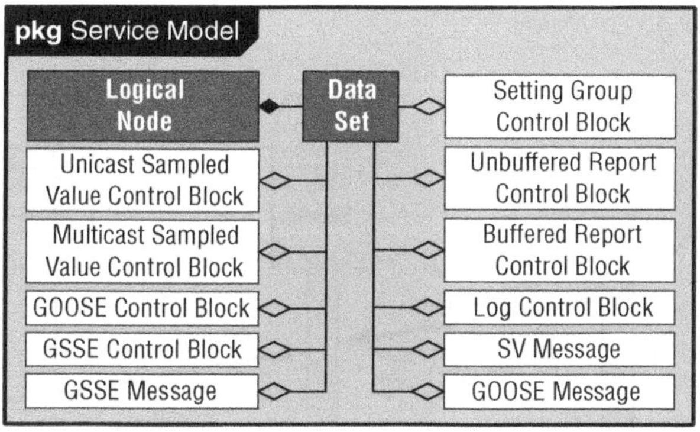

Figure 9.16 Data set multiple use.

Table 9.7 DATA-SET class definition.

DATA-SET class		
Attribute name	**Attribute type**	**Value/value range/explanation**
DSName	*ObjectName*	Instance name of an instance of ***DATA-SET***
DSRef	*ObjectReference*	Path-name of an instance of ***DATA-SET***
DSMemberRef [1..n]	(*)	(*) Functionally constrained data (***FCD***) or functionally constrained data attribute (***FCDA***)

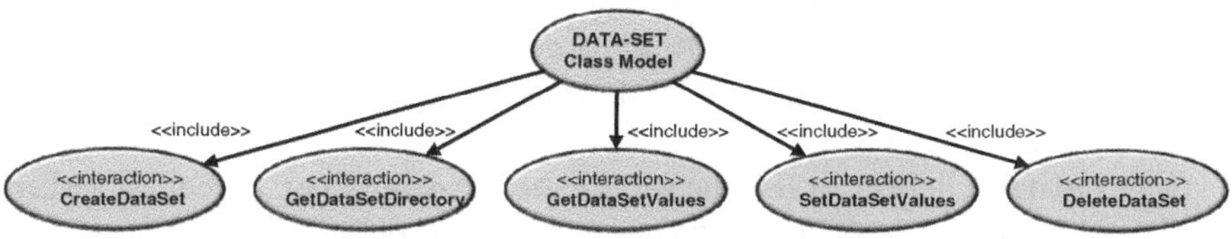

Figure 9.17 Data set model use case.

Table 9.8 DATA-SET class services.

Service	**Description**
GetDataSetValues	Retrieve all values of ***DATA*** referenced by the members of the ***DATA-SET***
SetDataSetValues	Write all values of ***DATA*** referenced by the members of the ***DATA-SET***
CreateDataSet	Create a ***DATA-SET*** by providing the ***FCD*** (***FCDA***) references or that form the ***DATA-SET***
DeleteDataSet	Delete a ***DATA-SET***
GetDataSetDirectory	Retrieve ***FCD*** references of all members referenced in the ***DATA-SET***

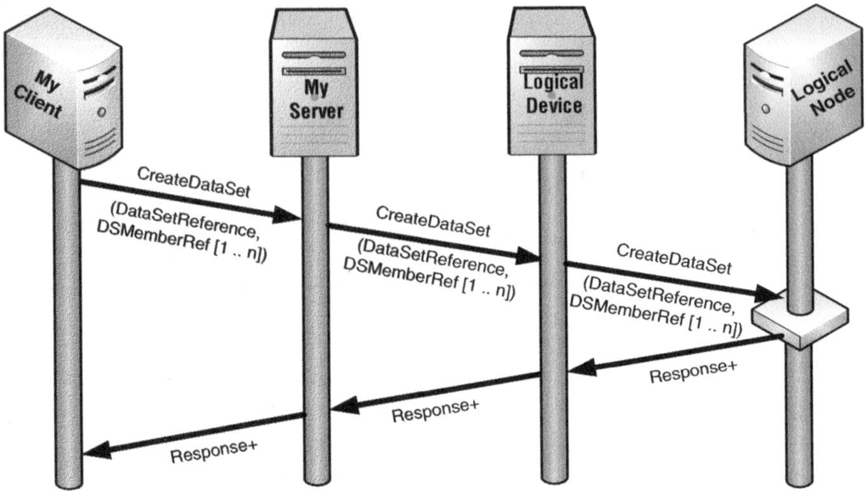

Figure 9.18 Normal CreateDataSet interaction.

ObjectReference of a ***DATA-SET*** that is to be made; a ***DSMemberRef [1..n]***—***data set*** member ***ObjectReference*** to identify the ***functionally constrained*** data (***FCD***) or ***functionally constrained data attribute*** (***FCDA***) of a ***DATA***; a ***Response+*** data to indicate that the service request succeeded; and a ***Response-*** data to suggest that the service request failed. Figure 9.18 shows a UML Sequence Diagram of the normal interaction for creating a new ***Data Set***.

Once created, clients can use the service ***DeleteDataSet*** to request servers to delete a ***DataSet***. It uses a ***DataSetReference***—***data set ObjectReference***—to specify the ***ObjectReference*** of ***DATA-SET*** to be deleted; a ***Response+*** to indicate that the service request succeeded; and a ***Response-*** to suggest that the service request failed. Figure 9.19 illustrates the UML Sequence Diagram of a typical interaction for deleting an existing ***Data Set***.

To retrieve the list of the ***ObjectReferences*** of all data and ***Data Attributes*** referenced by the ***DSMemberRef*** [1...n] attribute of a referenced ***DataSet***, clients can use the service ***GetDataSetDirectory***. It uses a ***DataSetReference***—data set ***ObjectReference***—to specify the ***ObjectReference*** of the ***DATA-SET***; a ***Response+*** and a ***DSMemberRef*** [1..n]—data set member ***ObjectReference***—that contains the ***ObjectReferences*** of the members of the ***DATA-SET*** in case the service request succeeded; and a ***Response-*** to indicate that the service request failed. Figure 9.20 illustrates the UML Sequence Diagram for a typical interaction of the ***GetDataSetDirectory*** service.

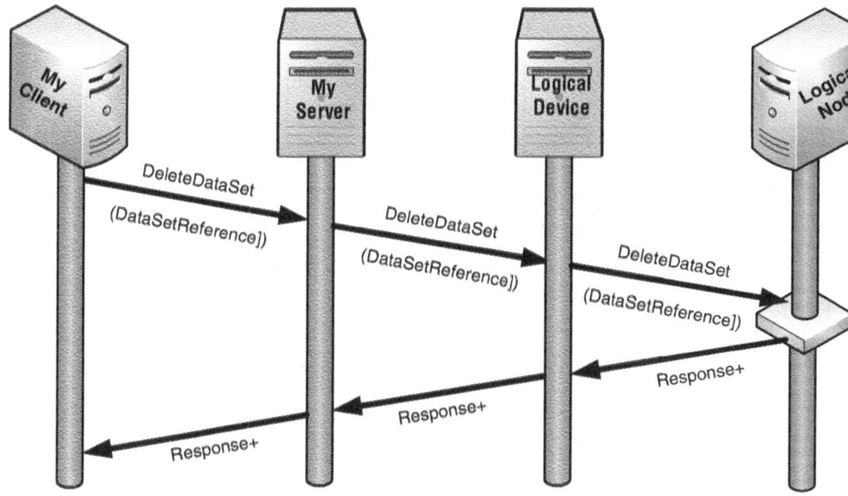

Figure 9.19 Normal DeleteDataSet interaction.

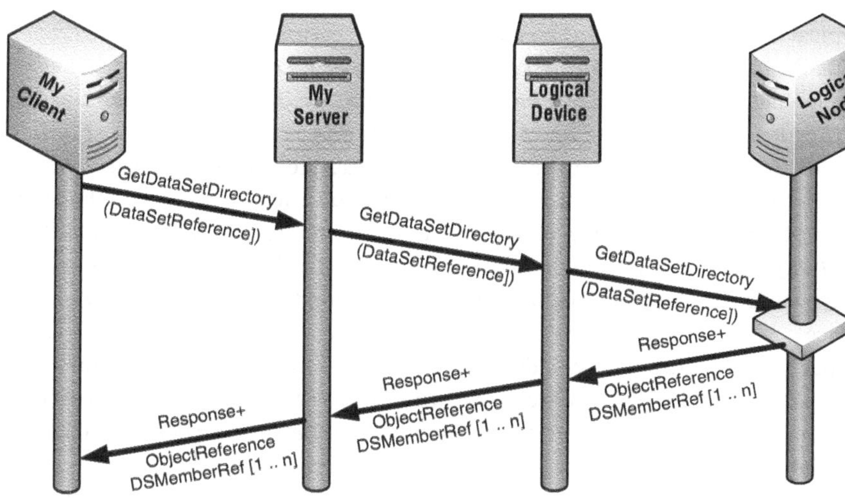

Figure 9.20 Normal GetDataSetDirectory interaction.

Similarly, clients can use the ***GetDataSetValues*** service to retrieve the values of all ***DataAttributes*** contained in the referenced ***DataSet***. It uses a Request as the ***ObjectReference*** of the ***DATA-SET***; a ***Response+*** with a ***DataAttributeValue*** [1..n] that contains values of a member of the ***DATA-SET*** in case the service request succeeded; and a ***Response-*** to indicate

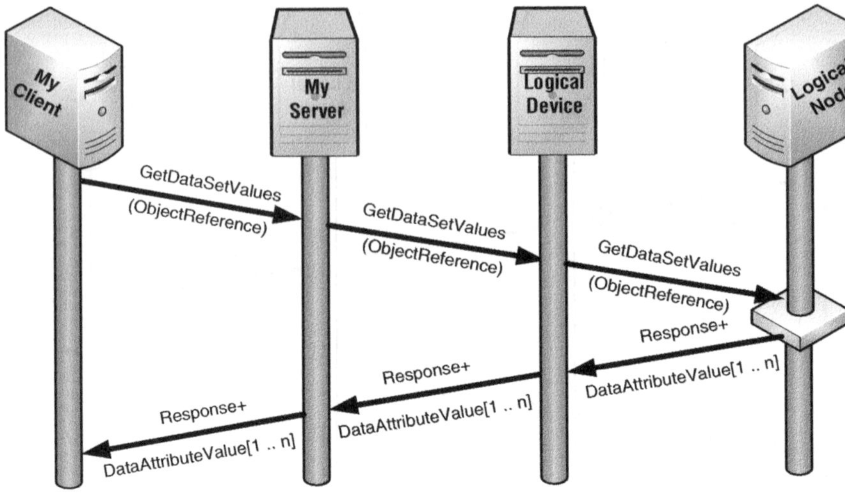

Figure 9.21 Normal GetDataSetValues interaction.

that the service request failed. Figure 9.21 shows the UML Sequence Diagram for a typical interaction for a ***GetDataSetValues*** service.

Finally, clients can use the service ***SetDataSetValues*** to set the values of all referenced ***DataAttributes*** within a ***DataSet***. It uses a ***Request*** as the ***ObjectReference*** of the ***DATA-SET*** and a ***DataAttributeValue [1..n]*** that contains values of a member of the ***DATA-SET***; it returns ***Response+*** to indicate that the service request succeeded, with a ***Result***, a list, specified in the order of the ***ObjectReferences*** of the ***DATA*** that are referenced in the ***DATA-SET***; or a ***Response-*** to indicate that the service request failed. Figure 9.22 illustrates the typical UML Sequence Diagram for the interaction for a ***SetDataSetValues*** service.

Once a ***Data Set*** has been defined, it can serve as the basis for several other services provided by IEC 61850 classes, primarily as the content to be transmitted in messages. Figure 9.23 illustrates an example of a ***Data Set*** being used as the base data list for ***GOOSE*** messages and report services across ***servers***.

In addition to services for controlling ***data sets***, IEC 61850 uses a control model to control devices and servers.

9.8 Control Model

The Control Model adopted by IEC 61850 describes the services used to control devices or parameter settings for server groups. The model provides services to operate ***DATA*** with ***DataAttribute***, subject to functional constraints

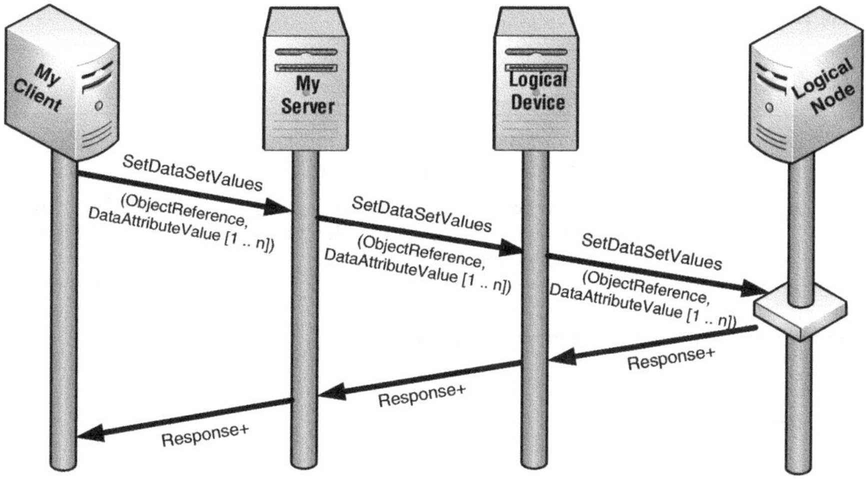

Figure 9.22 Normal SetDataSetValues interaction.

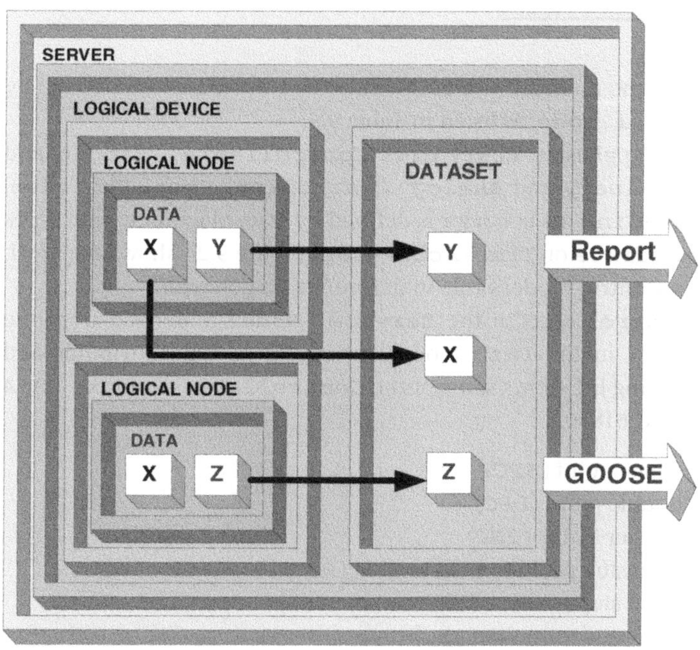

Figure 9.23 Relationship of data set model and signal list.

Table 9.9 Control model.

Mode		Description
CO	**Control**	`DataAttribute` shall represent control information whose value may be operated (control model) and read
SP	**Setpoint**	`DataAttribute` shall represent a set-point information whose value may be controlled (via a control model) and read. Values controlled shall become effective immediately

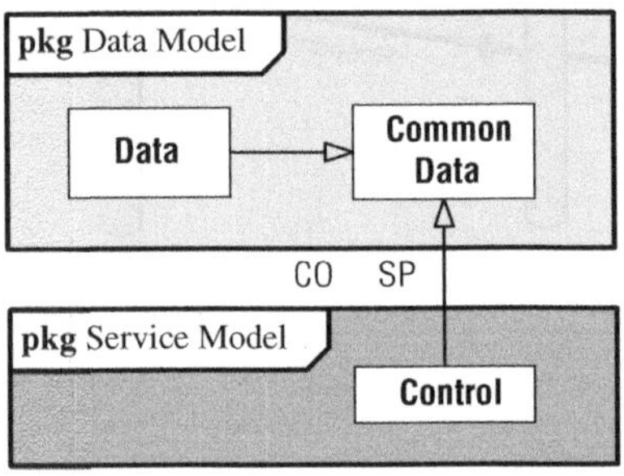

Figure 9.24 Control model.

(*FC* = *CO* or *SP*), for the intended use of the data. Two attributes are defined by IEC 61850 for ***control mode***, as listed in Table 9.9.

A Control model applies to object types ***Controllable Single*** and ***Double Points***, ***Binary*** and ***Analog Controlled Step Position***, and ***Analog Set Point***. Its behavior is defined by state machines, with types categorized as ***Immediate*** or ***Time-Activated***. Figure 9.24 shows the UML Class Diagram of a Control Model's role in defining data behavior.

Note that the ***Control*** class in the ***Service Model*** is derived from the ***Common DATA*** class in the ***Data*** model, inheriting its data attributes and functions. The following list shows some of the ***Controllable Common DATA*** classes defined by IEC 61850:

- Controllable single point (***SPC***)
- Controllable double point (***DPC***)
- Controllable integer status (***INC***)
- Binary-controlled step position information (***BSC***)
- Integer-controlled step position information (***ISC***)
- Controllable analogue set point (***APC***)

The sequence of services the Control Model offers can be (i) ***Direct Control***, where the requested service is executed directly, with no explicit selection of the object of action, and (ii) ***Select Before Operate***, where an explicit selection

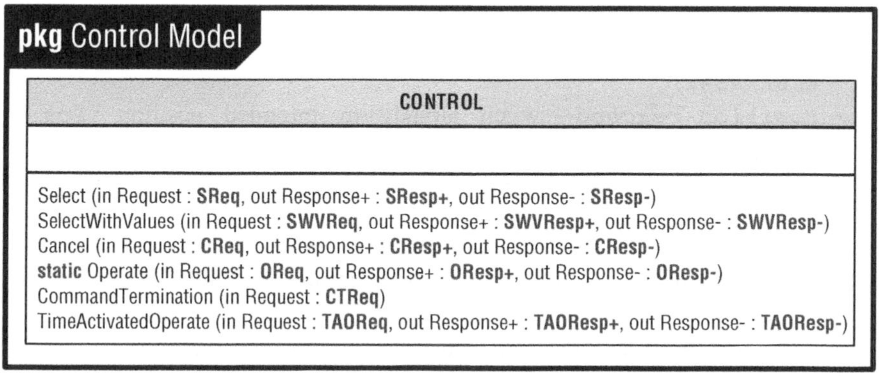

Figure 9.25 Control model package.

of the object of action is requested before the operation. The first is primarily used for direct switching of auxiliary equipment, while the second is mainly used for switching devices, with prior exclusive selection of equipment. The Control Model offers six services, as illustrated in the UML Package Diagram of Figure 9.25.

These services, when requested, use the following parameters:

- ***ControlObjectReference—ObjectReference*** of the controllable ***DATA*** to be accessed (Ex: ***Pos***)
- ***Value***—values for all implemented ***DataAttributes*** of a controllable common ***DATA*** class
- ***T***—control time-stamp—time when the client sends the control request
- ***Test***—test status (pass-through parameter)—define whether the information is caused by normal operation or by test
- ***Check***—check condition—specify the kind of checks a control object shall perform before issuing the control operation if the standard ***DATA*** class is ***DPC***
- ***AddCause***—additional cause diagnosis—reason for failure in a negative control service-specific response.
- ***TimOperRsp—TimeActivatedOperate*** response—specify the details of the positive response on the service ***TimeActivatedOperate***.

When there is a failure in the execution of a control action, an additional cause can be reported on the ***AddCause*** parameter, according to the following list:

- ***ServiceError type***—enumerated type of Service Error (common to ***ACSI***)
- ***Blocked-by-switching-hierarchy***—a ***Loc*** switch has the value ***True***

- ***Select-failed***—cancelled due to an unsuccessful selection
- ***Invalid-position***—aborted due to invalid switch position (***Pos*** in ***XCBR/XSWI***)
- ***Position-reached***—switch already in intended position (***Pos*** in ***XCBR/XSWI***)
- ***Parameter-change-in-execution***—blocked due to running parameter change
- ***Step-limit***—tap changer has reached the limit
- ***Blocked-by-Mode***—***LN*** is in a mode (***Mod***) that does not allow any switching
- ***Blocked-by-process***—an external event prevents operation
- ***Blocked-by-interlocking***—from other switching devices (eg, ***CILO***)
- ***Blocked-by-synchrocheck***—missing synchronism condition or time limit
- ***Command-already-in-execution***—control action already running
- ***Blocked-by-health***—internal event prevents operation
- ***1-of-n-control***—another control action already running
- ***Abortion-by-cancel***—due to a canceled service
- ***Time-limit-over***—exceeding a time limit
- ***Abortion-by-trip***—a trip aborts the control action.

Depending on configuration parameters, different behaviors are exposed by a Control Object:

- **Case 1**: (***direct-operate***)—Direct control with standard security
- **Case 2**: (***operate-once*** or ***operate-many***)—***Select-Before-Operate*** (***SBO***) control with standard security
- **Case 3**: (***direct-operate***)—Direct control with enhanced security
- **Case 4**: (***operate-once*** or ***operate-many***)—***SBO*** control with enhanced security.

In Case 1—***Direct Control with Normal Security***, the control object has no additional supervision of the status value. No failure information is generated for the client. This model should use the services ***Operate*** and ***TimeActivatedOperate***. Additionally, a change in the control object's status may trigger a report. Upon receipt of an ***Operate*** request, the control object shall verify that the control has been executed. If unsuccessful, the object control shall respond negatively to the requesting client. If successful, the object control shall respond positively to the requesting client and initiate the requested action. Figure 9.26 illustrates the UML Sequence Diagram depicting the interaction between a client and a server to execute a ***Direct Control with Normal Security***.

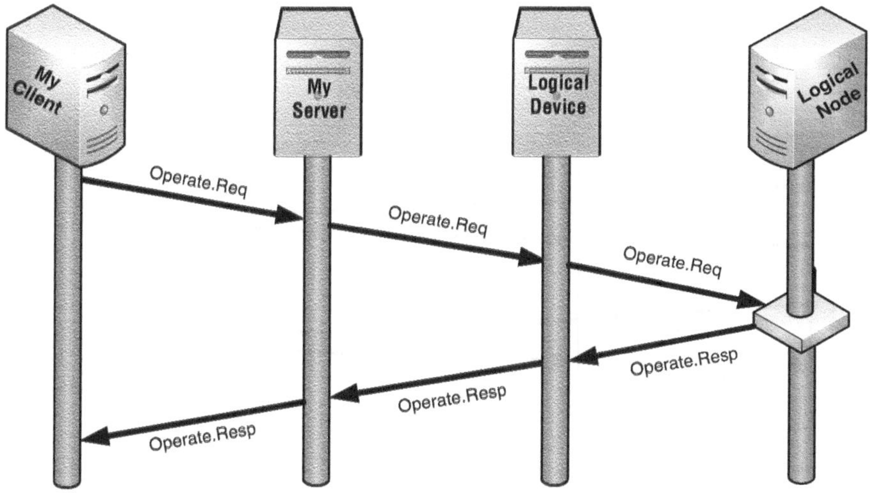

Figure 9.26 Direct control normal security.

In Case 2—***SBO Control with Normal Security***, the model shall utilize the services ***Select***, ***Cancel***, ***Operate***, and ***Time-Activated Operate***. A change in the control object's status may generate a report. Upon receipt of a ***Select*** request, the control shall determine whether the client has the appropriate access authority, whether the control object is not currently selected, whether the device represented by the LN is operable, and whether it is not tagged to restrict its operation. If the deselect timer expires, the control object shall change the state to unselected. If an ***Operate*** request is received while the state is not ***Ready***, the operation shall be denied. On receipt of an ***Operate*** request, the control object shall verify the control execution. If unsuccessful, it should respond negatively to the requesting client. If successful, it should issue a positive response with the cause of the requested action. Figure 9.27 illustrates the UML Sequence Diagram for the interaction between a client and a server to execute an ***SBO Control with Normal Security***.

In Case 3—***Control with Enhanced Security***, the control object shall additionally monitor the status value. Each command sequence shall be terminated by a ***CommandTermination*** service primitive. It should be used to control meaningful actions outside the device that contains the accessed control object. Upon receipt of a ***SelectWithValue*** request, it should determine whether the client has the appropriate access authority, whether a different client currently selects the control object, and whether the device is operable and not tagged to restrict operation. If the deselect timer expires before an ***Operate*** request is received, the state shall be changed to unselected. If an ***Operate*** request is received while the state is not ***Ready*** the operation shall be denied. Upon receipt

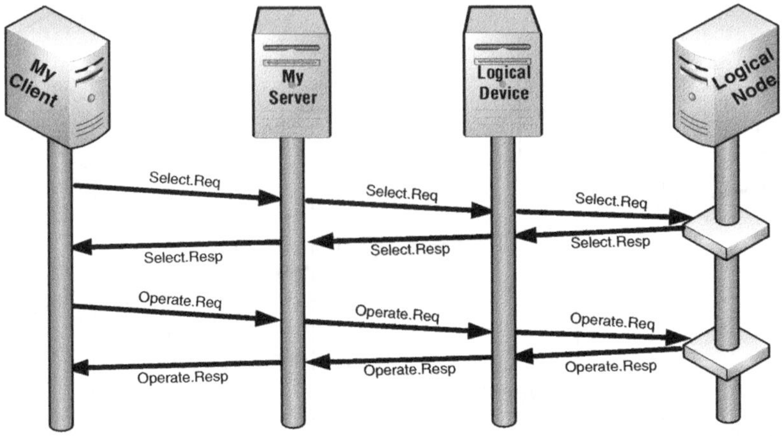

Figure 9.27 SBO control with normal security.

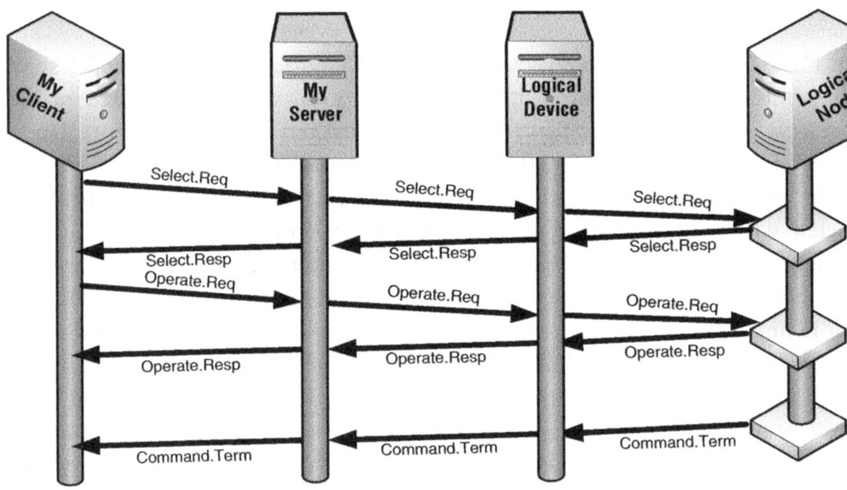

Figure 9.28 SBO control with enhanced security.

of an ***Operate*** request, the control execution should be validated. When leaving the ***WaitForChange*** state, if ***thsboClass*** is ***operate-once***, the new state shall be unselected. If ***sboClass*** is ***operate-many***, the new state shall be ***Ready***. Figure 9.28 illustrates the UML Sequence Diagram for the interaction between a client and a server to execute an ***SBO Control with Enhanced Security***.

Case 4—***Time-Activated-Operate Control***—shall consist of a ***TimeActivatedOperate*** request and response. The response shall inform

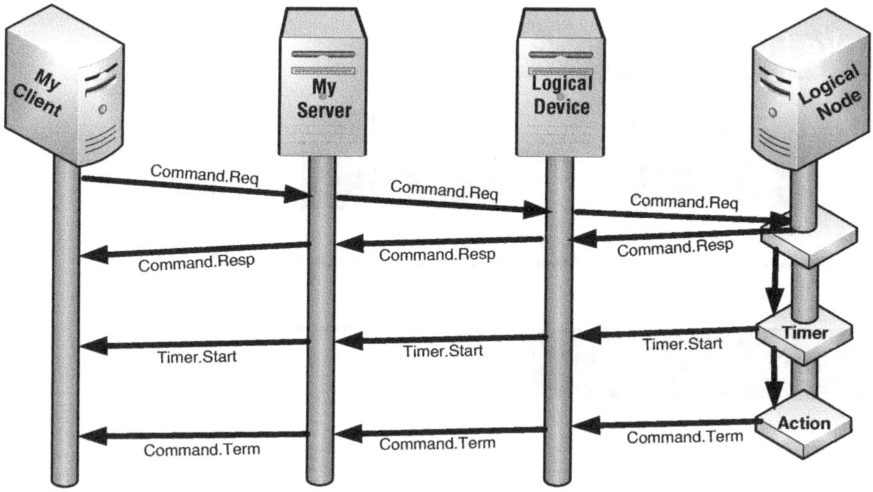

Figure 9.29 Sequence of Time-Activated-Operate control.

the requesting client whether the command succeeded and, if it triggered a time-activation process, whether that process succeeded or failed. Upon receipt of a ***TimeActivatedOperate*** request, it should verify its validity. If not successful, send a negative response. If successful, activate the timer, respond positively, and inform them that the timer has started. Upon the timer expiring, the desired action shall be executed, and a response shall be sent to the client. The ***Control with Enhanced Security*** model shall describe all further information exchange. Figure 9.29 illustrates the interaction between a client and a server to execute a ***Time-Activated Operate Control***.

In addition to controlling servers and physical devices, IEC 61850 also provides abstract services for managing files across servers, using a File Transfer Model.

9.9 File Transfer Model

The File Transfer Model of IEC 61850 defines ***ACSI*** services for transferring files between and within file stores, as well as managing file stores. It facilitates the exchange of large data blocks, such as programs and settings. The ***ACSI*** file store uses a single format—sequential, unstructured binary—that may contain programs, data, or both. Any interpretation of the contents is by mutual agreement of the systems involved. Figure 9.30 illustrates a UML Package Diagram showing the relationship between the service model and the functional model, where a ***Server*** can contain several ***File*** objects.

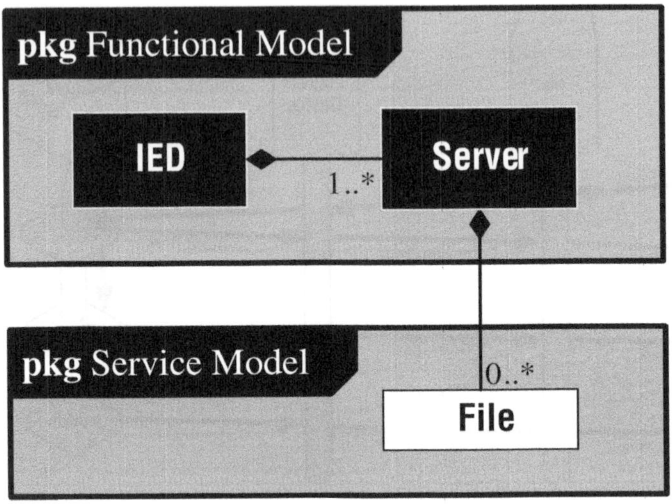

Figure 9.30 File transfer model.

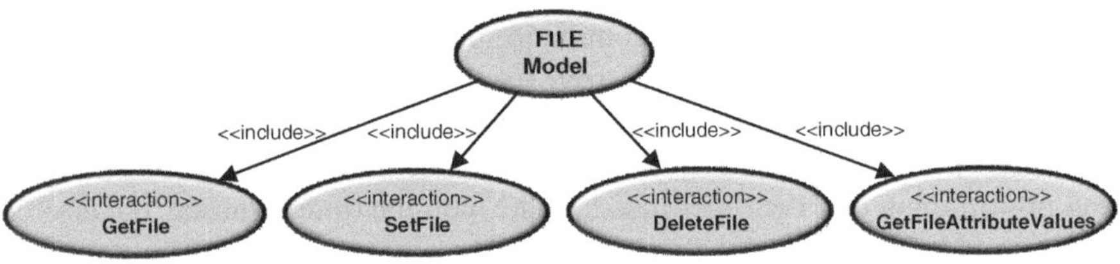

Figure 9.31 File model use case.

The ***File*** class offers services for the standardized transfer of files, such as fault records, among servers. It includes a uniform procedure for transmitting and managing files, where no data content is specified and no security mechanisms for data access are defined. Fault records should be saved consistently in Comtrade format, as defined by IEEE standard C37.111. Its attributes include:

- ***FileName***—Name in the ***ACSI*** file store, which may be structured to differentiate file types, for example, disturbance records, programs, and parameter and configuration data.
- ***FileSize [0..1]***—Length of a file in the file store (in octets)
- ***LastModified***—Time when the file was last modified.

The services offered by a ***File*** class are listed on the UML Use Case diagram in Figure 9.31.

A ***GetFile*** service transfers a file's contents from the server to the client. It requires a ***FileName***, which is the name of the file being transferred, and returns a **`Response+`** if the service succeeds, with a **`File-Data`** containing the transferred data, or a **`Response-`** if the service request fails. Figure 9.32 illustrates the UML Sequence Diagram of events associated with a typical **`GetFile`** interaction between a client and a server.

A ***DeleteFile*** service allows a client to delete files from the server's file store. It requires a **`FileName`** with the name of the deleted file and returns a **`Response+`** if the service succeeds, or a **`Response-`** if the service request fails. Figure 9.33 illustrates the UML Sequence Diagram of events related to a normal **`DeleteFile`** interaction between a client and a server.

With the **`GetFileAttributeValues`** service a client can obtain the name and attributes of a file in the server's file store. It needs to provide the **`FileName`** parameter with the file name whose attributes the client requests. A **`Response+`**

Figure 9.32 Normal GetFile interaction.

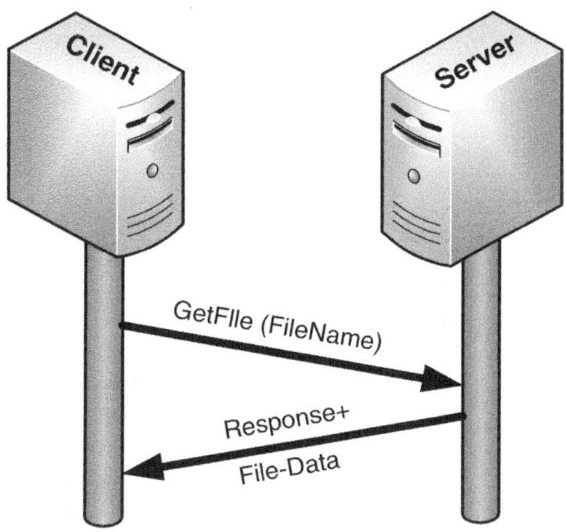

Figure 9.33 Normal DeleteFile interaction.

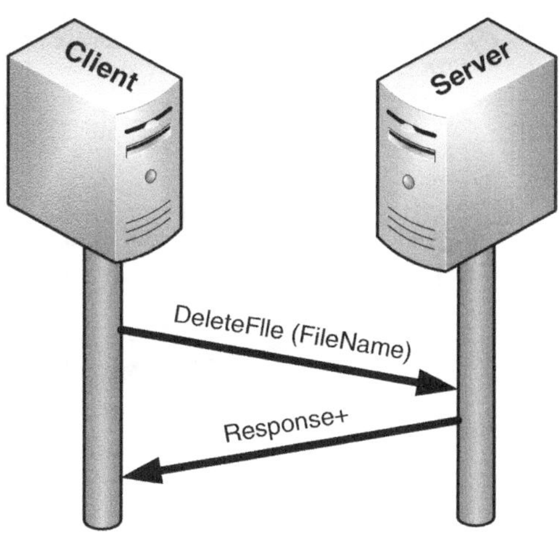

result will be returned if the service request succeeds, with the **`FileName`** of the file whose attributes are returned, the **`FileAttribute [1..n]`** structure with information describing the selected file. Otherwise, a **`Response-`** will be returned if the service request failed. Figure 9.34 illustrates the UML Sequence Diagram of events related to a normal **`GetFileAttributeValues`** interaction between a client and a server.

With the **`SetFile`** service, it is possible to transfer a file's contents from a client to a server. The service requires the **`FileName`** parameter to transfer the file's name and the **`File-Data`** structure to transfer the data. If the service request succeeds, a **`Response+`** will be returned. Otherwise, a **`Response-`** will be returned if the service request fails. Figure 9.35 illustrates the UML Sequence Diagram of events related to a normal **`SetFile`** interaction between a client and a server.

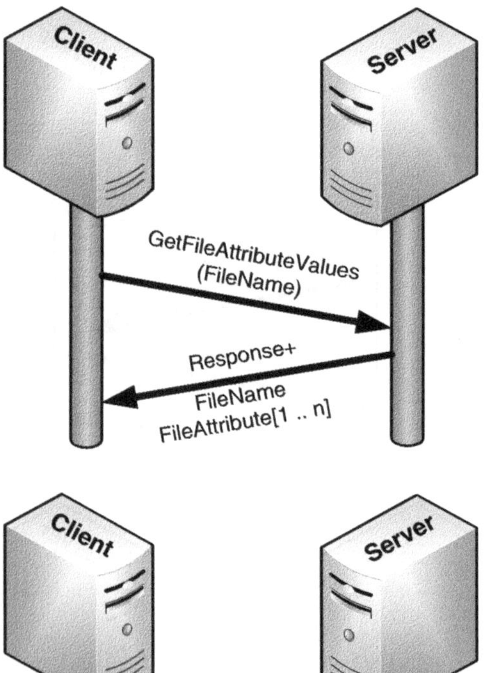

Figure 9.34 Normal GetFileAttributeValues interaction.

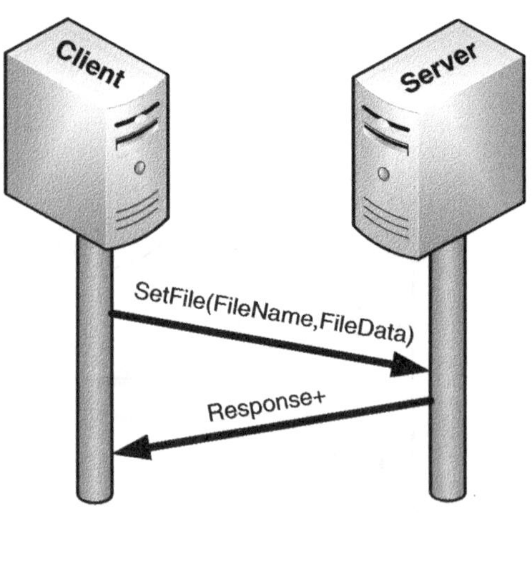

Figure 9.35 Normal SetFile interaction.

Managing files has many similarities with the reporting services provided by IEC 61850 in the Reporting Model.

9.10 Reporting Model

The Reporting Model of IEC 61850 defines the procedures for reporting data values from one or more ***logical nodes*** to a single client. One or more instances of a ***report control*** must be configured on the server at configuration time, according to the specific installation's needs. Examples of reporting models include the immediate reports of change-of-state notifications to clients, sequence-of-events tracking by keeping reports in sequence or storing and querying sequences of log entries, and polling data at any time in various formats to conserve bandwidth.

Using the Reporting Model, a ***Logical Node*** can transfer data values to a client immediately or after a buffer period. The model describes the conditions for generating reports based on parameters set by the client. Reports may be triggered by changes in process data values (for example, state changes or deadbands) or quality changes and can be sent immediately or deferred (buffered). Reports can also facilitate information exchange on changes of state and sequences of events, reporting entries in the event log (history) based on the parameters specified by the host. Event logs can be queried later, while messages can be sent immediately or with a delay (buffered).

The advantages of the ***Reporting*** and ***Logging*** services include timely reports that serve as an indication to clients under real-time constraints (optionally keeping a sequence of events for the client) and event logging for later retrieval (sequence of events stored on the server). This model minimizes the impact on network bandwidth by sending reports only when required or when a client-initiated general interrogation is enabled.

The rules for logging and reporting are defined in the ***Log Control Block*** (***LCB***) and ***Report Control Block (RCB)*** of the ***server***, respectively. Each log has an associated ***LCB***, and each report has an associated ***RCB***. These rules determine which ***Data Sets*** will be included and under what conditions. Services are provided so a client can subscribe to reports defined on the device. In contrast, reports can be buffered so that if communications are temporarily disrupted, all the reports are still sent to the client when communications are reestablished. Figure 9.36 illustrates the UML Package Diagram, which includes classes related to the IEC 61850 reporting model.

To provide its services, the Reporting Model uses C/S communication across the full seven-layer stack of the ISO model. It has a confirmed transmission layer that is very reliable but relatively time-consuming. As such, it is not suited for time-critical data transmission, but is well suited for communication with an operator,

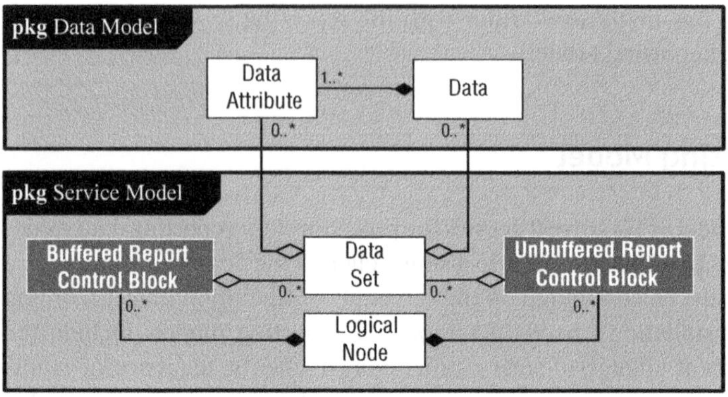

Figure 9.36 Reporting Model.

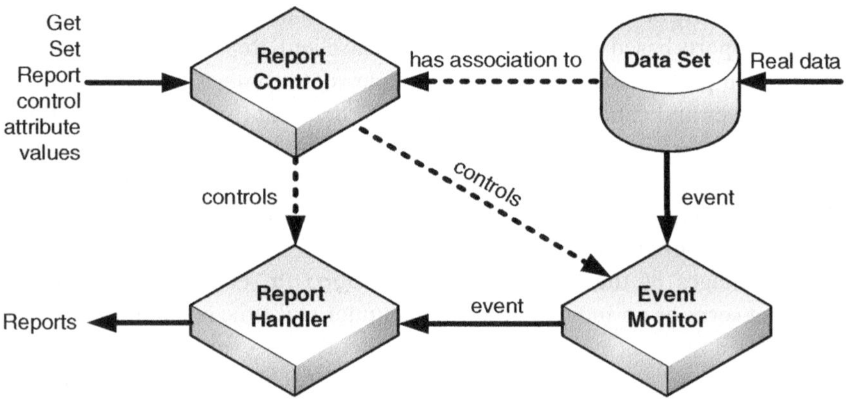

Figure 9.37 Basic building blocks for reporting model.

with a response time of the order of 1 second. In this system, the server is the source of all data for the client, and where a `data set` defines each report. In contrast to the master-slave relationship, IEC 61850 allows multiple C/S systems. The client requests information from the server and can modify the server's behavior by configuring the ***`Report Control Block`*** to send reports automatically.

Figure 9.37 shows the elemental composition of the Reporting Model. It consists of a ***`Report Control Block`*** that sets or reads the attribute values that control the operation of the ***`Event Monitor`*** and ***`Report Handler`***; an ***`Event Monitor`*** that observes the values and state of the data Attributes and data, and informs the ***`Report Handler`*** when changes occur; and a ***`Report Handler`*** that filters and formats the data values into a report structure and decides when to forward the report to the subscribed client.

Reporting services can be buffered or unbuffered, depending on the settings of the ***BRCB*** and ***UBRCB*** classes. Both allow the reporting, setting, and retrieval of values using the services provided by the ***RCB*** class. Figures 9.38 and 9.39 illustrate the UML Use Case Diagrams for these classes, described in Tables 9.10 and 9.11, respectively.

A ***Buffered Report*** is intended to help clients implement a well-defined functionality, such as a SCADA master. The client may know the ***Object Reference*** of the ***BRCB*** by configuration or using a naming convention. The visibility of these instances may be a subject of access control. When a ***BRCB*** is

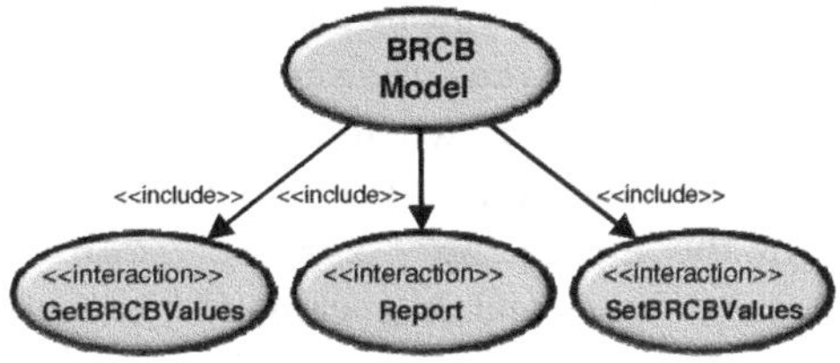

Figure 9.38 BRCB use cases.

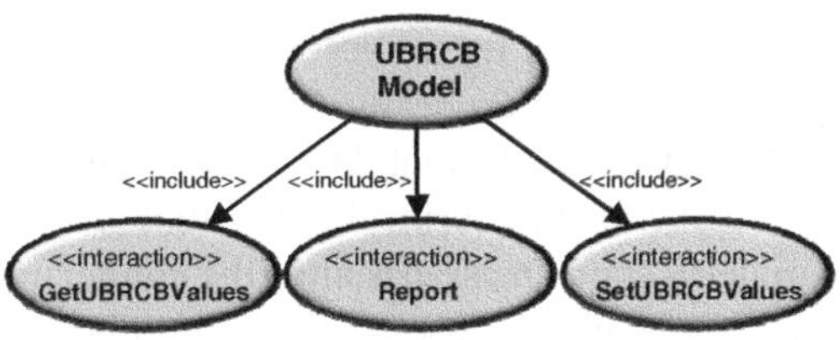

Figure 9.39 UBRCB use cases.

Table 9.10 BRCB class services.

Service	Description
Report	Send a buffered report
GetBRCBValues	Read an attribute of a ***BRCB***
SetBRCBValues	Write an attribute of a ***BRCB***

Table 9.11 UBRCB class services.

Service	Description
Report	Send an unbuffered report
GetUBRCBValues	Read an attribute of a ***UBRCB***
SetUBRCBValues	Write an attribute of a ***UBRCB***

enabled, all other clients have no access right to set its parameters until an explicit request by the client disables it.

Conversely, with an ***Unbuffered Report***, a server can make multiple instances of a report control class available and visible to all clients, which may use a specific instance or browse for one that is disabled and hence available. A client can view only one example of the report control class based on the connection or authentication view.

Several conditions can be used to generate reports. A ***Data-change*** triggered by a change in a value of a ***DataAttribute*** representing process-related data, where the ***data-change*** trigger option (***TrgOp*** = ***dchg***) signifies such a change; a ***Quality-change*** by a change in quality of a ***DataAttribute*** (***TrgOp*** = ***qchg***); and a ***Data-update*** by a freeze event in a value of a ***DataAttribute*** (***TrgOp*** = ***dupd***), where a change or update in a value of a ***DataAttribute*** with the same value as before represents a freeze event.

In the ***Buffered Report Control Block (BRCB)***, changes to DataAttributes and data, caused by trigger options, result in immediate or buffered transmission of those values. It provides the Sequence-Of-Events (SOE) functionality of IEC 61850. No events are lost because the reports are buffered. In this sequence, the server has one control block per client and sends reports spontaneously or cyclically. If interrupted, the messages are buffered in a limited buffer, ensuring optimal data throughput with no loss. As a disadvantage, it is unsuitable for time-critical applications, as historical data is transmitted, which can delay status messages after the connection has been restored. Also, the total reporting time increases with the number of clients served. Table 9.12 lists the attributes of the *BRCB* class.

An alternative is the ***Unbuffered Report Control Block (URCB)***, which sends reports immediately when changes to ***DataAttributes*** or data are caused by trigger options, on a "best efforts" basis. Depending on network traffic, some events may be lost as the reports are not buffered. In this sequence, the server maintains one control block per client and sends reports either spontaneously or cyclically, resulting in optimal data traffic. As a disadvantage, it is not well suited to time-critical applications, as status changes are lost during transmission interruptions. In addition, the total reporting time increases with the number of clients involved. Figure 9.40 shows how these services act on the data values of a ***BRCB*** control block.

BRCB uses a ***Report Service*** to send reports from the server to the client. It includes a ***ReportFormat*** parameter specifying the format of the information to be included in the report. Figure 9.41 shows events related to a normal ***Report*** interaction between a client and a server. ***BRCB*** shall use the report service to send reports from the server to the client. The ***ReportFormat*** specifies the information to be included in the report.

Table 9.12 *BRCB* class attributes.

Attribute	Description
BRCBName	Buffered report control name
BRCBRef	Buffered report control ***ObjectReference***
RptID	Report identifier
RptEna	Report enable
DatSet	Data set reference
ConfRev	Configuration revision count
OptFlds	Optional fields to include in report
BufTm	Buffer time between spontaneous reports
SqNum	Sequence number
TrgOp	Trigger options
IntgPd	Integrity period
GI	Request to start the general-interrogation process
PurgeBuf	Request to purge buffer
EntryID	Entry identifier of a sequence of events
TimeOfEntry	Time of entry is added to the buffer

Service ***SetBRCBValues*** defines the data that a ***BRCB*** will collect and retrieve. Clients can use this service to request servers to create ***BRCBs*** or configure ***BRCB*** attribute values. The typical sequence used by this service is shown on Figure 9.42, starting from a request from a server, through the logical device of an ***IED*** server, to a specific ***logical node***. After setting the ***BRCB*** values, the ***logical node*** sends a confirmation response to the requesting server through the logical device of its ***IED*** server. A similar interaction is used by the service ***GetBRCBValues*** to retrieve the ***BRCB*** of a ***logical node***.

An ***Unblocked Report Control Block (URCB)*** is like a ***BRCB***, except that ***URCBName*** is now the unbuffered report control name that unambiguously identifies the ***URCB*** within ***LOGICAL-NODE***. In contrast, ***URCBRef***, the unbuffered report control ***ObjectReference***, defines a unique pathname to ***URCB***. A flag named ***RptEna*** (report enable) is set to ***TRUE*** if the ***URCB*** is currently enabled to report DATA-SET values. In contrast, the flag ***Resv*** (reserve ***URCB***), when set to ***TRUE***, indicates that the URCB is currently exclusively reserved for the client that set it to ***TRUE***.

URCB services are like ***BRCB*** services, except for parameters specific to buffered reports, including the ***Report***, ***GetURCBValues***, and ***SetURCBValues***

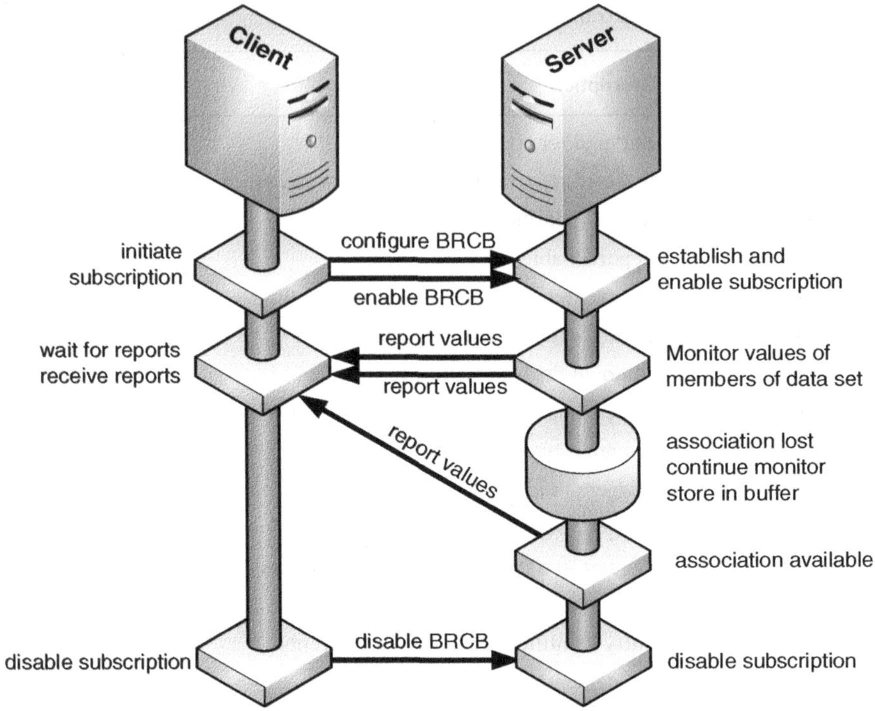

Figure 9.40 Buffered report control block mechanism.

Figure 9.41 Normal report interaction.

services. For the **`Report`** service, the same parameters apply, except that **`BufOvfl`** is not available. The service **`GetURCBValues`** aims to retrieve attribute values of a **`URCB`** made visible and thus accessible, using the same parameters as **`GetBRCBValues`**, except that **`BRCBReference`** shall be **`URCBReference`**, **`PurgeBuffer`** shall not be available, and **`Functional Constraint`** shall be **`RP`**. The service **`SetURCBValues`** is used to set attribute values of **`URCB`**

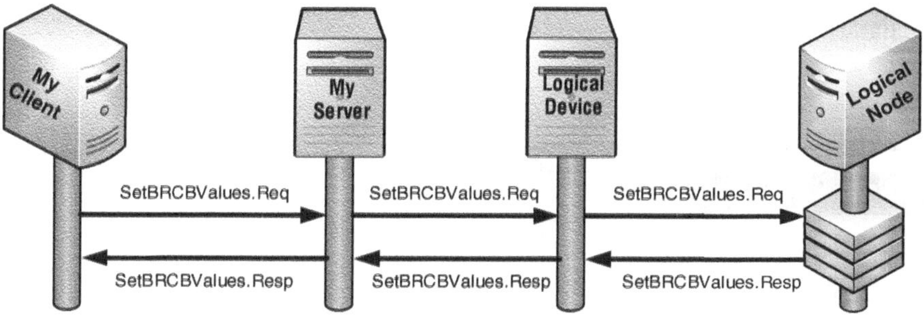

Figure 9.42 Normal SetBRCBValues interaction.

made visible and thus accessible to the requesting client, with parameters like ***SetBRCBValues***, except that ***BRCBReference*** shall be ***URCBReference***, ***PurgeBuffer*** shall not be available, and ***Functional Constraint*** shall be ***RP***. The reporting services can also be used to report the sequence of events stored in the Logging Model defined by IEC 61850.

9.11 Logging Model

The IEC 61850 logging model is designed to store data in the event log for future enquiries based on selected parameters. Message logging can be triggered by changes to process data values or quality information, allowing event logs to be queried later. Messages can be sent immediately or with a delay (buffered), following the same conditions as for report generation. The logs are time-ordered collections of data grouped into defined ***Data Sets***, usually related to essential aspects of a physical device or its core function. Clients can retrieve information from the log using queries that can be filtered by time range or named attributes.

Logging shall be independent of external application associations or other communication transactions to be effective. Even if communication is lost, login should continue, as it is asynchronous with communication-based retrieval, and the logging rate can be much faster than communication processes can report. Record retrieval can be by subsets to maintain an external, complete time or event-sequenced historical record. Records have relative significance with respect to time or ordering and may require sequence numbers to maintain their relative order.

Two classes are involved in the logging service. As part of a ***logical node***, the ***LCB*** controls the selection and triggering of logging information into a ***LOG*** object; and the ***LOG*** class, also a part of ***Logical Node 0*** and ***Logical Device***, for storage of logging information. Each ***LLN0*** is allowed only a single log that multiple ***LCB***s can use for data storage. Figure 9.43 shows the UML Class

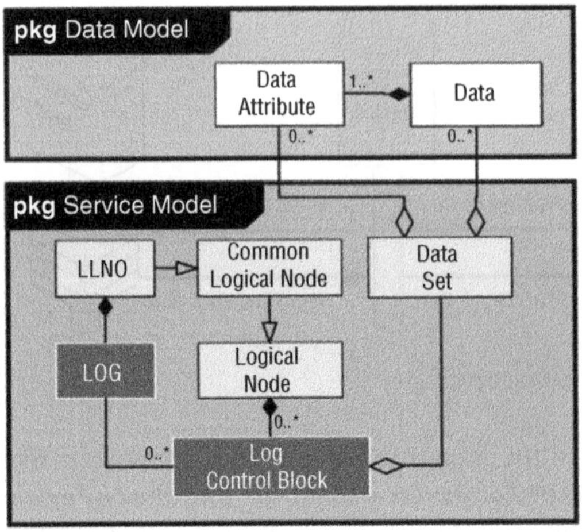

Figure 9.43 Logging model.

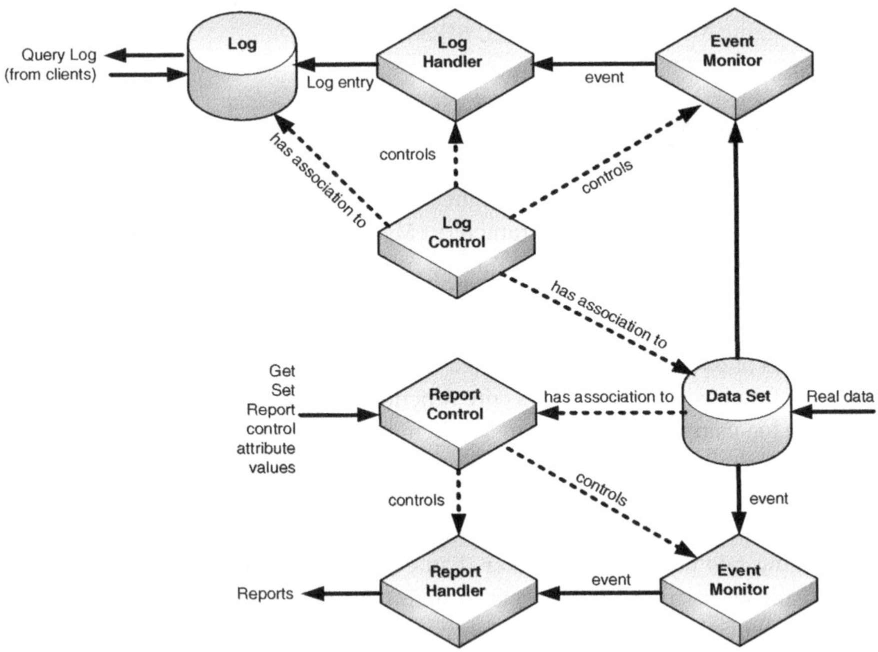

Figure 9.44 Basic building blocks for logging and reporting.

Diagram for the association of these classes with the `Service` and `Data` models of IEC 61850.

Typically, an implementation of the logging model is composed of four main components (Figure 9.44):

- ***Event monitor***—that checks the values and state of the ***Data Attributes*** and data referenced within a specified ***DataSet***
- ***Log handler***—that carries out the task of filtering and formatting data values as log entries, storing them in the log
- ***Log control***—used to set/get log control attributes, which control the operation of the log handler and event monitor
- ***Buffer***—a circular buffer (first in, first out) that overwrites the oldest values in the ***LOG***

The class ***LCB*** offers two services for configuring the logging process: ***GetLCBValues*** and ***SetLCBValues***, as shown in the UML Use Case Diagram of Figure 9.45. The class ***LOG*** provides three services for managing the logged data, illustrated in the UML Use Case Diagram of Figure 9.46: ***QueryLogByValue***, ***QueryLogAfter*** and ***GetLogStatusValues***.

An archive (***LOG***) is generated on the server and sent to the client upon request. As an advantage, data is transferred only as required and does not burden the operational data traffic. As a disadvantage, memory resources are needed on the server, and the logging timing may not be suitable for time-critical applications. ***Logs*** are members of ***data sets***, with the same triggering as in the Report Model, being logged to a circular buffer that supports multiple ***data sets***. These ***data sets*** can be retrieved by various clients using either the entry number or the ***timestamp***.

The client views the ***LOG*** as a linear buffer, where the ***LOG*** entries are identified by an ***EntryID*** - a unique ***LOG*** entry identifier; and a ***TimeOfEntry*** - the time when the ***LOG*** entry was added to the ***LOG***.

The conditions and constraints used for log generation are the same as for report generation, triggered by data changes, quality changes, or data updates. When an ***LCB*** is notified due to the integrity of the trigger options, the ***LCB*** creates a ***LOG*** entry for each member of the referenced ***DATA-SET***. The following attributes are part of the ***LCB*** class:

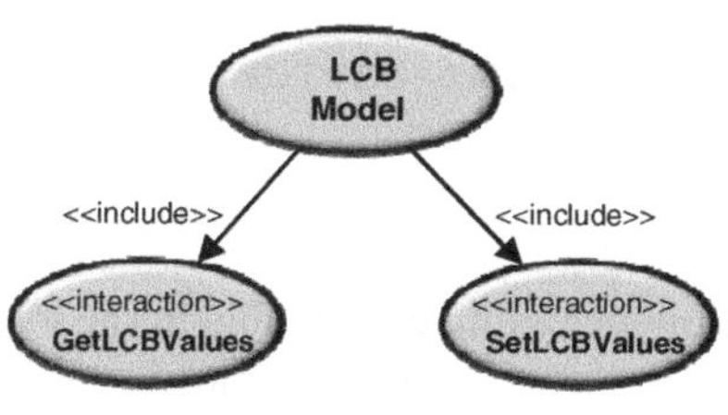

Figure 9.45 LCB use cases.

Figure 9.46 LOG use cases.

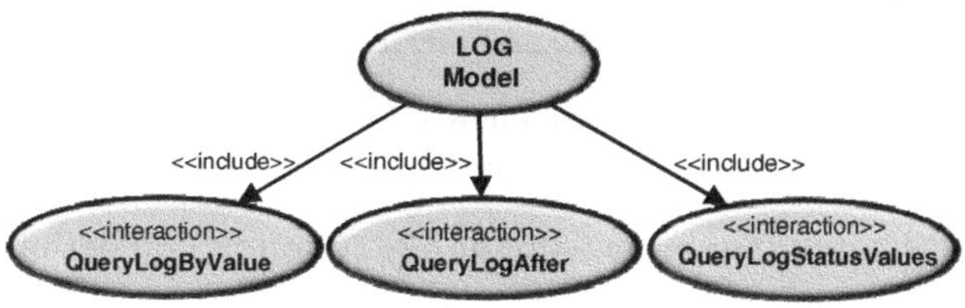

- ***LCBName***—log control name
- ***LCBRef***—log control ***ObjectReference***
- ***LogEna***—log enable
- ***DatSet***—data set reference
- ***OptFlds***—optional fields to include in log
- ***TrgOp***—trigger options
- ***IntgPd***—integrity period in ms for logging
- ***LogRef***—log reference

These attributes can be changed or retrieved using two ***LCB*** services, with the following parameters to create, change, or retrieve the ***LCB*** attributes:

- ***LCBReference***—ObjectReference of the ***LCB***
- ***FunctionalConstraint***—parameter to filter the respective instances of attributes of a ***LCB***
- ***DataSetReference***—value for the corresponding attribute ***DatSet*** of the referenced ***LCB***
- ***TriggerOptions***—value for the corresponding attribute ***TrgOp*** of the referenced ***LCB***
- ***IntegrityPeriod***—value for the corresponding attribute ***IntgPd*** of the referenced LCB
- ***LogReference***—value for the corresponding attribute ***LogRef*** of the referenced ***LCB***
- ***Response+***—service request succeeded
- ***Response-***—service request failed.

Similarly, the ***LOG*** class has the following attributes:

- ***LogName***—log name set to the name of the ***LOGICAL-DEVICE***
- ***LogRef***—log reference as a unique pathname of a ***LOG***
- ***OldEntrTm***—oldest log entry time stored
- ***NewEntrTm***—newest log entry time stored
- ***OldEntr***—oldest log entry ***EntryID*** sequence number available in the log
- ***NewEntr***—newest log entry ***EntryID*** sequence number in the log
- ***Entry [1..n]*** formed by:
  - ***TimeOfEntry***—time of log entry
  - ***EntryID***—entry identifier
  - ***EntryData [1..n]***—Data of Entry

These attributes can be changed or retrieved using the ***LOG*** services, with the following parameters to create, change, or retrieve the ***LOG*** attributes:

- ***LogReference***—***ObjectReference LogRef*** of a ***LOG***
- ***RangeStartTime***—range start time to retrieve log entries

- **RangeStopTime**—range stop time to retrieve log entries
- **ListOfLogEntries**—list of log entries between **RangeStartTime** and **RangeStopTime** of the service request
- **FunctionalConstraint**—value of the functional constraint parameter to filter a LOG's respective instances of attributes
- **Response+**—service request succeeded
- **Response-**—service request failed

Complementing these service sets, IEC 61850 defines a Setting Model for changing and querying **IED** settings.

9.12 Setting Model

Using the Setting Model, it is possible to switch over setting group values and edit the setting groups of **IEDs** in an automation system. For instance, it allows several values to be used one at a time, providing mechanisms to switch between several values of one or more **DATA**. Figure 9.47 illustrates how this is done.

Values that belong together in a setting form the **Setting Group** (**SG**). **SGs** enable simultaneous switching of multiple parameters, including numerous copies of each, with exactly one copy of each active and exactly one copy editable.

The services provided by the setting model allow clients to selectively switch among setting groups, with the advantage of implicit connection monitoring, in which the behavior used to establish the connection is defined on the client side. In this model it is possible to change (i) configuration parameters that define the global behavior of the whole SAS and its **IEDs**; (2) operating parameters that define the behavior of partial functions of the SAS and can be changed on-line during the regular operation of the SAS; (3) system parameters that determine the co-operation

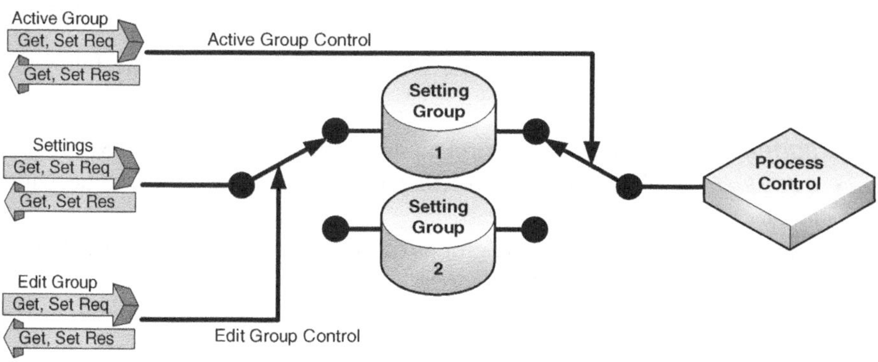

Figure 9.47 Setting group model.

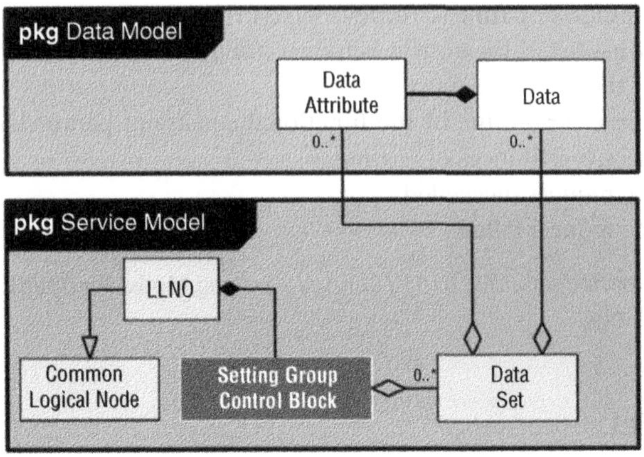

Figure 9.48 Setting Model.

of ***IEDs*** including the internal structures and procedures of an SAS about its technological limits and available components; (4) process parameters that describe all types of information that is exchanged between the process and the SAS; and (5) functional parameters that describe the qualitative and quantitative features of functionality used by the customer, typically changeable on-line.

The ***Setting Group Control Block*** (***SGCB***) model is a special structure for setting data contained in ***LNs***. Even if an instance of data can only have a single value, it might be necessary to store several values for that instance that can be used one at a time. The ***SGCB*** model stores and edits multiple values for one or more data sources, switching between them as needed. Several ***SGs*** can be defined with values for various data settings, which can only be set when the group is in the "***EDIT***" state. Once the values are set, the application can select them by switching that group to the "***ACTIVE***" state. This mechanism is illustrated in the UML Class Diagram of Figure 9.48.

To allow the control of settings, the ***SGCD*** structure contains the following attributes:

- ***SGCBName***—setting group control name within the scope of a ***LLN0***
- ***SGCBRef***—setting group control ***ObjectReference*** as a unique pathname of an ***SGCB***
- ***NumOfSG***—number of setting groups equal to the total number of ***SGs*** that are available in a ***LOGICAL-DEVICE***
- ***ActSG***—active setting group that identifies the values of the ***SG*** that are in the active buffer
- ***EditSG***—edit setting group that identifies the values of the ***SG*** in the edit buffer

- ***CnfEdit***—confirm the editing process
- ***LActTm***—last activation time that identifies when the last service ***SelectActiveSG*** has been processed.

This data is used to manage settings using six services, as illustrated in the UML Use Case Diagram of Figure 9.49.

The following descriptions apply to these services:

- ***SelectActiveSG***—select which ***SG*** shall become the active ***SG***
- ***SelectEditSG***—select which ***SG*** shall become the ***SG*** that can be edited after selecting
- ***SetSGValues***—write values to the ***SG*** that has been selected for editing
- ***ConfirmEditSGValues***—confirm that the new values to the ***SG*** that has been selected for editing become the values of the ***SG***
- ***SetSGValues***—read values from the ***SG*** that has been selected for editing (***FC=SE***) or of the active ***SG*** (***FC=SG***)
- ***GetGCBValues***—read all attribute values of the ***SGBD***.

To use these services, clients can select a combination of the following parameters:

- ***SGCBReference***–contains the ***ObjectReference LDName/LLN0.SGCB***
- ***Response+***—indicates that the service request succeeded
- ***Response-***—indicates that the service request failed
- ***FunctionalConstraint***—contains the value of the functional constraint parameter to identify the functional constraint of the respective attribute of ***SGCB*** contained in the ***LLN0***. The value shall be ***SP***.

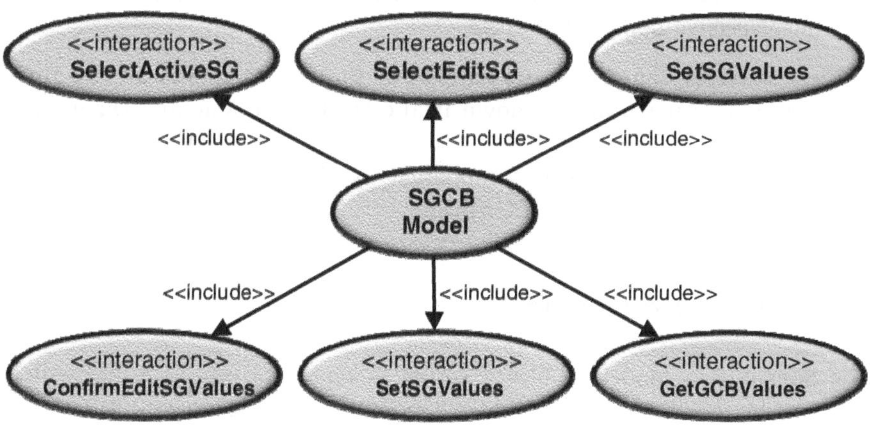

Figure 9.49 Setting model use cases.

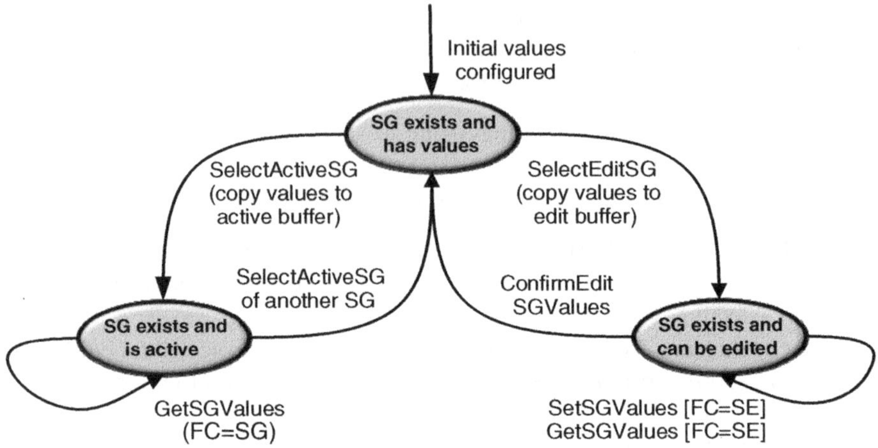

Figure 9.50 Setting group state machine.

- ***Reference***-—specifies the functionally constrained data (***FCD***) or functionally constrained data attributes (***FCDA***) of the ***DATA*** whose ***DataAttribute*** values are to be retrieved. The ***Reference*** shall be ***FCD*** or ***FCDA***. The ***FC*** value of the ***FCD*** or ***FCDA*** shall be
  - ***SE*** to retrieve the values of the ***SG*** in the edit buffer; and
  - ***SG*** to retrieve the values of the active ***SG***.
- ***DataAttributeValue [1..n]***—contains the values of all ***Data Attributes*** of a ***DATA*** referenced by ***FCD***; or the value of a ***Data Attribute*** referenced by ***FCDA***.
- ***SettingGroupNumber***—specifies the number ***ActSG*** of the ***SG*** (between 1 and ***NumOfSG***) that shall be used to determine the new values of ***DATA*** of the respective ***LOGICAL-NODEs***.

These services control the transitions of the setting model among three states in a state machine, as shown in the UML State Machine Diagram of Figure 9.50.

The setting model is further supported by the services provided by the Substitution Model defined by IEC 61850.

9.13 Substitution Model

The Substitution Model enables a server to replace a process value with a value set by the client, for example, when an invalid measurement is detected. It allows replacing a process value with manually entered data. Using the

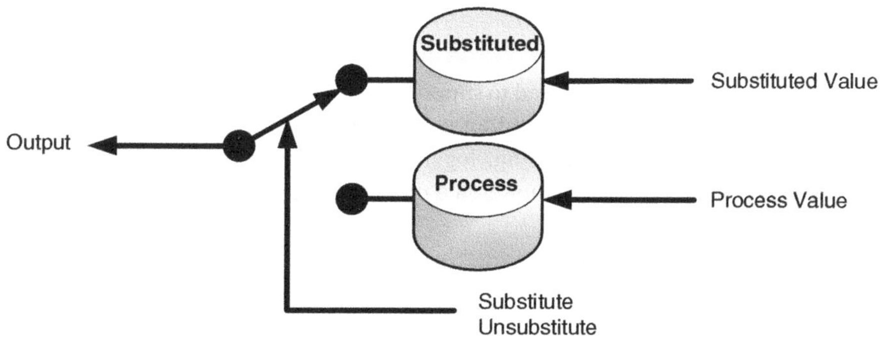

Figure 9.51 Substitution Model.

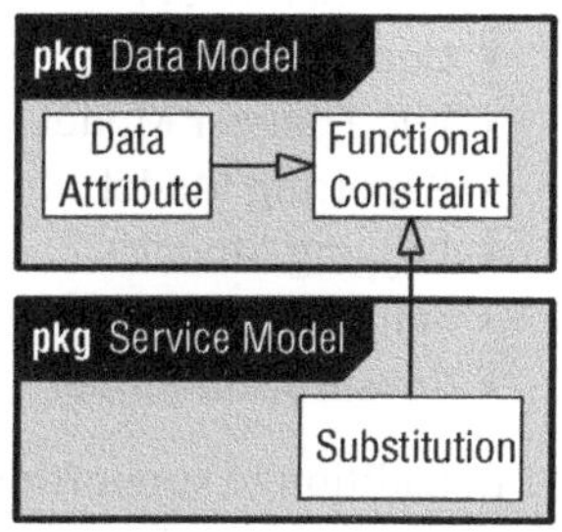

Figure 9.52 Substitution class diagram.

SetDataValues service, a client writes substitute values into the process image, implicitly including the connection monitor, and with no alternative possible. As requirements, the behavior for establishing the connection must be defined in the client, and after restarting the server, the substitute value must remain active.

The Substitution Model allows replacing values of ***DataAttributes*** whose functional constraint equals ***MX*** (for analog values) or ***ST*** (for status values). The ***DATA*** object provides the substituted values to clients instead of the process value. To achieve this, the client sets the ***DataAttribute*** to the entered value (using the service ***SetDatavalues***) so that when a client accesses the value of that ***DataAttribute***, it receives the manually entered value (substituted) instead of the value from the process, as shown in Figure 9.51.

Figure 9.52 shows the UML Class Diagram for the Substitution Model. Both classes, ***Data Attribute*** and ***Substitution***, inherit their behavior from the class ***Functional Constraints***.

The following data attributes are used in the Substitution Model class:

- ***subEna*** (enable substitution)—The current process value shall be replaced by the value provided in the ***DataAttribute subVal***.
- ***subVal***, ***subMag***, and ***subCMag*** (values for substituting process values)—The current process value shall be replaced by the value provided by the ***DataAttribute subVal***, ***subMag***, and ***subCMag***, respectively.
- ***subQ*** (value for substitution of quality)—The current process value shall be replaced by the value provided by the ***DataAttribute subQ***.
- ***subID***—Value to indicate the initiator of the substitution.

9.14 Summary

IEC 61850 service models are used to support typical engineering, operational, and maintenance requirements, including configuration settings, their substitution, association, file transfer, reporting, logging, timing, and control. This chapter introduced the main topics of the service models of IEC 61850, including:

- Abstract Services
- Association Model
- Logical Node Model
- Server Model
- Logical Node 0
- Data Set Model
- Control Model
- File Transfer Model
- Reporting Model
- Logging Model
- Setting Model
- Substitution Model

In addition to supporting the engineering, maintenance, and operation of automation systems, these services facilitate message exchange among servers and users, including remote management of ***IED*** settings. To synchronize these messages and events, the Time Model provides a specific set of services, described in Chapter 10.

9.15 Review Questions

1 Explain the purpose of the ***ACSI*** in IEC 61850. How does ***ACSI*** help separate object models from communication-specific implementations?

2 Describe the three main types of ***ACSI*** services—C/S, peer-to-peer, and time synchronization. For each category, explain which SAS operations they are best suited for and why.

3 Explain the role of the Association Model in enabling communication among IEC 61850 devices. Compare the features and typical applications of ***TPAA*** and ***Multi-Party*** application associations.

4 Using the ***Logical Node*** Model, analyze how the ***Mod*** and ***Beh*** attributes impact the behavior of protection or control functions. Provide an example of how test modes influence system operation.

5 Explain how the Server Model and ***Logical Node Zero*** (***LLN0***) facilitate device-wide configuration and supervision. What kinds of information and control functions are centralized in ***LLN0***?

6 Assess the advantages and limitations of utilizing ***Data Sets*** in IEC 61850. How do ***Data Sets*** enhance communication efficiency, and what challenges emerge in time-sensitive applications?

7 Consider a situation where a client needs to switch a high-voltage disconnector using ***SBO***. Describe the sequence of services involved and explain why ***SBO*** is necessary instead of direct control.

8 Analyze how the Control Model handles failures during command execution. Please select at least three ***AddCause*** diagnostics and describe the operational issues they relate to.

9 Discuss the main differences between ***Buffered Reporting (BRCB)*** and ***Unbuffered Reporting*** (***URCB***). How does each model impact reliability, bandwidth consumption, and suitability for different SAS applications?

10 Explain how the Logging Model guarantees reliable recording of historical events even during poor network conditions. Describe the functions of the ***LCB*** and ***LOG*** classes in handling stored events.

11 Use the Setting Model in a practical scenario where a protection relay transitions from an "urban grid" to an "islanded microgrid" configuration. What services and setting group attributes are involved in ensuring this transition occurs safely?

12 Examine the purpose of the Substitution Model and its importance during measurement failures. How does value substitution help ensure operational continuity, and what safeguards are in place to regulate its use?

10

Time Models

10.1 Introduction

As a standard for real-time information exchange in automation systems, IEC 61850 depends on an efficient timing model to sync distributed activities, messages, and events. The model requires a time-synchronization setup that supports real-time peer-to-peer communication, including a transparent clock mode for process-level exchange of discrete events, signals, commands, sampled values, and synchronous phasor data within a secure environment. It should offer a synchronized time base for applications in server and client ***Intelligent Electronic Devices (IEDs)***, with services provided by ***SCSM*** and time data shared through standardized network protocols.

10.2 Learning Objectives

This chapter outlines the primary service models in IEC 61850 for timing management, covering requirements for real-time systems, time sources, protocols, clock synchronization, and the specific ***logic nodes*** provided by IEC 61850 for time modeling and control.

10.3 Time Requirements

Among the primary requirements for real-time systems is the ability to respond to events within a prespecified time frame. This is particularly important in power system protection and automation, where the time to decide and act, such as controlling a process or stopping a dangerous condition (e.g., a short circuit), is vital and strictly required to accomplish their mission.

In distributed real-time systems, in addition to the time required for data and event processing on distributed servers, there is a need to transfer information and actions across a communication network, with precise time recording for decision-making, action, and logging. In IEC 61850, this is referred to as the event ***timestamp***, or a record of the exact instant of its occurrence. Based on these characteristics, several requirements can be listed for the time services provided by automation of real-time systems:

- The event ***timestamps*** shall be based on an existing time standard.
- The ***timestamp*** accuracy depends on the application requirements.
- Leap seconds shall be processed to adjust the mean solar time.
- The ***timestamp*** model shall allow computation of date and time.
- The ***timestamp*** shall be easily derived from commercially available sources.
- The overall time model shall allow computation of local time.
- The model of the time shall allow for half-hour offsets for local time zones.
- The time model shall indicate whether daylight saving is in effect or not.
- The ***Timestamp*** format shall last at least 100 years.
- The format shall be compact and easily manipulated by a machine.

To meet these requirements, a timing model requires an external, precise time source for the time master to synchronize distributed servers and client ***IEDs***, a time server to provide a source for substation internal time synchronization, a timestamping source, and a time management protocol to synchronize IED timestamps. The ***timestamps*** must be presented according to the chosen ***SCSM***. The following paragraph starts with a discussion of time sources available for power system automation.

10.4 Time Sources

A uniform ***timestamp*** format is required to synchronize events in real-time distributed systems. Automation systems based on IEC 61850 utilize Coordinated Universal Time (UTC), a standard established by the International Telecommunication Union (ITU) and maintained by the Bureau International des Poids et Mesures (BIPM) and the International Earth Rotation and Reference Systems Service (IERS). It originated as the basis for worldwide timekeeping and is maintained using a combination of atomic clocks and the Earth's rotation. UTC provides atomic precision, based on the vibrations of cesium atoms, which are highly stable and accurate. It occasionally adjusts using leap seconds to maintain synchronization with Earth's rotation. It is the Universal Reference for the global base time zone, with other time zones offset from it (e.g., UTC+1, UTC-5). Daylight saving time is not applied to UTC.

A ***timestamp*** in the format of UTC follows the ISO 8601 (International Standard for Date and Time Representation):

YYYY-MM-DDThh:mm:ssZ

where:

- *YYYY* represents the four-digit year
- *MM* represents the two-digit month (01–12)
- *DD* represents the two-digit day of the month (01–31)
- *T* represents the literal character T separating date and time
- *hh* represents the two-digit hour
- *mm* represents the two-digit minutes
- *ss* represents the two-digit seconds
- *Z* indicates UTC (Zulu time); means no time offset

Example: *2025-05-21T14:30:00Z* means 2:30 PM UTC on May 21, 2025.

10.5 Time Distribution

The global distribution of UTC signals for time reference is provided by satellite constellations that form part of the Global Navigation Satellite Systems (GNSS). These systems provide highly accurate timing signals, synchronized to atomic clocks onboard the satellites, which are crucial for navigation, communications, scientific research, and global timekeeping. Figure 10.1 illustrates the 253 central

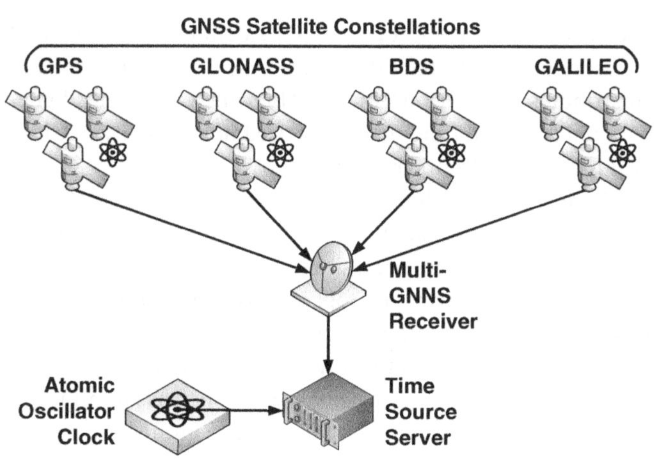

Figure 10.1 GNSS time sources.

satellite systems used as time references in GNSS, located in Medium Earth Orbit (MEO). This orbit lies between Low Earth Orbit (LEO) and Geostationary Orbit (GEO), at an altitude of ~2,000 to 35,786 km (typically around 20,000 km), with an orbital period of ~12 hours. Each constellation transmits over multiple frequency bands for additional precision, protection, and reliability to the timing system. The following is a description of the main characteristics of the constellations GPS, GNNS, BDS, and GALILEO.

Global Positioning System (GPS) is a constellation of ~30 operational satellites in MEO operated by the US Space Force from the United States. It distributes GPS time signals globally, one pulse per second with an accuracy of 1 μs, closely aligned with UTC, but does not include leap seconds. GPS time was synchronized with UTC in 1980, but has since diverged by the number of leap seconds. It is the primary timing source for telecom networks, financial systems, and power grids in the Western world, providing time with nanosecond-level accuracy.

Global Navigation Satellite System (GLONASS) is a constellation of ~24 operational satellites in MEO operated by the Russian Aerospace Forces from the Russian Federation. It distributes GLONASS time, synchronized with UTC(SU)—the Russian national UTC scale. It includes leap seconds and offers an alternative to GPS for timing in critical infrastructures.

GALILEO is a constellation of ~28 operational satellites in MEO operated by the European Union Agency for the Space Program. It distributes Galileo System Time (GST), which is steered to be close to UTC (ITU) with a fixed offset. It is maintained by European atomic clocks and synchronized with UTC through European metrology institutes, providing redundancy and enhanced accuracy when used in conjunction with GPS. It is designed to support high-precision timing and critical applications.

BDS (BeiDou) is a constellation of ~30 operational satellites in MEO, GEO, and Inclined Geosynchronous Orbit (IGSO) operated by the China Satellite Navigation Office. It distributes the BeiDou Time (BDT), which is closely aligned with UTC, the international standard time scale. It is used domestically in China and is increasingly used in the Asia-Pacific region.

GNSS satellites provide precise time signals globally, ensuring consistent synchronization across continents. Users can receive precise time without transmitting signals, enhancing security and accessibility. GNSS is a standard for telecommunications, finance, and power grid operations. Their atomic clocks (cesium, rubidium, or hydrogen maser) offer nanosecond-level timing accuracy, ensuring robust timekeeping even if some fail. However, they are not immune to failure, mainly due to antenna faults or cybersecurity threats such as jamming and spoofing. For backup purposes, an automation system can use multiple antennas, a local atomic clock, or synchronize to the Telecom backhaul time source after losing all GNSS sources.

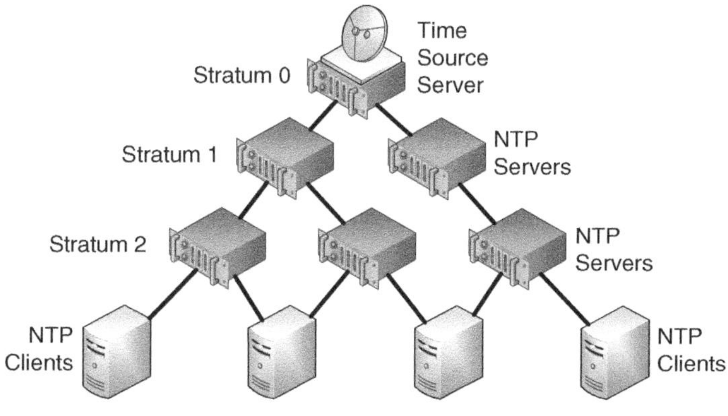

Figure 10.2 Time hierarchy.

10.6 Time Servers

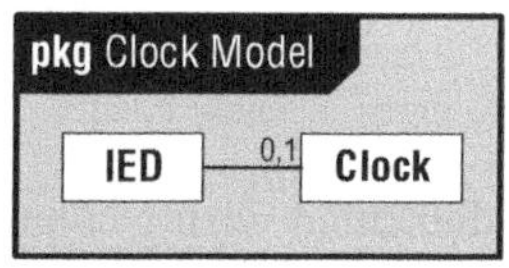

Figure 10.3 Clock model package.

Once captured by an antenna or a terrestrial clock in an automation system, time information can be distributed throughout the system via a hierarchy of time ***servers***. The high-precision source time ***server*** is at the highest stratum (0), fed by an atomic clock or GNSS clocks (Figure 10.2). Stratum 0 distributes time information to the next stratum, 1, which is formed by Network Time Protocol (NTP) servers that synchronize with the stratum 0 source ***server***. Stratum 2 is formed by NTP ***servers*** that sync with stratum 1 ***servers***, and so on. NTP clients or ***IEDs*** sync their clocks to the lowest stratum of NTP servers, using the NTP protocol.

In IEC 61850, each ***IED*** is associated with an optional internal clock to keep local time information, as shown in the UML Class Diagram in Figure 10.3.

These classes are part of the UML Class Diagram in Figure 5.5 and form the Product Model package of IEC 61850, which is part of the Strategic View on layer 2 of the general UML layered model shown in Figure 5.2. Depending on the implementation technology, ***timestamps*** can be distributed to ***IEDs*** using different time code formats.

10.7 Time Code Formats

A time protocol ensures that all systems on a network reference the same time, which is crucial for tasks such as logging events, authentication, and coordinating functions across distributed systems. The distribution of timing signals can be via

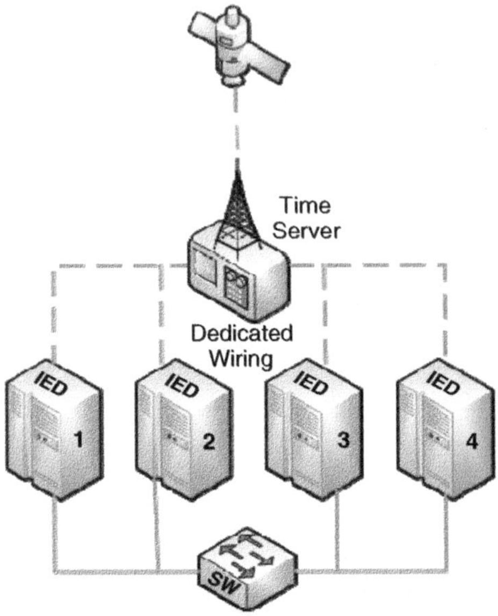

Figure 10.4 Time synchronization via dedicated wiring.

dedicated wiring (Figure 10.4) or an Ethernet network (Figure 10.5). Three protocols are commonly used to transfer time information in automation systems:

- **IRIG-B**—Inter-Range Instrumentation Group
- **NTP**—Network Time Protocol
- **PTP**—Precision Time Synchronization Protocol

IRIG-B is the most common time protocol for synchronizing servers using a coaxial or twisted-pair dedicated cable, with limited numbers of devices per output, depending on cable length and device load, and with an accuracy in the 100 μs range. GNSS can also be used, but every device needs an antenna. Today's most common architecture utilizes a GNSS receiver with an IRIG-B output, which is distributed to ***IEDs*** via a dedicated timing wire. This requires dedicated wiring, which introduces propagation delays that can affect accuracy, or serial communication such as RS232, RS422, or RS485. IRIG-B has the advantages of being simple to understand and implement, achieving microsecond precision, and being supported by many ***master clocks*** and ***IEDs***. Its disadvantages stem from the dedicated cable infrastructure required, with the total input impedance of ***IEDs*** not allowed to exceed the clock drive capability. In contrast, the ***IEDs*** and the source ***clock*** must be optically isolated to prevent ground loops. Microsecond-level time synchronization is typically achieved by distributing IRIG-B-encoded time signals or a precise one-pulse-per-second timing signal deployed as a separate network.

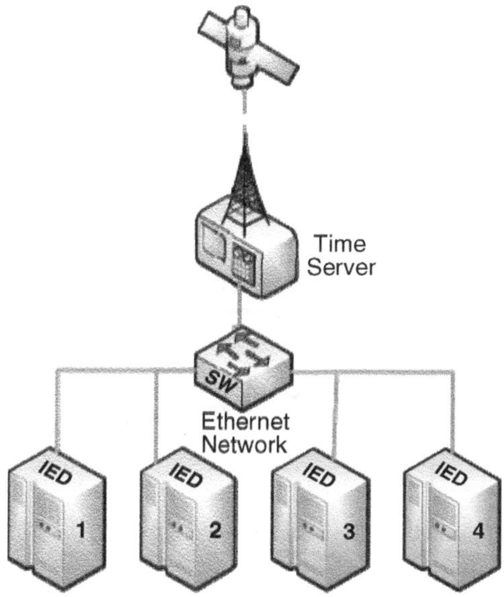

Figure 10.5 Time synchronization via Ethernet network.

Due to the stricter requirements of IEC 61850-based systems, time synchronization via Ethernet network is the preferred method for power system automation. The following paragraphs describe the two most common methods, NTP and PTP.

10.8 Network Time Protocol

NTP is the most common protocol for distributing a timing signal over Ethernet. It synchronizes ***servers*** across a local network with an accuracy of 2–3 ms, is indeterministic under heavy load, and is insufficient for IEC 61850 ***Process Bus*** and synchrophasors. Its main advantages are that it utilizes the Ethernet network, regardless of the network configuration, and does not require impedance matching or optical isolation. NTP can also use authentication (e.g., symmetric keys or network time security) to prevent tampering. But NTP time accuracy (0.1–1 ms) is insufficient for sample values (***SV***) applications, which require <1 μs accuracy.

NTP synchronization between a ***client*** and a ***server*** uses the ***timestamp*** method, as shown in the UML Sequence Diagram of Figure 10.6. NTP clients periodically contact NTP ***servers*** to calculate the offset and delay, correcting their local clocks. They use a four-***timestamp*** exchange to compute time offset and round-trip delay when interacting with an NTP ***server***:

- T_1: Time when the client sends the request
- T_2: Time when the ***server*** receives the request

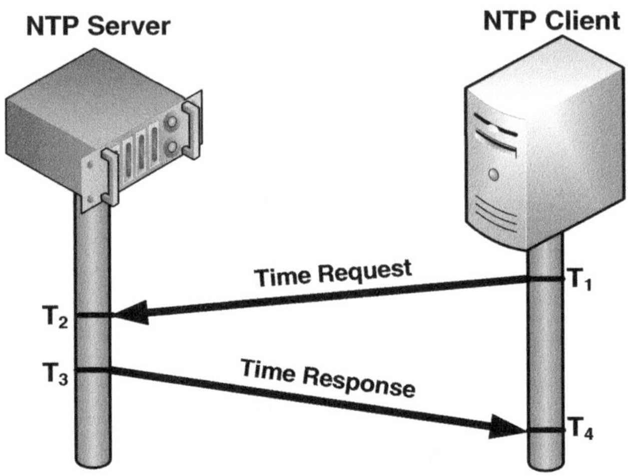

Figure 10.6 Time synchronization.

- T_3: Time when the ***server*** sends the response
- T_4: Time when the client receives the response

Timestamps T_1 and T_4 are collected locally from the client's internal clock, while the NTP server's time response provides *T*2 and *T*3 for each time request.

Using these ***timestamps***, the client can estimate the network round-trip delay by the expression:

$$d = (T_4 - T_1) + (T_3 - T_2)$$

and the offset to synchronize the local clock to the network:

$$\theta = (T_2 - T_1) + (T_3 - T_4).$$

On a Local Area Network (LAN), NTP can synchronize time to within a few milliseconds. Over the Internet, it typically achieves accuracy within tens of milliseconds, which is sufficient for most client–server interactions. A Simple Network Time Protocol (SNTP) is a reduced version of NTP, specified by IEC 61850 for simple networks with limited real-time requisites near 1 ms. For precise real-time services, PTP is the recommended protocol.

10.9 Precision Time Protocol

For IEC 61850-based real-time systems where accurate timing is essential, the IEEE 1588 (PTP) standard defines methods for synchronizing clocks across ***IEDs*** with sub-microsecond accuracy using multicast methods over standard Ethernet networks. It enables high-precision time synchronization between `IEDs` without requiring multiple GNSS receivers on the `IEDs`.

PTP can also be used to synchronize `servers` on a local network, with advanced features such as compensation for switching time and peer-to-peer propagation. This standard provides scalable time distribution over Ethernet and other networks by combining bidirectional communication with hardware-level timestamping to achieve precise clock synchronization. It can compensate for transmission medium delays and automatically elect the best master clock device. The Best Master Clock Algorithm selects the clock with the highest reported accuracy as the network's time source, based on the current grandmaster's accuracy relative to the new one.

When PTP packets traverse a network with multiple switches or routers, each hop introduces a variable network delay (due to queuing, processing, etc.), which can degrade synchronization accuracy. A `Transparent Switch` or `Transparent Clock` addresses this problem by measuring the residence time—the amount of time a PTP packet spends inside the `switch`, updating a field in the PTP packet called `correctionField`, which accumulates the delays introduced by intermediate devices (hops), passing the packet along without changing its final `timestamp`, but with the postponement accounted for. Figure 10.7 shows in a UML Sequence Diagram how PTP compensates by adjusting the internal `Slave Clock` of each `IED` (`merging unit` or `server`) in the network to the `Master Clock`, which serves as the reference time source. The reference time for the `Master Clock` may be obtained from an atomic `clock` or from a GNNS signal from another `clock` in the network

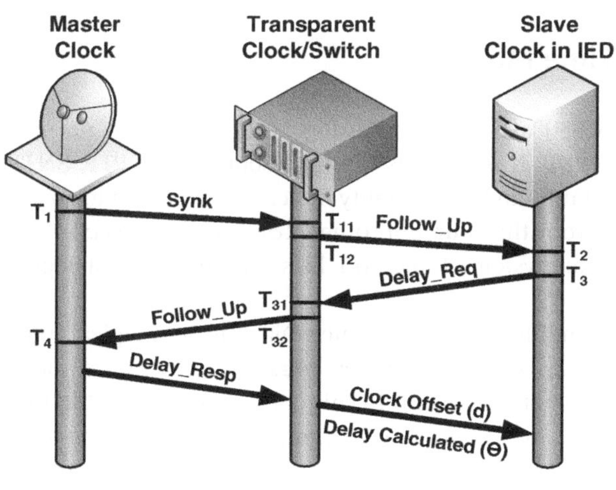

Figure 10.7 Precision time synchronization.

via NTP. The ***Slave Clock*** synchronizes with IEEE PTP messages broadcast by the ***Master Clock*** and retransmitted by transparent switches/clocks to the ***IEDs***.

To start a synchronization cycle, the ***Master Clock*** broadcasts a ***Sync*** message with the current time (T_1). Each ***Transparent Clock/Switch*** carries forward the precise ***timestamp*** of the ***Sync*** message (T_1) in a ***Follow_Up*** message to all subsequent switches and subscriber ***IEDs***, adding its internal processing delay ($CF_1 = T_{12} - T_{11}$) to the ***correctionField*** in the PTP message. Upon receipt of this message, the ***Slave Clock*** of each subscriber ***IED*** records the incoming time (T_2) and sends a ***Delay_Request*** message back to measure round-trip delay, with ***timestamp*** (T_3), received at the ***Master Clock*** at ***timestamp*** (T_4), updated by the internal processing delay ($CF_2 = T_{32} - T_{31}$) of the ***Transparent Clock/Switch*** added to the ***correctionField***. The ***Master Clock*** sends a ***Delay_Response*** message with the ***timestamp*** (T_4), allowing the ***Slave Clock*** to synchronize to the ***Master Clock***. Using these ***timestamps***, the ***Slave Clock*** can estimate the network delay by the expression:

$$d = \left[(T_2 - T_1 - CF_1) + (T_4 - T_3 - CF_2)\right]/2$$

and the offset to synchronize its internal clock to the ***Master Clock***:

$$\theta = \left[(T_2 - T_1 - CF_1) + (T_3 - T_4 + CF_2)\right]/2.$$

This mechanism allows each ***clock*** in the network to be precisely synchronized with a ***Master Clock*** for use by the IEC 61850 time model.

10.10 IEC 61850 Time Modeling

For time modeling, IEC 61850 uses mainly the logical node ***Time Source Synchronization (TSYN)***. It represents the time source (e.g., PTP, SNTP, GPS), the synchronization status, and time-quality indicators. It is used to ensure accurate time distribution from the source to other ***logical devices*** and ***nodes*** within an automation system. Table 10.1 lists the attributes of logical node ***TSYN***.

Figure 10.8 illustrates a simplified UML Sequence Diagram of a typical interaction between this ***logical node*** and ***time servers***, as well as other ***logical nodes*** in an automation system. In this configuration, an ***IED*** uses its instance of the ***TSYN logical node*** to synchronize its internal time reference with a GNSS Clock signal distributed by a ***Time Server***. An example of a ***logical node (LN)*** class uses ***TSYN*** to timestamp critical events, such as

Table 10.1 TSYN class attributes.

TSYN Logical Node				
Attribute	**Type**	**Explanation**	**T**	**M/O**
Common to all LNs				
NamPlt	*LPL*	Nameplate information		*M*
Beh	*ENS*	Behavior mode	*d*	*M*
Health	*ENS*	Health status	*d*	*M*
Mod	*ENC*	Mode control	*d*	*M*
Loc	*SPS*	Local/remote control selection	*d*	*O*
LocKey	*SPC*	Local control key	*d*	*O*
Optional Logical Node Information				
Proxy	*SPS*	Proxy indication	*d*	*O*
SboClass	*SPS*	SBO class indication	*d*	*O*
Plt	*LPL*	Additional nameplate information	-	*O*
OpCnt	*INS*	Operation count	*du*	*O*
Data Sets (see IEC 61850-7-2)				
t	*TS*	Timestamp of last synchronization	*q, t*	*M*
q	*Quality*	Quality of synchronized time	*q*	*M*
stVal	*ENS*	Current synchronization status	*d*	*M*
SynSta	*ENS*	Synchronization status	*d*	*M*
TmsStat	*ENS*	Time master status	*d*	*O*
NtpSrc	*ING*	NTP source identification	*d*	*O*
LeapSec	*ENS*	Leap second information	*d*	*O*
SynFail	*SPS*	Synchronization failure indicator	*d*	*O*
SynMode	*ENS*	Synchronization mode	*d*	*O*

circuit breaker operations or fault detection, facilitating event correlation across multiple devices.

In this configuration, the GNSS Clock sends a time signal to a ***Time Server*** that synchronizes with the GNSS signal and maintains the reference time. The ***IEDs*** in the automation system use Simple Network Time Protocol (SNTP) for

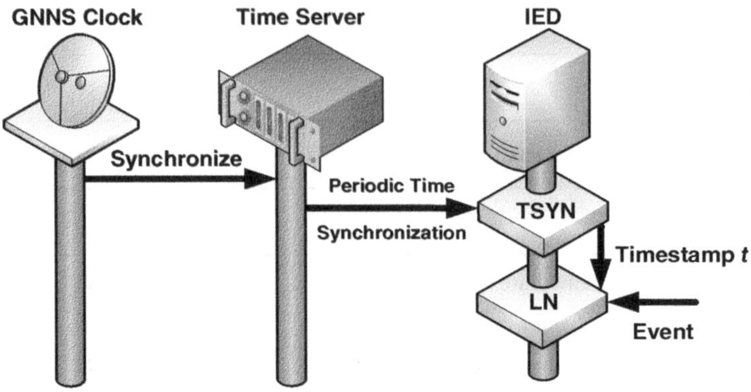

Figure 10.8 Time modeling.

network-based synchronization to the ***Time Server***. Each ***IED*** contains a ***TSYN logical node*** with the ***NtpSrc*** attribute configured to GNSS as the synchronization source. During operation, the attribute ***SynSta*** shows the synchronization status as "synchronized." The ***Time Server*** broadcasts time updates periodically to all subscribing ***IEDs***, allowing them to adjust their internal time references accordingly. Meanwhile, the logical node ***TSYN*** monitors the status and accuracy of these updates. When an event related to a ***logical node*** occurs, such as a breaker operation or a fault detection, the ***IED*** uses the ***TSYN*** attribute t to record the exact timestamp of the event and the attribute q to determine the timestamp's quality. ***IEDs*** can send this data over ***GOOSE*** or ***SV*** messages for real-time processing.

10.11 Summary

Precision time synchronization is a mandatory requirement for distributed real-time systems. IEC 61850 provides time models and services to distribute ***timestamp*** information to distributed ***IEDs*** in power system automation. This chapter introduced the main topics related to the time models of IEC 61850, including:

- **Time Requirements**—for real-time automation systems
- **Time Sources**—for precise sources of clock signals
- **Time Distribution**—for broadcasting clock signals
- **Time Servers**—for providing synchronized local clocks
- **Time Code Formats**—for transmitting precise time information
- **Network Time Protocol**—for synchronizing events using a network

- **Precision Time Protocol**—for distributing precise clock signals to ***IEDs***
- **IEC 61850 Time Models**—for managing time-related attributes

In addition to supporting the engineering, maintenance, and operation of automation systems, these time services facilitate information exchange in IEC 61850-based systems, following the message models introduced in Chapter 11.

10.12 Review Questions

1 Identify the key requirements for timestamps in distributed real-time systems according to IEC 61850. Which features ensure that time information is accurate, reliable, and interoperable across ***IEDs***?

2 Explain why UTC is used as the universal reference in IEC 61850 automation systems. Discuss how leap seconds, offsets, and the ISO 8601 format support consistent event representation.

3 Compare the timing characteristics, strengths, and limitations of IRIG-B, NTP, and PTP when used in IEC 61850 substations. When would each method be suitable or inadequate?

4 A utility needs to deploy ***Sampled Values*** (***SV***) over a ***Process Bus*** that requires sub-microsecond accuracy. Choose the appropriate time synchronization method and explain your choice based on protocol behavior and network architecture.

5 Explain the function of time servers and the hierarchy of strata in distributing synchronized time. How do devices at Stratum 0, 1, and 2 interact to keep accurate time across an automation system?

6 Assess the impact of GNSS vulnerabilities—such as jamming, spoofing, or antenna failure—on time synchronization in substations. Explore engineering methods for ensuring reliable time service in these conditions.

7 Summarize the information exchanged during the NTP four-timestamp method (T1–T4). How are delay and clock offset calculated from these timestamps?

8 Explain how do transparent clocks in PTP improve synchronization accuracy compared to standard Ethernet switches? What is the role of the ***correctionField*** in this process?

9 Consider a scenario where two protection ***IEDs*** need to synchronize fault events with millisecond accuracy. Explain how the ***TSYN*** logical node supports this requirement and how the quality of timestamps is communicated.

10 Compare the suitability of NTP and PTP for station-bus versus process-bus applications. How do bandwidth, latency, and determinism affect protocol choice?

11 In a mixed-vendor substation, one ***IED*** reports inconsistent timestamps despite receiving ***SNTP*** updates. Propose a systematic approach to diagnose and fix the synchronization problem using concepts from the chapter.

12 Explain how the IEC 61850 time model combines physical time sources, network protocols, and ***TSYN*** **`logical`** ***node*** attributes into a unified framework. How does this integration enhance support for distributed protection, event logging, and operator functions?

11

Message Models

11.1 Introduction

Data must be exchanged between servers and ***Intelligent Electronic Devices (IEDs)*** to perform the functions outlined in a Substation Automation System (SAS), as well as the wide-area functions necessary among substations. This data should be transmitted in messages supported by the current middleware, mapped to the resources provided by IEC 61850. To support both real-time and asynchronous communication in an SAS, the IEC 61850 standard offers several message models for data exchange and enabling functionality in equipment models.

11.2 Learning Objectives

This chapter introduces the primary message models defined by IEC 61850, including message types used for direct peer-to-peer rapid data transfer and client–server communication within and between digital installations. These include the ***Generic Substation Event*** (***GSE***) message, the ***Generic Object-Oriented Substation Event*** (***GOOSE***) message, the ***Generic Substation State Event*** (***GSSE***) message, and the ***Sampled Value*** (***SV***) message models, with their routable versions (***R-GOOSE*** and ***R-SV***). For easy reference, the chapter summary features a comparison table with recommendations on the main types and applications of IEC 61850 messages, as well as service selection.

11.3 Message Types

IEC 61850 classifies messages into six types based on performance classes and transfer times required by substation automation applications for protection, control, metering, and power quality. The end-to-end delay in transferring and

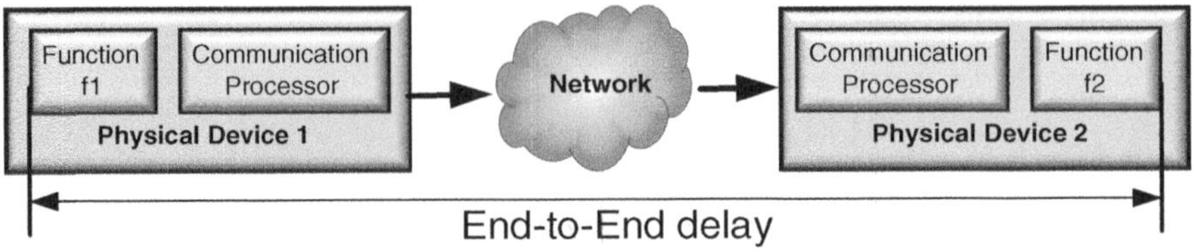

Figure 11.1 Message transfer time.

processing a message between two physical devices includes delays in each device's functions, the communication processor, and the physical transfer of the message across a network, as shown in Figure 11.1.

According to their intended application, messages are classified by IEC 61850 into six classes, gathered in two main groups:

- **Control and protection**
  - Class ***P1*** typically applies to a distribution bay or bays where low requirements can be accepted.
  - Class ***P2*** typically applies to a transmission bay, or if not otherwise specified by the customer.
  - Class ***P3*** typically applies to a transmission bay with top performance synchronizing features and breaker differential.
- **Metering and power quality**
  - Class ***M1*** refers to revenue metering with accuracy class 0.5 and 0.2 and up to the 5th harmonic.
  - Class ***M2*** refers to revenue metering with accuracy class 0.2 and 0.1 up to the 13th harmonic.
  - Class ***M3*** refers to quality metering up to the 40th harmonic.

Table 11.1 summarizes the data types transmitted by messages of class ***P*** (Protection and Control), with their transmission time, resolution, and rate frequency.

Table 11.2 summarizes the data types transmitted by messages of class ***M*** (Metering and Power Quality), including their accuracy, time, harmonics, resolution, and rate frequency.

In addition, IEC 61850 classifies messages into six types, according to performance level:

- **Type 1**—Fast messages
- **Type 2**—Medium-speed messages
- **Type 3**—Low-speed messages
- **Type 4**—Raw data messages
- **Type 5**—File transfer functions

Table 11.1 Raw data for protection and control messages.

Data type	Class	Transmission time (ms) defined by trip time	Resolution (bits) amplitude	Rate (samples[s]) frequency
Voltage	`P1`	10.0	13	480
Current			13	
Voltage	`P2`	3.0	16	960
Current			16	
Voltage	`P3`	3.0	16	1920
Current			16	

Table 11.2 Raw data for metering messages.

Data type	Class	Accuracy classes and harmonics	Resolution (bits) amplitude	Rate (samples[s]) frequency
Voltage	`M1`	Class 0.5 (IEC 62053-22)	12	1500
Current		Class 0.2 (IEC 60044-8) Up to 5th harmonic	14	
Voltage	`M2`	Class 0.2 (IEC 62053-22)	14	4000
Current		Class 0.1 (IEC 60044-8) Up to 13th harmonic	16	
Voltage	`M3`	Class 0.1	16	12000
Current		(not defined by IEC) Up to 40th harmonic	18	

- **Type 6**—Time synchronization messages
- **Type 7**—Command messages with access control

Fast messages of Type 1 transfer simple binary code containing data, commands, or simple messages. They are further divided into two subtypes:

- **Type 1A "Trip"**
  - For Performance Class `P1`, the total transmission time shall be half a cycle. Therefore, 10 ms is defined.
  - For Performance Class `P2/3`, the total transmission time shall be below the order of a quarter of a cycle. Therefore, 3 ms is defined.
- **Type 1B "Others"**
  - For Performance Class `P1`, the total transmission time shall be less than or equal to 100 ms.

- For Performance Class ***P2/3***, the total transmission time shall be in the order of one cycle. Therefore, 20 ms is defined.

Medium-speed Type 2 messages are those in which the time of origin is essential but the transmission time is less critical. They may include a single measurand, such as an RMS value, but the total transmission time shall be less than 100 ms.

Low-speed Type 3 messages are complex and may require time tagging. They should be used for slow-speed auto-control functions, transmission of event records, reading or changing set-point values, and general presentation of system data, with a total transmission time less than 100 ms.

Row-data messages of Type 4 include the digitized output from transducers and instrument transformers, independent of the transducer technology, as well as continuous streams of synchronized data from each ***IED***, interleaved with data from other ***IEDs***.

File transfer messages of Type 5 are used to transfer large data files, such as those for recording, information, and settings. The ***DDA*** must be divided into blocks of limited length to accommodate other communication activities. Typically, ***PICOM*** bit lengths are greater than or equal to 512 bits, and transfer times are not critical. Typically, they are greater than or equal to 1000 ms. For remote access, transferring these messages typically needs some authorization.

Time synchronization messages of Type 6 are used to synchronize the internal clocks of the ***IEDs***. Depending on the purpose (time tagging of events or sampling accuracy), different classes of time synchronizing accuracy are required, typically in accordance with the functional requirements. No direct requirements for synchronization are defined, except for the resulting time accuracy of the entire system. Table 11.3 shows the standard IEC synchronizing message accuracy for control and protection events, while Table 11.4 shows the required accuracy for instrument transformers.

Command messages with Access Control of Type 7 transfer control orders from local or remote human–machine interface functions, where a higher degree of security is required. They are based on message Type 3, with additional password and/or verification procedures, and may be converted to Type 1 at the process level.

Table 11.3 Message accuracy for protection and control.

Time performance class	Accuracy (ms)	Purpose
T1	± 1	Time tagging of events
T2	± 0,1	Time tagging of zero crossings and of data for the distributed synchro check. Time tags to support point-on-wave switching.

Table 11.4 Message accuracy for instrument transformers.

Time performance class	Accuracy (µs)	Reference		Phase angle (′) 50 Hz	Phase angle (′) 60 Hz	Fault location (m)
T3	± 25	*P1*		27	32	7500
T4	± 4	*P2*	*M1*	4	5	1200
T5	± 1	*P3*	*M2/3*	1	1	300

Figure 11.2 Message models.

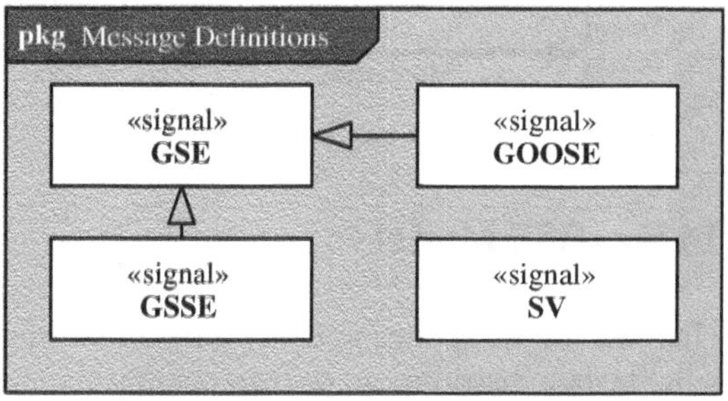

Figure 11.3 Message relations.

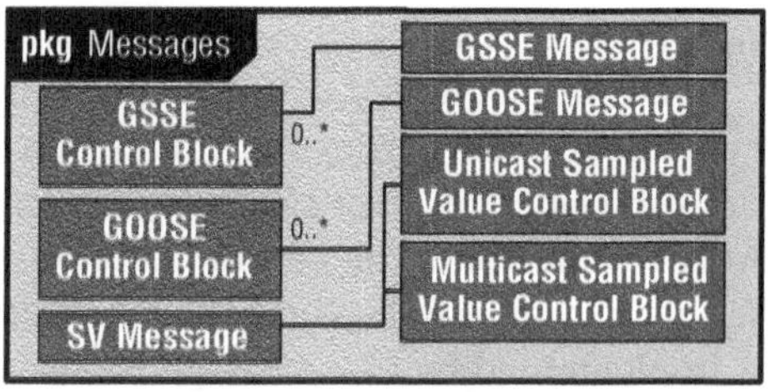

IEC 61850 messages can be further classified, based on their content and the mechanisms of generation and transmission, into six models, as illustrated in the UML Class Diagram in Figure 11.2.

- ***GSE*** model
- ***GOOSE*** model
- ***R-GOOSE*** model
- ***GSSE*** model
- ***SV*** model
- ***R-SV*** model

These messages are further related to other classes that control their functions, as shown in the UML Class Diagram of Figure 11.3.

The remaining paragraphs of this chapter describe the characteristics and applications of each message model supported by IEC 61850.

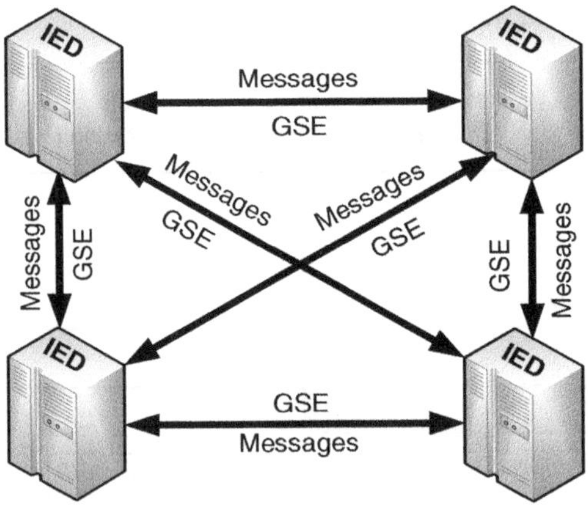

Figure 11.4 Generic Substation Event model.

11.4 GSE Model

The ***GSE*** model applies to many types of substation events. It is used for fast and reliable data distribution, peer-to-peer exchange of ***IED*** binary status, and simultaneous data distribution to multiple devices through multicast/broadcast services (Figure 11.4).

GSE is implemented using the publisher–subscriber mechanism, where the publisher/sender writes the values in a local buffer on the sending side and the subscriber/receiver reads them from a local buffer on the receiving side. At the same time, the communication/middleware system updates the subscriber's local buffers, controlled by a ***GSE*** control class in the publisher. ***GSE*** is implemented by two message services, ***GOOSE*** and ***GSSE***, discussed in the following paragraphs.

11.5 GOOSE Model

GOOSE stands for ***Generic Object-Oriented Substation Event***. It is used for quick and reliable system-wide data distribution by peer-to-peer data exchange of object-oriented information (Figure 11.5). It supports exchanging a wide range of possible common data organized by a ***DATA-SET*** and provides flexible means to specify which information will be exchanged.

A ***GOOSE*** model is implemented by specialized communication mapping to achieve performance, reliability, and multi-peer data exchange. It replaces hardwired ***IED*** input and output connections with ***IED*** multicasting ***GOOSE*** messages across a network, where subscribers receive ***GOOSE*** messages and take appropriate actions. Typical applications include transfer tripping and interlocking in

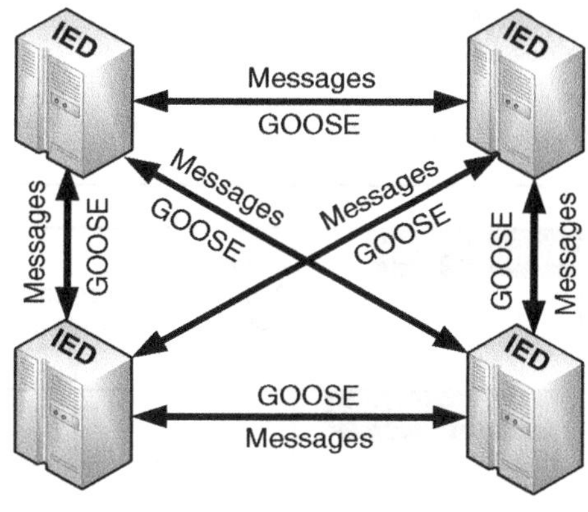

Figure 11.5 GOOSE model.

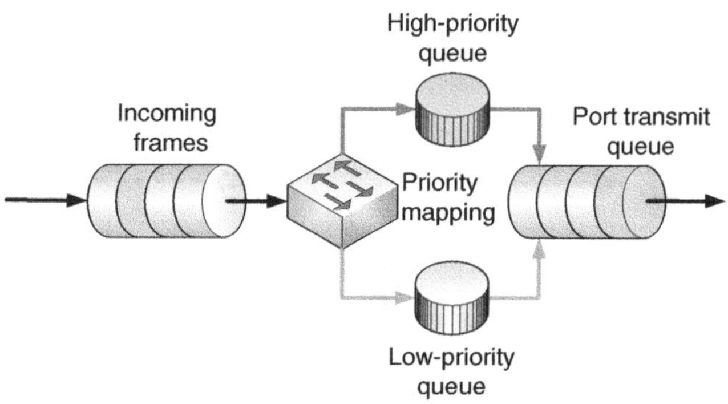

Figure 11.6 GOOSE message inside the switch.

substations. On any monitored state change, an ***IED*** can multicast a high-speed, binary object in a ***GOOSE*** report, typically containing the double command state of each of its status inputs, starters, output elements, and relays, actual and virtual.

The ***GOOSE*** model enables cyclical/spontaneous, real-time, and event-driven multicast (one-to-many) transmission of datasets without requiring acknowledgment of receipt from the subscriber server. It results in fast transmission because it is mapped directly to the link layer (Ethernet) of the ISO stack, is prioritized in switches via VLAN (Figure 11.6), and is configured via ***SCL*** (***Substation Configuration Language***) based on predefined ***datasets***. As a disadvantage, it lacks direct connection monitoring, which makes debugging and monitoring more challenging. Additionally, it requires a strict engineering discipline and offers no upper layer benefits. Data backup evaluation must be performed in the application.

Its main advantages include reduced wiring, simplified engineering, and shorter installation and commissioning times. Additionally, there is a decrease in I/Os on the ***IEDs***, resulting in reduced metal and implementation costs.

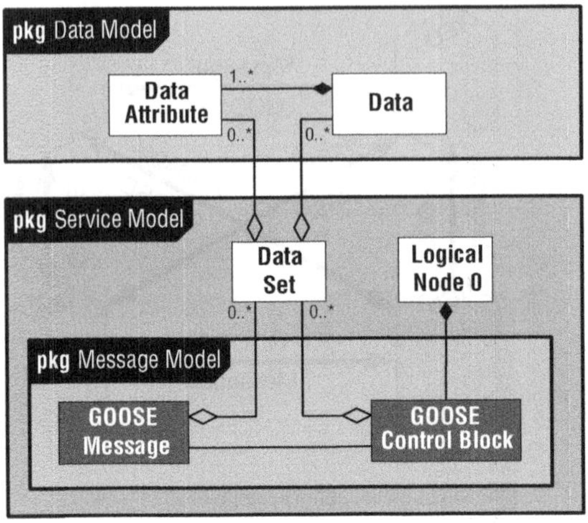

Figure 11.7 GOOSE model classes.

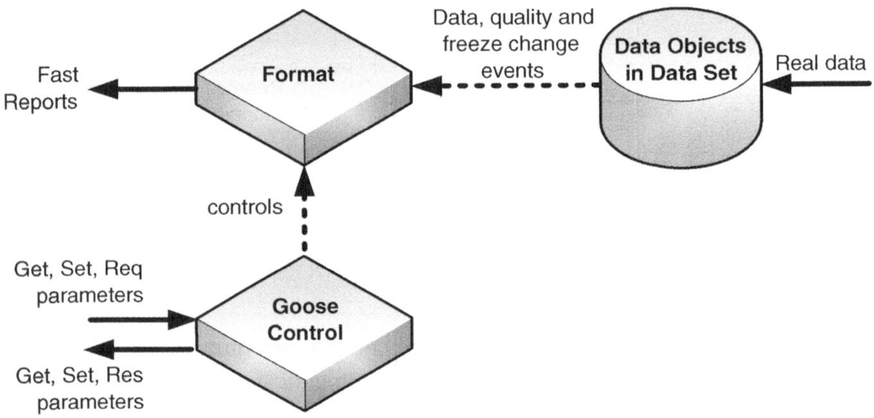

Figure 11.8 GOOSE model components.

The system also offers simplified testing, communication supervision, and redundant-channel support. The message content is defined using a configurable ***dataset***, and the configuration can be performed either online (via MMS services) or offline (via XML).

The ***GOOSE*** model comprises two control classes: ***DataSets*** and ***GOOSE Control Blocks***, as illustrated in the UML Class Diagram in Figure 11.7.

A ***DataSet*** defines ***DataAttributes*** for the ***GOOSE*** model (Figure 9.13). When changes occur in these ***DataAttributes***, they are formatted into a ***GOOSE*** message structure and transmitted to multiple recipients. The class ***GOOSE Control Block*** (***GoCB***) controls and regulates the publishing of ***GOOSE*** messages, subject to one of three conditions in the ***IED*** server (Figure 11.8):

- **Data change**
  - Triggered by a change in the value of a ***DataAttribute*** representing process-related data
  - The data-change trigger option (***TrgOp*** = ***dchg***) signifies such a change
- **Quality change**
  - A change in quality of a ***DataAttribute*** (***TrgOp*** = ***qchg***)
- **Data update**
  - A freezing event in the value of a ***DataAttribute*** (***TrgOp dupd***)
  - A change or update in the value of a ***DataAttribute*** with the same value as before, representing a freezing event

In addition to publishing fast events, ***GOOSE*** messages are also used to convey continuous messages to update new or returning subscribers who need to determine quickly the state of ***GOOSE*** values to which they were subscribed, to mimic continuous connections among ***IEDs***, to allow quick updates of logic and substation status, and to self-monitor the LAN. For example, if expected messages are missing from any subscriber, it triggers an alarm for maintenance attention. Figure 11.9 shows a UML Sequence Diagram of repeated ***GOOSE*** messages before and after an event or data change in the ***DATASET*** defined in the ***GOOSE***

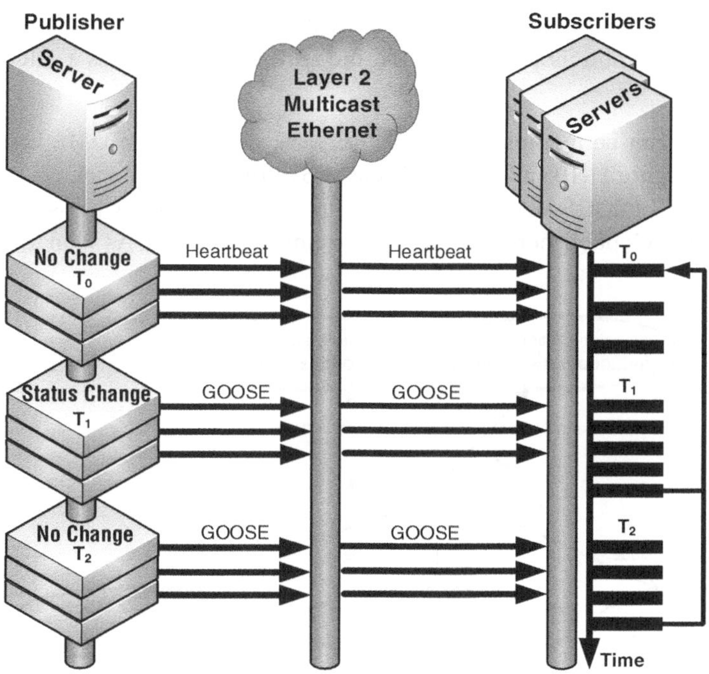

Figure 11.9 Time-critical communication with GOOSE.

Control Block. There is no acknowledgment from the subscribers. **GOOSE** messages start immediately and repeat at a short interval of T_1. The interval will increase (either rapidly or slowly) to a heartbeat interval T_0, optionally slowing to an intermediate, adjustable interval T_2, so that $T_0 > T_2 > T_1$. The heartbeat is a periodic short message published to allow subscribers to check the communication medium without relying on **GOOSE** events.

To orchestrate this model, a **GOOSE Control Block** (**GoCB**) class has the following attributes:

- **GoCBName**—**GOOSE** control name—unambiguously identify a **GoCB** within the scope of a **LLN0**
- **GoCBRef**—**GOOSE** control reference—unique pathname of a **GoCB** within the **LLN0**
- **GoEna**—**GOOSE** enable (if set to **TRUE**) indicates that the **GoCB** can send **GOOSE** messages
- **AppID**—application identification—visible string that represents a **LOGICAL-DEVICE** in which the **GoCB** is located
- **DatSet**—data set reference—represents the reference of the **DATA-SET** whose values of members shall be transmitted
- **ConfRev**—configuration revision—count of the number of times that the configuration of the **DATA-SET** referenced by **DatSet** has been changed
- **NdsCom**—needs commissioning–**TRUE** if the attribute **DatSet** has a value of **NULL**

These attributes can be manipulated by the services shown in the UML Use Case Diagram in Figure 11.10 and listed in Table 11.5 of the **GOOSE** model.

Servers use the SendGOOSEMessage Service to multicast **GOOSE** messages using the middleware's publisher/subscriber communication model. As soon as a

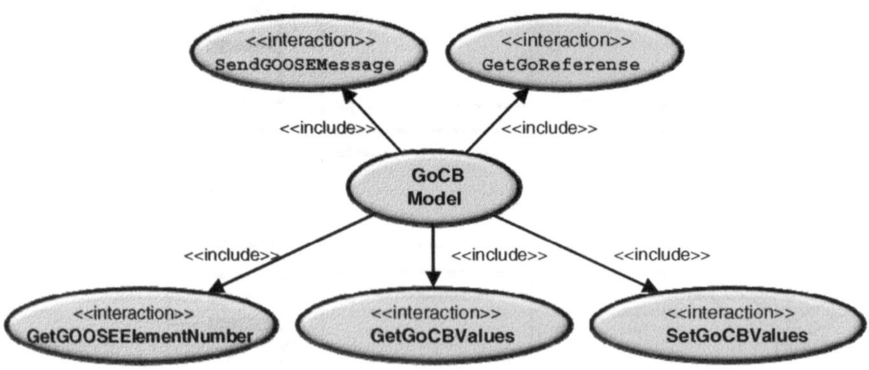

Figure 11.10 GoCB model use cases.

Table 11.5 GoCB service definitions.

Service	Description
SendGOOSEMessage	Send *GOOSE* message
GetGoReference	Retrieve the *FCD/FCDA* of a specific member of *DATA-SET* associated with the *GOOSE* message
GetGOOSEElementNumber	Retrieve the position of the member in the *DATA-SET* associated with the *GOOSE* message of an *FCD/FCDA*
GetGoCBValues	Retrieve the attributes of a *GoCB*
SetGoCBValues	Write the attributes of a *GoCB*

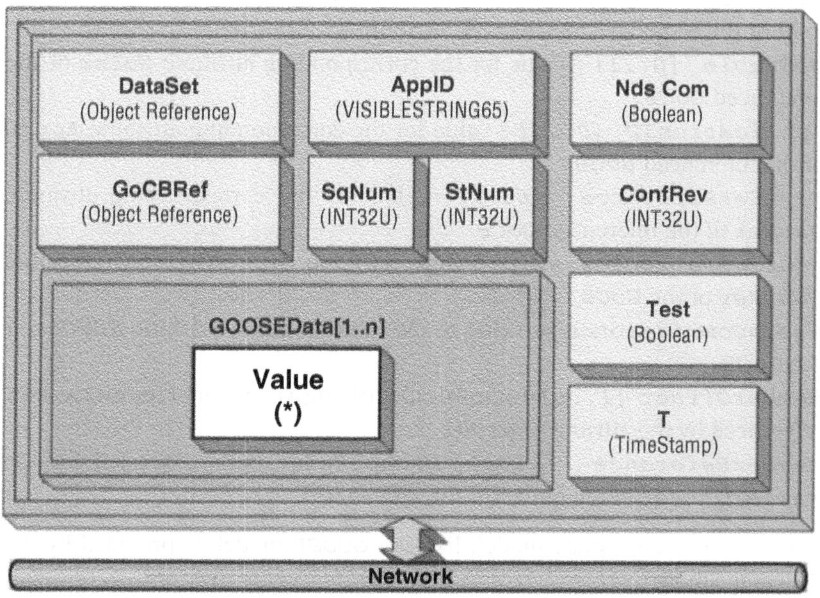

Figure 11.11 GOOSE message composition.

GOOSE message is triggered on the server, this service is called to forward it to the network, using the *GOOSE* message as a parameter. Figure 11.11 shows the internal composition of a *GOOSE* message, where the following components are identified:

- *AppID*—identifier of the *LD*
- *DatSet*—*DataSetReference* of the *DataSet* to be transmitted
- *ConfRev*—number of times the *DataSet* has been changed

- ***SqNum***—the sequence number of each ***GOOSE*** generated by this ***GoCB***
- ***StNum***—counter number of ***GOOSE*** messages sent by changes in a DataAttribute within the referenced ***DataSet***
- ***GoCBRef—ObjectReference*** of the ***GoCB***
- ***T***—time when the ***StNum*** was incremented
- ***Test***—if ***TRUE***, indicates not to use for operational purposes
- ***NdsCom***—indicates ***GoCB*** needs commissioning
- ***GOOSEData [1...n]***—values of the ***DataAttribute*** of ***DataSet***

A suitable selection of the following parameters defines the remaining services of the ***GOOSE*** model:

- ***GoCBReference***—value of the ***ObjectReference*** of the ***GoCB***
- ***FunctionalConstraint***—value of the functional constraint parameter to filter the respective instances of attributes of a ***GoCB***
- ***GoEnable [0..1]***—value for the corresponding attribute ***GoEna*** of the referenced ***GoCB***
- ***ApplicationID [0..1]***—value for the corresponding attribute ***AppID*** of the referenced ***GoCB***
- ***DataSetReference [0..1]***—value for the corresponding attribute ***DatSet*** of the referenced ***GoCB***
- ***ConfigurationRevision***—value of the corresponding attribute ***ConfRev*** of the ***GoCB***
- ***NeedsCommissioning***—value of the corresponding attribute ***NdsCom*** of the ***GoCB***
- ***MemberOffset [1..n]***—number identifying a member of the ***DATA-SET*** referenced by the attribute ***DatSet***
- ***MemberReference [1..n]—MemberReference*** requested for the ***MemberOffset*** of a member of the ***DATA-SET***

A more restrictive message model, like the ***GOOSE*** model, is provided by the ***GSSE*** Message model.

11.6 GSSE Model

GSSE stands for ***Generic Substation State Event***. It provides the capability to convey state change information (bit pairs) as a simple list of status and to exchange status information in bit pairs (Figure 11.12).

The ***GSSE*** model enables rapid, reliable system-wide data distribution via peer-to-peer exchange of binary status information. It differs from the ***GOOSE*** model by restricting the contained data to several double-command (bit-pair) status values,

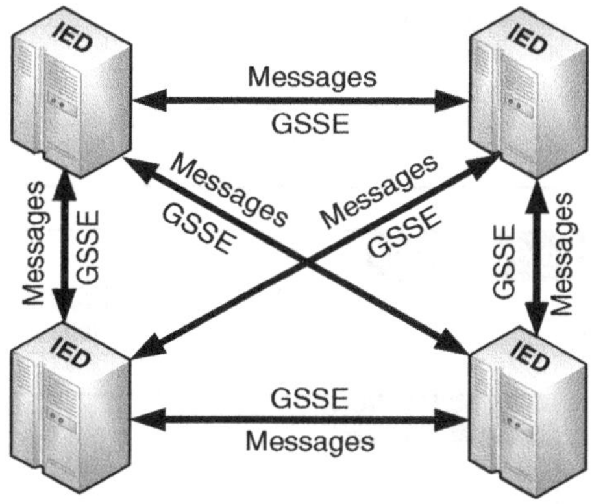

Figure 11.12 GSSE model.

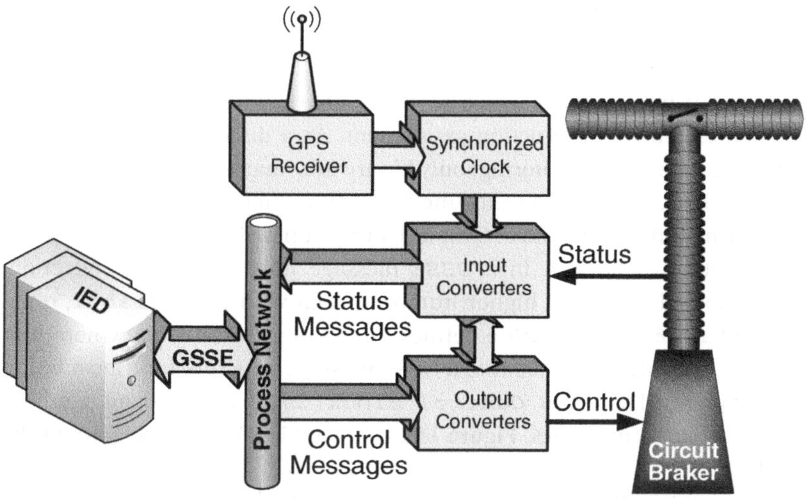

Figure 11.13 Architecture of a control unit.

such as open, closed, in transition, or invalid states. Typical applications of the ***GSSE*** model include the communication of status and command messages to and from switchgear equipment using a ***control unit***, as shown in Figure 11.13. A ***control unit*** is an ***IED*** that converts electrical commands or switchgear status into ***GSSE*** messages. As such, they can be used to control and monitor transformer tap changers, disconnecting switches, circuit breakers, and related equipment.

GSSE messages are cyclical/spontaneous multicast transmission of binary information as bit pairs without receipt acknowledgment. It leverages fast transmission by being mapped directly to the link layer of the OSI model, prioritized

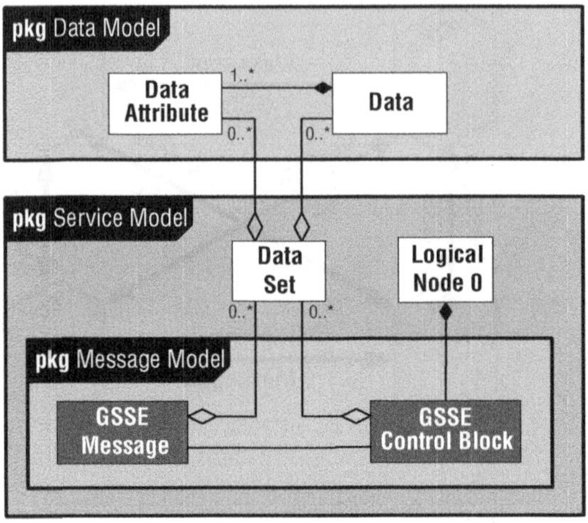

Figure 11.14 GSSE model classes.

according to user priority as specified in IEEE 802.1Q, and configured via ***IED*** name, bit-pair number, and function assignment. As a disadvantage, it does not provide direct connection monitoring; only binary information can be transmitted, with no quality byte, and it is not well-suited for substation interlocking because no two-pole information is transmitted. Simple data backup is also done using bit pairs.

The information to be sent in a ***GSSE*** message must be a data collection, uniquely numbered from 1 to higher numbers, each with a ***DataLabel***, organized in a ***DataSet***. The ***DataSet*** defines ***DataAttributes***, and when their values change, they are formatted into a GSSE message structure for transmission to several recipients. The ***GSSE Control Block*** (***GsCB***) controls and regulates the exchange of ***GSSE*** messages. Figure 11.14 shows a UML Class Diagram of the ***GSSE*** model.

The behavior of the ***GSSE*** model is almost identical to that of the ***GOOSE*** model; the only difference is the information format. ***GSSE*** only provides a simple list of status information expressed in bit pairs. The same concept of initiation and transmission of ***GOOSE*** messages applies to ***GSSE***, whose ***Control Block*** (***GsCB***) Class has the following attributes:

- ***GsCBName***—***GSSE*** control name unique within ***LLN0***
- ***GsCBRef***—***GSSE*** unique reference within ***LLN0***
- ***GsEna***—***GSSE*** enable
- ***AppID***—application identification string = ***LD***
- ***DataLabel [1..n]***—string references for each entry in ***LastSentData***
- ***LSentData [1..n]***—last sent data values

These attributes can be manipulated by the services shown in the UML Use Case Diagram of Figure 11.15 and listed in Table 11.6 from the ***GSSE*** model.

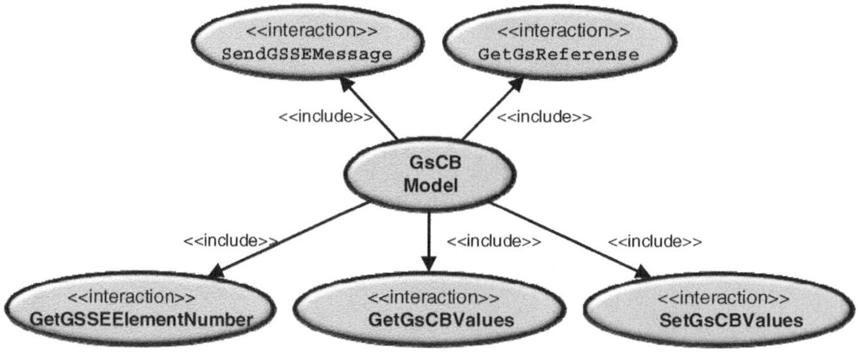

Figure 11.15 GsCB model use cases.

Table 11.6 GSSE control block services.

Service	Description
SendGSSEMessage	Send *GSSE* message
GetGsReference	Retrieve the *DataLabel* of a specific value associated with the *GSSE* message
GetGSSEElementNumber	Retrieve the position of the specific value associated with the *GSSE* message of a *DataLabel*
GetGsCBValues	Retrieve the attributes of a *GsCB*
SetGsCBValues	Write the attributes of a *GsCB*

The *SendGSSEMessage* service is used by class *GsCB* to multicast *GSSE* messages via the middleware's publisher–subscriber communication model. As soon as a *GSSE* message is triggered on the server, this service is called to forward it to the network, using the *GSSE* message as a parameter. Figure 11.16 shows the internal composition of a *GSSE* message, where the following components are identified:

- *AppID*—application identifier—identifier *LOGICAL-DEVICE* (taken from the *GsCB*) in which the *GsCB* is located
- *T*—time stamp—time at which the *StNum* attribute was incremented
- *SqNum*—sequence number—counter that shall increment each time a *GSSE* message has been sent
- *StNum*—state number—counter that increments each time a *GSSE* message is sent, and a value change is detected within the data values of *LSentData*
- *Test*—test—value of *TRUE* that the values of the message shall not be used for operational purposes

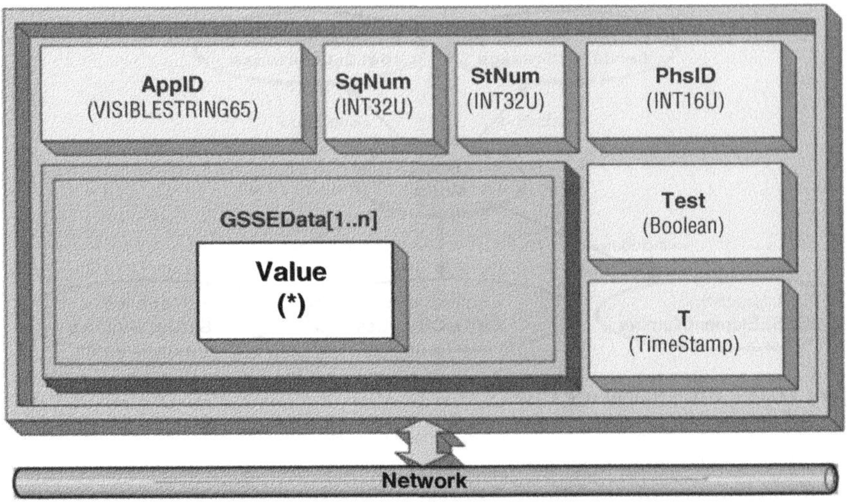

Figure 11.16 GSSE message composition.

- ***PhsID***—phase identification—faulted phases
- ***GSSEData [1..n]***—status value of four values coded as ***CODED ENUM***

A suitable selection of the following parameters defines the specific services of the ***GSSE*** model:

- ***GsCBReference***—identify the attribute ***GsCBRef*** of the ***GsCB*** for which ***DataLabels*** are being requested
- ***DataOffset [1..n]***—contains a number identifying a member of the Collection
- ***GsCBReference***—identifies the attribute ***GoCBRef*** of the ***GsCB*** for which ***DataLabels*** are returned
- ***DataLabel [1..n]***—contains the ***DataLabel*** requested for the ***Data Offset*** of the Collection
- ***Response-***—service request failed
- ***FunctionalConstraint***—contains the value of the functional constraint parameter to filter the respective instances of attributes of a ***GsCB***
- ***GsEnable***—value of the corresponding attribute ***GsEna*** of the referenced ***GsCB***
- ***ApplicationID***—value of the corresponding attribute ***AppID*** of the referenced ***GsCB***
- ***LastSentData [1..n]***—value of the attribute ***LSentData*** of the ***GsCB***
- ***Response+***—service request succeeded
- ***Response-***—service request failed.

Complementing the ***GSSE*** and ***GOOSE*** event-based models, IEC 61850 provides the ***SV*** model for the continuous transmission of ***SVs*** of analog quantities.

11.7 SV Model

SV messages are the rapid, cyclic transfer of samples of analog values from switchyard equipment, such as instrument transformers. The messages are composed of cyclical/spontaneous multicast transmission of SV information, represented as binary equivalents of analog values, without receipt acknowledgment. They result in fast transmission because they are mapped directly to the link layer of the OSI model (Figure 11.23). They are prioritized according to user priority, as specified in IEEE 802.1Q, but they do not offer direct connection monitoring. Synchronization is necessary for multiple sampled signals.

In this aspect, ***SV*** messages are very similar to ***GOOSE*** messages. Their start event is a continuous clock pulse, with a high degree of synchrony required for phasors of about 1 ms. Figure 11.17 shows how the ***SV*** model collects and publishes this data.

These messages are typically transported in a process network, near the switchyard. It provides improved services to transmit analog ***SVs***, eliminating complex wiring between ***IEDs*** and switchyard equipment. Part 9-1 of IEC 61850 specifies point-to-point transmission of ***SVs*** over serial links, while Part 9-2 specifies a multicast service over Ethernet. ***SV*** messages must have highly accurate time synchronization to support protection functions. ***Merging Units*** (***MUs***) are ***IEDs*** that provide sampling and time synchronization, serving as an interface to process buses via analog-to-digital conversion and sampling rates of up

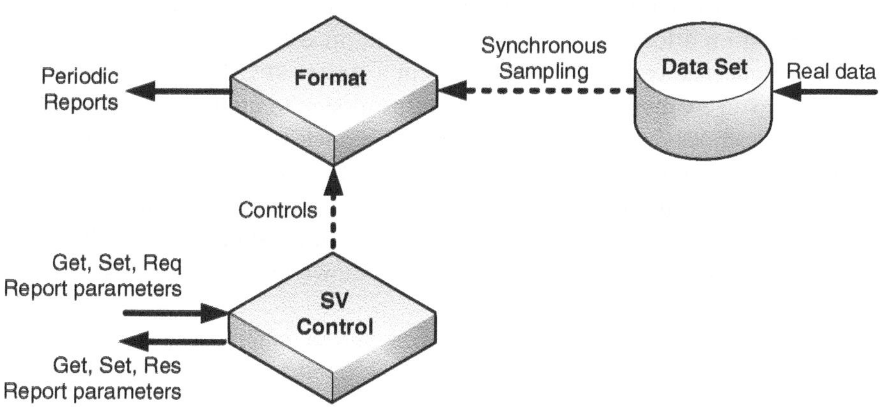

Figure 11.17 Sampled value model.

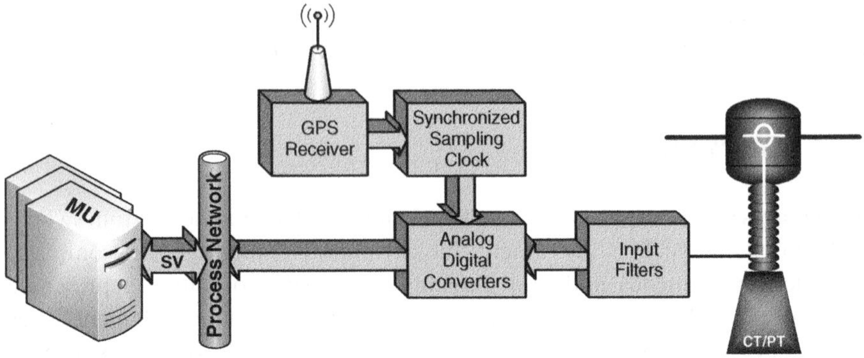

Figure 11.18 Architecture of an MU.

to 256 samples/cycle, and multicast the SV across the process network so that subscribers receive it and take appropriate action. Figure 11.18 shows the typical architecture of an ***MU***.

Many advantages are expected from using ***SV*** messages, including reduced implementation time, streamlined application development and integration, lower wiring costs, easier equipment upgrades, and the ability to migrate applications to new technologies. Additionally, ***SV*** offers a broader selection of equipment, improved availability of engineering tools, standardized naming semantics, and flexibility across current and future physical technologies. Due to the process used to transmit ***SV*** messages, there is no time for acknowledgment of receipt and repetition after loss detection, so it is expected that a few samples may be lost without impacting the function to be performed.

In addition to being used at the process level to retrieve synchronized samples, it can be used at the Bay/Unit level for Synchrocheck, and the samples can be multicast on a local network segment. Data in ***SV*** messages is of type ***CDC SAV*** and collected as ***DataAttributes*** in a ***DATA-SET***. These values are formatted into an ***SV*** message structure for transmission to multiple recipients. The exchange operates on a publisher–subscriber model, with ***timestamps*** added to the values. A ***Sampled Value Control Block*** (***SVCB***) class in the publisher controls communication and regulates the exchange of ***SV*** messages and their sample rates. These can be used to control multicast or unicast publishing, using ***MSVCB*** or ***USVCB*** blocks, respectively, as shown in the UML Class Diagram in Figure 11.19.

Multicast mode is based on the publish/subscribe communication model, in which subscribers must add themselves to the publisher's subscriber list. Each subscriber must associate with the publisher to create and configure an ***MSVCB*** class instance. So, sample multicasting is configured on the producer, and data

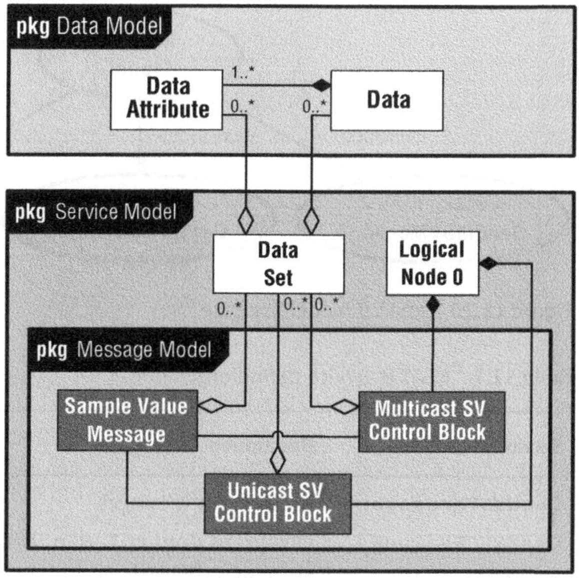

Figure 11.19 Sampled value model class diagram.

exchange is based on the ***multicast application association***. For self-descriptive capabilities, any client may read the attributes of the ***SVCB***, while authorized clients may modify the attributes of the ***SV*** control. The following attributes are part of an ***MSVCB*** class:

- ***MsvCBNam***—multicast sampled value control name—unambiguously identify a ***MSVCB*** within the scope of an ***LLN0***
- ***MsvCBRef***—multicast sampled value control reference—unique pathname of a ***MSVCB*** within an ***LLN0***
- ***SvEna—sampled value enable***—indicates that the ***MSVCB*** is currently enabled to send values of the ***MSVCB***
- ***MsvID***—multicast sampled value identifier—unique identification of the ***SV*** buffer related to updating the ***SV***
- ***DatSet***—reference of the ***DATA-SET*** whose members' values will be transmitted in the ***MSVCB*** message
- ***ConfRev***—configuration revision—count of the number of times that the configuration about the ***MSVCB*** has been changed
- ***SmpRate***—sample rate in units of samples per nominal period
- ***OptFlds***—optional fields to include in ***SV*** message—client-specified optional fields to be included in the ***SV*** message issued by this ***MSVCB***

The services offered by the ***MSVCB*** class are listed on the UML Use Case diagram in Figure 11.20 and described in Table 11.7.

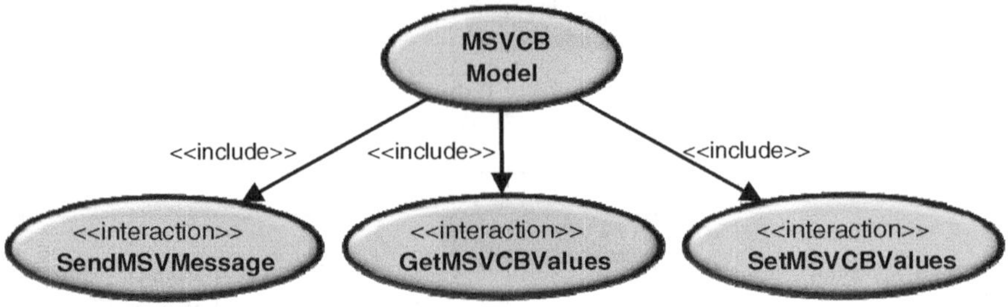

Figure 11.20 MSVCB model use case.

Table 11.7 MSVCB service definitions.

Service	Description
SendMSVMessage	Send of ***MSV*** messages
GetMSVCBValues	Obtain the ***Control Block*** (***CB***) values of ***MSV*** messages
SetMSVCBValues	Configure or modify the parameters of the ***MSVCB*** block

The ***SendMSVMessage*** service is used by an ***MSVCB*** class to multicast ***SV*** values to the client using the middleware's publisher/subscriber communication model over a ***MULTICAST-APPLICATION-ASSOCIATION***. The ***MSV*** message specifies the values of the members of the referenced ***DATA-SET*** of the ***MSVCB***, as defined in the abstract ***SV*** format. Figure 11.21 shows the internal composition of an ***MSV*** message, where the following components are identified:

- ***MsvID*** or ***UsvID***—values of the attributes ***MsvID*** or ***UsvID*** of the ***MSVCB*** or ***USVCB*** to be included in the message
- ***OptFlds***—which of the optional fields (***RefrTm***, ***SmpSynch*** and ***SmpRate***) are included in the message
- ***DatSet***—contains the ***ObjectReference*** of the ***DATA-SET*** whose values of the members are transmitted in the message
- ***Sample [1..n]***—value of ***DATA-SET*** sampled at a given time
- ***SmpCnt***—values of a counter increased for each sample
- ***RefrTm***—time when the transmission buffer was refreshed locally
- ***ConfRev***—value of the attribute ***ConfRev*** of the control block
- ***SmpSynch***—indicates whether the samples are synchronized
- ***SmpRate***—value of the attribute ***SmpRate*** of the control block

A suitable selection of the following parameters must parameterize the remaining services of the ***MSVCB*** model:

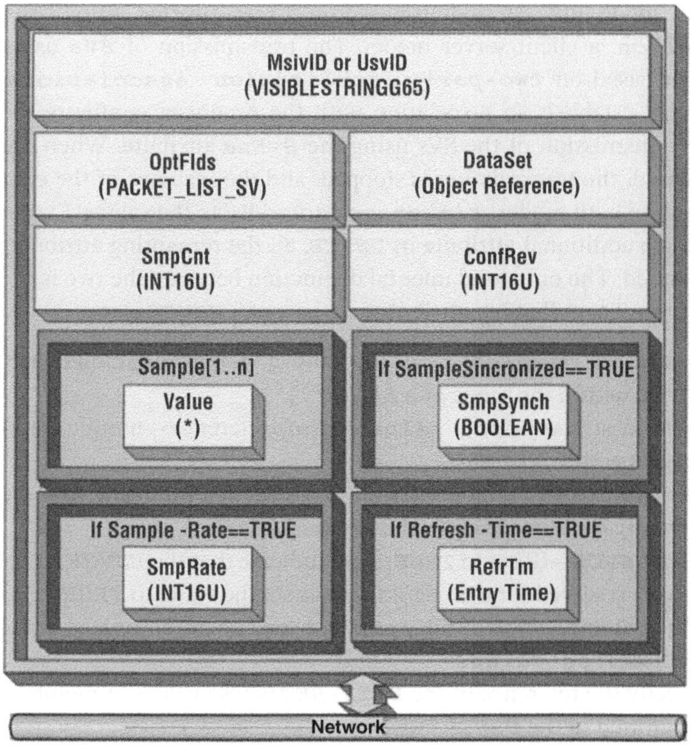

Figure 11.21 Sampled value message composition.

- ***MsvCBReference***—specifies the ***ObjectReference*** of the ***MSVCB***
- ***FunctionalConstraint***—contains the value of the ***functional constraint*** parameter to filter the respective instances of attributes of an ***MSVCB***
- ***SvEnable***—value of the corresponding attribute ***SvEna*** of the referenced ***MSVCB***
- ***MulticastSampleValueID***—value of the corresponding attribute ***MsvID*** of the referenced ***MSVCB***
- ***DataSetReference***—value of the corresponding attribute ***DatSet*** of the referenced ***MSVCB***
- ***ConfigurationRevision***—value of the corresponding attribute ***ConfRev*** of the ***MSVCB***
- ***SampleRate***—value of the corresponding attribute ***SmpRate*** of the ***MSVCB***
- ***Response+***—service request succeeded
- ***Response-***—service request failed

Unlike multicast mode, unicast mode is based on a **two-party application association**, a client/server model. The transmission of ***SVs*** using unicast (***USVCB***) is based on **two-party application associations**. The subscriber must establish an association with the producer, configure the class, and enable transmission of the SVs using the ***SvEna*** attribute. When the association is released, the transmission is stopped, and the instance of the control class is released. In both modes, ***timestamps*** are added to the values. Except for including a single additional attribute in ***USVCB***, all the remaining attributes and services are shared. The only fundamental distinction between the two is the mode of transmission. The following attributes are part of a ***USVCB*** class:

- ***UsvCBNam***—unicast **sampled value** control name—unambiguously identify a ***USVCB*** within the scope of a ***LLN0***
- ***UsvCBRef***—unicast **sampled value** control reference—unique path-name of a ***USVCB*** within a ***LLN0***
- ***SvEna***–**sampled value** enable—(if set to ***TRUE***) shall indicate that the ***USVCB*** is currently enabled to send values of the ***USVCB***
- ***Resv***—reserve ***USVCB***—(if set to ***TRUE***) shall indicate that the ***USVCB*** is currently exclusively reserved for the client that has set the value to ***TRUE***
- ***UsvID***—unique identification of the **sampled value** buffer related to the update of the **sampled values**
- ***DatSet***—specify the reference of the ***DATA-SET*** whose values of members are to be transmitted in the ***USVCB*** message
- ***ConfRev***—configuration revision—a count of the number of times that the configuration regarding the ***USVCB*** has been changed
- ***SmpRate***—specify the sample rate in units of samples per nominal period
- ***OptFlds***—optional fields to include in ***SV*** message—client-specified optional fields to be included in the ***SV*** message issued by this ***USVCB***

Similarly, these attributes can be manipulated by the services included in the UML Use Case Diagram in Figure 11.22 and listed in Table 11.8 for the ***USVCB*** class.

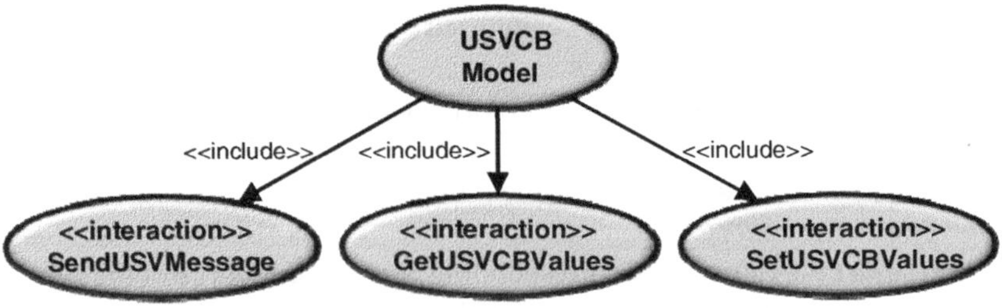

Figure 11.22 USVCB model use case.

Table 11.8 USVCB service definitions.

Service	Description
SendUSVMessage	Send of ***USV*** type messages
GetUSVCBValues	Obtain the ***Control Block*** (***CB***) values of ***USV*** messages
SetUSVCBValues	Configure or modify the parameters of the ***USVCB*** block

A ***USVCB*** uses the ***SendUSVMessage*** service to unicast ***SV*** values to the client using the publisher/subscriber communication model provided by the middleware over a ***UNICAST-APPLICATION-ASSOCIATION***. The ***USV*** message specifies the values of the members of the referenced ***DATA-SET*** of the ***USVCB*** as specified in the abstract ***SV*** format definition. A suitable selection of the following parameters must parameterize the remaining services of the ***USVCB*** model:

- ***UsvCBReference***—specifies the ***ObjectReference*** of the ***USVCB***
- ***FunctionalConstraint***—value of the functional constraint parameter to filter the respective instances of attributes of a ***USVCB***
- ***SvEnable***—value of the corresponding attribute ***SvEna*** of the referenced ***USVCB***
- ***CBReserved***—value of the corresponding attribute ***Resv*** of the referenced ***USVCB***
- ***UnicastSampleValueID***—value of the corresponding attribute ***UsvID*** of the referenced ***USVCB***
- ***DataSetReference***—value of the corresponding attribute ***DatSet*** of the referenced ***USVCB***
- ***ConfigurationRevision***—value of the corresponding attribute ***ConfRev*** of the ***USVCB***
- ***SampleRate***—value of the corresponding attribute ***SmpRate*** of the ***USVCB***.
- ***Response+***—service request succeeded
- ***Response-***—service request failed

Event-based intra-substation communication messages are processed at Layer 2 (Data) of the OSI model, and ***GOOSE*** and ***SV*** messages are dropped from the router. Their reachability is limited to a local subnet (broadcast/multicast Ethernet), requiring a Virtual Private Network (VPN) with tunnel security to extend beyond a substation's local subnet. To overcome this limitation, ***GOOSE*** and ***SV*** models were expanded to include routable ***GOOSE*** and ***SV*** messages (***R-GOOSE*** and ***R-SV***) to enable inter-substation or grid-wide fast communication.

11.8 R-GOOSE/SV Model

The ***R-GOOSE/SV*** model operates at Layer 3 (Network) of the OSI stack (Figure 11.23), but with a payload similar to local ***GOOSE*** and ***SV***, allowing messages to be routed over WANs, after being structured using Abstract Syntax One (ASN.1) at the Application layer, and coded into the Ethernet frame using some Basic Encoding Rules (BER) defined by IEC 61850, at the Presentation layer. The routable messages were created by adding a User Datagram Protocol (UDP) multicast Internet Protocol (IP) header to the original messages, which are processed at Layer 4 (Transport) of the OSI stack. They are intended to transport synchrophasor measurements, analog data, wide-area protection and control signals, and are similar in content to the ***GOOSE*** and ***SV*** messages.

The native IP at Layer 3 enables them to be processed by routers and traverse across different networks and substations, with no VPN required. It is scalable across multiple sites, covering large geographical areas. This is particularly attractive for many kinds of wide-area automation systems, such as:

- **WAMPAC**—Wide-Area Monitoring and PAC Systems
- **WAMS**—Wide-Area Measurement Systems
- **SCADA**—Supervisory Control and Data Acquisition Systems
- **RAS**—Remedial Action Systems
- **SIPS**—System Integrity Protection Schemes
- **DER**—Distributed Energy Resources

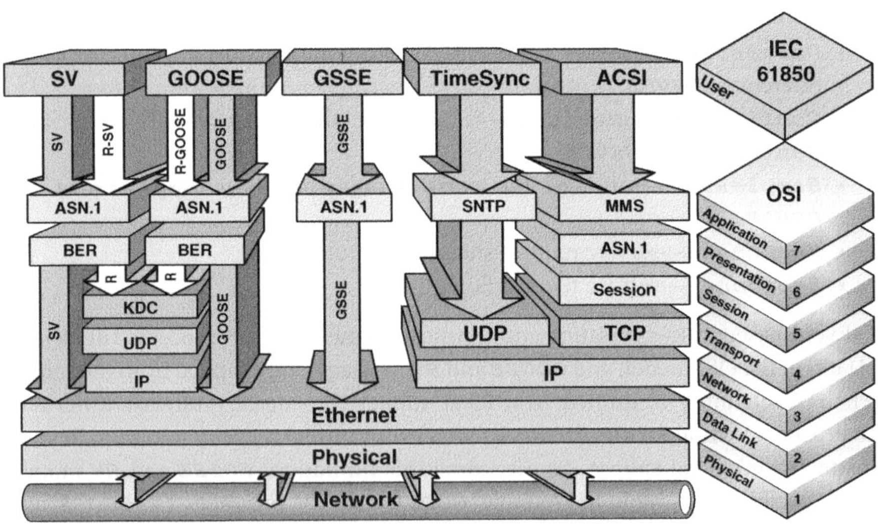

Figure 11.23 Routable GOOSE and SV messages.

Since they operate on IP networks, latency and cybersecurity must be taken into consideration. ***R-GOOSE*** and ***SV*** messages may encounter delays when routed over WANs, so proper network engineering is necessary to optimize their traffic and reduce latency. In cybersecurity, data interception (the unauthorized interception of data as it's transmitted over a network or channel) and data tampering (the deliberate modification of data in transit) are the main threats to ***R-GOOSE*** and ***SV*** messages. IEC 62351 provides policies and procedures for creating, managing, distributing, using, storing, and revoking Identity Digital Certificates (IDC) to secure the transmission of these messages (Figure 11.23). These IDCs are encrypted and authenticated by a Key Distribution Center (KDC) at Layer 5 (Session) of the OSI model (Figure 11.23). The KDC is a central component of symmetric key-based authentication systems used to secure the transmission of ***R-GOOSE*** and ***SV*** messages across a network. Its primary role is to authenticate users and services securely and to distribute temporary session keys that enable secure communication between entities. Encryption and signature offer protection against most attacks; encryption works against data interception and eavesdropping, while a signature works against data tampering. Using Advanced Encryption Standard (AES) and Hash Message Authentication Code (HMAC), KDC stores secret keys for all clients and services and issues encrypted tickets that contain client identities, session keys, and validity periods, which are readable only by the intended clients, ensuring message authenticity and integrity. This eliminates the need for each pair of servers to share individual keys, thereby reducing the risk of password exposure by using temporary tickets and enabling centralized authentication and access control across the network.

Figure 11.24 illustrates the structure of the standard ***GOOSE/SV*** messages and the ***R-GOOSE/R-SV***, as well as their relationship to the OSI stack. As can be seen, ***R-GOOSE/R-SV*** messages are longer, as they also utilize the Network, Transport, and Session layers and headers, requiring the corresponding IP, UDP/TCP, and KDC identifiers to secure transmission.

Session layer data is encapsulated in the UDP, which transports messages at the Transport layer. In the Network layer, IP is used to route and multicast ***R-GOOSE/ R-SV*** messages over a communication network. Ethernet is used for device communication at the Data Link layer. These real-time messages can also support the local and wide-area transmission of synchrophasor measurements as described in the following paragraph.

11.9 Synchrophasor Model

Phasor Measurement Units (***PMUs***) are high-precision measurement devices used in power systems to capture synchrophasors, which play a central role in wide-area automation systems listed in the previous paragraph. ***PMUs*** compute

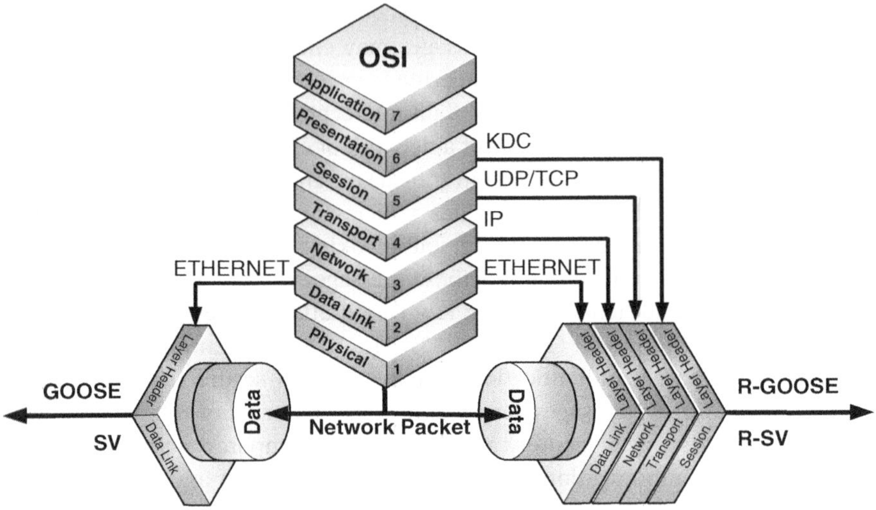

Figure 11.24 Structure of R-GOOSE/SV messages.

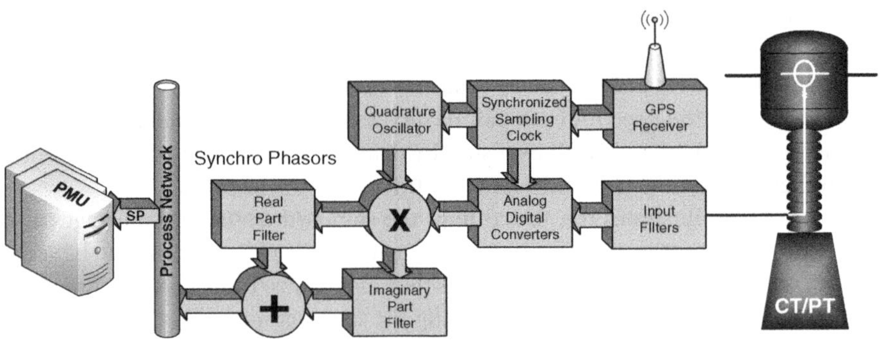

Figure 11.25 Architecture of a phasor measuring unit.

the magnitude and phase angle of voltage and current phasors using a standard time reference, providing a time-aligned picture of the power system's state. Figure 11.25 shows the typical architecture of a ***PMU***.

PMUs require low end-to-end latency to feed wide-area protection and control schemes that depend on fast, deterministic synchronized message delivery, typically at 30, 50, or 60 frames per second, as defined by the IEEE C37.118 standard. These messages are transmitted to local or remote ***Phasor Data Concentrators*** (***PDCs***) or directly to control and analytics applications.

Although IEC 61850 does not define a ***PMU*** logical node, it establishes a set of generic measuring logical nodes capable of modeling electrical quantities, such as:

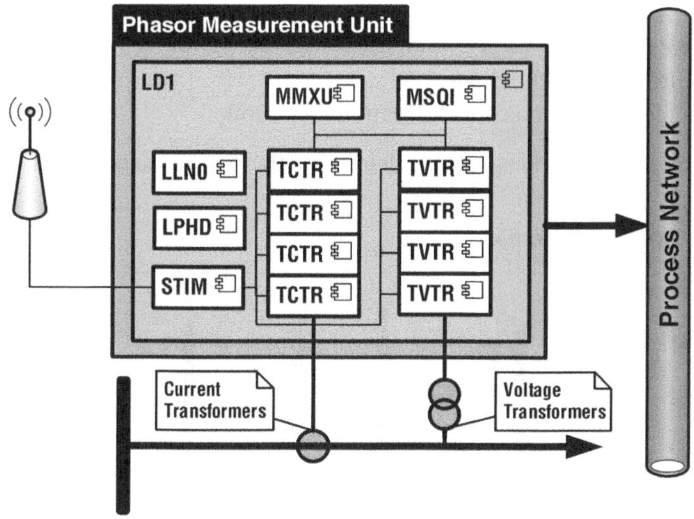

Figure 11.26 IEC 61850 PMU model.

- ***MMXU***—Measurement Unit
- ***MMTR***—Metering Unit
- ***TCYR***—Current Transformer
- ***TVTR***—Voltage Transformer
- ***MSQI***—Sequence and Imbalance

These logical nodes can be grouped into an ***IED*** to model a ***PMU***, where an instance of the ***MMXU*** logical node acts as the container for synchrophasor values, as described in the technical report IEC 61850-90-5. Figure 11.26 shows a possible ***PMU*** architecture modeled using IEC 61850.

Once modeled in the ***MMXU logical node***, synchrophasor data may be sequenced by instances of the ***MSQI logical node*** and streamed to local and wide-area ***PDC*** subscribers via ***GOOSE***, ***SV***, ***R-GOOSE***, ***R-SV***, or ***MMS***, according to the intended application requirements. It is possible to transport ***PMU***-type data within a fully IEC 61850-native infrastructure, following IEEE C37.118 format.

11.10 Summary

Selecting the best message model to use in an IEC 61850-based project should consider several criteria:

- Returning a reception acknowledgment
- Reception by several clients (multicast)

- Time-critical information exchange
- Continuous data traffic
- System load directly after the event
- Sending buffered data after a communication interruption

Table 11.9 summarizes how these criteria determine the best message model.

Table 11.9 IEC 61850 service selection.

IEC 61850 Service	Return of reception acknowledgment	Reception of several clients (multicast)	Time-critical information exchange	Continuous data traffic	System load directly after the event	Send buffered data after a communication interruption
GetDataValues (Poling per Request / Response)	Satisfied	Not satisfied	<500 ms	Low	Low	Not satisfied
SetURCBVValues / **SetBRCBValues**	Satisfied	Not satisfied	<500 ms	Low	Low	Not satisfied
Substitution per Request / Response	Satisfied	Not satisfied	≤1 s	Very low	Low	Not satisfied
Setting Group Control per Request / Response	Satisfied	Not satisfied	≤1 s	Very low	Low	Not satisfied
Control via Request / Response	Satisfied	Not satisfied	≤100 ms	Very low	Low	Not satisfied
Unbuffered Reporting	Satisfied	Not satisfied	≤100 ms	Low	Average	Not satisfied
Buffered Reporting	Satisfied	Not satisfied	≤100 ms	Low	Average	Satisfied
Logging	Not satisfied	Not satisfied	>1 s	Very low	Very high	Not satisfied
(R) GOOSE Message	Not satisfied	Satisfied	<20 ms	Average	High	Not satisfied
GSSE Message	Not satisfied	Satisfied	<20 ms	Average	High	Not satisfied
(R) SV Message	Not satisfied	Satisfied	<20 ms	Very high	Very high	Not satisfied
File Transfer	Not satisfied	Not satisfied	>1 s	Very low	Very high	Not satisfied

These criteria should be given primary consideration in the engineering models used to build IEC 61850-based systems, as described in Chapter 12.

11.11 Review Questions

1 Define the six IEC 61850 message classes (P1–P3 and M1–M3) and explain the types of data and performance requirements linked to each class.

2 Explain the differences between Type 1, Type 2, and Type 3 IEC 61850 messages. How do their timing characteristics reflect the needs of protection, control, and monitoring functions?

3 A protection ***IED*** must send a high-speed trip signal within 3 ms in a transmission-level setup. Identify which message type and performance class meet this requirement and explain your choice.

4 Compare the ***GOOSE*** and ***GSSE*** models in terms of data content, engineering complexity, and suitability for different protection and control applications. What trade-offs are involved in choosing ***GSSE*** over ***GOOSE***?

5 Explain how the publisher–subscriber mechanism facilitates ***GSE***-based communication. What functions do **DataSets** and **Control Blocks** serve in controlling event-driven message exchange?

6 Consider a substation where intermittent loss of ***GOOSE*** messages has been observed. Outline a diagnostic approach that analyzes message repetition, heartbeat intervals, and configuration attributes such as **GoEna**, **DatSet**, and **ConfRev**.

7 Explain how ***SV*** messages are different from ***GOOSE*** messages in their purpose, data features, and timing needs. Why is exact clock synchronization crucial for ***SV***-based protection functions?

8 An ***MU*** must transmit 256 samples per cycle to multiple ***IEDs*** on a **process bus**. Identify the suitable control block type (***MSVCB*** or ***USVCB***), explain the reasoning behind the choice, and discuss the effects on network traffic and system engineering.

9 Explain how ***R-GOOSE*** and ***R-SV*** enhance the capabilities of standard ***GOOSE*** and ***SV***. How do OSI layer mappings, UDP/IP encapsulation, and ASN.1/BER encoding facilitate inter-substation communication?

10 Evaluate the cybersecurity challenges linked to routable message models. How do IEC 62351 mechanisms—such as digital certificates, session keys, and authenticated encryption—protect ***R-GOOSE*** and ***R-SV*** traffic?

11 A system operator needs to transmit synchrophasor data from a ***PMU*** to a wide-area protection scheme using IEC 61850. Discuss which message models could be used (***GOOSE***, ***SV***, ***R-GOOSE***, ***R-SV***, or ***MMS***), and provide reasoning for the most appropriate choice.

12 Using the service selection criteria in Table 11.9, develop a message model strategy for a digital substation architecture that needs to support fast protection, synchronized measurements, control commands, and event reporting. Describe how each chosen model fulfills its specific functional requirement.

12

Engineering Models

12.1 Introduction

The ability to thoroughly engineer, describe, and configure an entire Substation Automation System (SAS) using an object-oriented language is a key feature of IEC 61850. The hardware independence, enabled by an open standard understandable by both humans and computers, introduces high efficiency and creates opportunities to optimize the engineering design and maintenance of these systems.

12.2 Learning Objectives

This chapter explains the configuration model and language used by IEC 61850 to specify and set up ***Intelligent Electronic Devices (IEDs)*** and SAS. It briefly describes the eXtensible Markup Language (XML) as the basis of the ***Substation Configuration Language(SCL)***, as standardized by IEC 61850, for defining system configuration and settings.

The chapter ends with a discussion of the engineering cycles for planning digital substations and how the IEC 61850 standard ***SCL*** files are incorporated into the Waterfall, V-Model, and Agile engineering frameworks.

12.3 Extensible Markup Language

XML is a standardized method developed by the World Wide Web Consortium (W3C) for representing structured information in a text file, independent of its presentation, using markup. It resembles the HyperText Markup Language (HTML), which is also supported by the W3C, but is more verbose, machine-readable, and human-readable. XML comprises a family of relatively new technologies with honorable roots. It is license-free, platform-independent, and well supported by both open and proprietary specialized tools, enabling it to be extended to meet specific needs.

An XML document is formed by its content, structure, and presentation information. Its syntax is based on the systematic use of tags, or text delimited by the characters "<" and ">," to demarcate each element of the file. Each open tag must be matched by a close tag, with the same name, preceded by a slash (/), as is shown in the definition of a "business card" in the following XML code:

```
<business_card>
    <name>
        <given_name>Iony</given_name>
        <family_name>Patriota</family_name>
    </name>
    <company>Tecnix Engineering</company>
</business_card>
```

The fundamental unit of XML content is the Element. Elements represent a tree structure, as shown in the previous code by text that is not underlined and delimited by tags. XML also allows the definition and use of attributes to the elements defined as metadata. The following code shows the addition of the attribute ***TYPE*** and its values to the element "phone" of a "business card."

```
<business_card>
    <name>
        <given_name>Iony</given_name>
        <family_name>Patriota</family_name>
    </name>
    <company>Tecnix Engenharia</company>
    <phone TYPE="Business">+55 81 32294145</phone>
    <phone TYPE="CEL">+55 81 99919907</phone>
</business_card>
```

A Document Type Definition (DTD) or an XML schema file defines element names, structure, and attribute names. A DTD file is one of several Standard Generalized Markup Language (SGML) and XML schema languages used to define the legal building blocks of an XML document. An XML schema is a description of a type of XML document, typically expressed as constraints on its structure and content beyond the basic syntactic constraints of XML. An XML schema can describe features beyond the structure of the XML document, such as value ranges or the number of times an element may appear (e.g., exactly one, at least one, etc.).

The whole structure of the language used by IEC 61850 to configure an SAS is defined by a set of XML schemas, published by IEC in the following files:

- ***SCL_Enums.xsd***—The used XML schema enumerations
- ***SCL_BaseSimpleTypes.xsd***—The basic simple types used by the other parts
- ***SCL_BaseTypes.xsd***—The basic complex type definitions used by the other parts
- ***SCL_Substation.xsd***—The Substation-related syntax definitions
- ***SCL_Communication.xsd***—The Communication-related syntax definitions
- ***SCL_IED.xsd***—The ***IED***-related syntax definitions
- ***SCL_DataTypeTemplates.xsd***—The data type template related to syntax definitions
- ***SCL.xsd***—The primary SCL schema syntax definition

These files define the syntactical conventions used by the XML-based language to specify systems based on IEC 61850, such as the following:

- Schema type names—start with the small letter "t" (e.g., ***tSubstation***)
- Attribute group definitions—start with the acronym ag (e.g., ***agAuthorization***)
- Attribute names—start with a small letter (e.g., ***name***)
- Element names—start with a capital letter (e.g., ***Substation***)

The use of XML provides a formal, unambiguous description of an automation system, including all communication links, ***IED*** capabilities, and applicable communication services, along with their relationships to the switchgear and the data used by the automation system, all of which are defined using the ***SCL***.

12.4 Substation Configuration Language

A configuration language is a file format describing configurations, parameters, communication schemes, and connections, used to exchange data between engineering tools. In IEC 61850, the ***SCL*** describes ***IED*** configurations and parameters, communication systems, switchyard (function) structures, and their relations. It is also used to exchange ***IED*** capability descriptions, ***IED*** system parameters, and automation system descriptions between engineering tools and ***IEDs*** from different manufacturers in a compatible manner.

The intended applications of ***SCL*** are to maintain consistency in distributed systems while supporting system maintenance through protection parameter handling, gateway engineering, and application configuration wizards. Additionally, it is used as a system specification in the single-line diagram, with the allocation of logical nodes (LNs), to preconfigure ***IEDs*** with a fixed number of ***LNs*** without binding to a specific process. It can be used for process configuration, with all ***IEDs*** bound to individual process functions, enhanced by access point connections and possible access paths in subnetworks for all potential clients. It can also predefine associations and client–server connections when an ***IED*** cannot dynamically build them, using a set of standardized file types.

12.5 SCL File Types

To support the full stages of the engineering cycle for the design of an automation system, IEC 61850 defines six types of ***SCL*** files, each identified with a three-letter suffix, formed by a hierarchy of XML schema files shown in Figure 12.1:

- *IED Capability Description (ICD)*
- *System Specification Description (SSD)*
- *Substation Configuration Description (SCD)*
- *Configured IED Description (CID)*
- *Instantiated IED Description (IID)*
- *Application Specification Description (ASD)*

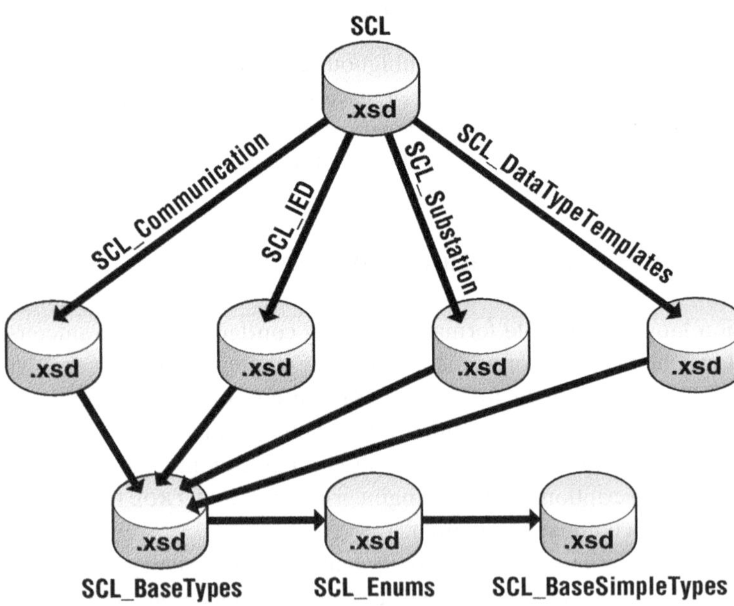

Figure 12.1 Hierarchy of SCL schema files.

SSD files contain the source requirements for an entire automation system. They encode the data exchange from a ***System Specification Tool (SST)*** to the ***System Configuration Tool (SCT)***, where the design is performed. The ***SSD*** file describes the single-line diagram of the substation and the required ***LNs*** that represent the intended automation functions. The ***Substation section*** contains the ***data type*** templates and ***LN*** type definitions. The ***IED*** and ***Communication sections*** are optional.

SCD files contain the data exchanged between the ***SCT*** and the ***ICT***, including descriptions of all ***IEDs***, communication configurations, and descriptions of a single substation.

CID files contain data exchanged from the ***ICT*** to each ***IED*** included in the design. The Communication section contains the ***IED's*** current address. A ***CID*** is an ***SCD*** file stripped down to what the concerned ***IED*** shall know.

IID files contain data exchanged for a single ***IED*** preconfigured specifically for a project. They are identical to a ***CID*** file, but only concerning the actual ***IED***, which is an interface between an ***IED*** tool and a system tool.

ICD files contain the data exchanged from the ***ICT*** to the ***SCT***. It describes the capabilities or items supported by an ***IED***, specifically one ***IED*** section per ***IED***, along with its data type templates and ***LN*** type definitions. Additionally, it includes an optional Substation section that binds the LN instances to primary equipment and an optional Communication section with possible default addresses for the ***IED***. Additional information can be included about the communication service capabilities, such as directory services, or if file transfer is supported, configuration capabilities such as how many ***data sets*** or ***control blocks*** can be configured dynamically or using an ***SCD*** file, and the provided functionality and data objects in terms of ***LNs*** and the contained data objects (***DATA***). The contents of an ***ICD*** file can be included in an ***IED*** section of a system ***SCD*** file, where the instance receives a system-specific IED name, and the ***IED*** section is enhanced with all project-specific communication definitions.

The ***ASD*** file contains a specification of a ***Basic Application Profile (BAP)*** of a single elementary application that can be instantiated by an ***SST*** or ***SCT*** in a project-specific application as needed. A ***BAP*** is a user-agreed-upon selection and interpretation of relevant parts of IEC 61850, intended to be used as building blocks for interoperable user/project specifications. A ***BAP*** typically includes the following information about an application:

- Use cases
- Functional description
- Logical architecture
- Functional variants
- Performance requirements

- Description of data model
- Communication services
- Device-related requirements
- Naming rules
- Capabilities for testing

All these files are managed through the engineering cycle for designing a digital substation and are modeled by the following packages of classes, shown in Figure 12.2:

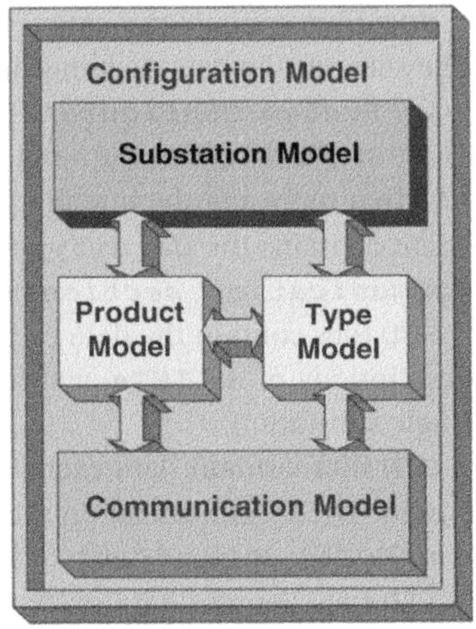

Figure 12.2 Configuration model components.

- **Substation Model**—a package of classes used to model the substation structure by a one-line diagram and the primary equipment configuration and functions of switchyard equipment (process devices) and their designation
- **Product Model**—a package of classes used to model the ***IED*** used to automate a station, its implementation, functions, and communication capabilities
- **Communication Model**—a package of classes used to model the networks with their topologies that connect the automation equipment, subnetworks, and access points to clients and servers
- **Type Model**—a package of classes used to model the ***data types*** used on the other models, with signal interfaces, data objects, and attributes

Even though XML is human-readable, it may become too verbose and complex to work with directly in its textual format. Suitable tools are available to read and edit XML files graphically, allowing exploration of their tree-like structure. This representation, as a structured tree of text, will be used as a graphical representation of the corresponding ***SCL*** file structure, optionally followed by a lane listing the values of each tree leaf. The following paragraphs will examine the internal structure of each XML file, using the detailed UML Class Diagram shown in Figure 16.1 of Annex 16.1 as a reference for all IEC 61850 configuration model packages, starting from the substation model.

12.6 Substation Model

The substation model is an object hierarchy based on the functional structure of a substation or power plant. It aims to relate an ***LN*** and its function to a substation function and to derive a functional designation for the ***LN*** from the substation structure. The ***SCL*** Substation Model Object Hierarchy comprises the following objects:

- ***Substation***—the object identifying a whole substation
- ***VoltageLevel***—an identifiable, electrically connected substation part having an identical voltage level
- ***Bay***—part or subfunction of the switchyard within one voltage level
- ***Equipment***—an apparatus within the switchyard
- ***SubEquipment***—a part or phase of an ***Equipment***
- ***ConnectivityNode***—the (electrical) connectivity node object connecting different primary devices
- ***Terminal***—an electrical connection point of a primary apparatus at the single line level

These elements are related by the UML Class Diagram shown in Figure 12.3.

A hierarchical view of a substation can be built by inheriting objects from these abstract classes, as shown in Figure 12.4. In this view, a ***Substation*** may be described by its ***Voltage Levels***, formed by ***Bays***, with their ***Equipment***. Each description level can contain its ***LNs***, related or not to specific ***Equipment***.

Figure 12.5 illustrates an example of a one-line diagram of a transformer bay in a substation, including the designation of all components, and a tree view representation in the ***Substation section*** of an ***SCL*** file. These tree-like views display the hierarchical structure of an XML file, making it easier to navigate and read than a pure XML file, and are supported by most XML and ***SCL*** editors.

Attaching ***LNs*** to switchyard equipment describes the connection between the power process and the SA system. This can be done at any level, from the ***Substation*** down to the phases of primary ***Equipment*** and to the connections within the single-line topology. Figure 12.6 illustrates the addition of a ***LN*** type, ***PDIF*** (differential protection), to the ***SCL*** file describing the automation of the power transformer in the tree view of Figure 12.5.

LNs and ***logical devices*** are allocated in ***IEDs*** according to the product model defined by IEC 61850.

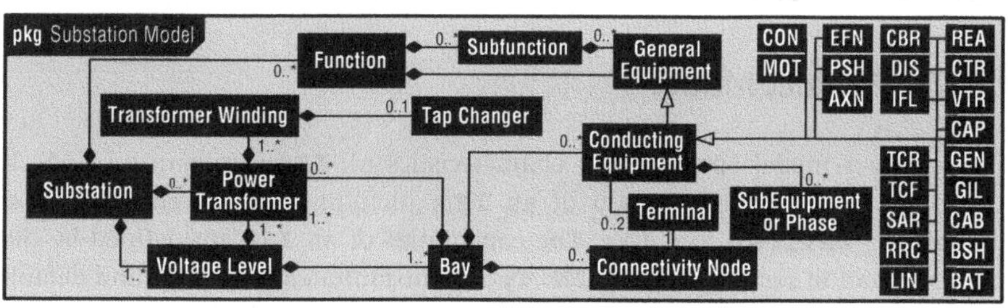

Figure 12.3 Substation model UML Class Diagram.

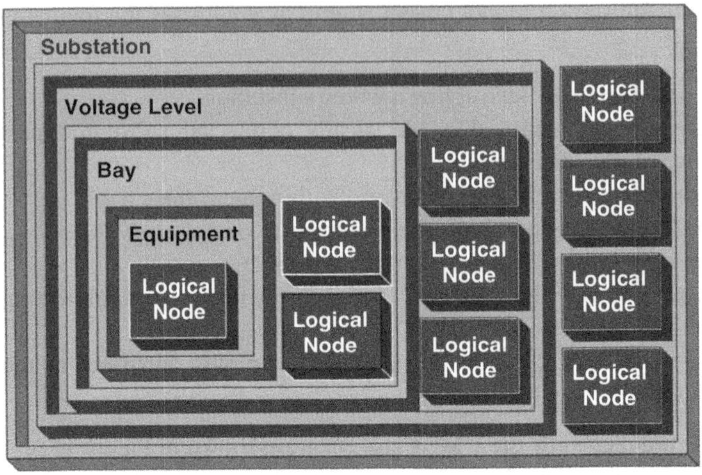

Figure 12.4 Substation section.

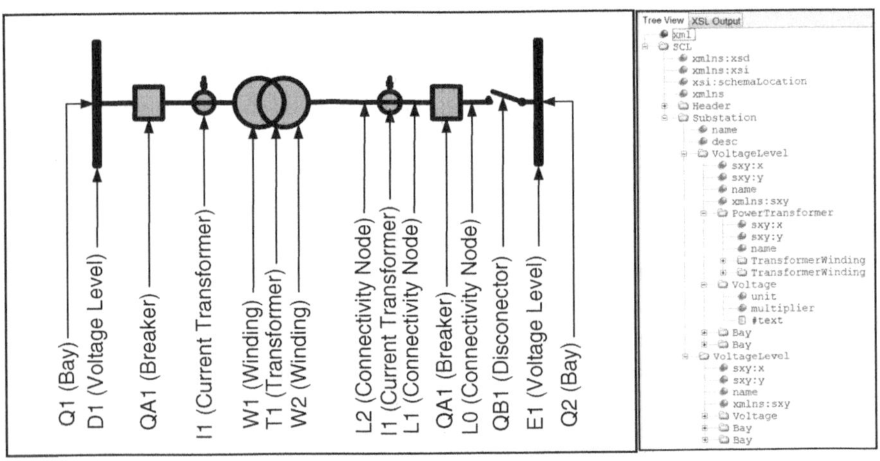

Figure 12.5 SCL Substation section of a transformer bay.

12.7 Product Model

The product model specifies the characteristics of ***IEDs*** used in an SAS. It describes the (pre)configuration of an ***IED***, including its ***access points***, ***logical devices***, and ***LNs***. The capabilities of an ***IED*** are defined by the communication services offered, ***LN Types***, instantiated data (***DO***), and default or configuration values. The ***SCL*** Product Model describes the following components of an SAS as an object hierarchy:

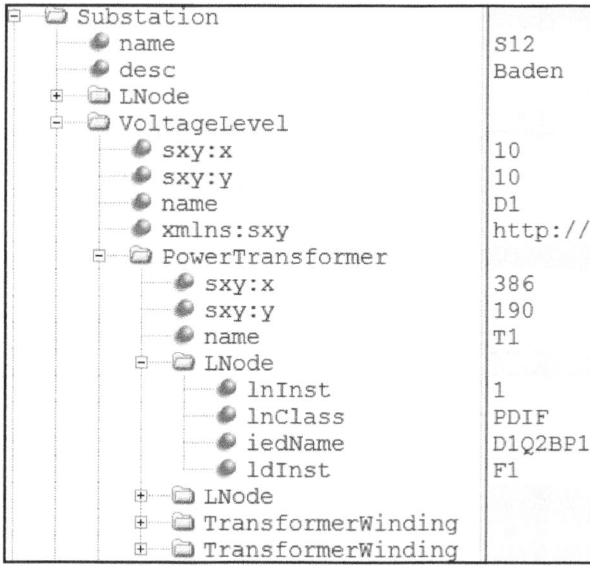

Figure 12.6 Association of logical nodes to equipment.

- ***IED***—a substation automation device performing SA functions by means of ***LNs***
- ***Server***—a communication entity within an ***IED***
- ***LDevice***—a logical device (***LD***) contained in a server
- ***LNode***—an ***LN*** contained in a logical device
- ***DO***—the ***DATA*** contained in the LNs
- ***Router***—a function of a communication network, connects different subnetworks, blocks real-time messages, outside the scope of the standard
- ***Clock***—function to indicate where a subnetwork master clock is located

These elements are related by the UML Class Diagram shown in Figure 12.7, from which the objects describing the products used in an automation system can be instantiated.

As with the Substation section, a hierarchical description of the products used in an automation system can be built by inheriting from these classes, as shown in Figure 12.8. In this view, an ***IED*** contains an ***Access Point*** to its ***Server***, which is formed by a ***Logical Device*** with several ***LNs***, each with its own services.

In the ***Product*** section of an ***SCL*** file, it is possible to specify typical or individual values for data attributes of an ***IED***. This can be used to determine values for configuration attributes and setting parameters, state values used during the engineering process or operation, and load or archive protection parameter values in a standardized way. Consider, for instance, the UML Communication

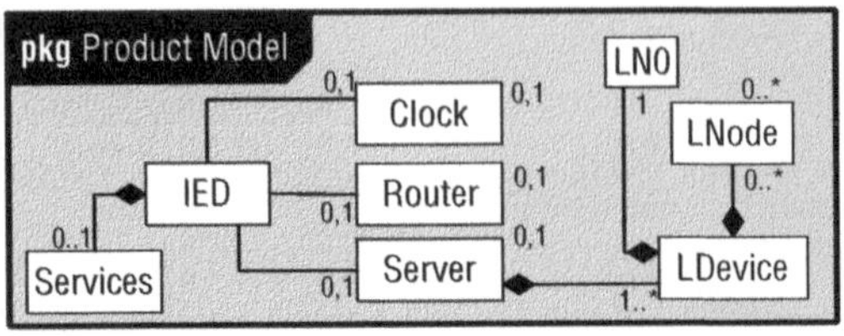

Figure 12.7 Product model UML Class Diagram.

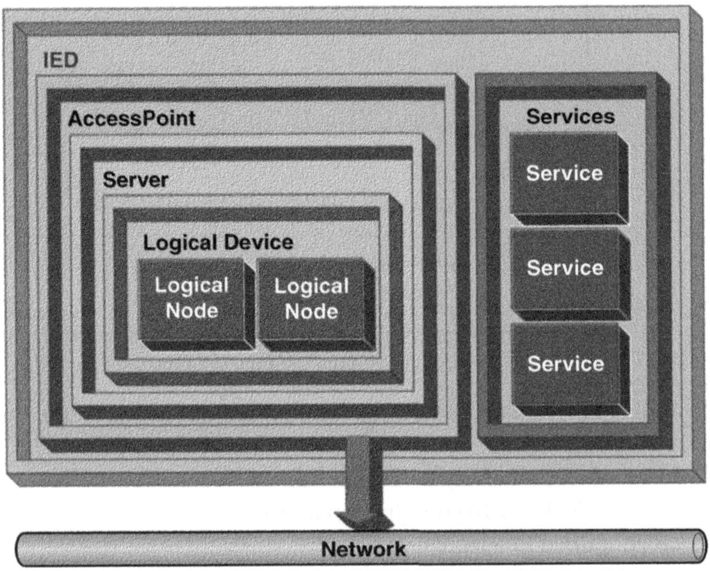

Figure 12.8 Product section.

Diagram of the protection system for a transformer bay shown in Figure 12.9, where the numbers on the links are references to ***PICOM*** types used for the data communication among the LNs.

Figure 12.10 shows a UML Deployment Diagram that illustrates the physical allocation of these functions across ***IEDs***. A code identifies each ***IED***. The picture also shows their description in a tree view of the ***SCL*** Product section.

For instance, the services offered by IED D1Q2SB1 and the number of available control blocks are shown in the ***SCL*** file tree view in Figure 12.11, as part of the ***Product section***.

A similar insertion can be made to specify the ***AccessPoint*** S1 for ***IED*** D1Q2SB1, as well as its ***Logical Device*** C1 and ***LNs*** of types ***LN0***, ***LPHD***, and ***XCBR***, as shown in the SCL file tree in Figure 12.12.

Access points are named and distributed throughout the network, following the communication model defined by IEC 61850.

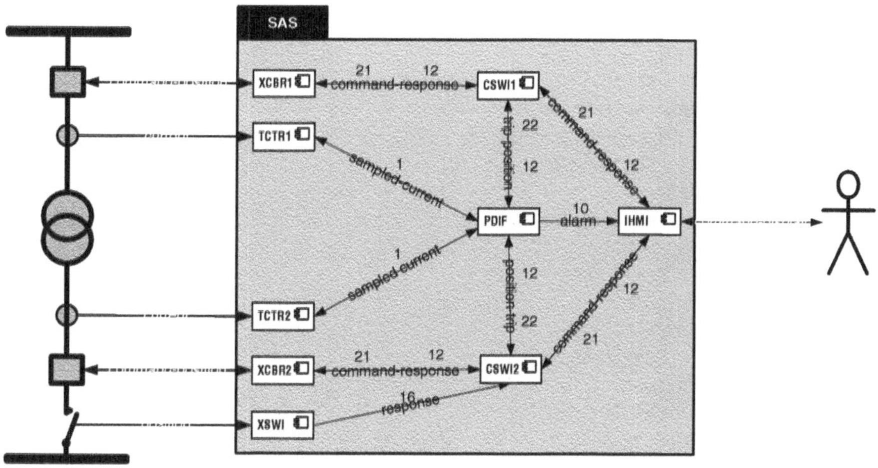

Figure 12.9 Power transformer protection.

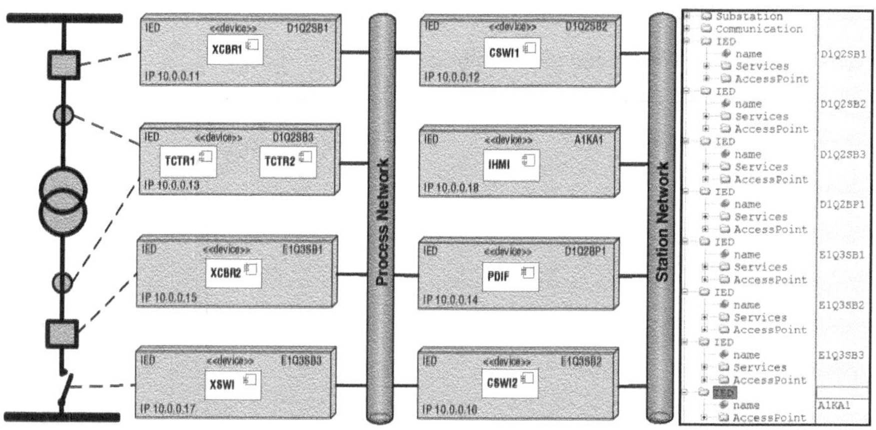

Figure 12.10 Power transformer protection deployment diagram.

12.8 Communication Model

The Communication Model is used to specify the characteristics of networks and access points of an automation system. It describes the direct connection possibilities between ***LNs*** using logical buses (***SubNetworks***) and ***IED*** access points. It defines which ***logical devices*** and ***LNs*** are reachable via a

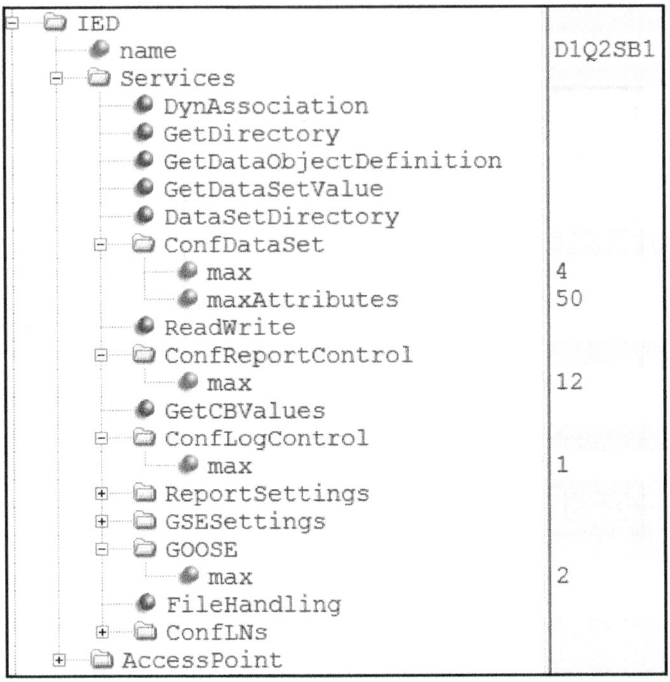

Figure 12.11 IED services and control blocks.

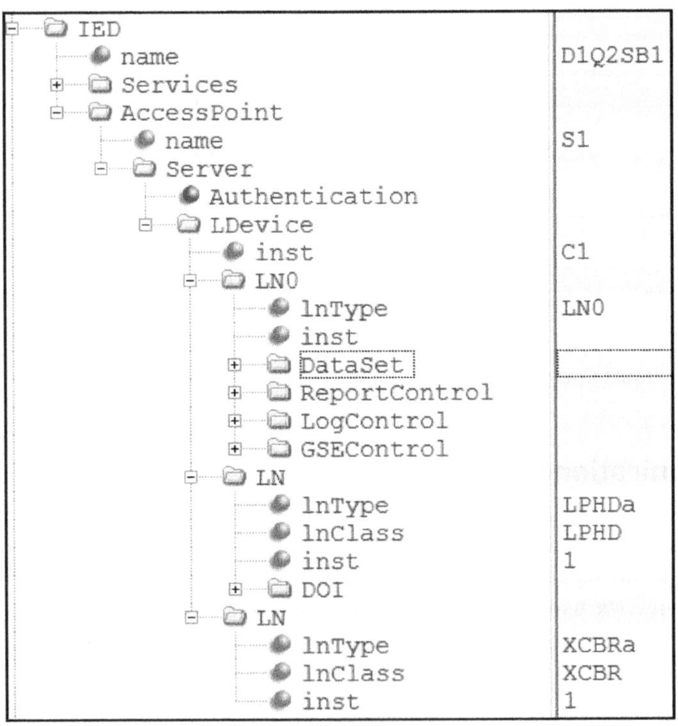

Figure 12.12 IED AccessPoint and LNs.

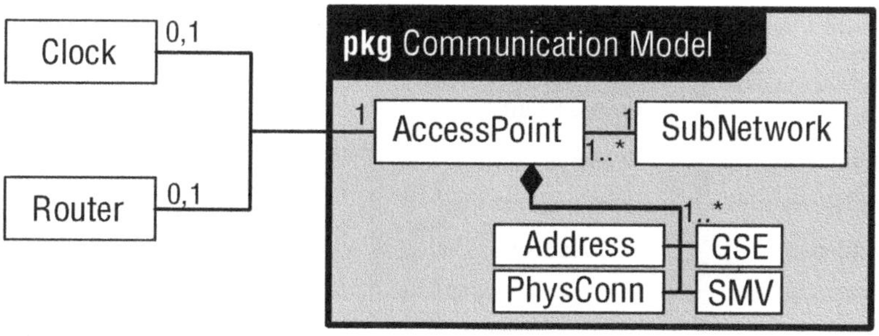

Figure 12.13 Communication model UML Class Diagram.

particular access point, and which ***IED*** access points are connected to a sub-network. The following classes are described in the UML Class Diagram of the Communication Model (Figure 12.13):

- ***Subnetwork***—a connecting node for direct (link layer) communication between ***access points***. It contains all access points that can (logically) communicate with the ***SubNetwork*** protocol, and without an intervening ***router***, and defines a logical connection with a specific protocol
- ***Access point***—a communication ***access point*** of the ***logical device***(s) of an ***IED*** to a ***subnetwork***
- ***Router***—a function to extend access to ***servers*** connected to another ***subnetwork*** at another ***access point*** of that ***IED***, which hosts the ***router*** function.
- ***Clock***—a master clock at this ***subnetwork*** is used to synchronize the internal ***clocks*** of all (other) ***IEDs*** connected to this ***subnetwork***.

Access Points are further detailed in the following inherited classes:

- ***PhysConn***—physical address of the server
- ***Address***—logical address of the server
- ***GSV***—addresses of ***GOOSE*** and ***GSSE*** control blocks
- ***SMV***—addresses of Sampled Value control blocks

As with the Substation and Product sections, a hierarchical description of the communication networks deployed in an automation system can be built by instantiating objects from these classes, as shown in Figure 12.14. In this view, a ***Subnetwork*** contains several ***AccessPoints***, specified by their physical and logical addresses on the ***Server***, as well as the addresses for ***GOOSE***, ***GSEE***, and ***Sampled Values*** messages.

An example of a description of Subnetwork W01, type 8-MMS and bit rate 10, can be seen in the ***Communication section*** of the tree view of the ***SCL*** file

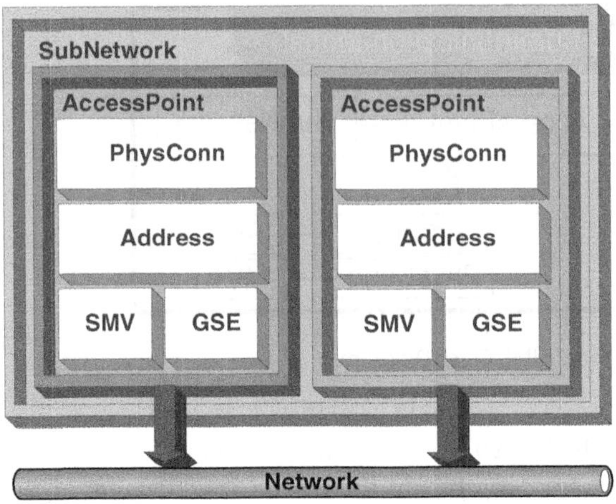

Figure 12.14 Communication section.

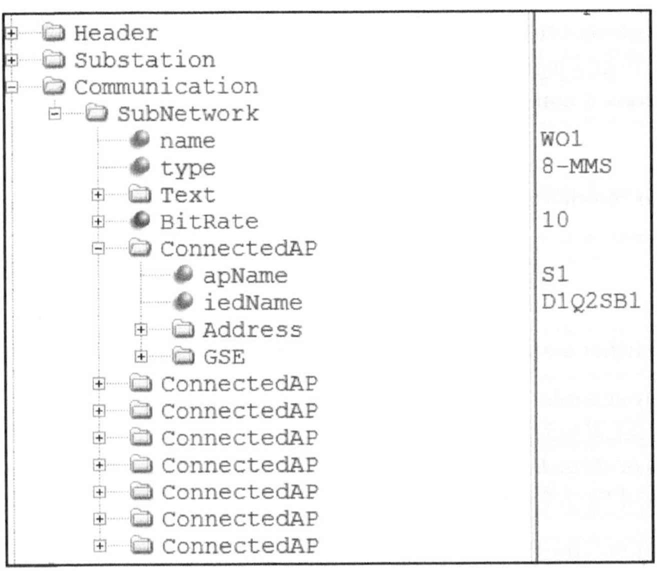

Figure 12.15 Communication networks and IED addresses.

shown in Figure 12.15. ***IED*** D1Q2SB1 is also shown to be connected to this network, as indicated by its logical address and ***GSE*** message addresses.

This information is distributed across several ***SCL*** files, standardized according to IEC 61850, for use in the engineering cycle of digital installations.

12.9 Generic Engineering Cycle

The Waterfall method is one of the earliest and most traditional approaches to the engineering and project development cycle for complex systems. It is a linear, sequential model that describes the lifecycle of a project, where each phase must be completed before proceeding to the next. The typical stages include (1) planning, (2) specification, (3) design, (4) deployment, and (5) operation, as depicted in Figure 12.16. This structured flow resembles a waterfall, where progress cascades steadily downward. Its strengths lie in clear documentation, well-defined stages, and ease of management, making it effective for projects with stable requirements.

Accordingly, the steps are performed by different actors and stakeholders (Figure 12.16):

- **Planner**—interprets the user's desires into a User Requirement Specification
- **Specifier**—converts the User Requirement into a Functional Specification
- **Designer**—translates the Functional Specification into a Design Specification
- **Builder**—compiles the Design Specification into an As-Built Product
- **Operator**—exercises the built system for conformance and user validation

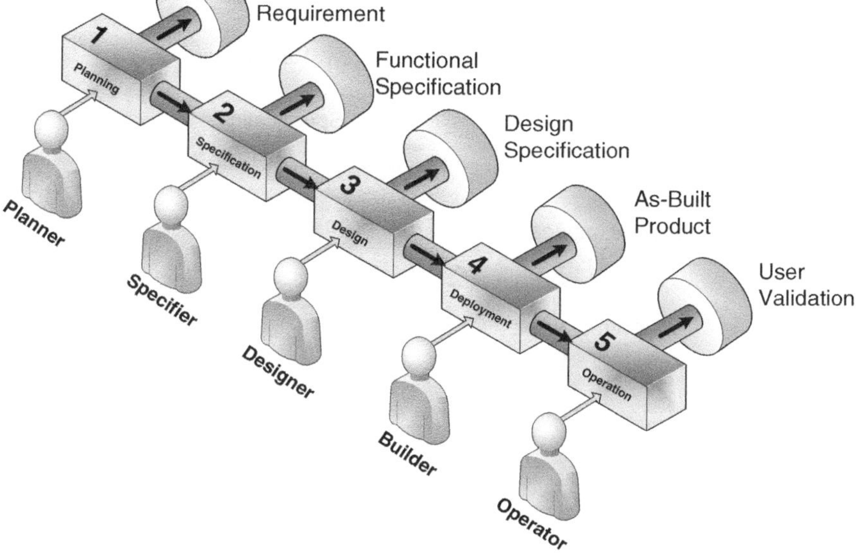

Figure 12.16 Waterfall engineering cycle.

These steps or phases produce, sequentially, the following products (Figure 12.16):

- **User Requirement**—defines what a user wants from the system
- **Functional Specification**—defines what functions the system should perform
- **Design Specification**—converts the Functional Specification into design rules
- **As-Built Product**—converted the Design Specification into building blocks of hardware and software
- **User Validation**—check the correctness of the Implementation against the Functional Specification and User Requirements

When applied to an IEC 61850-based system, the requirements and specifications are (digital) documents that detail the configuration of a digital system progressively, using the corresponding SCL models, as illustrated in Figure 12.17:

- **Requirements**
  - of the Power System
  - of the Substation and Power Plant
  - of the Automation Functions

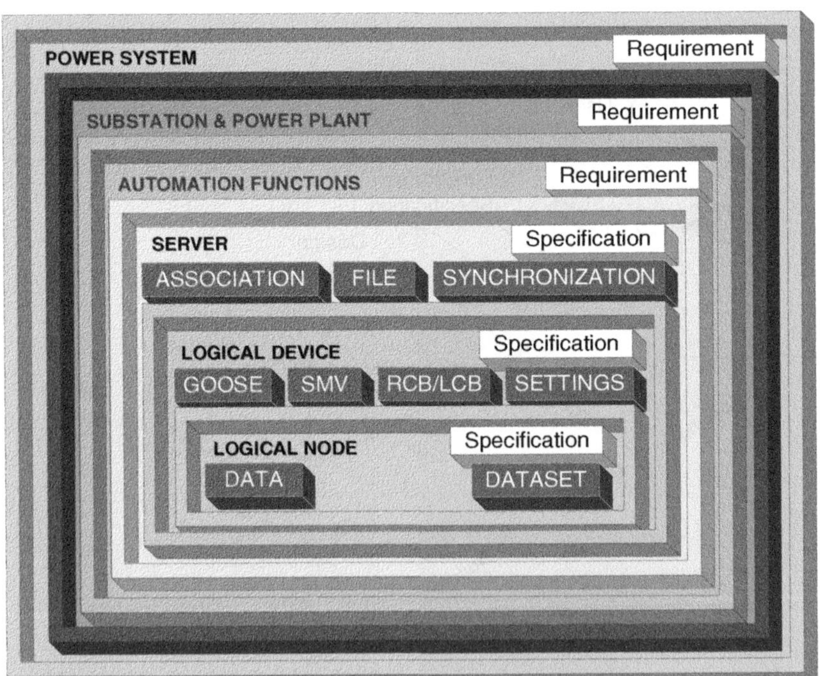

Figure 12.17 IEC 61850-based requirements and specifications.

- **Specifications**
  - of the Servers and Network
  - of the Logical Devices
  - of the LNs.

These requirements and specifications are related by a progressively detailed definition, starting with the power system and substation requirements and ending with the building specification for the automation functions, as illustrated in Figure 12.17.

The starting point is a user requirements document that describes the intended functions to be implemented in the automation system.

12.10 User Requirements

IEC 61850 does not standardize a format for these user requirements, except as examples of ***BAP***. Utilities have traditionally used text, table, and graphical formats to specify their requirements, usually for inclusion in a bidding process. Some independent organizations have proposed standard formats for user functional requirements, as described in the following sections.

This topic has been addressed by CIGRE Working Group B5.64 (Brochure 926), entitled "Methods for Specification of Functional Requirements of Protection, Automation, and Control," and Working Group B5.32 (Brochure 401), entitled "Functional Testing of IEC 61850 Based Systems," both available on the digital platform e-CIGRE.org. In the later brochure, an informal format is proposed for a Functional Implementation Conformance Statement, as shown in Annex 16.9, based on the IEC 61850 conformance statement format and following the UML Use Case format standardized by the OMG. This format is intended to describe the functional requirements of a system—what the system should do, from the user's perspective, composed of the following parts:

- **Actors:** stakeholders and external entities (people, systems, devices) that interact with the system
- **Function:** specific goals or tasks that actors want to accomplish using the system
- **Use Case:** flow of events performed by the function, optionally with a diagram

Conceptually, this format aligns with the direction outlined in Intent-Directed Network requirements, where the user's focus is on formally defining the objectives and desired performance of a system, leaving the design details to integrators, developers, manufacturers, and specific tools. In addition to these informal requirements, the CIGRE Brochure 926 also suggests a Domain-Specific

Language (DSL) for the formal specification of the functional requirements of automation systems. Formal methods are system design techniques that use rigorously specified mathematical models to build software and hardware systems. They allow the use of mathematical proofs as validation methods to ensure correct behavior and are suitable for automatic interpretation or for compilation to lower-level languages or technologies. They can also support design validation and model checking before deployment.

To be useful as a formal specification language, a DSL should provide a near-natural language (not XML) that is easy to learn (not thousands of pages like IEC 61850), using a computer and human-readable syntax, adequate for documentation and maintenance. It should use well-defined formal grammar and semantics (not natural language), with a limited vocabulary common to the PAC domain, but sufficient to describe the behavior of switchyard equipment, PAC functions, human operators, and distributed remote systems. The description of a formal language includes its:

- **Lexicon**—a vocabulary or symbols (lexemes) used by the language
- **Sintaxe**—a set of rules to combine the symbols in well-formed phrases
- **Semantics**—a set of rules to convey the meaning of any well-formed phrase
- **Pragmatics**—a set of methods for the practical use of the language

Ideally, a formal requirement language should be agnostic to the target implementation technology and be oriented towards the user's requirements. A formal user requirement for an automation system can then be compiled or interpreted to different target technologies and specification languages, such as SCL/XML for IEC 61850, CIM/XML for ISO/IEC 61960, ST/XML for ISO/IEC 61599, or ST/IL for ISO/IEC 61113 (Figure 12.18). Additionally, a requirement for an automation system can instantiate a library of predefined models or requirements, documented as templates or BAPs, coded in the formal language DSL of the user requirement.

Once a formal user requirement (written in text or in a DSL) is compiled to a formal specification language (such as SCL for IEC 61850), the remaining standard engineering cycle can be followed as described in the following paragraphs.

12.11 IEC 61850 Engineering Cycle

A future compiler or interpreter for a user requirement is proposed by IEC 61850 to be processed by a ***`Concept Definition Tool`*** (***CDT***). This tool produces an ***ASD*** file, as part of the family of XML-based specification and configuration files defined in the standard. The ***ASD*** file describes the functional and communication requirements of a particular application or system use case (for example,

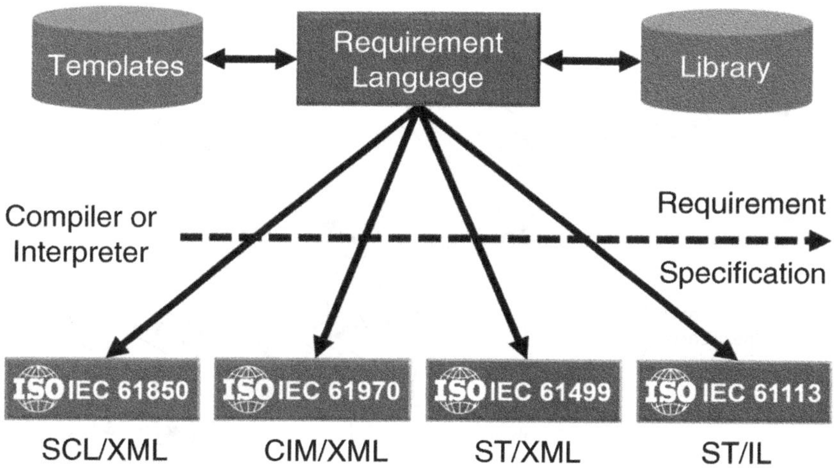

Figure 12.18 Compilers and interpreters.

protection, control, monitoring, or automation functions in a substation). It is not tied to a specific device yet—instead, it specifies what the application needs in terms of ***LNs***, ***Data Objects*** (***DOs***), and services. In a typical engineering cycle, at the requirements/specification stage, the ***ASD*** defines what the system must be capable of doing using IEC 61850. Later, these requirements are mapped into concrete devices through an ***ICD*** and then into a complete ***SCD***.

Once compiled, the ***SCL*** files defined by IEC 61850 can be used throughout the lifecycle of an automation system, from user requirements through planning, design, configuration, deployment, and maintenance, with support from appropriate software tools. They can be mapped, for instance, to the traditional phases of the Waterfall model of system engineering design, as shown in Figure 12.19, comprising four main stages, supported by the corresponding tools defined by IEC 61850:

0. ***CDT***
1. ***SST***
2. ***SCT***
3. ***ICT***

Note that the information flow is bidirectional in the central duct of Figure 12.19. These tools generate configuration files downward and allow them to be modified and updated upward in the Waterfall model. Starting from the user functional requirements compiled in ***ASD*** files generated by a ***CDT***, the design is further translated by an ***SST*** into an ***SSD*** file. This is further detailed in an ***SCD*** file by an ***SCT***,

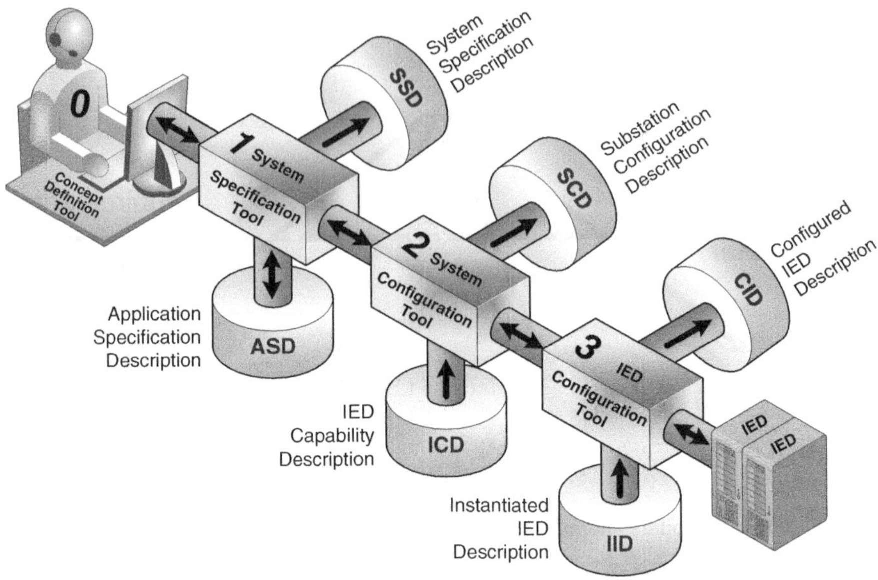

Figure 12.19 SCL file types and the engineering cycle tools.

using a library of available ICD files provided by the manufacturer. From the ***SCD*** file, ***ICT*** generates the ***CID*** files to be uploaded to an ***IED***, using a library of available ***IID*** files imported from the ***IEDs***.

In addition to the Waterfall model, a similar sequence can be adapted to other system engineering design methodologies, such as the V-Model (Figure 12.20), where testing is added to each design phase of the Waterfall model to verify and validate requirements and successive designs throughout the development cycle.

The V-Model adds the following testing phases for user acceptance of the final product against the user requirements definition:

- **Concept Testing**—to verify and validate the implementation against the user concepts in the engineering cycle.
- **System Testing**—to verify and validate the system against the specification produced in the engineering cycle.
- **Integration Testing**—to verify and validate the integration against the system design produced in the engineering cycle.
- **Component Testing**—to verify and validate each component according to the configuration produced in the engineering cycle.

Due to the widespread acceptance of IEC 61850, which enables active participation by final users and stakeholders in the upgrade, refurbishment, planning, and design of digital substations, the Agile development process, primarily used

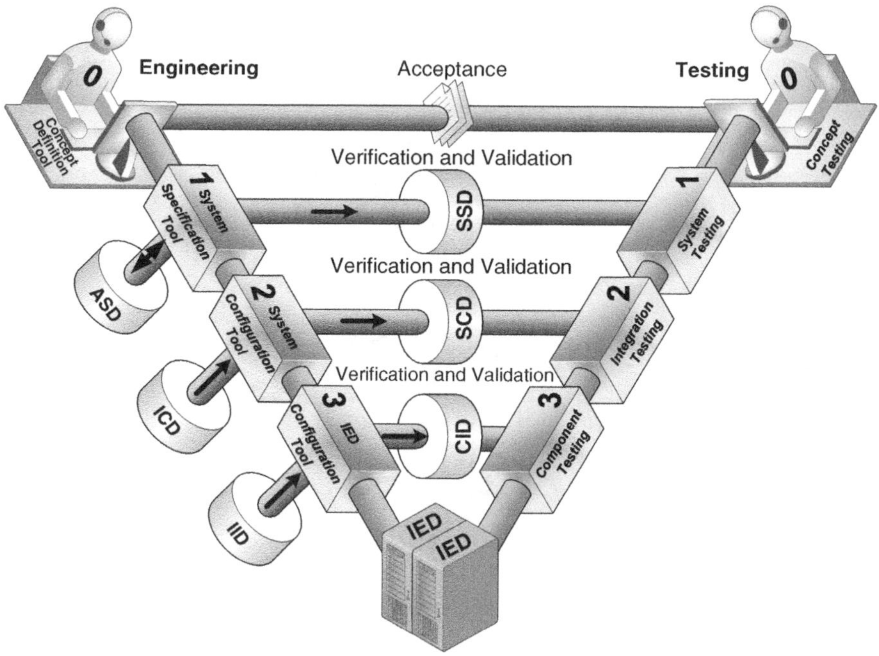

Figure 12.20 V-Model engineering cycle.

in the software industry, is increasingly adopted in the engineering cycle of IEC 61850-based systems. Agile projects are developed using smaller iterations (typically called Sprints) that deliver a potentially shippable product increment to gather user feedback and ensure the product meets their needs. This is particularly important for the progressive upgrade of legacy automation systems and for the addition of new IEC 61850-based functions. Figure 12.21 shows the typical phases of the Agile engineering cycle, and their relation to the tools and *SCL* files defined by IEC 61850.

Agile introduces the following interaction phases to facilitate user acceptance of incremental product changes within each Sprint:

- **Design**—how the software will be structured and interact with other parts
- **Build**—coding, configuring, and development of the software
- **Test**—to ensure it meets the defined requirements and works as expected
- **Review**—feedback to make any adjustments for the next iteration

Note that at each Sprint, changes may be made to all *SCL* files throughout the project, using the tools defined by IEC 61850. Waterfall and V-Model can be used in each Sprint to review the design. Bidirectional changes to the *SCL*

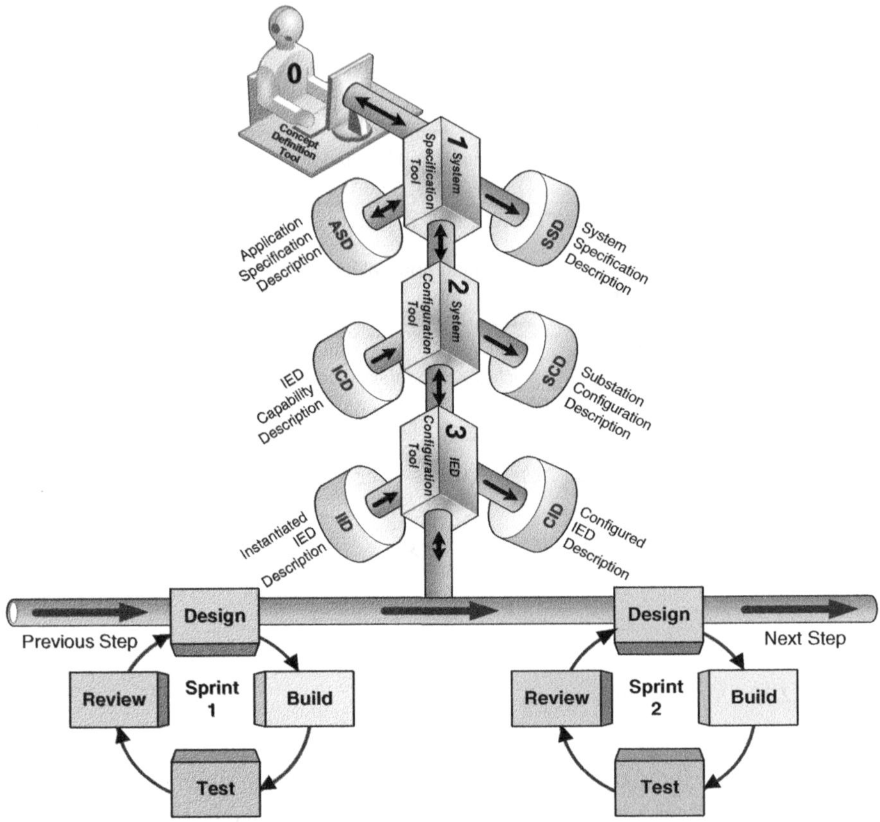

Figure 12.21 Agile engineering cycle.

files in the central duct between Sprints are vital to maintaining consistency. To ensure continuity, traceability, and integrity throughout the Agile development cycle, a centralized, version-controlled repository for all *SCL* source code should be established. This repository is preserved across Sprint phases using Version Control Management in a secure repository, where every change is tracked through commits, branches, and merge requests. This enables full historical traceability, facilitates rollback when necessary, and ensures that all Sprint deliverables are captured in a controlled environment.

The Agile approach is particularly suitable for projects where requirements change during development or integration with legacy systems. Common Agile frameworks include Scrum, Kanban, and Extreme Programming (XP). As IEC 61850 matures as a software-based automation solution, Agile methods are expected to become common design frameworks for digital installations.

12.12 Summary

The primary advantage of the IEC 61850 engineering cycle and configuration model is the use of a standardized object-oriented language that is independent of hardware and supplier. An open standard that humans and computers can understand offers high efficiency and opportunities to optimize engineering design, tool support, and maintenance of these systems.

This chapter introduced the configuration model, tools, and language standardized by IEC 61850 for specifying and configuring ***IEDs*** and SAS. The XML was briefly described as the basis of the ***SCL*** adopted by IEC 61850, which defines the configuration and settings of any automation system. The standardized tools and ***SCL*** files were introduced, highlighting their role in the engineering cycle of digital installations, which can use either the Waterfall, V-Model, or Agile frameworks. These frameworks must be complemented by the testing models described in Chapter 13.

12.13 Review Questions

1 Describe the role of XML in IEC 61850 and explain why it is appropriate as the basis for the ***SCL***.

2 Explain how the hierarchical structure of ***SCL*** (Substation Model, Product Model, Communication Model, and Type Model) facilitates hardware-independent engineering of SAS.

3 Summarize the purpose and typical contents of each of the following ***SCL*** file types: ***SSD***, ***SCD***, ***CID***, ***IID***, ***ICD***, and ***ASD***.

4 A utility plans to add new protection ***IEDs*** to an existing digital substation. Identify which ***SCL*** files and engineering tools (***CDT***, ***SST***, ***SCT***, ***ICT***) are involved in this process and explain how they interact.

5 Compare the Waterfall, V-Model, and Agile engineering cycles in the context of IEC 61850 projects. What advantages and limitations arise when applying each model to designing digital substations?

6 Discuss how the Substation Model in ***SCL*** represents the physical layout of a substation. How do elements such as ***VoltageLevel***, ***Bay***, ***Equipment***, and ***LNs*** assist with functional mapping?

7 An engineer must set up communication among multiple ***IEDs*** on a process bus using ***GOOSE*** and ***SV*** messages. Explain how the ***SCL*** Communication Model and **AccessPoint** definitions facilitate this setup.

8 Evaluate the importance of ***ICD*** files in enabling interoperability among multi-vendor ***IEDs***. Why are capability descriptions crucial for system integration and device setup?

9 Given a single-line diagram of a new transformer bay, outline the steps to create the corresponding ***Substation section*** in an ***SSD*** file, including assigning ***LNs*** to primary equipment.

10 Explain the concept of a ***BAP*** within the ***ASD*** file and describe how it helps formalize user requirements for IEC 61850-based applications.

11 Discuss the significance of version control and change traceability in Agile engineering cycles that depend on ***SCL*** files. How do centralized repositories and organized commits promote consistency across Sprints?

12 Suggest a workflow for developing a protection function that starts with user requirements and ends with configured ***IEDs*** deployed in the field. Identify the ***SCL*** files generated at each stage and describe their role in the engineering lifecycle.

13

Testing Models

13.1 Introduction

Like any computerized system, Substation Automation Systems (SAS) can encounter both visible and hidden failures that happen during manufacturing, integration, and commissioning or are acquired during operation due to human, environmental, hardware, or software issues. Besides formal verification of the design and configuration, testing is an effective way to ensure the reliability of an SAS and its compliance with requirements. As an object-oriented standard, IEC 61850 offers detailed specifications for testing distributed automation systems, mainly to ensure the reliability of the testing process while reducing its impact on the System Under Test (SUT).

13.2 Learning Objectives

This chapter describes the main testing models defined by IEC 61850, including factory, type, system, and Site Acceptance Tests (SATs), as well as conformance and interoperability demonstrations essential for ensuring SAS reliability. After reviewing general software testing principles, it explains an object-oriented approach for IEC 61850-based systems, using the UML Test Profile proposed by the Object Management Group (OMG) to automate both test execution and formal design validation.

13.3 Testing and Verification

Testing is an empirical investigation that provides stakeholders with information about the quality of a product or service, or its conformance to specifications or to the context in which it is intended to operate. The need for testing and verification

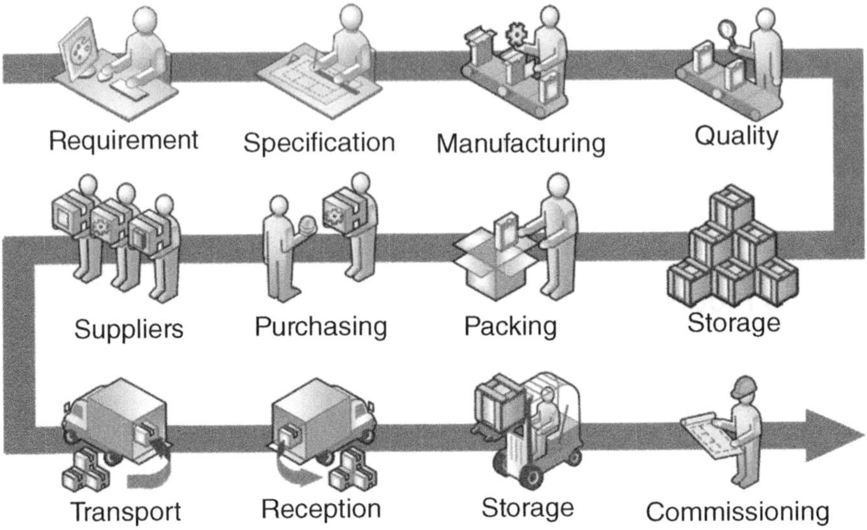

Figure 13.1 Steps in the development of a digital system.

of a digital system arises from the diverse phases of its production, where opportunities abound for the accidental or intentional introduction of bugs and failures. Figure 13.1 illustrates a typical production cycle for a digital installation, comprising 12 distinct steps performed by different people at various locations and times, which are cascaded, thereby introducing opportunities for cumulative failures.

To validate a specific stage in the development of a product, two approaches are usually adopted:

- **Verification**—Checking that the system behaves as expected for *all conditions*, before implementation, with the following characteristics:
  - Usually employing a formal proofing method
  - Detect some errors but not their absence
  - Cannot find all errors
  - Much cheaper than testing
  - Requires fewer mathematical skills
  - Requires good tools and practical skills
- **Testing**—Checking that the system behaves as expected for *some conditions*, after implementation, with the following characteristics:
  - Usually employing a simulation method
  - Demonstrate absence of errors in a model

- Cannot prove their absence on a real system
- Often very expensive
- Requires highly qualified engineers
- Automated techniques are somewhat limited

Figure 13.2 helps in understanding the fundamental difference between these two methods, exemplified by the validation of the impedance limit of a (mho) distance protection, represented in a resistance (R) and reactance (X) diagram. Testing consists of simulating the relay's behavior at points along the characteristic curve—three points in this example. Verification, on the contrary, is the confirmation, by some formal method based on the implementation of the relay, that the impedance characteristic is a circumference.

Two typical user requirements for automation systems are *safety* (nothing bad ever happens) and *liveness* (something good eventually happens). An example is the specification for a protection system for the transformer bay illustrated in a one-line diagram in Figure 13.3.

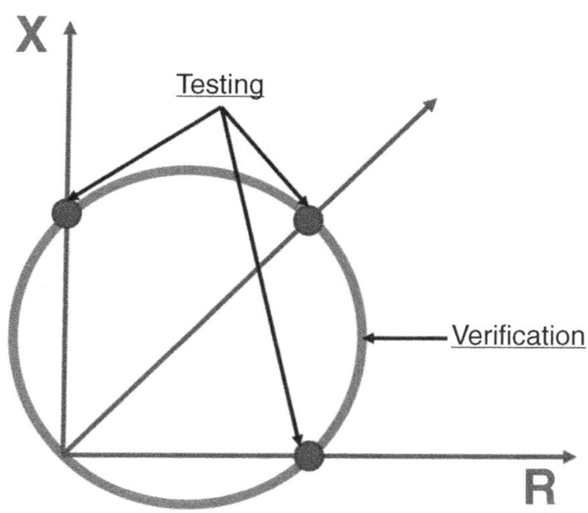

Figure 13.2 Testing and verification of a distance protection.

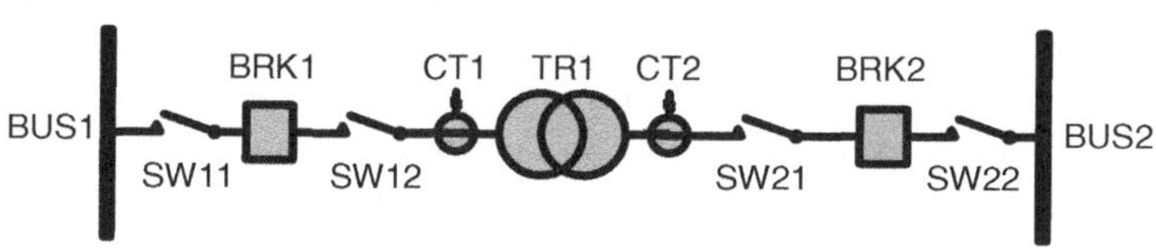

Figure 13.3 Transformer bay one-line diagram.

The safety and liveness user requirements for this system could look like the following:

- **Liveness**—Opening or closing of switches SW11 and SW12 shall be blocked whenever breaker BRK1 stays closed.
- **Safety**—Transformer TR1 should be tripped in no more than 100 ms after any overload greater than 120% of any of its coil nominal current, with a duration of at least 50 ms.

Both requisites can be validated in a design through testing or verification to ensure the system works correctly according to its design and meets all specified requirements. This may involve checking the entire system—including hardware, software, and communication—as a whole, with a focus on functionality, performance, security, reliability, and interoperability. Specifically, for the final product to conform to the user requirements, the validation process should address the user's needs, as specified in a document such as the Functional Implementation Conformance Statement (FICS), described in Section 12.10, in the actual operational environment, including operators, field conditions, and regulatory constraints. In digital systems, validation is primarily performed through software testing.

13.4 Software Testing

SAS, primarily based on IEC 61850, are model-driven software systems that run on distributed hardware. Testing of these systems also requires adopting object-oriented concepts. The following list summarizes the evolution of software testing from manual testing to model-based testing:

- Manual testing
- Capture/replay testing
- Script-based testing
- Keyword-driven testing
- Model-based testing

Manual testing is essentially human (user-oriented) functional testing. Figure 13.4 illustrates the primary concepts of this type of testing. Based on a set of requirements and a test plan, a test designer generates a set of test cases that a test executor uses to exercise the SUT and produce testing results.

For IEC 61850-based systems, this type of testing suffers from limited functional coverage and often lacks regression testing capabilities. It is a very costly process (every execution is manual), resulting in no effective measurement of test coverage.

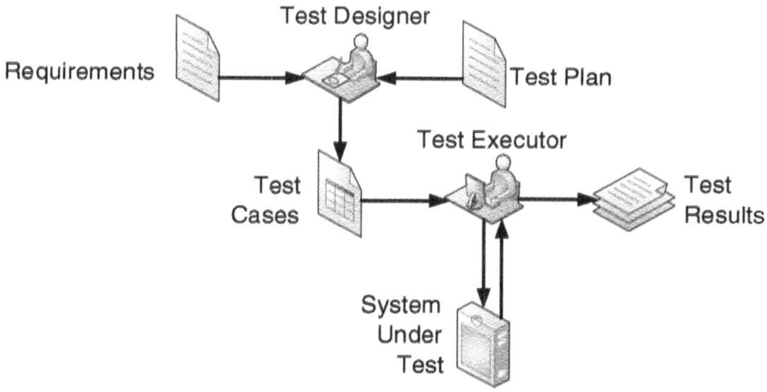

Figure 13.4 Manual testing.

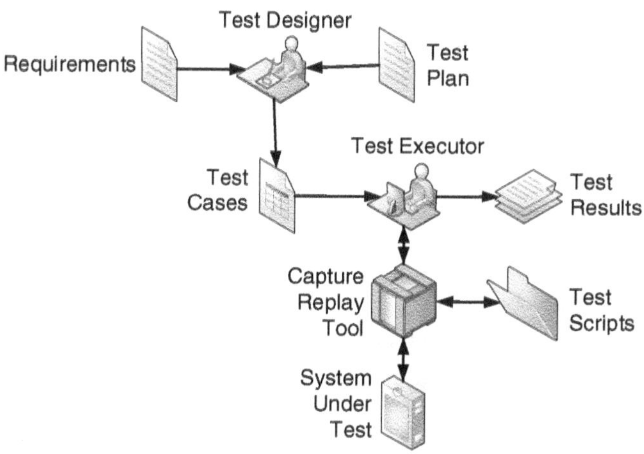

Figure 13.5 Capture/replay testing.

The next evolution of testing concepts introduced process automation, utilizing a capture/replay tool to execute predefined, stored test scripts. This concept is depicted in Figure 13.5.

In this scheme, test scripts are automatically executed from captured test cases. Again, for IEC 61850-based systems, it suffers from incomplete coverage of SUT functionality, weak regression testing capabilities, and high sensitivity to SUT changes. It is a costly process, as each change requires manual recapturing of test cases.

To address some of these disadvantages, scripting-based testing introduced the role of a script implementor, who translates test cases into a scripting language, which a test executor tool executes and generates test results. Figure 13.6 illustrates the typical flow of this type of testing.

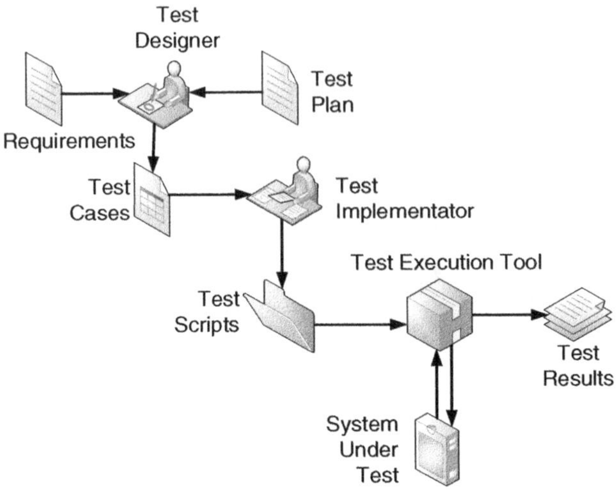

Figure 13.6 Script-based testing.

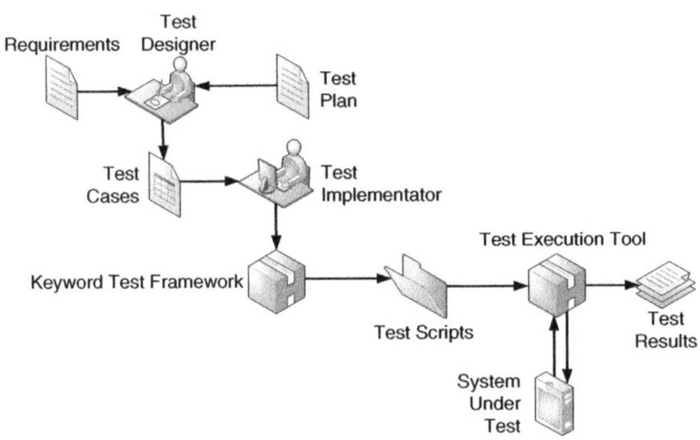

Figure 13.7 Keyword-driven testing.

The main advantage of this scheme is the automatic execution and repetition of test scripts, which are not necessarily captured from previous tests. However, they still provide only limited coverage of SUT functionality for IEC 61850-based systems. Complex scripts are challenging to write and maintain, and the requirement traceability must be developed manually, which is costly.

The keyword-driven testing concept was the next evolution, introducing a new resource: the test implementor generates test scripts using a keyword-driven test framework. This scheme is shown in Figure 13.7.

Although it is easier to develop high-level test scripts, available from many relay test tools, this scheme also suffers from imprecise coverage of SUT functionality, requiring manual creation of requirements traceability, which is costly. Following the tendency in software design, this aspect naturally led to the development of model-based testing.

13.5 Model-based Testing

Model-based testing followed naturally from the introduction of model-based software development and its use in IEC 61850-based systems. In this scheme, the test designer produces an SUT model that a test case generator uses to generate test cases. A digital twin is a virtual, real-time model of a physical object (an SUT), process, or system that mirrors its real-world counterpart, enabling it to predict its behavior and even to autogenerate test cases. It closely mimics the concept of a virtual IED (***vIED***) of IEC 61850. A test script generator uses test cases to generate test scripts that are simulated in the digital twin and then run by a test execution tool. This setup is shown in Figure 13.8.

The main advantages of this scheme are the independence of manual test generation and the automation of functional test case design, which result in reduced design and maintenance costs. Additionally, it provides systematic coverage of the model's functionality and automatically generates a traceability matrix. A SUT model and requirement fault detection are natural outcomes of model-based testing, resulting in reduced testing costs and time, improved test quality, easier requirements evolution, and traceability. Its primary disadvantage is that it requires knowledge of modeling to model SUT functionality. Outdated

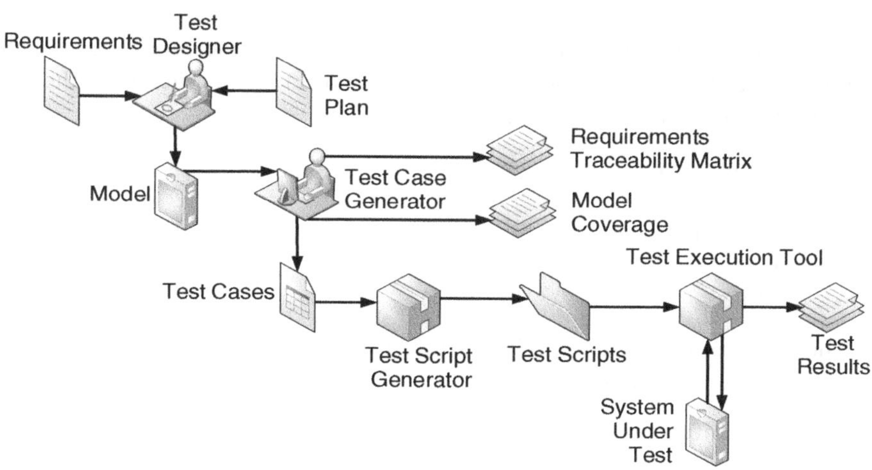

Figure 13.8 Model-based testing.

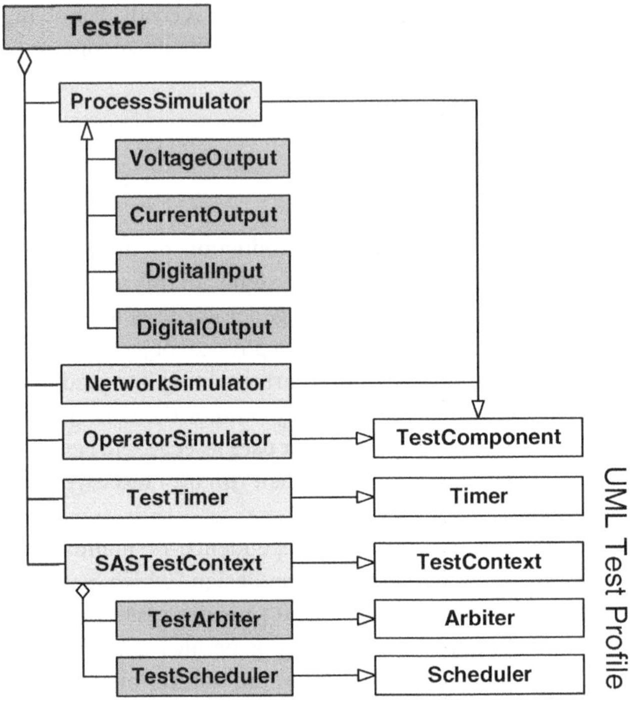

Figure 13.9 Test architecture based on UML Test Profile.

requirements may lead to the inappropriate use of model-based testing, resulting in excessive time spent analyzing failed tests (diagnoses) and a tendency toward useless metrics.

To perform these tests, an abstract object-oriented architecture is suggested, based on the UML Test Profile of the OMG (Figure 13.9), inherited from the following abstract classes:

- TestComponent
- Timer
- TestContext
- Arbiter
- Scheduler

These classes, inherited from the UML Test Profile, perform the following main functions in a test scheme:

- **Test architecture**—main test structure and test configuration
- **Test behavior**—dynamic aspects of test procedures
- **Test data**—structures and meaning of values to be processed in a test
- **Test time**—concepts for a time-quantified definition of test procedures

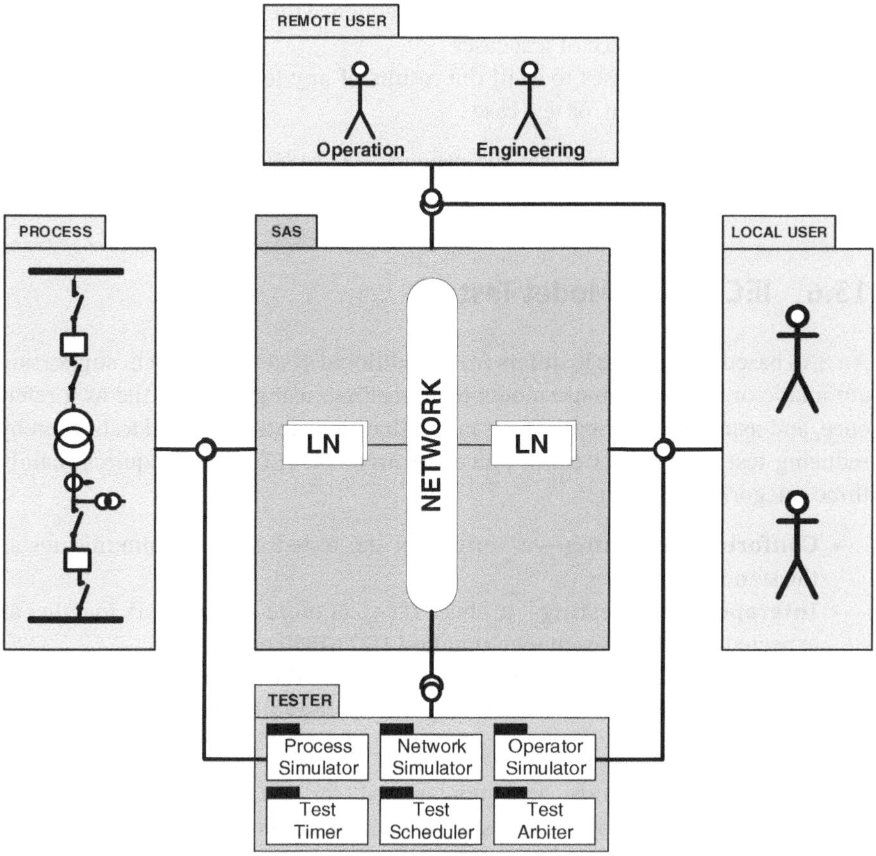

Figure 13.10 Functional test architecture.

Jointly, they enable the definition of a comprehensive test architecture comprising classes that simulate the operation of the primary process, the remote user, the local user, and the test tool, as illustrated in Figure 13.10.

The following packages are part of the Tester package, inherited from the UML Test Profile:

- **Process simulator**—classes to emulate the signals that are received and sent from and to the process, to monitor and send analog, digital, and ***`sampled values`*** and messages
- **Network simulator**—classes to supervise and generate network messages related to any ***`logical node`***, to monitor and send network messages containing sampled and digital values
- **Operator simulator**—classes to emulate network messages related to an operator logical node, to monitor and send operator messages

- **Test timer**—classes to start, stop, and sequence the steps of a functional test, to guide the sequence of test cases
- **Test arbiter**—classes to avail the results of any test sequence, publish the results of a test plan, or test case

This architecture can perform the primary IEC 61850 tests, including factory, system, site, conformance, interoperability, and performance tests.

13.6 IEC 61850 Model Test

An SAS based on IEC 61850 differs from traditional systems mainly in supporting automatic or semi-automatic model-based testing, using the *SCD* file as a reference, and using object-oriented tests rather than conventional signal tests, thereby reducing test effort. As a communication protocol, IEC 61850 requires mainly three categories of testing:

- **Conformance testing**—to verify that the tested device communicates as the standard specifies
- **Interoperability testing**—to check if two or more devices work together as expected when they exchange standard IEC 61850 messages
- **Performance or stress testing**—to evaluate the attainment of device or system performance specifications, often to establish boundaries for their capabilities

Only conformance tests are standardized for IEC 61850-based devices. Interoperability and performance testing are not standardized because they depend on specific system requirements and implementation details. The way conformance tests are used in product development is shown in Figure 13.11. IEC TC 57, the Technical Committee responsible for IEC 61850, maintains the standard used by developers to create products, publishes the test cases used by test developers to design systems, and requires test laboratories to verify product conformance with the standard. The results of the conformance tests are used to certify the product's adherence to the standard or to support the product development.

Similar roles are performed by utilities and other agents while producing specifications and test cases for new SAS, as shown in Figure 13.12. System designers and integrators select among available products to architect systems that comply with the utility specification. These systems are tested in a laboratory or the field to certify the design with the specifications, report the results to the utility, and support the development process.

As a model-driven standard, IEC 61850, in addition to physical testing of IEDs, provides a formal way to validate a design before implementation.

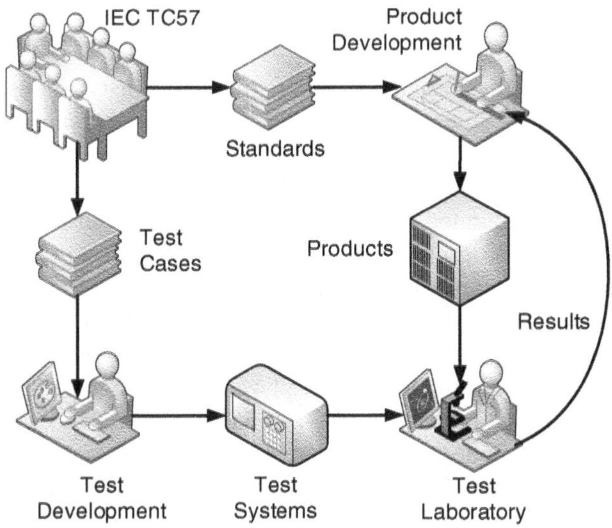

Figure 13.11 Standards, products, and test system relations.

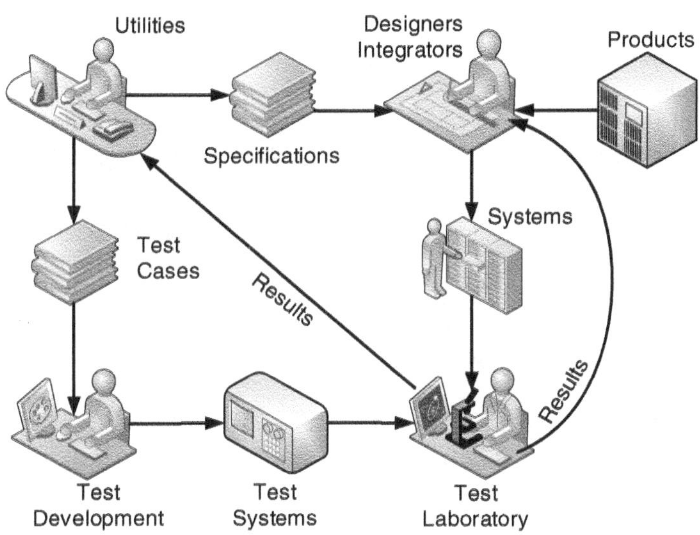

Figure 13.12 Roles and agents in testing and development.

13.7 IEC 61850 Model Validation

IEC 61850 plays a key role in the design validation of digital installations by providing standard models for integrating all roles and agents, as shown in Figure 13.13. Utilities create models (possibly using a DSL as described in Section 11.9) to specify their requirements and to validate the solution against them. Integrators use the code generated from these models (possibly utilizing a DSL compiler to *SCL*) to create a design that meets the specification. Finally, testers use the same models to generate test cases (perhaps using a model-based formal language as described in the UML Test Profile, Section 13.5) and to verify the design against the specification. This concept can be applied throughout the engineering design chain, connecting the four major players in the engineering cycle—utilities, integrators, testers, and validators—by enabling them to access a shared model of the digital installation. Ultimately, even the textual version of IEC 61850 will be autogenerated from the UML model of the standard, avoiding misinterpretation and easing interoperability among tools.

Model-driven testing of IEC 61850 can be incorporated by inserting model checkers into the engineering cycle. This approach validates each phase using the corresponding model defined in the previous phase, generating a verdict on its validity. Figure 13.14 illustrates a possible chain of testing and validation, generating successive verdicts as part of the engineering cycle of an IEC 61850-based system. These verdicts can be checked and integrated into the Waterfall, V-Model, or Agile design cycle.

At each phase of the engineering cycle, a model checker validates the design against the previous step (or Agile Sprint) or a standard model (e.g., UML),

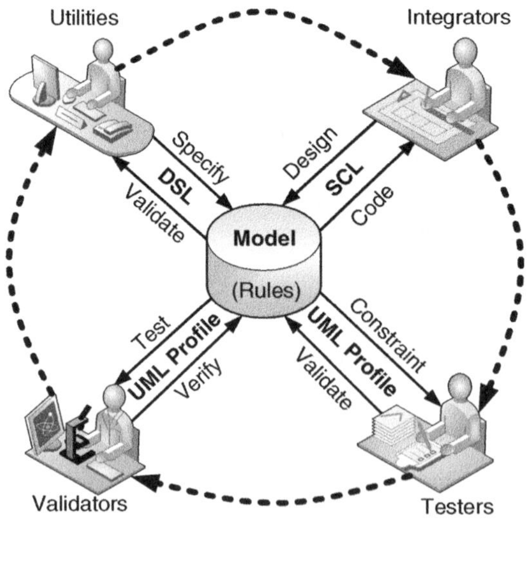

Figure 13.13 Models in testing and validation.

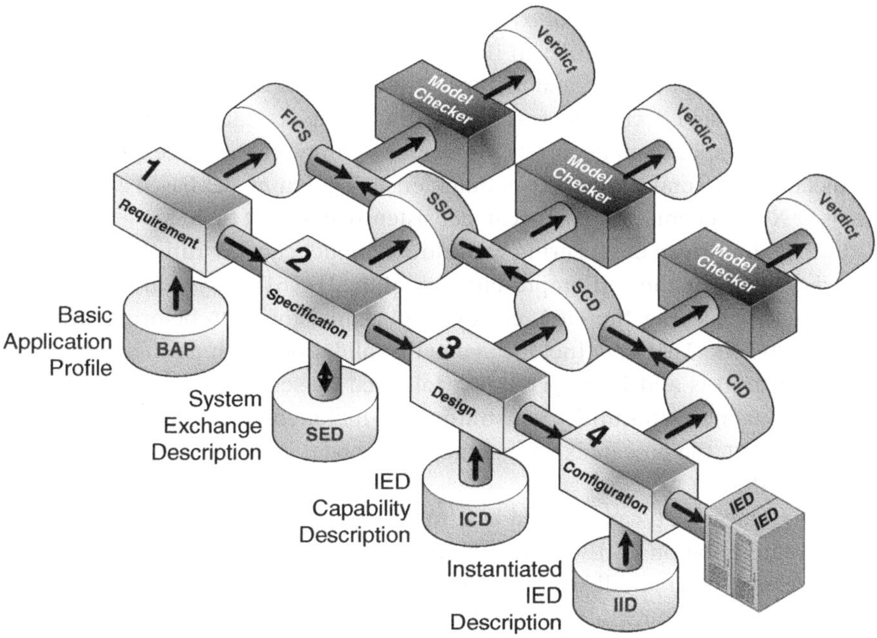

Figure 13.14 IEC 61850 model checking.

generating a verdict on its adherence. In the example of Figure 13.14, three model checkers are used to validate (i) the SSD file against a FICS file, (ii) the SCD file against an SSD file, and (iii) the CID file against the SCD file. The model checker automates the verification of these constraints within the model at every stage of development, using, for instance, an Object Constraint Language (OCL).

13.8 Object Constraint Language

As IEC 61850 is based on UML, the restrictions can be expressed using the OCL. This precise, declarative textual language is part of the UML standard and is used to specify constraints, preconditions, postconditions, invariants, and queries on object-oriented models. Good open-source and proprietary tools, both textual and graphical, are available to validate UML model-based designs against formal constraints. OCL overcomes the limitations of UML's graphical notation by providing textual, formal, declarative, and unambiguous definitions for rules and conditions within a model. These definitions extend beyond structural or syntactic definitions and can be used across various phases of the engineering cycle, including analysis and model-based testing. Using OCL with IEC 61850 enables you to verify the correctness of your system model (e.g., ***SCL*** description, ***ASD*** model, or a UML representation of ***LNs*** and ***DOs***) before or after its implementation, for instance, conformance to rules in IEC 61850 that are not easily captured in ***XSD***; consistency of models (e.g., mandatory attributes, valid data type ranges); or verification of design decisions or utility standards (e.g., certain ***Logical Nodes*** must coexist, specific data objects must not be empty, etc.). OCL expressions are embedded in several IEC 61850 modules, ensuring that model-based engineering tools or XML schema generators can consistently interpret them.

In a model-driven engineering workflow, a model checker runs OCL queries/checks to validate the UML representation of the IEC 61850 system at each stage by directly checking the OCL constraints against the ***SCL*** before generating ***SCD/ICD*** files. This may include syntactic validation, such as checking structural constraints and interoperability, followed by semantic validation, which involves business and utility constraints not included in a model. In this process, any ***SCL*** file is seen as an instance of a model and, as such, must comply with its rules.

In summary, OCL can be used as a formal rule-checking layer on top of the UML representation of IEC 61850 models, verifying semantic constraints that XSD files and schema validation alone cannot enforce. Additionally, it can encode limitations and enforce utility standards, including the user requirements to be checked during the engineering cycle of an SAS. Model checkers based on OCL can guide the review and early correction of bugs at each stage of the engineering cycle. They are prerequisites for implementation validation, followed by unit and system tests before final deployment.

13.9 IEC 61850 Unit Tests

In software design, a unit test is a small, automated test that verifies the smallest testable part of an application. Following this definition, a general algorithm for unit testing an IEC 61850-based ***IED*** or system may be formed by four steps:

- **Injection of messages**—(***GOOSE/SMV/MMS/GSSE/Analog/Discrete***) at points of an ***IED***, or station, bay, or process networks
- **Recording of messages**—(***GOOSE/SMV/MMS/GSSE Analog/Discrete***) at points of an ***IED***, or station, bay, or process networks
- **Evaluation of functional/performance criteria**—comparing records with stated requirements
- **Issuing a verdict**—based on a classification of the evaluation result

These steps can be completed by following the general flow depicted in Figure 13.15: checking the preconditions before the test, performing the test, checking the postconditions after the test, and finally, issuing a verdict about the test result.

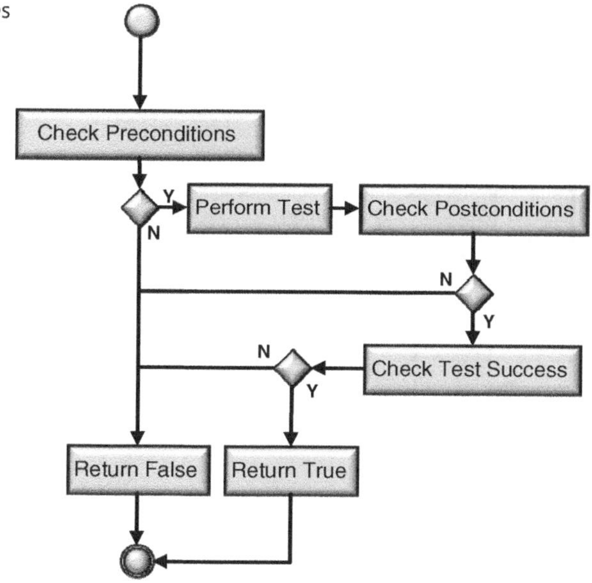

Figure 13.15 Basic activities of a test.

This algorithm involves the collaboration of the author of the test script that creates and revises the test plan, including test cases, expected results, and pre- and post-test setup; the tester that executes the test plan by performing actions listed in each test case and records actual results; and the reviewer that avails the test results by comparing with the expected results to determine whether the test case passed or failed the functional requirements. This general test setup can be used to test ***IEDs***, ***merging units (MUs)***, and distributed components in accordance with IEC 61850.

Testing of ***MUs*** involves the following main steps, as shown in Figure 13.16:

- Generate analog values as input to the ***MU***.
- Receive the sampled analog values from the tested ***MU***.
- Ensure that they provide the required sample measured values.
- Analyze the individual samples' phase (time) and magnitude differences and compare these to the ***MU*** calibration specifications.

A similar setup can be used to test a generic ***IED***, as shown in Figure 13.17, following these steps:

- Subscribe to and monitor the ***GOOSE*** messages received from the tested ***IED***.
- If the tested device has relay outputs, wire them into the test device, so that their operation (time tag) will be compared with the ***GOOSE*** received messages.

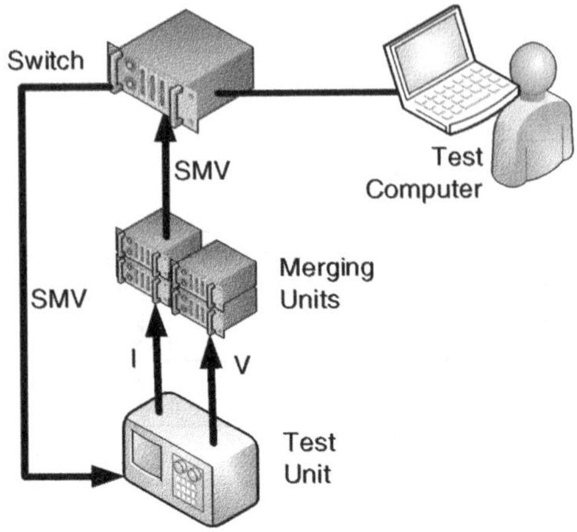

Figure 13.16 Testing of merging units.

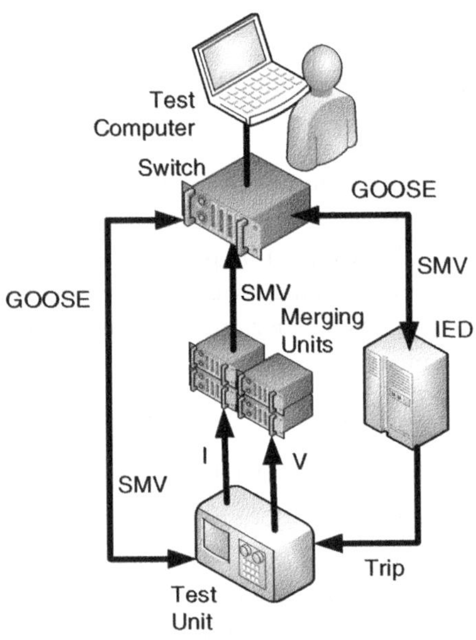

Figure 13.17 Testing of IED with process bus and hard-wired interface.

- Retrieve the waveform records from the tested device.
- Compare with the original waveforms from the simulation tool.

This can be compared with the traditional relay testing method shown in Figure 13.18, where simulated or recorded waveforms are stored on a test computer that drives a test unit to apply these waveforms to an IED while checking the trip messages.

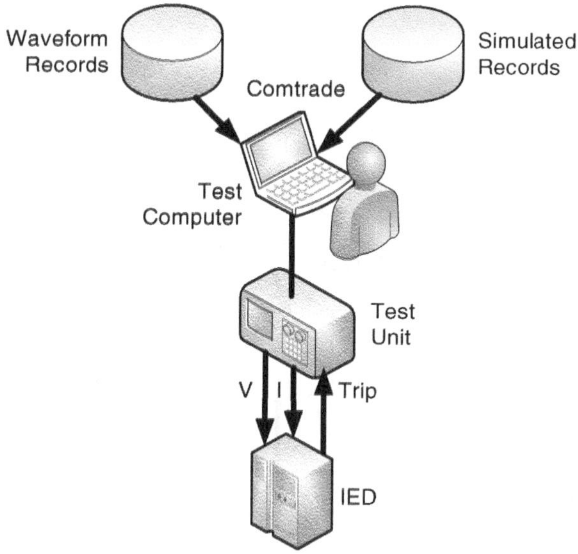

Figure 13.18 Conventional test setup.

These same tools can be used to test the requirements of distributed applications, which comprise multiple devices connected by a communication network, in an IEC 61850-based system.

13.10 IEC 61850 System Tests

To illustrate testing a more complex system, consider the scheme in Figure 13.19 for a simple distributed application involving two ***IEDs*** connected to a switch. A test computer is used to coordinate the following actions:

- Command of multiple test devices with virtual simulators
- Simulation of multiple ***MUs*** and ***IEDs***
- Simulation on the computers of all the required sampled analog values and ***GOOSE*** messages
- Split the simulation results and distribute them between the individual physical devices
- Subscription to the test components to ***GOOSE*** messages from different ***IEDs***

Specific measures are defined by IEC 61850 to allow the systematic testing of selected functions in an energized SAS, by injection and monitoring of test messages, without affecting the entire system. This is provided by setting an object mode attribute (***Mod***) of a ***logic device*** (***LLN0***) or any ***LN*** part of the function under test to a different mode. These modes can be set to the ***On***, ***Off***,

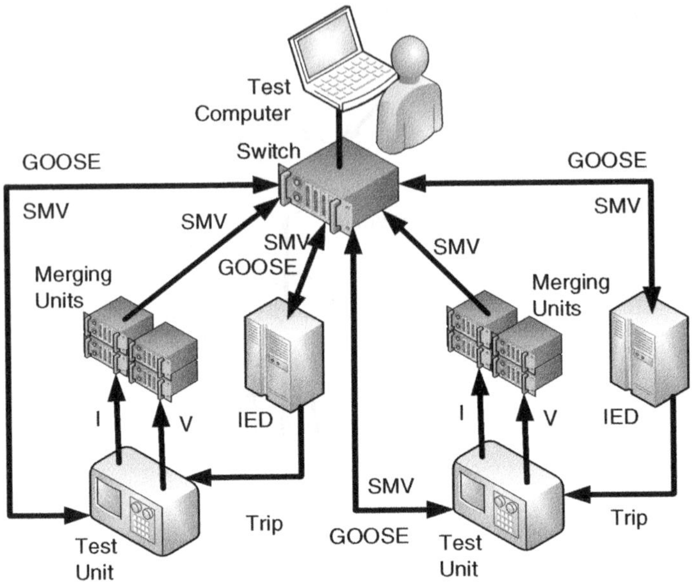

Figure 13.19 Testing distributed applications.

`On-blocked`, or **`Test/blocked`** state in both ***LLN0*** and ***LN***, resulting in various behaviors of the corresponding **`logical node`**, as listed in Table 13.1.

The standard operating mode of a **`logical node`**, when not under test (with ***Mod=On*** **`andBeh.stVal=on`**), being a subscriber to ***GOOSE*** message from another ***LN***, with the **`Test`** attribute set to ***False***, is to perform the intended function, that is, to generate the standard output, as shown in Figure 13.20.

On the other hand, if the ***GOOSE*** message has a test flag set to **`True`**, it will not be executed or propagated by the subscriber ***LN***, as shown in Figure 13.21. This is particularly important during maintenance tests of existing systems.

All these tests are usually performed during the development of a system, forming a chain of engineering tests, as in the Waterfall design cycle described in the following paragraph.

13.11 Engineering Tests

In addition to model validation, engineering tests, whether unit- or system level, are intended to ensure the system performs as intended throughout the engineering cycle. They are usually performed sequentially during the development of a digital system, as illustrated in the chain of Figure 13.22. The figure also shows

Table 13.1 Mode and behavior of logical nodes.

LDMode	LNMode	LNBeh
On	On	On
On-blocked	On	On-blocked
Test	On	Test
Test/blocked	On	Test/blocked
Off	On	Off
On	On-blocked	On-blocked
On-blocked	On-blocked	On-blocked
Test	On-blocked	Test/blocked
Test/blocked	On-blocked	Test/blocked
Off	On-blocked	Off
On	Test	Test
On-blocked	Test	Test/blocked
Test	Test	Test
Test/blocked	Test	Test/blocked
Off	Test	Off
On	Test/blocked	Test/blocked
On-blocked	Test/blocked	Test/blocked
Test	Test/blocked	Test/blocked
Test/blocked	Test/blocked	Test/blocked
Off	Test/blocked	Off
On	Off	Off
On-blocked	Off	Off
Test	Off	Off
Test/blocked	Off	Off
Off	Off	Off

the stakeholders involved (client, integrator, manufacturer, and certifier) and their respective objectives for the following tests:

- **CAT**—Conformance Acceptance Test by a Certifier
- **TAT**—Type Acceptance Test by a Manufacturer
- **FAT**—Factory Acceptance Test by an Integrator
- **SAT**—Site Acceptance Test by the Client

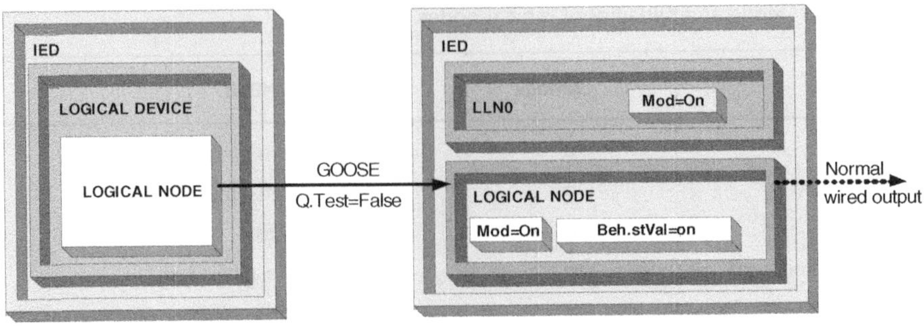

Figure 13.20 GOOSE message in the normal operating mode.

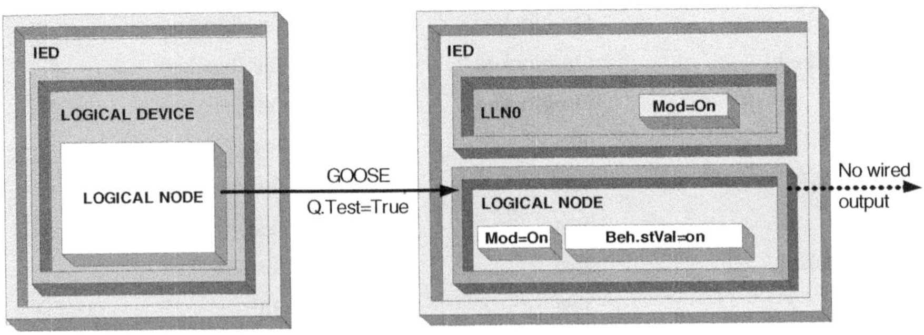

Figure 13.21 GOOSE message in the test operating mode.

Conformance Acceptance Test (CAT) checks whether the system design documents (functional specifications, architecture, diagrams, interface definitions) meet the contractual, *standard*, and technical requirements. Today, it is typically a paper-based process, sometimes with review and simulations, possibly conducted by a certifier; however, it can also be performed through model validation using OCL. It aims to check the *adequacy* (at planning time) of the design by answering the question "Did the design conform to the user requirements?" before implementation/fabrication, after the customer has approved the design baseline.

Type Acceptance Test (TAT) tries to validate that a specific product, device, or ***IED*** type has *consistency* (at design time) with standards, design, and vendor specifications. It is typically performed in accredited laboratories or *manufacturer* facilities, with a focus on compliance with international/industry standards (IEC, IEEE, etc.); electrical, thermal, mechanical, and environmental stress tests; functional tests of the device type (e.g., relay, switch, router); and interoperability with reference implementations (e.g., IEC 61850 communication profiles), resulting in a certified type-tested equipment that can be integrated to the project. It can also be supported by model-based verification using OCL.

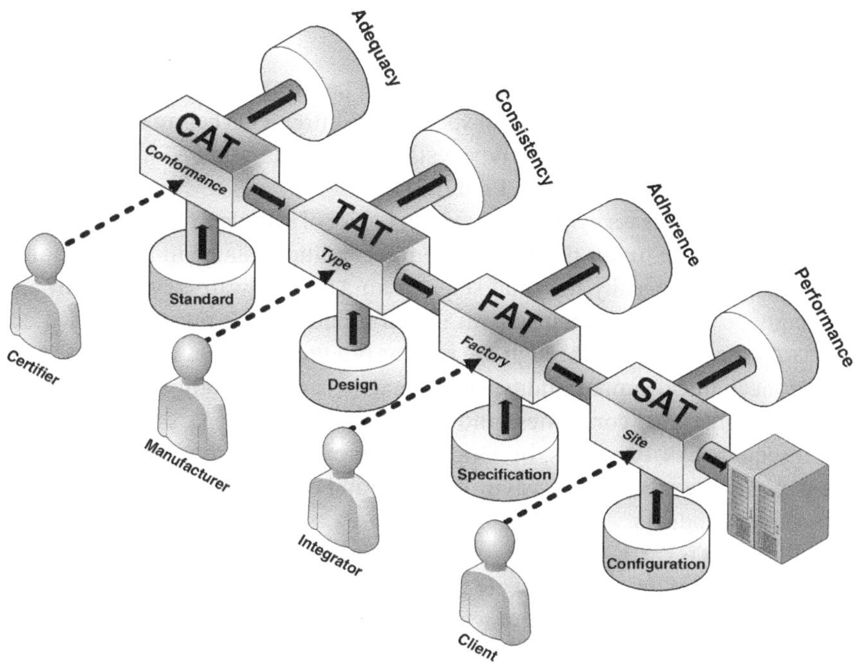

Figure 13.22 Engineering testing sequences.

Factory Acceptance Test (FAT) intends to verify the *adherence* (at production time) of hardware, software, and system integration by an *integrator* to the user's *specification* in the supplier's environment (factory or lab) before shipping to the site. It focuses on hardware functionality, communication protocols, software logic, protection algorithms, interoperability (if IEC 61850 or multi-vendor), and performance under simulated conditions, before the system is ready for delivery. It can also be supported by model-based verification using OCL.

Site Acceptance Test (SAT) aims to demonstrate full system functionality in the real operational environment by validating performance (at deployment time) for the *client* after the site *configuration*. It focuses on installation verification (cabling, input/output signals, and equipment), checking system operation under real-world conditions, and verifying failover, redundancy, and cybersecurity checks, as well as contractual specifications, training, and operator acceptance. The output is a formal approval from the end-user/owner before the system is handed over for operation. It can also be supported by model-based verification using OCL.

These tests are also classified as factory or site tests, depending on the location where they are performed, or as conformance, interoperability, or performance tests, based on their objectives within the engineering cycle.

13.12 Factory Tests

Factory tests are custom-agreed functional tests performed at the manufacturer's facilities to ensure a system meets all specified requirements before it's shipped to the client. It includes three types: type tests, routine tests, and FATs, as illustrated in the UML Use Case Diagram of Figure 13.23.

Type test comprises verifying the correct behavior of sampled ***IEDs*** by exercising the system software under the environmental conditions stated in their technical data sheets. It is typically the final stage of an ***IED*** hardware development and a prerequisite for the commencement of full production. It must be carried out with ***IEDs*** manufactured through the regular production cycle. Typical type tests include mechanical supportability, electromagnetic compatibility, climatic influences, and functional correctness and completeness. Figure 13.24 illustrates the overall sequence of type tests, in which an approved firmware serves as a reference to verify the mechanical, environmental, and electromagnetic compatibility of a series of products.

A routine test is carried out for each product before leaving the manufacturer. It is the final stage of an ***IED*** hardware production and a precondition for customer delivery. It may also be carried out with ***IEDs*** manufactured through the regular

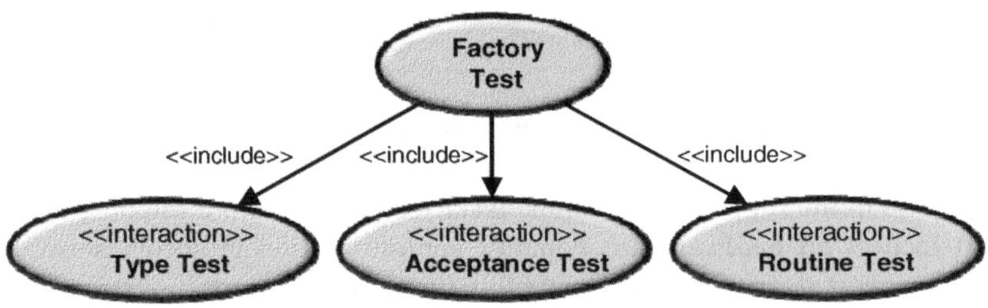

Figure 13.23 Contents of a factory test.

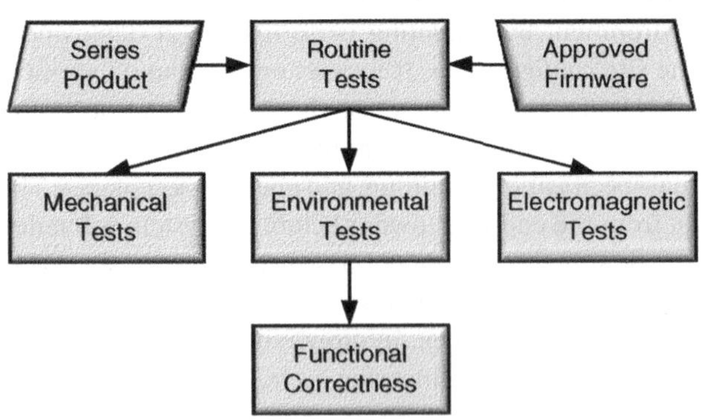

Figure 13.24 Contents of a type test.

production cycle. Figure 13.25 shows a typical UML Use Case Diagram of a routine test, comprising the insulation, function, and burn-in tests.

Factory or system acceptance tests are customer-agreed functional tests of an SAS or its parts, using the parameter set for the planned application. It should be done in the factory or by a system integrator using process-simulating test equipment. The FAT and SAT are based on customer requirements for an SAS, usually done by the system integrator, and are generally witnessed by the customer. FAT of IEC 61850 *IEDs* checks that the data model, the communication services, and the performance defined in the standard and implemented in the system follow the project specification. The precondition for this phase is the complete assembly of the system, full documentation of the system on paper and in files (if applicable), selection of simulator(s) for the missing parts, and a test plan negotiated between the system integrator and the user. These tests differ from traditional systems in that they support automatic or semi-automatic testing or model verification using the *SCD* file and facilitate the easy simulation of missing parts. Compared with conventional signal tests, object-oriented tests may reduce test effort.

System tests are intended to check the correct behavior of the *IEDs* and the overall SAS under various application conditions. They mark the final stage in the development of *IEDs* within the SAS product family. They mainly consist of testing each function, interoperability among *IEDs*, and performance of the whole system, as shown in the UML Use Case Diagram of Figure 13.26.

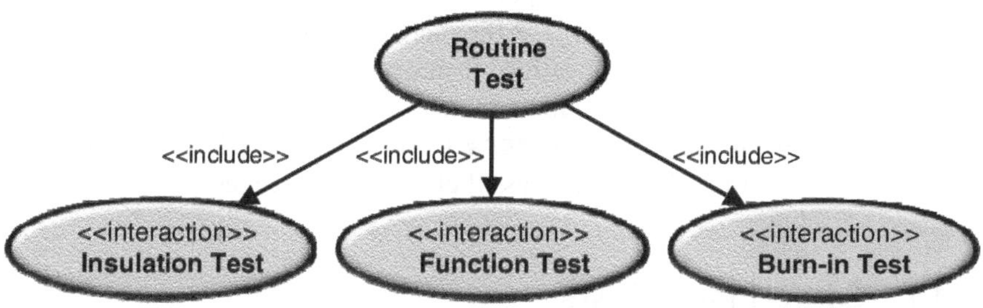

Figure 13.25 Contents of a routine test.

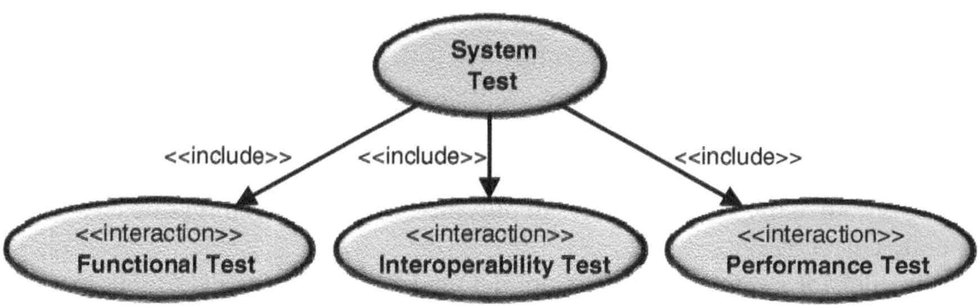

Figure 13.26 Contents of a system test.

Among these tests, interoperability is perhaps the main requirement for IEC 61850-based systems.

13.13 Interoperability Tests

Interoperability tests aim to demonstrate whether ***IEDs*** exchange data appropriately. They are primarily used to ensure interoperability between partners, thereby avoiding complex integration and acceptance testing when schedules are tight, visibility is high, nerves are raw, and the situation is less ideal for troubleshooting and repair. As there is no interoperability testing standard, the results are based on an agreement between the parties and are primarily used to demonstrate interoperability within each scheme.

Typically, they are performed by connecting two or more ***IEDs*** to a LAN, stimulating the exchange of IEC 61850 messages, and exercising their interactive behavior. The test mainly simulates faults with relay test sets to check the exchange of ***GOOSE/SV*** messages or ***C/S*** control requests from operators or to simulate the behavior of devices not connected by generating system service messages and background traffic. The test setup can be similar to the scheme for testing a distributed application (Figure 13.19).

The main difficulties with interoperability tests are that there is no standard to certify their results, and no third party is entitled to verify them. UCA, the International Users Group (UCAIug), is the main body responsible for IEC 61850 interoperability testing and certification. It maintains the official Conformance Test Procedures (CTP) and accredits test laboratories, issuing the IEC 61850 Certificate of Conformance (CoC) for ***IEDs***. Certificates are publicly listed on the UCAIug website for those items that pass their conformance tests.

13.14 Conformance Tests

A conformance test is a type test for device communication, intended to demonstrate that the device's physical interface and data flow conform to the rules defined in the standard. The main objective is to illustrate the interaction among ***IEDs*** for a given communications architecture and specific network load, to reduce the risk of failed interoperability between devices when put in service, to determine if a relay or ***IED*** conforms to the specifications of the standard, and to enhance the ability of users to purchase systems that integrate easily and operate correctly.

The rules for conformance tests are detailed in Part 10 of IEC 61850. In principle, they do not replace SAT and FAT, which are dedicated to testing a design against customer requirements. Conformance tests are devoted to checking devices against IEC 61850 requirements. As such, they reduce costs and interoperability issues, especially when using IEDs from different suppliers, thereby increasing confidence in the solution.

Following conformance testing terminology, a Device Under Test (DUT) can be checked by a static review, to examine its implementation statements for conformance, mainly to check if sufficient requirements were declared, or by a dynamic test, by running a set of tests against the device, primarily to check if it was implemented correctly. Typically, a test is performed by exchanging messages between a test system and the DUT. The test system sends an array of test messages to the DUT and records the responses. Messages are selected to exercise all DUT communication features and verify or certify them.

Two categories of test cases are used to confirm the conformance of a device to the IEC 61850 standard:

- **Positive test case**—for verification of normal conditions, by sending the correct messages, and typically resulting in a ***response+*** from the device
- **Negative test case**—verifying abnormal conditions, by checking the correct error messages, and typically resulting in a ***response-*** from the device

IEC 61850 defines conformance test cases for different standard devices, models, and classes, including ***Server***, ***Logical Device***, ***Data***, ***Attribute*** models, ***Data Set*** model, ***Setting Group Model***, ***Log Control Model***, ***GOOSE*** events, ***Control Model***, ***Substitution Model***, transmission of ***Sample Values***, ***Time*** and ***Time*** synchronization, ***File*** transfer, etc. This enables the application of conformance tests to system components, relays, ***IEDs***, gateway servers, client/server software, and integration tools, as well as for software certification of IEC 61850 products, before their performance tests of adequacy to a specific user-defined function.

13.15 Performance Tests

A performance test is different from conformance or interoperability tests. Instead of checking whether an ***IED*** complies with the standard, performance testing verifies whether the system meets, for instance, the timing, reliability, and scalability requirements defined by the user. A performance test of an IEC 61850 system evaluates how well the system performs under realistic or stressed operating conditions, including end-to-end latency, jitter and synchronization accuracy, throughput and bandwidth usage on the ***process bus*** and ***station bus***, system behavior under load, and recovery time after faults.

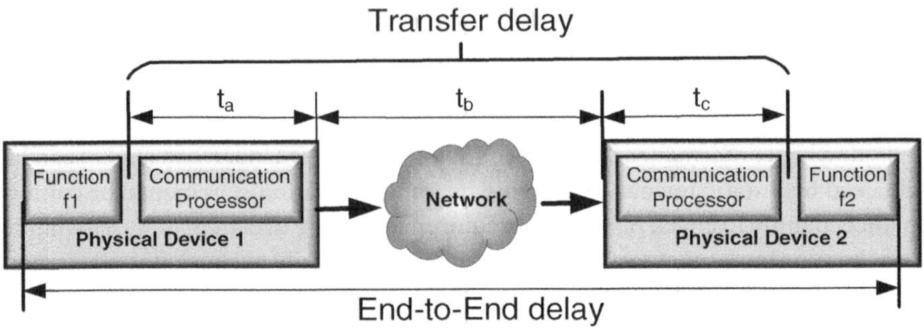

Figure 13.27 Transfer time composition.

Being a real-time system, one of the main objectives of performance tests is to evaluate the time needed for a critical control message from the initiating event to result in outputs from the subscriber ***IEDs***. They depend mainly on network communications latency, time synchronization, and accuracy.

Communication latency, or transfer delay, is the time it takes the network to deliver a process value from a sending physical device to the process logic of a receiving device. It is composed of the following parcels, as shown in Figure 13.27.

- t_a: the time required for the sending device to transmit the process value (estimated)
- t_b: the time required for the network to deliver the message (measured)
- t_c: the time the receiving device requires to deliver the value to its process logic (estimated)

Accordingly, there are two main types of latency:

- **Output latency**—a time interval between a physical input (or message) change and the appearance of a message on the output media (or physical output)
- **Input latency**—a time interval between the appearance of a message on the input media (or physical input) and a physical (or message) output change

Both apply to ***GOOSE***, ***GSSE***, ***SV*** input and output messages, and C/S report and control messages in IEC 61850-based systems.

Performance tests for time synchronization and accuracy aim to verify the ***IED's*** ability to communicate timestamp information for an instrumented event. Accordingly, they are classified into two types of tests:

- **Time from external source**—The first accuracy measurement is made with the ***IED*** directly receiving time from the same external source used by the test system

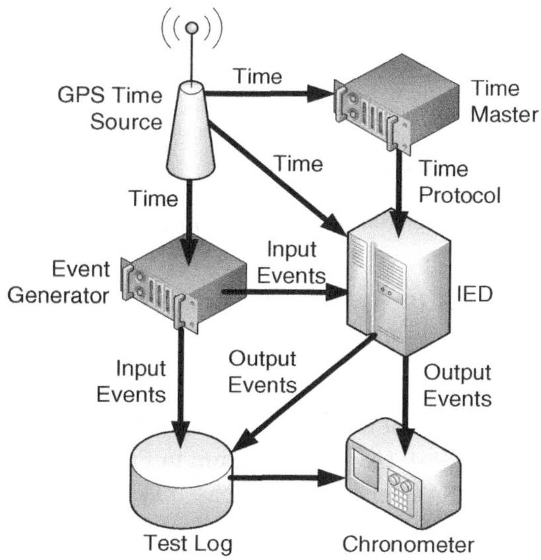

Figure 13.28 Time synchronization and accuracy test setup.

- **Time from time synchronization protocol**—The second accuracy measurement is made with the ***IED*** using the time synchronization protocol with the Time Master function in the test system.

Figure 13.28 shows a general test setup for time synchronization and accuracy, using a universal time source (GPS) that feeds the same time signal to a time master, an event generator, and the ***IED*** under test. The time master distributes these time signals in the network in a suitable protocol to all connected ***IEDs***. At the same time, the event generator simulates input events to the ***IED***, which generates timed signals and messages as output events. All input and output events are recorded in a test log and a chronometer that checks time synchronization and accuracy.

After testing all performance requirements, the ultimate test can be executed by the user as part of the site tests.

13.16 Site Tests

SAT are performed at the customer's facilities to verify that installed ***IEDs*** or systems function correctly and meet all technical, functional, and performance requirements in their final environment. They include verifying each data and control point and the correct functionality within and between SAS and its operating environment, covering the entire installed plant using the final parameter set.

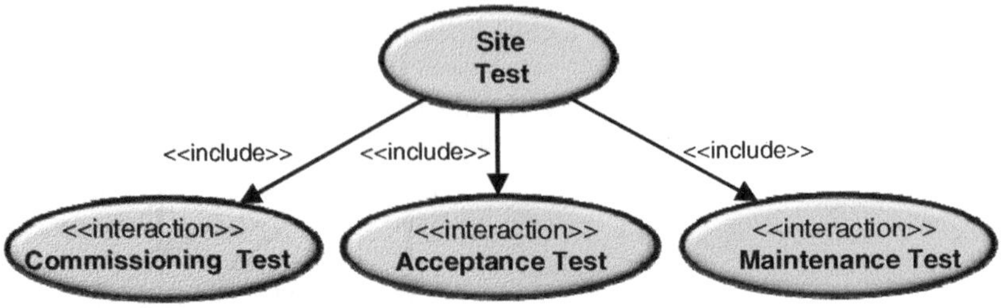

Figure 13.29 Contents of a site acceptance test.

The SAT is a contractual customer-agreed functional test, a precondition for the SAS being accepted, put into operation, and kept in operation, usually comprising three types of tests: acceptance, commissioning, and maintenance tests, as shown in the UML Use Case Diagram in Figure 13.29.

The SAT for IEC 61850-based systems primarily verifies that the data model, communication services, and performance defined in the standard are implemented and adhere to the project specification. The precondition for the SAT is the on-site availability of all physical parts of the SA system, with complete documentation on paper and in files, if applicable. Depending on the actual system design, many wires may be replaced by serial and network connections. The starting condition for the commissioning test involves finalizing in-site installations, including initial tests such as power supply, cabling verification, and the provision of all serial links, as seen in traditional systems, to check that the system was installed correctly. The starting condition for the acceptance test is the finalization of the commissioning phase, with the updated as-built documentation available in either paper or digital form, if applicable, and a test plan negotiated between the system integrator and the user. It aims to check that the as-built systems meet the client's requirements and business needs.

Maintenance tests may be performed periodically throughout the SAS's useful life, or after major updates or upgrades, to verify that the system continues to operate and perform as expected. These tests are primarily intended to uncover hidden failures not detected by online monitoring, typically used in software-based systems, or by post-fault analysis of protection systems. Most of these tests are also intended to verify the conformance of statements, certifications, and interoperability declarations provided by vendors and certification authorities.

13.17 Conformance Statements

A conformance statement is a formal declaration, provided by a vendor, associated with a specific implementation of a standard in a product or ***IED***. Among the conformance statements, an Interoperability Declaration is a document issued by a vendor or competent authority stating that the supplied good or service meets the required specifications to operate with other vendor goods or services. It can be a manufacturer's declaration of interoperability testing for different devices. Unlike a conformance certification, an interoperability declaration is not standardized by the IEC; it is usually provided by manufacturers and requested by clients.

A Conformance Certification is a document certified by a competent authority that the supplied good or service meets the required specifications. It is a declaration from an independent certification entity that the device has been tested for conformity. It is also called a certificate of conformity. For the IEC 61850, the procedures for performing certification tests are defined and maintained by Utility Communications Architecture (UCA), the International Users Group designated by IEC. In contrast, the required tests are described in IEC 61850 module 10.

To guide the process of conformance testing, the International Organization for Standardization (ISO) defines several types of documents to be supplied by manufacturers of IEC 61850-based products or systems:

- ***PICS—Protocol Implementation Conformance Statement***
- ***MICS—Model Implementation Conformance Statement***
- ***PIXIT—Protocol Implementation eXtra Information for Testing***
- ***ACSI Basic Conformance Statement***
- ***ACSI Models Conformance Statement***
- ***ACSI Service Conformance Statement***
- ***GOOSE Conformance Statement***
- ***GSSE Conformance Statement***
- ***SCL Conformance Statement***

A ***PICS*** document summarizes the standardized communication capabilities of the system or device to be tested. It contains information regarding the ***ACSI***, optional parts, specific restrictions, or add-ons. Its primary use is selecting the appropriate set of tests, providing the basis for conformance tests. It also refers to the implementation of the communication stack and the model mapping to it. The ***PICS*** serves three purposes: (1) selecting the appropriate set of tests; (2) ensuring that the tests appropriate to a claim of conformance are performed; and (3) providing the basis for the review of the static conformance.

A ***MICS*** document outlines the standard data object model elements supported by the system or device and provides information about the data models that are part of the ***ACSI***.

A ***PIXIT*** document provides specific information about the system or device that is outside the scope of IEC 61850. As such, it is not subject to standardization. Its main objectives are to provide information on the physical setup not covered by the ***ACSI***, as well as details on hardware, communication sockets, and other relevant information.

An ***ACSI*** Model Conformance Statement details the standard data object models supported by the system or device. It includes definitions of the specific ***logical nodes***, standard data classes, and attribute types. These definitions are also found in the ***ICD*** file and the response to the service ***getDirectory***, if applicable.

A ***GOOSE*** or ***GSSE*** Conformance Statement defines the publisher and subscriber services provided by the ***IED*** to test IED communication.

SCL Conformance Statements define the capabilities of the ***IED*** or system configurator for exporting ***ICD*** and ***IID*** files, importing and using ***SCD*** files, and data flow engineering.

In addition to these statements, the supplier must confirm that the design adheres to the FICS and meets the user requirements, as described in Section 12.10.

These documents are used jointly across all system testing phases, including factory, site, interoperability, performance, and conformance tests, supporting the development of IEC 61850 tests and tools, conformance certification, and interoperability declarations.

13.18 Summary

Testing is a significant part of design and integration, as well as of the commissioning and maintenance of any extensive software system, such as an SAS. The ***IED*** manufacturer typically performs unit testing on physical hardware, software, or logical nodes, while accredited labs conduct conformance testing in accordance with IEC 61850. Functional tests are applied to the assembled system during commissioning and maintenance, designed to verify its behavior in accordance with an accepted specification or requirement document.

Testing tools must have the necessary resources to exercise the specific functional requirements of IEC 61850-based systems, and, as such, they are treated as ***IEDs*** with specialized capabilities. This includes the ability to simulate external and internal components of the SAS. A testing architecture was described in this chapter, using UML, with all resources modeled in an object-oriented approach. As an example, classes and software packages are specified for a process simulator to mimic the behavior of switchyard equipment, such as instrument transformers, breakers, and switches, during the test. Similar classes were listed for a network simulator to exercise the behavior of any ***logical node*** on the station or process network. An operator simulator was also included to model the behavior of local and remote human–machine interfaces to the SAS. The UML Test Profile, as defined by the OMG, was used to model all test components and to specify a test scheduler, a timer, and an arbiter. These objects sequence the test, measure event times, and decide on test verdicts.

Due to their inherent complexity and dimension, the deployment and maintenance of IEC 61850-based systems require a structured approach to testing. This includes verification during the design and commissioning phases and routine maintenance during the operational phase. The primary objective is to compare the system's actual performance with its intended functionality. In this respect, semantic and syntactic design validation using model checkers based on formal methods, such as the OMG's OCL, is the obvious choice. However, it requires learning additional (textual and graphical) languages and new software packages, in addition to the already defined IEC 61850 tools. Many new concepts, such as Artificial Intelligence (AI) and Large Language Models (LLMs), are being proposed and developed to reduce this complexity.

This chapter introduced the main testing models defined by IEC 61850, including FAT, TAT, system acceptance test, and SAT, as well as the validation, conformance, and interoperability demonstrations necessary to guarantee SAS's reliability.

13.19 Review Questions

1. Define the difference between verification and testing in the context of digital SAS. What does each method aim to demonstrate about the system?

2. Explain why IEC 61850-based SAS particularly benefit from model-based testing instead of manual, capture–replay, or script-driven testing.

3. Evaluate the limitations of traditional signal-based testing when applied to object-oriented IEC 61850 systems. How does object-oriented testing improve coverage and reduce test effort?

4. Consider a transformer protection bay with safety and liveness requirements. Explain how model-based testing can be used to verify these requirements before implementation.

5. List and briefly describe the primary factory test types—type tests, routine tests, and FATs—and explain their roles in the product lifecycle.

6. Discuss the importance of the `logical node` attribute ***`Mod`*** (`mode`) and the related ***`LN`*** behaviors in enabling safe testing within energized SAS

environments. How do these modes help prevent unintended operations during testing?

7 Outline a test procedure for verifying the proper operation of a ***MU*** using ***SV*** messages. Which signals need to be injected, and which outputs should be analyzed?

8 Compare conformance testing with interoperability testing for IEC 61850 devices. Why can conformance be standardized while interoperability cannot?

9 Describe the roles of ***PICS***, ***MICS***, and ***PIXIT*** documents during conformance testing. How does each one help in choosing and carrying out the right test cases?

10 A system integrator must conduct a FAT for a multi-vendor IEC 61850 station. Identify the key elements that need to be simulated or validated, and explain how the ***SCD*** file supports this process.

11 Explore the role of model checkers and the OCL in validating IEC 61850 engineering artifacts such as ***SSD***, ***SCD***, and ***CID*** files. What types of constraints can OCL verify that XML schemas alone cannot?

12 Suggest a comprehensive testing process for an IEC 61850 project—from initial design validation to on-site acceptance—explaining the roles of CAT, TAT, FAT, and SAT within the entire engineering cycle.

14

Security Models

14.1 Introduction

Current power networks have a large surface area that is vulnerable to cybersecurity threats because of their extensive communication systems within and between utilities, as well as the widespread use of distributed, multivendor software-based devices and functions. Any security breach in these systems can cause widespread impacts, such as power outages over large regions, emphasizing the need for a structured plan of preventative measures. Security should be a fundamental part of the automation architecture of substations, power plants, and wide-area systems, and it should be integrated into their specifications from the start.

Security, reliability, and dependability are vital for substation and control systems, especially for protection functions that depend on these networks. The shift to digital and Ethernet devices has fundamentally changed the main pathways for tripping and control signals both inside and outside a substation, replacing the traditional copper wiring that used to connect these devices and now exposing these paths to both internal and external threats.

14.2 Learning Objectives

This chapter provides a layered overview of power system cybersecurity requirements, structured according to hierarchical domains and the Purdue Enterprise Reference Architecture and Methodology (PERA). It includes the common domains and typical policies recommended for each automation level, primarily based on IEC 62351—Cyber Security Series for Smart Grid, the standard recommended for securing IEC 61850-based systems. The requirements span from local substations and power plants to higher levels of System Operation, Business, and Corporate functions, covering the entire attack surface exposed by power systems.

The chapter ends with a review of reliability measures, mainly for digital substations, along with cybersecurity countermeasures to maintain the original reliability and dependability of protection and control functions, as well as specific standard recommendations for IEC 61850-based systems.

14.3 Cybersecurity Requirements

In cybersecurity of Operation Technology (OT), the traditional principles of confidentiality, integrity, and availability—often referred to as the CIA triad in Information Technology (IT) systems—are complemented by the principle of Accountability, forming the foundational framework for protecting automation systems and data, with the following objectives:

- **Confidentiality**—protects information from unauthorized access and disclosure
- **Integrity**—guarantees that data is accurate, complete, and has not been altered without authorization
- **Availability**—ensures that systems, services, assets, and data are accessible and usable when needed by authorized users
- **Accountability or Non-repudiation**—prevents the denial of an action that took place or the claim of an action that did not take place. It is also required for IT systems, but is less common in OT systems.

For power system automation, each term of the CIA triad has specific means and objectives, mainly related to latency, assurance, and secrecy of grid/market information, as listed as follows:

- **Confidentiality (customer information):**
  - Privacy of customer information
  - Electric market information
  - Corporate information
- **Integrity (assurance):**
  - Data has not been modified without authorization
  - The source of data is authenticated
  - Timestamp is known and authenticated
  - Quality of data is known and authenticated
- **Availability (latency needs):**
  - ≤ 4 ms for protective relaying
  - Sub-seconds for transmission of situational awareness
  - Seconds for substation and feeder (SCADA) data
  - Minutes for monitoring noncritical equipment
  - Hours for meter reading and longer-term market pricing
  - Days/weeks/months for power quality

- **Non-repudiation or accountability**
  - Identification of audit logging
  - Event recording
  - Network management

Due to the utility's wide-area communication system, these requirements typically span a vast geographic area, making them increasingly crucial for IEC 61850-based automation systems.

14.4 Communication Architecture

The communication architecture of an electricity utility can be represented as a layered structure composed of different domains, each with its own objective. A domain is a set of related assets, usually located in a specific space, with predefined perimeters, such as:

- **Physical perimeter**—delimited by walls and geographical location
- **Electronic perimeter**—delimited by logical borders among networks
- **Domain perimeter**—delimited by organizational responsibilities
- **Functional perimeter**—delimited by functionality, organized as systems

For cybersecurity analysis of automation systems, six domains are typically classified in a utility, as shown in Figure 14.1:

1. Substation Domain
2. Control Room Domain
3. Wide-Area Domain
4. Control Center Domain
5. Corporate Domain
6. External Domain

The following paragraphs contain a bottom-up description of these domains.

The Substation Domain gathers all local communication switches and installation automation resources at the lowest level, near the switchyard. It usually encompasses the substation and ***process networks***, linking the ***IEDs*** and ***control/merging units*** that monitor and control the power equipment. Subdomains can be defined inside the substation, for the ***substation***, ***bay***, and ***process network***, or for specific parts of the local area network.

The next level refers to the Control Room Domain, which typically includes a local demilitarized zone (DMZ) to support management processes, segregated from the automation network that connects the operator and engineering stations, as well as the switches and routers for local and remote communications.

The Wide-Area Domain's third level uses a long-distance wide-area network (WAN) of routers and communication channels to connect substations, power

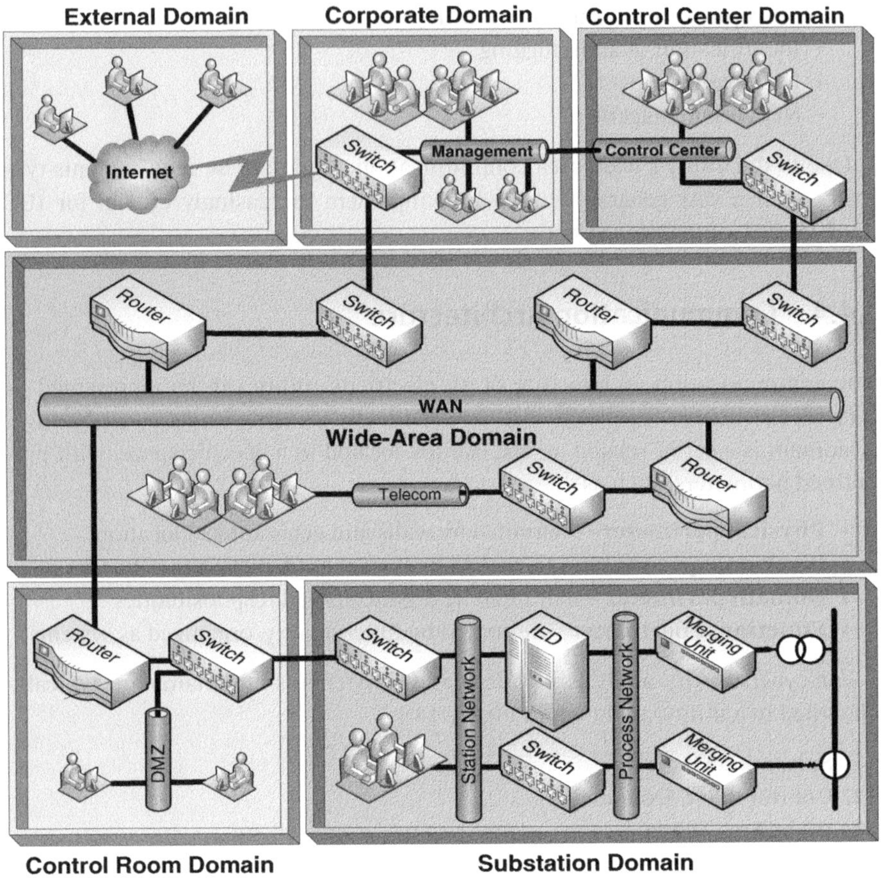

Figure 14.1 Utility automation domains.

plants, and corporate offices. Depending on the utility's size, a telecommunication control center will monitor, control, and maintain this company-wide network. This domain also connects the installations to the utility control center.

The fourth level, the Control Center Domain, is where the utility electrical grid is controlled from a central point, using the WAN of the Wide-Area Domain. External communication to the national grid dispatch is also located in this domain.

The fifth level, the Corporate Domain, comprises the company's IT resources for management purposes. This level also connects to the corporate WAN, extending its administrative and management processes to the power plant and substation domains.

Finally, the sixth level, the External Domain, encompasses companies that utilize external IT resources to communicate and access external processes. This may include cloud services such as Infrastructure as a Service (IaaS) or Platform as a Service (PaaS), as well as market transactions, grid operation, and communication services for external users or employers.

These layers can be divided into subdomains for segregating services and security measures. A utility's physical IT/OT assets can be represented in a more detailed layered architecture, modelled and adapted from the original Purdue model (PERA). Figure 14.2 shows a generic view of a utility's IT/OT physical assets and their connections to external entities. This figure is just conceptual. It does not intend to represent all aspects or precise domains of a specific utility data network.

According to this model, modern electrical power systems form a linked network of power plants and substations, needing a hierarchy of communication networks to convey information from the field equipment and switchgear, through merging and control units accessible by a process network local to each station, up to a station network where Intelligent Electronic Devices (***IED***) are interconnected to station computers and engineering stations for operational functions. Station and process switches from Local Area Networks (LAN) are necessary to deploy the local distributed automation functions. These ***station networks*** are connected by routers, forming a Wide-Area Network (WAN) that spans several stations and eventually the entire corporate communication system, with external access to the Internet for operational and administrative functions. Control centers and internal and external users use this network to perform wide-area functions and remote actions on each station's local systems.

Following the Purdue model, the physical IT/OT asset architecture is divided into six hierarchical layers, identified by six numerical levels shown in Figure 14.2, that interact or are related vertically and horizontally:

- **Level 0**—Field Network
- **Level 1**—Process Network
- **Level 2**—Station Network
- **Level 3**—Control Center Network
- **Level 4**—Corporate Network
- **Level 5**—External Network

The lowest layer, at level 0, also known as the Field Network, comprises all physical items that communicate directly with switchyard equipment, such as circuit breakers, transformers, and reactors. Generically, this level refers to any installation at Generation, Transmission, Distribution, or Prosumer (Consumers and/or Producers) stations. Industrial protocols such as IEC 61850, IEC 61131, Modbus, and OPC/UA are typically used to communicate directly with these assets.

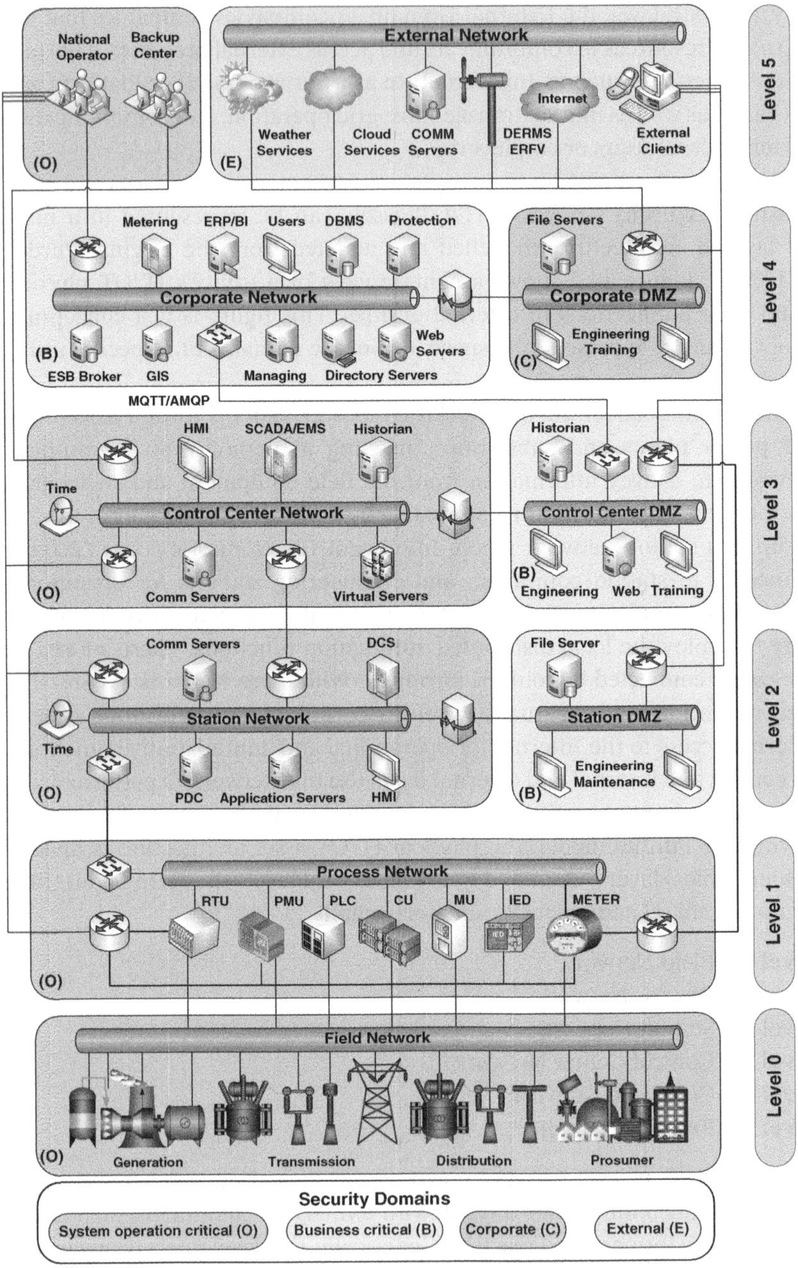

Figure 14.2 Power system architectural levels.

The second layer, at level 1, also known as the Process Network, comprises all physical items that directly monitor, meter, or control power system equipment such as busbars, feeders, circuit breakers, transformers, reactors, etc. Industrial protocols, such as IEC 61850 (***process bus***), IEC 61131, Modbus, and OPC/UA, are typically used to communicate locally among these assets and with Level 0 assets. Typical items in this layer include Remote Terminal Unit (RTU), Phasor Measurement Unit (***PMU***), Programmable Logic Controller (PLC), Intelligent Electronic Device (***IED***), ***Merging Units*** (***MU***), ***CU*** (***Control Units***), and Meters. Switches and Routers can be used to communicate locally and remotely from this layer, typically using protocols such as DNP, IEC 104, IEC 61850, and OPC.

The third layer, at level 2, also known as the Station Network, comprises all physical items that centrally supervise, monitor, and control the entire substation or power plant. Currently, this level is primarily based on the IEC 61850 protocol (***station bus***). Still, protocols such as IEC 61131, Modbus, and OPC/UA have also been adopted to facilitate communication with lower levels of the system. Typical items included in this layer comprise Communication Servers, Digital Control System (DCS), Phasor Data Concentrator (PDC), Engineering Stations, Human–Machine Interface (HMI), Gateways (GW), Application Servers, and Time Servers. Switches and Routers can communicate locally and remotely at this layer, using typical protocols such as IEC 61850, DNP, and IEC 104. Optionally, this level may include a station DMZ segregated from the rest of the local assets by a Gateway, connecting Engineering, Maintenance, and File servers, that can be remotely accessed from other layers.

The fourth layer, at level 3, also known as the Control Center Network, comprises all physical items that centrally supervise, monitor, and control the utility substations and power plants. Again, this is just a conceptual view and does not intend to represent a specific utility's existing or required assets. This includes the primary and backup Generation and Transmission Control Centers. Typically, this level primarily uses VLANs and protocols such as DNP3, routable IEC 61850 messages, IEC 104, and ICCP to communicate with lower levels (RTU and SCADA in substations and power plants), and IEC 870-6/ICCP protocols to the National or Regional Control Center at the upper level. The main items included in this layer are communication servers, virtual servers, historians, SCADA/EMS, HMI (human-machine interface), gateways, application servers, and time servers. Switches and Routers can communicate locally and remotely from this layer. Typically, a Gateway separates one or more Control Center DMZ from the rest of the Control Center assets, connecting Engineering, Training, and Web servers, and Historians, which are remotely accessed from other layers.

The fifth layer, at level 4, also known as the Corporate Network, comprises all IT physical items that interact with the Control Centers to process business, engineering, and administrative tasks. This typically includes ERP (Enterprise

Resource Planning), BI (Business Intelligence), DBMS (Database Management Systems), ESB (Enterprise Service Bus), Directory Services, and Web Servers. Other corporate services that operate at this level may include servers for revenue metering, platforms for acquiring information from mobile equipment, remote management of protection systems, and business and accounting systems. Typically, this level uses mainly VLAN or Real-Time Streaming Protocol (RTSP) (e.g., MATT or AMQP) to communicate with the Control Center Network, and other protocols to communicate with the National or Regional Control Center at the upper level. The main physical assets included in this layer are communication servers, virtual servers, historians, gateways, application servers, and time servers. Switches and Routers can communicate locally and remotely from this layer. One or more Corporate DMZs are usually segregated from the rest of the corporate assets by a Gateway, which connects Engineering, Training, and File servers and can be remotely accessed from other layers.

The sixth layer, at top level 5, also known as the External Network, comprises all external entities that communicate with the utility for business, operation, engineering, and administrative tasks. This includes the grid or National Control Center, market operators, External Backup Center, Cloud Services, Communication Servers, DERMS (Distributed Energy Resource Management Systems), External Clients, and Internet users. Specific corporate clients include employees who need to access internal resources from an external site. Typically, this level uses mainly VLAN, HTTP, and WS (Web Services) to communicate with the Corporate Network and lower levels.

All these internal and external connections expose a vast attack surface for hackers, offering many types of threats, as described in the following paragraphs.

14.5 Power System Threats

A power system cybersecurity threat is any potential danger or malicious act that seeks to damage, disrupt, steal, or gain unauthorized access to utility system data, networks, or digital systems. As such, they can be classified into two main categories:

- **Inadvertent Threats**, resulting from:
  - Safety Failures
  - Software/Firmware Malfunctions
  - Equipment Failures
  - Carelessness
  - Natural Disasters
- **Deliberate Threats**, resulting from:
  - Disgruntled Employees

- Industrial Espionage
- Vandalism
- Cyber Hackers
- Viruses and Worms
- Theft
- Terrorism

These deliberate threats can originate from various sources, including hackers, cybercriminal organizations, insiders, or even nation-states, and they target existing vulnerabilities in software, hardware, or human behavior. The threats to software and hardware used in PAC systems can occur across all seven layers of the OSI stack and target all types of IEC 61850 communication and messages, due to the typical vulnerabilities of each layer, as shown in Figure 14.3.

Depending on the attack's effects and objectives, different types of cyberattacks may target PAC systems, as listed in Table 14.1.

Many sources of information are available to support a cyberattack on a utility automation system, such as:

- Books on attack techniques
- Websites with free attack software
- Hired hackers to write sophisticated attacks
- Dark web resources
- Target information shared among hackers
- Cyber-warfare groups funded by nations
- Annual conventions of attackers
- Security tool developers

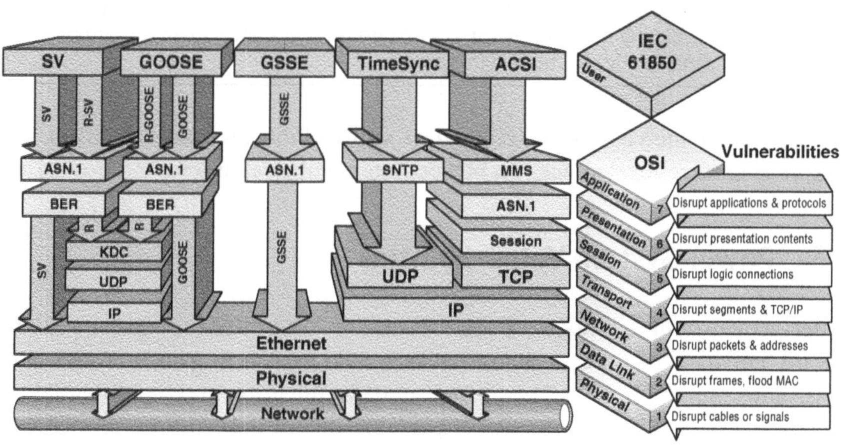

Figure 14.3 OSI stack and IEC 61850 vulnerabilities.

Table 14.1 Types of cyberattacks.

Attack	Description
Sniff	Unauthorized traffic analysis
Replay	Unauthorized replay of captured traffic
Spoof	Impersonating an authorized user
Dos	Deny service or overload the network
Error	Operator error
Social	Social engineering of authorized users
Virus	Virus infection of system components
Destroy	Destruction of control/business/configuration data
Modify	Modification of control/business/configuration data
Bypass	Bypass of system security functions and mechanisms
Physical	Compromise of physical security mechanisms
Nature	Acts of nature that cause the system's unavailability

Table 14.2 Definitions of vulnerability.

Technology	Vulnerability
Information technology	A weakness in information system security design, procedures, implementation, or internal controls that could be exploited to gain unauthorized access to information or an information system
Operation technology	The characteristics of a system that cause it to suffer a definite degradation (incapability to perform the designated mission) because of having been subjected to a certain level of effects in an unnatural (manmade) hostile environment

These sources increase the likelihood of vulnerability exploration, given the widespread surface-level attacks on power system vulnerabilities.

14.6 Power System Vulnerabilities

A cybersecurity vulnerability is a weakness or flaw in a utility's computer system, software, network, or process that a hacker could exploit to gain unauthorized access, cause disruption, or compromise data integrity and confidentiality. Depending on the IT/OT technological domains, different definitions of the term vulnerability apply, as provided by The Free Dictionary (www.thefreedictionary.com), as shown in Table 14.2.

Specifically for electrical power systems, the following common types of vulnerabilities can be listed, for inadvertent and deliberate cybersecurity threats:

- **Vulnerabilities to Inadvertent Threats**
  - Equipment vulnerabilities and inadequacies
  - Complexity, degraded, or inadequate analysis
  - Lack of standardized operating procedures
  - Incorrect settings and testing
  - Inability to detect loss of grid power
  - Inadequate personnel training
  - Manipulated or mistaken market prices
  - Inadequate governance, organization, and procedures
- **Vulnerabilities to Deliberate Threats**
  - Inadequately protected access
  - Poor management of passwords
  - Poor security maintenance
  - Inadequate security training
  - Inadequate re-testing procedures
  - Security management failures

Many vulnerabilities are caused by human actions or by poor PAC system design. Table 14.3 lists some examples of sources of power system vulnerabilities found in utility PAC systems.

All these vulnerabilities are amplified by the vast attack surface presented by utility distributed, wide-area PAC systems, which attract the attention of power system hackers.

14.7 Power System Hackers

A cybersecurity hacker is an individual or organization that uses their technical knowledge and skills to identify and exploit vulnerabilities in computer systems, networks, or software. The attack surface exposed by an electricity utility can be mapped to the layered communication structure described in the previous paragraph. At each level, a hacker may be interested in having access to the assets of each domain to perpetrate an attack. Hackers can have diverse motivations and ethical stances, which typically categorize them into groups, as listed in Table 14.4.

Table 14.3 Sources of power system vulnerabilities.

Vulnerability	Description
Plaintext	Use of clear text protocols
Services	Unnecessary services enabled
Remote	Uncontrolled remote access
Architecture	Poor system architecture
Development	Poor system implementation
Nopolicies	Inadequate security policies
Spof	Single points of failure
Notraining	Inadequate user training
3rdparty	Unauthorized third party access
Norisk	Lack of risk assessment

Table 14.4 Types of hackers.

Type	Name	Description
	White Hats	Good guys, computer security experts, attest that information systems are secure.
	Black Hats	Bad guys, just plain hackers, break into networks or computers, or create computer viruses.
	Script Kiddies	Black hat hackers who use borrowed programs to attack networks and deface websites to make names for themselves.
	Hacktivists	Motivated by politics or religion, or to expose wrongdoing, or to take revenge, or to harass their target.
	State Sponsored	Governments with limitless time and funding to target civilians, corporations, and governments.
	Spies	Corporate hired hackers to infiltrate the competition and steal trade secrets.
	Cyber Terrorists	Motivated by religion or politics, try to create fear and chaos by disrupting critical infrastructures.

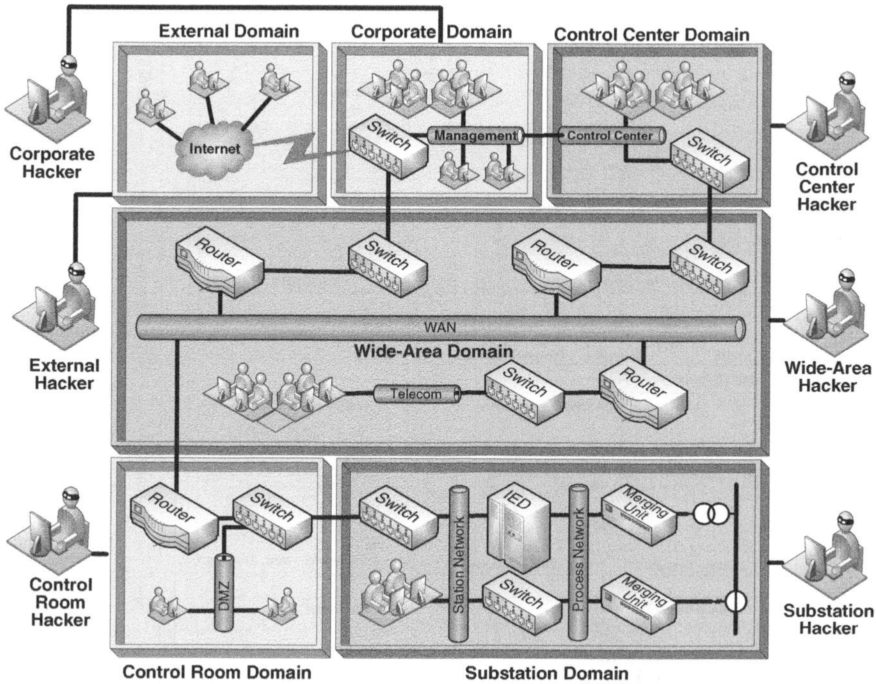

Figure 14.4 Utility hackers.

Following the utility hierarchical communication architecture of Figure 14.1, six types of hackers are typically related to assaults on the attack surface of each utility domain, as shown in Figure 14.4:

1. Substation Hacker
2. Control Room Hacker
3. Wide-Area Hacker
4. Control Center Hacker
5. Corporate Hacker
6. External Hacker

A similar association exists for power system hackers to the levels of the Purdue model, as depicted in Figure 14.5, classified accordingly as:

0. Field Hacker
1. Process Hacker
2. Station Hacker
3. Control Center Hacker
4. Corporate Hacker
5. External Hacker

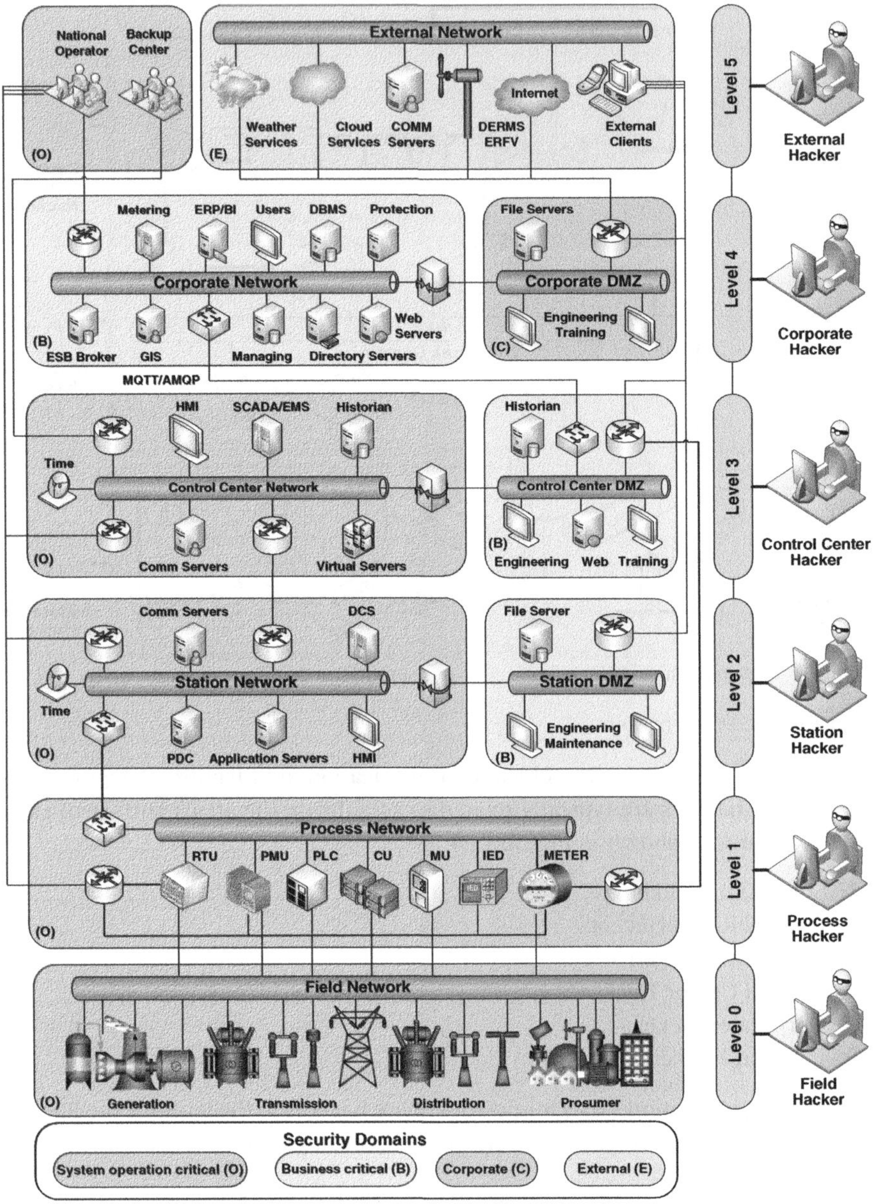

Figure 14.5 Power system hackers.

Field Hackers operate directly at the lowest levels of the Purdue Model (Level 0)—the physical process, where they explore the vulnerabilities of field devices, instrumentation, sensors, actuators, valves, drives, relays, transmitters, and switchyard equipment, to replace or rewire sensors, bypass limit switches, safety relays, or interlocks. Internal personnel may have physical access to the switchyard and usually do not require hands-on ability to manipulate the field process, which is not directly supervised. External hackers may also interfere with the physical level by using magnetic bombs to disrupt wireless and time-source communications.

Process Hackers act directly at Level 1 of the Purdue Model, where they explore the vulnerabilities of process devices, such as reprogramming PLCs using engineering software, uploading/downloading ladder logic, function blocks, ***merging unit*** settings, ***control unit*** settings, changing setpoints, PID parameters, or timing logic. Internal personnel may have physical access to process ***IEDs*** by-passing firewalls and network monitoring, and possess the hands-on ability to manipulate the automated process. External hackers may also interfere with the process level by exploring exposed communication vulnerabilities in the devices.

Station Hackers attack directly at Level 2 of the Purdue Model, where they explore the vulnerabilities of station automation devices. This includes reprogramming SCADA, HMI, and engineering stations; historians; protection and automation ***IEDs***; uploading and downloading SCL files; changing logic nodes, logical devices, and network settings; and changing setpoints and timing logic. Internal personnel may have direct local or remote access to station ***IEDs*** bypassing firewalls and network monitoring, and possess the specialized hands-on ability to manipulate the automated process. External hackers may also get access to the station level by exploring exposed vulnerabilities.

Control Center Hackers target Level 3 of the Purdue Model, exploiting vulnerabilities in control center devices and communication networks to disrupt operations. This includes reprogramming EMS (Energy Management Systems), AGC (Automatic Generation Control), SCADA, HMI, communication servers, and engineering stations, as well as historians, protection, and wide-area systems such as SIPS (System Integrity Protection Systems) and RAS (Remedial Action Systems), utilizing specialized OT engineering software. This also involves remotely changing ***SCL*** files and network settings, as well as adjusting setpoints and timing logic. Internal personnel may have direct local or remote access to the control center devices, bypassing firewalls and network monitoring, but require specialized knowledge to manipulate the control process. External hackers may also get access to the control center level by exploring exposed vulnerabilities.

Corporate Hackers focus directly on Level 4 of the Purdue Model, exploring the vulnerabilities of corporate offices, devices, and communication networks.

This includes reprogramming MMS (Metering Management Systems), directory services, DBMS (Database Management Systems), ERP (Enterprise Resource Planning), BI (Business Intelligence), AMS (Asset Management Systems), including ***IED*** settings, communication servers, firewalls, DMZs, and network access, utilizing specialized IT engineering software. Internal personnel may have direct local or remote access to the corporate stations and switches, bypassing firewalls and network monitoring, but require specialized knowledge to manipulate the corporate processes. External hackers may also gain access to the corporate level by exploiting exposed vulnerabilities and social engineering through social networks.

External Hackers primarily focus on Level 5 of the Purdue Model, targeting vulnerabilities in the corporation's external services and communication channels to disrupt its business operations. This includes cloud services such as weather services, DERMS (Distributed Energy Resource Management Systems), clients, market platforms, third-party rental infrastructure, and partners. External personnel may also target vulnerabilities across all other levels, using local or remote access to distributed devices to bypass firewalls and network monitoring, but require specialized knowledge or internal support to manipulate each level.

The cybersecurity of each domain must be managed in an integrated approach, possibly managed by a corporate-wide Security Operations Center (SOC), to guarantee the security of the automation systems.

14.8 Automation Security

By their very constitution, digital substations represent potential targets for cyberattacks, from internal or external sources. Its distribution over extensive geographic areas, in a constant process of evolution, with multiple owners, amplifies the attack surface and the number of typical vulnerabilities associated with digital assets. The economic and social consequences of a successful attack on these assets amplify the risk.

As digital systems, ***IED*** and communication networks used in the protection and automation of digital substations expose some well-known vulnerabilities associated with these assets, imported from IT assets:

- **Plaintext**—using open text protocols
- **Services**—unnecessary services enabled
- **Remote**—uncontrolled remote access
- **Architecture**—poor system architecture
- **Development**—poor implementation of the system
- **Nopolicies**—inadequate security policies

- **Spof**—common points of failure
- **Notraining**—inadequate user training
- **3rdparty**—unauthorized access by third parties
- **Norisk**—lack of risk assessment

As a result, digital substations can be targets of typical attacks associated with these assets, familiar to IT experts, such as:

- **Sniff**—unauthorized traffic analysis
- **Replay**—unauthorized replay of captured traffic
- **Spoof**—simulation of an authorized user
- **DoS**—denial of service or network overload
- **Error**—operator error
- **Social**—social engineering of authorized users
- **Virus**—system components virus infection
- **Destroy**—Control/Business/Configuration data destruction
- **Modify**—modification of control/business/configuration data
- **Bypass**—bypass of system functions and security mechanisms
- **Physical**—impairment of physical security mechanisms
- **Nature**—acts of nature that cause the system to become unavailable

Standardized methods are available to protect digital assets from these threats and secure various utility operation domains against cyberattacks, but specialized to SAS, such as implementing cybersecurity domains.

14.9 Cybersecurity Domains

The cybersecurity of IEC 61850-based systems usually follows the concepts defined by the standard IEC 62351 (Power systems management and associated information exchange—Data and communications security), where the following security domains are typically identified in the physical architecture of a utility asset:

- System Operation Critical
- Business Critical
- Corporate
- External

These domains may be physical or virtual and are identified by rounded colored rectangles around the network assets in Figure 14.5, which are used to define specific security policies for protecting a utility's physical assets. The perimeter of each security domain is maintained at a desired level of security, consistent across all assets within the domain. The exchange of information to and from a security domain is validated with the security level requirements within the security domain before being allowed. The security domains comprise logical and physical assets that span more than one layer in the physical architecture and are also protected by logical and physical measures standard to each layer.

The System Operation Critical security domain, identified by the letter (O) in Figure 14.2, applies to all assets directly related to the availability and reliability of power generation, transmission, distribution, and direct connection infrastructure, as well as to major clients. It comprises part of the Field, Process, Station, and Control Center networks and layers, at levels 0–5 of the asset architecture. Typical assets in this domain include power equipment at Generation, Transmission, Distribution, or Prosumer (Consumers and/or Producers) stations, and industrial protocols such as IEC 61850, IEC 61131, Modbus, and OPC/UA, which are typically used to communicate locally with these assets.

The Business Critical security domain, identified by the letter (B) in Figure 14.2, applies to all assets supporting the critical operation of the electrical network, which are not essential to the power system's reliability and availability. It comprises part of the Station, Control Center, and Corporate networks and layers, at levels 2–5 of the asset architecture. Typical assets in this domain include for instance, station DMZ at level 2 segregated from the remaining local holdings by a Gateway, connecting Engineering, Maintenance and File servers; Control Center DMZ at level 3 segregated from the rest of Control Center assets by a Gateway, connecting Engineering, Training and Web servers, and mirror Historians; and ERP, BI, DBMS, ESB, Directory and Web Servers at level 4; and the related protocols for external domain communication.

The Corporate security domain, identified by the letter (C) in Figure 14.2, applies to all assets and supports business operations with baseline security that is not essential to power system reliability and availability. It comprises only part of the Corporate network and layer, at level 4 of the asset architecture. Typical assets in this domain include, for instance, a corporate DMZ segregated from the rest of local holdings by a Gateway, connecting Engineering, Maintenance, and File servers; a Control Center DMZ at level 3 segregated from the rest of Corporate assets by a Gateway, connecting Engineering, Training, and File servers, and the related protocols for external domain communication.

Finally, the External security domain, identified by the letter (E) in Figure 14.2, applies to all external assets and entities that support the corporation's business and market operations and utilize and support communication over public networks. It comprises only part of the External network and layer, at level 5 of the asset architecture. Typical assets and entities in this domain include the National Grid Control Center, Market Operator Control Center, the Backup Center, Cloud Services, Communication Servers, DERMS, External and Internet Clients, and the related protocols for external domain communication.

These domains aim to segregate each utility area by its function or role in the business objectives and to concentrate protection against cybersecurity threats.

14.10 Cybersecurity Threats

The behavior of each cyber-threat is a stochastic process, as its occurrence is impossible to anticipate. A general model of the dominant concepts of potential and functional incidents can be used to represent their inception and evolution, through the temporal degradation of the security of a domain or asset during an attack, divided into three stages. The first stage corresponds to the normal state, in which a hacker probes the asset or domain. It is followed by a second stage, after a detectable event of the start of a functional degradation, also known as an infection from a cyber virus or the penetration of a cyber hacker, which is followed by the third or failed stage: the inability of the domain to perform its required function fully, referred to as a cyber incident. These stages can be viewed as slices of areas under the graph of Figure 14.6, representing the degradation of the domain's functional capacity or resistance to cyber incidents along its operating cycle, measured by a suitable performance index, delimited by the following conditions:

- **Normal**—or during a probing cyberattack, before a penetration or potential incident
- **Infected**—or during the cyber penetration stage, before the perpetration of an incident
- **Failed**—or during the perpetration of a cyberattack, after a functional incident

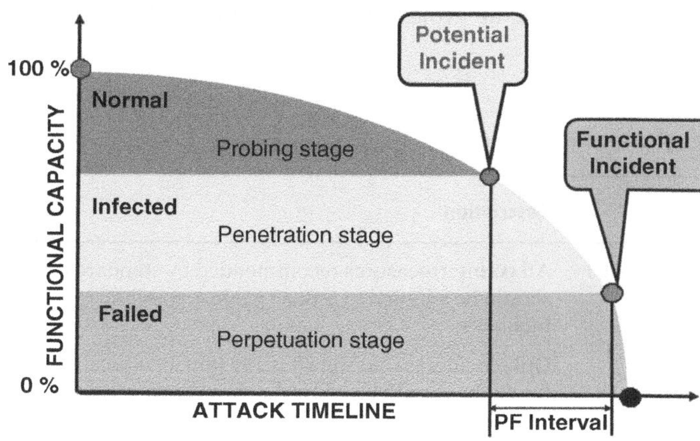

Figure 14.6 Cybersecurity resistance curve.

In this figure, the Potential Functional (PF) interval represents the expected duration of the penetrating stage of a cyberattack to a domain or asset, before a functional incident is provoked. These concepts serve to classify the cybersecurity policies applicable to automation systems.

14.11 Cybersecurity Policies

Due to its unique characteristics, the cybersecurity of OT assets requires distinct policies compared to those of IT domains. Depending on the IT/OT domain, two types of policies are typically adopted to protect against cyberattacks, as shown in Table 14.5.

For both domains, the recommended policy will depend on the characteristics of the cyber-threat and the consequent incident. An incident is any event that compromises or poses an imminent threat to any of the CIA triad (Confidentiality, Integrity, or Availability) of information, systems, networks, or data. In simpler terms, it's when something goes wrong in a PAC environment that either causes harm or could do so. Following these definitions, a classification can be applied to incidents of cybersecurity using the following criteria:

- **Unreliable**—impossible to protect or accept the consequences of incidents
- **Measurable**—possible to evaluate the level of threat penetration by inspection
- **Predictable**—possible to estimate, based on past cyberattacks, the expected time to occur
- **Controllable**—possible to change the attack rate with countermeasures
- **Hidden**—impossible to know without a functional inspection or a second incident
- **Uncontrollable**—impossible to avoid, but supportable without a cyber countermeasure

Table 14.5 Types of cybersecurity policies.

Domain	Policy	Description
IT	Compliance-based	All countermeasures recommended by standards should be adopted to protect against possible incidents.
OT	Risk-based	Only incidents that significantly impact critical functions should be addressed by cybersecurity countermeasures, based on a thorough risk analysis.

A set of consistent actions and countermeasures can be selected for each cyber-threat, among a standardized set of policies, according to the following list:

- **Avoidance**—modify the design of the cyber asset or domain to reduce cyber incidents
- **Recovery**—reduce the threat before a cyber incident with a routine countermeasure
- **Detection**—assess potential cyber incidents by suitable probing, inspection or measurement
- **Assurance**—uncover hidden incidents by suitable domain functional testing
- **Assumption**—recover the domain from a cyber incident after its occurrence
- **Limitation**—required countermeasures from the user, other than the IT or OT people

Based on these classifications, the recommended policy for a domain may be selected according to the incident type, as shown in the flowchart in Figure 14.7.

Typically, these policies are recommended at different points in the cyberattack timeline of a cybersecurity process, as shown in Figure 14.8.

Implementing a policy requires selecting a set of specific countermeasures, as described in the following paragraph.

14.12 Cybersecurity Countermeasures

Cybersecurity countermeasures can be taken to prevent incidents caused by cyberattacks on the domains of electrical power systems, or otherwise, to reduce their impacts to acceptable levels.

Once a cybersecurity policy is selected for a given threat, a set of countermeasures should be chosen from the options available in current cybersecurity technologies. The choice should be based on appropriate criteria of applicability and effectiveness for each threat type. The following is a list of typical criteria used to select cybersecurity countermeasures:

- **Applicability**
  - Eliminates threats
  - Prevents attacks
  - Reduces vulnerabilities
  - Detects incidents
  - Discovers hidden incidents
  - Restores consumables
  - Recovers after incidents

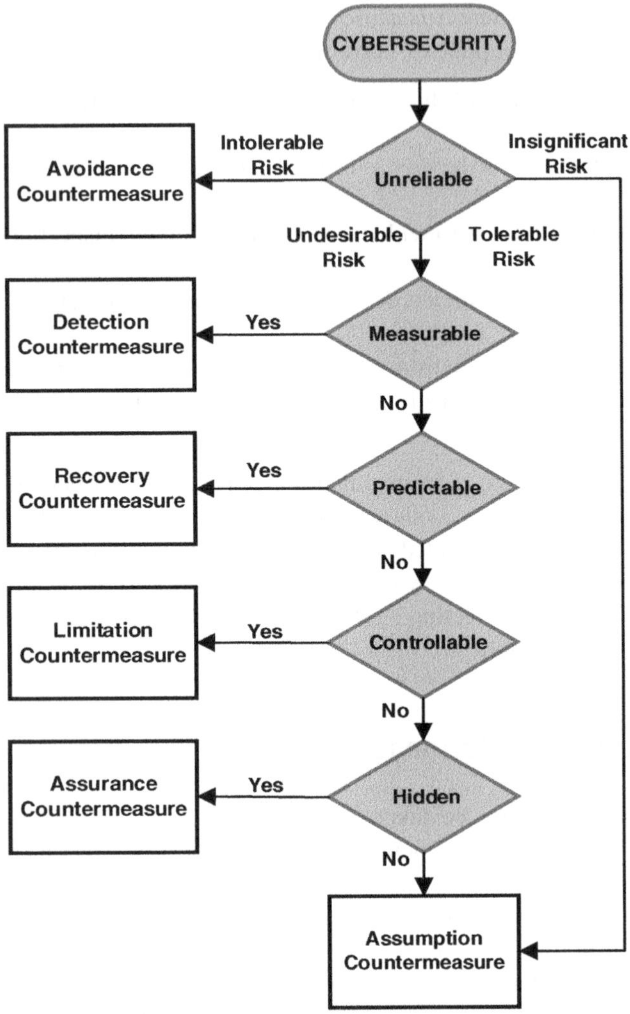

Figure 14.7 Cybersecurity policy selection.

- **Effectiveness**
  - Economic (cost-effective)
  - Mandatory (environmental or legal requirement)
  - Required (by design)
  - Viable (by technology)

Figure 14.9 shows some possible countermeasures that can be applied at each OSI layer to mitigate common threats in communication networks. Some or most of them can be used to protect the domains of IEC 61850-based systems.

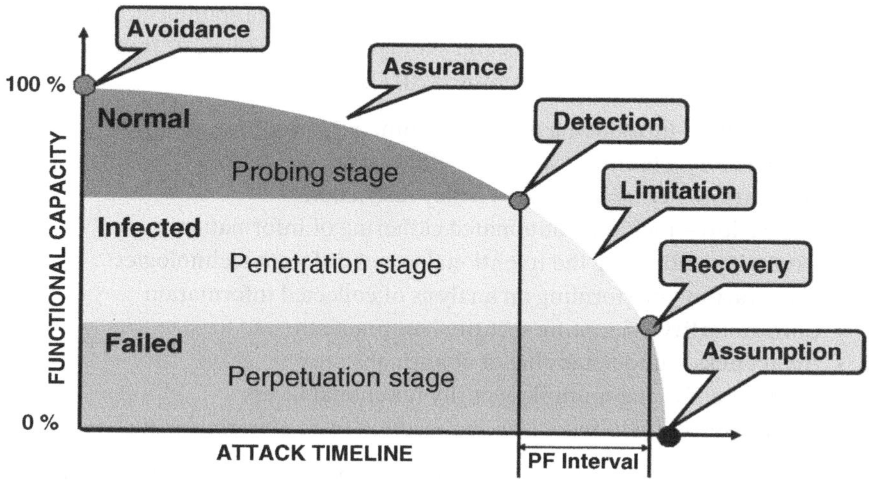

Figure 14.8 Cybersecurity policy timeline.

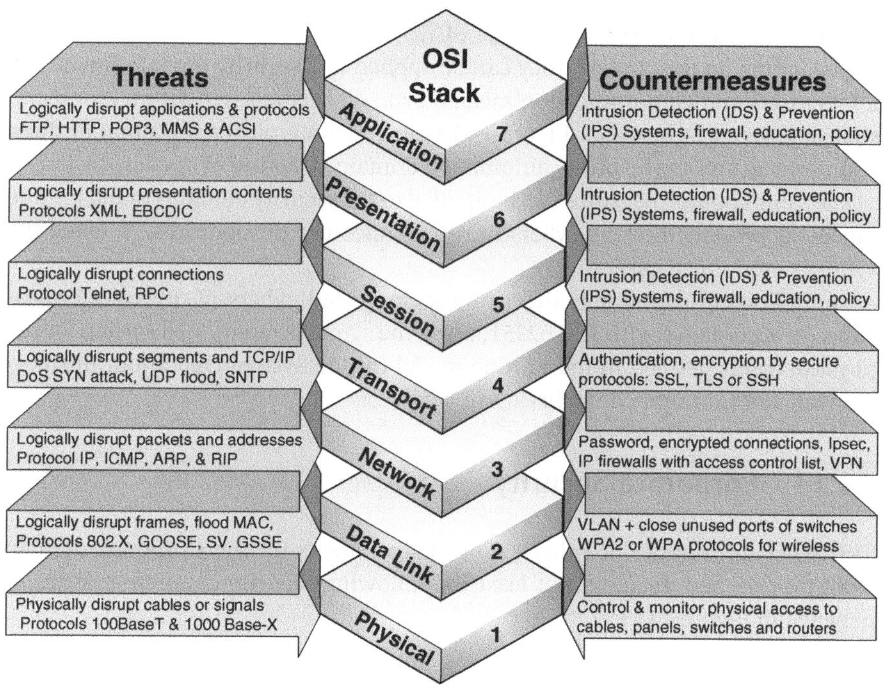

Figure 14.9 OSI stack threats and countermeasures.

Many lists of countermeasures can be used to choose the countermeasures, recommended by regulatory agencies and standardization bodies, or from a generic list, such as those proposed by Amoroso (2011):

- **Deception**—introducing misleading functionality/information
- **Discretion**—obscuring sensitive information
- **Separation**—enforcing access policy restrictions
- **Collection**—including automated gathering of information
- **Diversity**—adopting the intentional use of different technologies
- **Correlation**—performing an analysis of collected information
- **Commonality**—adopting security best practices
- **Awareness**—understanding of abnormal status
- **Depth**—enforcing multiple security functional layers
- **Response**—scheduling a planned reaction to an abnormal status

Using this list, suitable cybersecurity countermeasures can be mapped to each selected policy, as is shown in Table 14.6, as an example of a cybersecurity plan.

Following the recommendations of the standard IEC 62351 for IEC 61850-based systems, for each security domain, specific safety measures and controls are required from utility policies, which can be selected from a standardized set of countermeasure classes, identified by standardized graphic symbols, derived from IEC 62351-10, as represented in Table 14.7.

Depending on the context, they can be applied to a security domain (including all its assets and communication means) or to a specific asset within a domain, such as a server or protocol. Figure 14.10 illustrates a typical application of these countermeasures to the utility automation domain structure of Section 14.4.

The same countermeasures can be applied to the security domains of the Purdue model, as presented in the cybersecurity architecture of Figure 14.11, using the symbols mentioned earlier.

The following paragraphs describe the suggested cybersecurity countermeasures, in accordance with IEC 62351, using the symbols mentioned earlier, for the physical assets defined in the Purdue model for the System Operation, Business Critical, and Corporate domains.

14.13 Corporate Security

The Seller or Supplier of (physical or logical) assets for the Corporate domain shall provide and document at least the following security countermeasures as depicted in Figure 14.11:

- Traffic restrictions for forbidden communication (Firewalls) with external entities, including weather services, cloud services, DERMS, the Internet, and external clients

Table 14.6 Cybersecurity policies and countermeasures.

		Policy					
		Avoidance	**Assurance**	**Detection**	**Limitation**	**Recovery**	**Assumption**
Countermeasure	Deception	Misleading functionality/ information	Scan available ports and resources	Check honey pot deception traps	Periodic updating of honey pots	Clean honeypot traps and database	No misleading functionality/ information
	Discretion	Obscuring sensitive information	Try disclosing sensitive information	Check the disclosure of sensitive data	Periodic updating of password	Replace broken passwords/sensitive data	Allow disclosing public information
	Separation	Enforced access policy restrictions	Try unauthorized access	Check unauthorized access tentative	Periodic review of security domains	Rework broken firewall rules	Unrestricted open access policy
	Collection	Automated gathering of information	Simulate incident to gather information	Check collected log information	Periodic emptying of logs	Restore overloaded database	No information gathering
	Diversity	Intentional use of different technologies	Try to substitute a supplier	Check diversity of suppliers	Periodic renewing of suppliers	Change disrupted technologies	Use identical technologies
	Correlation	Analysis of collected information	Try injecting correlated information	Check correlation of logged information	Periodic analysis of collected data	Identify and block the source of attacks	No analysis of incidents or information
	Commonality	Adoption of security best practices	Try nonstandard practices	Check conformance audit records	Periodic updating of security policies	Reinforce broken security best rules	Nonstandardized practices
	Awareness	Understanding of abnormal status	Simulate perception of abnormal status	Check perception of incidents	Periodic renewing of operator training	Retrain after undetected incidents	No understanding of abnormal status
	Depth	Enforcing multiple security functional layers	Try unauthorized cross of security layers	Check logs for partial security layer breaking	Periodic review of firewall rules	Reinforce broken depth defenses	None or single security functional layer
	Response	Misleading functionality/ information	Simulate reaction to abnormal status	Check response to simulated failures	Periodic review of disaster/recovery plan	Run disaster recovery plans	Unplanned reaction to abnormal status

Table 14.7 Cybersecurity countermeasures.

Symbol	Name	Description
	Firewalls	Traffic restrictions for forbidden communication
	Strong Authentications	Multifactor authentication or challenge responses
	Domains	Administrative grouping of multiple private networks
	RBAC	Role-based access control
	Security Option	Specific protocol safety alternatives
	DMZ	Demilitarized zone to separate LANs from untrusted networks
	Data Cryptography	Disguising information from unauthorized entities
	Traffic Segregation	Virtual private network
	Monitoring	Logging and event recording for auditing
	Virus Protection	Detection and removal of viruses

- Multifactor authentication or challenge responses (Strong Authentication) in all servers in the corporate DMZ
- Administrative grouping of multiple private networks (Domains) in the corporate DMZ
- RBAC to all assets of the corporate DMZ
- Specific protocol safety alternatives (Security Option) of the protocols used to connect to external clients and entities
- Traffic Segregation—(Virtual Private Network [VPN]) to external clients that need to access corporate IT assets
- Logging and event recording for auditing (Monitoring) of all internal and external accesses
- Detection and removal of viruses (Virus Protection)

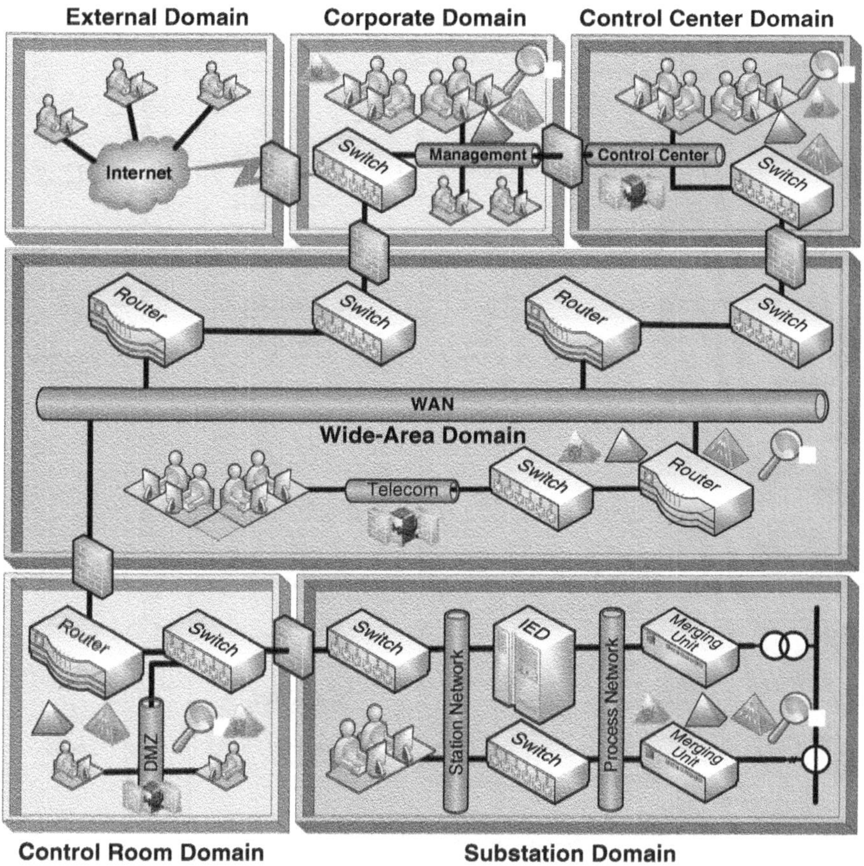

Figure 14.10 Utility cybersecurity domains.

These countermeasures are typically deployed in a utility Security Operations Center (SOC), which may also centralize its management to protect internal system operations.

14.14 Operation Security

The Seller or Supplier of (physical or logical) assets for the System Operation Critical domain shall provide and document at least the following security countermeasures as depicted in Figure 14.11:

- Traffic restrictions for forbidden communication (Firewalls) with internal entities like backup control centers, substations, power plants, and corporate users, as well as with external entities

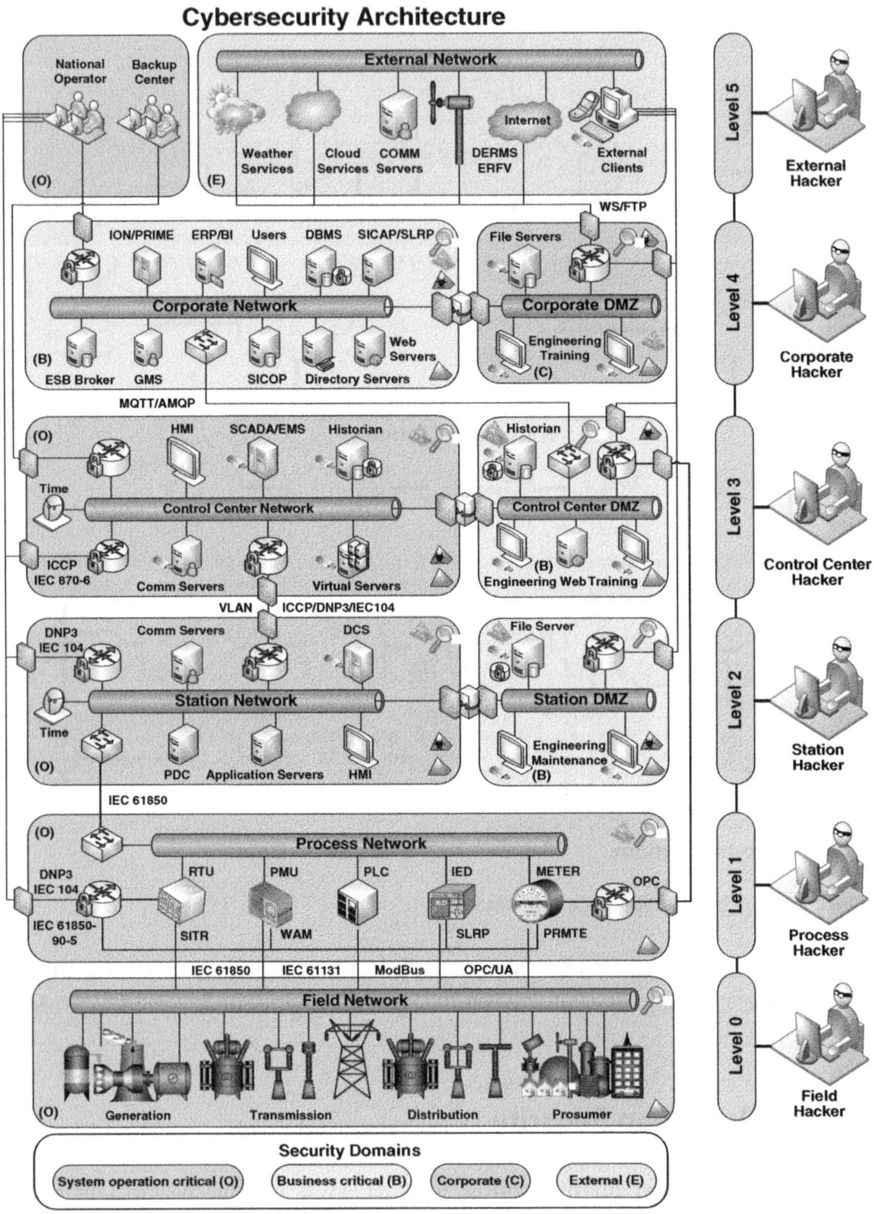

Figure 14.11 Cybersecurity architecture.

- Multifactor authentication or challenge responses (Strong Authentication) in all servers
- Administrative grouping of multiple private networks (Domains) for the real-time assets of the control center
- RBAC to all assets of the control center
- Specific protocol safety alternatives (Security Option) of the protocols used to connect to an independent operator, the back-up control center, substations, and power plants
- DMZs to separate LANs from untrusted networks, mainly to exchange data with corporate users and external clients
- Disguising information to unauthorized entities (Data Cryptography), mainly for historians
- Traffic Segregation—(VPN) to further protect the communication with internal entities
- Logging and event recording for auditing (Monitoring) of interactions with all real-time assets
- Hardware hardening of servers and operational stations

These measures are necessary to maintain the security of the utility operation, which is considered the most critical domain. They support business continuity and further preserve its security.

14.15 Business Security

The Seller or Supplier of (physical or logical) assets for the Business Critical domains shall provide and document at least the following security countermeasures as depicted in Figure 14.11:

- Traffic restrictions for forbidden communication (Firewalls) with internal and external entities, and mainly with the real-time domain
- Multifactor authentication or challenge responses (Strong Authentication) in all servers in the control center DMZ
- Administrative grouping of multiple private networks (Domains) for the DMZ assets of the control center and corporate network
- RBAC to all assets of the control center DMZ and corporate network
- Specific protocol safety alternatives (Security Option) of the protocols used to connect to the corporate network and external clients
- Traffic Segregation—(VPN) to further protect the communication with internal and external entities

- Logging and event recording for auditing (Monitoring) of interactions with all real-time assets and DMZ assets
- Detection and removal of viruses (Virus Protection)

The security of the operational and business domains provides external protection for digital substations and power plants, necessitating additional internal countermeasures to maintain their security and reliability.

14.16 Substation Security

The reliability of protection and automation in digital substations is now dependent not only on the redundancy and quality of their devices but also on the architecture and reliability of the local communication networks and the security domains to which they belong. Previous communication in conventional substations was deterministic and reliable, carried out over metallic wires, and inherently secure. In digital substations, the network's reliability is probabilistic, dependent on the nondeterministic, concurrent transmission of messages in Ethernet networks, and subject to overload, cybersecurity threats, and message collisions. For comparison, Figure 14.12 illustrates, in a simplified manner, the typical configuration of a conventional protection system, comprising an instrument transformer (*IT*), a protection ***IED***, an auxiliary relay, and a circuit breaker, with dedicated metallic connections, as well as some possible vulnerabilities of these systems.

For comparison, Figure 14.13 illustrates, also in a simplified way, the typical configuration of a digital protection system, with a non-conventional current instrument transformer (***NCIT***), two segments of a ***process network***, a

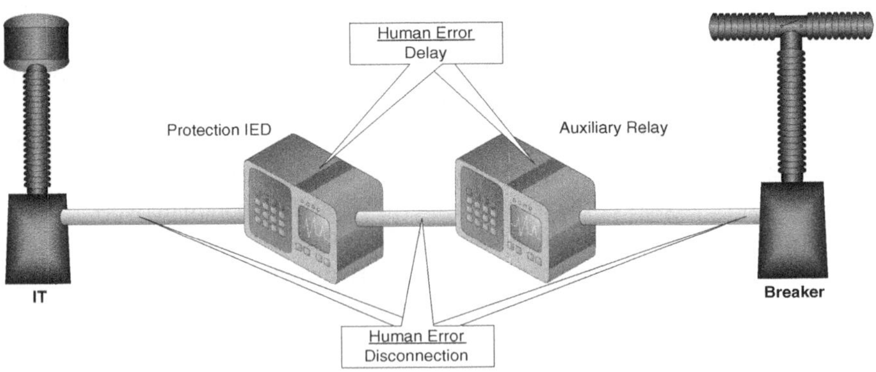

Figure 14.12 Conventional system failure modes.

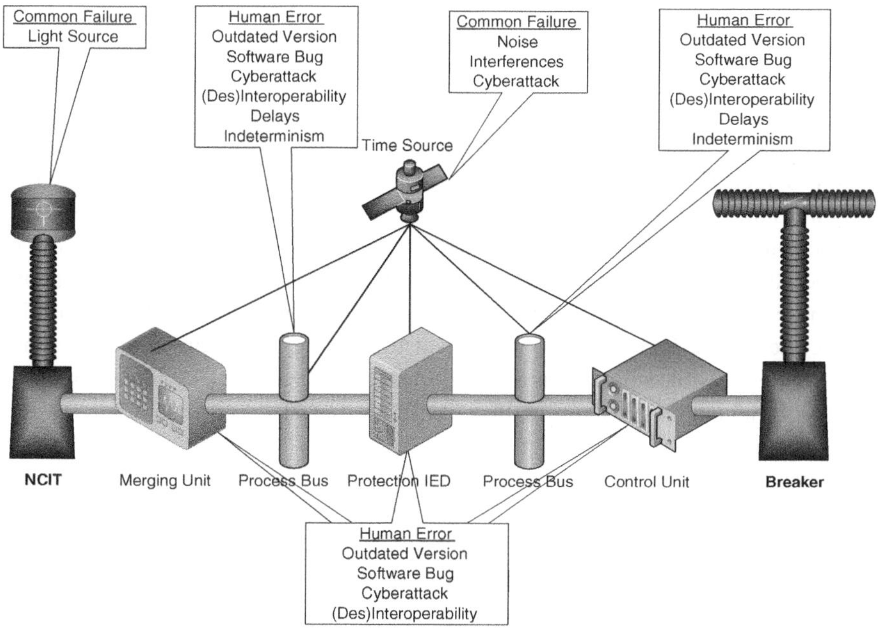

Figure 14.13 Typical failure modes of a digital system.

merging unit, a protection relay, a ***control unit***, and a circuit breaker, and the associated main failure modes. Note the difference in the number of possible vulnerabilities and the increase in surface area exposed to attack.

The way device redundancy is implemented directly affects the resulting reliability. The two most common configurations are the *hot-hot* and hot-standby topologies. In the first, both protections are active simultaneously and are invariably identical or perform the same functions. They are usually called primary and alternate to distinguish them since they perform the same functions. In the *hot-standby* configuration, one of the protections is the main, which acts as the primary during defects, while the other acts only if the primary fails. In this case, it is often referred to as backup protection. In both cases, they mustn't have common vulnerabilities or failure modes for the result to be effective. In the case of digital protection, for example, they cannot act or receive signals through a shared local communication network. It is also necessary to implement network redundancy for the results to be effective.

In digital substations, ***process networks*** (which collect and transmit data to and from primary equipment) and station networks (which transmit data between ***IEDs*** and operators for decision-making) can introduce vulnerabilities standard to various protection systems, since in principle they can span the entire substation, or be segmented into fractions of the facility. They are in series with ***IEDs*** and signal sensors (CT and TP), so they directly impact reliability. Its redundancy should be treated similarly to protection devices and ***IEDs***, to ensure the reliability of the entire protection and teleprotection system.

A common vulnerability in these networks is the reference time source, usually provided by Global Positioning System (GPS) satellite signals captured by antennas and distributed to ***IEDs***. It can affect all of them simultaneously as a single source, such as during a satellite failure, an atmospheric phenomenon, or a cyberattack, representing a common vulnerability. Special preventive measures for these phenomena need to be incorporated into the facilities' design to minimize the risk of incorrect action or even the failure of the protection systems. Among the possible solutions is distributing clock signals via PTP (Precision Time Protocol), which enables automatic reconfiguration of the time reference source in such situations.

However, they do not eliminate vulnerabilities typical of local networks, such as loss of auxiliary power, physical failures in switches, and programming errors, which pose reliability weaknesses. Additionally, many substations are at an intermediate stage of modernization, featuring a mix of digitized and electromechanical components and multiple protocols, including Modbus and IEC 60870-5-103. These reasons diminish their usefulness as an alternative to physical duplication of local networks, regardless of the protocols employed, for increasing reliability. Due to its reliance on communication systems, IEC 61850 warrants special attention regarding cybersecurity.

14.17 IEC 61850 Security

IEC 61850 does not directly address cybersecurity aspects. The cybersecurity of automation systems, including those based on IEC 61850, is primarily addressed by IEC 62351 (Cybersecurity Series for Smart Grids). This standard provides mechanisms such as authentication, encryption, integrity, and access control for the protocols used in power system automation. Table 14.8 shows the recommended security measures detailed by IEC 62351 for each communication service provided by IEC 61850.

For real-time high-resolution waveform messages within substations, IEC 61850-90 recommends a lightweight security mechanism for Authentication and Tamper Detection. For ***GOOSE/SV*** multicast messages, IEC 62351-6 recommends using digital signatures and integrity checks to minimize their impact on message latency. Authentication and encryption are recommended for client-server communication due to their less restrictive time requirements.

Table 14.8 IEC 62351 cybersecurity measures.

IEC 61850 Services	IEC 62351 Security Measures
GOOSE/*SV* multicast messages	Digital signatures and integrity checks
R-GOOSE/*R-SV* messages	Authentication, encryption, and digital signatures
Client–server communication	Authentication and encryption
Human–machine Interfaces	RBAC
Synchrophasor messages	Same as for *R-GOOSE*/*R-SV* messages

For inter-substation messages of moderate resolution, an optional encryption mechanism is suggested at the publisher side, depending on application requirements, as adopted for the broadcasting of *R-SV* and *R-GOOSE* messages, complemented by audit trails and a chain of trust at the edges and subscribers of the applications. The former is usually provided by the Key Distribution Center (KDC), which manages symmetric key coordination between the publisher and subscribers, as described in Section 11.8. For the latter, RBAC is recommended to protect all human access to the automation system and an auditing system. This should allow the secure transit of sample values and synchrophasors across different utility domains.

14.18 Summary

The digitalization of control and protection systems, along with their associated communication, has implications for the safety and operation of the electrical system. The primary change involves replacing deterministic communication over metallic wires with optical and wireless probabilistic communication over Ethernet networks, as used in fourth-generation architectures. The biggest challenge is ensuring that the benefits of digitalization, such as interoperability, communication, open protocols, storage, flexible configuration, and fault logging, are achieved without compromising the reliability and security of conventional substations.

This chapter reviewed the main consequences of this transition for the safety and reliability of utility operations, as well as its impact on the power system's maintenance, operation, projects, reliability, and security. Cybersecurity policies and countermeasures were recommended for all major utility communication domains, following the Purdue architecture and the IEC 62351 recommendations for IEC 61850-based systems.

14.19 Review Questions

1 Define the four core cybersecurity objectives in OT environments (Confidentiality, Integrity, Availability, Accountability) and explain how each one specifically relates to power system automation.

2 Explain how the layered communication architecture of a utility—from the Substation Domain to the External Domain—shapes cybersecurity requirements and expands the potential attack surface.

3 Compare the vulnerabilities of traditional wired protection systems with those of digital substations using Ethernet-based architectures. How does transitioning from deterministic to probabilistic communication impact reliability and security?

4 Given the Purdue Model (Levels 0–5), identify one plausible cyberattack scenario at each of three layers (Field, Station, Corporate) and describe the vulnerabilities that enable these attacks.

5 Discuss the differences between unintended and intentional cybersecurity threats in power systems, providing examples of common vulnerabilities linked to each type.

6 Evaluate how various hacker profiles (e.g., script kiddie, hacktivist, state-sponsored actor) might target different utility domains and necessitate different defensive strategies.

7 Summarize the role of security domains specified in IEC 62351, including System Operation Critical, Business Critical, Corporate, and External, and explain the reasoning behind dividing assets into these domains.

8 A utility must secure its System Operation Critical domain. Propose a set of countermeasures based on IEC 62351 recommendations, explaining why each measure is appropriate for real-time operational assets.

9 Examine the cybersecurity policy models for IT (compliance-based) and OT (risk-based). Why does OT require a risk-based approach, and how does the PF incident curve support this distinction?

10 Explain how cybersecurity measures across various OSI layers, such as encryption, RBAC, VPNs, and firewalls, work together to safeguard IEC 61850 communication services.

11 Consider a substation deploying ***GOOSE*** and SV traffic for protection functions. Discuss the trade-offs involved when applying security measures such as digital signatures or encryption, with particular emphasis on latency and system availability.

12 Propose a multi-layer cybersecurity strategy for an IEC 61850-based substation that addresses threats from Level 0 (Field) to Level 5 (External). Your answer should incorporate device redundancy, time-source protection, network segmentation, and IEC 62351 controls.

15

Automation Models

15.1 Introduction

The automation of substations, power plants, and transmission lines is currently carried out using software-based digital ***Intelligent Electronic Devices (IEDs)*** and local area networks, primarily relying on the IEC 61850 protocol. Extensions to the IEC 61850 standard are now available for hydropower, wind power, and Distributed Energy Resources (DER), with many others in development for different devices. Although its concepts are well established, many utilities and engineers still look for concrete examples of how these principles are applied in real-world projects.

15.2 Learning Objectives

This chapter demonstrates the specification and implementation of various automation functions in accordance with IEC 61850 standards. One specification is fully formatted as an Functional Implementation Conformance Statement (FICS) to illustrate the Unified Modeling Language (UML) Use Case template recommended in CIGRE Technical Brochure 401 (Annex 16.9). All implementations are presented as UML diagrams but can also be expressed using the FICS format. Examples include protection, teleprotection, interlocking, control, switching, remote operation, fault recording, condition monitoring, line transfer, breaker failure, and load shedding in power stations. All these functions rely on ***merging units (MUs)*** and ***control units (CUs)***, as specialized IEDs, to communicate with switchyard equipment. Additional examples related to monitoring and controlling hydropower and wind power plants, as well as DER, are included in the Annexes.

15.3 Merging and Control Functions

As a model-driven technology, IEC 61850 depends on models of each power system component for automation, utilizing predefined ***logical nodes (LNs)***. Figure 15.1 shows the specific ***LNs*** used to represent each high-voltage piece of equipment in a transformer bay, which are installed as separate devices for each circuit breaker, disconnector switch, and current transformer. The physical architecture of a typical ***MU*** is depicted in Figure 11.18 and that of a ***CU*** in Figure 11.13.

MUs and ***CUs*** can typically be combined in a single ***server***, as shown in the UML Package Diagram of Figure 15.2 of an ***IED*** with four ***TCTR LNs*** modeling four current transformers (three phases plus neutral) and four ***TVTR LNs*** modeling four voltage transformers (three phases plus neutral), in addition to an external clock ***STIM*** and LN zero ***LLN0***.

Once modeled, these monitoring and control functions can be used to implement protection and other automation functions, as described in the following paragraphs.

15.4 Protection Functions

A typical protection function in a power station involves measuring external and internal signals of the protected zone, including the breakers that control the energy flow into and out of the zone, as shown in Figure 15.3. During an internal

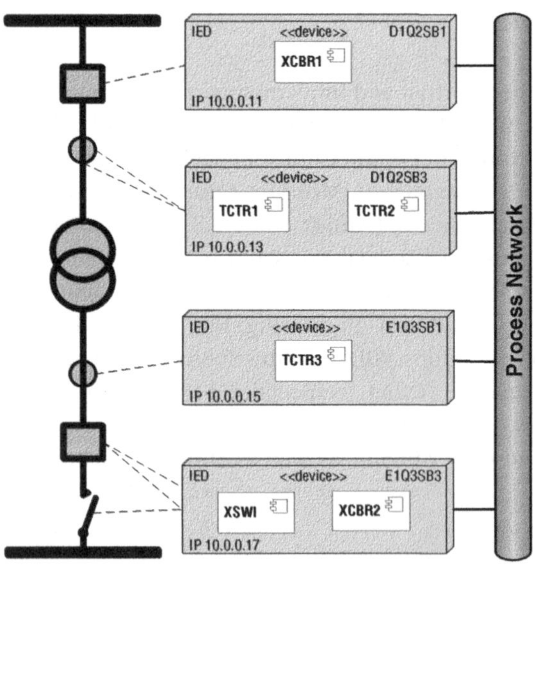

Figure 15.1 Logical nodes of MU and CU.

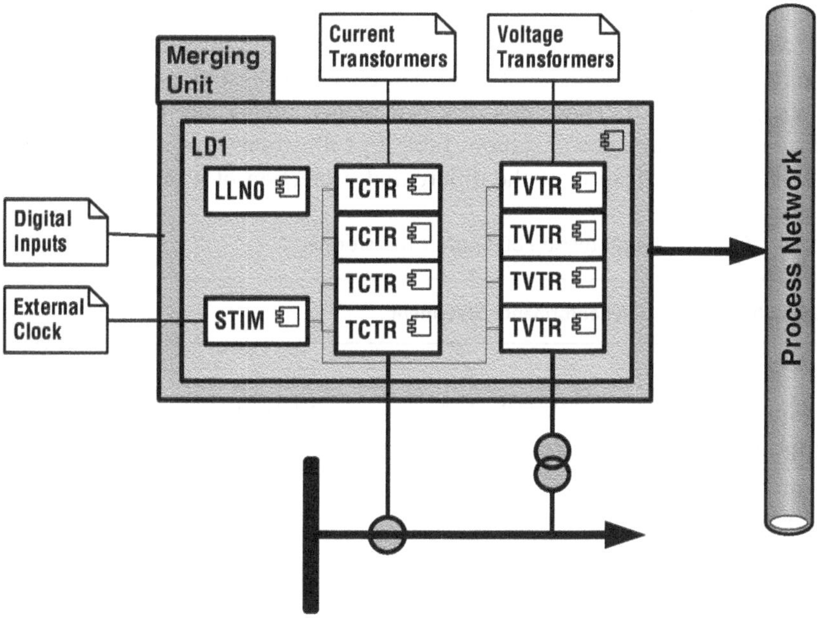

Figure 15.2 Typical combined MU and CU.

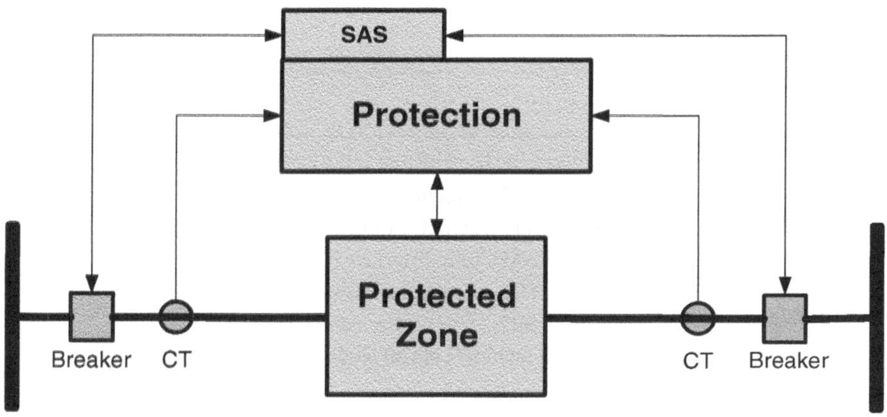

Figure 15.3 Protection function.

fault, to completely isolate the protected zone from other zones, all energy inflow and outflow should be interrupted by circuit breakers. Based on the measured signals, Substation Automation Systems (***SAS***) ***LNs*** detect internal faults and command the tripping of the related breakers.

Depending on the equipment within the protected zone, different types of IEC 61850 ***LNs*** can be instantiated to implement the protection function. Annex 16.5 contains a list of ***LNs*** defined by IEC 61850 related to substations, hydropower, wind power, and DER. These modules can model almost any protection and automation system in a power station. Table 15.1 illustrates how an FICS can be developed as a specification of the differential protection of a two-wind power

Table 15.1 FICS for the protection of a power transformer.

Functional Implementation Conformance Statement	
Code	PTR 1
Name	Differential Protection of a Power Transformer
Description	To trip the transformer in case of an internal fault
Customer	Client 1
Substation	Substation 1
SCL File	To be defined
Primary User (Actor)	TR1—Power Transformer
Secondary User (Actor)	Station Operator Breaker Failure Protection (to be described in another FICS)
Stakeholder and Interest	Owner
Function Description	
Trigger	Internal fault in the transformer (short-circuit)
Components or Logical Nodes	PDIF—Differential Protection (Logical Node) CSWI1 and CSWI2—Switch Controllers (Logical Nodes) IHMI—Human–Machine Interface (Logical Node) TCTR1 and TCTR2—Current transformer (Logical Node) XCBR1 and XCBR2—Circuit Breaker (Logical Node) XSWI—Circuit Switch (Logical Node)
Process Equipment	TR1—Power Transformer CBR1 and CBR2—Circuit Breakers TC1 and TC2—Current Transformers SW—Disconnecting Switch
Performance	The transformer is isolated from the grid 20 ms after an internal fault The station operator is notified in 5 ms after isolation or breaker failure The breaker failure scheme is triggered 3 ms after a failure

Preconditions	The transformer is energized and in service CT ratios and protection settings are configured
Post conditions on Success	The transformer is fully isolated from the grid after an internal fault The station operator is notified about the internal fault
Post conditions on Failure	Breaker failure activated (to be described in another FICS) The station operator is notified about the breaker failure

Use Case Description

Use Case Name	**US1 (Internal short circuit)**		
Basic Course Description	**1**	TR1	Internal short circuit
	2	TC1&2	Increase measured current
	3	TCTR1&2	Detect an increase in current
	4	PDIF	Detect current unbalance, send trip, notify IHMI
	5	CSWI1&2	Receive trip, send command to XCBR1 and XCBR2
	6	XCBR1&2	Receive command, send trip to CBR1 and CBR2
	7	CBR1&2	Receive the trip and open
	8	IHMI	Show status and alarm
	9	Operator	Recognize status and alarm
Extensions	**Flow of events for external short circuit**		
	1	TR1	External short circuit (outside the protected zone)
	2	TC1&2	Increase measured current
	3	TCTR1&2	Detect an increase in current
	4	PDIF	No unbalance, do not send trip, do not notify IHMI
	Flow of events for breaker failure during an internal short circuit		
	1	TR1	Internal short circuit
	2	TC1&2	Increase measured current
	3	TCTR1&2	Detect an increase in current
	4	PDIF	Detect current unbalance, send trip, notify IHMI
	5	CSWI1&2	Receive trip, send command to XCBR1 and XCBR2
	6	XCBR1&2	Receive command, send trip to CBR1 and CBR2
	7	CBR1&2	Do not open; activate breaker failure protection
	8	IHMI	Show status and alarm

transformer. Similar specifications can be applied to all automation functions within an installation.

According to this specification, Figures 15.4 and 15.5 show possible compositions of differential protection functions for two- and three-winding power transformers in a substation, respectively, using a UML Communication Diagram. In

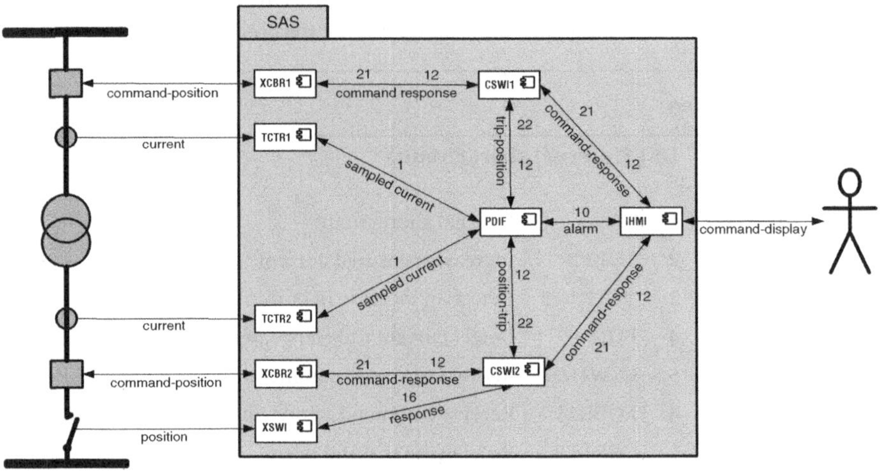

Figure 15.4 Two-winding transformer protection.

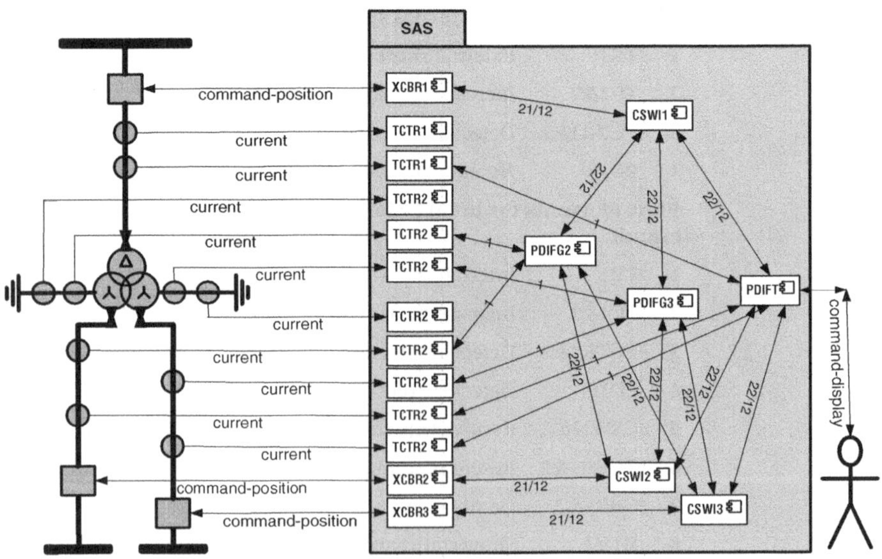

Figure 15.5 Three-winding transformer protection.

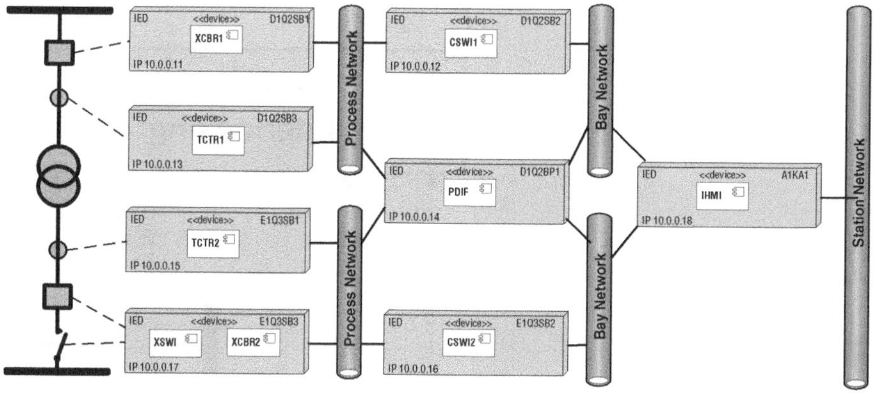

Figure 15.6 Station-level network and logical nodes.

addition to the ***LNs***, the types of information exchanged between them are shown with their corresponding ***PICOM*** numbers.

Note that ***LNs*** are used not only to convey signals to and from high-voltage equipment (current, voltage, commands, etc.) but also to model the different kinds of decisions and information exchange within the SAS and with external users. ***LNs TCTR*** and ***XCBR*** model the high-voltage current transformers and circuit breakers surrounding the protected transformer, while ***PDIF*** models the differential protection. Note also the ***CSWI LN***, which controls the switching logic of circuit breakers.

Physically, IEC 61850 allows the deployment of these ***LNs*** in different ***IEDs*** and network segments, as shown in the UML Deployment Diagram of Figure 15.6. The process network typically connects the ***LNs*** for controlling circuit breakers (***XCBR***) and switches (***XSWI***), as well as for modeling current instrument transformers (***TCTR***). The bay level includes the ***LNs*** for bay control (***CSWI***) and transformer differential protection (***PDIF***). The station-level network comprises a ***LN*** for the human interface (***IHMI***) and ***gateways*** for the upper external levels.

15.5 Interlocking Functions

In SAS, interlocking functions are required whenever it is necessary to block one function during the operation of another. A typical example of interlocking function is the reverse interlocking of radial feeders in a substation. This function aims to prevent the infeed busbar breaker from tripping due to overcurrent devices on the outgoing feeders (Figure 15.7) during a fault on the outgoing feeders.

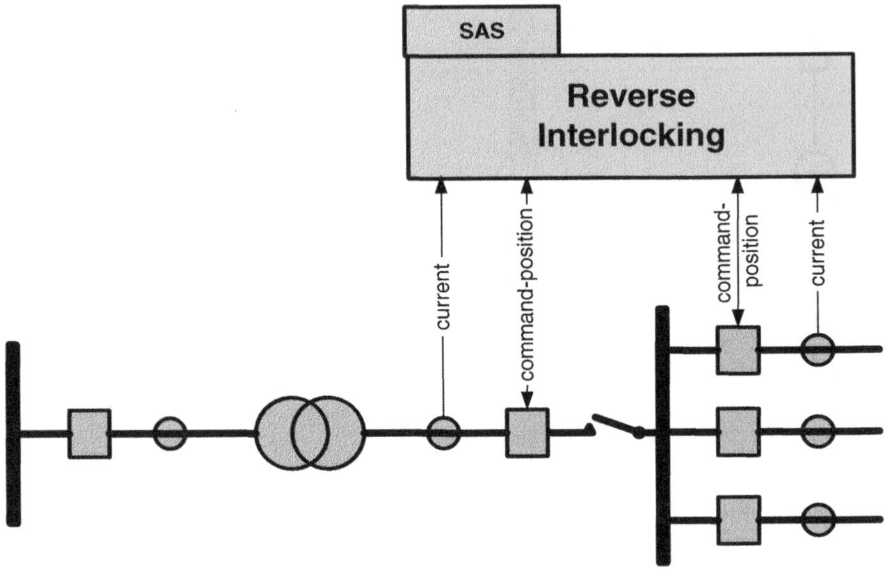

Figure 15.7 Reverse interlocking of radial feeders.

The interlocking can be fully implemented in IEC 61850 by exchanging ***GOOSE*** messages between the time-overcurrent ***LNs*** (***PTOC***) of the server running the feeder automation system and the transformer automation system, as shown in the UML Communication Diagram in Figure 15.8, which depicts the ***PICOM*** data exchanged between the ***LNs***. The sending information from the ***LN PTOC*** in the feeder SAS is the overcurrent pickup operation and direction information during a feeder fault, taken from the ***Str*** data, which is used in the ***LN PTOC*** in the transformer SAS to block its operation. At the inception of a fault in the feeder, the ***PTOC LN*** picks up and sends a ***GOOSE*** message to the transformer ***IED***, thereby blocking the transformer ***IED's*** instant overcurrent protection. When the fault is removed, another ***GOOSE*** message is sent, thereby unblocking the instantaneous overcurrent function.

15.6 Transfer Functions

Transfer functions are required in substation automation to allocate a function to another function, primarily during maintenance or when a function or asset is unavailable. A typical application involves transferring the protection functions from a feeder breaker to a bus coupler or transfer breaker, as shown in Figure 15.9. In normal conditions, the busbar is connected to the circuit breakers A and B, and

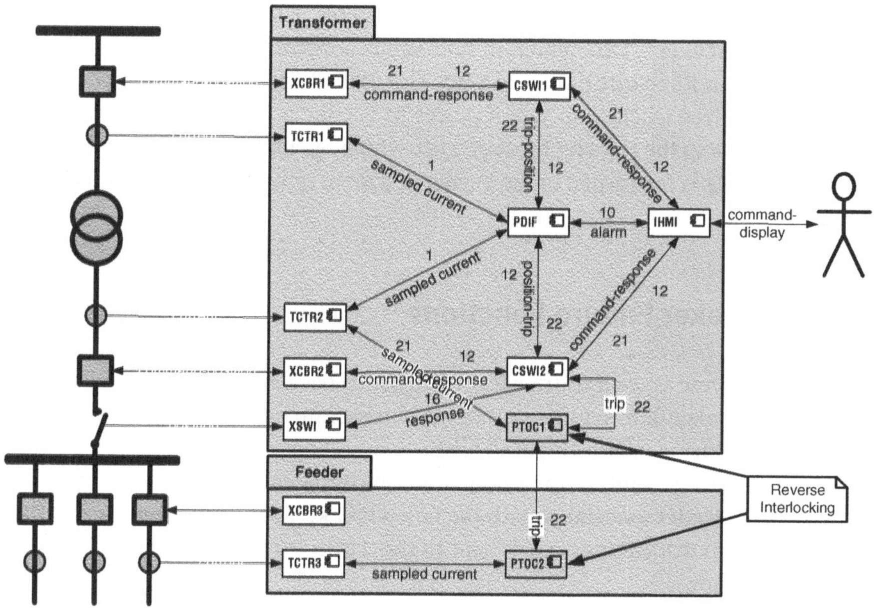

Figure 15.8 Reverse interlocking with GOOSE messages.

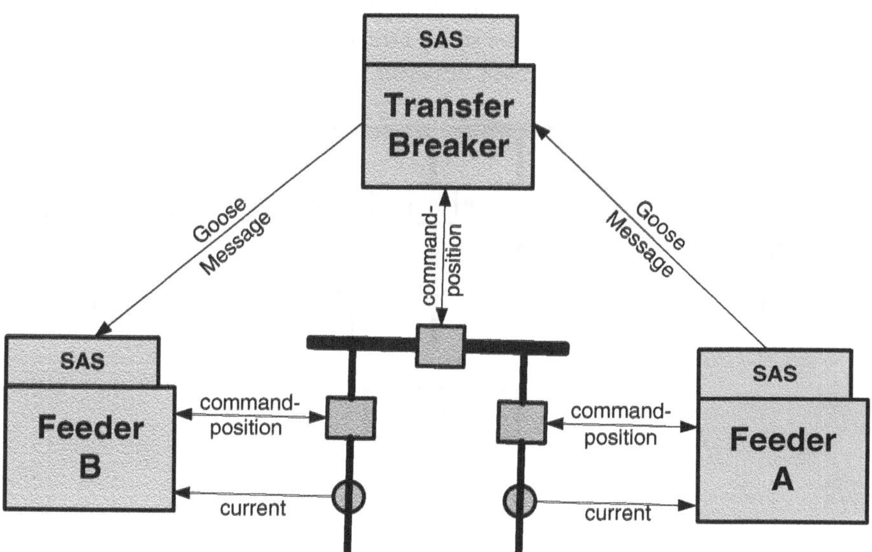

Figure 15.9 Line transfer to bus coupler breaker.

the transfer breaker is open. When Feeder A opens, a ***GOOSE*** telegram is sent to the transfer breaker's ***IED***, which in turn sends a ***GOOSE*** to the ***IED*** of circuit B, switching to another ***setting group***. The ***IED*** of the transfer breaker verifies and synchronizes its closing. When power in Feeder A is re-established, its ***IED*** sends a ***GOOSE*** to the transfer breaker ***IED***, which opens the transfer breaker, and another ***GOOSE*** is forwarded to the Feeder A ***IED*** to return it to its previous group of settings.

15.7 Breaker Failure Functions

A similar scheme is used to transfer functions to backup protection during malfunctions. Breaker failure functions aim to trip backup breakers if the main circuit breaker fails during a fault (Figure 15.10).

While detecting a fault in the feeder, the ***IED*** initiates the protection algorithm for the faulty feeder associated with the failed breaker. The circuit breaker fault is detected; a trip ***GOOSE*** message is sent to the ***IEDs*** of circuit breakers A and B to clear the fault.

15.8 Monitoring Functions

In addition to supporting the automation and protection of digital substations, IEC 61850 defines a comprehensive set of ***LNs*** for condition monitoring of most types of switchyard equipment used in power systems. Following is a list of the

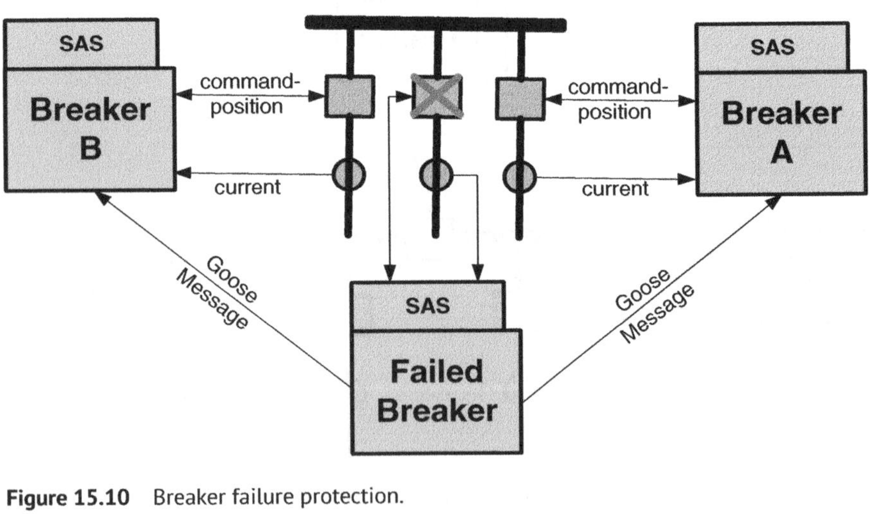

Figure 15.10 Breaker failure protection.

leading power system equipment for which IEC 61850 and IEC 61400 define standardized ***LNs*** for condition monitoring and control:

- Power Transformers
- Wind Power Plants
- Hydropower Plants
- Distributed Energy Resources
- Circuit Breakers
- Disconnectors and Isolators
- Earthing Switches
- Current Transformers
- Voltage Transformers
- Surge Arresters
- Shunt Capacitor Banks
- Shunt Reactors
- Busbars
- Transmission Line/Feeders
- Grounding Grid/Earthing Systems
- Capacitive Voltage Dividers
- High-Voltage Cables
- Switchyard Auxiliary Systems

The following paragraphs describe the typical organization of Condition Monitoring Systems (CMSs) for some of these switchyard equipment, using IEC 61850.

15.9 Transformer Functions

Power transformers are perhaps the most important and expensive assets in a substation, deserving extensive monitoring for protection purposes and asset management. A CMS for a power transformer under IEC 61850 can be deployed using a data model-centric architecture, in which each phenomenon, diagnostic estimate, and alarm in the transformer is monitored via standardized ***LNs***. The architecture of the CMS can be organized, for instance, into the following systems:

- Electrical Measurement System
- Thermal Cooling System
- Dissolved Gas and Oil Chemistry System
- On-Line Tap Changer System
- Computed Health Diagnostics System

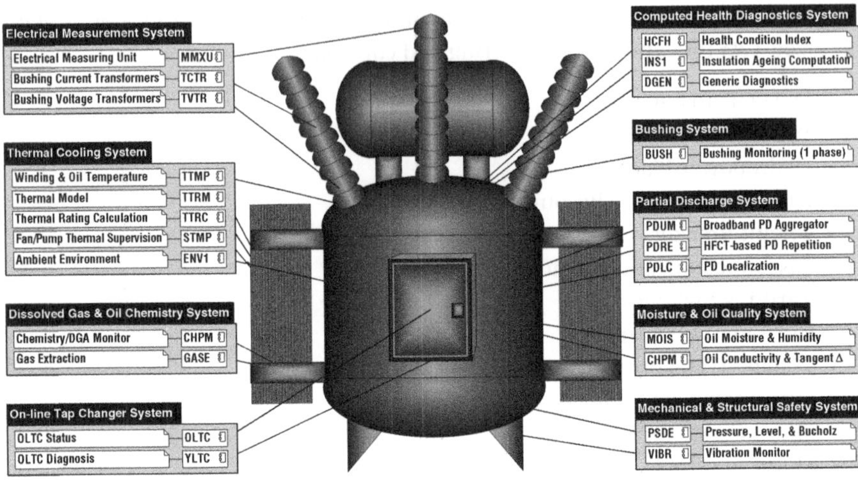

Figure 15.11 Power transformer monitoring.

- Bushing System
- Partial Discharge System
- Moisture and Oil Quality System
- Mechanical and Structural Safety System

Figure 15.11 shows a UML Package Diagram grouping the standardized ***LNs*** that can be used for each system in a power transformer. Every package contains the class of each ***LN*** and a note with its purpose in the monitoring system.

These packages can be distributed across several ***CUs*** and ***MUs*** within the transformer control cabinet, into a field cabinet near the transformer, or grouped into a set of **`logical devices`** in a transformer monitoring ***IED***. ***`Report Control Blocks`*** and ***`Data Sets`*** can be defined using ***SCL*** to gather specific data from these ***LN*** for event publishing via ***GOOSE*** messages and for periodic or on-demand reporting on thermal trending, gas alarms, partial-discharge spikes, bushing trends, OLTC history, etc., required for asset management.

15.10 Circuit Breaker Functions

The same concept can be used to specify a CMS for circuit breakers. Like power transformers, these are critical primary equipment that safely interrupt fault currents to preserve the stability of the electric power system and to change the grid topology. They are subject to several failure modes, including mechanical

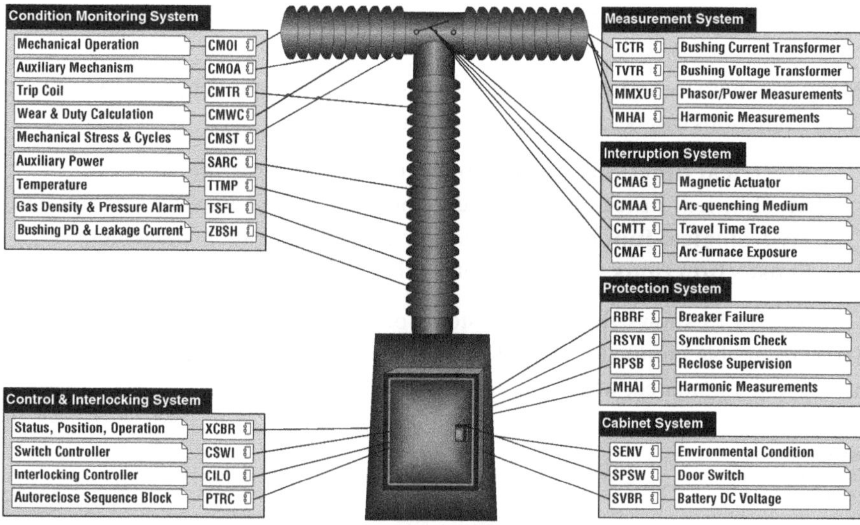

Figure 15.12 Circuit breaker monitoring.

wear, insulation degradation, gas leakage, and auxiliary system failures. A CMS provides continuous, real-time assessment of key breaker parameters—such as operating times, coil currents, contact travel, mechanism pressure, insulation condition, and number of operations. It can be organized, for instance, into the following systems:

- CMS
- Control and Interlocking System
- Measurement System
- Interruption System
- Projection System
- Cabinet System

Figure 15.12 shows a UML Package Diagram grouping the standardized ***LNs*** that can be used for each system in a circuit breaker. Every package contains the class of each ***LN*** and a note with its purpose in the monitoring system.

These packages can be embedded as ***CUs*** and ***MUs*** within an existing cabinet at the circuit breaker or grouped into a set of ***logical devices*** in an ***IED*** at the process or ***station network***.

Using IEC 61850, it is possible to mimic this process to monitor and control entire digital installations, as illustrated in the following paragraphs for hydropower and wind power plants.

15.11 Hydropower Functions

Many automation and monitoring systems exist in a typical hydropower plant. These functions can be classified into four types:

- **Electrical functions**—mainly protection and control functions
- **Mechanical functions**—related to the turbines and associated equipment
- **Hydrological functions**—water flow control and dam management
- **Sensor functions**—measurements other than electrical

Figure 15.13 shows the major systems of a typical Gas-Insulated Substation (GIS) reversible pump-storage hydropower plant. All these systems must be monitored and automated, which can be done using IEC 61850.

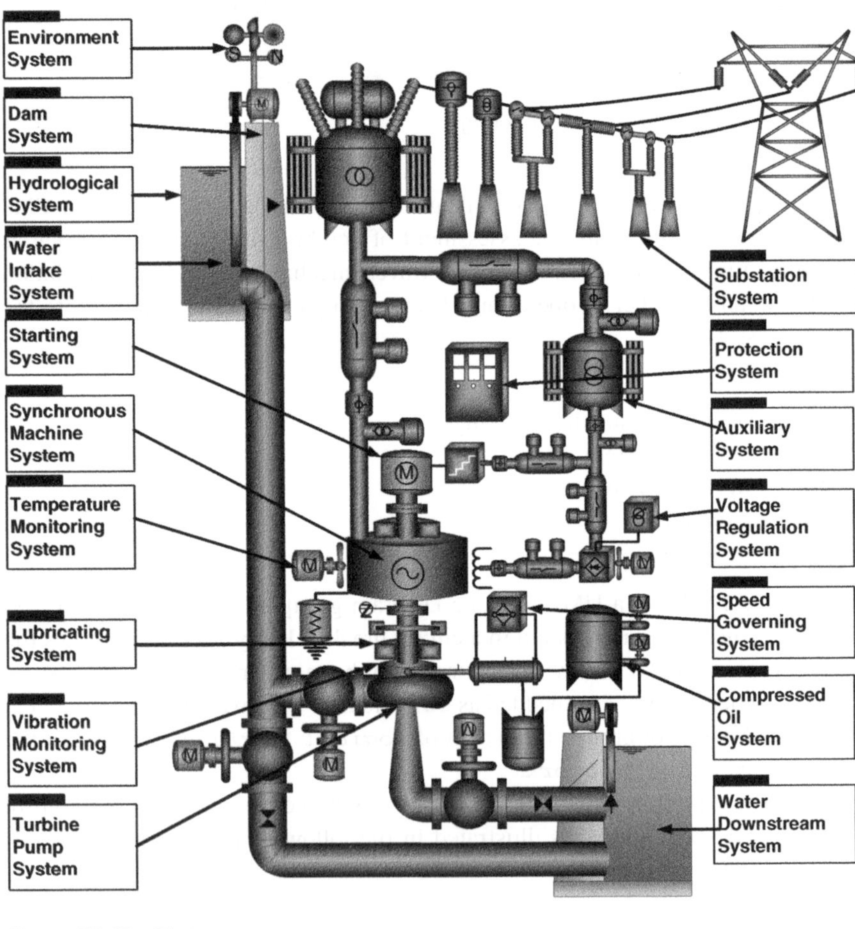

Figure 15.13 Hydropower systems.

Each system can be modeled and automated using IEC 61850, with the specific ***LNs*** standardized in IEC 61850 Part 7-410, dedicated to hydropower plants. Annex 0 contains a comprehensive gas-insulated hydropower plant model, along with its corresponding ***LNs***. The following paragraphs describe the possible ***LNs*** for modeling typical hydropower systems, including the starting system, synchronous machine system, temperature monitoring system, lubrication monitoring system, vibration monitoring system, turbine pump system, chimney system, and water downstream system.

Figure 15.14 illustrates how the starting system can be modeled using ***LNs*** that represent the unit sequencer and operating status, including the starting breaker (***XCBR***), starting current transformer (***TCTR***), starting motor (***ZMOT***), and synchronizing device (***RSYN***).

A similar model can be developed using ***LNs*** for the synchronous machine generator (***ZSMC***), including the breaker (***SCBR***) and neutral resistor (***ZRES***), as shown in Figure 15.15. ***LN ZSMC*** models any synchronous machine, including its rating data, controls, and operational status.

Another standard system in hydropower plants is temperature monitoring. It models devices that monitor the temperature of major plant components and

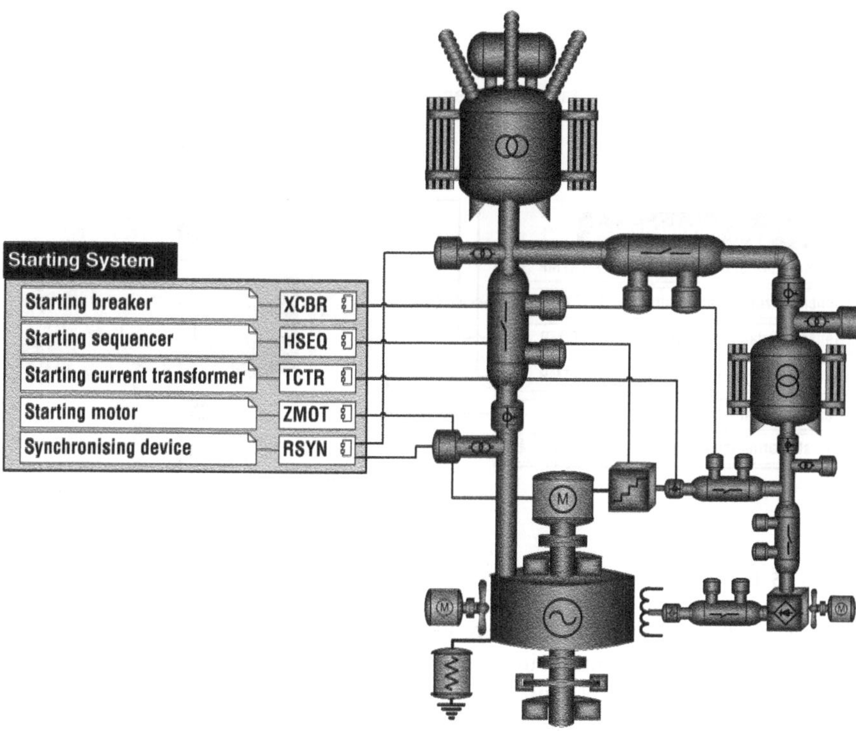

Figure 15.14 Hydropower starting system.

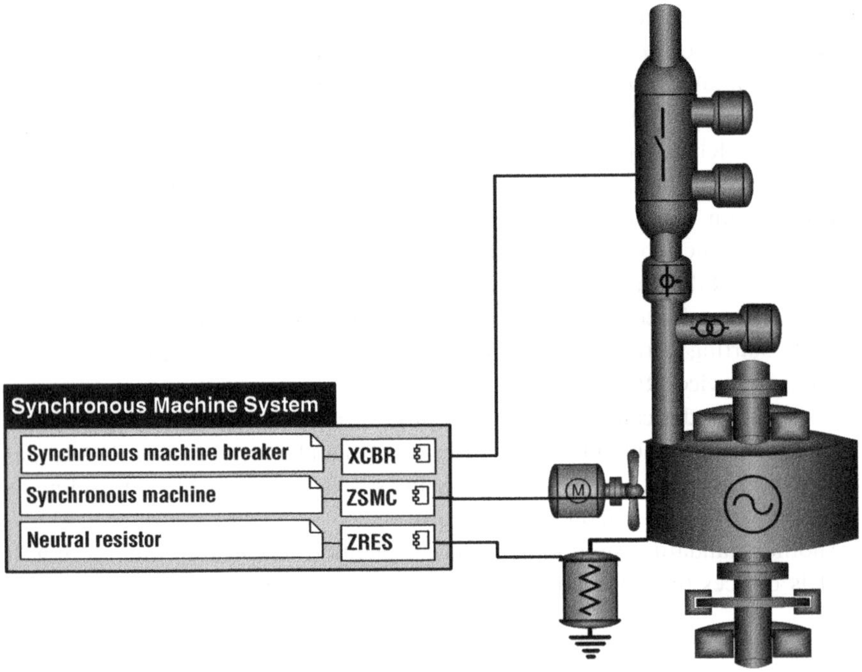

Figure 15.15 Synchronous machine system.

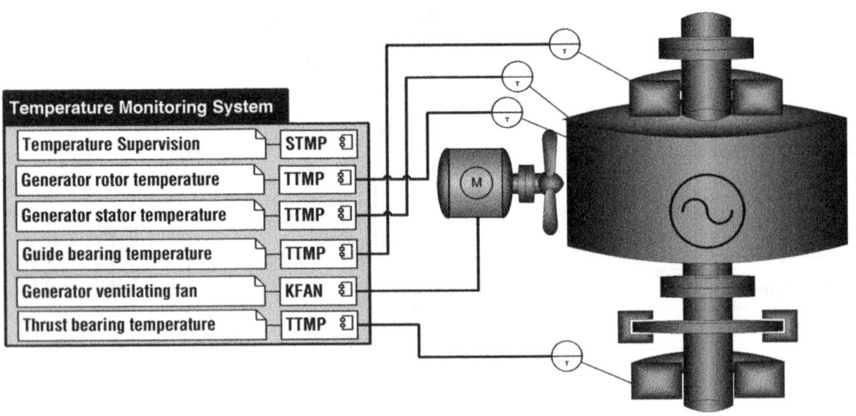

Figure 15.16 Temperature monitoring system.

provide alarm, trip/shutdown, and cooling control functions. Figure 15.16 shows a typical temperature monitoring system, with specific ***LNs*** to monitor the heat content of the generator (***STMP***), ventilating fans (***KFAN***), and instances of the ***LN TTMP*** to monitor the rotor, stator, guide bearings, and thrust bearings of the hydro generator.

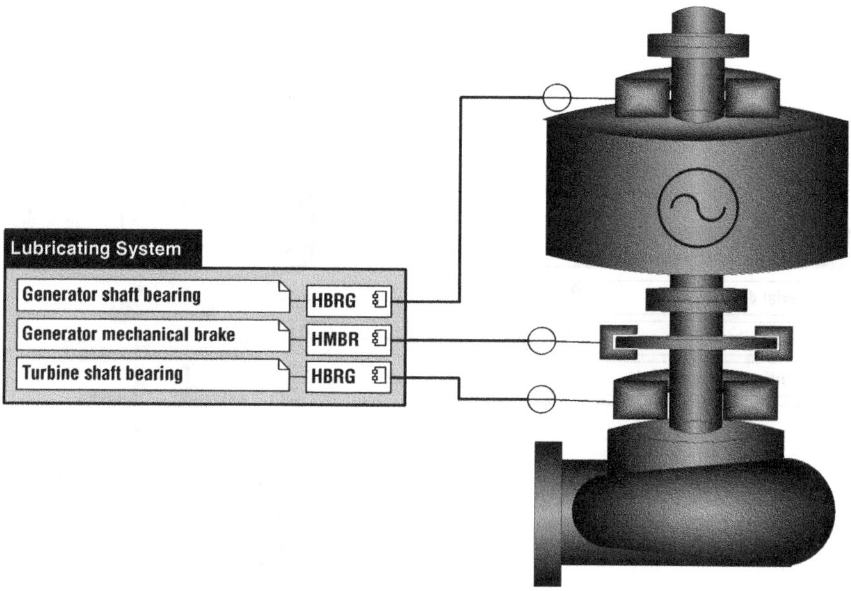

Figure 15.17 Lubricating monitoring system.

Due to their importance in hydropower plants, lubricating systems are typically independent and autonomous. They model the physical devices for thrust, guide bearings, and brakes of the turbine/pump system using instances of the ***LN HMBR***, as shown in Figure 15.17.

Vibration is also an important system to model and monitor, as it is one of the main failure modes of hydro generators. A dedicated vibration monitoring system is usually included in the power plant SAS and modeled as shown in Figure 15.18. ***LNs*** are instantiated to model the shaft's axial and vertical displacement (***TAXD***) and shaft axial vibration (***TVBR***), which are used for monitoring, alarm, and protection functions.

The waterways of the turbine/pump system can also be modeled in IEC 61850 in most hydropower plants, as shown in Figure 15.19. In addition to the ***LN HTUR*** used to model the turbine, the ***LN KVLV*** is instantiated to model the bypass or relief valves, as well as the intake and suction valves. Pressure sensors are modeled by different instances of ***LN TPRS*** for the intake, outflow, and bypass waterways. Flow sensors can also be added by instantiating the ***LN HDLS***. These ***LNs*** enable a comprehensive model of the waterways at the power plant and their control.

Chimneys and other pressure- and water-hammer-limiting hydraulic structures are usually monitored by a LN HLVL to supervise the water level, as shown in Figure 15.20 for penstock and draft-tube chimneys. Similar models can be implemented to monitor other pressure control structures, such as compressed air chambers.

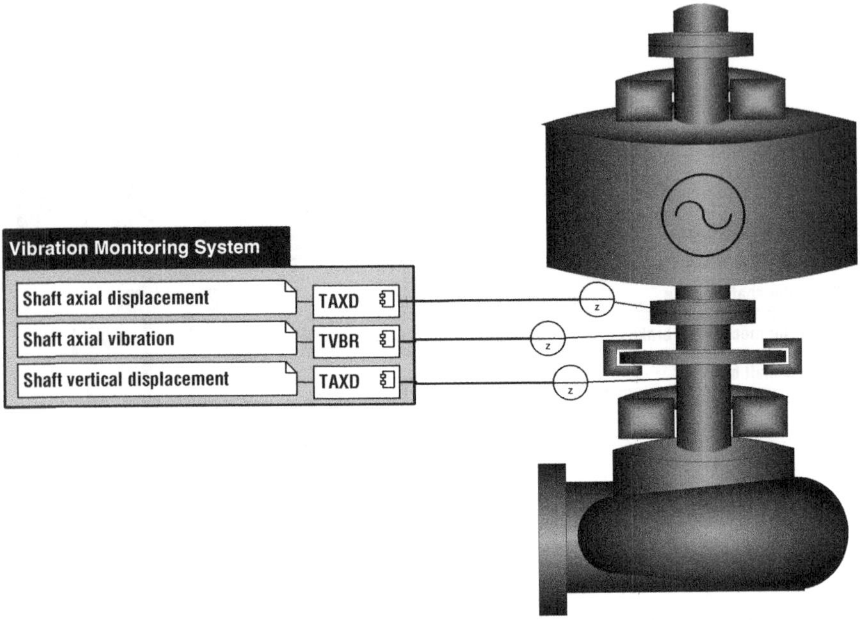

Figure 15.18 Vibration monitoring system.

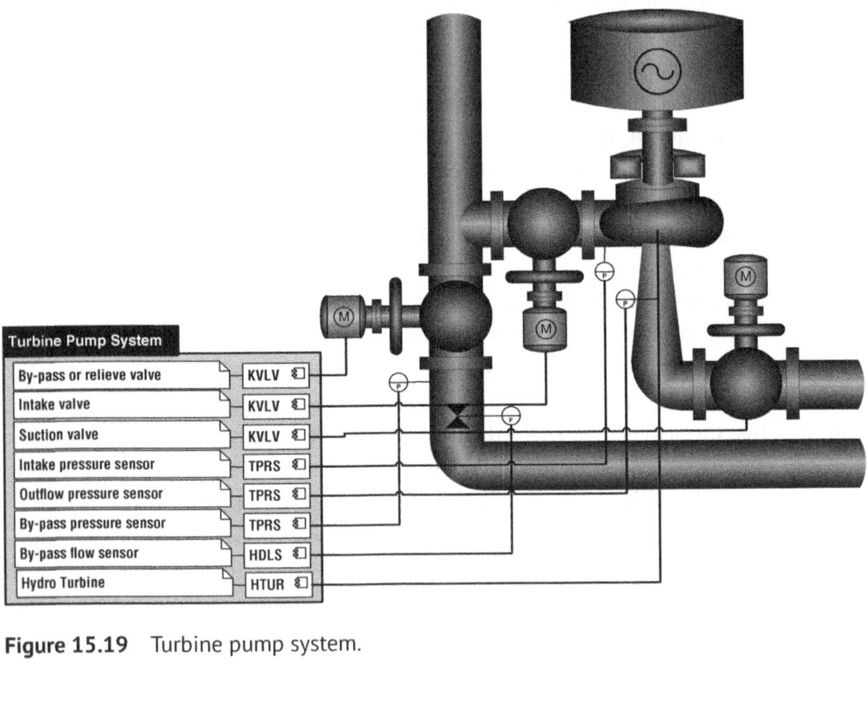

Figure 15.19 Turbine pump system.

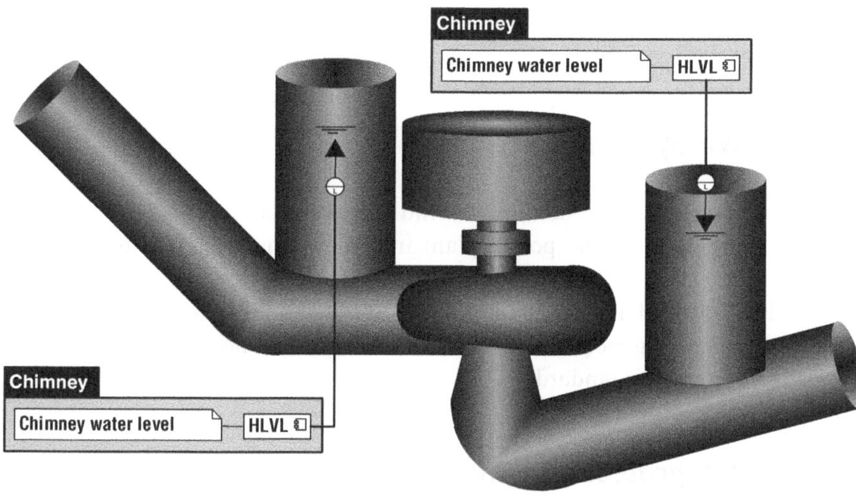

Figure 15.20 Chimney system.

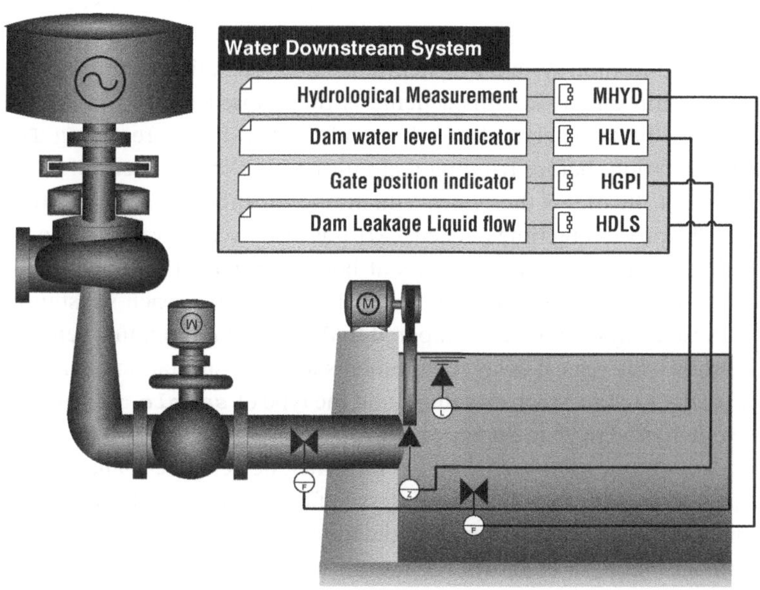

Figure 15.21 Water downstream system.

Specific ***LNs*** monitor the remaining water flues, as shown in Figure 15.21 for the water downstream system. In addition to the ***LN*** for downstream flow hydrological measurement (***MHYD***), ***LNs*** are instantiated to model the lower reservoir level (***HLVL***), the draft tube gate position (***HGPI***), and the dam leakage liquid flow (***HDLS***). A similar system can be used to model the water upstream system.

15.12 Windpower Functions

Following the same approach, most wind power functions can be modeled in IEC 61850 by dividing the power plant into functional systems, as shown in Figure 15.22.

For wind power plants, the standard IEC 61400 defines a complete set of ***LNs*** suitable for modeling most of these systems. Annex 16.3 shows the application of typical ***LNs*** from this standard.

15.13 Teleprotection Functions

IEC 61850 can be used to model telecommunication schemes for a transmission line differential teleprotection function, as shown in Figure 15.23. In this scheme, ***SV*** and ***GOOSE*** messages must be exchanged between the two-line terminals using a telecommunication system to synchronize their operation.

An essential requirement for this scheme is the elapsed time for a ***GOOSE*** or ***SV*** message to be transferred from the sending ***IED*** to the receiving ***IED*** at the other substation, before tripping a circuit breaker in the event of a line fault. Figure 15.24 illustrates the typical timeframe for this transfer. Note that, in addition to the processing time of each ***IED***, it is also necessary to include the processing times of the telecom gateways at both terminals, the transmission time of the network link/LAN, and the local area network at each substation. The sum of these delays should be compared to the protection requirements.

Table 15.2 shows the typical delay requirements for inter-substation communications, the size of each message exchange, and the type of ***sample value*** (***SV***) or ***GOOSE*** method used to code the messages.

Substation communication architectures may include separate managed networks and protocols other than IP, requiring specific routing and gateway configurations. The architecture may be based on the tunneling of messages or gateways at both terminals. Figure 15.25 shows a communication architecture for tunneling ***GOOSE/SV*** messages between two substations using multicast routers (***MROUTER***) at the network layer of the OSI protocol stack. Several routing protocols can be used at this layer, including PPTP, L2F, L2TP, IPsec, and MPLS.

If different protocols are used on the substations, ***gateways*** are required at each end of the communication channel to translate the messages. Figure 15.26 shows a typical configuration for communication using ***gateways***. Note that this arrangement can also connect parts of an SAS that uses different protocols.

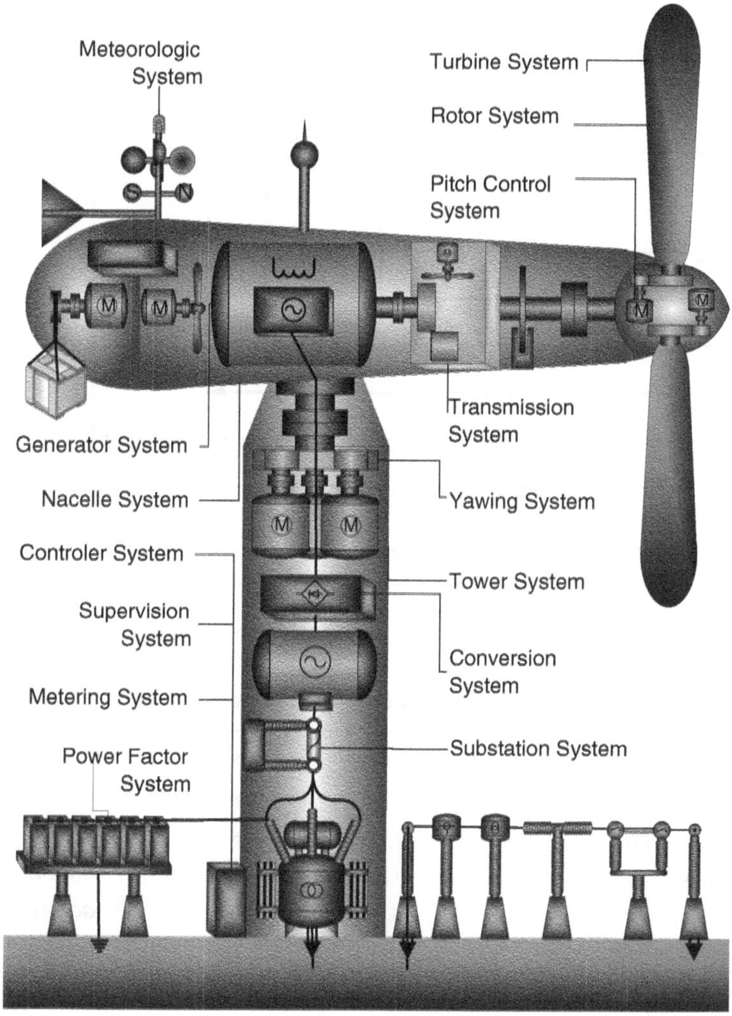

Figure 15.22 Windpower systems.

Figure 15.23
Teleprotection functions.

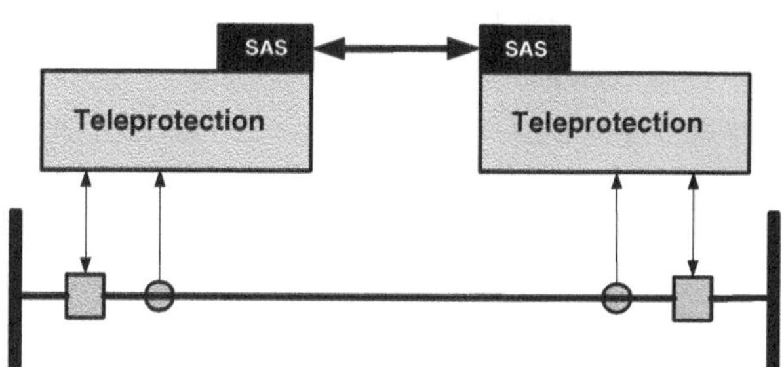

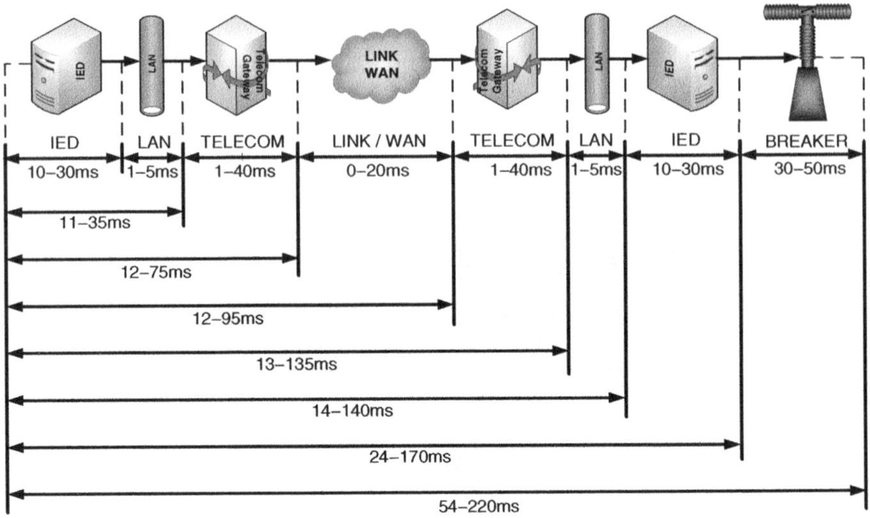

Figure 15.24 Teleprotection time requirements.

Table 15.2 Inter-substation communication requirements.

Application	Delay	Content	Message
Permissive tele-protection scheme	5 ms	7 bits	*GOOSE*
Blocking tele-protection scheme	5 ms	7 bits	*GOOSE*
Directional comparison protection	5 ms	7 bits	*GOOSE*
Transfer/direct tripping	5 ms	3 bits	*GOOSE*
Interlocking	≤100 ms	10 bits	*GOOSE*
Multiphase auto-reclosing	10 ms	6 bits	*GOOSE*
Current differential line protection	¼ cy	3 × 8 × 12 bits	*SV+GOOSE*
Phase comparison protection	¼ cy	4 bits	*GOOSE*
System integrity protection	¼ cy	3 × 8 × 12 bits	*SV+GOOSE*
Real-time generator shedding	¼ cy	3 × 8 × 12 bits	*SV+GOOSE*
Out-of-step detection	1 cy	1 × 8 × 12 bits	*SV+GOOSE*
Synchrophasors	¼ cy	6 × 8 × 12 bits	*SV+GOOSE*
Remedial action schemes	¼ cy	6 × 8 × 12 bits	*SV+GOOSE*

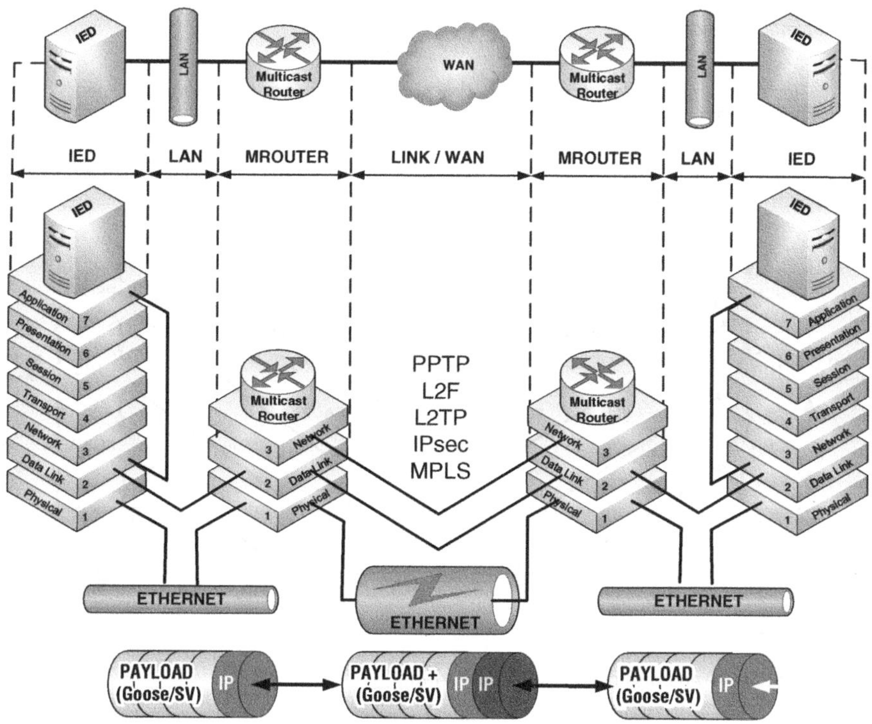

Figure 15.25 Multicast tunneling between substations.

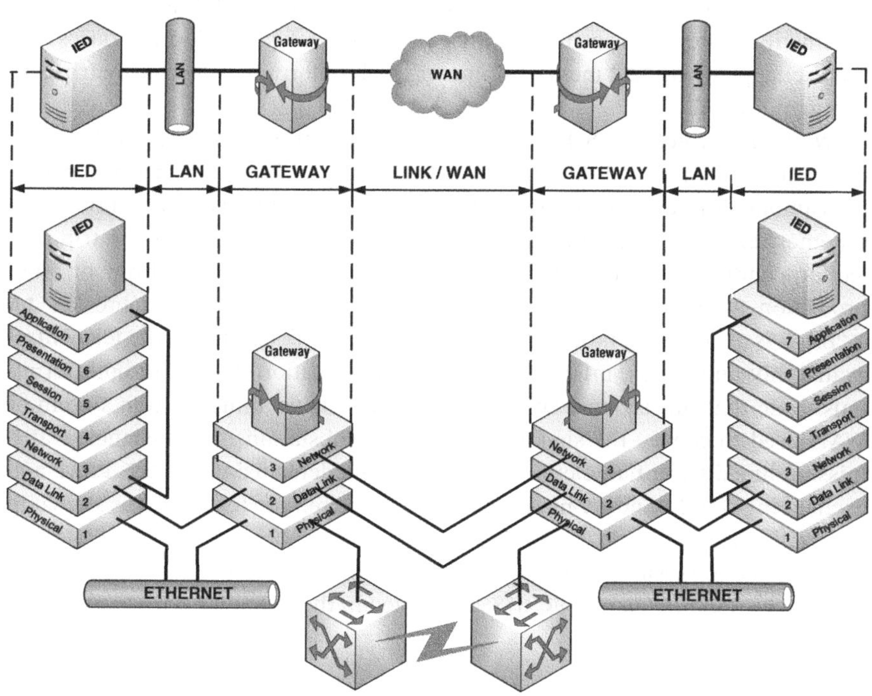

Figure 15.26 Gateway between substations.

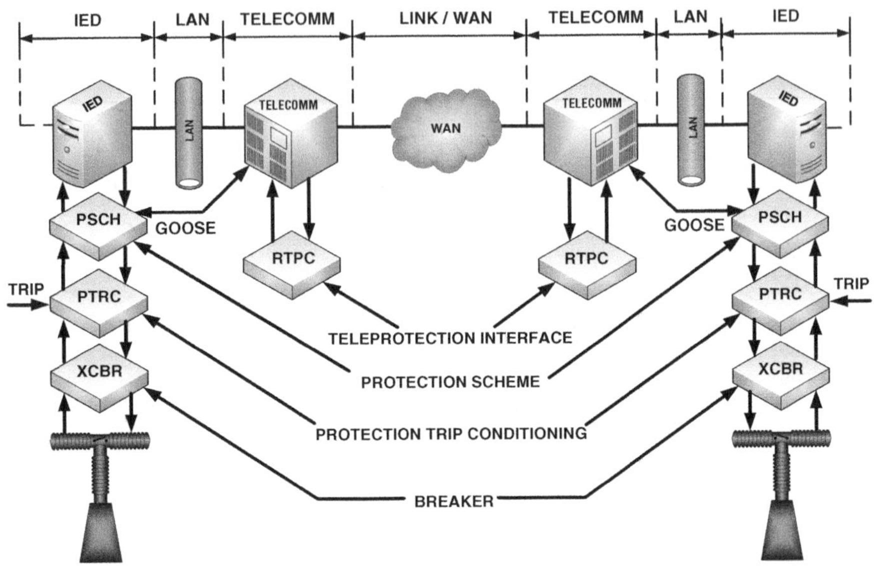

Figure 15.27 Transmission line teleprotection.

Figure 15.27 shows a typical IEC 61850-based teleprotection system for a transmission line. In addition to the ***LNs*** used to protect each line terminal, this scheme illustrates the specific ***LNs*** that model the teleprotection interfaces and the exchange of ***GOOSE*** messages among the line terminals to convey trip and command signals.

LN PSCH (Protection Scheme) models the teleprotection scheme for line-protection function coordination, conveying the exchange of ***operate*** outputs among different protection functions and the conditions for line-protection schemes. ***LN PTRC*** (Remote Telecontrol Point Controller) models the trip protection conditioning required to connect the ***operate*** outputs of one or more protection functions to a typical ***trip*** transmitted to the circuit breaker ***LN XCBR***. It is also used to model the communication link and to handle telecontrol availability and status, interacting with communication devices in both terminals. Note that this scheme abstracts the type of telecommunication system or WAN used to convey the signals between the substations. For instance, transmission line differential teleprotection can be modeled using the ***LN PDIF*** and exchanging ***GOOSE*** and ***SV*** messages between the remote terminals, as shown in Figure 15.28.

Teleprotection systems are examples of a much larger set of wide-area functions that can be deployed using IEC 61850, as listed in the following paragraph.

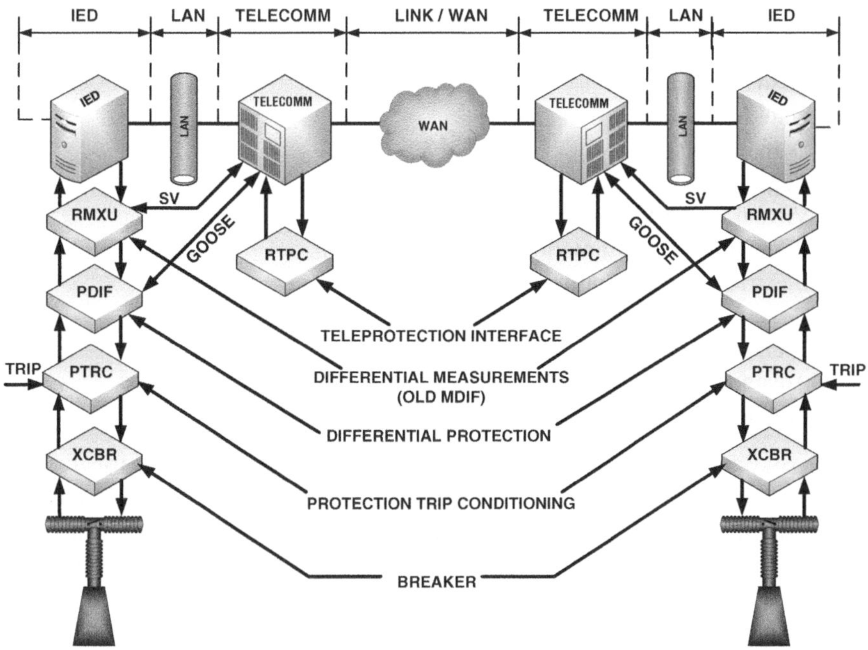

Figure 15.28 Transmission line differential teleprotection.

15.14 Wide-area Functions

The following list summarizes some types of wide-area automation systems required to operate an electrical grid, in which the standard IEC 61850 can be used, mainly at the lower level near the power devices and at the upper levels using routable ***GOOSE/SV***:

- Wholesale Energy Market
- Retail Energy Market
- Transmission Operation
- Distribution Operation
- Economic Dispatch
- Demand Side Management
- Wide-Area Network Video, Voice, and Data
- Generation Shedding
- Automatic Generation Control (AGC)
- Automatic Voltage Regulation (AVR)

- Reactive Energy Regulation
- Supervisory Control and Data Acquisition (SCADA)
- Load Shedding
- State Estimation
- Demand Response
- Aggregators
- Virtual Power Plants
- Protection and Automation and Teleprotection
- Electrical Vehicle Stations
- Governor Control
- HVDC Control
- Advanced Metering
- Mobile Workforce

These systems are distributed vertically at different levels of the electrical power system, from the field layer, through the station, operation, and enterprise levels, up to the market layer, and horizontally across the different sectors, from generation through the transmission, distribution, and consumer, as shown in the matrix of Figure 15.29. Several communication networks are required to operate these systems, ranging hierarchically from the (0) local power network, through the (1) process, (2) station, (3) corporate, and (4) external networks.

A significant part of a utility business's operations is deployed on corporate and external networks, where IEC 61968 (Enterprise Business Function Interfaces

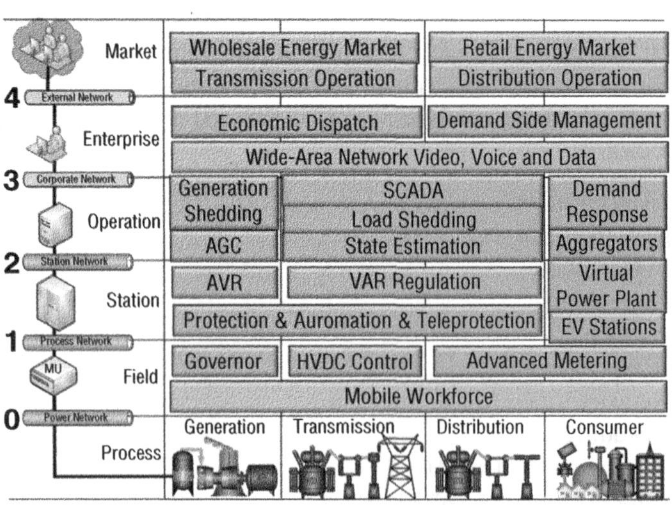

Figure 15.29 Basic grid automation systems.

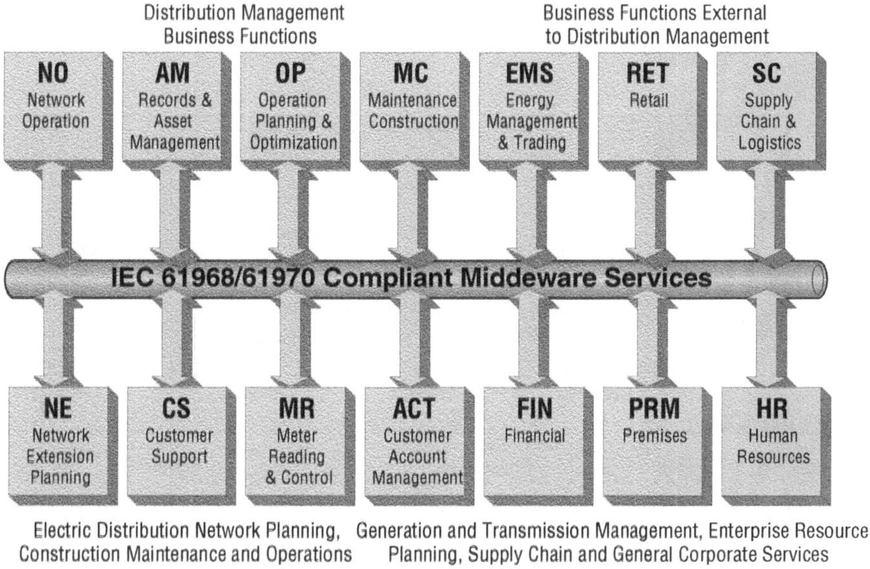

Figure 15.30 Basic business automation systems.

for Utility Operations) and IEC 61970 (Energy Management System Application Program Interface) are the primary standards for implementing these systems, primarily at the upper network layers. Figure 15.30 shows the main set of artifacts defined by these standards.

At the lower layers, IEC 61850 is the leading candidate for implementing these systems, which encompass the process and station networks, as well as portions of the corporate network. The introduction of routable ***GOOSE/SV*** messages extends the application of IEC 61850 as the preferred method for implementing long-distance protection and control systems, such as Inter-Substation Protection Schemes (ISPS), System Integrity Protection Systems (SIPS), Remedial Action Systems (RAS), Centralized Remedial Action Systems (CRAS), and Wide-Area Metering, Protection, Automation, and Control (WAMPAC) systems. These are distributed decision applications that require the exchange of information and control signals between ***IEDs*** located in different substations and power plants. Figure 15.31 illustrates a possible architecture of a wide-area PAC system based on IEC 61850. In this scheme, ***Sample Values*** (***SV***) and ***Phasor Measurements*** (***PM***) are collected from ***MUs*** and ***Phasor Measuring Units*** (***PMU***) at the process network of substations and transmitted to local ***Phasor Data Concentrators*** (***PDC***) at the station network of substations. The ***PDCs*** of different substations can exchange signals and controls via ***R-GOOSE/SV*** messages with other ***PDCs*** in remote substations,

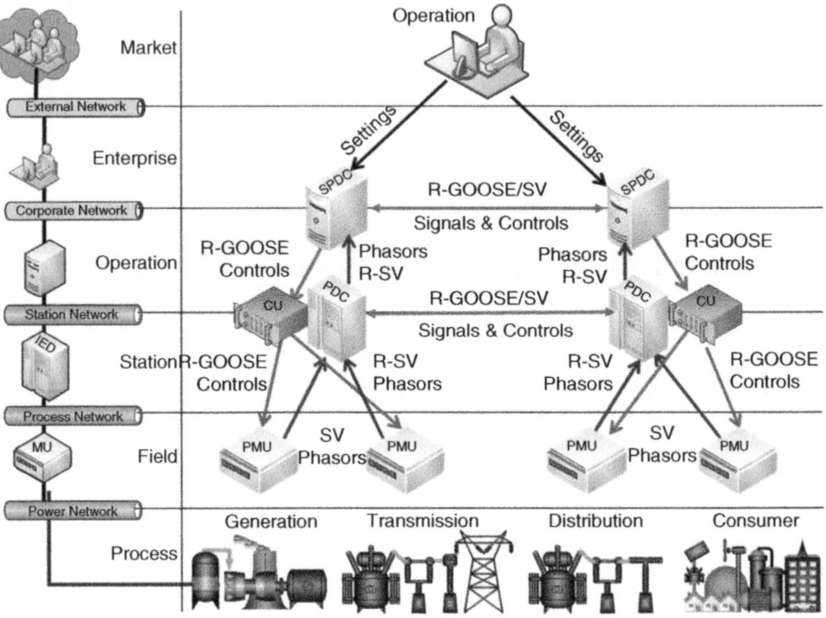

Figure 15.31 Wide-area PAC systems.

supporting distributed protection decisions that generate ***R-GOOSE*** messages in the local ***CUs*** and trip signals to the field network. The local PDCs can exchange information with ***Super PDCs*** (***SPDCs***) on the Corporate Network or with ***Centralized PDCs*** (***CPDCs***) on the External Network to support wide-area protection schemes, generating control signals that are sent back to the local ***PDCs*** via ***R-GOOSE*** messages.

The standards IEC 61968 and IEC 61970 define object-oriented classes that model the significant artifacts and processes performed by utility business functions, using a Common Information Model (CIM). An active effort is underway within IEC to harmonize these standards with IEC 61850, as both adopt an object-oriented approach to represent the power system.

15.15 Summary

The large number of ***LNs*** defined in the IEC 61850 standard and related documents enables the modeling of most systems used in power plants, transmission lines, and substations. For functions not defined by existing ***LNs***, the standard allows the definition of new functions, subject to predefined communication rules. This chapter introduced several examples of application of the standard IEC 61850 for the automation of power system functions, including:

- **Protection**—for differential protection
- **Interlocking**—for reverse interlocking of radial feeders
- **Transfer**—from a feeder breaker to a bus coupler or transfer breaker
- **Breaker Failure**—to trip backup breakers in case a breaker fails
- **Transformer**—for condition monitoring
- **Circuit Breaker**—for condition monitoring and control
- **Hydropower**—for automation and monitoring
- **Windpower**—for automation and monitoring
- **Teleprotection**—for inter-substation differential protection
- **Wide Area**—for remote operation and automation systems

According to IEC 61850, several object models for automation functions in substations and power plants were described. The annexes list additional cases related to monitoring and controlling hydropower and wind power plants and DER.

15.16 Review Questions

1 Explain how creating ***LNs*** in IEC 61850 can represent ***MUs and CUs***.

2 Using the example of the combined ***MU*** and ***CU***, explain how ***TCTR***, ***TVTR***, ***STIM***, and ***LLN0*** interact to provide measurement and synchronization services for protection and automation functions.

3 Given the differential protection FICS example, explain how the ***PDIF***, ***CSWI***, ***TCTR***, and ***XCBR LNs*** work together to detect an internal transformer fault and isolate the protected zone.

4 Compare how ***LNs*** are deployed across ***process***, ***bay***, and ***station*** networks. How does the physical layout of ***LNs*** impact performance, reliability, and cybersecurity in digital substations?

5 Explain the principle of reverse interlocking in radial feeders and discuss how ***GOOSE*** messaging facilitates its implementation in an IEC 61850-based substation.

6 A feeder protection ***IED*** must temporarily switch its protection settings to a bus coupler during maintenance. Explain how transfer functions and ***GOOSE*** signaling can be designed to guarantee correct and safe operation.

7 Breaker failure protection demands quick backup tripping via multiple ***IEDs***. Assess the challenges posed by digital communication networks and propose strategies to reduce delays and prevent misoperation.

8 List the main categories of CMS for power transformers under IEC 61850, and briefly explain the purpose of each category.

9 Hydropower automation involves modeling electrical, mechanical, hydrological, and sensor systems. Select two of these areas and explain how IEC 61850 ***LNs*** represent their main components and functions.

10 For a wind power plant modeled with IEC 61400 ***LNs***, suggest how to integrate turbine status, environmental data, and electrical controls into a single monitoring system.

11 Teleprotection schemes must meet strict delay requirements for ***GOOSE*** and ***SV*** messages. Explain how telecommunication architectures (e.g., tunneling, gateways, multicast routers) influence latency and reliability in long-distance differential protection.

12 Considering the wide-area automation model (WAMPAC), explain how ***MUs***, ***PMUs***, ***PDCs***, and ***R-GOOSE*** messages communicate across process, station, corporate, and external networks to enable coordinated protection and control actions.

Annexes

The following figures include an integrated UML class diagram of IEC 61850 (Figure A.1) and examples of its application for implementing substations (Figure A.2), hydropower plants (Figure A.3), wind power plants (Figure A.4), and DERs (Figure A.5). Tables A.1 and A.2 list the UML, SysML, network, and security symbols used in the book. A functional UML use case template is provided in Table A.3.

A.1 IEC 61850 Class Diagram

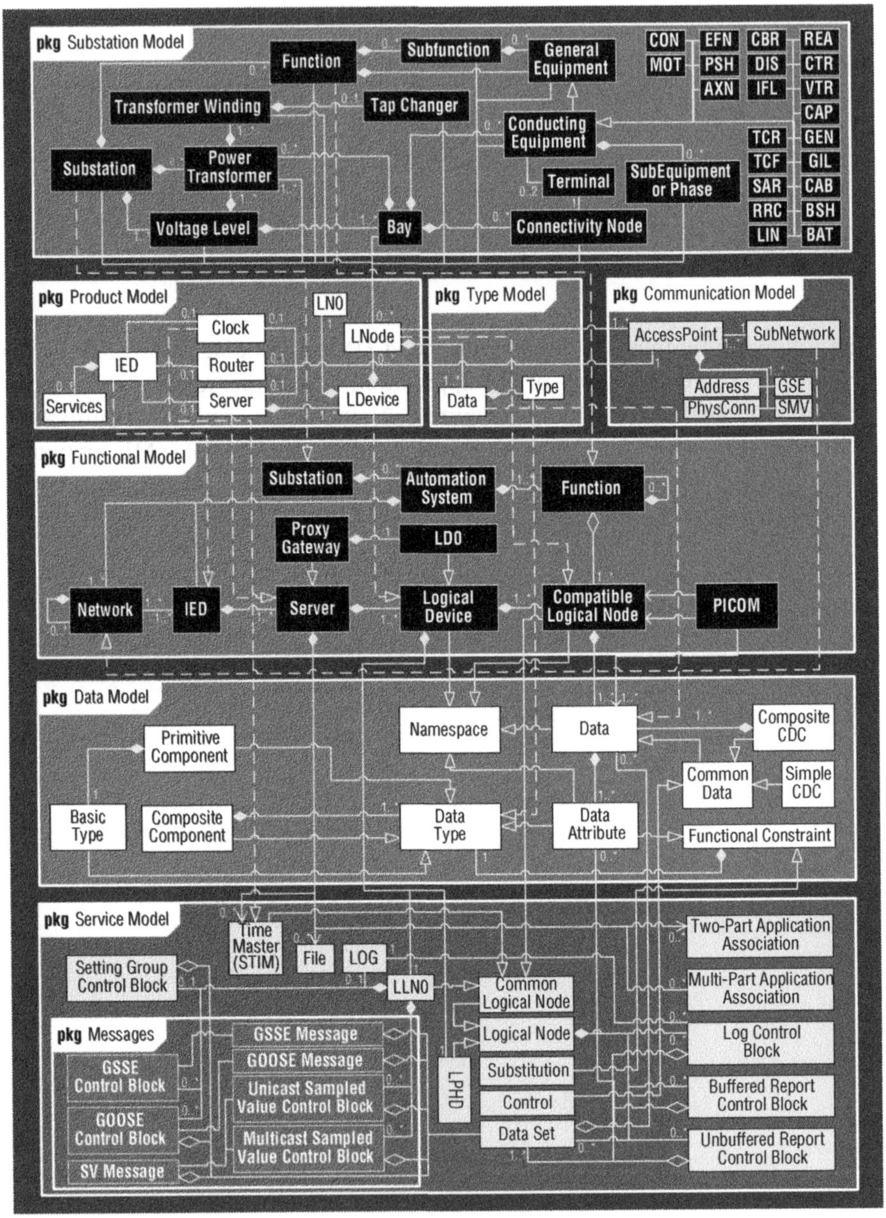

Figure A.1 Layered hierarchical object-oriented view of IEC 61850.

A.2 IEC 61850 Substation Model

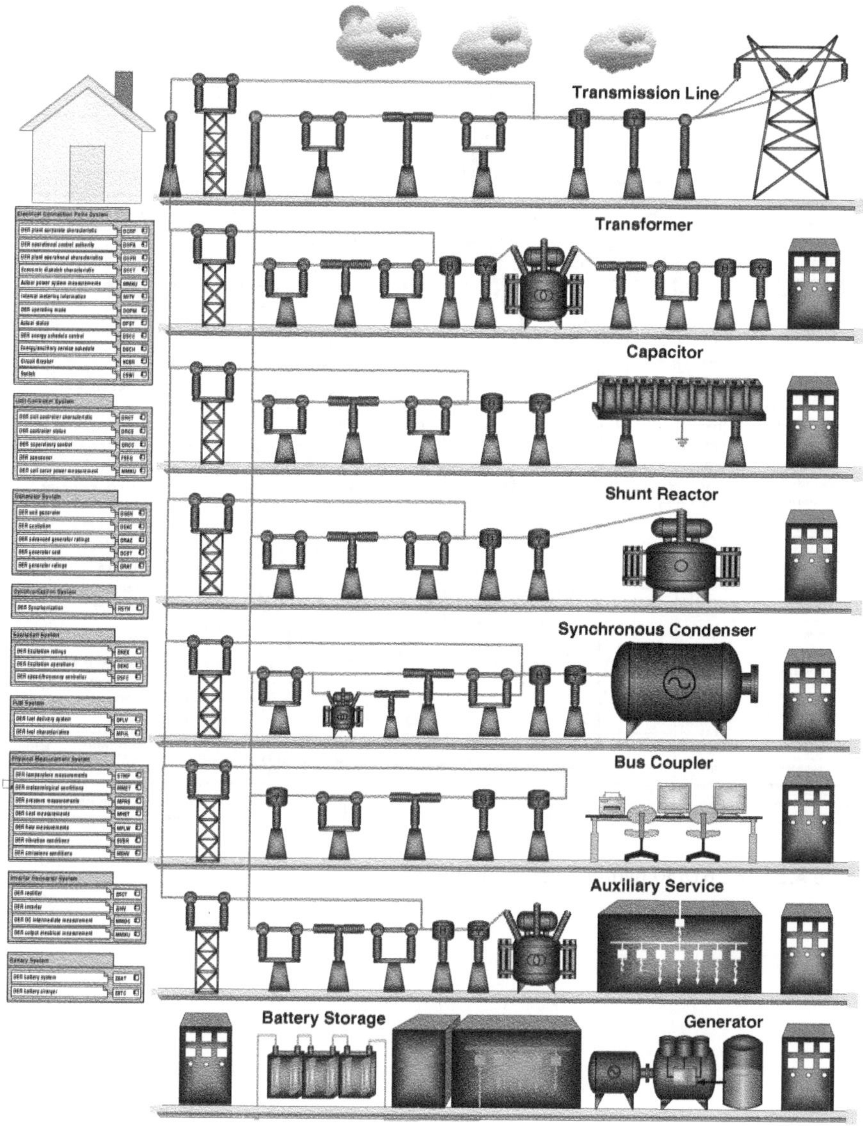

Figure A.2 IEC 61850 substation model.

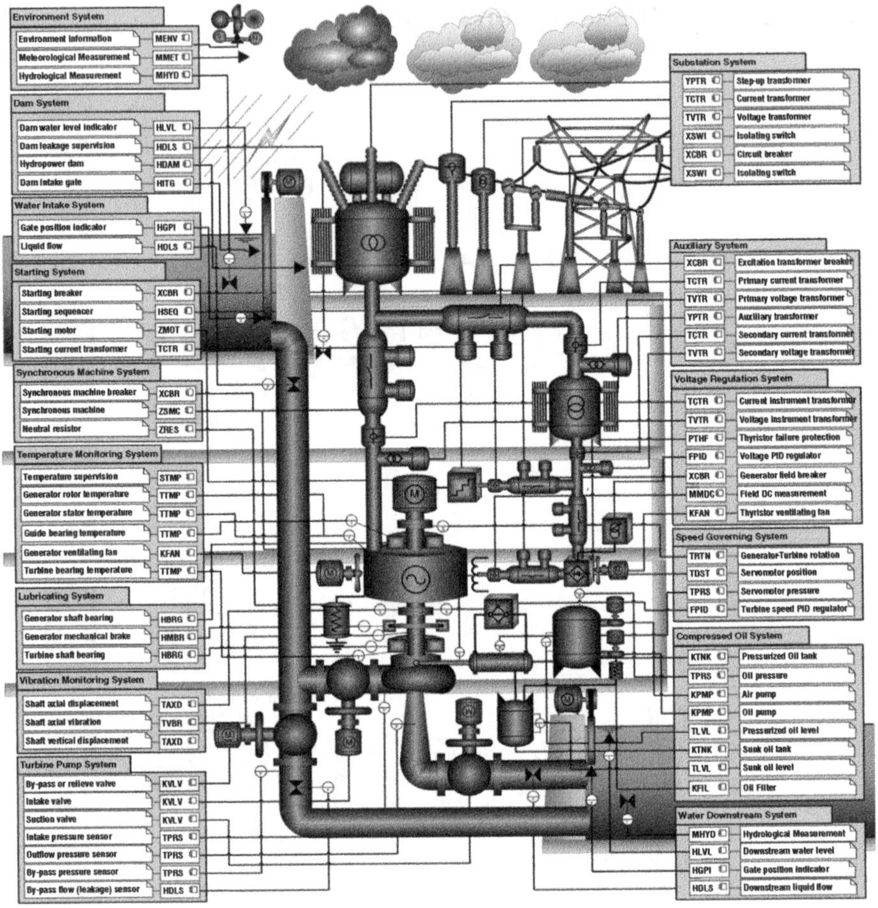

Figure A.3 IEC 61850 hydropower plant model.

A.3 IEC 61850 Windpower Plant Model

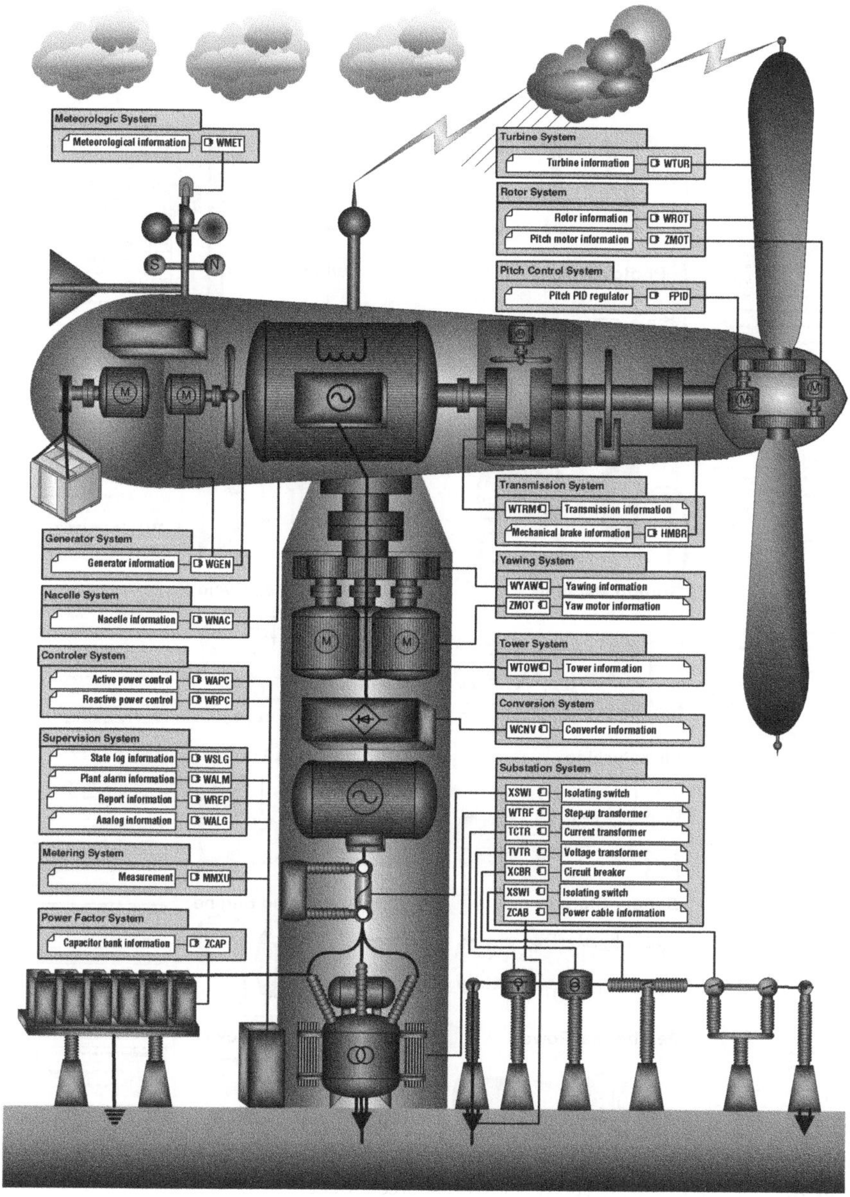

Figure A.4 IEC 61850 windpower plant model.

A.4 IEC 61850 Distributed Energy Resource Model

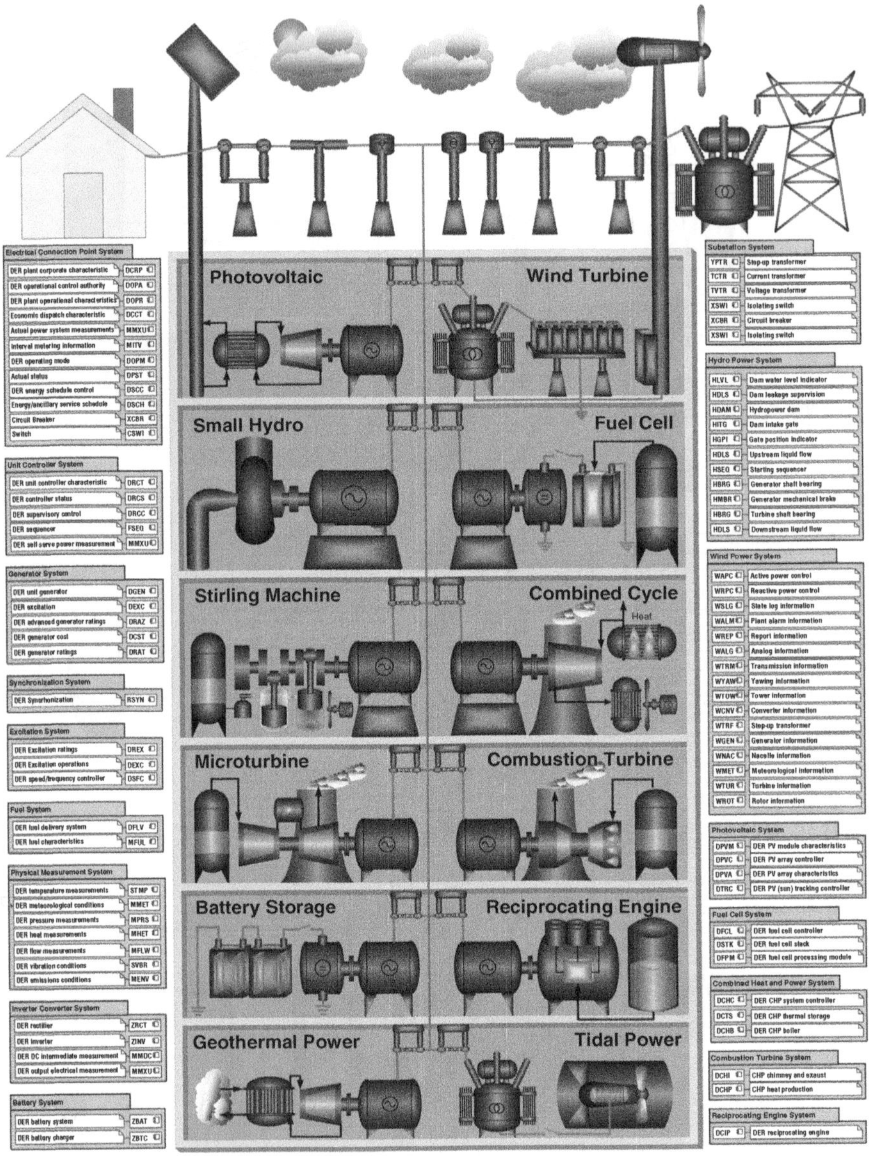

Figure A.5 IEC 61850 distributed energy resource model.

A.5 IEC 61850 Logical Nodes

ANCR	Neutral current regulator
ARCO	Reactive power control
ATCC	Automatic tap changer controller
AVCO	Voltage control
CALH	Alarm handling
CCGR	Cooling group control
CILO	Interlocking
CLN	Common logical node
CPOW	Point-on-wave switching
CSWI	Switch controller
CSYN	Synchronizer controller
DCCT	DER economic dispatch parameters
DCHC	CHP system controller
DCIP	Reciprocating engine
DCRP	DER plant corporate characteristics at the ECP
DCST	Generator cost
DCTS	Thermal storage
DEXC	Excitation
DFCL	Fuel cell controller
DFLV	Fuel delivery system
DFPM	Fuel processing module
DFTK	Excitation ratings
DGEN	DER unit generator
DOPA	DER operational authority at the ECP
DOPM	Operating mode at ECP
DOPR	Operational characteristics at ECP
DPST	Status information at the ECP
DPVA	Photovoltaic array characteristics
DPVC	Photovoltaic array controller
DPVM	Photovoltaic module ratings
DRAT	DER generator ratings
DRAZ	DER advanced generator ratings
DRCC	DER supervisory control
DRCP	DER plant corporate characteristics at the ECP

(Continued)

DRCS	DER controller status
DRCT	DER controller characteristics
DSCC	DER energy and/or ancillary services schedule control
DSCH	DER energy and/or ancillary services schedule
DSFC	Speed/frequency controller
DSTK	Fuel cell stack
DTRC	Tracking controller
FCNT	Counter
FCSD	Curve shape description
FFIL	Generic filter
FLIM	Control function output limitation
FPID	PID regulator
FRMP	Ramp function
FSEQ	Sequencer
FSPT	Set-point control function
FXOT	Action at over threshold
FXUT	Action at under threshold
GAPC	Generic automatic process control
GGIO	Generic process I/O
GLOG	Generic log
GSAL	Generic security application
HBRG	Turbine – generator shaft bearing
HCOM	Combinator (3D-CAM or 2D-CAM)
HDAM	Hydropower dam
HDLS	Dam leakage supervision
HGPI	Gate position indicator
HGTE	Dam gate
HITG	Intake gate
HJCL	Power plant joint control function
HLKG	Leakage supervision
HLVL	Dam water level indicator
HMBR	Mechanical brake for the generator shaft
HNDL	Needle control
HNHD	Net head data
HOTP	Dam overtopping protection

HRES	Water reservoir
HSEQ	Start/stop sequencer
HSPD	Speed monitoring
HUNT	Hydropower production unit
HWCL	Water control function
IARC	Archiving
IHMI	Human–machine interface
ISAF	Safety alarm function
ITCI	Telecontrol interface
ITMI	Telemonitoring interface
KFAN	Fan
KFIL	Filter
KPMP	Pump
KTNK	Tank
KVLV	Valve control
LLN0	Logical node zero
LPHD	Physical device information
LTRK	Logical node service tracking
MADV	Advanced measurement unit
MDIF	Differential measurements
MENV	Environmental information
MFLK	Flicker measurement unit
MFLW	Flow measurements
MFUL	Fuel characteristics
MHAI	Harmonics or interharmonics
MHAN	Non-phase-related harmonics or interharmonics
MHET	Heat measured values
MHYD	Hydrological information
MMDC	DC measurement
MMET	Meteorological information
MMTN	Metering
MMTR	Metering
MMXN	Non-phase-related measurement
MMXU	Measurement
MPRS	Pressure measurements

(Continued)

MSQI	Sequence and imbalance
MSTA	Metering statistics
MVBR	Vibration conditions
PDIF	Differential
PDIR	Direction comparison
PDIS	Distance
PDOP	Directional overpower
PDUP	Directional underpower
PFRC	Rate of change of frequency
PHAR	Harmonic restraint
PHIZ	Ground detector
PIOC	Instantaneous overcurrent
PMRI	Motor restart inhibition
PMSS	Motor starting time supervision
POPF	Overpower factor
PPAM	Phase angle measuring
PRTR	Rotor protection
PSCH	Protection scheme
PSDE	Sensitive directional earth fault
PTEF	Transient earth fault
PTHF	Thyristor protection
PTOC	Time overcurrent
PTOF	Over frequency
PTOV	Overvoltage
PTRC	Protection trip conditioning
PTTR	Thermal overload
PTUC	Undercurrent
PTUF	Underfrequency
PTUV	Undervoltage
PUPF	Underpower factor
PVOC	Voltage-controlled time overcurrent
PVPH	Volts per Hz
PZSU	Zero speed or under speed
QFVR	Frequency variation
QITR	Current transient

QIUB	Current unbalance variation
QVTR	Voltage transient
QVUB	Voltage unbalance variation
QVVR	Voltage variation
RADR	Disturbance recorder channel analog
RBDR	Disturbance recorder channel binary
RBRF	Breaker failure
RDIR	Directional element
RDRE	Disturbance recorder function
RDRS	Disturbance record handling
RFLO	Fault locator
RPSB	Power swing detection/blocking
RREC	Auto reclosing
RSOF	Switch-on-to-fault function
RSYN	Synchronism check
RTPC	Teleprotection communication interfaces
SARC	Monitoring and diagnostics for arcs
SCBR	Circuit breaker wear supervision
SIMG	Insulation medium supervision (gas)
SIML	Insulation medium supervision (liquid)
SLTC	Tap changer supervision
SOPM	Supervision of operating mechanism
SPDC	Monitoring and diagnostics for partial discharges
SPTR	Power transformer supervision
SSWI	Circuit switch supervision
STMP	Temperature supervision
SVBR	Vibration supervision
TANG	Angle
TAXD	Axial displacement
TCTR	Current transformer
TDST	Distance
TFLW	Liquid flow
TFRQ	Frequency
THUM	Humidity
TLVL	LMedia level

(Continued)

TMGF	Magnetic field
TMVM	Movement sensor
TPOS	Position indicator
TPRS	Pressure sensor
TRTN	Rotation transmitter
TSND	Sound pressure sensor
TTMP	Temperature sensor
TTNS	Mechanical tension/stress
TVBR	Vibration sensor
TVTR	Voltage transformer
TWPH	Water acidity
WALG	Wind turbine analog log information
WALM	Windpower plant alarm information
WAPC	Windpower plant active power control
WCNV	Wind turbine converter information
WGEN	Wind turbine generator information
WMET	Windpower plant meteorological information
WNAC	Wind turbine nacelle information
WREP	Wind turbine report information
WROT	Wind turbine rotor information
WRPC	Windpower plant reactive power control
WSLG	Wind turbine state log information
WTOW	Wind turbine tower information
WTRF	Wind turbine transformer information
WTRM	Wind turbine transmission information
WTUR	Wind turbine general information
WYAW	Wind turbine yawing information
XCBR	Circuit breaker
XFUS	Fuse
XSWI	Circuit switch
YEFN	Earth fault neutralizer (Petersen coil)
YLTC	Tap changer
YPSH	Power shunt
YPTR	Power transformer
ZAXN	Auxiliary network

ZBAT	Battery
ZBSH	Bushing
ZBTC	Battery charger
ZCAB	Power cable
ZCAP	Capacitor bank
ZCON	Converter
ZGEN	Generator
ZGIL	Gas insulated line
ZINV	Inverter
ZLIN	Power overhead line
ZMOT	Motor
ZRCT	Rectifier
ZREA	Reactor
ZRES	Neutral resistor
ZRRC	Rotating reactive component
ZSAR	Surge arrestor
ZSCR	Semi-conductor-controlled rectifier
ZSMC	Synchronous machine
ZTCF	Thyristor-controlled frequency converter
ZTCR	Thyristor-controlled reactive component

A.6 IEC 61850 Acronyms

A	Current in Amperes (Amps)
a.c.	alternating current
ACD	ACtivation information of Directional protection
acs	Access
ACSE	Application Common Service Element
ACSI	Abstract Communication Service Interface
ACT	Protection ACTivation information
Acu	Acoustic
Age	Aging
AIS	Air Insulated Switchgear
Alm	Alarm

(Continued)

ALPDU	Application Layer Protocol Data Unit
Amp	Current—non-phase-related
An	Analog
Ang	Angle
A-Profile	Application Profile
APCI	Application Protocol Control Information
APDU	Application Protocol Data Unit
API	Application Program Interface
ASDU	Application Service Data Unit
ASG	Analog SettinG
ASN.1	Abstract Syntax Notation One
AUI	Attachment Unit Interface, Transceiver, or connecting cable
Auth	Authorisation
Auto	Automatic
Aux	Auxiliary
Av	Average
B	Bushing
Bat	Battery
Beh	Behavior
BER	Basic Encoding Rules ASN.1
Bin	Binary
Blk	Block, or Blocked
Bnd	Band
Bo	Bottom
BR	Buffered Report (Functional Constraint)
BRC	Buffered Report Control class
BRCB	Buffered Report Control Block
CAD	Computer Aided Design
Cap	Capability
Car	Carrier
CB	Circuit Breaker
CD	ROM Compact Disc Read Only Memory
CDC	Common Data Class
CDCAName	Common Data Class Attribute Name
cdcNs	common data class Name space

CDCNSpace	Common Data Class Name Space
CE	Cooling Equipment
Cf	Crest factor
CF	ConFiguration (Functional Constraint)
Cfg	Configuration
CFI	Canonical Format Identifier
CG	Core Ground
Ch	Channel
Cha	Charger
Chg	Change
Chk	Check
Chr	Characteristic
CIM	Common Information Model of IEC 61970-301
Cir	Circulating
CL	Connectionless
Clc	Calculate
Client-CR	Client Conformance Requirement
Clk	Clock or Clockwise
Cls	Close
Cnt	Counter
CO	ContrOl (Functional Constraint)
Col	Coil
ConNode	Connectivity Node
Cor	Correction
CRC	Cyclic Redundancy Check
Crd	Coordination
Crv	Curve
CSMA/CD	Carrier Sense Multiple Access/Collision Detection
CT	Current Transformer/Transducer
Ctl	Control
Ctr	Centre
Cyc	Cycle
d.c.	direct current
DA	Data Attribute
DANP	Doubly Attached Node with PRP

(Continued)

DAT	Data Attribute Type
dataNs	Data Name Space
DataRef	Data Reference
DatAttrRef	Data Attribute Reference
DC	DesCription (functional constraint)
dchg	Trigger option for data-change
Dea	Dead
Den	Density
Det	Detected
DEX	De-EXcitation
DF	Data Frame
Diag	Diagnostics
Dif	Differential/Difference
Dir	Directional
Dl	Delay
Dlt	Delete
Dmd	Demand
Dn	Down
DO	Data Object
DORef	Data Object Reference
DPC	Double Point Control
DPS	Double Point Status information
DPSCO	Double Point Controllable Status Output
DQ0	Direct, Quadrature and Zero (0) axis quantities
Drag	Drag Hand
Drv	Drive
DS	Data Set
Dsch	Discharge
DSG	Data Set Group
DTD	Document Type Definition
dupd	trigger option for data update
Dur	Duration
DUT	Device Under Test
EC	Earth Coil
ECT	Electronic Current Transformer or transducer

EF	Earth Fault
EMC	Electromagnetic Compatibility
EMI	Electromagnetic Interference
Ena	Enabled
EPRI	Electric Power Research Institute
Eq	Equalization or Equal
Ev	Evaluation
EVT	Electronic Voltage Transformer or transducer
Ex	Excitation
EX	EXtended definition (Functional Constraint)
Exc	Exceeded
Excl	Exclusion
F/S	Functional Standard
FA	Fault Arc
Fact	Factor
FAT	Factory Acceptance Test
FC	Functional Constraint
FCD	Functionally Constrained Data
FCDA	Functionally Constrained Data Attribute
fchg	Trigger option for filtered-data change
FD	Fault Distance
Flt	Fault
Flw	Flow
FPF	Forward Power Flow
Fu	Fuse
Fwd	Forward
Gen	General
GI	General Interrogation
GIS	Gas Insulated Switchgear
Gn	Generator
Gnd	Ground
GO	Goose Control
GoCB	Goose Control Block
GOMSFE	Generic Object Models for Substation and Feeder Equipment
GOOSE	Generic Object-Oriented Substation Events

(Continued)

GPS	Global Positioning System (time source)
Gr	Group
Grd	Guard
Gri	Grid
GS	GSSE Control (Functional Constraint)
GsCB	GSSE Control Block
GSE	Generic Substation Event
GSEM	Generic Substation Event Model
GSSE	Generic Substation Status Event
H	Harmonics (phase-related)
H2	Hydrogen
Ha	Harmonics (non-phase-related)
Hi	High or Highest
HMI	Human–Machine Interface
HP	Hot Point
HSR	High-availability Seamless Redundancy
Hz	Hertz – frequency cycles/second
I/O	Status Inputs/Output contacts, or channels
ICD	IED Configuration Description
IEC	International Electrotechnical Commission
IED	Intelligent Electronic Device
IEEE	Institute of Electrical and Electronic Engineers
IETF	Internet Engineering Task Force
IF	Interface (serial)
Imb	Imbalance
Imp	Impedance (non-phase-related)
In	Input
Ina	Inactivity
INC	INteger status – Controllable
Incr	Increment
Ind	Indication
Inh	Inhibit
Ins	Insulation
Int	Integer
IntgPd	Integrity Period

IP	Internet Protocol
ISC	Integer Step Controlled position information
ISCSO	Integer Status Controllable Status Output
ISI	Integer Status Information
ISO	International Standards Organization
IT	Current x Time product
L	Lower
LAN	Local Area Network
LC	LOG CONTROL Class
LCB	Log Control Block
LD	Logical Device
Ld	Lead
LD0	Logical Device Zero (0)
LDC	Line Drop Compensation
LDCR	Line Drop Compensation Resistance
LDCX	Line Drop Compensation Reactance (X)
LDCZ	Line Drop Compensation Impedance (Z)
ldNs	logical device Name space
LED	Light Emitting Diode
Len	Length
Lev	Level
Lg	Lag
LG	LoGging (Functional Constraint)
Lim	Limit
Lin	Line
Liv	Live
LLC	Logical Link Control
LLN0	Logical Node Zero (0)
LN	Logical Node IEC 61850-1
LN	Name Logical Node Name
LNC	Logical Node Class
LNData	Logical Node Data
LNG	Logical Node Group
lnNs	logical node Name space
Lo	Low

(Continued)

LO	LockOut
Loc	Local
Lod	Load or Loading
Lok	Locked
Los	Loss
LPHD	Logical Node PHysical Device
LSAP	Link Service Access Point
LSDU	Link layer Service Data Unit
Lst	List
LTC	Load Tap Changer
m	Minutes
M	Mandatory
M/O	Data Object is Mandatory or Optional
MAC	Media Access Control
MAU	Medium Attachment Unit (Transceiver)
Max	Maximum
MCAA	MultiCast Application Association
Mem	Memory
MICS	Model Implementation Conformance Statement
Min	Minimum
MMS	Manufacturing Message Specification (ISO 9506)
Mod	Mode
Mot	Motor
ms	Milliseconds
MS	Multicast Sampled value control (Functional Constraint)
Mst	Moisture
MSVC	Multicast Sampled Value Control
MSVCB	Multicast Sampled Value Control Block
MT	Main Tank
MTTF	Mean Time To Failure
MTTR	Mean Time To Repair
MU	Merging Unit
MX	Measurand analog value X (functional constraint)
N	Neutral
Nam	Name

NCC	Network Control Centre
Net	Net sum
Ng	Negative
Nom	Nominal, Normalizing
NPL	Name PLate
Num	Number
O	Optional
Ofs	Offset
Op	Operate/Operating
Opn	Open
OSI	Open Systems Interconnection
Out	Output
Ov	Over/Override/Overflow
Pa	Partial
Par	Parallel
PC	Physical Connection
Pct	Percent PD Physical Device
PDU	Protocol Data Unit
PE	Process Environment
Per	Periodic
PF	Power Factor
Ph	Phase
PHD	PHysical Device
PhPh	Phase to Phase
Phy	Physical
PICOM	Piece of Information for COMmunication
PICS	Protocol Implementation Conformance Statement
PIXIT	Protocol Implementation eXtra Information for Testing
Pls	Pulse
Plt	Plate
Pmp	Pump
Po	Polar
Pol	Polarizing
pos	Position
POW	Point On Wave Switching

(Continued)

PP	Phase to Phase
PPV	Phase to Phase Voltage
Pres	Pressure
Prg	Progress
Pri	Primary
Pro	Protection
PRP	Parallel Redundancy Protocol
Ps	Positive
Pst	Post
Pwr	Power
qchg	Trigger option for quality-change
Qty	Quantity
R0	Zero Sequence Resistance
R1	Positive Sequence Resistance
Ra	Raise
Rat	Ratio
Rcd	Record or Recording
Rch	Reach
Rcl	Reclaim
Re	Retry
React	Reactance
Rec	Reclose
Red	Reduction
Rel	Release
Rem	Remote
Res	Residual
Rest	Resistance
RFC	Request For Comments
Ris	Resistance
Rl	Relation
Rms	Root mean square
Rot	Rotation
RP	Unbuffered RePort (functional constraint)
RPF	Reverse Power Flow
Rs	Reset, Resettable

Rsl	Result
Rst	Restraint
RSTP	Rapid Spanning Tree Protocol
Rsv	Reserve
Rte	Rate
Rtg	Rating
RTU	Remote Terminal Unit
Rv	Reverse
Rx	Receive/Received
S1	Step one
S2	Step two
SA	Substation Automation
SAN	Singly Attached Node
SAP	Service Access Point
SAS	Substation Automation System
SAT	Site Acceptance Test
SAV	Sampled Analog Value
SBO	Select Before Operate
SC	Secondary Converter
SCADA	Supervisory Control And Data Acquisition
SCD	Substation Configuration Description
Sch	Scheme
SCL	Substation Configuration description Language
SCO	Supply Change Over
SCSM	Specific Communication Service Mapping
SE	Setting Group Editable (functional constraint)
Sec	Security
Seq	Sequence
Server-CR	Server-Conformance Requirement
Set	Setting
SF6	Sulphur HexaFluoride gas
SG	Setting Group (functional constraint)
SGC	Setting Group Control class
SGCB	Setting Group Control Block
Sh	Shunt

(Continued)

SIG	Status Indication Group
SMV	Sampled Measured Value
SMVC	Sampled Measured Value Control IEC
SNTP	Simple Network Time Protocol
SoE	Sequence of Events
Sp	Speed
SP	SetPoint (functional constraint)
SPC	Single Point Control
SPCSO	Single Point Controllable Status Output
SPS	Single Point Status information
Src	Source
ST	STatus information (functional constraint)
Stat	Statistics
Std	Standard
Str	Start
Sts	Stress
Sup	Supply
SUT	System Under Test
SV	Sampled Value
Svc	Service
SVC	Sampled Value Control
Sw	Switch
Swg	Swing
Syn	Synchronization
T	Transient data
TCI	TeleControl Interface
TCP	Transmission Control Protocol
TCP/IP	Transmission Control Protocol/Internet Protocol
Td	Total distortion
Tdf	Transformer derating factor
TE	Telecommunication Environment
Thd	Total harmonic distortion
Thm	Thermal
Tif	Telephone influence factor
Tm	Time

Tmh	Time in hours
TMI	TeleMonitoring Interface
Tmm	Time in minutes
Tmms	Time in milliseconds
Tmp	Temperature
Tms	Time in seconds
To	Top
Tot	Total
T-Profile	Transport Profile
TP	Three Pole
TPAA	Two-Party Application Association
TPID	Tag Protocol Identifier
Tr	Trip
Trg	Trigger
TrgOp	Trigger Option
TrgOpEna	Trigger Option Enabled
Ts	Total signed
Tu	Total unsigned
Tx	Transmit/Transmitted
Typ	Type
UCATM	Utility Communications Architecture
UML	Unified Modeling Language
Un	Under
URC	Unbuffered Report Control
URCB	Unbuffered Report Control Block
URI	Universal Resource Identifier
US	Unicast Sampled value control (functional constraint)
USMVC	Unicast Sampled Measured Value Control
USVC	Unicast Sampled Value Control
USVCB	Unicast Sampled Value Control Block
UTC	Coordinated Universal Time
V	Voltage
VA	Volt Amperes
Vac	Vacuum
Val	Value

(Continued)

Var	Volt Amperes reactive
V-Get	Virtual Get function (ISO 9506-1)
VID	VLAN IDentifier
VLAN	Virtual Local Area Network
Vlv	Valve
VMD	Virtual Manufacturing Device
Vol	Voltage (non-phase-related)
vPAC	Virtual Protection, Automation and Control
V-Put	Virtual Put function (ISO 9506-1)
VT	Voltage Transformer/Transducer
W	Watts active power
Wac	Watchdog
Watt	active power (non-phase-related)
Wei	Week infeed
Wh	Watt hours
Wid	Width
Win	Window
Wrm	Warm
X0	Zero sequence reactance
X1	Positive sequence reactance
XML	eXtensible Mark-up Language
XX	Wildcard characters (e.g., all functional constraints)
Z	Impedance
Z0	Zero sequence impedance
Z1	Positive sequence impedance
Zer	Zero
Zn	Zone
Zro	Zero sequence method

A.7 UML and SysML Graphical Symbols

Table A.1 UML and SysML graphical symbols.

Shape	Name	Description
	Package	Collection of interfaces and classes
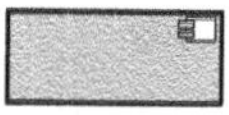	Package	Collection of object interfaces and classes
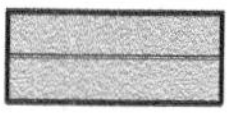	Class	Collection of data and methods
	Note	Descriptive text attached to any item
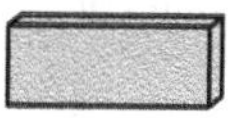	Deployment	Collection of physical processors or structures
	Server	Intelligent Electronic Device (IED) or processor
	Lifeline	An individual participant in a sequence diagram
	User	An actor in a use-case diagram
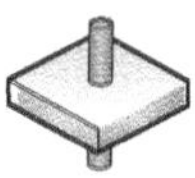	Process	A series of activities
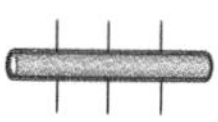	Network	A collection of nodes, links, and traffic streams
	Cloud	Shareable physical or virtual resources, usually over the Internet
	Use case	A description of a system's function to achieve a user's goal
	Composition	A "whole part" relationship where the part is strongly dependent upon the whole
	Association	A structural relationship where objects of one class are connected to objects of another
	Aggregation	A "whole part" relationship where the part can exist independently of the whole

(Continued)

Table A.1 (Continued)

Shape	Name	Description
	Inheritance	An "is–a" relationship where a subclass inherits from a superclass
	Dependency	A weaker relationship indicating that one class depends on another
	Directed association	A relationship between two classifiers that only allows navigation in one direction
	Realization	A relationship between an interface and the class that implements it
1,0...*,1...*n*	Multiplicity	Specifies how many objects of one class are associated with objects of another
<<include>>	Inclusion	When a base use case includes the functionality of another use case
<<extend>>	Extension	When one use case (extension) extends the behavior of another use case (base)

A.8 Network and Security Graphical Symbols

Table A.2 Network and security graphical symbols.

Shape	Name	Description
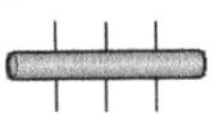	LAN	Local area network
	WAN	Wide-area network
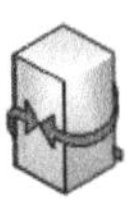	Gateway	Connection of networks with different protocols
	Server	A computer that provides information or services
	Mainframe	Large high-speed server

Shape	Name	Description
	Channel	Physical transmission medium in a network
	Switch	A device that connects devices in a network
	Hub	A device that broadcasts data in a network
	Bridge	A device that connects segments in a network
	Router	A device that transfers data between networks
	Protocol	Formal rules for exchanging data in a network
	Firewall	Traffic restrictions for forbidden communication
	Authentication	Strong multifactor authentication
	Domain	Administrative grouping of multiple networks
	RBAC	Role-based access control
	Security Option	Specific protocol safety alternatives
	DMZ	Demilitarized zones to separate LANs
	Cryptography	Disguising information to unauthorized entities
	VPN	Virtual private network
	Monitoring	Logging and event recording for auditing

(Continued)

Table A.2 (Continued)

Shape	Name	Description
	Virus Protection	Detection and removal of viruses
	HMI	Human–machine interface
	Time Source	Satellite clock
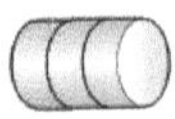	Payload	Packet contents of messages
	Data or Queue	Data storage or message queue

A.9 Functional UML Use Case Template

Table A.3 Functional UML use case template.

Functional Implementation Conformance Statement	
Code	Short distinctive name of the function from the SAS
Name	Phrase that declares the main objective of the function
Description	Longer description or summary of the function objective
Customer	Identification of the owner or integrator of the substation
Substation	Identification of the substation
SCL file	Substation configuration language file and version, if available
Primary user (actor)	Role name or description of the primary functional actor/user of the use case among people, system, etc. (e.g., Operation, Engineering, Process, Dispatch)
Secondary user (actor)	Role name or description of the secondary functional actor/user of the use case among people, system, etc. (e.g., Operation, Engineering, Process, Dispatch)
Stakeholder and interest	Name of the stakeholder and interest of the stakeholder in the use case

Function Description	
Trigger	Which action(s)/event(s) of the primary/secondary users initiate the use case
Components or logical nodes	(Codes of) Component(s) architecture or logical node(s) that implement or realize the function or use case, taken from the SCL file, if available
Process equipment	(Codes of) Associated substation process equipment, affected by the function
Performance	Goal or quantification of function objectives (e.g., execution time, record accuracy, etc.)
Preconditions	Expected state of the automation system, substation, or its environment before the use case may be applied (e.g., closed breakers, switches, etc.)
Post conditions on success	Expected state of the automation system, substation, or its environment after successful completion of the use case (e.g., tripped breakers, alarms, recordings, etc.)
Post conditions on failure	Expected state of the automation system, substation, or its environment after unsuccessful completion of the use case (e.g., breaker failure, etc.)

Use Case Description			
Basic course description	Flow of events performed during the normal state		
	1	Actor	Event, step, or condition of successful execution
	2	System	Event, step, or condition of successful execution
	...	...	...
	N	System	Event, step, or condition of successful execution
Extensions	Alternative flow of events performed during the normal state		
	1	Actor	Event, step, or condition of successful execution
	2	System	Event, step, or condition of successful execution
	...	...	...
	N	System	Event, step, or condition of successful execution

Bibliography

A. Tutorials

Siqueira, I., Slides from Tutorial Cybersecurity of Electric Power System, Brazilian National Committee of CIGRE, Rio de Janeiro.

Siqueira, I., Slides from Tutorial IEC 61850-based Automation Systems, Institute for Innovation and Applied Technology (ITAI), Foz do Iguaçu.

Siqueira, I., Slides from Tutorial Power Plant Automation, PUCMinas, Belo Horizonte.

B. Books

Amoroso, E., Cyber Attacks: Protecting National Infrastructure, Elsevier, Amsterdam, 2011.

Apostolov, A., IEC 61850 Digitizing the Electric Power Grid, Artech House, London, 2023.

Bishop, P. and Nair, N., Eds., IEC 61850 Principles and Applications to Electric Power Systems, Second Edition, CIGRE Study Committee B5: Protection and Automation, Springer, Paris, France, 2020.

Bradley, N., The XML Schema Companion, Addison-Wesley, Boston, 2004.

Brand, K-P., Lohmann, V., and Wimmer, W., Substation Automation Handbook, Utility Automation Consulting Lohmann, Bengarten, Switzerland, 2003.

Douglass, B. P., Real-time UML: Advances in the UML for Real-time Systems, Third Edition, Addison-Wesley Professional, New York, 2004.

Falk, H., IEC 61850 Demystified, Artech House, London, UK, 2019.

Fowler, M., UML Distilled: A Brief Guide to the Standard Object Modelling Language, Third Edition, Addison-Wesley Professional, New York, 2003.

Ozansoy, C., Modelling and Object-oriented Implementation of IEC 61 850 – The New International Standard on Substation Communications and Automation, Lambert Academic Publishing, Strasburg, Germany, 2010.

Padilla, E. Substation Automation Systems – Design and Implementation, Wiley, New York, 2016.

Siqueira, I., Advanced Control of Hydroelectric Power Plants, Second Edition, Tecnix Engineering and Architecture, ISBN BOB3M5YNR8, 2022.

Siqueira, I. and Hatziargyriou, N., Eds., Electricity supply systems of the future, Springer and CIGRE – International Council on Large Electric Systems, Paris, FR, 2020.

Tsai, J. J. P., Bi, Y., Yang, S. J. H., and Smith, R. A. W., Distributed Real-time Systems: Monitoring, Visualization, Debugging, and Analysis, John Wiley & Sons, Inc., New York, 1996.

Yuan, Y. and Yang, Y., Eds, IEC 61850-Based Smart Substations – Principles, Testing, Operation and Maintenance, Academic Press, London, UK, 2019.

C. Standards

IEC 60870-5-101: Telecontrol equipment and systems – Part 5-101: Transmission protocols: Companion standard for basic telecontrol tasks, International Electrotechnical Commission, Switzerland.

IEC 60870-5-103: Telecontrol equipment and systems – Part 5-103: Transmission protocols: Companion standard for the informative interface of protection equipment, International Electrotechnical Commission, Switzerland.

IEC 60870-5-104: Telecontrol equipment and systems – Part 5-104: Transmission protocols: Network access for IEC 60870-5-101 using standard transport profiles, International Electrotechnical Commission, Switzerland.

IEC 60870-6: Telecontrol equipment and systems – Part 6: Telecontrol protocols compatible with ISO standards and ITU-T recommendations, International Electrotechnical Commission, Switzerland.

IEC 61346: Industrial systems, installations and equipment and industrial products – Structuring principles and reference designations, International Electrotechnical Commission, Switzerland.

IEC 61850-1: Communication networks and systems in substations – Part 1: Introduction and Overview, International Electrotechnical Commission, Switzerland.

IEC 61850-10: Communication networks and systems in substations – Part 10: Conformance , International Electrotechnical Commission, Switzerland.

IEC 61850-3: Communication networks and systems in substations – Part 3: General requirements, International Electrotechnical Commission, Switzerland.

IEC 61850-4: Communication networks and systems in substations – Part 4: System and project management, International Electrotechnical Commission, Switzerland.

IEC 61850-5: Communication networks and systems in substations – Part 5: Communication requirements for functions and device models, International Electrotechnical Commission, Switzerland.

IEC 61850-6: Communication networks and systems in substations – Part 6: Configuration description language for communication in electrical substations related to ***IEDs***, International Electrotechnical Commission, Switzerland.

IEC 61850-7-1: Communication networks and systems in substations – Part 7-1: Basic communication structure for substation and feeder equipment – Principles and models, International Electrotechnical Commission, Switzerland.

IEC 61850-7-2: Communication networks and systems in substations – Part 7-2: Basic communication structure for substation and feeder equipment – Abstract communication service interface (ACSI), International Electrotechnical Commission, Switzerland.

IEC 61850-7-3: Communication networks and systems in substations – Part 7-3: Basic communication structure for substation and feeder equipment – Common data classes, International Electrotechnical Commission, Switzerland.

IEC 61850-7-4: Communication networks and systems in substations – Part 7-4: Basic communication structure for substation and feeder equipment – Compatible logical node classes and data classes, International Electrotechnical Commission, Switzerland.

IEC 61850-8-1: Communication networks and systems in substations – Part 8-1: Specific Communication Service Mapping (SCSM) – Mappings to MMS (ISO 9506-1 and ISO 9506-2) and to ISO/IEC 8802-3, International Electrotechnical Commission, Switzerland.

IEC 61850-9-1: Communication networks and systems in substations – Part 9-1: Specific Communication Service Mapping (SCSM) – Sampled values over serial unidirectional multidrop point to point link, International Electrotechnical Commission, Switzerland.

IEC 61850-9-2: Communication networks and systems in substations – Part 9-2: Specific Communication Service Mapping (SCSM) – Sampled values over ISO/IEC 8802-3, International Electrotechnical Commission, Switzerland.

IEC 61882: Analysis techniques for system reliability – Procedure for failure mode and effects analysis (FMEA), International Electrotechnical Commission, Switzerland.

IEC 61882: Hazard and Operability Studies (HAZOP Studies) – Application Guide, International Electrotechnical Commission, Switzerland.

IEC 62351-1: Cyber Security Standards for Communication Standards – Introduction to the standard, International Electrotechnical Commission, Switzerland.

IEC 62351-10: Cyber Security Standards for Communication Standards – Security Architecture, International Electrotechnical Commission, Switzerland.

IEC 62351-11: Cyber Security Standards for Communication Standards – Security for XML Files, International Electrotechnical Commission, Switzerland.

IEC 62351-2: Cyber Security Standards for Communication Standards – Glossary of terms, International Electrotechnical Commission, Switzerland.

IEC 62351-3: Cyber Security Standards for Communication Standards – Security for any profiles including TCP/IP, International Electrotechnical Commission, Switzerland.

IEC 62351-4: Cyber Security Standards for Communication Standards – Security for any profiles including MMS, International Electrotechnical Commission, Switzerland.

IEC 62351-5: Cyber Security Standards for Communication Standards – Security for any profiles including IEC 60870-5, International Electrotechnical Commission, Switzerland.

IEC 62351-6: Cyber Security Standards for Communication Standards – Security for IEC 61850 profiles, International Electrotechnical Commission, Switzerland.

IEC 62351-7: Cyber Security Standards for Communication Standards – Security through network and system management, International Electrotechnical Commission, Switzerland.

IEC 62351-8: Cyber Security Standards for Communication Standards – Role-based access control, International Electrotechnical Commission, Switzerland.

IEC 62351-9: Cyber Security Standards for Communication Standards – Key Management, International Electrotechnical Commission, Switzerland.

IEC TS 61850-2: Communication Networks and Systems in substations – Part 2: Glossary, International Electrotechnical Commission, Switzerland.

IEEE Std C37.118:2024, IEEE Standard for Synchrophasor Data Transfer for Power System.

IEEE Std C37.2:1996, IEEE Standard Electrical Power System Device Function Numbers and Contact Designations.

ISO/IEC. IEC 61131 – Programmable controllers, International Electrotechnical Commission, Switzerland.

ISO/IEC. IEC 61499 – Function Blocks, International Electrotechnical Commission, Switzerland, Geneva.

OMG SysML – System Modeling Language, http://www.omgsysml.org/

OMG UML – Unified Modeling Language, http://www.omg.org/spec/UML/

OMG, UML Testing Profile, The Object Management Group, available on www.omg.org, 2005.

W3C, Extensible Markup Language (XML), The World Wide Web Consortium, available on www.w3.org, 2006.

D. Reports

Apostolov, A., Convenor, CIGRE Brochure 949, Experience Gained and Recommendations for Implementation of Process Bus in Protection, Automation and Control Systems, CIGRE – International Council on Large Electric Systems, Paris, FR, 2024.

Apostolov, A., Convenor, CIGRE Technical Brochure 326, The Introduction of IEC 61850 and its Impact on Protection and Automation within Substations, CIGRE – International Council on Large Electric Systems, Paris, FR, 2007.

Apostolov, A., Convenor, CIGRE Technical Brochure 760, Test Strategy for Protection, Automation and Control (PAC) functions in a Fully Digital Substation based on IEC 61850 Applications, CIGRE – International Council on Large Electric Systems, Paris, FR, 2019.

Castellanos, J., Convenor, CIGRE Technical Brochure 466, Engineering Guidelines for IEC 61850 Based Digital SAS, CIGRE – International Council on Large Electric Systems, Paris, FR, 2011.

Holstein, D., Convenor, CIGRE Technical Brochure 427, The Impact of Implementing Cyber Security Requirements using IEC 61850, CIGRE – International Council on Large Electric Systems, Paris, FR, 2010.

Huon, G., Convenor, CIGRE Technical Brochure 819, IEC 61850-based substation automation systems – Users expectations and stakeholders interactions, CIGRE – International Council on Large Electric Systems, Paris, FR, 2020.

IEC TR 61850-1-2: Communication networks and systems in substations – Guidelines for Cybersecurity in IEC 61850, Systems International Electrotechnical Commission, Switzerland.

IEC TR 61850-7-5: Communication networks and systems in substations – Extended Data Model for Specific Applications, Systems International Electrotechnical Commission, Switzerland.

IEC TR 61850-7-500: Communication networks and systems in substations – Guide for Modelling Substation Automation Functions, Systems International Electrotechnical Commission, Switzerland.

IEC TR 61850-90-1: Communication networks and systems in substations – Communication Between Substations, Systems International Electrotechnical Commission, Switzerland.

IEC TR 61850-90-10: Communication networks and systems in substations – Modelling of Functions for Hydropower Plants, Systems International Electrotechnical Commission, Switzerland.

IEC TR 61850-90-11: Communication networks and systems in substations – Application of IEC 61850 for Microgrids, Systems International Electrotechnical Commission, Switzerland.

IEC TR 61850-90-12: Communication networks and systems in substations – Modelling for Active Distribution Networks, Systems International Electrotechnical Commission, Switzerland.

IEC TR 61850-90-2: Communication networks and systems in substations – Communication Between Control Systems and Operation Centers, Systems International Electrotechnical Commission, Switzerland.

IEC TR 61850-90-3: Communication networks and systems in substations – Condition Monitoring of Equipment, Systems International Electrotechnical Commission, Switzerland.

IEC TR 61850-90-4: Communication networks and systems in substations – Ethernet-Based Communication Network Requirements, Systems International Electrotechnical Commission, Switzerland.

IEC TR 61850-90-5: Communication networks and systems in substations – Application of IEC 61850 for GOOSE and Sampled Values Transmission over IP Networks, Systems International Electrotechnical Commission, Switzerland.

IEC TR 61850-90-6: Communication networks and systems in substations – Modelling of Demand Response Resources, Systems International Electrotechnical Commission, Switzerland.

IEC TR 61850-90-7: Communication networks and systems in substations – Data Models for Photovoltaic Inverters, Batteries, and Other Distributed Energy Resources (DERs), Systems International Electrotechnical Commission, Switzerland.

IEC TR 61850-90-8: Communication networks and systems in substations – Distribution Automation, Systems International Electrotechnical Commission, Switzerland.

IEC TR 61850-90-9: Communication networks and systems in substations – Application of IEC 61850 for Smart Metering Systems, Systems International Electrotechnical Commission, Switzerland.

IEC TS 61850-6-3: Communication networks and systems for power utility automation – Part 6-3: Format of machine-processable rules for validation of IEC 61850 XML-based files, Systems International Electrotechnical Commission, Switzerland.

Siqueira, I., Convenor, CIGRE Brochure 401, Functional Testing of IEC 61850-Based Systems, CIGRE – International Council on Large Electric Systems, Paris, FR, 2009.

Siqueira, I., Convenor, CIGRE Brochure 926, Methods for Specification of Functional Requirements of Protection, Automation, and Control, CIGRE – International Council on Large Electric Systems, Paris, FR, 2024.

Tholomier, D., Convenor, CIGRE Brochure 540, IEC 61850 Standard to Protection Schemes, CIGRE – International Council on Large Electric Systems, Paris, FR, 2013.

E. Papers

Aftab, M. A., Hussain, S. M. S., Ali, I., and Ustun, T. S., A Novel SCL configuration method for modeling microgrids With IEC 61850. IEEE Systems Journal, vol. 14, no. 2, pp. 2676–2683, 2020a.

Aftab, M. A., Hussain, S. M. S., Ali, I., and Ustun, T. S., IEC 61850-Based communication layer modeling for electric vehicles: Electric vehicle charging and discharging processes based on the international electrotechnical commission 61850 standard and its extensions. IEEE Industrial Electronics Magazine, vol. 14, no. 2, pp. 4–14, 2020b.

Aftab, M. A., Hussain, S. M. S., Ali, I., and Ustun, T. S., IEC 61850 based substation automation system: A survey. International Journal of Electrical Power and Energy Systems, vol. 120 p. 106008, 2020c.

Aftab, M. A., Hussain, S. M. S., Ali, I., and Ustun, T. S., IEC 61850 and XMPP communication based energy management in microgrids considering electric vehicles. IEEE Access, vol. 6 pp. 35657–35668, 2018.

Aftab, M. A., Hussain, S. M. S., Kumar, V., Ustun, T. S., and Ali, I., IEC 61850 communication assisted synchronization strategy for microgrids. In: Proceedings of the ICIIS 2018 – International Conference on Industrial and Information Systems, 2018.

Aftab, M. A., Hussain, S. M. S., Latif, A., Das, D. C., and Ustun, T. S., IEC 61850 communication based dual stage load frequency controller for isolated hybrid microgrid. International Journal of Electrical Power and Energy Systems, vol. 130 p. 106909, 2021.

Apostolov, A. P., Distributed protection, control, and recording in IEC 61850-based substation automation systems. In: Proceedings of the 8th IEE International Conference on Developments in Power System Protection (DPSP 2004), 2004.

Apostolov, A. and Vandiver, B. IEC 61850 GOOSE applications to distribution protection schemes. In: Proceedings of the 64th Annual Conference for Protective Relay Engineers (CPRE 2011), College Station, TX, USA, pp. 178–184, 2011.

Apostolov, A., Efficient maintenance testing in digital substations based on IEC 61850 edition 2. Protection and Control of Modern Power Systems, vol. 2, article 37, 2017.

Apostolov, A., IEC 61850 9-2 process bus applications and benefits. In: Proceedings of the 10th IET International Conference on Developments in Power System Protection (DPSP 2010) – Managing the Change, Manchester, UK, p. 78, 2010.

Apostolov, A., IEC 61850 9-2 process bus: Basics, applications and benefits. In: Western Protective Relay Conference (WPRC 2009), Spokane, WA, USA, 2009.

Apostolov, A., IEC 61850 Fundamentals. Seminar Notes/Tutorial Material, OMICRON, 2006.

Apostolov, A., Substation automation systems. In: Wiley Encyclopedia of Electrical and Electronics Engineering, Wiley, Hoboken, 2016.

Apostolov, A., Testing of complex IEC 61850-based substation automation systems, International Journal of Reliability and Safety in Power Systems (exact journal title varies slightly by source), vol. 2, no. 2, pp. 233–244, 2008.

Apostolov, A., The role of IEC 61850 reporting in faults and disturbance analysis. In: TRUC – The Relay Users Conference, c. 2012–2013.

Apostolov, A., Time in IEC 61850-based substation protection and control systems. PAC World Magazine, c. 2019. (Online technical article on timing aspects in IEC 61850-based systems.)

Brand, K. P., Maeda, T., Oestrich, K., and Riedman, P., First experiences with customer specifications of IEC 61850-based substation automation systems. In: CIGRE SC B5 Colloquium, 2005, Paper 203.

Brand, K. P., The Introduction of IEC 61850 and its impact on protection and automation within substation, CIGRE Electra Magazine, n. 233, 2007.

Brunner C. and Bloch, C., IEC 61850 – introduction to an interoperability standard, webinar presentation (OSMOSE project), 2021.

Brunner, C., How the IEC 61850 supports the migration phase, paper presented at CIGRÉ Session, Paris, France, 2002.

Brunner, C., IEC 61850 for power system communication, tutorial presentation, IEEE PES T&D Conference, Chicago, IL, USA, 2008.

Brunner, C., IEC 61850 process connection – a smart solution to connect the primary equipment to the substation automation system. In: Proceedings of the 15th Power Systems Computation Conference (PSCC), Liège, Belgium, 2005, Session 13, Paper 3.

Brunner, C., IEC 61850 standard update, Presentation at IEC 61850 Europe Conference, Amsterdam, Netherlands, 2017.

Brunner, C., IEC 61850 update – why do top-down engineering? PAC World Magazine, Issue 49, 2019.

Brunner, C., Introduction to system specification for IEC 61850 from a standards perspective, workshop presentation, 2021.

Brunner, C., Schimmel, G., and Schubert, H., Standardisation of serial links replacing parallel wiring to transfer process data – approach, state and practical experience. In: Proceedings of the CIGRÉ Session, Paris, France, 2002.

Brunner, C., The impact of IEC 61850 on protection. In: Proceedings of the 9th IET International Conference, Developments in Power System Protection (DPSP 2008), Glasgow, U.K., 2008, pp. 14–19.

Brunner, C., TISSUES, PAC World Magazine, column explaining the IEC 61850 TISSUES process, 2019.

Brunner, C., Will IEEE 1588 finally leverage the IEC 61850 process bus. In: Proceedings of the 10th IET International Conference, Developments in Power System Protection (DPSP 2010), Manchester, U.K., 2010.

Farooq, S. M., Hussain, S. M. S., Kiran, S., and Ustun, T. S., Certificate based security mechanisms in vehicular Ad-Hoc networks based on IEC 61850 and IEEE WAVE standards. Electronics, vol. 8, no. 1, art. 96, 2019.

Hussain, S. M. S., Aftab, M. A., Ali, I., and Ustun, T. S., IEC 61850 based energy management system using Plug-In Electric vehicles and distributed generators during emergencies. International Journal of Electrical Power and Energy Systems, vol. 119, art. 105873, 2020a.

Hussain, S. M. S., Aftab, M. A., Nadeem, F., Ali, I., and Ustun, T. S., Optimal energy routing in microgrids with IEC 61850 based energy routers. IEEE Transactions on Industrial Electronics, vol. 67, no. 6, pp. 5161–5169, 2020b.

Hussain, S. M. S., Ustun, T. S., Nsonga, P., and Ali, I., IEEE 1609 WAVE and IEC 61850 standard communication based integrated EV charging management in smart . IEEE Transactions on Vehicular Technology, vol. 67, no. 8, pp. 7690–7697, 2018.

Nadeem, F., Aftab, M. A., Hussain, S. M. S., Ali, I., Tiwari, P. K., Goswami, A. K., and Ustun, T. S., Virtual power plant management in smart with XMPP based IEC 61850 communication. Energies, vol. 12, no. 12, art. 2398, 2019.

Schwarz, K., 61850: A single standard for the engineering, automation, and supervision of power systems on all voltage levels. In: Industrial Communication Technology Handbook, 2nd ed., R. Zurawski, Ed. Boca Raton, FL, USA: CRC Press, c. 2014.

Schwarz, K., Advanced condition monitoring of primary equipment with the standard series IEC 61850 and IEC 61400-25. In: Proceedings of the CEPSI 2008, Macau, China, 2008a.

Schwarz, K., Comparison of IEC 60870-5-101/-103/-104, DNP3, and IEC 60870-6-TASE.2 with IEC 61850, tech. report, SCC (Schwarz Consulting Company), Edition 2012-07-21, p. 23.

Schwarz, K., IEC 61850 also outside the substation for the whole electrical power system. In: Proceedings of the 15th Power Systems Computation Conference (PSCC), Liège, Belgium, 2005.

Schwarz, K., IEC 61850 beyond substations – The standard for the whole energy supply system. In Proceedings of the CEPSI 2008, Macau, China, 2008b.

Schwarz, K., IEC 61850, IEC 61400-25, and IEC 61970: Information models and information exchange for electric power systems. In Proceedings of the DistribuTECH, Orlando, FL, USA, 2004, pp. 1–5.

Siqueira, I., A Importância dos Testes Funcionais e de Interoperabilidade para a Integração de Sistemas de Proteção e Automação Utilizando a Norma IEC61850, X Seminário Técnico de Proteção e Controle, CIGRE, Belo Horizonte, MG, Brasil.

Siqueira, I., A Layered Hierarchical Object-oriented View of IEC 61850. PAC World Conference, Dublin, Ireland, 2011.

Siqueira, I., A Tool for Testing and Fault Diagnosis in IEC 61850–Based Systems, International Conference on Actual Trends in Development of Power System Protection and Automation, CIGRE, Moscow, Russia.

Siqueira, I. and Pereira, A. T. A., Commissioning test of IEC 61850-based substation automation systems, International Conference on Actual Trends in Development of Power System Protection and Automation, CIGRE, Yekaterinburg, Russia, 2013.

Siqueira, I., Design and Automatic Testing of IEC 61850 Substation Automation Systems, PAC World Magazine, Los Angeles, US, 2010a.

Siqueira, I., Diretrizes para Ensaios de Interoperabilidade e Testes Funcionais em Relés Multifuncionais Baseados na Norma IEC61850, X Seminário Técnico de Proteção e Controle, CIGRE, Belo Horizonte, MG, Brasil.

Siqueira, I., et al., Coordination of protection and automation in future networks, CIGRE Symposium, Bologna, Italy, 2011a.

Siqueira, I., et al., On the Fast Evolution towards the Optimization of Simulation, Software and Hardware for SIPS in Brazil, PAC World Conference, Dublin, Ireland, 2011b.

Siqueira, I., et al., Structure of data and information for PAC and operation applications, International Conference on Actual Trends in Development of Power System Protection and Automation, Saint Petersburg, Russia, 2011c.

Siqueira, I., Faarooqui, N., and Nair, N. A., Review of international industry practices for specification of functional requirements of protection, Automation and Control, CIGRE Science & Engineering, n. 11, 2018.

Siqueira, I., Functional and interoperability tests using the IEC61850 standard applied to substations – Research and development in Brazil, CIGRE Biennial Session, Paris, France, 2008.

Siqueira, I., Model-based Testing and Diagnosis of IEC 61850 Systems, PAC World Magazine, Los Angeles, US, 2010b.

Siqueira, I., Paulino, M. D. C., and Chesf, U. A. C., Requisitos para Interoperabilidade de ***IEDs*** e Sistemas Baseados na Norma IEC61850, X STPC – Seminário Técnico de Proteção, CIGRE Brasil, Recife, Brasil, 2010.

Siqueira, I., Perspective, Strategy and Applications of IEC 61850 in Brazil, PAC World Magazine, Los Angeles, US, 2009.

Siqueira, I., System for Integration of Protection and Control Devices, CIGRE Biennial Session, CIGRE, Paris, France, 2010c.

Siqueira, I., Uma visão hierárquica e orientada a objetos de sistemas de automação baseados na norma IEC 61850, XXII SNPTEE Seminário Nacional de Produção e Transmissão de Energia Elétrica – CIGRE – Brasília – DF, 2013.

Ustun, T. S., A critical review of IEC 61850 testing tools. Sustainability, vol. 13, no. 11, art. 6213, 2021.

Ustun, T. S., Aftab, M. A., Ali, I., and Hussain, S. M. S., A novel scheme for performance evaluation of an IEC 61850-based active distribution system substation. IEEE Access, vol. 7 pp. 123893–123902, 2019.

Ustun, T. S. and Hussain, S. M. S., IEC 61850 modeling of UPFC and XMPP communication for power management in microgrids. IEEE Access, vol. 8 pp. 141696–141704, 2020.

Ustun, T. S., Farooq, S. M., and Hussain, S. M. S., A novel approach for mitigation of replay and masquerade attacks in Smartgrids using IEC 61850 standard. IEEE Access, vol. 7 pp. 156044–156053, 2019.

Ustun, T. S., Hussain, S. M. S., Syed, M. H., and Dambrauskas, P., IEC-61850-based communication for integrated EV management in power systems with renewable penetration. Energies, vol. 14, no. 9, art. 2493, 2021.

Ustun, T. S., Hussain, S. M. S., Ulutas, A., Onen, A., Roomi, M. M., and Mashima, D., Machine learning-based intrusion detection for achieving cybersecurity in smart using IEC 61850 GOOSE messages. Symmetry, vol. 13, no. 5, art. 826, 2021.

Ustun, T. S., Hussain, S. M. S., Yavuz, L., and Onen, A. Artificial intelligence based intrusion detection system for IEC 61850 sampled values under symmetric and asymmetric faults. IEEE Access, vol. 9 pp. 56486–56495, 2021.

Ustun, T. S., Ozansoy, C., and Zayegh, A., Simulation of communication infrastructure of a centralized microgrid protection system based on IEC 61850-7-420. In: Proceedings of the 3rd IEEE International Conference on Smart Grid Communications (SmartGridComm), Tainan, Taiwan, 2012, pp. 492–497.

Zhu, Z., Xu, B., Brunner, C., Yip, T., and Chen, Y., IEC 61850 configuration solution to distributed intelligence in distribution grid automation, Energies, vol. 10, no. 4, p. 528, 2017.

F. Videos

Baumgartner, B., Time Synchronization for IEC 61850. In: Route to IEC 61850 Power Utility Communication Tutorial and Workshop, OMICRON, Germany, 2016.

Brunner, C., The Concept of IEC 61850. In: Route to IEC 61850 Power Utility Communication Tutorial and Workshop, it4power, Germany, 2016.

Jenkner, M., Redundancy Concepts in IEC 61850. In: Route to IEC 61850 Power Utility Communication Tutorial and Workshop, Moxa, Germany, 2016.

Reuter, J., Engineering IEC 61850 Systems. In: Route to IEC 61850 Power Utility Communication Tutorial and Workshop, Helinks, Germany, 2016.

Schossig, T., Testing IEC 61850 Systems. In: Route to IEC 61850 Power Utility Communication Tutorial and Workshop, OMICRON, Germany, 2016.

Siqueira, I., Electricity Supply System of the Future, available at https://www.youtube.com/watch?v=SQuCMXgZcAg.

G. Websites

CIGRE, https://www.cigre.org
IEC TC 57, https://www.tc57.iec.ch
IEEE, https://www.ieee.org
PAC World Magazine, https://www.pacw.org
Satoshi – IEC 61850 Master, https://www.chatGPT.com

Index

g

h

i

m

n

Printed and bound by CPI Group (UK) Ltd, Croydon, CR0 4YY

17/09/2026

14964235-0007